D1441451

The Fourfold Gospel

OR

A HARMONY *of the* FOUR GOSPELS

Resulting in a complete chronological life
of Christ, divided into titled sections and
sub-divisions, with comments interjected in
the text; especially designed for the use of
Sunday-school teachers and advanced
pupils.

J.W. McGARVEY
and
PHILIP Y. PENDLETON

GUARDIAN OF TRUTH

Bowling Green, Kentucky

INTRODUCTION.

We feel that in placing this work before the public we should accompany it with some words of explanation. It is unique, presenting a combination of features never before collected in one work. Harmonies and Fourfold Gospels are plentiful, and we have examined a large number of them, beginning with the pioneer work of Tatian. We have sought to utilize all the good features employed by others, and to introduce several new and helpful inventions of our own.

PRESERVING THE TEXT.

Believing fully and firmly that the Scriptures are the word of God, we have sought to preserve all that is contained in them, and have, in combining them, regarded it as wrong to take liberties with them. To carry out this reverential idea we have introduced the *variant readings* of each Gospel, enclosing them in braces, so that they will not confuse the reader. By doing this we have, according to our count, except in the cases of a few redundant pronouns, only omitted five words of the text, which, if we remember correctly, are three "ands," one "but" and one "with." To accomplish this almost absolute conservation of the wording of the text without involving the reader in hopeless confusion, has been no easy task, especially in cases where all four Gospels are combined in a single section.

TO DISTINGUISH THE GOSPELS.

Then, to enable the reader to discriminate as he reads, we have indicated the particular Gospel from which our word or words are taken, by the several superior letters; viz.: a, b, c and d, which stand respectively for the four Gospels, Matthew, Mark, Luke and John. We have followed the punctuation of each Gospel as we have used its words, also giving the punctuation mark which followed the last word taken.

COMBINATION ILLUSTRATED.

To illustrate our method of combination, let us take Section 36, which is a fitting together of the following passages, viz.:

9 And as Jesus passed by from thence, he saw a man, called Matthew, sitting at the place of toll: and he saith unto him, Follow me. And he arose, and followed him.—Matt. ix. 9.

13 And he went forth again by the sea side; and all the multitude resorted unto him, and he taught them. 14 And as he passed by, he saw Levi the *son* of Alphaeus sitting at the place of toll, and he saith unto him, Follow me. And he arose and followed him.—Mark ii. 13, 14.

27 And after these things he went forth, and beheld a publican, named Levi, sitting at the place of toll, and said unto him, Follow me. 28 And he forsook all, and rose up and followed him. — Luke v. 27, 28.

Which three passages are combined as follows:

c 27 And after these things he went forth, ᵇ again by the sea side; and all the multitude resorted unto him, and he taught them. 14 And as he ᵃ Jesus passed by from thence, he saw ᶜ and beheld ᵃ a man, ᶜ a publican, named {ᵃ called} Matthew, ᶜ Levi, ᵇ the son of Alphaeus sitting at the place of toll, and he saith {ᶜ said} unto him, Follow me. 28 And he forsook all, ᵇ and he arose {ᶜ rose up} and followed him.

Now, in this passage we have retained the redundant pronoun "he" in the phrase he Jesus. Where Luke has the phrase **named Matthew,** Matthew has the variant reading **called Matthew.** Where Mark says **saith,** Luke gives the variant **said,** and where Mark says **arose,** Luke says **rose up.** By variant reading we mean one which can not be combined with the other texts so that the combined text will read smoothly.

LESSER AND FULLER FORMS.

Moreover, we have endeavored to use the fullest form, including the words of those Gospels which have the lesser forms of sentences, except where the sentence ends in a period, in which case we have given the least form, so that the larger form of the other Gospels might be made apparent; as, for instance, this sentence, taken from Matthew xii. 47; Mark iii. 32; Luke viii. 20: [c] **20 And it was told him,** [a] **Behold, thy mother and thy brethren** [b] **seek for thee.** [c] **stand without desiring to see thee.** [a] **seeking to speak to thee.** Here Mark has the short form, Luke a longer form, and Matthew a trifle the longest form; all of which is indicated by the order in which each part is placed, and the several periods which close the thought of each evangelist.

But in compiling the work we have bound ourselves by no inflexible rule; for to do so would, in many instances, make the reading very complex, whereas our first study has been to make the work simple, and to avoid confusing the mind of the reader.

SECTIONS AND SUBDIVISIONS.

We have divided the work into sections for analytical purposes, and in order to aid in the work of indexing and giving cross references. We have arranged the sections in what we believe to be the best chronological order, but have not attempted to justify our chronology, because space would not permit. We have also given the time and place of each section, where these things could be ascertained with any degree of accuracy. In this matter, however, we are liable to dis-

appoint many of our readers, because we have been conserva-
tive. The dates and places given in similar works are too
often mere arbitrary assumptions: there being so little ground
or reason back of them that they do not even justify one in
calling them speculative. Unless we have had some reason
for fixing a date or assigning a locality, we have refrained
from doing either, though we have found them freely and positively asserted in such places in similar works.

FOUR POINTS OF ECONOMY.

By the use of pronounced black letter type we enable the
reader to follow the Scripture text, omitting the comments if
he chooses. But by thus combining the four Gospels and
interjecting the comment into the text, we have produced the
most labor-saving, time-saving, condensed commentary ever
placed before the people. Those familiar with commentaries
can best realize what this means. Incidents told in one Gospel are repeated in other Gospels, and when a commentator
has given his annotations on Matthew, and comes to the same
facts recorded in Mark, or Luke, or John, he wastes his space
by printing the duplicate text, and he wastes his reader's time
by referring him to his comments in the volume on Matthew.
By combining the Gospels for commentary purposes we have
saved this space and time.

Again, in most commentaries a fifth or a sixth of the space
is taken up in drawing distinctions between the texts of the
four Gospels, while in this work these distinctions are placed
before the reader's eye, where he can see them for himself at
a glance. Moreover, in other commentaries, which give the
text, another sixth or seventh of the work is taken up in
reprinting in the notes that portion of the text concerning
which the commentator wishes to speak. Our interjected
method avoids all this needless repetition, and makes it possible for us to present the comment with the least preliminary
verbiage or introductory setting. Time is also saved because
the reader does not have to look back and forth from the text
at the top to the comment at the bottom of the page. Again,

other commentaries lose a large amount of space by using the King James text. Those which preceded the revision waste space correcting the translation and modernizing its English: those published since the revision suffer a similar waste by drawing endless comparisons between the two texts. By choosing the American revision as the basis for our work, we have a text which needs but little explanation or apology, and we are thereby enabled to employ the reader's time and strength to his best advantage.

CARE IN PREPARING THIS WORK.

In preparing the work there has been no sparing of time, labor or expense. While we have carefully avoided all conceits, quibblings and useless refinements, and have studied to present only that which was useful, helpful and practical, we have endeavored to put into the work the results of careful investigation and studious research. Besides theological treatises and works of reference, a full line of commentaries has been used. In some few cases, where the sections have been simple, from thirty to fifty commentaries have been consulted; but in the vast majority of sections between eighty and one hundred commentaries have been searched and sifted. To these painstaking labors of the junior editor, there has been added the results of the wider researches of the senior editor, effected during a half century of continuous Bible study and teaching. We have not aimed to produce a commentary for the textual critic, the theologian, or the professor; but a plain and simple work for all readers of God's word.

AN OBJECT IN VIEW.

Moreover, having in view the preparation of a new series of Sunday-school lessons, we have prepared this work as a basis for such series. As the present International Series handles mere scraps of the Bible, it is practicable to print the text in the quarterlies; but with a series which deals with the whole Bible, larger portions must be assigned for the lessons, and such printing of the text in the quarterlies becomes impossible. In such a series the pupil must be referred to the Bible itself, and in order that he may have a Bible with comments, we have prepared the present work, intending to follow it with similar volumes, until the entire Bible is given to the public in this annotated form, if God permit. J. W. McGARVEY.

PHILIP Y. PENDLETON.

The Fourfold Gospel.

PART FIRST.

THE PERIOD OF CHRIST'S LIFE PRIOR TO HIS MINISTRY.

I.

LUKE'S PREFACE AND DEDICATION.

cLUKE I. 1-4.*

c1 **Forasmuch as many** [of whom we know nothing and have even no tradition] **have taken in hand to draw up a narrative concerning those matters which have been fulfilled** [completed, or accomplished according to the divine will] **among us, 2 even as they delivered them unto us, who from the beginning were eyewitnesses** [the apostles were necessarily such and there were some few others—Acts i. 21-23] **and ministers of the word** [the apostles were ministers, and not ecclesiastical dignitaries], **3 it seemed good to me also, having traced the course of all things accurately from the first** [and being therefore thoroughly fitted to write the gospel], **to write unto thee in order** [not in chronological but in topical order], **most excellent Theophilus** [Luke also dedicated the Book of Acts to this man. Nothing is known of Theophilus, but he is supposed to have been a Greek of high official rank]; **4 that thou mightest know the certainty** [might have a

---

*NOTE.—The four Gospels are respectively represented in this volume by the superior letters a, b, c and d; and variations in the readings of the four Gospels are inserted in braces, thus: { }

fixed written record, and not trust to a floating, variable tradition or a treacherous memory] concerning the things
[the gospel facts] wherein thou wast instructed.

II.

JOHN'S INTRODUCTION.

ᵈJohn i. 1–18.

ᵈ1 In the beginning was the Word [a title for Jesus
peculiar to the apostle John], **and the Word was with God**
[not going before nor coming after God, but with Him at the
beginning], **and the Word was God.** [Not more, not less.]
**2 The same was in the beginning with God. 3 All
things were made through him** [the New Testament
often speaks of Christ as the Creator—see ver. 10; I. Cor.
viii. 6; Col. i. 13, 17; Heb. i. 2]; **and without him was
not anything made that hath been made.** [This shows
that Jesus himself is not a creature.] **4 In him was life**
[As in the Father (chap. v. 26). As this life animates the
living, so can it reanimate the dead—John xi. 25]; **and the
life was the light of men.** [The life of Jesus is the light
of men, because from that life we get our intellect and understanding, and because that life formed and governs the creation around us by which we become enlightened as to the
existence and power of God—Rom. i. 18–21; Acts xiv. 16,
17.] **5 And the light shineth in the darkness** [an
ignorant, benighted world]; **and the darkness apprehended it not.** [Did not receive or admit it. Jesus, the
Light of the world, was despised and rejected by men.]
**6 There came a man, sent from God, whose name
was John. 7 The same came for witness, that he
might bear witness of the light** [that he might tell men
that Jesus was the Messiah], **that all** [who heard his testi-
mony] **might believe** [in Jesus] **through him. 8 He
was not the light** ["He was the lamp that burneth and
shineth "(chap. v. 35); but not the Sun of righteousness—

Mal. iv. 2], but *came* that he might bear witness of the light. 9 There was the true light [as opposed to the imperfect, incomplete and transitory lights], *even the light which lighteth every man* [all men are enlightened in some degree and enlightened of Christ: some by nature, some by conscience, and some by Bible revelation], coming into the world. 10 He was in the world [invisibly present, renewing and sustaining his creation], and the world was made through him, and the world knew him not. [Though it might and should have known him—Rom. i. 18–21; Acts xiv. 16, 17.] 11 He came [visibly in the flesh] unto his own [his own land or possessions—Hos. ix. 3; Jer. ii. 7; Zech. ii. 12], and they that were his own [the children of Israel—Ex. xix. 5; Deut. vii. 6; xiv. 2] received him not. 12 But as many as received him [whether Jew or Gentile], to them gave he the right to become children of God [comp. Rom. iii. 14–17; Gal. iii. 26; iv. 6, 7; I. John iii. 1, 2], *even* to them that believe on his name: 13 who were born, not of blood [descent from Abraham, David or any other godly person does not make a man a child of God—Luke iii. 8; Matt. iii. 9; ch. viii. 39, 40; Gal. iii. 6, 7, 29], nor of the will of the flesh [the efforts and exertions of our own human hearts and natures may reform, but can not regenerate, the life—ch. iii. 6], nor of the will of man [we are not begotten of God by the acts and deeds of our fellow-men, however much they may aid us in leading right lives], but of God. [Ch. iii. 5; I. John iv. 7; v. 1.] 14 And the Word became flesh [by being born at Bethlehem of the Virgin Mary], and dwelt among us, (and we beheld his glory [in his miracles, and especially in his transfiguration—ch. ii. 11; II. Pet. i. 16–18], glory as of the only begotten from the Father) [such glory as was suitable to the Son of God], full of grace and truth. [The glory of Christ was not in pomp and worldly grandeur, but in the holiness, grace and truth of his daily life.] 15 John [the Baptist] beareth witness of him [the words of John still witness to unbelieving Jews and Gentiles], and crieth,

saying, This was he of whom I said [John had preached about Jesus before Jesus appeared; he now points to Jesus as the one about whom he had preached], **He that cometh after me** [he for whom I as a forerunner have prepared the way—Matt. iii. 3] **is become before me** [is worthy of more honor and reverence than am I]: **for he was before me.** [Though born into the world six months later than John, Jesus, as the Word, had existed from eternity. (In verse 16 the words are the apostle John's, and not John the Baptist's.)] **16 For of his fulness** [Jesus was full of grace and truth—and all the attributes of God—Eph. i. 23; iii. 19; iv. 13; Col. i. 19; ii. 9] **we all received** [by union with him all his perfection and righteousness became ours—Phil. i. 10, 11; iii. 8, 9; I. Cor. i. 30], **and grace for grace.** [This may mean that we receive a grace kindred to or like each several grace that is in Christ (Rom. viii. 29; xii. 2; Eph. iv. 11-13). But it more probably means fullness of grace, or fresh grace daily added to the grace already bestowed.] **17 For the law** [the Old Dispensation with its condemnation (Rom. iii. 20; Gal. ii. 21) and its types and shadows—Col. ii. 16, 17; Heb. viii. 4, 5; x. 1] **was given through Moses** [by angels at Mt. Sinai—Heb. ii. 2]; **grace and truth** [the New Dispensation with its justification (Rom. iii. 21-26) and its realities—Heb. ix. 1-15] **came through Jesus Christ.** [Heb. i. 1, 2; ii. 3.] **18 No man hath seen God at any time** [I. John iv. 12, 20; ch. i. 18; I. Tim. vi. 16]; **the only begotten Son** [the word "only begotten" indicates that none other bears with Christ a like relationship to God], **who is in the bosom of the Father** [who bears the closest and tenderest relationship and fellowship as to the Father], **he hath declared** *him.* [Ch. iii. 11; ch. xv. 9; Col. i. 15.]

III.

GENEALOGY OF JESUS ACCORDING TO MATTHEW.

^a MATT. I. 1–17.

^a 1 **The book of the generation** [or genealogy] **of Jesus Christ, the son of David** [the Messiah was promised to David—II. Sam. vii. 16; John vii. 42], **the son of Abraham.** [Messiah was also promised to Abraham—Gen. xxii. 18; Gal. iii. 16.] 2 **Abraham begat Isaac; and Isaac begat Jacob; and Jacob begat Judah and his brethren** [mentioned here because they were the heads of the tribes for whom especially Matthew wrote his Cospel]; 3 **and Judah begat Perez and Zerah** [these two were twins] **of Tamar** [she was the incestuous daughter-in-law of Judah]; **and Perez begat Hezron; and Hezron begat Ram; 4 and Ram begat Amminadab; and Amminadab begat Nahshon; and Nahshon begat Salmon; 5 and Salmon begat Boaz of Rahab** [she had been a heathen and a harlot of Jericho]; **and Boaz begat Obed of Ruth** [she was a heathen Moabitess]; **and Obed begat Jesse; 6 and Jesse begat David the king.** [These fourteen were patriarchs. The second fourteen were all kings.] **And David** [we may count David twice, first as a patriarch, second as one of the kings; and thus make up the full number of the second fourteen] **begat Solomon of her** *that had been the wife* [the adulteress Bathsheba] **of Uriah; 7 and Solomon** [a wise but sinful king] **begat Rehoboam** [a foolish king, from whose kingdom of twelve tribes God cut off ten tribes]; **and Rehoboam begat Abijah** [a sinful king, like his father Rehoboam]; **and Abijah begat Asa** [a godly king who reformed his kingdom of Judah]; 8 **and Asa begat Jehoshaphat** [a good king, much like his father Asa; but he displeased God somewhat by being too friendly with Ahab, the wicked king of Israel]; **and Jehoshaphat begat Joram**

[Joram married Athaliah, the wicked daughter of Ahab, **and** followed Ahab in all his ungodly practices]; **and Joram** [Joram begat Ahaziah, and Ahaziah begat Joash, and Joash begat Amaziah; and Amaziah begat Uzziah. The names of Ahaziah, Joash and Amaziah were probably omitted for the sake of symmetry, but may have been dropped because they were the wicked descendants of Ahab unto the fourth generation—Ex. xx. 4, 5] **begat Uzziah** [he was a good king, but was smitten with leprosy for presumptuously entering the temple]; **9 and Uzziah begat Jotham** [a good king like Uzziah, his father]; **and Jotham begat Ahaz** [one of Judah's worst kings]; **and Ahaz begat Hezekiah** [a royal, godly king, like David]; **10 and Hezekiah begat Manasseh** [an evil king, like Ahaz, but, being punished of God, he repented]; **and Manasseh begat Amon** [an evil king like his father Manasseh; who waxed worse and worse till his people conspired against him and slew him]; **and Amon begat Josiah** [a good king, much like Hezekiah]; **11 and Josiah begat** [Jehoiakim, and Jehoiakim begat] **Jechoniah and his brethren** [So far as is known, Jechoniah had no literal brothers. We may, therefore, take the word "brethren" as meaning his royal kindred; viz.: his father, Jehoiakim, and his uncles, Jehoahaz and Zedekiah, the three sons of Josiah], **at the time** [probably about B. C. 599] **of the carrying away** [into captivity] **to Babylon. 12 And after the carrying away to Babylon Jechoniah** [If we do not count David twice, as above indicated (as a patriarch and a king), we must count Jechoniah twice (as a king who became a citizen). But if we count Jehoiakim as properly included in the phrase "his brethren" at verse 11, we need count no one twice] **begat Shealtiel** [Luke calls Shealtiel the son of Neri. Jechoniah may have been the natural, and Neri the legal, father of Shealtiel—Deut. xxv. 5-10; Matt. xxii. 24. Or Luke's Shealtiel and Zerubbabel may have been different persons from the Shealtiel and Zerubbabel of Matthew]; **and Shealtiel begat Zerubbabel** [the governor of Jerusalem, who rebuilt the temple, as told by Ezra, Haggai and Zechariah]; **13 and**

Zerubbabel begat Abiud; and Abiud begat Eliakim; and Eliakim begat Azor; 14 and Azor begat Sadoc; and Sadoc begat Achim; and Achim begat Eliud; 15 and Eliud begat Eleazar; and Eleazar begat Matthan; and Matthan begat Jacob; 16 and Jacob begat Joseph the husband of Mary, of whom was born Jesus [the name Jesus means Saviour], who is called Christ. [The word "Christ" is a title. It means the anointed One. Prophets, priests and kings were anointed; Jesus was all three.] 17 So all the generations, from Abraham unto David, are fourteen generations; and from David unto the carrying away to Babylon fourteen generations; and from the carrying away to Babylon unto the Christ fourteen generations. [The Jews, to whom Matthew wrote his Gospel, were extremely fond of such groupings and divisions as this.]

IV.

GENEALOGY ACCORDING TO LUKE.

ᶜ LUKE III. 23–38.

ᶜ 23 And Jesus himself [Luke has been speaking about John the Baptist, he now turns to speak of Jesus himself], when he began *to teach*, was about thirty years of age [the age when a Levite entered upon God's service— Num. iv. 46, 47], being the son (as was supposed) of Joseph, the *son* [this may mean that Jesus was grandson of Heli, or that Joseph was counted as a son of Heli because he was his son-in-law] of Heli, 24 the *son* of Matthat, the *son* of Levi, the *son* of Melchi, the *son* of Jannai, the *son* of Joseph, 25 the *son* of Mattathias, the *son* of Amos, the *son* of Nahum, the *son* of Esli, the *son* of Naggai, 26 the *son* of Maath, the *son* of Mattathias, the *son* of Semein, the *son* of Josech, the *son* of Joda, 27 the *son* of Joanan, the *son* of Rhesa, the *son* of Zerubbabel, the *son* of Shealtiel, the *son* of Neri [Matthew calls Shealtiel the son of Jechoniah.

Jechoniah may have been the natural, and Neri the legal, father of Shealtiel—Deut. xxv. 5–10; Matt. xxii. 24], **28 the** *son* **of Melchi, the** *son* **of Addi, the** *son* **of Cosan, the** *son* **of Elmadam, the** *son* **of Er, 29 the** *son* **of Jesus, the** *son* **of Eliezer, the** *son* **of Jorim, the** *son* **of Matthat, the** *son* **of Levi, 30 the** *son* **of Symeon, the** *son* **of Judas, the** *son* **of Joseph, the** *son* **of Jonam, the** *son* **of Eliakim, 31 the** *son* **of Melea, the** *son* **of Menna, the** *son* **of Mattatha, the** *son* **of Nathan, the** *son* **of David, 32 the** *son* **of Jesse, the** *son* **of Obed, the** *son* **of Boaz, the** *son* **of Salmon** [he was probably one of the two spies who were sent to Jericho by Joshua—Judg. ii. 1–24], **the** *son* **of Nahshon** [he was prince of the tribe of Judah during the wanderings in the wilderness—Num. i. 4–7; x. 14], **33 the** *son* **of Amminadab, the** *son* **of Arni, the** *son* of **Hezron, the** *son* **of Perez, the** *son* **of Judah, 34 the** *son* **of Jacob, the** *son* **of Isaac, the** *son* **of Abraham, the** *son* **of Terah, the** *son* **of Nahor, 35 the** *son* **of Serug, the** *son* **of Reu, the** *son* **of Peleg, the** *son* **of Eber** [it is thought that the name "Hebrew" comes from this man—Gen. x. 21; xl. 15; Ex. ii. 6], **the** *son* **of Shelah, 36 the** *son* **of Cainan, the** *son* **of Arphaxad, the** *son* **of Shem, the** *son* **of Noah** [the hero of the flood], **the** *son* **of Lamech, 37 the** *son* **of Methuselah** [who lived to be the oldest man on record, dying when 969 years old], **the** *son* **of Enoch** [whom God translated], **the** *son* **of Jared, the** *son* **of Mahalaleel, the** *son* **of Cainan, 38 the** *son* **of Enos, the** *son* **of Seth** [the third son of Adam], **the** *son* **of Adam, the** *son* **of God.** [Adam was the son of God, being not merely a creature, but a creature made in God's image and likeness—Gen. i. 26, 27.]

V.

ANNUNCIATION TO ZACHARIAS OF THE BIRTH OF JOHN THE BAPTIST.

(At Jerusalem.   Probably B. C. 6.)

ᶜ LUKE I. 5–25.

ᶜ **5 There was in the days of Herod, king of Judaea** [a Jewish proselyte, an Idumæan or Edomite by birth, founder of the Herodian family, king of Judæa from B. C. 40 to A. D. 4, made such by the Roman Senate on the recommendation of Mark Antony and Octavius Cæsar], **a certain priest named Zacharias, of the course** [David divided the priests into twenty-four bodies or courses, each course serving in rotation one week in the temple (I. Chron. xxiv. 3–19). Of these courses that of Abijah was the eighth] **of Abijah: and he had a wife of the daughters of Aaron** [The Baptist was of the priestly race by both parents, a family distinction much esteemed among the Jews. He who was thus doubly a priest proclaimed Him who changed the priesthood], **and her name was Elisabeth.** [She was named after her ancestress Elisheba, the wife of Aaron.] **6 And they were both righteous before God** [that is, truly righteous, or righteous in God's judgment, and not in mere appearance—Gen. vii. 1], **walking in all the commandments and ordinances** [Strictly construed, commandments would refer to moral, and ordinances to ceremonial laws. The two words include all the positive and negative precepts] **of the Lord blameless. 7 And they had no child** [this fact was a reproach and shame to her, barrenness being considered even a punishment for sin by many], **because that Elisabeth was barren** [the births of Isaac, Samson, Samuel and the Baptist were all contrary to nature, and were faint foreshadowings of the greater miracle which took place in the birth of our Lord], **and they both were *now* well stricken in years. 8 Now it came to pass,**

**while he executed the priest's office before God in the
order of his course** [that is, when it came the turn of his
course to minister in the temple], **9 according to the
custom** [there were many duties in the temple service, and
the priests in each course daily drew lots for these duties] **of
the priest's office, his lot was to enter into the temple**
[not that group of buildings, courts and enclosures which
was all called temple ; but the real sanctuary itself, the small
but holy building which took the place of the tabernacle of
the wilderness] **of the Lord and burn incense.** [Made of
a mixture of sweet spices. The temple incense was made
of stacte, onycha, galbanum and pure frankincense, in equal
parts, beaten very small—Ex. xxx. 7, 8, 34–38.] **10 And
the whole multitude** [the presence of the multitude indicates that it was a sabbath or feast day] **of the people were
praying** [Incense is a symbol of prayer (Ps. cxli. 1, 2; Rev.
viii. 3). Each of the multitude prayed in silence] **without**
[outside the sanctuary, in the temple courts, particularly the
court of the women] **at the hour of incense.** [Incense
was offered evening and morning (Ex. xxx. 1–8). Probably at
9 A. M. and at 3 P. M.   Compare Acts iii. 1.   The text favors
the idea that Zacharias' vision came in the morning.] **11 And
there appeared unto him** [one of God's invisible messengers who came visibly—II. Kings vi. 17; Ps. xxxiv. 7] **an
angel of the Lord** [Luke frequently tells of the ministration of angels (ch. i. 26; ii. 9, 13, 21; xii. 8; xv. 10;
xvi. 22; xxii. 43; xxiv. 4, 23).   They are also often mentioned
in the Book of Acts.   There had been no appearance of an
angel for about four hundred years] **standing on the right
side** [the place of honor and dignity—Acts vii. 56] **of the
altar of incense.** [The altar on which Zacharias was burning
incense.   It stood in the Holy Place in front of the veil which
hung between the holy and most holy places.   It was a small
table twenty-two inches in breadth and length and forty-four
inches in height.   It was made of acacia wood, and overlaid
with gold—Ex. xxxvii. 25.]   **12 And Zacharias was
troubled** [as men always are at the sight of heavenly beings

—Gen. iii. 9, 10; Dan. x. 7–12; Rev. i. 17, 18] **when he saw** *him*, **and fear fell upon him. 13 But the angel said unto him, Fear not** [these are the first words of the gospel which began at that hour to unfold itself], **Zacharias: because thy supplication is heard, and thy wife Elisabeth shall bear thee a son, and thou shalt call his name John.** [This name means "The Lord is gracious," or the Lord is merciful.] **14 And thou shalt have joy and gladness** [thou shalt feel as Abraham did when he named his new-born son Isaac; that is, "Laughter"]; **and many** [but not all] **shall rejoice at his birth. 15 For he shall be great in the sight of the Lord** [compare verse 6], **and he shall drink no wine nor strong drink** [Strong drink is any other fermented liquor. Wycliffe's version calls it "syder," and the Anglo-Saxon version calls it "beor," of which palm wine was the most common kind. As to the temperance of the Baptist, compare the history of Samson (Judg. xiii. 3–5), and the law of the Nazarites—Num. vi. 2–4]; **and he shall be filled with the Holy Spirit** [the stimulation of the Spirit is elsewhere thus contrasted with alcoholic stimulants—Acts ii. 15–18; Eph. v. 18], **even from his mother's womb.** [See verse 41.] **16 And many of the children of Israel shall he turn unto the Lord their God.** [These words were quoted from Mal. iv. 6, and resumed the thread of prophecy which had been broken nearly four centuries before. Roman rule had brought in the vices and profligacy of Italy and Greece, and the nation needed to turn back to its former godly life.] **17 And he shall go before his face** [the face of Messiah, who is also the Lord God—Mal. iii. 1] **in the spirit and power of Elijah** [And thus in fulfillment of the prophecy that Elijah should come again (Mal. iv. 6; Matt. xvii. 9–30). The Jews still expect Elijah as the forerunner of Messiah. John showed the spirit of Elijah in his ascetic dress and life (II. Kings i. 8; Matt. iii. 4) and in his message of repentance —I. Kings xviii. 21–40], **to turn the hearts of the fathers to the children** ["These are the last words of the Old Testament, there used by a prophet; here expounded by an angel: there concluding the law; here beginning the gospel." The phrase may mean: 1. John will restore unity to the families of Israel, now divided into political factions, as Herodians or friends of Rome, and zealots or patriots; and into religious factions, as Pharisees, Sadducees, Essenes, etc.; or more likely it may mean, 2. That John would restore the broken relationship between the patriarchs Abraham, Isaac and Jacob, and their degenerate descendants—Isa. xxix. 22, 23; lxiii. 16; John viii. 37–40], **and the disobedient** *to walk* **in the wisdom of the just; to make ready for the Lord a people prepared** *for him.* [As in the East the "friend," or go-between, prepares the bride to understand and appreciate her bridegroom—John iii. 28, 29]. **18 And Zacharias said unto the angel, Whereby shall I know this?** [In asking for a sign Zacharias showed his unbelief (Matt. xii. 38, 39). His question in the original is in four words. Four faithless words cost him forty weeks of silence] **for I am an old man** [So said Abraham (Gen. xvii. 17). The law which retired Levites from service at the age of fifty years (Num. viii. 25, 26) did not apply to priests. They served to extreme old age], **and my wife well stricken in years. 19 And the angel answering said unto him, I am Gabriel** [This name means "hero, or mighty one, of God." Gabriel announced to Daniel the time of Christ's birth and death, and the overthrow and final restoration of the Jewish nation (Dan. vii.–xii.). He also announced the birth of Jesus to Mary (verse 26). The Bible gives the name of but one other angel; viz.: Michael, meaning "Who is like God?" Since Gabriel was the messenger who announced God's merciful and gracious purposes, and Michael the one who executed his decrees and punishments, the Jews had a beautiful saying that "Gabriel flew with two wings, and Michael with only one." The very ancient book of Enoch (Jude 14) gives us the name of two other archangels; viz.: Uriel, meaning "God is light;" and Raphael, meaning "healer of God"], **that stand in the presence of God** [Seven angels are

spoken of as standing in the presence of God (Rev. viii. 2),
and may probably be called "angels of the presence" (Isa.
lxiii. 9). But to see the face of God is no doubt accorded
to all angels (Matt. xviii. 10). One who stands in the presence of God should be believed by men without approving
signs]; **and I was sent to speak unto thee, and to bring
thee these good tidings.** [Our word "gospel" means good
tidings.] **20 And behold, thou shalt be silent** [it was a
sign; and also a punishment for having sought a sign] **and
not able to speak, until the day that these things shall
come to pass, because thou believedst not my words,
which shall be fulfilled in their season. 21 And the
people were waiting for Zacharias, and they marvelled
while he tarried** [The Jews considered slow service as irreverent and displeasing to God. The punishment attached to
displeasing service made them fearful—Lev. xvi. 13] **in the
temple. 22 And when he came out, he could not
speak unto them** [Could not dismiss them with the usual
blessing (Num. vi. 23–26). Disbelief is always powerless to
bless]: **and they perceived** [probably by his excited man-
ner] **that he had seen a vision** [the most vivid and objec-
tive of all spiritual phenomena—ch. xxiv. 23; Acts xxvi. 19; II.
Cor. xii. 1; Dan. ix. 23] **in the temple: and he continued
making signs unto them, and remained dumb. 23
And it came to pass, when the days of his ministration** [They are said to have lasted from the evening of one
Sabbath (Friday at sundown) to the morning of the next.
Though doubtless chagrined at the punishment which had
come upon him, the old priest remained at his post, and dwelt
in the temple until his week was finished] **were fulfilled, he
departed unto his house.** [Some guess that he lived at
Hebron, others at Jutta, five miles south of Hebron, others at
Ain Karim, four miles west of Jerusalem, but no one knows.]
**24 And after these days Elisabeth his wife conceived;
and she hid herself** [probably through mingled feelings of
modesty, humility, devotion and joy] **five months** [at the
end of which time her seclusion was interrupted by the visit

of Mary], **saying, 25 Thus** [graciously and mercifully] **hath the Lord done unto me in the days wherein he looked upon** *me*, **to take away my reproach** [the reproach of being childless—Gen. xxx. 23] **among men.**

VI.

ANNUNCIATION OF THE BIRTH OF JESUS.

(At Nazareth, B. C. 5.)

ᶜLUKE I. 26–38.

ᶜ**26 Now in the sixth month** [this is the passage from which we learn that John was six months older than Jesus] **the angel Gabriel was sent from God unto a city of Galilee, named Nazareth** [Luke alone tells us where Mary lived before the birth of Jesus. That Nazareth was an unimportant town is shown by the fact that it is mentioned nowhere in the Old Testament, nor in the Talmud, nor in Josephus, who mentions two hundred and four towns and cities of Galilee. The way in which Luke introduces Galilee and Nazareth shows that he wrote to those unfamiliar with Palestine. Compare the conversation at John i. 45, 46. Galilee comprised the lands of Zebulun, Naphtali, Issachar and Asher. It was rich in trees and pastures. Its people were hardy and warlike], **27 to a virgin betrothed** [In the East, the betrothal or engagement was entered into with much ceremony, and usually took place a year before the marriage. It was so sacred that the parties entering into it could not be separated save by a bill of divorcement—Matt. i. 19] **to a man whose name was Joseph, of the house of David** [that is, Joseph was of the house of David]; **and the virgin's name was Mary.** [The same name as Miriam—Ex. xv. 20.] **28 And he came in unto her, and said, Hail, thou that art highly favored, the Lord** *is* **with thee. 29 But she was greatly troubled at the saying, and cast in her mind what manner of salutation this might be.** [Whether it meant a present sorrow or joy, for God's salutations all mean joy, but usually that joy is in the distant future—Heb. xii. 11; II. Cor. iv. 17, 18.] **30 And the angel said unto her, Fear not** [the gospel is full of " Fear nots "; it teaches us that perfect love which casts out fear—I. John iv. 18], **Mary: for thou hast found favor with God. 31 And behold, thou shalt conceive in thy womb, and bring forth a son, and shalt call his name JESUS.** [The same as Hoshea (Num. xiii. 8); Joshua and Jeshua (Zech. iii. 1). It means the " salvation of Jehovah." It was one of the most common Jewish names, but was given to Jesus by divine direction because of its fitness—Matt. i. 21.] **32 He shall be great, and shall be called the Son of the Most High** [A common Hebrew way of saying "He shall be." Even the evil spirits called Jesus by this name—Mark v. 7]: **and the Lord God shall give unto him** [he shall not receive his kingdom as a bribe from Satan (Matt. iv. 9), nor win it by force of arms (John xviii. 10, 11, 36; Matt. xxvi. 53), but as the gift of God—Acts ii. 32–36; Phil. ii. 9–11; Matt. xxviii. 18] **the throne** [see Ps. cxxxii. 11] **of his father David** [this must refer to Mary's descent from David, for she is expressly told in verse 35 that her son would have no earthly father]: **33 and he shall reign over the house of Jacob** [That is, over the family or descendants of Jacob; but the expression includes his spiritual, rather than his carnal, descendants (Gal. iii. 7, 28, 29). This name therefore includes the Gentiles as the name of a river includes the rivers which flow into it] **forever** [Dan. ii. 44; vii. 13, 14, 27; Mic. iv. 7; Ps. xlv. 6; Heb. i. 8; Rev. xi. 15]; **and of his kingdom there shall be no end.** [Isa. vii. 9. Christ shall resign his mediatorial kingdom to the Father at the close of this dispensation (I. Cor. xv. 24–28); but as being one with his Father he shall still rule forever.] **34 And Mary said unto the angel, How shall this be** [Her question indicates surprise, not disbelief. Unlike Zacharias, she asked no sign. The youthful village maiden, amid her humble daily duties, shows a more ready faith in the far more startling message than the aged priest in the holy place of the temple in the atmosphere

of the sacred incense], **seeing I know not a man? 35
And the angel answered and said unto her, The Holy
Spirit shall come upon thee, and the power of the
Most High shall overshadow** [the Spirit of God is thus
spoken of as "brooding over" or overshadowing creation to
develop it—Gen. i. 2] **thee** [This indicates that the Holy
Spirit himself created the body of Christ (Heb. x. 5). The
spirit, or divine nature, of Christ was from the beginning,
and was unbegotten—that is, in the sense of being created]:
wherefore also the holy thing [the body of Jesus—Heb.
vii. 26; I. Pet. ii. 22] **which is begotten** [Gal. iv. 4] **shall
be called the Son of God.** [As the Evangelist is here talking
about the bodily and human nature of Jesus, it is possible that
he may here speak of Jesus as the Son of God in the same
sense in which he called Adam the son of God (ch. iii. 38);
that is, his body and human nature were the direct and miraculous production of the divine power. If so, we find Jesus
called the Son of God in three several senses: 1. Here, because he was born into the world in a supernatural manner.
2. Elsewhere, because by his resurrection he was begotten
from the dead (Rom. i. 4; Acts xiii. 33; Ps. ii. 7). 3. Also
elsewhere, because of the eternal, immutable and unparalleled relationship which he sustains to the Father—John i. 1, 14,
18.] **36 And behold, Elisabeth thy kinswoman, she also
hath conceived a son in her old age; and this is the
sixth month with her that was called barren.** [The angel
tells of Elisabeth's condition, that it may encourage the faith
of Mary, and lead her to trust in Him with whom nothing is
impossible—Jer. xxxii. 17, 27; Gen. xviii. 14; Matt. xix. 26.]
37 For no word from God shall be void of power.
[Isa. lv. 11.] **38 And Mary said, Behold, the handmaid**
[Literally, slave or bondservant. It is the feminine form of
the word which Paul so often applies to himself (Rom. i. 1;
Tit. i. 1). Mary uses it to indicate her submissive and obedient spirit] **of the Lord; be it unto me according to thy
word.** [In great faith she not only believes the promise, but
prays for its fulfillment. She bowed to the will of God like

Eli (I. Sam. iii. 18), and became the mother of Him who prayed, " Not my will, but thine, be done "—Luke xxii. 42.] **And the angel departed from her.**

VII.

MARY, FUTURE MOTHER OF JESUS, VISITS ELISABETH, FUTURE MOTHER OF JOHN THE BAPTIST.

(In the Hill Country of Judæa, B. C. 5.)

^c LUKE I. 39–56.

^c **39 And Mary arose in these days** [within a week or two after the angel appeared to her] **and went into the hill country** [the district of Judah lying south of Jerusalem, of which the city of Hebron was the center] **with haste** [she fled to those whom God had inspired, so that they could understand her condition and know her innocence—to those who were inspired as Joseph needed to be inspired, that he might understand—Matt. i. 18–25], **into a city of Judah** [where Zacharias dwelt—see verse 23]; **40 and entered into the house of Zacharias and saluted Elisabeth. 41 And it came to pass, when Elisabeth heard the salutation of Mary, the babe leaped in her womb** [see verse 15]; **and Elisabeth was filled with the Holy Spirit** [sufficiently to have a supernatural knowledge of things and to utter prophecy]; **42 and she lifted up her voice with a loud cry** [Indicating intense, ecstatic joy. What joy must have filled the hearts of these two women as they realized that one was to be the mother of the long-expected Messiah, and the other of his Elijah-like forerunner!], **and said, Blessed** [see verse 28] *art* **thou among women, and blessed** *is* **the fruit of thy womb. 43 And whence is this to me** [why am I thus honored?—Matt. viii. 7, 8], **that the mother of my Lord** [This word imported sometimes divinity, and sometimes mere superiority. The Jews employed this term in connection with the Messiah; but in which sense can not

now be determined. Inspired writers employ it in the higher sense when applying it to Jesus (Matt. xxii. 41-45), and in that sense it is no doubt used here] **should come unto me? 44 For behold, when the voice of thy salutation came into mine ears, the babe leaped in my womb for joy. 45 And blessed** *is* **she that believed** [Elisabeth may have here remembered how her own husband failed to believe]; **for there shall be a fulfilment of the things which have been spoken to her from the Lord. 46 And Mary said** [She speaks in poetic strain. Her song closely resembles that of Hannah—I. Sam. ii. 1-10], **My soul doth magnify** [Mary's song is called "The Magnificat" from this word] **the Lord, 47 and my spirit hath rejoiced in God my Saviour. 48 For he hath looked upon the low estate** [this refers to the contrast between her present condition and that of the former glories of David's house, from which she sprang] **of his handmaid: For behold, from henceforth all generations shall call me blessed.** [Here ends the first section of her song. In it she speaks of herself, and her adoration toward God for his condescending blessing. Mary was blessed in her motherhood, Abraham in his covenants and promises, Paul in his apostleship, etc., but none of these human beings are to be worshiped because of the blessings which they received. Rather should we bestow the more worship on God, from whom these their blessings flow— Jas. i. 17.] **49 For he that is mighty hath done to me great things; And holy is his name.** [Ex. xx. 7.] **50 And his mercy is unto generations and generations** [that is, it is unceasing—Ex. xx. 6] **On them that fear him.** [Here ends the second division of her song. In it Mary glorifies God for his power, holiness and mercy.] **51 He hath showed strength with his arm** ["God's efficacy is represented by his finger (Ex. viii. 19); his great power by his hand (Ex. iii. 20); and his omnipotence by his arm—Ex. xv. 16"]; **He hath scattered the proud in the imagination of their heart. 52 He hath put down princes from their thrones, And hath exalted them of low degree.**

53 The hungry he hath filled with good things; And the rich he hath sent empty away. [These expressions are hyperboles for the disappointment of the proud, the princely and the rich, in whose families the Messiah was expected. God has passed these by, and exalted a lowly one. Here ends the third section or verse of the hymn. It speaks of the changes which the Messiah should work as if he had already worked them.] **54 He hath given help to Israel his servant, That he might remember mercy 55 (As he spake unto our fathers) Toward Abraham** [Mic. vii. 20; Gal. iii. 16] **and his seed for ever.** [The hymn closes with an expression of gratitude to God for his faithfulness in keeping his covenants.] **56 And Mary abode with her about three months** [or until John was born], **and returned** [a favorite word with Luke, used twenty-one times in his Gospel] **unto her house.**

VIII.

THE BIRTH AND EARLY LIFE OF JOHN THE BAPTIST.

(Hill Country of Judæa, B. C. 5.)

c LUKE I. 57–80.

c **57 Now Elisabeth's time was fulfilled that she should be delivered; and she brought forth a son. 58 And her neighbors and her kinsfolk heard that the Lord had magnified his mercy toward her** [mercy in granting a child; great mercy in granting so illustrious a child]; **and they rejoiced with her. 59 And it came to pass on the eighth day** [See Gen. xvii. 12; Lev. xii. 3; Phil. iii. 5. Male children were named at their circumcision, probably because at that time the names of Abram and Sarai had been changed (Gen. xvii. 5, 15). Females were named when they were weaned], **that they came to circumcise the child; and they would have called him Zacharias, after the name of his father. 60 And his mother answered and said, Not so** [Zacharias had evidently written, and thus communicated to his wife all that the angel had told him, and how the child was to be named John]; **but he shall be called John. 61 And they said unto her, There is none of thy kindred** [Family names were even more thought of, and honored, among the Jews than among us. They had no taste for romantic and eccentric names] **that is called by this name. 62 And they made signs** [this seems to indicate that Zacharias was deaf as well as dumb] **to his father, what he would have him called. 63 And he asked for a writing tablet** [tablets were sometimes made of lead, but were usually small wooden boards, either smeared with wax, or having sand sprinkled over them, on which words were written with an iron stylus or pencil], **and wrote, saying, His name is John. And they marvelled all.** [Being surprised that both parents should thus unite upon an unexpected name.] **64 And his mouth was opened immediately** [See verse 20. The angel's words were now completely fulfilled, therefore the punishment for disbelief was removed], **and his tongue** *loosed,* **and he spake, blessing God.** [Probably in the words recorded in verses 68–79.] **65 And fear came** [The miraculous phenomena attending the birth of John made the people so conscious of the presence of God as to fill them with awe. The influence of this fear spread far and wide until the chills and tremors of expected changes and revolutions were felt even by the citizens of Rome, as their poets and historians testify] **on all that dwelt round about them: and all these sayings were noised abroad throughout all the hill country of Judaea. 66 And all that heard them laid them up in their heart, saying, What then shall this child be?** [We probably find an echo of this question thirty years later when John entered upon his ministry—John i. 19.] **For the hand of the Lord was with him. 67 And his father Zacharias was filled with the Holy Spirit, and prophesied** [This his prophecy is the last of the old dispensation, and the first of the new, or Christian, era. It also is poetry, and is a hymn of thanksgiving for the time of Messiah's advent], **saying, 68 Blessed** [the hymn gets its name from this word, and is called the Benedictus] *be* **the Lord, the God of Israel; For he hath visited** [Come back, in the person of his Spirit, to his people. After some four hundred years of absence the Holy Spirit, as the spirit of prophecy, had again returned to God's people. Malachi, the last of the prophets, had been dead about four centuries] **and wrought redemption for his people, 69 And hath raised up a horn** [the horn is a symbol of power—Dan. vii. 7, 8; viii. 21] **of salvation for us In the house of his servant David** [this also indicates that Mary was of the house of David] **70 (As he spake by the mouth of his holy prophets that have been from of old)** [Gen. iii. 15; xxii. 18; xlix. 10; Num. xxiv. 17; II. Pet. i. 21; Heb. i. 1], **71 Salvation from our enemies** [not only Rome, the enemy of Israelitish prosperity, but also those evil agencies which wage ceaseless warfare against the souls of men—Eph. vi. 12], **and from the hand of all that hate us; 72 To show mercy towards our fathers, And to remember his holy covenant** [contract or agreement]; **73 The oath which he sware unto Abraham our father** [see Gen. xii. 3; xvii. 4; xxii. 16, 17], **74 To grant unto us that we being delivered out of the hand of our enemies Should serve him without fear, 75 In holiness and righteousness** [holiness is good conduct toward God, righteousness is good conduct toward men] **before him all our days. 76 Yea and thou, child** [the rest of the psalm is addressed to the infant John], **shalt be called the prophet** [see Matt. xi. 9; Luke xx. 6] **of the Most High: For thou shalt go before the face of the Lord** [the Lord Jesus Christ] **to make ready his ways** [Isa. xl. 3; Matt. iii. 3]; **77 To give knowledge of salvation unto his people** [Israel had a false idea that the Messiah's salvation would be from political evil. John was needed to tell them that it was from sin that God proposed to deliver them. Perdition does not consist in political wrongs, but in divine condemnation] **In the remission of their sins** [through Christ's work—Acts v. 31],

78 Because of the tender mercy of our God, Whereby the dayspring from on high [One of the many names for Jesus or his kingdom. The prophets loved to picture Messiah's advent as a sunrise (Isa. ix. 2; lx. 1–3; Mal. iv. 2; Matt. iv. 16; John i. 4, 5). Christ's coming was the dawn of a new day for Israel and for mankind] **shall visit us, 79 To shine upon them that sit in darkness and the shadow of death; To guide our feet into the way of peace.** [Travelers in the Judæan mountains often waited patiently for the morning light, lest they should lose their lives by a false step taken in the darkness—Isa. lix. 8.] **80 And the child grew, and waxed strong in spirit** [I. Sam. ii. 26; Luke ii. 40, 52], **and was in the deserts** [The thinly settled region west of the Dead Sea. In I. Sam. xxiii. 19 it is called Jeshimon, or "the Horror"] **till the day of his showing unto Israel.** [The day when he commenced his ministry and declared his commission as Messiah's forerunner.]

IX.

ANNUNCIATION TO JOSEPH OF THE BIRTH OF JESUS.

(At Nazareth, B. C. 5.)

ᵃ MATT. I. 18–25.

ᵃ **18 Now the birth** [The birth of Jesus is to be handled with reverential awe. We are not to probe into its mysteries with presumptuous curiosity. The birth of common persons is mysterious enough (Eccl. xi. 5; Ps. cxxxix. 13–16), and we do not well, therefore, if we seek to be wise above what is written as to the birth of the Son of God] **of Jesus Christ was on this wise: When his mother Mary had been betrothed** [The Jews were usually betrothed ten or twelve months prior to the marriage. So sacred was this relationship that unfaithfulness to it was deemed adultery, and was punishable by death—death by stoning (Deut. xxii. 23–28; Lev. xx. 10; Ezek. xvi. 38; John viii. 5). Those betrothed

were regarded as husband and wife, and could only be separated by divorcement. Hebrew betrothals set the world a
good example. Hasty marriage is too often followed by
hasty repentance. " No woman of Israel was married unless
she had been first espoused "] **to Joseph, before they
came together** [Before Joseph brought his bride to his own
home. An espoused maiden lived in her father's house until
the marriage, as is our own custom] **she was found with
child of the Holy Spirit.** [The two evangelists (Matthew
and Luke) which give the earthly genealogy of Jesus are
each careful to mention his miraculous conception through the
Holy Spirit (comp. Luke i. 35). All New Testament writers
recognize Jesus as at once both human and divine. Christ's
physical nature was begotten of the Holy Spirit, but the
Christian's *spiritual* nature is begotten of him (John i. 13).
The act of the Holy Spirit in this case indicates that he is a
personality, and not a mere influence, as some are disposed to
imagine. Influences do not create physical bodies.] **19 And
Joseph her husband, being a righteous man** [As a righteous man he could not complete his marriage, and thus stain
his family name. As a merciful man he did not wish to
openly disgrace the one to whom he was so fondly attached.
He wished to act justly toward his own reputation, and mercifully toward the reputation of Mary], **and not willing to
make her a public example** [he did not wish to expose her
to the shame of a public trial before the court, nor to punish
her as the law permitted], **was minded to put her away
privily.** [The law of Moses gave the husband the power of
divorce (Deut. xxiv. 1). The bill or writing certifying
the divorce usually stated the cause, and was handed to the
wife in the presence of witnesses. Joseph evidently intended
to omit stating any cause in the bill, that there might be no
record to convict her of shame. The law of divorce applied to
betrothed as well as to married persons. In his kindness Joseph
anticipates the special teaching of Christ (Matt. xix. 8) and
the general instruction of Paul (Gal. vi. 1). How different
the conduct of the innocent Joseph from that of guilty Judah

(Gen. xxxviii. 24). Judah needed some one to point out his unfitness—John viii. 7.] **20 But when he thought on these things** [God guides the thoughtful, not the unthinking], **behold, an angel of the Lord appeared unto him** [The Lord looks after the good name of those who honor his name, and he serves those who serve him (I. Sam. ii. 30; John xii. 26). The sufferings of both Mary and Joseph must have been very extreme at this time—one being forced to suspect the chief object of his affections, and the other being compelled to rest under the unjust suspicions of loved ones, because of a condition which God alone could explain. But God does explain where we can not understand without his revelation, and where we absolutely need to know] **in a dream** [A mode of communication frequently used by God (Gen. xx. 3; xxxi. 11, 24; xxxvii. 5; xli. 1; I. Kings iii. 5; Dan. vii. 1; Job iv. 13–15). It is difficult to say how men determined between ordinary and divine dreams, but doubtless the latter came with a glory and vividness which gave assurance of their supernatural nature. Matthew mentions four divine dreams; viz.: this one; the second one given to Joseph (Matt. ii. 13); the dream of the Magi (Matt. ii. 12); and the dream of Pilate's wife—ch. xxvii. 19], **saying, Joseph** [We are known to angels, and they address us by name (Acts x. 3, 13; xvii. 24). Much more does the Lord know our names—John x. 3; Luke xix. 5], **thou son of David** [the name of David was calculated to waken the memories of God's promises, and helped to prepare Joseph to receive the wonderful news that Messiah was about to be born, for Messiah was the promised heir of David], **fear not to take unto thee Mary thy wife** [Have no fear as to Mary's virtue and purity. Fear no disgrace in taking her. Joseph feared as a son of David that this marriage would sully his genealogy. But it was that which gave point and purpose to an otherwise barren and uninteresting record. He feared as a man lest he should share Mary's apparent disgrace; but he had infinitely more reason to fear his unworthiness to share with her the exalted responsibilities of parentage to our

Lord]: **for that which is conceived in her is of the Holy Spirit. 21 And she shall bring forth a son** [the angel does not say "shall bear thee a son," as he said to Zacharias—Luke i. 13]; **and thou shalt call his name JESUS** [Joseph was to take the position of a legal father to the child and name it. The name means " Salvation of Jehovah," or " Jehovah is the Saviour." Would we could all bear our names, such as Christian, pastor, magistrate, father, mother, child, etc., as Jesus bore that wonderful and responsible name of Saviour]; **for it is he that shall save his people from their sins** [Thus from before his very birthhour the nature of Christ's salvation is fully set forth. He came to save from the guilt, power and punishment of sin. He saves from the guilt of sin by having shed his blood, that sins may be remitted or washed clean. He saves from the power of sin by bestowing the gift of the Spirit, who regenerates, comforts and strengthens, and ultimately he saves from the punishment of sin by giving us a resurrection from the dead, and an abundant entrance into the home of glory. That is no salvation at all which fails to free us from this triple bondage of sin.] **22 Now all this is come to pass, that it might be fulfilled which was spoken by the Lord** [It was not fulfilled because predicted, but was rather predicted because sure to take place. Prophecies are fulfilled in four ways; namely, 1. When a thing clearly predicted comes to pass. 2. When that which has been pictured in type and shadow is at last shown forth in substance and reality. 3. When an event which has been described in language more elevated and elaborate than it demands is followed by another similar event to which the said language is more perfectly suited. 4. When parabolic or figurative language may be applied to some subsequent event. The prophecy of Isaiah was fulfilled after this third fashion, which was spoken by the Lord. In innumerable passages the divine origin and inspiration of the Scriptures are clearly and unmistakably set forth. The same Spirit which foretold through the lips of the prophet now interprets the foretelling through the lips of the angel] **through the prophet** [Isa. vii. 14. Isaiah's name is not given. The ancients were studious readers, and had few books, so that there was little need to cite authors by name], **saying** [About the year 740 B. C. While Ahaz was king of Judah, his land was threatened with an invasion by the united armies of Syria and Israel. Isaiah came to the frightened Ahaz, promised divine aid, and told Ahaz to seek from God a sign confirming this promise. This, Ahaz refused to do; whereupon Isaiah replied that God would grant a sign anyway. The sign was that a virgin should have a son, and before the son reached the age of discretion, the kingdoms of Syria and Israel should be destroyed. The sign given Ahaz was one of deliverance, and prefigured the birth of Christ, the great Deliverer, in four ways: 1. A virgin bearing a child. 2. A male child (Rev. xii. 5). 3. The divinely ordered naming of the child. 4. The significance of the name given. Jesus fulfilled in his ministry many predictions; but many more such as this one were fulfilled upon him without his volition], **23 Behold, the virgin shall be with child** [The Sonship of Jesus demands a miraculous birth. If we doubt the miracle of his conception, we can never solve the perplexing problem of his marvelous life and death], **and shall bring forth a son, and they shall call his name** [rather, title: under the head of "name" the titles of Jesus are also set forth at Isa. ix. 6] **Immanuel; which is, being interpreted, God with us** [Nature shows God above us; the Law shows God against us; but the Gospel shows God with us, and for us. The blessing of the church militant is Christ, God with us: that of the church triumphant is Christ, us with God. In this world Jesus walked "with us" in human form (John i. 14); and because he did so, we, in the world to come, shall walk "with him" in divine form (I. John iii. 2; I. Cor. xv. 49). In a personal sense Jesus may fitly be called "God with us," for he was God and man united in one body.] **24 And Joseph arose from his sleep, and did as the angel of the Lord commanded him** [he followed the instructions, though contrary to his first inclination. Blessed are they who permit God to guide them. As Joseph appears to have acted at once upon the angel's instruction, the marriage must have taken place several months prior to the birth of Jesus], **and took unto him his wife** [thus becoming the legally recognized father of Jesus, and though he bestowed upon Jesus but a humble name (Luke iv. 22; Matt. xiii. 55), he nevertheless rescued him from the reproach of an illegitimate birth]; **25 and knew her not till she brought forth a son** [Romish teachers contend for the doctrine of the perpetual virginity of Mary, that she may be regarded as an object of worship. This doctrine can not be proved by Scripture. But there are weightier reasons than this which forbid us to worship her; namely, it can not be proven from Scripture either that she was *divine* or that she was *sinless*. Moreover, the fact that she entered the marital state at all, shows that she was perfectly human, and comported herself as such] : **and he called his name JESUS.** [Two Old Testament heroes bore the name Jesus under the form Joshua. One was captain of Israel for the conquest of Canaan, the other was high priest of Israel for rebuilding the temple (Zech. vi. 11, 12). Christ was both the Captain of our salvation and the High Priest of our profession.]

X.

THE BIRTH OF JESUS.

(At Bethlehem of Judæa, B. C. 5.)

ᶜ LUKE II. 1-7.

ᶜ **1 Now it came to pass in those days** [the days of the birth of John the Baptist], **there went out a decree** [a law] **from Caesar Augustus** [Octavius, or Augustus, Cæsar was the nephew of and successor to Julius Cæsar. He took the name Augustus in compliment to his own greatness; and our month August is named for him; its old name being Sextilis], **that all the world should be enrolled.** [This enrollment or census was the first step in the process of taxation.] **2 This was the first**

enrollment. [Publius Sulpicius Quirinius was **governor of**
Syria, A. D. 6–11, and made a census of his province at
that time, as Luke well knew (Acts v. 7). We have no other
record showing either his governorship or a census made by
him *at the time of the birth of Christ.* But he was held
in high favor by the Emperor, and was, about the time
of the birth of Christ, carrying on a war just north of
Syria, in Cilicia, and it is therefore easy for us to accept
Luke's statement that as imperial commissioner or as
governor of Syria he made such a census. Quirinius was
doubtless twice governor of Syria, his first term being about
B. C. 5–1. The Greek word *hegemon*, which Luke uses for
governor, would be used for either of the Roman titles; viz.:
Proprætor, or senatorial governor; or Quæstor, or imperial
commissioner. Quirinius may have commenced the enrollment as Quæstor and finished it ten years later as Proprætor.
He was a well-known character in that age. Harsh and
avaricious as a governor, but an able and loyal soldier, earning a Roman triumph for successes in Cilicia, and being honored by a public funeral in A. D. 21] **made when Quirinius
was governor of Syria.** [A Roman province including
all Palestine, and a tract four or five times as large lying
to the northeast of Palestine.] **3 And all went to enroll
themselves** [The enrollment may have had no reference
to taxation. It was more probably to ascertain the military
strength of the various provinces. The Romans enrolled
each person at the place where he was then residing; but
permitted the Jews to thus return to their ancestral or tribal
cities and enroll themselves as citizens of these cities], **every
one to his own city.** [The city where his ancestors had been
settled by Joshua when he divided the land—Josh. xiii.–xviii.]
**4 And Joseph also went up from Galilee, out of the
city of Nazareth** [see ch. i. 26], **unto Judaea, to the city
of David** [after the lapse of ten centuries the name of David
still cast its fragrance over the place of his birth—I. Sam.
xvii. 12], **which is called Bethlehem** [Meaning "house
of bread." It was the later or Jewish name for the old

Canaanitish village of Ephrath, the Ephrath near which Rachel died (Gen. xxxv. 19). It was marked by Micah as the birthplace of Messiah—Mic. v. 2; Matt. ii. 5, 6], **because he was of the house and family of David; 5 to enroll himself with Mary, who was betrothed to him** [see Matt. i. 25], **being great with child. 6 And it came to pass, while they were there, the days were fulfilled that she should be delivered.** [The early Christians made no record of the date of Christ's birth; we find no mention of December 25 earlier than the fourth century. The Eastern church celebrated Christ's birth by a feast called Epiphany, which means manifestation. They chose January 6 as the date for this feast, for they reasoned that if the first Adam was born on the sixth day of creation, the second Adam must have been born on the sixth day of the year! The Western church celebrated Christ's birth on the 25th of December by a feast called Natalis, which means Nativity. But Pope Julius I. (A. D. 337–352) designated December 25 as the proper day, and the Eastern churches soon united with the Western churches in observing this day; and the custom has become universal. We do not observe this day because of the Pope's decree, but because of the tradition on which the Pope's decree was founded.] **7 And she brought forth her firstborn** [This word in no way implies that the Virgin subsequently had other children. Jesus, the only begotten, is also called the firstborn — Heb. i. 6] **son; and she wrapped** [having none to help her, she swathed him in bands with her own hands] **him in swaddling clothes** [the new-born Jewish child was washed in water, rubbed with salt, and then wrapped in bands or blankets, which confined the limbs closely—Ezek. xvi. 4], **and laid him in a manger** [Justin Martyr, who was born about the beginning of the second century and suffered martyrdom A. D. 165, first tells us the tradition that the stable in which Jesus was born was a cavern. Caves, however, were never used for stables except when they opened on the sides of hills. The one at Bethlehem is a cellar fourteen feet under the level

surface. Justin must, therefore, be mistaken], **because
there was no room for them in the inn.** [Eastern inns
had landlords like our own. The inn was full at this time
because of the number who had come to be enrolled.
Inns contained rooms for persons and stalls for animals: there
was no room in the former, but there was in the latter.]

XI.

THE BIRTH OF JESUS PROCLAIMED BY ANGEl S
TO THE SHEPHERDS.

(Near Bethlehem, B. C. 5.)

c LUKE II. 8-20.

᪣**8 And there were shepherds in the same country**
[they were in the same fields from which David had been
called to tend God's Israel, or flock] **abiding in the field,
and keeping watch by night over their flock.** [When
the flock is too far from the village to lead it to the fold at
night, these shepherds still so abide with it in the field, even
in the dead of winter.] **9 And an angel of the Lord
stood by them** [He stood upon the earth at their side, and
did not float above them in the heavens, as he is usually pictured. His standing upon the earth shows a fuller fellowship
and sympathy with men—comp. Acts i. 10], **and the glory
of the Lord shone round about them** [The Shechinah,
or bright cloud, which symbolizes the divine presence (Ex.
xxiv. 16; I. Kings viii. 10; Isa. vi. 1-3; Rom. ix. 4). It was
seen by the three apostles upon the mount of transfiguration
(Matt. xvii. 5), by Stephen (Acts vii. 55), and by Paul—Acts
xxii. 6-11]: **and they were sore afraid. 10 And the
angel said unto them, Be not afraid; for behold, I
bring you good tidings of great joy** [Christianity is a
religion of present joys, and leads onward to joy eternal]
**which shall be to all the people: 11 for there is born
to you** [born as a gift to us—John iii. 16] **this day in the
city of David a Saviour** [the angel omits the name of

Jesus; but gives the meaning of his name], **who is Christ**
[Messiah is the Hebrew and Christ is the Greek for our
English word "anointed." Prophets, priests and kings were
anointed. Jesus held all these three offices for all our race
for all eternity] **the Lord. 12 And this** *is* **the sign** [The
token by which to identify the child. A babe in a manger
was no ordinary sight] **unto you: Ye shall find a babe
wrapped in swaddling clothes, and lying in a manger.**
["What fearful odds! What a strange contrast! Idolatry on
the throne (in the person of Augustus Cæsar), and the founder
of a new religion and a new empire lying in a manger!"]
**13 And suddenly there was with the angel a multi-
tude** [The event was too important to be heralded by any one
angel. All heaven was interested in the departure of its
Prince, and marveled at the grace of the Father who sent him
—I. Pet. i. 12] **of the heavenly host** [God's army (I. Kings
xxii. 19; Ps. xxiii. 20, 21). The Deity is called "God of
Sabaoth"; that is, God of hosts or multitude (Rom. ix. 29;
Jas. v. 4; Dan. vii. 10; Rev. v. 11, 12); but at this time God's
army appeared to announce the coming of eternal peace]
**praising God, and saying, 14 Glory to God in the
highest** [in the highest heavens—Job xvi. 9; Ps. cxlviii. 1],
And on earth peace among men [The angels invoke
blessing on God and peace upon man. Peace between God
and man, and ultimately peace between man and man] **in
whom he is well pleased.** [The love of God is shed
abroad upon all, even the vilest of sinners (Rom. v. 8; I. Tim.
i. 15); but his peace comes upon those who have accepted his
Son, and in whom he is therefore especially well pleased
(Rom. ix. 11). Peace is the unfailing apostolic salutation
toward Christians (Rom. i. 7; I. Cor. i. 3; II. Cor. i. 2, etc.),
and is attainable in the highest degree by Christians only
—John xiv. 27; xvi. 33; Col. iii. 15; Phil. iv. 7.] **15 And
it came to pass, when the angels went away from them
into heaven, the shepherds said one to another, Let us
now go even unto Bethlehem, and see this thing that
is come to pass, which the Lord hath made known**

unto us. **16 And they came with haste, and found both Mary and Joseph, and the babe lying in the manger. 17 And when they saw it, they made known concerning the saying which was spoken to them about the child.** [They were the first evangelists. Among the heralds of Christ we note one great prophet, John the Baptist, and one learned Pharisee, Paul; the rest are shepherds, fishermen, and publicans, yet their gospel has triumphed over the wisdom of men (I. Cor. i. 26–29; II. Cor. iv. 7). The shepherds were moved to publish by the same spirit which actuated the lepers at Samaria—II. Kings vii. 9.] **18 And all that heard it wondered** [the gospel story excites wonder; the more we ponder it the more wonderful it becomes] **at the things which were spoken unto them by the shepherds. 19 But Mary kept all these sayings** [The silence of Mary contrasts with the talkativeness of the shepherds. But it is the duty of Christians both to ponder and to publish], **pondering them in her heart.** [Only Mary could know the fact here stated; and the statement indicates that Luke got the opening parts of his Gospel from the mother of our Lord. She had much to think about. The angelic messages to Zacharias, to herself and to the shepherds were full of significance, and her mind would search diligently to comprehend the fullness of their meaning. In her quiet thoughtfulness the beauty of the Virgin's character shines forth—I. Pet. iii 4.] **20 And the shepherds returned** [they did not make this glorious occasion an excuse for neglecting their humble duties], **glorifying** [because of the greatness of that which had been revealed] **and praising God** [because of the goodness of that which he revealed] **for all the things that they had heard and seen, even as it was spoken unto them.** [Jesus came in exactly the manner in which his coming had been spoken of or described by the angels a few hours before; and also just as his coming had been spoken of or described by the prophets centuries and centuries before. God's word holds good for eternity as truly as for one day. The shepherds doubtless passed to their reward during the thirty years which Jesus spent in seclusion prior to entering upon his ministry. But the rest of their commonplace life was now filled with music of praise, and their night watches lit by the glory of God, which could never entirely fade away.

XII.

CIRCUMCISION, TEMPLE SERVICE AND NAMING OF JESUS.

(The Temple at Jerusalem, B. C. 4.)

ᶜLUKE II. 21–39.

ᶜ**21 And when eight days** [Gen. xvii. 12] **were fulfilled for circumcising him** [The rite was doubtless performed by Joseph. By this rite Jesus was "made like unto his brethren" (Heb. ii. 16, 17); that is, he became a member of the covenant nation, and became a debtor to the law—Gal. v. 3], **his name was called JESUS** [see Luke i. 59], **which was so called by the angel before he was conceived in the womb.** [Luke i. 31.] **22 And when the days of their purification according to the law of Moses were fulfilled** [Purification took place on the fortieth day after the nativity in the case of males, and eighty days in the case of females (Lev. xii. 1–5). Until it was performed the mother was not permitted to go to the temple, take part in any public service, or even to leave her house. It seems that the members of her family were also ceremonially unclean, because they came in daily contact with her], **they brought him up to Jerusalem** [to the temple], **to present him to the Lord** [When God slew the firstborn of Egypt he spared the firstborn of Israel. For this reason all the firstborn cf Israel were regarded as being peculiarly the Lord's (Ex. xii. 29, 30; xiii. 2); and the firstborn male child of each family had to be redeemed with money (Ex. xiii. 11–15; Num. xviii. 15, 16). Originally the firstborn or eldest son was priest of the household after his father's death; but God chose the Levites to serve in his sanctuary in the place of these first-

born or household priests (Num. iii. 11-13; viii. 14-19); but
this choosing did not annul the statute which required the
payment of redemption money. The redemption money for
a male was five shekels of the sanctuary, or about $3.75—Lev.
xxvii. 6]. **23 (as it is written in the law of the Lord**
[for additional passages see Ex. xxii. 29; xxxiv. 19, 20],
**Every male that openeth the womb shall be called
holy to the Lord), 24 and to offer a sacrifice** [By redemption money and sacrifice the life of Jesus was ceremonially redeemed from God the Father, that his consecration of
it to the will of the Father might be perfect. We likewise
are redeemed by the blood of Christ, but are expected never-
**theless to be more consecrated than ever] according to
that which is said in the law of the Lord** [Lev. xii.
6-8; v. 11], **A pair of turtledoves, or two young pigeons.**
[The required offering was a yearling lamb for a burnt offering, and a young pigeon for a sin-offering. But the law
allowed a poor mother to substitute doves or pigeons for the
lamb. We see here an early trace of the poverty of Him who
had not where to lay his head. Knowing the greatness of the
child, Joseph and Mary would never have used the lesser
sacrifice if they could have afforded the regular and more
costly one. Poverty is not dishonorable in God's sight; for
Mary was honored of him above all women.]   **25 And
behold, there was a man in Jerusalem, whose name
was Simeon** [the name means "Hearing." Some think
that it was Rabbi Simeon, the son of the great teacher Hillel;
but the context forbids such an idea]; **and this man was
righteous and devout** [Right in outward and devout in his
inward life. The first prophet to tell the world that its Messiah had come was a thoroughly good man], **looking for**
[Waiting like Jacob (Gen. xlix. 18), and Joseph of Arimathea
(Mark xv. 43), he realized the truth of God's promise (Isa.
xlix. 23). The Jews waited for a coming Prince, local, carnal, finite, temporal; we wait for a KING universal, spiritual,
infinite, eternal, the Son of God. Hence the magnitude of
our expected consolation is to theirs as an ocean is to a drop of

water] **the consolation of Israel** [A common name for the era of the Messiah, which was so called because the advent of the Christ would bring comfort (Isa. xl. 1) to his people. Jews swore by the consolation of Israel, and the phrase, "May I see the consolation of Israel," was common among them. A prayer for the coming of the Messiah was daily used by them]: **and the Holy Spirit was upon him.** [Luke i. 68.] **26 And it had been revealed unto him by the Holy Spirit** [probably in a dream], **that he should not see death before he had seen the Lord's Christ.** [A remarkable favor, a notable blessing—Luke x. 23, 24.] **27 And he came in the Spirit** [moved by the impulses of inspiration—Matt. xxii. 14; Rev. i. 10] **into the temple** [those who go to church perfunctorily see little ; those who go in the Spirit—according to the measure in which He is given them—see and hear much]: **and when the parents brought in the child Jesus, that they might do concerning him after the custom of the law, 28 then he received him into his arms, and blessed God, and said, 29 Now lettest thou thy servant depart** [This hymn of Simeon is called the "*Nunc Dimittis*," from the two words with which the Latin translation of it begins. Simeon regards his death as now near, since he had seen that for which God had kept him alive. He represents himself as a sentinel who, seeing the rising of the day-star which is the signal that his watch is relieved, knows his weary waiting is at an end], **Lord, According to thy word** [God keeps his word, and never disappoints], **in peace** [to the living the Jews said, "Go to peace" (Leshalom), as Jethro said to Moses; to the dying they said, "Go in peace" (Beshalom)— Gen. xv. 15] ; **30 For mine eyes have seen thy salvation** [Only the eye which sees Christ is satisfied with seeing (Eccl. i. 18). To one who has Christ in his arms and salvation before his eyes the world looks poor indeed, and the loss of it appears gain—Phil. i. 21], **31 Which thou hast prepared** [God prepared the gospel in his counsels before Christ came into the world (Acts ii. 23), and foretold it by the proph-

ets—Acts iii. 18] **before the face of all peoples** [T
Jewish Scriptures were then scattered among all nations, a
all people were acquainted with the Hebrew expectations o
Messiah. Simeon saw in the Babe the initial step of G
toward fulfilling all these prophecies] ; **32 A light for reve**
tion [A reference to Isa. xlix. 6. Christ's light has reveal
the Father to the Gentiles. That Simeon should prophesy t
is an evidence of the large spiritual knowledge given hi
since even the apostles were slow to grasp the fullness
Christ's world-wide mission—see Ps. xcviii. 2, 3; Isa. lii.
xlii. 6] **to the Gentiles, And the glory** [Isa. xlv.
Israel is doubly glorified in Jesus, in that God chose this peo
to receive the Word, or divine Son, and in that Jesus, as a Je
presented to the world the picture of the perfect manho
In his divinity and his humanity Jesus glorified Israel] **of t**
people Israel. [The Gentiles and Israel are here co
trasted. The Gentiles refused the knowledge of God (Ro
i. 28), and Israel abused it (Rom. iii. 1-9.] **33 And**
father and his mother were marvelling at the thin
which were spoken concerning him [Not because th
heard anything which was really new, but because the wor
caused them to see the truth in a new way. They were al
doubtless surprised to find that an utter stranger should spe
thus about the child. Such manifestations of inspiration we
no more common then than now] ; **34 and Simeon bless**
them [While blessing the parents, he refrained from blessi
the child, lest it might appear that he did it as a superi
He could bless God in the heavens (see verse 28) without fe
of being misunderstood; but to bless this little Babe mig
seem to be presumptuous], **and said unto Mary his mot**
[thus distinguishing between Mary the real parent, a
Joseph the supposed one], **Behold, this *child* is set** [eit
as a stone of stumbling (Isa. viii. 14; Rom. ix. 32, 33; I. C
i. 23), or a precious cornerstone (I. Pet. ii. 7, 8; Acts iv.
I. Cor. iii. 11). Jesus is the cornerstone of true religi
Those who reject him fall over him and are broken; th
who accept him, build upon him, and are lifted up and edifie

for the falling and the rising of many in Israel [Jesus
has always wrought changes which are like fallings and ris-
ings. In his own earthly lifetime Pharisees, Herodians, Sadducees, Nazarenes, Gadarenes, etc., sank down before his
example and teaching; while fishermen, publicans and outcasts were elevated and encouraged by his sympathy. In the
ecclesiastical field Jesus has brought down the powers of
superstition and priestcraft, and exalted the common worshiper, giving him liberty of conscience. In the political
field Jesus has brought down the pride of kings and lifted up
the common people, and given them sovereign powers. In
the spiritual realm this work of Jesus is most clearly displayed.
Not only did he bring down the pride of Judah and lift up the
despised Gentiles (Rom. xi. 25); but he has worked a leveling
and a lifting work in the life of each of his followers. Those
proud of their manhood, he has made as children, that they
might become truly men (Matt. xviii. 3); those wise in their
own conceit, he approaches with the foolishness of preaching,
that they may become instructed in the true learning (I. Cor.
i. 26-31); those strong in self-confidence, he makes weak, that
he may fill them with the divine power (II. Cor. xii. 10; Phil.
iv. 13). Like Paul, we fall and rise in Christ—Acts ix. 4-6];
and for a sign [Something which challenges attention, and
is full of significant meaning. Signs were intended to allay
controversy, and to exclude contradiction, but Jesus provoked
both. When he was thus first in the temple, opposition was
prophesied; when he was last there it was fully realized—
Matt. xxiii. 38] **which is spoken against** [during his
earthly lifetime Jesus was called "deceiver," "Samaritan,"
"demoniac," etc., and subsequently his followers were abused
(Acts xxviii. 22); later the Jews wrote of him as "the
deceiver," "that man" and "the hung." Early Christians
were charged by the pagans with committing cannibalism,
incest, and every conceivable atrocity, and in this day "Christian" is—after Jew—the most stinging term of reproach
known to the Eastern tongue]; **35 yea and a sword shall
pierce through thine own soul** [Simeon had read and un-

derstood the prophecies which told of the suffering Messiah (Isa. xlii. 14-xliii. 12). Hence, to prepare the soul of Mary he touches this minor chord. By as much as the prophecies and annunciations concerning Jesus, led Mary to expect honor and glory for her son; by so much did the rejection, persecution and cruel death of Jesus overwhelm her with piercing anguish and disappointment. It is also probable that at the time of the crucifixion Mary shared with the apostles the doubts as to the mission of Jesus, and these doubts must have been unspeakably bitter to her]; **that thoughts out of many hearts may be revealed.** [The word here trans-lated " thoughts " is generally used to signify bad or evil thoughts. Jesus often revealed such (John ix. 16); but the context shows that Simeon had in mind the evil thoughts which were revealed by the sufferings inflicted on Christ. The human heart is desperately wicked (Jer. xvii. 9); but its wickedness was never more manifest than when it chose a murderer and crucified its Creator (Acts iii. 14, 15). Men are still revealed by their attitude toward Christ, the sincere being drawn to him, and the hypocrites being repelled from him. But at the judgment he shall shine forth as the perfect revealer of all thoughts and actions—Matt. x. 26.] **36 And there was one Anna** [the same name as Hannah (I. Sam. i. 10), meaning "He was gracious"], **a prophetess** [like Miriam, Deborah, Huldah—II. Chron. xxxiv. 22], **the daugh-ter of Phanuel** [the same as Peniel, meaning " Face of God"—Gen. xxxii. 30], **of the tribe of Asher** [Asher was the second son of Jacob and Zilpah (Gen. xxx. 12, 13). The name means "happy." Though the ten tribes were lost and scattered, many individuals belonging to them remained in Judah—Acts xxvi. 7; Jas. i. 1] **(she was of a great age, having lived with a husband seven years from her vir-ginity, 37 and she had been a widow even unto four-score and four years)** [She had been married seven years, and was now eighty-four years old. Her long widowhood is mentioned, because young widows who did not remarry were held in especial honor. Anna was about twenty-four years

old when Jerusalem was conquered by Pompey, and came
under the power of Rome], **who departed not from the
temple** [This may simply mean that she was unusually assidu-
ous in her attendance at all the temple services (Acts ii. 46);
or it may be taken literally, in which case we may suppose
that her prophetic talents had secured for her the right of
living in one of the temple chambers. Those who patiently
frequent God's house will sooner or later obtain a blessing],
worshipping with fastings [Moses appointed one yearly
fast; viz.: that on the day of Atonement; but the Pharisees
introduced the custom of fasting twice a week, to commem-
orate the days when Moses was supposed to have ascended
and descended Mt. Sinai; viz.: on Monday and Thursday.
They had also otherwise multiplied the fasts—Luke v. 33] **and
supplications night and day.** [In Hebrew idiom night is
mentioned before day, following the example of Moses (Gen.
i. 5). The Hebrew theory that "God made the world in six
days and seven nights," may have given birth to this idiom.
For instances of this idiom see Acts xxvi. 7; I. Tim. v. 5.
There were probably night services of sacred music held in
the temple, at which priests sung anthems—Ps. cxxxiv. 1, 2;
cxix. 62.] **38 And coming up at that very hour she
gave thanks unto God, and spake of him** [Jesus] **to all
them that were looking for the redemption of Jerusalem.   39 And when they** [the parents of Jesus] **had
accomplished all things that were according to the
law of the Lord, they returned.** [Luke here adds the
words "into Galilee, to their own city, Nazareth." We have
omitted these words from the text here, and carried them forward to Section XV., where they rightfully belong.   Luke
omits to tell that Jesus returned to Nazareth by way of Bethlehem and Egypt.   Such omissions are common in all biog-
raphies, and this one is paralleled by Luke himself in his life
of Paul.   Compare Acts ix. 19-26 with Gal. i. 17, 18.]

XIII.

EASTERN WISE-MEN OR MAGI VISIT JESUS, THE NEW-BORN KING.

(Jerusalem and Bethlehem, B. C. 4.)

^aMATT. II. 1–12.

^a1 Now when Jesus was born in Bethlehem [It lies five miles south by west of Jerusalem, a little to the east of the road to Hebron. It occupies part of the summit and sides of a narrow limestone ridge which shoots out eastward from the central chain of the Judæan mountains, and breaks down abruptly into deep valleys on the north, south and east. Its old name, Ephrath, meant "the fruitful." Bethlehem means "house of bread." Its modern name, Beitlahm, means "house of meat." It was the home of Boaz and Ruth, of Jesse and David. The modern town contains about five hundred houses, occupied by Greek-church Christians. Over the rock-hewn cave which monks point out as the stable where Christ was born, there stands a church built by the Empress Helena, A. D. 325–327, which is the oldest monument to Christ known to men. Bethlehem was a suitable birthplace for a spiritual king; as suitable as Rome would have been for a temporal king. We do not know when the town received its name, nor by whom the name was given, but as God had chosen it as the birthplace of Jesus for many centuries before the incarnation, he may have caused it to be named Bethlehem, or "house of bread," with prophetic reference to Him who is the "Bread of Life"] of Judaea [called thus to distinguish it from Bethlehem of Zebulon —Josh. xix. 15] in the days [It is difficult to determine the exact year of Christ's birth. Dionysius the Small, an abbot at Rome, in A. D. 526, published an Easter cycle, in which he fixed the birth of Christ in the year 754 of the city of Rome (A. U. C.). This date has been followed ever since. But Jesus was born before the death of Herod, and Josephus

and Dion Cassius fix the death of Herod in the year 750
A. U. C. Herod died that year, just before the Passover,
and shortly after an eclipse of the moon, which took place on
the night between the 12th and 13th of March. Jesus was
born several months previous to the death of Herod, either
toward the end of the year 749 A. U. C. (B. C. 5), or at the
beginning of the year 750—B. C. 4] **of Herod** [This man
was born at Ascalon, B. C. 71, and died at Jericho, A. D. 4.
His father was an Edomite, and his mother an Ishmaelite.
He was a man of fine executive ability and dauntless courage,
but was full of suspicion and duplicity, and his reign was
stained by acts of inhuman cruelty. He enlarged and
beautified the temple at Jerusalem, and blessed his kingdom
by many other important public works] **the king** [The life
of Herod will be found in Josephus' Antiquities, Books 14–17.
He was not an independent monarch, but a king subject to the
Roman Empire], **behold, Wise**-**men** [This word designates
an order, or caste, of priests and philosophers (called magi),
which existed in the countries east of the Euphrates, from
a very remote period. We first find the word in Scripture at
Jer. xxxix. 13, in the name rab-mag, which signifies chief magi.
This class is frequently referred to in the Book of Daniel,
where its members are called magicians, and it is probable
that Daniel himself was a rab-mag (Dan. v. 11). The order
is believed to have arisen among the Chaldeans and to have
come down through the Assyrian, Medean and Persian kingdoms. The magi were, in many ways, the Levites of the
East; they performed all public religious rites, claimed exclusive mediatorship between God and man, were the authority on
all doctrinal points, constituted the supreme council of the
realm, and had charge of the education of the royal family.
They practiced divination, interpreted auguries and dreams,
and professed to foretell the destinies of men. They were
particularly famous for their skill in astronomy, and had kept
a record of the more important celestial phenomena, which
dated back several centuries prior to the reign of Alexander
the Great. They were probably originally honest seekers

after truth, but degenerated into mere imposters, as the Bible record shows (Acts viii. 9-11 and xiii. 8). Nothing is said as to the number who came nor as to the country from whence they came. The number and quality of the gifts has become the foundation for a tradition that they were three kings from Arabia, and during the Middle Ages it was professed that their bodies were found and removed to the cathedral at Cologne. Their shrine is still shown there to credulous travelers, and their names are given as Caspar, Melchior and Balthazar] **from the east** [Probably from Persia, the chief seat of the Median religion. Jews dwelling in Persian provinces among the Parthians, Medes and Elamites (Acts ii. 9) may have so prepared the minds of the magi as to set them looking for the star of Bethlehem. But in addition to the knowledge carried by captive Israelites, the men of the East had other light. The great Chinese sage, Confucius (B. C. 551–479), foretold a coming Teacher in the West, and Zoroaster, the founder of the Persian religion, who is thought to have been a contemporary of Abraham, had predicted the coming of a great, supernaturally begotten Prophet. To these Balaam had added his prophecy (Num. xxiv. 17). Moreover, the Septuagint translation made at Alexandria about 280 B. C. had rendered the Old Testament Scriptures into Greek, the language of commerce, and had carried the knowledge of Hebrew prophecy into all lands, and had wakened a slight but world-wide expectation of a Messiah. The Roman writers, Suetonius (70–123, A. D.) and Tacitus (75–125, A. D.) bear witness to this expectation that a great world-ruling king would come out of Judæa. But all this put together can not account for the visit of the magi. They were guided directly by God, and nothing else may have even influenced them] **came to Jerusalem** [They naturally sought for the ruler of the state at the state's capital. They came to Jerusalem after Jesus had been presented in the temple, and taken back to Bethlehem, and, therefore, when the infant Jesus was more than forty days old. They must have come at least forty days before the death

of Herod, for he spent the last forty days of his life
at Jericho and the baths of Callirrhoe; but the wise men
found him still at Jerusalem. Jesus must, therefore, have
been at least eighty days old when Herod died], **saying,
2 Where is he** [They seem to have expected to find all
Jerusalem knowing and worshiping this new-born King.
Their disappointment is shared by many modern converts from
heathendom who visit so-called Christian countries, and are
filled with astonishment and sadness at the ignorance and
unbelief which they discover] **that is born King of the
Jews?** [These words were calculated to startle Herod, who
was by birth neither king nor Jew. This title was accorded
to Jesus by Pilate, who wrote it in his inscription, and caused
it to be placed over the head of Christ upon the cross. None
has borne the title since; so Jesus has stood before the world
for nearly two thousand years as the last and only king of the
Jews. The king of the Jews was the prophetically announced
ruler of all men] **for we saw** [Those in the pagan darkness of the East rejoiced in the star. It was as a light that
shineth in a dark place (II. Pet. i. 10). But those in Jerusalem appear not to have seen it, and certainly ignored it] **his
star** [The great astronomer Kepler, ascertaining that there was
a conjunction of the planets Jupiter and Saturn in 747 A. U.
C., to which conjunction the planet Mars was also added in
the year 748, suggested that this grouping of stars may have
formed the so-called star of Bethlehem. But this theory is
highly improbable; for these planets never appeared as one
star, for they were never nearer to each other than double
the apparent diameter of the moon. Moreover, the magi
used the word " *aster*," star, not " *astron*," a group of stars.
Again, the action of the star of Bethlehem forbids us to think
that it was any one of the ordinary heavenly bodies. It was
a specially prepared luminous orb moving toward Bethlehem
as a guiding sign, and resting over the house of Joseph as an
identifying index] **in the east** [the magi were in the east,
the star was in the west], **and are come** [if the reign of
Edomite Herod began to fulfill the first part of Jacob's

prophecy by showing the departure of the scepter from Judah (Gen. xlix. 10), the coming of the Gentile magi began the fulfillment of the second part by becoming the firstfruits of the gathering of the people] **to worship him.** [Was their worship a religious service or a mere expression of reverence for an earthly king? More likely the former. If so, the boldness with which they declared their purpose to worship proved them worthy of the benediction of Him who afterwards said, "And blessed is he whosoever shall find no occasion of stumbling in me."] **3 And when Herod the king heard it** [his evil heart, full of suspicions of all kinds, caused him to keep Jerusalem full of spies; so that knowledge of the magi soon reached his ears], **he was troubled, and all Jerusalem with him.** [Herod was troubled because his succession to the throne was threatened, and Jerusalem was troubled because it dreaded a conflict between rival claimants for the throne. A short time before this, certain Pharisees had predicted that "God had decreed that Herod's government should cease, and his posterity should be deprived of it." In consequence, six thousand Pharisees had refused to take the oath of allegiance to Herod, and a great commotion had ensued (Josephus xvii. 2, 4). Herod was determined to maintain his rule at any cost. To secure himself against the claims of the house of the Maccabees, he had slain five of its princes and princesses, including his favored wife Mariamne, thus extirpating that line of pretenders. Of course, prophecy predicted that Messiah should have the kingdom; but Herod's sinful heart hoped that these prophecies would not be fulfilled in his own time. Modern Herods know concerning Christ's second coming, but hope that it will be postponed till their own career is finished. Modern Jerusalemites prefer their Herods with peace to Messiah with revolution. Multitudes rest under the dominion of Satan, because they fear the revolutionary conflict and struggle necessary to enthrone the Christ in his stead. Christ is the peace of the righteous, the trouble of the wicked. Imperfect knowledge of him troubles, but perfect knowledge and love cast out fear—I. John iv. 18.] **4 And gathering**

together all the chief priests and scribes of the people
[This is one of several expressions which designate the whole
of or a portion of the Sanhedrin or Jewish court. This body
consisted of seventy-one or seventy-two members, divided
into three classes; namely, chief priests, scribes, or lawyers,
and elders, or men of age and reputation among the people.
The Sanhedrin was probably formed in imitation of the body
of elders appointed to assist Moses (Num. xi. 16). It is
thought to have been instituted after the Babylonian captivity.
As the scribes transcribed the Scriptures they were naturally
familiar with their contents, and well skilled in their inter-
pretation], **he inquired of them** [Herod shows that common
but strange mixture of regard and contempt for the word of
God which makes men anxious to know its predictions, that
they may form their plans to defeat them. The first inquirers
for Jesus were shepherds, the second were wise men, the third
was a king, the fourth were scribes and priests. He wakens
inquiry among all classes; but each uses a different means of
research. The shepherds are directed by angels; the wise
men by a star; the scribes by Scripture; the king by counsel-
ors] **where the Christ** [the fact that these foreigners came
thus wondrously guided, coupled with the fact that the King
they sought was one by birth (David's line having been so
long apparently extinct), led Herod to the conclusion that this
coming King could be none other than the Messiah] **should
be born.** [Thus, by light from different sources, king and
priests and people were informed of the fact that Messiah was
newly born into the world, and the very time and place of his
birth were brought to notice. God gave them the fact, and
left them to make such use of it as they would.] **5 And
they said unto him, In Bethlehem** [It was generally known
that Christ should be born in Bethlehem (John vii. 42). The
very body or court which officially announced the birthplace
of Jesus subsequently condemned him to death as an imposter]
of Judaea: for thus it is written [The quotation which
follows in the sixth verse is taken from Mic. v. 2–4, but is
freely translated. The translation sets the words of Micah in

the language of the times of Herod, and therefore resembles some of our modern attempts at Biblical revision. The use which the scribes made of this prophecy is very important, for it shows that the Jews originally regarded this passage of Scripture as fixing the birthplace of Messiah, and condemns as a fruit of bigotry and prejudice the modern effort of certain rabbis to explain away this natural interpretation] **through the prophet, 6 And thou Bethlehem, land of Judah, Art in no wise least among the princes of Judah: For out of thee shall come forth a governor, Who shall be shepherd of my people Israel. 7 Then Herod privily** [Herod did not wish to give the infant claimant the honor and prestige of an open and avowed concern about him. Moreover, had he openly professed a desire to worship the new King, all Jerusalem would have been conscious of his hypocrisy, and some would have found it hard to keep silent] **called the Wise-men, and learned of them** [Though Herod sought Christ from improper motives, yet he used the best methods. He asked aid of those versed in the Scriptures, and also of those proficient in science] **exactly what time the star appeared.** [That he might ascertain, if possible, exactly on what night Christ had been born.] **8 And he sent them to Bethlehem** [thus answering their question asked in verse 2], **and said, Go and search out exactly concerning the young child; and when ye have found** *him*, **bring me word, that I also may come and worship him.** [His meaning was, That I may come with my Judas kiss to betray and to destroy. Duplicity was a well-known characteristic of Herod. He had Aristobulus, the high priest, drowned by his companions while bathing, though they seemed to be only ducking him in sport. In this case Herod concealed fraud beneath an appearance of piety. Religion is one of the favorite masks of the devil (II. Cor. xi. 13–15). It is as hard for the ambitious to avoid hypocrisy as it is for the rich to shun avarice.] **9 And they, having heard the king, went their way** [No scribes were with them. The scribes were content with the *theory* as to the place of

Christ's birth, but desired no practical knowledge of the Babe himself]; **and lo, the star, which they saw in the east, went before them** [guiding them], **till it came and stood** [thus stopping them] **over where the young child was.** [A real or ordinary star would have stood indiscriminately over every house in Bethlehem, and would have been no aid whatever toward finding the right child. For planets to stand over any place, they must be in the zenith and have an altitude of ninety degrees. This star, therefore, could not have been a conjunction of planets, for their altitude at Bethlehem is fifty-seven degrees, and seen at this angle they would have led the magi on down into Africa. The magi were undoubtedly favored with a special revelation as to the Babe and the star. It was probably given in a dream similar to that spoken of in verse 12. The star, as one of the temporary incidentals of Christianity, faded away; but the Sun of righteousness which took its place in the spiritual firmament shines on, and shall shine on forever.] **10 And when they saw the star, they rejoiced** [a comfort restored is a comfort multiplied] **with exceeding great joy.** [The return of the star assured them that God would lead them safely and surely to the object of their desires. Their joy was such as comes to those who come from seasons of dark doubt to the glories of light and faith. The star enabled them to find Jesus without asking questions, and bringing such public attention to him as would aid Herod in preventing his escape. Since the magi were guided by a star, they were forced to enter Bethlehem by night, and this contributed to the privacy of their coming and the safety of Jesus.] **11 And they came into the house** [the humble home of the carpenter might have shook their faith in the royalty of the son, but the miraculous honors accorded him in the star and the Scripture raised him in their estimation above all the humiliation of external circumstances], **and saw the young child with Mary his mother** [she was the only attendant in this King's retinue—the retinue of him who became poor that we, out of his poverty, might be made rich]; **and they**

fell down [the usual Oriental method of showing **either rev-erence or worship**] **and worshipped him** [It is safe to think that the manner in which they had been led to Jesus caused them to worship him as divine. Their long journey and their exuberant joy at its success indicate that they sought more than the great king of a foreign nation. The God who led them by a star, would hardly deny them full knowledge as to the object of their quest. Had their worship been mere rever-ence, Mary would, no doubt, have been included in it. We should note their faith. They had known Christ but one day; he had performed no miracles; he had none other to do him homage; he was but a helpless Babe, yet they fell down and worshiped him. Their faith is told for a memorial of them. They worshiped him not as one who must win his honors; but as one already invested with them. When we come to Christ let us come to worship, not to patronize, not to employ him for sectarian uses, not to use him as an axiom on which to base some vapid theological speculation]; **and opening their treasures, they offered unto him gifts** [Oriental custom requires that an inferior shall approach his superior with a gift. These gifts probably contributed to the sustenance of the parents and the child while in Egypt], **gold and frankin-cense** [A white resin or gum obtained by slitting the bark of the *Arbor thuris*. The best is said to come from Persia. It is also a product of Arabia. It is very fragrant when burned] **and myrrh.** [It also is obtained from a tree in the same manner as frankincense. The tree is similar to the acacia. It grows from eight to ten feet high, and is thorny. It is found in Egypt, Arabia and Abyssinia. Myrrh means bitterness. The gum was chiefly used in embalming dead bodies, as it prevented putrefaction. It was also used in oint-ments, and for perfume; and as an anodyne it was sometimes added to wine.] **12 And being warned** *of God* **in a dream** [this suggests that as they came by night, so they were aroused and caused to depart by night, that their coming and going might, in no way, betray the whereabouts of the infant King] **that they should not return to Herod, they de-**

parted into their own country another way. [They took the road from Bethlehem to Jericho, and thus passed eastward without returning to Jerusalem.]

XIV.

FLIGHT INTO EGYPT AND SLAUGHTER OF THE BETHLEHEM CHILDREN.

(Bethlehem and Road thence to Egypt, B. C. 4.)

ᵃ MATT. ii. 13–18.

ᵃ **13 Now when they were departed** [The text favors the idea that the arrival and departure of the magi and the departure of Joseph for Egypt, all occurred in one night. If so, the people of Bethlehem knew nothing of these matters], **behold, an angel of the Lord appeareth to Joseph in a dream, saying, Arise** [this command calls for immediate departure] **and take the young child and his mother, and flee into Egypt** [This land was ever the refuge of Israel when fleeing from famine and oppression. One hundred miles in a direct line from Bethlehem would carry Joseph well over the border of Egypt. Two hundred miles would bring him to the river Nile. In Egypt he would find friends, possibly acquaintances. There were at that time about one million Jews in the Nile valley. In Alexandria, a city of 300,000, from one-fifth to two-fifths of the population were Jews, two of the five wards being given over to them; and the Talmud describes how, in its great synagogue, all the men of like craft or trade sat together. Thus Joseph might there find fellow-craftsmen, as did Paul in Corinth—Acts xviii. 3], **and be thou there until I tell thee: for Herod will seek the young child to destroy him.** [Thus joy at the honor of the magi's visit and worship gives place to terror at the wrath of Herod. The quiet days at Bethlehem are followed by a night of fear and flight. The parents of Jesus were experiencing those conflicting joys and sorrows which characterize the lives of all who have to do with Christ—Mark. x. 30; II.

Tim. iii. 12.] **14 And he arose and took the young child and his mother by night, and departed into Egypt** [What a criticism upon Israel when Egypt, the house of bondage, the seat of tyranny, the land of the immemorial enemies of God's people, was regarded as a place of refuge from its ruler. Jesus was saved by flight. God invariably prefers the ordinary to the extraordinary means]; **15 and was there until the death of Herod** [as Herod died soon after the flight into Egypt, the sojourn of the family of Jesus in that land must have been brief, for they returned after his death] : **that it might be fulfilled which was spoken by the Lord** [the message is the Lord's, the words and voice are the prophet's] **through the prophet** [see Hos. xi. 1], **saying, Out of Egypt did I call my son.** [This prophecy, no doubt, had a primary reference to the Exodus, and was an echo of the words of Moses at Ex. iv. 22, 23. In their type and antitype relationship the Old and New Testaments may be likened to the shell and kernel of a nut. Israel was Israel, and God's Son, because it included in itself the yet unformed and unborn body which was later to be inhabited by the spirit of the Word or Son of God. The seed of Abraham was called out of Egypt, that the promised seed enveloped within it might have a body and nature prepared in the land of liberty, and not in that of bondage. Israel was the outer shell, and Christ the kernel, hence the double significance of the prophecy—the twice repeated movement of the nation and the Man.] **16 Then Herod, when he saw that he was mocked** [the magi, no doubt, intended to return to Herod, and would have done so but for the dream, but when they failed to return, they seemed to Herod to have taken pleasure in deceiving him, and the very honesty of their conduct passed for the lowest depth of cunning] **of the Wise-men, was exceeding wroth** [wroth at being made sport of, and doubly wroth because of the serious matter as to which they presumed to jest], **and sent forth** [murderers, suddenly], **and slew** [Thus early did persecution attend those associated with Christ (Matt. x. 24, 25). This brutality was in keeping with

Herod's character. Jealousy as to his authority led him to murder two high priests, his uncle Joseph, his wife, and three of his own sons, besides many other innocent persons. Fearing lest the people should rejoice at his departure, he summoned the leading citizens out of all the cities of his realm, and, shutting them up in the circus grounds at Jericho, ordered his sister Salome and her husband to have them all put to death at the moment when he died, that the land might mourn at his death] **all the male children that were in Bethlehem** [As Bethlehem was not a large place, the number of martyrs could not have been large. It is variously estimated that from twelve to fifty were slain. Had the parents of Bethlehem known that Jesus was on the way to Egypt, they might have saved their own children by giving information as to the whereabouts of the right child; that is, if we may assume that they were told why their children were being butchered], **and in all the borders** [Adjacent places; settlements or houses around Bethlehem. The present population of the town is fully five thousand; it was probably even larger in Christ's time] **thereof, from two years old and under** [according to Jewish reckoning this would mean all children from birth up to between twelve and thirteen months old, all past one year old being counted as two years old], **according to the time which he had exactly learned of the Wise-men.** [That is, he used their date as a basis for his calculations. It is likely that six months had elapsed since the star appeared, and that Herod doubled the months to make doubly sure of destroying the rival claimant. Not knowing whether the child was born before or after the appearing of the star, he included all the children of that full year in which the star came.] **17 Then was fulfilled** [Verses 6, 15 and 18 give us three different kinds of prophecy. The first is direct, and relates wholly to an event which was yet future; the second is a case where an *act* described is symbolic of another later and larger act; the last is a case where *words* describing one act may be taken as fitly and vividly describing another later act, though the acts them-

selves may bear small resemblance.   Matthew does not mean
that Jeremiah predicted the slaughter at Bethlehem ; but that
his words, though spoken as to another occasion, were so
chosen of the Spirit that they might be fitly applied to this latter occasion] **that which was spoken through Jeremiah
the prophet** [Jer. xxxi. 15], **saying, 18 A voice was
heard in Ramah** [This word means " highland " or " hill."
The town lies six miles north of Jerusalem.   It was the birthplace and burial-place of the prophet Samuel.   It is also supposed to be the Aramathea of the New Testament. See Matt.
xxvii. 57], **Weeping and great mourning, Rachel weeping for her children** [Why these tearful mothers in Bethlehem ?   Because that which Christ escaped remained for his
brethren, their children, to suffer.   If he would escape death,
all his brethren must die.   But he died that all his brethren
might live] ; **And she would not be comforted, because
they are not.**   [The words here quoted were originally written concerning the Babylonish captivity (Jer. xxxi. 15).
Ramah was a town of Benjamin (Josh. xviii. 25).   Jeremiah
was carried thither in chains with the other captives, but was
there released by order of Nebuchadnezzar (Jer. xl. 1 ; xxxix.
11, 12).   Here he saw the captives depart for Babylon, and
heard the weeping of the poor who were left in the land
(xxxix. 10) ; hence the mention of Ramah as the place of
lamentation.   He represents Rachel as weeping, because the
Benjamites were descendants of Rachel, and, perhaps, because the tomb of Rachel was "in the border of Benjamin,"
and not far away (I. Sam. x. 2).   The image of the ancient
mother of the tribe rising from her tomb to weep, and refusing to be comforted because her children were not around her,
is inimitably beautiful ; and this image so strikingly portrayed
the weeping in Bethlehem that Matthew adopts the words of
the prophet, and says that they were here fulfilled.   It was the
fulfillment, not of a prediction, properly speaking, but of certain *words* spoken by the prophet.]

XV.

THE CHILD JESUS BROUGHT FROM EGYPT TO NAZARETH.

(Egypt and Nazareth, B. C. 4.)

ᵃ MATT. II. 19–23; ᶜ LUKE II. 39.

ᵃ **19 But when Herod was dead** [He died in the thirty-seventh year of his reign and the seventieth of his life. A frightful inward burning consumed him, and the stench of his sickness was such that his attendants could not stay near him. So horrible was his condition that he even endeavored to end it by suicide], **behold, an angel of the Lord** [word did not come by the infant Jesus; he was "made like unto his brethren" (Heb. ii. 17), and being a child, "he spake as a child" (I. Cor. xiii. 11), and not as an oracle] **appeareth in a dream to Joseph in Egypt** [Joseph had obeyed the command given at verse 13, and God kept the promise contained therein. God ever keeps covenant with the obedient], **saying, 20 Arise** [Happy Joseph! his path was ordered of God. Let us also seek such ordering. "In all thy ways acknowledge him, And he will direct thy paths"— Prov. iii. 6] **and take the young child and his mother, and go into the land of Israel** [The phrase "land of Israel" originally meant all Palestine, but during the period of the kingdom of the ten tribes it was restricted to their portion of the country. After the captivities and the return of Judah from Babylon the phrase resumed its original meaning, and hence it is here used to include all Palestine. As Jesus "was not sent but unto the lost sheep of the house of Israel" (Matt. xxv. 24), it was fitting that he return thither from Egypt]; **for they** ["They" is doubtless the plural of majesty ; though it may include others unknown to us, who were employed by him or advised him] **are dead** [How prophetic the words! Christ's enemies die, but he lives on. How innumerable this host of opposers! Persecutors, oppressors, infidels, critics, literatures, organiza-

tions, principalities and powers, a vast and motley array of
forces, have sought the life of Jesus, have made a great noise
in the world, and died away in silence.   Pharaohs, Neros,
Diocletians, many a Charles, Torquemada and Bloody Mary
have come up and gone down, but the King of Israel lives on]
**that sought the young child's life. 21 And he arose
and took the young child and his mother, and came**
[The length of his sojourn in Egypt is uncertain. It is variously estimated at from two weeks to more than seven months]
into the land of Israel. 22 But when he heard [Joseph
heard this on entering Palestine.   As he knew of Herod's
death by revelation, and hence before any one else in Egypt,
there was no one there to tell him who succeeded Herod]
that Archelaus [By his last will and testament Herod
divided his kingdom among three of his sons, and Augustus
Cæsar consented to the provisions of this will.   Archelaus,
under the title of Ethnarch, received Judæa, Idumæa and
Samaria; Antipas, under title of Tetrarch, received Galilee
and Peræa; and Philip, under title of Tetrarch, received
Trachonitis (with Ituræa), Batanæa and Auranitis.   Each of
these sons bore the name of Herod, like their father.   Augustus withheld from Archelaus the title of king, promising it to
him " if he governed that part virtuously."   But in the very
beginning of his reign he massacred three thousand Jews at
once, in the temple, at the time of the Passover, because they
called for justice upon the agents who performed the barbar-
ities of his father's reign.   Not long after this a solemn embassy of the Jews went to Rome, and petitioned Augustus to
remove Archelaus, and make his kingdom a Roman province.
After a reign of nine years, Archelaus was banished to
Vienne, in Gaul, where he died A. D. 6.   After him Judæa
had no more native kings, and the scepter was clean departed
from Judah.   The land became a Roman province, and its
governors were successively Quirinius, Coponius, Ambivius,
Annius Rufus, Valerius Gratus and Pontius Pilate] **was
reigning over Judaea in the room of his father Herod**
[These words sound like an echo of those employed by the

embassy just referred to, for it said to Augustus concerning this man, "He seemed to be so afraid lest he should not be deemed Herod's own son, that he took special care to prove it"], **he was afraid to go thither** [As Matthew has spoken of Joseph residing at Bethlehem (and he did reside there for quite awhile after the birth of Jesus), the use of the word "thither" implies that Joseph planned to return to that town. Mary had kindred somewhere in the neighborhood (Luke i. 36, 39, 40), and doubtless both parents thought that David's city was the most fitting place for the nurture of David's heir]; **and being warned of God in a dream** [God permitted Joseph to follow the bent of his fear. Joseph's obedience shows him a fit person for the momentous charge entrusted to him], {c **they returned**} a **he withdrew** [From the territory of Archelaus to that of Antipas, who was a man of much milder disposition. As the brothers were on no good terms, Joseph felt sure that in no case would Antipas deliver him and his to Archelaus] **into the parts of Galilee** [It means "circuit." It is the northern of the three divisions of the Holy Land. Its population was very dense, and was a mixture of Jews and Gentiles. Hence all Galileans were despised by the purer Jews of Judæa], **23 and came and dwelt in a city called Nazareth ;** c **their own city** [This town lies on a hillside, girt in by fifteen higher hills. It is a secluded nook. Here Jesus grew up in obscurity till he reached his thirtieth year. Here he spent about nine-tenths of his earthly life. Sweet humility! Lowliness is as rare and precious a virtue as pride is a plentiful and repugnant vice] a **that it might be fulfilled which was spoken through the prophets** [Matthew uses the plural, "prophets," because this prophecy is not the actual words of any prophet, but is the general sense of many of them. We have noted three kinds of prophecy; this is the fourth kind, viz.: one where the very trend or general scope of Scripture is itself a prophecy], **that he should be called a Nazarene.** [The Hebrew word *netzer* means "branch" or "sprout." It is used figuratively for that which is lowly or despised (Isa. xiv. 9; Ezek. xv. 1–6; Mal. iv. 1).

See also John xv. 6; Rom. xi. 21. Now, Nazareth, if derived
from *netzer*, answered to its name, and was a despised place
(John i. 45, 46), and Jesus, though in truth a Bethlehemite,
bore the name Nazarene because it fitly expressed the contempt of those who despised and rejected him.]

XVI.

JESUS LIVING AT NAZARETH AND VISITING JERUSALEM IN HIS TWELFTH YEAR.

(Nazareth and Jerusalem, B. C. 7 or 8.)

ᶜLUKE II. 40–52.

ᶜ**40 And the child grew** [This verse contains the history
of thirty years. It describes the growth of our Lord as a natural, human growth (compare Luke i. 80); for, though Jesus
was truly divine, he was also perfectly man. To try to distinguish between the divine and human in Jesus, is to waste
time upon an impracticable mystery which is too subtle for our
dull and finite minds], **and waxed strong** [His life expanded
like other human lives. He learned as other boys; he obeyed
as other children. As he used means and waited patiently for
growth, so must each individual Christian, and so must the
church. Though the latter is a mystical body, and ani-
mated by the Holy Spirit, it must nevertheless make increase
of itself before coming to the perfect man—Eph. iv. 16],
**filled with wisdom : and the grace of God was upon
him.** [These words describe briefly the life of Christ during
all the preparatory period at Nazareth. It was a quiet life, but
its sinless purity made the Baptist feel his own unworthiness
compared to it (Matt. iii. 14), and its sweet reasonableness
inspired in Mary, the mother, that confidence which led her
to sanction, without reserve, any request or command which
Jesus might utter—John ii. 5.] **41 And his parents** [Males
were required to attend the Passover (Ex. xiii. 7); but women
were not. The great rabbi, Hillel (born about B. C. 110,
died A. D. 10), recommended that they should do so, and the

LIVING AT NAZARETH. 57

practice was esteemed an act of admirable piety] **went every year** [regular attendance upon worship is likewise enjoined upon us— Heb. x. 25] **to Jerusalem at the feast of the passover.** [The Passover, one of the three great Jewish feasts, commemorated the mercy of God in causing his angel to "pass over" the houses in Israel on the night that he slew all the firstborn of Egypt. It took place at the full moon which occurred next after the vernal equinox. At it the firstfruits of the harvest were offered (Lev. xxiii. 10–15). The second feast, Pentecost, occurred fifty days later, and commemorated the giving of the law. At it the firstfruits of the wheat harvest, in the form of bread (Lev. xxiii. 17), were offered. The third feast, or Tabernacles, occurred near the end of September, or beginning of October, and commemorated the days when Israel dwelt in tents in the wilderness. It was observed as a thanksgiving for the blessings of the year. Every adult male Jew dwelling in Judæa was required to attend these three feasts. Josephus tells us that the numbers assembled at them in Jerusalem often exceeded two millions.] **42 And when he was twelve years old** [The incident which Luke here reports is the only one given in the period between the return from Egypt and Jesus' thirtieth year. It shows that Jesus did not attend the school of the rabbis in Jerusalem (Mark vi. 2; John vi. 42; vii. 15). But we learn that he could write (John viii. 6), and there is little doubt but that he spoke both Hebrew and Greek], **they went up** [the altitude of Jerusalem is higher than that of Nazareth, and the distance between the two places is about seventy miles] **after the custom of the feast** [the custom was that the feast was celebrated annually in Jerusalem]; **43 and when they had fulfilled the days** [eight days in all; one day for killing the passover, and seven for observing the feast of unleavened bread which followed it—Ex. xii. 15; Lev. xxiii. 56], **as they were returning, the boy Jesus** [Luke narrates something about every stage of Christ's life. He speaks of him as a babe (ii. 16), as a little child (ii. 40), here as a boy, and afterwards as a man] **tarried behind in Jerusalem** [to take advantage of the opportunity to

hear the great teachers in the schools]; **and his parents
knew it not** [As vast crowds attended the Passover, it was
easy to lose sight of a boy amid the festal throng. Indeed, the
incident is often repeated even to this day during the feast
seasons at Jerusalem]; **44 but supposing him to be in the
company** [We see here the confidence of the parents, and the
independence of the child. The sinlessness of Jesus was not
due to any exceptional care on the part of his parents. Jews
going to and from their festivals traveled in caravans for
pleasure and safety. In the daytime the young folks mingled
freely among the travelers, and sought out whatever companionship they wished. But in the evening, when the camp was
formed, and the tents were pitched, the members of each
family came together], **they went a day's journey** [They
probably returned by the way of Jericho to avoid passing
through Samaria, because of the hatred existing between Jews
and Samaritans. In more modern times the first day's journey
is a short one, and it was probably so then. It was made so in
order that the travelers might return to the city whence they
had departed, should they discover that they had forgotten
anything—should they find that they had forgotten a sack
of meal, a blanket or a child]; **and they sought for him
among their kinsfolk and acquaintance** [those with
whom he was most likely to have traveled during the day]:
**45 and when they found him not, they returned to
Jerusalem, seeking for him.** [Parents who have temporarily suffered the loss of their children can easily imagine their
feelings. Christ, though a divine gift to them, was lost. So
may we also lose him, though he be God's gift to us.] **46
And it came to pass, after three days** [Each part of a
day was reckoned as a day when at the beginning and ending
of a series. The parents missed Jesus on the evening of the first
day, returned to Jerusalem and sought for him on the second
day, and probably found him on the morning of the third day.
The disciples of Jesus also lost him in the grave for part of one
day, and all of the next, and found him resurrected on the
morning of the third day—Luke xxiv. 21] **they found him**

in the temple [Probably in one of the many chambers which tradition says were built against the walls of the temple and its enclosures, and opened upon the temple courts. The sacred secret which they knew concerning the child should have sent them at once to the temple to seek for him], **sitting** [Jewish scholars sat upon the ground at the feet of their teachers] **in the midst** [the teachers sat on semi-circular benches and thus partially surrounded their scholars] **of the teachers** [these teachers had schools in which they taught for the fees of their pupils, and are not to be confounded with the scribes, who were mere copyists], **both hearing them, and asking them questions** [He was not teaching : the God of order does not expect childhood to teach. He was among them as a modest scholar, and not as a forward child. The rabbinical method of instruction was to state cases, or problems, bearing upon the interpretation or application of the law, which cases or problems were to be solved by the pupils. For typical problems see Matt. xxii. 15–46]: **47 and all that heard him were amazed at his understanding and his answers. 48 And when they** [his parents] **saw him, they were astonished** [Mary and Joseph stood as much in awe of these renowned national teachers as peasants do of kings, and were therefore astonished that their youthful son presumed to speak to them]; **and his mother said unto him, Son, why hast thou thus dealt with us?** [Her language implies that Jesus had been fully instructed as to the time when his parents and their caravan would depart for Galilee, and that he was expected to depart with them. Obedience to his higher duties constrained him to appear disobedient to his parents] **behold, thy father** [As legal father of Jesus, this expression would necessarily have to be used when speaking of Joseph. But Jesus does not accept Joseph as his father, as we see by his answer] **and I sought thee sorrowing.** [Because they thought him lost.] **49 And he said unto them** [What follows are the first recorded words of Jesus; he here speaks of the same being—the Father—to whom he commended his spirit in his last words upon the cross (Luke xxiii. 46). His last recorded words on earth are found at Acts i. 7, 8; his last recorded words in heaven are found in Rev. xxii. 10–20, but these last words are spoken through the medium of an angel], **How is it that ye sought me?** [Mary, knowing all that had been divinely revealed to her concerning Jesus, should have expected to find him in the temple] **knew ye not that I must** [In this oft-repeated phrase, "I must," Jesus sets forth that devotion (John iv. 34) to the will of the Father by which his whole life was directed] **be in my Father's** [Literally "the Father of me." Jesus invariably used the article in speaking of himself, and said "the Father of me," and invariably omitted the article, and said " Father of you," when speaking of his disciples. His relationship to the Father differed from ours, and God, not Joseph, was his father] **house?** [See John ii. 16, 17; viii. 35.] **50 And they understood not** [It may seem strange that Mary, knowing all that she did concerning the birth of Jesus, etc., did not grasp the meaning of his words, but we are all slow to grasp great truths ; and failure to be understood was therefore a matter of daily occurrence with Jesus. (Luke ix. 45; xviii. 34; Mark ix. 32; John x. 6.) Christ spoke plainly, but human ears were slow to comprehend his wonderful sayings. We need to be watchful lest our ears be censured for a like slowness] **the saying which he spake unto them. 51 And he went down with them** [Jerusalem was among the mountains, Nazareth among the hills], **and came to Nazareth** [A beautiful and healthful town, but so lacking in piety and learning as to form the "dry ground" out of which it was prophetically predicted that the glorious and fruitful life of Jesus would spring. Here Christ rose above all times and schools and revealed to man that "life more abundant" than all kings, lawgivers or sages had ever discovered. His character, like the New Jerusalem, descended from God out of heaven, and no education obtained in Nazareth will explain it. The struggle of self-made men with their early environment is noticeable to the last, but it is not so with him. The discourses of Jesus are the outpourings of divine knowledge, and not the result of study or self-culture]; **and he was subject** [Our example in all things, he here set before us that pattern of obedience which children should observe toward their parents. In these years Jesus learned the trade of his supposed father (Mark vi. 3). Christ was a laborer, and thereby sanctified labor, and showed that dignity and glory belong to inward and not to outward conditions] **unto them** [His parents, Joseph and Mary. We find no mention of Joseph after this, and the probability is that he soon died]: **and his mother kept all** *these* **sayings in her heart.** [She had many treasured sayings of angels, shepherds, wise men and prophets. She now began to add to these the sayings of Christ himself.] **52 And Jesus advanced in wisdom and stature, and in favor with God and men.** [He did not *literally* grow in favor with God. This is a phenomenal expression. The favor of God and man kept company for quite awhile; but the favor of God abode with Jesus when man's good will was utterly withdrawn. Men admire holiness until it becomes aggressive, and then they feel an antagonism against it as great, or intense, as their previous admiration.]

PART SECOND.

BEGINNING OF THE MINISTRY OF JOHN THE BAPTIST, THE FORERUNNER.

XVII.

JOHN THE BAPTIST'S PERSON AND PREACHING.

(In the wilderness of Judæa, and on the banks of the Jordan, occupying several months, probably A. D. 25 or 26.)

ᵃ MATT. III. 1–12; ᵇ MARK i. 1–8; ᶜ LUKE III. 1–18.

ᵇ 1 **The beginning of the gospel** [John begins his Gospel from eternity, where the Word is found coexistent with God. Matthew begins with Jesus, the humanly generated son of Abraham and David, born in the days of Herod the king. Luke begins with the birth of John the Baptist, the Messiah's herald; and Mark begins with the ministry of John the Baptist. While the three other evangelists take a brief survey of the *preparation* of the gospel, Mark looks particularly to the period when it began to be *preached*. Gospel means good news, and news is not news until it is proclaimed. The gospel began to be preached or proclaimed with the ministry of John the Baptist (Luke xvi. 16). His ministry was the dawn of that gospel of which Christ's preaching was the sunrise] **of Jesus** [this is our Lord's *name* as a human being; it means " Saviour "] **Christ** [Though this is also sometimes used as a name, it is in reality our Lord's *title*. It means "the Anointed," and is equivalent to saying that Jesus is our Prophet, Priest and King] **the Son of God.** [This indicates our Lord's eternal *nature ;* it was divine. Mark's Gospel was written to establish that fact, which is the foundation of the church (Matt. xvi. 18). John's Gospel was written for a like purpose (John xx. 31). John uses the phrase " Son of

God" twenty-nine times, and Mark seven times. As these two evangelists wrote chiefly for Gentile readers, they emphasized the divinity of Jesus, and paid less attention to his Jewish ancestry. But Matthew, writing for Hebrews, prefers the title "Son of David," which he applies to Jesus some nine times, that he may identify him as the Messiah promised in the seed of David—II. Sam. vii. 12; Ps. lxxii. 1–17; lxxxix. 3, 4; cxxxii. 11, 12.] ᶜ1 **Now in the fifteenth year of the reign** [Tiberius Cæsar, stepson of and successor to Augustus, began to reign as joint ruler with Augustus in August, A. U. C. 765 (A. D. 11). On Aug. 19, 767, Augustus died and Tiberius became sole ruler. Luke counts from the beginning of the joint rule, and his fifteen years bring us to 779. In August, 779, Tiberius began his fifteenth year, and about December of that year Jesus would have completed his thirtieth year] **of Tiberius Caesar** [He was born B. C. 41, died March 16, A. D. 37. As a citizen he distinguished himself as orator, soldier and public official. But as emperor he was slothful, self-indulgent, indescribably licentious, vindictive and cruel. He was a master of dissimulation and cunning, and was a veritable scourge to his people. But he still found flatterers even in Palestine, Cæsarea Philippi and the town Tiberias being named for him], **Pontius Pilate** [see mention of him in account of our Lord's trial] **being governor of Judaea** [The province of Judæa was subdued by Pompey and brought under Roman control in B. C. 63. Its history from that date till the governorship of Pilate can be found in Josephus], **and Herod** [Also called Antipas. The ruler who murdered John the Baptist and who assisted at the trial of Jesus] **being tetrarch** [this word means properly the ruler of a fourth part of a country, but was used loosely for any petty tributary prince] **of Galilee** [This province lay north of Samaria, and measured about twenty-five miles from north to south, and twenty-seven miles from east to west. It was a rich and fertile country], **and his brother** [half-brother] **Philip** [He was distinguished by justice and moderation, the one decent man in the Herodian family. He married Salome, who obtained John the Baptist's head for a dance. He built Cæsarea Philippi, and transformed Bethsaida Julius from a village to a city, and died there A. D. 44. After his death his domains became part of the Roman province of Syria] **tetrarch of the region of Ituraea** [A district thirty miles long by twenty-five broad, lying north of Batanæa, east of Mt. Hermon, west of Trachonitis. It received its name from Jetur, son of Ishmael (Gen. xxv. 15). Its Ishmaelite inhabitants were conquered by Aristobulus, king of Judæa, B. C. 100, and forced by him to accept the Jewish faith. They were marauders, and famous for the use of the bow] **and Trachonitis** [A district about twenty-two miles from north to south by fourteen from east to west. Its name means "rough" or "stony," and it amply deserves it. It lies between Ituræa and the desert, and has been infested with robbers from the earliest ages. It is called the Argob in the Old Testament, "an ocean of basaltic rock and boulders, tossed about in the wildest confusion, and intermingled with fissures and crevices in every direction"], **and Lysanias** [Profane history gives us no account of this man. It tells of a Lysanias, king of Chalcis, under Mt. Lebanon, who was put to death by Mark Antony, B. C. 36, or sixty-odd years before this, and another who was tetrarch of Abilene in the reigns of Caligula and Claudius twenty years after this. He probably was son of the first and father of the second] **tetrarch of Abilene** [The city of Abila (which comes from the word "abel," meaning meadow) is eighteen miles from Damascus and thirty-eight from Baalbec. The province lying about it is mentioned because it subsequently formed part of the Jewish territory, being given to Herod Agrippa I. by the Emperor Claudius about A. D. 41], **2 in the high priesthood of Annas and Caiaphas** [Annas had been high priest 7–14 A. D., when he was deposed by the procurator, Gratus. Caiaphas was son-in-law of and successor to Annas. Luke gives both names, one as the rightful and the other as the acting high priest. Compare Acts iv. 6. Gentile innovations had made sad havoc with the Jewish law as to this office. In the last one hundred and seven years of the temple's existence there were no less than twenty-eight high priests. Luke is the only one who fixes the time when Jesus began his ministry. He locates it by emperor and governor, tetrarch and high priest, as an event of world-wide importance, and of concern to all the kingdoms of men. He conceives of it as Paul did—Acts xxvi. 26], **the word of God** [The divine commission which bade John enter his career as a prophet (Jer. i. 1; Ezek. vi. 1). Prophets gave temporary and limited manifestations of God's will (Heb. i. 1, 2). Jesus is the everlasting and unlimited manifestation of the divine purpose and of the very Godhead—John xiv. 9; xii. 45; Col. i. 15; Heb. i. 3; II. Cor. iv. 6] **came unto John, the son of Zacharias, in the wilderness.** [The wilderness of Judæa is that almost uninhabitable mass of barren ridges extending the whole length of the Dead Sea, and a few miles further north. It is from five to ten miles wide.] **ᵃ 1 And in those days** [Some take this expression as referring to the years when Jesus dwelt at Nazareth. But it is better to regard it as a Hebraism equivalent to "that age" or "that era" (Ex. xii. 11). It contrasts the era when the Baptist lived with the era when Matthew wrote his Gospel, just as we say "in these days of enlightenment" when we wish to contrast the present time with the days of the American Revolution] **cometh John** [he was cousin to Jesus] **the Baptist** [So called because God first gave through him the ordinance of baptism. It has been erroneously thought by some that John borrowed this ordinance from the Jewish practice of proselyte baptism. This could not be, for John baptized his converts, but Jewish proselytes baptized themselves. The law required such self-baptism of all persons who were unclean (Lev. xiv. 9; Num. xix. 19; viii. 7; Lev. xv., xvi.). More than twenty distinct cases are specified in which the law required bathing or self-baptism, and it is to these Paul refers when he states that the law consisted in part "of divers baptisms" (Heb. ix. 10). But the law did not require this of proselytes, and proselyte baptism was a human appendage to the divinely given Jewish ritual, just as infant baptism is to the true Christian ritual. Proselyte baptism is not mentioned in history till the third century of the Christian era. Neither Josephus, nor Philo, nor the Apocrypha, nor the Targums say anything about it, though they all mention proselytes. In fact, the oldest mention of it in Jewish writings is in the Babylonian Gemara, which was completed about five hundred years after Christ. The New Testament implies the non-existence of proselyte baptism (Matt. xxi. 25; John i. 25, 33). John could hardly have been called the *Baptist*, had he used an old-time rite in the accustomed manner. The Baptist was a link between the Old and the New Testament. Belonging to the Old, he announced the New], **preaching** [Not sermonizing, but crying out a message as a king's herald making a proclamation, or a policeman crying " Fire! " in a slumbering town. His discourse was brief and unembellished. Its force lay in the importance of the truth announced. It promised to the Hebrew the fulfillment of two thousand years of longing. It demanded repentance, but for a new reason. The old call to repentance had wooed with the promise of earthly blessings, and warned with the threat of earthly judgments; but John's repentance had to do with the kingdom of heaven and things eternal. It suggested the Holy Spirit as a reward, and unquenchable fire as the punishment] **in the wilderness of Judaea** [that part of the wilderness which John chose for the scene of his ministry is a desert plain lying along the western bank of the Jordan, be-between Jericho and the Dead Sea], **saying, 2 Repent ye** [to repent is to change the *will* in reference to *sin*, resolving to sin no more] **for** [John sets forth the motive for repentance. Repentance is the duty, and the approach of the kingdom is the motive inciting to it. Only by repentance could the people be prepared for the kingdom. Those who are indifferent to the obligations of an old revelation would be ill-prepared to receive a new one] **the kingdom of heaven is at hand.** [Dan. ii. 44. " Kingdom of heaven " is peculiar to Matthew, who uses it thirty-one times. He also joins with the other evangelists in calling it the kingdom of God. We know not why he preferred the expression, "kingdom of heaven."] **3 For this is he that was spoken of through Isaiah the prophet,** ᶜ **3 And he came** [he made his public appearance, and, like that of Elijah, it was a sudden one—I. Kings xvii. 1] **into all the region round about the Jordan** [The Jordan valley is called in the old Testament the Arabah, and by the modern Arabs the Ghor. It is the deepest valley in the world, its lowest part being about thirteen hundred feet below the level of the ocean] **preaching the baptism of repentance unto the remission of sins** [as a change leading to remission or forgiveness of sins] ᵇ **even** ᶜ **4 as it is written in the book of the words of Isaiah the prophet** [Isaiah flourished from about 759 to 699 B. C.], ᵃ **saying,** ᵇ **Behold** [The clause beginning with "Behold," and ending with "way," is taken from Mal. iii. 1. The Revised Version makes Mark quote this passage as if it were from Isaiah, the reading being "written in Isaiah the prophet," but the King James' version gives the reading, "written in the prophets." Following the reasoning of Canon Cook, we hold that the latter was the original reading —see Speaker's Commentary, note at the end of Mark i.] **I send my messenger** [John the Baptist was that messenger] **before thy face** [Malachi says, "my face." "Thy" and "my" are used interchangeably, because of the unity of the Deity—John x. 30], **who shall prepare thy way** [Mark says little about the prophets, but at the outset of his Gospel he calls attention to the fact that the entire pathway of Jesus was the subject of prophetical prediction]; ᶜ **The voice** [Isaiah xl. 3, 4, quoted from the LXX. The words were God's, the voice was John's. So Paul also spake (I. Thess. ii. 1–13). It was prophesied before he was born that John should be a preparing messenger for Christ—Luke i. 17] **of one crying in the wilderness** [This prophecy of Isaiah's could relate to none but John, for no other prophet ever made the wilderness the scene of his preaching. But John always preached there, and instead of going to the people he compelled the people to come out to him. John was the second Elijah. The claims of all who in these days profess to be reincarnations of Elijah may be tested and condemned by this prophecy, for none of them frequent the wilderness], **Make ye ready the way** [See also Isa. xxxv. 8–10. Isaiah's language is highly figurative. It represents a band of engineers and workmen preparing the road for their king through a rough, mountainous district. The figure was familiar to the people of the East, and nearly every generation there witnessed some such road-making. The haughty Semiramis leveled the mountains before her. Josephus, describing the march of Vespasian, says that there went before him such as were to make the road even and straight, and if it were anywhere rough and hard, to smooth it over, to plane it, and to cut down woods that hindered the march, that the army might not be tired. Some have thought that Isaiah's prophecy referred primarily to the return of the Jewish captives from Babylon. But it refers far more directly to the ministry of the Baptist; for it is not said that the way was to be prepared for the people, but for Jehovah himself. It is a beautiful figure, but the real preparation was the more beautiful transformation of repentance. By inducing repentance, John was to prepare the people to receive Jesus and his apostles, and to hearken to their preaching] **of the Lord, Make his paths straight. 5 Every valley shall be filled, And every mountain and hill shall be brought low ; And the crooked shall become straight, And the rough way smooth** [The literal meaning of this passage is expressed at Isa. ii. 12–17. See also Zech. iv. 7. Commentators give detailed application of this prophecy, and, following their example, we may regard the Pharisees and Sadducees as mountains of self-righteousness, needing to be thrown down, and thereby brought to meekness and humility; the outcasts and harlots as valleys of humiliation, needing to be exalted and filled with hope ; and the publicans and soldiers as crooked and rough byways, needing to be straightened and smoothed with proper ideals of righteousness. But the application is general, and not to be limited to such details. However, civil tyranny and ecclesiastical pride must each be leveled, and the rights of the common people must be exalted before the kingdom of God can

enter in]; **6 And all flesh shall see the salvation of God.**
[This last clause of the prophecy is added by Luke alone. He
loves to dwell upon the universality of Christ's gospel.] ᵇ**4
John came, who baptized in the wilderness and
preached the baptism of repentance unto remission
of sins.** [Pardoning mercy was to be found in Christ, and
all rites then looked forward to the cleansing effected by
the shedding of his blood, as all rites now look back to it. But
in popular estimation John's baptism was no doubt regarded as
consummating an immediate forgiveness.] ᵃ**4 Now John
himself** [Himself indicates that John's manner of life differed
from that of his disciples. He did not oblige them to practice
the full measure of his abstinence] **had his raiment of**
[John's dress and food preached in harmony with his voice.
His clothing and fare rendered him independent of the rich
and great, so that he could more freely and plainly rebuke
their sins. Calling others to repentance, he himself set an
example of austere self-denial. So much so that the Pharisees
said he had a demon—Matt. xi. 18] ᵇ**6 And was clothed
with** ᵃ**camel's hair** [Camels were plentiful in the East.
Their finer hair was woven into elegant cloths; but that
which was coarser and shaggier was made into a fabric
like our druggets, and used for the coats of shepherds
and camel-drivers, and for the covering of tents. Prophets often wore such cloth (Zech. xiii. 4), and no doubt
it was the habitual garb of John's prototype (Mal. iv. 5), the
prophet Elijah (II. Kings i. 8). In Elijah's day there was
demand for protest against the sad havoc which Phœnician luxury and licentiousness were making with the purer morals of
Israel; and in John's day a like protest was needed against a
like contamination wrought by Greek manners and customs.
Both prophets, by their austerity, rebuked such apostasy, and
Jezebel answered the rebuke by attempting Elijah's life,
while Herodias actually took the life of John. As a herald
John was suited to the King whose appearing he was to announce, for Jesus was meek and lowly (Zech. ix. 9), and had
no form nor comeliness that he should be desired—Isa. liii. 2],

and a leathern girdle about his loins [The loose skirts worn in the East required a girdle to bind them to the body. This was usually made of linen or silk, but was frequently more costly, being wrought with silver and gold. John's girdle was plain, undressed leather]; **and his food was** {ᵇ**and did eat**} ᵃ**locusts** [Locusts, like Western grasshoppers, were extremely plentiful (Joel i. 4; Isa. xxxiii. 4, 5). The law declared them clean, and thus permitted the people to eat them for food (Lev. xi. 22). Arabs still eat them, and in some Oriental cities they are found for sale in the market. But they are regarded as fit only for the poor. They are frequently seasoned with camel's milk and honey] **and wild honey.** [Canaan was promised as a land flowing with milk and honey (Ex. ii. 8–17; xiii. 15; I. Sam. xiv. 26). Many of the trees in the plains of Jericho, such as the palm, fig, manna, ash and tamarisk, exuded sweet gums, which went by the name of tree honey, but there is no need to suppose, as some do, that this was what John ate. The country once abounded in wild bees, and their honey was very plentiful. We have on the record an instance of the speed with which they could fill the place which they selected for their hives (Judg. xiv. 5–9). The diet of the Baptist was very light, and Jesus so speaks of it (Matt. xi. 18). He probably had no set time for his meals, and all days were more or less fastdays. Thus John gave himself wholly to his ministry, and became a voice—all voice. John took the wilderness for a church, and filled it. He courted no honors, but no Jew of his time received more of them, and by some he was even regarded as Messiah—Luke xiii. 15.] ᵇ**5 And there** ᵃ**5 Then went out unto him** ᵇ**all** [A hyperbole common with Hebrew writers and such as we use when we say, " the whole town turned out," "everybody was there," etc. Both Matthew and Luke show that some did not accept John's baptism (Matt. xxi. 23–25; Luke vii. 30). But from the language of the evangelist we might infer that, first and last, something like a million people may have attended John's ministry] **the country of Judaea, and all they of Jerusalem; and**

all the region round about the Jordan [This last phrase includes the entire river valley. On both sides of the river between the lake of Galilee and Jericho, there were many important cities, any one of which would be more apt to send its citizens to John's baptism than the proud capital of Jerusalem] ; **6 and they were baptized of him** [Literally, immersed of him. In every stage of the Greek language this has been the unquestioned meaning of the verb *baptizo*, and it still retains this meaning in modern Greek. In accordance with this meaning, the Greek Church, in all its branches, has uniformly practiced immersion from the earliest period to the present time. Greek Christians never speak of other denominations as "baptizing by sprinkling," but they say "they sprinkle *instead* of baptizing." John's baptism was instituted of God (John i. 33), just as Christian baptism was instituted by Christ (Matt. xxviii. 19). The Pharisees recognized John's rite as so important as to require divine authority, and even then they underestimated it, regarding it as a mere purification—Josephus Ant. xviii. 5, 2] **in the river Jordan, confessing their sins.** [As John's baptism was for the remission of sins, it was very proper that it should be preceded by a confession. The context indicates that the confession was public and general. There is no hint of such auricular confession as is practiced by the Catholics. See also Acts xix. 18. John, writing to baptized Christians, bids them to confess their sins, that Jesus may forgive them (I. John i. 9). Christian baptism being also for the remission of sins (Acts ii. 38), the ordinance itself is a very potent confession that the one baptized has sins to be remitted, and it seems to be a sufficient public expression of confession as to sins; for while John's baptism called for a confession of sins, Christian baptism calls only for a confession of faith in Christ—Acts xxii. 16; Rom. x. 9, 10; Mark xvi. 16.] **7 But when he saw many of the Pharisees and Sadducees** [Josephus tells us that these two leading sects of the Jews started about the same time in the days of Jonathan, the high priest, or B. C. 159–144. But the sentiments which at that time divided the

people into two rival parties entered the minds and hearts of
the Jews immediately after the return from the Babylonian
captivity.   These returned Jews differed as to the attitude
and policy which Israel should manifest toward the neighboring heathen.   Some contended for a strict separation between
the Jews and all pagan peoples.   These eventually formed the
Pharisee party, and the name Pharisee means "the separate."
Originally these men were genuine patriots and reformers, but
afterwards the majority of them became mere formalists.
As theologians the Pharisees represented the orthodox party,
and were followed by the vast majority of the people.   They
believed (1) in the resurrection of the dead; (2) a future state
with rewards and punishments; (3) angels and spirits; and
(4) a special providence of God carried out by angels and
spirits.   As a sect they are said to have numbered six thousand at the time of Herod's death.   They were the patriotic
party, and the zealots were their extreme section.   They covered an extremely selfish spirit with a pious formalism, and by
parading their virtues they obtained an almost unbounded influence over the people.   By exposing their hypocrisy, Jesus
sought to destroy their power over the multitude, and incurred
that bitter enmity with which they pursued him to his death.
But certain other of the captives who returned from Babylon
desired a freer intercourse with the pagans, and sought to
break away from every restraint which debarred therefrom.
These became Sadducees.   They consented to no other restraint
than the Scriptures themselves imposed, and they interpreted
these as laxly as possible.   Some take their name to mean
"the party of 'righteousness,'" but more think that it comes
from their founder, Zadok, and is a corruption of the word
Zadokite.   Zadok flourished 260 B. C.   His teacher, Antig-
onus Sochæus, taught him to serve God disinterestedly—that
is, without hope of reward or punishment.   From his teaching
Zadok inferred that there was no future state of rewards or
punishment, and on this belief founded his sect.   From this
fundamental doctrine sprang the other tenets of the Sadducees.
They denied all the four points of belief held by the Pharisees,

asserting that there was no resurrection; no rewards and punishments hereafter; no angels, no spirits. They believed that there was a God, but denied that he had any special supervision of human affairs (Matt. xxii. 23; Acts xxiii. 8). They were the materialists of that day. Considering all God's promises as referring to this world, they looked upon poverty and distress as an evidence of God's curse. Hence to relieve the poor was to sin against God by interfering with his mode of government. Far fewer than the Pharisees, they were their rivals in power; for they were the aristocratic party, and held the high-priesthood, with all its glories. Their high political position, their great wealth, and the Roman favor which they courted by consenting to foreign rule and pagan customs, made them a body to be respected and feared] **coming to his baptism, he said {ᶜtherefore to the multitudes that went out to be baptized of him} ᵃ unto them** [John spoke principally to the leaders, but his denunciation indirectly included the multitude who followed their leadership], **Ye offspring of vipers** [A metaphor for their *likeness* to vipers—as like them as if they had been begotten of them. The viper was a species of serpent from two to five feet in length, and about one inch thick. Its head is flat, and its body a yellowish color, speckled with long brown spots. It is extremely poisonous (Acts xxviii. 6). John here uses the word figuratively, and probably borrows the figure from Isa. lix. 5. It means that the Jewish rulers were full of guile and malice, cunning and venom. With these words John gave them a vigorous shaking, for only thus could he hope to waken their slumbering consciences. But only one who has had a vision of "the King in his beauty," should presume thus to address his fellow-men. The serpent is an emblem of the devil (Gen. iii. 1; Rev. xii. 9, 14, 15), and Jesus not only repeated John's words (Matt. xii. 35; Matt. xxiii. 23, 33), but he interpreted the words, and told them plainly that they were "the children of the devil" (John viii. 44). The Jewish rulers well deserved this name, for they poisoned the religious principles of the nation, and accomplished the crucifixion of the Son of God], **who warned**

you to flee [John's baptism, like that of Moses at the Red Sea (I. Cor. x. 2), was a way of escape from destruction, if rightly used. Christian baptism is also such a way, and whosoever will may enter thereby into the safety of the kingdom of Christ, but baptism can not be used as an easy bit of ritual to charm away evil. It must be accompanied by all the spiritual changes which the ordinance implies] **from the wrath to come?** [Prophecy foretold that Messiah's times would be accompanied with wrath (Isa. lxiii. 3–6; Dan. vii. 10–26); but the Jews were all of the opinion that this wrath would be meted out upon the Gentiles and were not prepared to hear John apply the prophecy to themselves. To all his hearers John preached the coming kingdom; to the impenitent, he preached the coming wrath. Thus he prepared the way for the first coming of the Messiah, and those who would prepare the people for his second coming would do well to follow his example, The Bible has a voice of warning and denunciation, as well as words of invitation and love. Whosoever omits the warning of the judgment, speaks but half the message which God would have him deliver. God's wrath is his resentment against sin—Matt. xviii. 34; xxii. 7; Mark iii. 5.] **8 Bring forth therefore fruit worthy of repentance** [John had demanded repentance, he now demands the fruits of it. By " fruit " or " fruits," as Luke has it, he means the manner of life which shows a real repentance] : **9 and think not {^cbegin not}** [John nips their self-excuse in the bud] ^a**to say within yourselves** [speaking to your conscience to quiet it], **We have Abraham to our father** [The Jews thought that Messiah would rule over them as a nation, and that all Jews would, therefore, be by birthright citizens of his kingdom. They thought that descent from Abraham was all that would be necessary to bring them into that kingdom. John's words must have been very surprising to them. The Talmud is full of expressions showing the extravagant value which Jews of a later age attached to Abrahamic descent. "Abraham," it says, " sits next the gates of hell, and doth not permit any wicked Israelite to go down into it." Again it represents God as saying to Abraham, "If thy children were like dead bodies without sinews or bones, thy merit would avail for them." Again, "A single Israelite is worth more before God than all the people who have been or shall be." Again, "The world was made for their [Israel's] sake." This pride was the more inexcusable because the Jews were clearly warned by their prophets that their privileges were not exclusive, and that they would by no means escape just punishment for their sins (Jer. vii. 3, 4; Mic. iii. 11; Isa. xlviii. 2). John repeated this message, and Jesus reiterated it (Matt. viii. 11, 12; Luke xvi. 24). We should note that in this preparation for the gospel a blow was struck at confidence and trust in carnal descent. Birth gives no man any privileges in the kingdom of God, for all are born outside of it, and all must be born again into it (John i. 13; iii. 3); yet many still claim peculiar rights from Christian parentage, and infant baptism rests on this false conception. The New Testament teaches us that we are children of Abraham by faith, and not by blood; by spiritual and not carnal descent (Rom. iv. 12-16; Gal. iii. 26; vi. 15; John viii. 39). It had been better for the Jews never to have heard of Abraham, than to have thus falsely viewed the rights which they inherited from him]: **for I say unto you, that God is able of these stones to raise up children unto Abraham.** [John meant that their being children of Abraham by natural descent gave them no more merit than children of Abraham made out of stones would have. He pointed to the stones along the bank of Jordan as he spoke.] **10 And even now the axe** c**also** a**lieth at the root of the trees: every tree therefore that bringeth not forth good fruit is hewn down** [the threatened cutting down means the end of the probation of each hearer, when, if found fruitless, he would be cast into the fire mentioned below], **and cast into the fire.** [Used as fuel.] c**10 And the multitudes asked him, saying, What must we do?** [This is the cry of the awakened conscience (Acts ii. 37; xvi. 30; xxii. 10). John answered it by recommending them to do the very reverse of what they

were doing, which, in their case, was true fruit of repentance.] **11 And he answered and said unto them, He
that hath two coats** [By coat is meant the tunic, or inner
garment, worn next to the skin. It reached to the knees, and
sometimes to the ankles, and generally had sleeves. Two
tunics were a luxury in a land where thousands were too poor
to own even one. Wrath was coming, and he that would obtain mercy from it must show mercy—Matt. v. 7), **let him
impart to him that hath none** [For a like precept given to
Christians, see II. Cor. viii. 13–15; Jas. ii. 15–17; I. John iii.
17]; **and he that hath food, let him do likewise. 12
And there came also publicans** [The Roman Government
did not collect its own taxes. Instead of doing so, it divided
the empire into districts, and sold the privilege of collecting the
taxes in these districts to certain capitalists and men of rank.
These capitalists employed agents to do the actual collecting.
These agents were usually natives of the districts in which
they lived, and those in Palestine were called publicans. Their
masters urged and encouraged them to make most fraudulent
and vexatious exactions. They systematically overcharged
the people and often brought false accusation to obtain money
by blackmail. These publicans were justly regarded by the
Jews as apostates and traitors, and were classed with the lowest and most abandoned characters. The system was bad, but its
practitioners were worse. The Greeks regarded the word
' publican " as synonymous with "plunderer." Suidas pictures the life of a publican as "unrestrained plunder, un-
blushing greed, unreasonable pettifogging, shameless business."
The Turks to-day collect by this Roman method. Being publicly condemned, and therefore continually kept conscious of
their sin, the publicans repented more readily than the self-
righteous Pharisees. Conscience is one of God's greatest
gifts, and he that destroys it must answer for it] **to be baptized, and they said unto him, Teacher** [The publicans,
though lowest down, gave John the highest title. Self-
abnegation is full of the virtue of reverence, but self-righteousness utterly lacks it], **what must we do? 13 And he**

said unto them, **Extort no more than that which is appointed you.** [Such was their habitual, universal sin. No man should make his calling an excuse for evil-doing.] **14 And soldiers** [These soldiers were probably Jewish troops in the employ of Herod. Had they been Romans, John would doubtless have told them to worship God] **also asked him, saying, And we, what must we do? And he said unto them, Extort from no man by violence** [The soldiers, poorly paid, often found it convenient to extort money by intimidation. Strong in their organization, they terrified the weak and enforced gratuities by acts of violence], **neither accuse *any one* wrongfully** [John here condemns the custom of blackmailing the rich by acting as informers and false accusers against them]; **and be content with your wages.** [The term wages includes rations and money. The soldiers were not to add to their receipts by pillage or extortion. Soldiers' wages were about three cents a day, so they were exposed to strong temptation. Yet John did not bid them abandon their profession, and become ascetics like himself. His teaching was practical. He allowed war as an act of government. Whether Christianity sanctions it or not, is another question.] **15 And as the people were in expectation** [expecting the Christ — see John i. 19–28], **and all men reasoned in their hearts concerning John, whether haply he were the Christ** [Prophecy induced a Messianic expectation. The scepter had departed from Judah, and Cæsar's deputies ruled. Tetrarchs and procurators held the whole civil government. In their hands lay the power of life and death from which only Roman citizens could appeal (Acts xxv. 11). The power of the Jewish courts was limited to excommunication or scourging. The seventy weeks of Daniel were now expiring, and other prophecies indicated the fullness of time. But distress, rather than prophecy, enhanced their expectation. Tiberius, the most infamous of men, governed the world. Pontius Pilate, insolent, cruel, was making life irksome and maddening the people. Herod Antipas, by a course of reckless apostasy and unbridled lust, grieved even the religious sense of the hypocrite.   Annas and Caiaphas, impersonators of materialism, sat in the chief seat of spiritual power.   Men might well look for a deliverer, and hasten with joy to hear of a coming King.   But, neverthe-less, we could have no more forceful statement of the deep impression made by John's ministry than that the people were disposed to take him for the Christ] ; **16 John answered, saying unto them all,** ᵇ **7 And he preached, saying,** ª **11 I indeed baptize** { ᵇ **baptized** } ª **you in** { ᶜ **with** } ª **water unto repentance** [That is, unto the completion of your repentance. Repentance had to begin before the baptism was admin-istered.   After the sinner repented, baptism consummated his repentance, being the symbolic washing away of that from which he had repented and the bringing of the candidate into the blessings granted to the repentant—Mark i. 4; Luke iii. 3] : ᶜ **but there** { ª **he that** } [John preached repentance be-cause of a coming King; he now announces who the King is.   He pictures this King as, first, administering a different baptism from his own ; second, as a judge who would separate the righteous from the wicked, just as a husbandman sifts the wheat from the chaff] ᵇ **cometh after me** [Subsequent to me in ministry.   But John indicates that the coming of Christ would be closely coupled with his own appearing.   One event was to immediately follow the other.   So Malachi binds to-gether in one time the appearing of both forerunner and judge —Mal. iii. 1–3] **he that is mightier than I** [mightier both to save and to punish], ª **whose shoes** [The sandal then worn was a piece of wood or leather bound to the sole of the foot to protect it from the burning sand or the sharp stones.   It was the forerunner of our modern shoe] **I am not worthy to bear** [To untie or carry away the shoe of the master or his guest was the work of the lowest slave of the household.   As a figure of speech, the shoe is always associated with subjugation and slavery (Ps. lx. 8).   John means, " I am not worthy to be his servant."   John was simply the forerunner of Jesus ; the higher office and honor of being Jesus' attendants was reserved for others—Matt. xi. 11] : ᵇ **the latchet** [the lace or strap] **of whose shoes I am**

not worthy to stoop down and unloose. ᶜhe shall baptize you in the Holy Spirit [That which is here referred to was foretold by the prophets (Isa. xliv. 3; Joel ii. 28). In the early church there was an abundant outpouring of the Spirit of God (Tit. iii. 5, 6; Acts ii. 3, 4, 17; x. 44). This prophecy began to be fulfilled on the day of Pentecost (Acts i. 5; ii. 4). In the choice of the word "baptize" God indicated through his prophet how full this flooding of the Spirit would be] **and *in* fire** [Many learned commentators regard the expression "in fire" as a mere amplification of the spiritual baptism added to express the purging and purifying effects of that baptism, but the context forbids this, for, in verse 10, casting the unfruitful trees into the fire represents the punishment of the wicked, and, in verse 12, the burning of the chaff with fire does the same, and consequently the baptizing in fire of the intervening verse must, according to the force of the context, have the same reference. True, the expression "he will baptize *you* in the Holy Spirit and fire," does not separate the persons addressed into two parties, and, if the context is disregarded, might be understood as meaning that the same persons were to be baptized in both; yet the context must not be disregarded, and it clearly separates them] : **17 whose fan** [Winnowing shovel. In the days of John the Baptist, and in that country at the present day, wheat and other grain was not threshed by machinery. It was beaten out by flails, or trodden out by oxen on some smooth, hard plat of ground called the threshing-floor. These threshing-floors were usually on elevations where the wind blew freely. When the grain was trodden out, it was winnowed or separated from the chaff by being tossed into the air with a fan or winnowing shovel. When so tossed, the wind blew the chaff away, and the clean grain fell upon the threshing-floor] **is in his hand** [Ready for immediate work. Both John and Malachi, who foretold John, are disposed to picture Jesus as the judge (Mal. iii. 19–24). Of all the pictures of God which the Bible gives, that of a judge is the most common and frequent], **thoroughly to {ᵃand he will thoroughly} ᶜcleanse his threshing-floor** [Removing the chaff is called purging the floor. Humanity is a mixture of good and bad, and to separate this mixture, save the good and destroy the bad, is the work of Christ. He partially purges the floor in this present time by gathering his saints into the church and leaving the unrepentant in the world. But hereafter on the day of judgment he will make a complete and final separation between the just and the unjust by sending the evil from his presence and gathering his own into the garner of heaven (Matt. xxv. 32, 33). He shall also winnow our individual characters, and remove all evil from us—Luke xxii. 31, 32; Rom. vii. 21–25], **and to {ᵃand he will} ᶜgather the {ᵃhis} ᶜwheat into his {ᵃthe} ᶜgarner** [Eastern garners or granaries were usually subterranean vaults or caves. Garnered grain rested in safety. It was removed from peril of birds, storms, blight and mildew. Christians are now on God's threshing-floor; hereafter they will be gathered into the security of his garner]; **but the chaff** [when the Bible wishes to show the worthlessness and the doom of the ungodly, chaff is one of its favorite figures—Job xxi. 18; Ps. i. 4; Isa. xvii. 13; Jer. xv. 7; Hos. xiii. 3; Mal. iv. 1] **he will burn up** [To prevent chaff from being blown back and mixed again with the wheat, it was burned up. All the chaff in the church shall be consumed on the day of judgment (I. Cor. iii. 12, 13), and there shall be no mixing of good and bad after death—Luke xvi. 26] **with unquenchable fire.** [In this and in other places (I. Thess. i. 8, 9; Mark ix. 48; Matt. xxv. 41), the future suffering of the wicked is taught in the Bible. He shows no kindness to his neighbor, no friendship toward mankind, who conceals the terrors of the Lord. These terrors are set forth in no uncertain terms. Many believe that God will restore the wicked and eventually save all the human race. Others hold that God will annihilate the wicked, and thus end their torment. This passage and the one cited in Mark would be hard to reconcile with either of these views; they indicate that there will be no arrest of judgment nor stay of punishment when once God begins to execute his condemnation. God purged the world with water at the time of the flood; he will again purge it with fire on the day of judgment—II. Pet. iii. 7–10.] **18 With many other exhortations** [The sermon here given is in the nature of a summary. It embodies the substance of John's preaching. Afterwards John preached Christ more directly—John i. 29–36] **therefore preached he good tidings unto the people** [but, like the good tidings of the angel at Bethlehem, it was good only to those who, by repentance, made themselves well pleasing to God].

PART THIRD.

BEGINNING OF OUR LORD'S MINISTRY.

XVIII.

JESUS BAPTIZED BY JOHN IN THE JORDAN.

(Jordan east of Jericho, Spring of A. D. 27.)

ᵃMATT. III. 13–17; ᵇMARK i. 9–11; ᶜLUKE iii. 21, 22.

ᵇ**9 And** {ᵃ**13 Then**} ᵇ**it came to pass in those days, that Jesus came** {ᵃ**cometh**} ᵇ**from Nazareth of Galilee, ᵃto the Jordan** [Tradition fixes upon a ford of Jordan east of Jericho as the place where Jesus was baptized. It is the same section of the river which opened for the passage of Israel under Joshua, and later for Elijah and Elisha. This ford is seventy or eighty miles from Nazareth] **unto John, to be baptized of him.** [He set out from Nazareth, intending to be baptized. Such was his intention before he heard John preach, and he was therefore not persuaded to do it by the preaching. His righteousness was not the result of human persuasion.] ᵇ**and was baptized of John in** [Greek "into." The body of Jesus was immersed or plunged into the river] **the Jordan.** ᵃ**14 But John would have hindered him** [It seemed to John too great an honor for him to baptize Jesus, and too great a humiliation for Jesus to be baptized. There is some dispute as to how John came to know this righteousness of Christ, which prompted his protest. The one natural explanation is, that the intimacy of the two families indicated at the beginning of Luke's account had been kept up, and John knew the history of his kinsman], **saying, I have need to be baptized of thee** [those are most fit to administer an ordinance who have themselves deeply experienced the need of it], **and comest thou to me?** [John felt that he needed Jesus' baptism, but could not think that Jesus needed his. The words " I," " thee," " thou," and " me," show that John contrasted the baptizers as well as the baptisms. As a human being he marveled that the Son of God should come to him to be immersed. The comings of Jesus and the purposes for which he comes are still the greatest marvels which confront the minds of men. Moreover, it should be noted that this protest of John's needed to be made, for it saved Jesus from being baptized without explanation, as if he were a sinner. Baptism without such explanation might have compromised our Lord's claims as the sinless one.] **15 But Jesus answering said unto him, Suffer** *it* **now** [Permit me for this moment to appear as your inferior. The future will make plain and clear the difference between us, both as to our missions and our natures. The words show a Messianic consciousness on the part of Jesus] : **for thus it becometh us** [some take the word " us " as referring to Jesus and John, but the clause " to fulfil all righteousness " shows that " us " refers to Jesus, and he uses the plural to show that it also becometh all of us] **to fulfil all righteousness.** [Jesus came not only to fulfill all the requirements of the law, but also all that wider range of righteousness of which the law was only a part. 1. Though John's baptism was no part of the Mosaic ritual, it was, nevertheless, a precept of God, given by his prophet (John i. 33). Had Jesus neglected or refused to obey this precept he would have lacked a portion of the full armor of righteousness, and the Pharisees would have hastened to strike him at this loose joint of his harness (Matt. xxi. 23–27). 2. It was the divinely appointed method by which the Messiahship of Jesus was to be revealed to the witness John (John i. 33, 34). We should note here that those who fail to obey God's ordinance of baptism, fail (1) to follow the example of Jesus in fulfilling the divine will and precepts; (2) to obey one of the positive commands of almighty God spoken by his own Son.] **Then he suffereth him.** [John's humility caused him to shrink from this duty, but did not make him willfully persist in declining it. Humility ceases to be a virtue when it keeps us from performing our allotted tasks.] ᶜ **21 Now it came to pass, when all the people were baptized** [This may mean that, on the day of his baptism, Jesus was the last candidate, and hence his baptism was the most conspicuous of all; but it more probably means that Jesus was baptized in the midst of John's work—at the period when his baptism was in greatest favor], **that, Jesus also having been** {ᵃ **16 And Jesus, when he was**} ᶜ **baptized, and praying** [All divine ordinances should be accompanied with prayer. Luke frequently notes the times when Jesus prayed. Here, at the entrance of his ministry, he prayed, and at the last moment of it he also prayed (Luke xxiii. 46). In his highest exaltation at the transfiguration (Luke ix. 29), and in the lowest depth of the humiliation in Gethsemane (Luke xxii. 41), he prayed. He prayed for his apostles whom he chose (Luke vi. 12), and for his murderers by whom he was rejected (Luke xxiii. 34). He prayed before Peter confessed him (Luke ix. 18), and also before Peter denied him—Luke xxii. 32], ᵇ **10 And straightway coming up out of** {ᵃ **went up straightway from**} ᵇ **the water** [the two prepositions, "out of" and "from," show that Jesus was not yet fully out of the river, and that the vision and the voice were immediately associated with his baptism], ᵃ **and lo,** ᵇ **he saw** [The statement that *he* saw the Spirit descending, which is also the language of Matthew, has been taken by some as implying that the Spirit was invisible to the multitude. But we know from John's narrative that it was also seen by John the Baptist (John i. 33, 34), and if it was visible to him and to Jesus, and if it descended, as Luke affirms, in a bodily shape like a dove (Luke iii. 22), it would have required a miracle to hide it from the multitude. Moreover, the object of the Spirit's visible appearance was to point Jesus out, not to himself, but to others; and to point him out as the person concerning whom the voice from heaven was uttered. No doubt, then, the Spirit was visible and the voice audible to all who

were present *] **the heavens rent asunder** [for], ᵃ **the
heavens were** {ᶜ **heaven was**} ᵃ **opened unto him** [The
heavens open at the beginning of Jesus' ministry to honor
him, and at the end of it to receive him. Christ is the opener
of heaven for all men], **and he saw the Spirit of God
descending** [the Spirit came upon Jesus to give him the
miraculous power which he afterward exerted—Luke iv. 14]
as a dove [That is, like a dove. All four evangelists are careful to inform us that it was not an actual dove], **and coming
upon him;** ᶜ **22 and the Holy Spirit descended in a
bodily form** [Lightfoot suggests that the Spirit thus descended
that he might be revealed to be a personal substance and not
merely an operation of the Godhead, and might thus make a
sensible demonstration as to his proper place in the Trinity], **as
a dove** [The descent of the Spirit upon Jesus was in accordance with prophecy (Isa. xi. 2; lxi. 1). The dove shape suggests purity, gentleness, peace, etc. Jesus makes the dove a
symbol of harmlessness (Matt. x. 15). In fact, the nature of
this bird makes it a fit emblem of the Spirit, for it comports
well with the fruits of the Spirit (Gal. v. 22, 23). The nations
of the earth emblazon eagles upon their banners and lions upon
their shields, but He who shall gather all nations into his kingdom, appeared as a Lamb, and his Spirit appeared under the
symbol of a dove. Verily his kingdom is not of this world. It

---

꙰ Recognizing the ꞷei ht of Bro. McGarvey's argument, I nevertheless
contend that the multitude only shared partia ly in such a vision, if they shared
in it at al ; for 1. There is no Scripture which even hints that the vision was seen
by more than the two *inspired* parties, Jesus and John; and, on the contrary, the
words of Jesus at John v. 37, thou⁀h not addressed to the specific audience
present at his baptism, were addressed to the Jews genera.ly. 2. Jesus was to
be manifested by his character and teaching rather than by heavenly sights
and sounds (Matt. xii. 39), and the mysteries of the kingdom (Matt. xiii. 11) and
the opened heave s (John i. 50, 51), with many other manifestations, were
reserved for believers (John xii. 28-30; Matt. xvii. 1, 2, 9; Acts i. 9; vii. 55, 59;
x 40, 41), and are still so reserved (I. Cor. ii. 14). As to the arguments given
above, we suggest that "bodily shape" does not insure universal sight. Balaam
did not see what the ass saw (Num. xxii. 21-31). Again, it may be true that
Jesus did not need to see the vision to "point him out to himself," but he must
have needed it for some purpose, for it is twice asserted that he saw it, and the
temptations which immediately follow show that assurances of his divinity at
this particular time were by no means misplaced.

is a kingdom of peace and love, not of bloodshed and ambition.   Noah's dove bore the olive branch, the symbol of peace,
and the Holy Spirit manifested Jesus, God's olive branch of
peace sent into this world—Ps. lxxii. 7; Luke ii. 14; John
xiv. 27; Eph. ii. 11–18], **upon him, ᵃ 17 and lo, a voice
ᶜ came ᵃ out of the heavens, {ᶜ heaven}** [Voices from
heaven acknowledged the person of Christ at his birth, his
baptism, his transfiguration and during the concluding days of
his ministry.   At his baptism Jesus was honored by the attestation of both the Spirit and the Father.   But the ordinance
itself was honored by the sensible manifestation of each several personality of the Deity—that the three into whose
name we ourselves are also baptized], **ᵃ saying, This is
{ᵇ thou art}** [The "this is," etc., of Matthew are probably the
words as John the Baptist reported them: the "thou art," etc.,
of Mark and Luke are the words as Jesus actually heard them.
The testimony of the Father is in unreserved support of the
fundamental proposition of Christianity on which the church of
Christ is founded (Matt. xvi. 15–18).   On this point no witness
in the universe was so well qualified to speak as the Father, and
no other fact was so well worthy the honor of being sanctioned
by his audible utterance as this.   The testimony of Christ's life,
of his works, of the Baptist and of the Scriptures might have
been sufficient; but when the Father himself speaks, who
shall doubt the adequacy of the proof?] **ᵃ my beloved Son**
[See also Matt. vii. 5.   The Father himself states that relationship of which the apostle John so often spoke (John i. 1).
Adam was made (Gen. i. 26), but Jesus was begotten (Ps. ii.
7).   Both were sons of God, but in far different senses.   The
baptism of Jesus bears many marked relationships to our own:
1. At his baptism Jesus was manifested as the Son of God.
At our baptism we are likewise manifested as God's children,
for we are baptized into the name of the Father, and are thereby
permitted to take upon ourselves his name.   2. At his baptism
Jesus was fully commissioned as the Christ.   Not anointed
with material oil, but divinely consecrated and qualified by the
Spirit and accredited by the Father.   At baptism we also

received the Spirit (John iii. 5; Acts ii. 38; xix. 1–6) who commissions and empowers us to Christian ministry—Acts i. 8; I. John iii. 24], **in whom** {ᶜ **in thee**} [Some make the phrases "in whom" and "in thee" to mean more than simply a declaration that God is pleased *with* Jesus. They see in it also the statement that the Father will be pleased with all who are "*in* Christ Jesus"—Eph. i. 6] ᵃ**I am well pleased.** [It is no slight commendation to be well pleasing to God (Job iv. 18). It is the Christian's joy that his Saviour had this commendation of the Father at the entrance upon his ministry.] ᶜ**23 And Jesus himself, when he began *to teach*, was about thirty years of age.** [The age when a Levite entered on God's service (Num. iv. 3, 47); at which Joseph stood before Pharaoh (Gen. xli. 46); and at which David began to reign (II. Sam. v. 4). Canon Cook fixes the date of Christ's baptism in the spring A. U. C. 780, Wiseler in the summer of that year, and Ellicott in the winter of that year.]

XIX.

JESUS TEMPTED IN THE WILDERNESS.

ᵃ MATT. IV. 1–11; ᵇ MARK I. 12, 13; ᶜ LUKE IV. 1–13.

ᶜ**1 And Jesus, full of the Holy Spirit, returned from the Jordan, ᵇ12 And straightway the Spirit driveth him forth ᶜand ᵃ1 Then** [Just after his baptism, with the glow of the descended Spirit still upon him, and the commending voice of the Father still ringing in his ears, Jesus is rushed into the suffering of temptation. Thus abrupt and violent are the changes of life. The spiritually exalted may expect these sharp contrasts. Afteᵣ being in the third heaven, Paul had a messenger of Satan to buffet him—II. Cor. xii. 7] **was Jesus led up** [The two expressions "driveth" and "led up" show that Jesus was drawn to the wilderness by an irresistible impulse, and did not go thither of his own volition (Ezek. xl. 2). He was brought into temptation, but did not seek it. He was led of God into temptation, but was not tempted of God. God

may bring us into temptation (Matt. vi. 13; xxvi. 31; Job i.
12; ii. 6), and may make temptation a blessing unto us, tem-
pering it to our strength, and making us stronger by the victory
over it (I. Cor. x. 13; Jas. i. 2, 12), but God himself never
tempts us—Jas. i. 13] **of the Spirit into the wilderness**
[The wilderness sets in back of Jericho and extends thence
along the whole western shore of the Dead Sea. The northern end of this region is in full view from the Jordan as one
looks westward, and a more desolate and forbidding landscape
it would be hard to find. It is vain to locate the temptation in
any particular part of it. Jesus may have wandered about
over nearly all of it] **to be tempted of the devil.** [As a second David, Jesus went forth to meet that Goliath who had so
long vaunted himself against all who sought to serve God, and
had as yet found none to vanquish him. The account of the
temptation must have been given to the disciples by Jesus himself, and as it pleased him to give it to us as an actual history
of real facts, it behooves us to so accept it without being presumptuously inquisitive. Of course it has supernatural features, but the supernatural confronts us all through the life of
Jesus, so there is nothing strange about it here. Jesus had
taken upon him our flesh, and hence he could be tempted, with
a possibility of falling. But his divinity insured his victory over
temptation. He became like us in ability to fall, that he might
make us like unto himself in power to resist. It behooved him
to be tempted, that thus sharing our nature with its weakness
and temptation he might bring us to share his nature with its
strength and sinlessness (Heb. ii. 17, 18; iv. 15, 16). Sinlessness does not preclude temptation, else Adam could not have
been tempted, nor could Satan himself have fallen. Moreover, temptation is in no sense sin. It is the yielding of the
will to temptation which constitutes sin. The spiritual history
of humanity revolves around two persons; namely, the first and
the second Adam. The temptation of Christ was as real as
that of Adam. He had taken upon himself our tempt-
able nature (Phil. ii. 7, 8), and he was tempted not as a
private soldier, but as the second Adam, the Captain of

our salvation (Heb. ii. 10–18). The failure of the first Adam brought sorrow, darkness and death; the success of the second Adam brought joy, light and immortality. One of the tenets of modern infidelity is the denial of the personality of the devil. It is asserted that the idea of a devil was not known to the early Hebrews, but was borrowed from Persian dualism. The Persians held that there were two contending deities —a good one and a bad one; and the Hebrews, according to these critics, learned this doctrine from the Persians during the days of their Babylonian captivity, and modified it so that the god of evil became the devil. But such a theory is based upon the absurd notion that all the books of the Old Testament were written after the return of the Jews from Babylon. Their theory requires this notion, for the books of Genesis and Job, which were written centuries before the captivity, both show a knowledge of this being, and the first connects him and his work with the very beginning of human history. Those who believe in the inspiration of the Scriptures must also believe in the personality of the devil, for they plainly teach it. The devil is a fallen angel (Jude 6; II. Pet. ii. 4). This doctrine need startle no one, for as there are good and bad spirits in the body, so there are good and bad spirits out of the body. Since God permits sinful spirits in the body, why should he not also permit them out of the body? If there can be a Herod, a Nero, a Judas, among men, why may there not be a Satan among evil spirits? Being but an angel, Satan is neither omnipresent, omniscient nor omnipotent. He is only a tolerated rebel, as we are tolerated rebels. He was the first sinner (I. John iii. 8), and was the originator of sin (John viii. 44). He is the perpetual tempter of mankind (Rev. xx. 2, 8), but he shall be conquered by the Redeemer (John xii. 31; Rev. xii. 9), and may be conquered by us also through the grace of Christ (I. Pet. v. 8, 9; Jas. iv. 7); but is, nevertheless, dangerous (Rev. ii. 10; iii. 9). Jesus, therefore, teaches us to pray for deliverance from him (Matt. vi. 13, R. V.). Jesus will destroy the works of Satan (I. John iii. 8), and Satan himself shall suffer eternal punishment

(Rev. xx. 10). There is but one devil in the spirit world. The word which our King James Version translates "devils" should be translated "demons." The word "devil" means false accuser or slanderer, and the word in the plural is twice applied, metaphorically, to men and women (II. Tim. iii. 3; I. Tim. iii. 11). The devil is called slanderer because he speaks against men (Rev. xii. 10–12) and against God (Gen. iii. 1–5). The word "devil" is Greek. The word "Satan" is Hebrew, and means adversary (Job ii. 1). Satan is referred to under many other terms, such as Beelzebub (Matt. xii. 24); serpent (Rev. xii. 9); prince of the powers of the air (Eph. ii. 2); Abaddon (Hebrew) and Apollyon (Greek), meaning destroyer (Rev. ix. 11); Belial, meaning good for nothing (II. Cor. vi. 15); murderer and liar (John viii. 44); prince of this world (John xii. 31); god of this world (II. Cor. iv. 4); and the dragon (Rev. xii. 7). These terms are always used in the Bible to designate an actual person; they are never used merely to personify evil. The devil may have appeared to Jesus in bodily form, or he may have come insensibly as he does to us. Our Lord's temptation makes the personality of the tempter essential, else Christ's own heart must have suggested evil to him, which is incompatible with his perfect holiness.] ᵇ **13 And he was** ᶜ **led in the Spirit** [that is, under the power of the Spirit] **in the wilderness** [Isolation from humanity is no security from temptation. In fact, our present passage of Scripture shows that it is highly favorable to temptation. The experience of all hermits shows that loneliness is the mother of a multitude of evil desires] **2 during forty days** [Matthew speaks of the temptation as coming "after" forty days. Evidently Mark and Luke regard the long fast as part of the process of temptation, seeing that without it the first temptation would have been without force. There is no evidence of any other specific temptations before the three], **being tempted of** ᵇ **Satan;** ᶜ **the devil,** ᵇ **and he was with the wild beasts** [A graphic touch, showing the dreariness and desolation of the wilderness, and indicating its peril. Lions,

wolves, leopards and serpents have been found in the
Judæan wilderness]; ^c **And he did eat nothing** [It used to
be thought that a forty days' absolute fast was a practical impossibility, and Luke's words were therefore modified to mean
that he ate very little. But as a forty days' fast has been safely
accomplished in modern times, and as it was Jesus who fasted,
we see no reason why we should not take Luke's statement
literally, as indicating an absolute fast] **in those days: and
when they were completed,** ^a**2 And when he had
fasted forty days and forty nights** [A forty days' fast was
accomplished by Moses (Ex. xxxiv. 28; Deut. ix. 18), and by
Elijah (I. Kings xix. 8), and it is a significant fact in this connection that these two men appeared with Christ at his transfiguration (Matt. xvii. 3). Those who share Christ's sufferings shall also share his glorification (Rom. viii. 17; II. Tim.
ii. 11, 12). The forty days' fast became a basis for the temptation. We are told that temptation results from the excitement
of desire (Jas. i. 14), and, as a rule, the greater the desire the
greater the temptation. Viewed from this standpoint the temptation of the second Adam greatly exceeded in strength that of
the first, for Adam abstained as to a particular fruit, but Christ
fasted as to all things edible], **he afterward hungered.**
[Here, for the first time, our Lord is shown as sharing our
physical needs. We should note for our comfort that one may
lack bread and suffer want, and still be infinitely beloved in
heaven.] **3 And the tempter came** [Satan is pre-eminently
the tempter, for other tempters are his agents. He may possibly have appeared as an angel of light (II. Cor. xi. 14), but
the purpose of his coming is more important than the manner
of it. He came to produce sin in Jesus, for sin would render
him forever incapable of becoming our Saviour—a sacrifice
for the sins of others] ^c**3 And the devil said unto him,
If thou art the Son of God, command this stone that
it** {^a**command that these stones**} **become bread.**
[The devil's "if" strikes at the faith of Christ, and faith is
the bond of union and accord between man and God. The
main sin of this temptation was therefore distrust, though it

had other sinful phases. The Father's voice had just declared the Sonship of Jesus, and Satan here boldly questions the truth of God's words, just as he did in the beginning (Gen. iii. 3–5). The temptation smacks of curiosity, and curiosity is the mother of many sins. Though Satan so glibly questioned the divinity of Christ, his kingdom soon began to feel the power of that divinity (Luke iv. 34–41), and shall continue to feel it until his kingdom is destroyed (Heb. ii. 14; I. John iii. 8). This temptation appealed to the present appetite, the impulse of the moment, as many of our temptations do. It has been quaintly said of the tempter that "he had sped so successfully to his own mind by a temptation about a matter of eating with the first Adam, that he practiced the old manner of trading with the second." This first temptation is still Satan's favorite with the poor. He suggests to them that if they were really the beloved objects of God's care, their condition would be otherwise. We should note that Jesus wrought no selfish miracle. Such an act would have been contrary to all Scripture precedent. Paul did not heal himself (I. Cor. xii. 7–9; Gal. iv. 13; Col. iv. 14); nor Epaphroditus (Phil. ii. 25-27), nor Trophimus (II. Tim. iv. 20). Denying himself the right to make bread in the wilderness, Christ freely used his miraculous power to feed others in the desert (Matt. xiv. 15–21), and merited as just praise those words which were meant as a bitter taunt—Matt. xxvii. 42.] **4 But he** {ᶜ**4 And Jesus**} ᵃ**answered and said,** ᶜ**unto him, It is written** [Jesus quotes Deut. viii. 3. It is a saying relative to the times when Israel was sustained by manna in the wilderness. The case of Jesus was now similar to that of Israel. He was in a foodless wilderness, but he trusted that as God had provided for Israel in its helplessness, so would he now provide for him. Israel sinned by doubt and murmuring, and proposing to obtain bread in its own way—that is, by returning to Egypt (Ex. xvi. 1–9). Jesus avoided a like sin. We should note the use which our Lord made of Scripture: in his hour of trial he did not look to visions and voices and special revelation for guidance, but used the written Word as the lamp for his feet (Ps. cxix. 105); in the conflict of temptation he did not defend himself by his own divine wisdom, but used that wisdom which God had revealed to all Israel through his prophets. Jesus fought as a man (Phil. ii. 6, 7), and used that weapon which, as God, he had given to man (Eph. vi. 17). Jesus used the Scripture as of final, argument-ending authority. Eve also started with "God hath said" (Gen. iii. 3); but she was not constant in her adherence to God's word. Jesus permitted Satan neither to question nor pervert the Scripture], **Man** [In using the word "man" Jesus takes his stand with us as a human being] **shall not live by bread alone.** [Called out of Egypt as God's Son (Matt. ii. 15), Jesus could well expect that he would be fed with manna after his forty days' fast. He trusted that God could furnish a table in the wilderness (Ps. lxxviii. 19). We, too, have abundant reason for a like trust. God gave us our lives, and gave his Son to redeem them from sin. He may let us suffer, but we can not perish if we trust him. Let us live by his word rather than by bread. It is better to die for righteousness than to live by sin. God fed Israel with supernatural bread, to show the people that they lived thus, and not by what they were pleased to call natural means. The stomach is a useful agent, but it is not the source of life, nor even the life sustainer. Those who think that the securing of bread is the first essential to the sustaining of life, will fail to seek any diviner food, and so will eventually starve with hunger—soul hunger.] [a] **but by every word that proceedeth out of the mouth of God.** [To satisfy our sense of duty is often more pleasant than to appease the pangs of hunger (John iv. 32–34; Job xxiii. 12; Jer. xv. 16). The trust of Jesus that God would speak in his behalf and save him, was like that of Job (Job xiii. 15). God can sustain our lives without food if he chooses. We shall live if God wills it, bread or no bread; and we shall likewise die at his word (Matt. vi. 25; John vi. 47–58; Acts xvii. 28). God can support our lives independent of our body—Matt. x. 28.] **5 Then the devil taketh him** [Matthew emphasizes the compulsory companionship of Satan. Jesus was in the hands of Satan as was Job (Job ii. 5, 6); but in Jesus' case Satan had the power of life and death, and he eventually took Jesus to the cross and slew him there] **into the holy city** [A common name for Jerusalem. The inscription on Jewish coins was "Jerusalem the Holy." Arabs to-day call it "el Kuds," "the Holy." The Holy City did not exclude the tempter nor temptations. The church may be the scene of man's sorest trial to resist wrong. But in the Holy City which is to come there will be no temptation]; ᶜ9 **And he led him to Jerusalem, ᵃand he set him** [the two verbs "taking" and "setting" imply that Satan exercised a control over the bodily person of our Lord] **on the pinnacle of the temple** [It is not known exactly what spot is indicated by the word "pinnacle." Hence three places have been contended for as the proper locality: 1. The apex of the temple structure itself. 2. The top of Solomon's porch. 3. The top of Herod's royal portico. As to the temple itself, Josephus tells us that its roof was covered with spikes of gold, to prevent even birds from alighting upon it, and, if so, men could not stand upon it. Solomon's porch, or the eastern portico, faced the Mount of Olives, and has been fixed upon by tradition as the place from which James, the Lord's brother, was hurled. The royal portico of Herod was at the southeast corner of the temple enclosure, and overlooked the valley of Kidron. Here was then, and is yet, the greatest height about the temple, and it was, therefore the most suitable place for Satan's proposal], **6 and saith** {ᶜ said} ᵃ **unto him, If** [Godly life rests on faith. The life the devil would have us lead rests on ifs and uncertainties, on doubt and skepticism. We should note that foolish men doubt the divinity of Jesus, but the temptations of our Lord show how positively Satan was convinced of it. The opening scenes of Christ's ministry are redolent with his divinity. The Baptist asserted his purity and might, the Spirit visibly acknowledged his worthiness, the Father audibly testified to his Sonship, and the devil twice assaulted him as the divine champion] **thou art the Son of God, cast thyself down**

[The first temptation was to under-confidence; the second to over-trust and presumption—two very dangerous conditions of the soul. Men begin by disparagingly doubting that Jesus can save them from their sins, and end by recklessly presuming that he will save them in their sins. Comparing this with Eve's temptation, we find that she was vainly curious to see if she might be like God (Gen. iii. 5), but Christ resisted such curiosity. It is urged by some as to this temptation that there is no hint of vainglory or display, because nothing is said about casting himself down in the presence of the people, and that Jesus was merely taken to the temple because the sacred locality would tend to heighten his trust in the protecting promise which Satan quoted. But this ground is not well taken, for: 1. The temple presumes a crowd. 2. We have a right to presume that this temptation would be like others to which Jesus was subjected. He was frequently invited to work miracles to satisfy curiosity, and he invariably refused to do so]: ^c**from hence: 10 for it is written** [The quotation is taken from Ps. xci. 11, 12, and applies to man generally. Note 1. The devil's head is full of Scripture, but to no profit, for his heart is empty of it. 2. By quoting it he shows a sense of its power which modern rationalism would do well to consider. 3. Satan's abuse of Scripture did not discourage Christ's use of it], **He shall give his angels charge concerning thee** [Regarding Satan's words as a quotation, we are struck with the fact that his knowledge of this particular passage was based upon his personal experience. He had been confronted by the presence of the guardian angels and had fretted at it (Job i. 10; II. Kings vi. 8, 17; Ps. xxxiv. 7; Jude 9). As a temptation, Satan's words appeal to Jesus to be more religious; to put more trust and reliance upon the promises of the Father; and he puts him in the place—the temple—where he might argue that God could least afford to let his promise fail], **to guard thee: 11 and, On their hands they shall bear thee up** [All who love pomp, display of artistic taste, gaieties of fashion, intoxication of fame, etc., fall by this temptation. Those who truly rest on God's promises, stand on a sure foundation, but those who rise on bubbles must come **down when they burst**], **Lest haply thou dash thy foot against a stone. 12 And Jesus answering said unto him, ᵃ again it is written {ᶜsaid,}** ["Written," "said;" the writings of Scripture are in general the sayings of God. But the Bible is not made up of isolated texts. To get a right understanding we must compare Scripture with Scripture. We could have no higher indorsement of the Old Testament than this use of it by Christ. It was sufficient for him in his temptations. and with the addition of the New Testament, it is sufficient for us in all things—II. Tim. iii. 16, 17; Col. iii. 3–16], ᵃ **Thou shalt not make trial** [Make experiment upon God, set traps for him, put one's self in dangerous situations, hoping thereby to draw forth some show of loving deliverance. Had Jesus cast himself down, he would have demanded of the Father a needless miracle to prove his Sonship, and would thereby have put the love of God to an unnecessary trial. All who jeopardize themselves without any command of God or call of duty, make trial of his love] **of the Lord thy God. 8 Again, the devil taketh him** [whether naturally or supernaturally, "whether in the body or out of the body" (II. Cor. xii. 2–4), we can not tell. But it was a real, practical trial and temptation] **unto an exceeding high mountain** [it is immaterial which mountain this was; for from no mountain could one see the whole earth with the natural eye], ᶜ **5 And he led him up, ᵃ and showeth {ᶜshowed} ᵃ him** [It is not said by either evangelist that Jesus saw the kingdoms from the mountain-top, but that Satan *showed* them to him. From any high Judæan mountain it would be easy for him to locate Rome, Greece, Egypt, Persia and Assyria, and as he pointed out their locality a few brief words of description would picture them to the imagination of Jesus, and cause their glories to move before his eyes. But it is very likely that to this description some sort of supernatural vision was added. It tempted the eye of Jesus as the luscious fruit did the eye of Eve—Gen. iii. 16] **all the kingdoms of the world** [It tempted Jesus to realize the dreams which the Jewish nation entertained. It was an appeal to him to reveal himself in the fullness of his power and authority as above generals, princes, kings and all beings of all ages. An appeal to obtain by physical rather than by spiritual power; by the short-cut path of policy rather than by the long road of suffering and martyrdom. Jesus came to obtain the kingdoms of the world. He was born King of the Jews, and confessed himself to be a King before Pilate. All authority is now given unto him, and he must reign until he puts all his enemies under his feet, and until all the kingdoms of the world become his kingdom. Satan's way to obtain this kingdom differed from God's way. He might obtain it by doing Satan's will and becoming his worshiper, or by worshiping God and doing his will. Satan would give the speedier possession, but God the more lasting. We also strive for a kingdom; but let us obtain ours as Christ did his], **and the glory of them** [That is, all their resources as well as their magnificence. Their cities, lands and people, their armies, treasures and temples, etc. Many parents, in encouraging their children to seek earthly glory and distinction, unconsciously assist Satan in urging this temptation]; ᶜ**in a moment of time.** [These words strongly indicate that the prospect must have been supernaturally presented. The suddenness of the vision added greatly to the power of the temptation.] ᵃ**9 and he** ᶜ**the devil said unto him, To thee will I give all this authority** {ᵃ**All these things will I give thee,**} [From the standpoint of Christ's humanity, how overwhelming the temptation! It was the world's honors to one who had for thirty years led the life of a village carpenter: it was the world's riches to him who had not where to lay his head. From the standpoint of Jesus' divinity the temptation was repulsive. It was a large offer in the sight of Satan, but a small one in the sight of him who made all the worlds. Such offers are large to the children of the world, but small to those who are by faith joint-heirs with Christ (Rom. viii. 17; Phil. iii. 7, 8). But the temptation was, nevertheless, very specious and plausible. The power of Jesus linked with that of Satan, and operating through Jewish fanaticism and pagan expectation would, in a few months, have brought the whole earth into one temporal kingdom, with Jesus as its head. But the kingdom of Christ rested upon a surer promise (Ps. ii. 8) than that here given by the "father of lies." God had promised, and, despite the pretensions of Satan, God had not yet retired from the government of the world. It was true that Satan and his emissaries had, by usurpation, gained an apparent possession of the world, but Jesus had right to it as the heir of God (Matt. xxi. 33–43). Being stronger than Satan, he had come to regain his kingdom, not by treaty, but by conquest (Luke xi. 19–22). Moreover, he would obtain it as a spiritual and not as a carnal kingdom. Servants of Christ should remember this. Every attempt to establish Messiah's kingdom as an outward, worldly dominion is an effort to convert the kingdom of heaven into the kingdom of the devil. God's kingdom can not be secularized. It should be noted also that Satan omits the words "if thou be the Son of God" in this instance, for their presence would have marred the force of the temptation. Note also that this was the only temptation wherein Satan evinced any show of generosity. He is slow to give anything, and most of us sell out to him for nothing—Isa. lii. 3], **and the glory of them: for it hath been delivered unto me** [Satan does not claim an absolute but a derivative right, and his claim is not wholly unfounded (John xii. 31; xiv. 30; xvi. 11). But the kingdom has been delivered unto him by men rather than by God (Eph. ii. 2). How much more quickly Jesus would have obtained power, had he received it from men by consenting to co-operate with them in their sinful practices as does Satan]; **and to whomsoever I will** [Not so Jesus. His giving is according to the Father's will—Matt. ix. 23] **I give it.** [The Emperor Tiberius then held it in the fullest sense ambition ever realized. Yet he was the most miserable and degraded of men. Satan knows how to take full toll for all that he gives.] **7 If** [In the temptations Satan uses three "ifs." The first "if" is one of despairing doubt; the second, one of vainglorious speculation; the third, one of moral and spiritual compromise] **thou therefore wilt ª fall down and worship ᶜ before me** [Satan and God each seek the worship of man, but from very different motives. God is holiness and goodness, and we are invited to worship him that we may thereby be induced to grow like him. But Satan seeks worship for vanity's sake. How vast the vanity which would give so great a reward for one act of worship! Verily the devil is fond of it. He gives nothing unless he obtains it, and all his generosity is selfishness. Worshiping before Satan is the bending of the soul rather than of the body. He holds before each of us some crown of success, and says: "Bend just a little; slightly compromise your conscience. Accept the help of Pharisee and Sadducee, and keep silent as to their sins. Mix a little diplomacy with your righteousness. Stoop just a little. If you do, I will aid you and insure your success. If you do not, I will defeat you and laugh at your failures." It is Satan's sin to make such suggestions, but it is not our sin until we comply with them. We may more quickly obtain by his wrong way, but more surely by God's right way. Let no Christian be humiliated or discouraged by gross temptation, since even the Son of God was tempted to worship the devil. What Jesus would not do, the Beast has done, and has received the kingdoms for a season (Rev. xiii. 1–9). Note, too, that it is all one whether we worship Satan, or mammon, the gift which he offers—Matt. vi. 24], **it shall all be thine. 8 And ª 10 Then ᶜ Jesus answered and said {ª saith} ᶜ unto him, ª Get thee hence** [The passionate utterance of an aroused soul. Indignation is as divine as patience (Eph. iv. 26). Satan's sweetest temptation was most disgusting to Christ, for its sin was so grossly apparent. It ran counter to the very first of the ten commandments. Jesus would give it no room in his thoughts; he spurned it, as being as heinous as the law describes it (Deut. iii. 6–11). Temptation must be peremptorily rejected. Jesus did not stop to weigh the worthiness of Satan; it was sufficient that God only is to be worshiped. As God, Jesus was himself an object of worship; but as man he worshiped the Father privately and publicly. Satan sought to command Jesus, but was commanded of him. **Step by step Satan has obeyed this command, and, foot after foot, earth's spiritual world has been yielded by his departing presence],** **Satan** [The first and second temptations were so subtle and covert, and their sin so skillfully disguised, as to suggest that Satan himself was disguised. If so, his pride and vanity, revealed in this last temptation, betrayed him so that Jesus tore off his mask and called him by his right name. When he tempted him in a somewhat similar matter, Jesus called Simon Peter by this name (Matt. xvi. 23), but he laid a different command upon each of them. To Satan he spoke as an enemy, saying: "Get thee hence." He ordered Satan from his presence, for he had no proper place there. To Peter he spoke as to a presumptuous disciple, saying: "Get thee behind me." The disciple is a follower of his master, and his proper place is in the rear] : **for it is written** [Jesus gives a free translation of Deut. vi. 13. He substitutes the word "worship" for the word "fears." Fear prohibits false and induces true worship, and loving worship is the source of all acceptable service. The three Scripture quotations used by Jesus are all from the Book of Deuteronomy. He struck Satan with that very part of the Spirit's sword which modern critical infidelity, in the name of religion, and often aided by so-called religious organizations, seeks to persuade us to cast away], **Thou shalt worship the Lord thy God, and him only shalt thou serve.** [By serving God, Jesus obtained all the earthly authority which the devil offered him, and heavenly authority in addition thereto (Matt. xxviii. 18). So much better are the rewards of God than Satan's.] ᶜ **13 And when the devil had completed every temptation,** ᵃ **11 Then the devil leaveth {ᶜ he departeth from} him for a season.** [See Jas. iv. 7. But Satan left to return many times. Here was the first being endowed with human nature who had defeated Satan under all circumstances for thirty years. This was Satan's first defeat under Christ's ministry. His last is yet to come, and it shall come by this same Christ Jesus. Temptations are battles. They leave the victor stronger and the

vanquished weaker. Hence Satan when resisted is represented as fleeing. But he only flees for a season. He never
despairs of the conflict so long as man is on the earth. Christ
was constantly tempted by the returning devil (Luke xxii. 28).
As Jesus hung upon the cross, all these three temptations with
their accompanying "ifs" were spread out before him—Matt.
xxvi. 39–43] ᵃ **and behold, angels came** [They had probably
witnessed the contest. Compare I. Cor. iv. 9; I. Tim. iii. 16.
Angels do not appear again visibly ministering unto Jesus until
we find him in Gethsemane (Luke xxii. 43). When Satan
finally departs from us, we, too, shall find ourselves in the presence of the angels—Luke xvi. 22] **and ministered unto
him.** [Jesus was probably fed by the angels, as was Elijah by
one of them (I. Kings xix. 4-7). Satan and suffering first,
then angels, refreshment and rest. God had indeed given his
angels charge, and they came to him who refused to put the
Father to the test. But they did not succor Jesus during his
temptation, for that was to be resisted by himself alone—Isa.
lxiii. 3.]

XX.

JOHN'S FIRST TESTIMONY TO JESUS.

(Bethany beyond Jordan, February, A. D. 27.)

ᵈ JOHN I. 19–34.

ᵈ **19 And this is the witness of John** [John had been
sent to testify, "and" this is the matter of his testimony],
when the Jews [The term "Jews" is used seventy times by
John to describe the ruling classes of Judæa] **sent unto him**
[In thus sending an embassy they honored John more than
they ever honored Christ. They looked upon John as a priest
and Judæan, but upon Jesus as a carpenter and Galilean. It
is probable that the sending of this investigating committee
marks the period when the feelings of the rulers toward John
changed from friendliness to hostility. At the first, probably
led on by the prophecies of Daniel, these Jews found joy in

John's coming (John v. 33-35). When they attended his ministry in person he denounced their wickedness and incurred their hatred] **from Jerusalem priests and Levites** [they were commissioned to teach (II. Chron. v. 3; Neh. viii. 7-9), and it was probably because of their wisdom as teachers that they were sent to question John about his baptism] **to ask him, Who art thou? 20 And he confessed, and denied not; and he confessed** [The repetition here suggests John's firmness under repeated temptation. As the questioners ran down the scale from "Christ" to "that prophet," John felt himself diminishing in their estimation, but firmly declined to take honors which did not belong to him], **I am not** [in this entire section (vs. 20-24) John places emphasis upon the pronoun "I," that he may contrast himself with Christ] **the Christ.** [When the apostle John wrote this Gospel it had become fashionable with many of the Baptist's disciples to assert that the Baptist was the Christ. (Recognitions of Clement i. 50, 60; Olshausen, Hengstenberg, Godet.) In giving this testimony of the Baptist, John corrects this error; but his more direct purpose is to show forth John's full testimony, and give the basis for the words of Jesus found at John v. 33. The fact that the Jews were disposed to look upon John as the Messiah gave all the greater weight to his testimony; for the more exalted the person of the witness, the weightier are his words. John's own experience doubtless caused him to feel the influence of the Baptist's testimony.] **21 And they asked him, What then? Art thou Elijah?** [Malachi had declared that Elijah should precede the Messiah (Mal. iv. 5). The Jews interpreted this prophecy literally, and looked for the return of the veritable Elijah who was translated (Matt. xvii. 10). This literal Elijah did return, and was seen upon the Mount of Transfiguration before the crucifixion of our Lord. But the prophecy of Malachi referred to a spiritual Elijah—one who should come "in the spirit and power of Elijah," and in this sense John fulfilled Malachi's prediction—Luke i. 17; Matt. xi. 14; xvii. 12.] **And he saith, I am not.** [He answered their question according to the sense in which they had asked it. He was not the Elijah who had been translated about nine hundred years before this time.] **Art thou the prophet?** [Moses had foretold a prophet who should come (Deut. xviii. 15–18), but the Jews appear to have had no fixed opinion concerning him, for some thought he would be a second Moses, others a second Elijah, others the Messiah. The Scriptures show us how uncertain they were about him (Matt. xvi. 14; John vi. 14; vii. 40, 41). As to Jeremiah being that prophet, see II. Macc. ii. 7. Even Christians disagree as to whether Moses refers to Christ or to a line of prophets. Though divided in opinion as to who this prophet would be, the Jews were fairly unanimous as to what he would do. Finding in their Scriptures two pictures of the Christ, one representing him as a great Conqueror, and the other of his priesthood, setting him forth as a great Sufferer, they took the pictures to refer to *two* personages, one denoting a king—the Messiah—and the other a prophet. The Jews to this day thus divide the Christ of prophecy, and seek to make him two personages.] **And he answered, No.** [He was not the prophet, either as he or as they understood that term. John gives us a beautiful example of humility. Like Paul, he would not be overvalued—Acts xiv. 13–15; I. Cor. i. 12, 13.] **22 They said therefore unto him, Who art thou? that we may give an answer to them that sent us. What sayest thou of thyself?** [Unable to guess his office, they asked him to state it plainly.] **23 He said, I am the voice** [It is as though John answered, "You ask who I am. My personality is nothing: my message everything. I shall pass away as a sound passes into silence; but the truth which I have uttered shall abide." In his answer John shows himself to be the spiritual Elijah, for he declares that he came to do the work of Elijah; viz.: to prepare the people for the advent of Messiah. There are many echoes in the world; but few voices] **of one crying in the wilderness, Make straight the way of the Lord** [prepare the minds and hearts of the people that Christ may freely enter in], **as said Isaiah the prophet.** [Isa. xl. 3.] **24 And they had been sent from**

the Pharisees. [Of all the Jewish sects the Pharisees were most attentive to external rites and ceremonies, and hence would notice John's baptism more than would others. It is interesting to notice that the Pharisees, who were Christ's most bitter opponents, were warned of John about the presence of Messiah from the very beginning.] **25 And they asked him, and said unto him, Why then baptizest thou, if thou art not the Christ, neither Elijah, neither the prophet?** [If you are no more important personage, why do you presume to introduce any other ordinance than those provided for by the law of Moses? The question shows that to them John's baptism was a new rite. Even if proselyte baptism existed at this time (of which there is certainly no sufficient evidence), it differed in two marked ways from John's baptism: 1. John baptized his converts, while proselytes baptized themselves. 2. John baptized Jews and not Gentiles.] **26 John answered them, saying, I baptize in water: in the midst of you standeth one whom ye know not, 27** *even* **he that cometh after me** [that is, follows in that way which I as forerunner am preparing for him], **the latchet of whose shoe I am not worthy to unloose.** [The words "standeth" and "shoe" showed that the person of whom the Baptist spoke had a visible, bodily form. To unloose the latchet was a peculiarly servile office. The Talmud says, "Every office a servant will do for his master, a scholar should perform for his teacher, except loosing his sandal-thong." The greatest prophet felt unworthy to render Christ this humble service, but unconverted sinners often presume to serve Christ according to their own will, and fully expect to have their service honored and rewarded. Taken as a whole, the answer of John appears indirect and insufficient. What was there in all this to authorize him to baptize? This appears to be his meaning: "You demand my authority for baptism. It rests in him for whom I prepare the way. It is a small matter to introduce baptism in water for one so worthy. If you accept him, my baptism will need no explanation; and if you reject him, my rite and its authority are both wholly immaterial.] **28 These things were done in Bethany beyond the Jordan** [Owing to variation in the manuscripts, we may read " Bethany " or " Bethabara," or even possibly " Bethabara in Bathania." Tradition fixes upon the Jericho ford, which is about five miles on an air line north of the Dead Sea, as the site of Jesus' baptism. But this spot is eighty miles from Cana of Galilee, and hence Jesus, leaving it on foot, could not well have attended the wedding in Cana on "the third day " (John ii. 1). We must therefore look for Bethany or Bethabara farther up the river. John the Baptist was a roving preacher (Luke iii. 3), and during the forty days of Jesus' temptation he seems to have moved up the river Jordan. Fifty miles above the Jericho ford, and ten miles south of the Sea of Galilee, Lieutenant Conder found a ford named 'Abarah (meaning " ferry "), which answers to Bethabara (meaning " house of the ferry "). It was in the land of Bashan, which in the time of Christ was called Bathania (meaning " soft soil "). This spot is only twenty-two miles from Cana. Being *beyond* the Jordan, it is not in Galilee, as Dr. Thomson asserts. Conder says: " We have collected the names of over forty fords, and no other is called 'Abarah; nor does the word occur again in all the nine thousand names collected by the survey party "], **where John was baptizing. 29 On the morrow he seeth Jesus coming unto him** [Jesus had just returned from the temptation in the wilderness. This is his first appearance in John's Gospel. The fact that John leaves out all the early history of Jesus shows that he wrote many years after the other evangelists, when all these facts were so well known as to need no mention by him], **and saith, Behold, the Lamb of God** [Lambs were commonly used for sin-offerings (Lev. iv. 32), and three of them were sacrificed in the cleansing of a leper (Lev. xiv. 10). A lamb was also the victim of the morning (9 A. M.) and evening (3 P. M.) sacrifice (Ex. xix. 38)—the hours when Jesus was nailed to the cross and when he expired. A lamb was also the victim at the paschal supper. The great prophecy of Isaiah, setting forth the vicarious sacrifice of Christ (Isa. liii. 1–23) depicts him as a lamb, and in terms which answer closely to the words here used by John. The Jews to whom John spoke readily understood his allusion as being to sacrificial lambs; but they could not understand his meaning, for they had no thought of the sacrifice of a person. Jesus is called the Lamb of God because he is the lamb or sacrifice which God provided and accepted as the true and only sin-offering—Heb. x. 4-14; I. Pet. i. 19], **that taketh away the sin of the world!** [The present tense, "taketh," is used because the expiatory effect of Christ's sacrifice is perpetual, and the fountain of his forgiveness never fails. Expiated sin is thus spoken of as being taken away (Lev. x. 17; Ex. xxxiv. 7; Num. xiv. 8). Some, seeking to avoid the vicarious nature of Christ's sacrifice, claim that the Baptist means that Jesus would gradually lift the world out of sin by his teaching. But lambs do not teach, and sin is not removed by teaching, but by sacrifice (Heb. ix. 22; Rev. v. 9). Jesus was sacrificed for the world, that is, for the entire human family in all ages. All are bought, but all do not acknowledge the purchase (II. Pet. ii. 1). He gives liberty to all, but all do not receive it, and some having received it return again to bondage (Gal. iv. 9). The Baptist had baptized for the remission of sins. He now points his converts to him who would make this promise good unto their souls. A Christian looks upon Christ as one who has taken away his past sin (I. Pet. ii. 24), and who will forgive his present sin—I. John i. 9.] **30 This is he of whom I said** [for this saying see John i. 15, 27], **After me cometh a man who is become before me: for he was before me.** [As a man John was six months older than Jesus, but Jesus was the eternal Word. The Baptist therefore asserts here the pre-existence of our Lord.] **31 And I knew him not** [had no such certain knowledge of him as would fit me to testify concerning him]; **but that he should be made manifest to Israel, for this cause came I baptizing in water.** [John baptized not only that he himself might know Christ by the spiritual sign, but also that through that knowledge duly published all Israel might know him.] **32 And John bare witness,**

saying, I have beheld the Spirit descending as a dove out of heaven; and it abode upon him. [The descent of the Spirit served at least two purposes: 1. It enabled John to identify the Messiah. 2. It was, so to speak, an official recognition of Jesus as Messiah similar to the anointing or crowning of a king. It is asserted by some that it was of no benefit to Jesus, since his own divine powers permitted of no addition; but the language of Scripture indicates otherwise — Isa. xi. 2, 3; Luke iv. 17–19; John iii. 34.] **33 And I knew him not** [John's assertions that he did not know Jesus are assertions that he did not know him to be the Messiah. He *believed* it, as appears from his reluctance to baptize him, but he did not know it. His language to the people shows this (John i. 26). Many of the people must have known Jesus, but none of them knew him to be the Messiah. Moreover, when John denied that he knew Jesus as Messiah we must not take it that he was ignorant of the past history of Jesus. No doubt he knew in a general way who Jesus was; but as the official forerunner and announcer of Jesus, and as the heaven-sent witness (John i. 6, 7), it was necessary that the Baptist should receive, by personal revelation from God, as here stated, an indubitable, absolute knowledge of the Messiahship of Jesus. Without this, John would not have been truly qualified as a witness. That Jesus is the Son of God must not rest on hearsay evidence. John kept silent till he could testify of his own knowledge]: **but he that sent me** [thus humbly does John claim his divine commission as a prophet] **to baptize in water, he said unto me, Upon whomsoever thou shalt see the Spirit descending, and abiding upon him** [John seems to emphasize the abiding of the Spirit. The Spirit of God was also bestowed upon the prophets and the apostles, but in them his power was intermittent, and not constant; visions came to them intermittently, but with Christ the fellowship of the Spirit was continuous], **the same is he that baptizeth in the Holy Spirit.** [Christ bestows the Spirit upon his own. If he himself received the Spirit at the time of his baptism, why should it be thought strange that he bestows the Spirit upon his disciples at the time of their baptism?—See Acts ii. 38; xix. 1–7; Tit. iii. 5.] **34 And I have seen** [that is, I have seen the promised sign], **and have borne witness that this is the Son of God.** [This is the climax of John's testimony. It was two-fold, embracing the results of the two senses of sight and hearing. 1. John *saw* the dove-like apparition of the Spirit, which convinced him that Jesus was the one to baptize in the Spirit. 2. He *heard* the voice of the Father, which convinced him that Jesus was the Son of God. As to each of these two facts he had a separate revelation, appealing to a different sense, and each given by that personage of the Deity more nearly concerned in the matter revealed. John was not only to prepare the people to receive Christ by calling them to repentance, and baptizing them for the remission of their sins; there was another work equally great and important to be performed. Their *heads* as well as their *hearts* needed his preparatory services. His testimony ran counter to and corrected popular opinion concerning Christ. We see that John corrected four errors. 1. The Jews looked for a Messiah of no greater spiritual worthiness than John himself, but the Baptist disclaimed even the right to unlace the Lord's shoe, that he might emphasize the difference between himself and the Messiah in point of spiritual excellency. 2. The Jews looked for one who would come after Moses, David, and the prophets, and lost sight of the fact that he would be before them, both in point of time and of honor (Matt. xxii. 41–46). 3. The Jews looked for a liberator from earthly bondage — a glorious king; John pointed them to a liberator from spiritual bondage, a perfect sacrifice acceptable to God. 4. The Jews looked for a human Messiah, a son of David. John enlarged their idea, by pointing them to a Messiah who was also the Son of God. When the Jews accept John's guidance as a prophet, they will believe in the Messiahship of Jesus.]

XXI.

JESUS MAKES HIS FIRST DISCIPLES.

(Bethany beyond Jordan, Spring, A. D. 27.)

^d JOHN I. 35–51.

^d **35 Again on the morrow** [John's direct testimony bore fruit on the second day] **John was standing, and two of his disciples** [An audience of two. A small field; but a large harvest]**; 36 and he looked** [Gazed intently. The word is used at Mark xiv. 67; Luke xxii. 61; Mark x. 21, 43. John looked searchingly at that face, which, so far as any record shows, he was never to see on earth again. The more intently we look upon Jesus, the more powerfully we proclaim him] **upon Jesus as he walked** [This detail seems to be introduced to show that the Baptist did not stop Jesus and enter into familiar conversation with him. The witness of John was wholly that of an inspired, unbiased prophet, and not that of a friend or a familiar acquaintance], **and saith, Behold, the Lamb of God!** [John repeats this testimony. He might have chosen another message, but preferred this one. Paul also had but one theme—I. Cor. ii. 2; Gal. vi. 14.] **37 And the two disciples** [Andrew and probably John, the writer of this Gospel. The following are indications that it was John: 1. From this time on he speaks as an eye-witness. 2. We have no other account in his Gospel of his call to discipleship. 3. On seven other occasions in this Gospel he withholds his name — John xiii. 26; xix. 26, 35; xxii.; xxi. 7, 20, 24] **heard him speak, and they followed Jesus.** [Here is the fountainhead of Christianity, for Christianity is following Jesus.] **38 And Jesus turned, and beheld them following, and saith unto them, What seek ye?** [They doubtless felt such awe and reverence for the person of Jesus as would make them hesitate to address him. Hence Jesus himself opens the way for intercourse with himself.] **And they said unto him, Rabbi (which is to say, being interpreted, Teacher)**

[By the way in which John explains Jewish words and customs, it becomes apparent that his Gospel was written for Gentiles as well as for Jews. Some take these explanations as
evidence that John's Gospel was written after the destruction
of the temple at Jerusalem. They are indeed a slight evidence
of this, for it is more expedient to explain a custom which has
ceased to exist than one which survives to explain itself],
**where abidest thou? 39 He saith unto them, Come,
and ye shall see.** [The fitting invitation of him who says:
" Seek, and ye shall find."] **They came therefore and
saw where he abode; and they abode with him that
day: it was about the tenth hour.** [It being a crisis in his
life, John remembered the very hour. If John reckoned time
according to the Jewish method, it was about 4 P. M. If
according to the Roman method, it was 10 A. M. We are
inclined to accept the latter as correct.] **40 One of the two
that heard John *speak*, and followed him, was Andrew,
Simon Peter's brother. 41 He findeth first** [before he
did anything else] **his own brother Simon** [The word
" own " is here coupled with " brother " to show that Simon
was not a mere relative (as the word " brother " might mean),
but was literally Andrew's brother] **and saith unto him,
We have found the Messiah (which is, being interpreted, Christ).** [" Messiah " is Hebrew, " Christ "
is Greek, "Anointed " is English. Jesus is the anointed of
God. In finding him, Andrew had made the greatest discovery which it is possible for a man to make.] **42 He brought
him unto Jesus.** [Thus Andrew had in a sense the honor of
being the first Christian evangelist.] **Jesus looked upon him,
and said, Thou art Simon** [this name means "hearing"]
**the son of John: thou shalt be called Cephas (which
is by interpretation, Peter).** [Cephas is Hebrew, Peter is
Greek, stone is English. It means a mass of rock detached
from the bed-rock or strata on which the earth rests. The
future tense, " thou shalt be," indicates that Peter was to win
his name. It is given prophetically to describe the stability to
which the then weak and vacillating Simon should attain.] **43**

On the morrow he was minded to go forth into Galilee, and he findeth Philip [In the synoptists, Philip is a mere name in the apostolic list. Through John we gain some true acquaintance with him—vi. 5; xii. 21; xiv. 8]: **and Jesus saith unto him, Follow me.** [The Lord's usual invitation to discipleship—Matt. viii. 22; xx. 9; xix. 21; Mark ii. 14; x. 21; Luke v. 21; ix. 59; John xxi. 19.] **44 Now Philip was from Bethsaida** [Bethsaida of Galilee, on the northwestern shore of the Lake of Galilee. It was a wicked place— Matt. xi. 41], **of the city of Andrew and Peter.** [It appears that Peter afterward removed to Capernaum—Mark i. 29.] **45 Philip findeth Nathanael** [Nathanael is commonly identified with Bartholomew for the following reasons: 1. The name Bartholomew is only a patronymic, and hence its bearer would be likely to have an additional name. (Compare Matt. xvi. 17; Acts iv. 36.) 2. John never mentions Bartholomew, and the Synoptists never mention Nathanael, though John mentions him among apostles at the beginning and at the close of Christ's ministry. 3. The Synoptists, in their list of apostles, invariably place Philip next to Bartholomew, and show a tendency to place brothers and friends together. 4. All the other disciples mentioned in this chapter become apostles, and none are so highly commended as Nathanael. 5. Bartholomew is connected with Matthew in the list at Acts i. 13, and the names Matthew and Nathanael both mean the same, and are equal to the Greek name Theodore, which means " gift of God." But even so the identification is not perfect], **and saith unto him, We have found him, of whom Moses in the law, and the prophets, wrote** [The whole law is full of symbolism which refers to Christ. The following references may be taken as more specific: Gen. xlix. 10; Num. xxiv. 17–19; Deut. xviii. 15. The passages in the prophets are too numerous to mention. For samples see Isa. vii. 14; ix. 6; lii. 13; liii. 1–12; Ezek. xxxiv. 23–31. In brief, Moses wrote of him as a Prophet, David as Lord, Isaiah as the Son of the virgin and suffering Servant, Jeremiah as the

Branch, Ezekiel as the Shepherd, Malachi as the Messenger of the Covenant, Daniel as the Messiah. Christ is the hero and subject-matter of both Testaments—I. Pet. i. 11; John v. 39], **Jesus of Nazareth, the son of Joseph.** [Philip knew no better at this time, and John did not change the words of Philip to suit his later knowledge of Christ's parentage. John has already declared the divine origin of Jesus (ver. 14), thereby agreeing with the detailed account of Matthew and Luke.] **46 And Nathanael said unto him, Can any good thing come out of Nazareth?** [Because of their want of culture, their rude dialect, and their contact with Gentiles, the Galileans were lightly esteemed by the inhabitants of Judæa (John vii. 52). But here Nathanael, a Galilean himself, speaks slightingly of Nazareth. Some think that Nazareth was no worse than the rest of Galilee, and that Nathanael speaks thus disparagingly because he dwelt in the neighboring town of Cana, and felt that jealousy which often exists between rival villages. But the guileless Nathanael had no such jealousy, and the persistency with which the enemies of Jesus called him the Nazarene indicates that there was more than a local odium attached to the name Nazareth. Moreover, it was the first city to offer violence to Christ, and was ready on one day's acquaintance with his preaching to put him to death.] **Philip saith unto him, Come and see.** [So said afterward the woman of Samaria (John iv. 23). Investigation removes prejudice.] **47 Jesus saw Nathanael coming to him, and saith of him, Behold, an Israelite indeed** [An Israelite in spirit as well as in flesh (Rom. ii. 28, 29; ix. 16). Such a character contrasted sharply with the prevalent formalism and hypocrisy of that day], **in whom is no guile!** Some see in the word guile a reference to Jacob. He was a man full of all subtlety and guile in his early years, but his experience at Peniel (Gen. xxxii. 22–31) changed his nature and his name, and he became Israel, the spiritual father of all true Israelites.] **48 Nathanael saith unto him, Whence knowest thou me?** [Nathanael's surprise clearly indicates that the knowledge which Jesus exhibited was miraculous.] **Jesus answered and said unto him, Before Philip called thee, when thou wast under the fig tree, I saw thee.** [The fig-tree affords the densest shade in Palestine—a shade where no sun-spot can be seen. This fact has made it immemorially a resting-place and a refuge from the fierce Syrian sunlight. Under such a cover Jesus saw Nathanael when he was alone. Such superhuman knowledge wrought faith in Nathanael, as it did afterward in the woman of Samaria.—See Prov. xv. 3.] **49 Nathanael answered him, Rabbi, thou art the Son of God; thou art King of Israel.** [Psalm ii. and Isa. ix. 6 prophetically announce Jesus as the Son of God. These and other prophecies had just been more clearly announced by the Baptist (ver. 34). It is clear, therefore, where Nathanael got his words; but it is not so clear how well he understood them. This is the first recorded uninspired confession of the divinity of Jesus, but Matt. xvi. 16, 17 indicates that it was but partially comprehended, else Peter might have been instructed by Nathanael. The expression "King of Israel" probably expressed the hope which Nathanael then entertained that Jesus would restore the ancient Jewish kingdom of David —Acts i. 6.] **50 Jesus answered and said unto him, Because I said unto thee, I saw thee underneath the fig tree, believest thou? thou shalt see greater things than these.** [Nathanael regarded the revelation of his character and whereabouts as a great thing, but he was destined to see yet greater miracles. Opportunities improved lead to larger privileges, and for those who believe, the evidences are increased.] **51 And he saith unto him, Verily, verily** [This word means "in truth." John twenty-five times represents the Saviour as thus using the double "verily." Matthew quotes the single "verily" thirty times, Mark fourteen times, and Luke seven times. The word is used to mark the importance of the truth about to be uttered], **I say unto you** ["you" is plural and includes all present as well as Nathanael], **Ye shall see the heaven opened, and the angels of God ascending and descending upon the Son of man.**

[Jesus having referred to Nathanael as a true Israelite, promises to him — and to those like him — a blessing answering to
Jacob's vision of the ladder; that is, that the ascent and descent of ministering angels shall be by means of Christ. Jesus
calls himself the Son of man upwards of eighty times. The
expression is found in all four Gospels, but is there invariably
used by Christ himself. Stephen (Acts vii. 56) and John (Rev.
i. 13) also use this title, to indicate that the glorious being
whom they saw was like Jesus—like him in his human estate.
In this chapter Jesus has been called by others "The Lamb of
God," "the Son of God," "the Messiah," and "the King of
Israel." Jesus chooses yet another title, "Son of man," for
himself. At this earliest dawning of their expectations, while
their minds were thus full of his titles of glory, Jesus introduces to his disciples this one which speaks of his humanity
and humility. The expression may have been suggested by
Dan. vii. 13, 14.]

XXII.

JESUS WORKS HIS FIRST MIRACLE AT CANA IN GALILEE.

ᵈJOHN II. 1–11.

ᵈ**1 And the third day** [From the calling of Philip (John
i. 43). The days enumerated in John's first two chapters constitute a week, and may perhaps be intended as a contrast to
the last week of Christ's ministry (John xii. 1). It took two
days to journey from the Jordan to Cana] **there was a marriage in Cana of Galilee** [In Palestine the marriage ceremony usually began at twilight. The feast after the marriage
was at the home of the bridegroom, and was sometimes prolonged for several days (Gen. xxix. 27; Judg. xiv. 12); but
in this case it seems likely that poverty limited the wedding
feast to one day. The site of Cana is disputed. From the
eighth century a place called Kefr-Kenna (village of Cana),
lying a little over three miles northeast of Nazareth, has been

regarded as John's Cana of Galilee. But recently some ruins called Khurbet-Cana, twelve miles north of Nazareth, which doubtfully are said to have retained the name of Kana-el-Jilil (Cana of Galilee), have been preferred by some as the true site. In our judgment Kefr-Kenna has the stronger claim. It is situated on the westward slope of a hill, with a copious and unfailing spring adjoining it on the southwest]; **and the mother of Jesus was there** [John never called our Lord's mother by her name. He assumes that she is known to his readers. This is one of the many points tending to show the supplemental character of John's Gospel. He avoids repeating what is found in the first three Gospels]: **2 and Jesus also was bidden** [being the Creator of woman, and the author of matrimony, it was fitting that the Son of God should grace a marriage feast with his presence], **and his disciples, to the marriage.** [This is the earliest use of the term "disciples" in the ministry of Jesus. His disciples were Andrew, Peter, Philip, Nathanael, and probably John and James.] **3 And when the wine failed** [Probably the arrival of Christ and his disciples helped to exhaust the supply. Shortage of provision when guests are invited is considered a sore humiliation the world over], **the mother of Jesus saith unto him, They have no wine.** [The interest which Mary took in the feast and the way in which she addressed the servants at verse 5, suggests that she was a close friend of the bridegroom's family. Though she merely states the unfortunate condition to Jesus, her statement is a covert petition to him that he would remedy it, as our Lord's answer shows. She practically requested him to work a miricle, nor is it strange that she should do this. Remembering the many early sayings about him which she had treasured in her heart (Luke ii. 19, 51), and doubtless being informed of what had occurred at his baptism, and of the proclamation which John the Baptist had made concerning him, and seeing a group of disciples gathered about him, it was very reasonable for her to expect him to do something which would reveal the high purposes for which he had been born.] **4 And Jesus saith unto her, Woman,**

what have I to do with thee? [Jesus did not call her "mother," but "woman," a term of courteous respect, but indicating no spirit of obedience. "As much as to say," says Augustine, "thou art not the mother of that in me which worketh miracles." Moses recognized that parental duties were subordinate to divine (Deut. xxxiii. 9); and Jesus emphasized the principle (Matt. x. 37). Jesus taught that relationship to him was spiritual, and not fleshly (Matt. xii. 46–50), and Paul coveted such relationship (II. Cor. v. 16, 17). The expression, "What have I," etc., is used frequently in the Scriptures and invariably indicates a mild rebuke (Judg. xi. 12; II. Sam. xvi. 10; I. Kings xvii. 18; II. Kings iii. 13; Matt. viii. 29; Mark i. 24; Luke viii. 28). It means, "leave me to act as I please," and Jesus uses it to assert that he is independent of all human relationships in the exercise of his Messiahship. It corrects two errors taught by the Catholic Church: 1. Catholicism says that our Lord's mother was immaculate, but if this were true she could not have incurred our Lord's rebuke. 2. Catholicism teaches that Mary's intercession is recognized by Christ. But this is the only instance on record of such intercession, and though it was addressed to Christ while in the flesh and was concerning a purely temporal matter, it was promptly rebuked.] **mine hour is not yet come.** [Our Lord's answer indicates that Mary's request had in it more than a desire for the gift of wine. What she principally wanted was to have Jesus manifest himself as Messiah. Now, Jesus gave many secondary, but only one supreme, manifestation of his glory or Messiahship. His miracles were secondary manifestations, but his Passion was the supreme manifestation (John viii. 28; ii. 18, 19; Matt. xii. 38–40). Jesus called this supreme sign his "hour" (John xii. 23, 27; xvii. 1; Matt. xxvi. 45; Luke xxii. 53; see also John vii. 30; viii. 20). His mother sought for a supreme sign, but at that time only a secondary sign could be fittingly given. The triumph at Pentecost was not to be achieved at Cana.] **5 His mother saith unto the servants** [though he had spoken words of rebuke, his mother was neither offended nor discouraged

because of them], **Whatsoever he saith unto you, do it.**
[She commands unlimited obedience. Though her words are
not addressed to us, they will prove of untold profit to us if we
obey them.] **6 Now there were six waterpots of stone
set there after the Jews' manner of purifying** [The
details of the account suggest that John was an eye-witness.
The Jews regarded themselves as ceremonially unclean if they
did not wash their hands before eating—Matt. xv. 2; Mark
vii. 3, 4], **containing two or three firkins apiece.** [At
Kefr-Kenna an old, one-story house near the lower edge of
the village is regarded by the Greeks as the one in which this
wedding feast was held. The room is a rude chapel, and at
one side stand two old stone mortars, one holding about eight
gallons and the other about ten, now used for immersing
infants, but said by the attending priest to be two of the identical waterpots here mentioned. The simple-minded old man
was not aware that the six waterpots held each two or three
firkins apiece—between eighteen and twenty-seven gallons, a
firkin being nine gallons—or double the quantity of his mortars. If he had known this, he might have chiseled out his
mortars a little deeper!] **7 Jesus saith unto them, Fill
the waterpots with water.** [The jars had been partially
emptied by the ablutions of the company.] **And they filled
them up to the brim.** [This statement serves two purposes.
1. It emphasizes the great quantity. 2. It shows that there
was no room to add anything whatever to the contents of the
jars. As to the quantity, it was between 106 and 162 gallons.
As we do not know the number of guests nor the duration of
the feast, we can not accurately measure the Lord's bounty.
But as twelve basketfuls were left after feeding the five thousand, there was doubtless here a like sufficiency, and the
surplus would serve as an acceptable gift to the married
couple.] **8 And he saith unto them, Draw out now**
[the word "now" seems to indicate the turning-point when
the water became wine], **and bear unto the ruler of the
feast.** [According to the custom of that age, one of the
guests was usually chosen to preside over such festivities, and

he was called the ruler. Our modern toastmaster is probably a relic of this ancient custom.] **And they bare it. 9 And when the ruler of the feast tasted the water now become wine, and knew not whence it was** (but the servants that had drawn the water knew), **the ruler of the feast calleth the bridegroom, 10 and saith unto him, Every man setteth on first** [when the taste is sharpest and most critical] **the good wine** [the adjective " good " refers rather to flavor than to strength]; **and when** *men* **have drunk freely** [The ruler was no disciple of Jesus, and he speaks in the merry spirit of the world. He gives his own experience as to the habits of feasts, and his words give no indication that those present indulged to excess]**,** *then* **that which is worse: thou hast kept the good wine until now.** [It is part of Christ's system to reserve the best until the last. Sin's first cup is always the sweetest, but with God that which follows is ever superior to that which has preceded it. As to the bearing of this miracle upon the question of temperance, the New Testament elsewhere clearly condemns the immoderate use of wine, and as these condemnations proceed from Christ we may rightly conceive of him, as in this instance, doing nothing contraıy thereto. The liquors of this land in the strength of their intoxicating properties differ so widely from the light wines of Palestine that even the most moderate use of them seems immoderate in comparison. In creating wine Jesus did no more than as Creator and Renewer of the earth he had always done. From the beginning God has always so created or replenished the earth as to allow the possibility of excess.] **11 This beginning of his signs did Jesus in Cana of Galilee, and manifested his glory** [This was the beginning or first of the miracles, and John's statement brands as false all the Catholic traditions which tell of miracles performed by Christ in his childhood. We should note also that it was a sign. The value of the miracle was in what it signified, not in what it wrought. It manifested the glory of Christ, part of which glory is his power to change the worse into the better, the simpler into the richer. It is the glory of Christ that he can transform sinners into his own like-ness—I. John iii. 2; I. Cor. xv. 42–44; Phil. iii. 20, 21]; **and his disciples believed on him.** [In this chapter John as a disciple three times gives us a disciple's point of view as to Christ's miracles; here, at verse 17 and at verse 22. They implanted faith in those whose hearts were right before God (John v. 38). The miracles of Christ created widespread excitement. There had been none of a notorious nature since Daniel had been cast to the lions, and had read the writing on Belshazzar's wall some five hundred and eighty years before.]

XXIII.

JESUS' FIRST RESIDENCE AT CAPERNAUM.

d JOHN II. 12.

d 12 After this he went down to Capernaum [The site of Capernaum is generally conceded to be marked by the ruins now called Tel-Hum. Jesus is said to have gone "down" because Cana is among the hills, and Capernaum was by the Lake of Galilee, about six hundred feet below sea level], **he, and his mother, and** *his* **brethren, and his disciples** [There is much dispute as to what the New Testament writers mean by the phrase "brethren of the Lord." This phrase, found in any other than a Jewish book, would be taken to mean either the full or the half brothers of Jesus, and it has probably that meaning here. The Catholic Church, contending for the perpetual virginity of our Lord's mother, has argued that his brethren were either the sons of Joseph by a former marriage, or that they were sons of Alphæus (also called Clopas) and a sister of our Lord's mother, who, like her, was also called Mary (John xix. 25). This latter view is based upon the fact that two of the sons of Alphæus bear the same names as those borne by two of our Lord's brethren, which is far from conclusive, since the names James and Judas were extremely common. Moreover, we learn from John vii. 5, that the Lord's brethren did not believe on him, and harmonists place the time of this unbelief late in our Lord's ministry, when the sons of Alphæus were not only believers, but some of them even apostles. Our Lord's brethren are mentioned nine times in the New Testament, and a study of these references will give us some light. Three of them, viz.: John vii. 3, 5, 10; I. Cor. ix. 5; Gal. i. 19, are rather non-committal. The other six (Matt. xii. 46; xiii. 55; Mark iii. 32; vi. 3; Luke viii. 19, 20; John ii. 12) speak of his brethren in connection with his mother, and strongly indicate that Jesus was the first-born son of Mary, and that she had at least four other sons, besides daughters. These brethren of Jesus are constantly represented as attending his mother, without a hint that they were not her children. Against this conclusion there is but one argument which has any force; namely, that our Lord committed his mother into the keeping of the apostle John, rather than to his brethren (John xix. 25-27), but this fact may be easily accounted for. Many mothers are but scantily and grudgingly supported by their sons]; **and there they abode not many days.** [Because the passover was at hand, and he went up to Jerusalem. This notice of the brief sojourn of Jesus at Capernaum throws light on several things: 1. It shows where Jesus spent most of his time between his baptism and the first passover. 2. It helps to explain how the nobleman, who afterwards sought him at Cana, became acquainted with him. 3. It prepares us to look for his first visit to Nazareth at a later period. 4. It also explains why Jesus sought Capernaum as his place of residence after leaving Nazareth. Moreover, it shows that the natural ties of kindred were not immediately snapped by Christ. Until he went up to the first passover, he abode with his mother and his brethren.

PART FOURTH.

FROM THE FIRST TO THE SECOND PASSOVER.

(Time: One Year.)

XXIV.

JESUS ATTENDS THE FIRST PASSOVER OF HIS MINISTRY.

(Jerusalem, April 9, A. D. 27.)

Subdivision A.

JESUS CLEANSES THE TEMPLE.

ᵈJOHN II. 13–25.

ᵈ**13 And the passover of the Jews was at hand**
[We get our information as to the length of our Lord's
ministry from John's Gospel. He groups his narrative
around six Jewish festivals: 1, He here mentions the first
passover; 2, another feast, which we take to have been also a
passover (v. 1); 3, another passover (vi. 4); 4, the feast of
tabernacles (vii. 2); 5, dedication (x. 22); 6, passover (xi. 55).
This gives the entire length of our Lord's ministry as three
years and a fraction], **and Jesus went up to Jerusalem.**
[It was fitting that he should enter upon his full ministry in
this city, as it was still the center of what was recognized as a
heaven-revealed worship. The fitness of Jerusalem for such
beginnings was afterwards recognized in the preaching of the
gospel of the New or Christian dispensation—Acts i. 8.] **14
And he found in the temple** [Our English word "temple"
includes two Greek words; namely, 1. The *naos,* or sanc-

tuary—the small structure which contained the holy and most holy places, and which answered to the tabernacle used in the wilderness. 2. The *hieron*, or entire court spaces which surrounded the *naos*, and which included some nineteen acres. This *hieron* was divided into four courts, and as one entered toward the *naos* from the east, he passed successively through them, as follows: 1, Court of the Gentiles; 2, of the women; 3, of Israel; 4, of the priests. It was in this outer or Gentiles' court that the markets described in this section were held] **those that sold oxen and sheep and doves, and the changers of money sitting** [This market in the temple was for the convenience of the people, and the nearness of the passover increased its size. Oxen and doves were constantly needed for sacrificial purposes, and as each family which ate the passover required a lamb, they would be in the market in great abundance. Josephus tells us it required about two hundred thousand lambs for a passover feast, but his exaggerations will stand a liberal discount] : **15 and he made a scourge of cords, and he cast all** [The rest of the verse shows that "all" does not refer to men, but to sheep and oxen. The scourge was used in driving them out] **out of the temple, both the sheep and the oxen; and he poured out the changers' money, and overthrew their tables** [The Jews were each required to pay, for the support of the temple service, one half-shekel annually (Ex. xxx. 13; Matt. xvii. 24). These money-changers sat at small tables, on which their coins were piled and counted] ; **16 and to them that sold the doves he said, Take these things hence** [As the doves were in cages of wicker-work, they could not be driven out; hence Jesus called upon their owners to remove them. Though Jesus cleansed the house, he wrought no waste of property. The sheep and oxen were safe outside the temple, the scattered money could be gathered from the stone pavement, and the doves were not set free from their cages] ; **make not my Father's house a house of merchandise.** [Jesus bases his peculiar authority over the temple on his peculiar relationship to Him for whom the temple was built.

As a Son, he purged the temple of his Father. In the beginning of his ministry he contested their right to thus appropriate
his Father's house to their uses, but in the end of his ministry
he spoke of the temple as "your house" (Matt. xxiii. 38),
thereby indicating that the people had taken unto themselves
that which truly belonged to God, even as the wicked husbandmen appropriated the vineyard (Luke xx. 14, 15). The
rebuke of Jesus was addressed to the priests, for the market
belonged to them, and the money-changers were their agents.
Edersheim says that this traffic alone cleared the priests about
three hundred thousand dollars a year. Though churches
differ widely from the temple, they are still God's houses, and
should not be profaned. Religion should not be mixed with
traffic, for traffic tends toward sin. Phariseeism is its fruit—a
wish to carry on profitable business, even with God. On this
occasion Jesus objected to the use of the temple for trade
without criticising the nature of the trade. When he purged
the temple three years later, he branded the traders as robbers
—Matt. xxi. 13.] **17 His disciples remembered that it
was written** [Ps. lxix. 9], **Zeal for** [loving concern for]
**thy house shall eat me up. 18 The Jews therefore
answered and said unto him, What sign showest thou
unto us, seeing that thou doest these things?** [The
Jews felt that only a divinely commissioned person could thus
interfere with the ordering of God's house. They therefore
called upon Jesus to give them a sign as an evidence that he
possessed such divine commission. The manner in which he
had cleansed the house of its trafficers was of itself a sign, if
they had only had eyes to see it. Jesus could not have thus
cleansed the temple unaided had he been a mere man. The
power which he showed in the temple was much like that
which he manifested in Gethsemane—John xviii. 6.] **19
Jesus answered and said unto them, Destroy this
temple, and in three days I will raise it up.** [John
here records this saying, and Matthew (ch. xxvi. 61) and Mark
(xiv. 58) tells us how at the trial it was twisted into a charge
against Christ: thus the Evangelists supplement each other.

For "temple" in this sentence Jesus uses the word "*naos,*" or sanctuary, the structure which was peculiarly the seat oï God's presence. The sanctuary was a figure or symbol of the body of Christ, and the words of Jesus were a covert prediction that as they were desecrating the symbol so would they destroy his body, which it symbolized. They reverenced the Spirit of God neither as it dwelt in the sanctuary nor as it dwelt in the body of Christ. The body of Jesus was a temple (Col. ii. 9), and Christians and the church are also temples (I. Cor. iii. 16, 17; vi. 19; II. Cor. v. 1; II. Pet. i. 13). God's temples can not be permanently destroyed. They are "raised up."] **20 The Jews therefore said, Forty and six years was this temple in building** [The temple which then stood upon Mt. Moriah was the third structure which had occupied that site. The first temple, built by Solomon (B. C. 1012-1005), was destroyed by Nebuchadnezzar. The second temple, built by Zerubbabel and Jeshua (B. C. 520), had been torn down and rebuilt by Herod the Great, but in such a manner as not to interfere with the temple service. The sanctuary was completed in one year and a half, while the courts required eight years. Josephus says eighteen thousand workmen were employed in its erection. Additional outbuildings and other work had been carried on from that time, and the whole was not completed until A. D. 64], **and wilt thou raise it up in three days?** [To put before him the difficulty of what he apparently proposed to do, they merely mention one item—time. They say nothing of the army of workmen, nothing of the variety and cost of material, nothing of the skill required in the process of construction. How impossible seemed his offer! Yet by no means so impossible as that real offer which they misunderstood. A man might rear a temple in three days, but, apart from Christ Jesus, self-resurrection is unknown to history.] **21 But he spake of the temple of his body.** [John differs from the other three Evangelists, in that he frequently comments upon the facts which he records. Both history and commentary are inspired.] **22 When therefore he was raised from the dead, his**

disciples remembered that he spake this [It was three years before they understood this saying. Thus truth often lies dormant for years before it springs up in the heart and bears fruit—I. Cor. xv. 58; Eccles. xi. 1]; **and they believed the scripture** [several passages foretell the resurrection—Ps. xvi. 9, 10; lxviii. 18], **and the word which Jesus had said.** [They believed that Jesus had meant to predict that the Jews would kill him, and that he would rise again on the third day.] **23 Now when he was in Jerusalem at the passover, during the feast** [the seven days' feast of unleavened bread—Lev. xxiii. 5, 6], **many believed on his name, beholding his signs which he did.** [We have no description of the miracles wrought at this time. See John iv. 45; xx. 30.] **24 But Jesus did not trust himself unto them, for that he knew all men** [The word here translated "trust" is the same as that translated "believe" in the preceding verse. They trusted him, but he did not trust them, for he knew them. He did not tell them anything of his plans and purposes, and the conversation with Nicodemus which follows is a sample of this reticence], **25 and because he needed not that any one should bear witness concerning man; for he himself knew what was in man.** [John gives us many examples of this supernatural knowledge which Jesus possessed. See i. 42, 47, 48; iii. 3; iv. 29; vi. 61, 64; xi. 4, 14; xiii. 11; xxi. 17. This chapter itself gives us a faithful picture of "what was in man." We find in it temple profaners, money-makers, signseekers, opposers of reform, false and weak professors of faith, etc.. but none to whom Jesus could trust himself.]

Subdivision B.

JESUS TALKS WITH NICODEMUS.

^dJOHN III. 1–21.

^d **1 Now there was a man of the Pharisees, named Nicodemus, a ruler of the Jews** [Nicodemus is mentioned only by John. His character is marked by a prudence amounting almost to timidity. At John vii. 50–52 he defends Jesus, but without committing himself as in any way interested in him: at John xix. 38, 39, he brought spices for the body of Jesus, but only after Joseph of Arimathæa had secured the body. Nicodemus was a ruler, or a member of the Sanhedrin]: **2 the same came unto him by night** [Thus avoiding the hostility of his colleagues, and also obtaining a more personal and uninterrupted interview with Jesus. That his coming by night revealed his character is shown by the fact that John repeats the expression when describing him at ch. xix. 39. But, in justice, it should be said that Nicodemus was the only one of his order who came at all during our Lord's life], **and said to him, Rabbi, we** [Nicodemus uses the plural, to avoid committing himself too much. Nicodemus would assert nothing but that which was commonly admitted by many. We learn from John xii. 42, 43, that late in the ministry of Christ, when hostility towards him was most bitter, many of the rulers still believed in him. No doubt, then, when Nicodemus said "we" he used the word advisedly and conscientiously] **know that thou art a teacher come from God** [The rulers knew that Jesus was not the product of any of the rabbinical schools, and his miracles marked him as a prophet and distinguished him from all who were guided merely by reason, no matter how learned]; **for no one can do these signs that thou doest** [John ii. 25], **except God be with him.** [These words show the effect of Christ's miracles. Miracles arrest attention and challenge investigation,

and prove that he who works them is from God—Acts x. 38.]
3 Jesus answered [Not the words, but the thoughts, of Nicodemus. The answers of Jesus often look rather to the
thoughts of the questioner than to the form of the question.
Nicodemus came seeking to know something about the kingdom of God, and Jesus opened at once upon the subject] **and
said unto him, Verily, verily, I say unto thee, Except
one be born anew, he cannot see the kingdom of God.**
[The word translated " anew " may also mean " from above,"
and some commentators seek to so translate it here, but it is
rightly translated " anew," for Nicodemus understood it to
mean a *second* birth. As to the import of the passage,
Luther's words are pertinent: " My doctrine is not of doing,
and of leaving undone, but of being and becoming; so that it
is not a new work to be done, but the being new created—not
the living otherwise, but the being new-born." To " see " the
kingdom means to possess or enjoy it—Ps. xvi. 10; xc. 15;
John viii. 51; Luke ii. 26.] **4 Nicodemus saith unto him,
How can a man be born when he is old? can he enter
a second time into his mother's womb, and be born?**
[Knowing that a man can not be literally born a second time,
Nicodemus states to Jesus the literal import of his words,
hoping thereby to draw from him an explanation of this new,
strange metaphor which he was using. So far as he did grasp
the meaning of Jesus, Nicodemus saw himself barred forever
from the kingdom by an impossible requirement. Many, like
him, need to learn that God asks of us nothing that is impossible;
that, on the contrary, the yoke is easy and the burden is light.]
**5 Jesus answered, Verily, verily, I say unto thee,
Except one be born of water and the Spirit, he cannot
enter into the kingdom of God.** [By far the vast majority
of scholars consider the word " water " in this verse as a reference to Christian baptism. The Cambridge Bible says " the
outward sign and inward grace of Christian baptism are here
clearly given, and an unbiased mind can scarcely avoid seeing
this plain fact. This becomes still clearer when we compare

John i. 26, 33, where the Baptist declares, 'I baptize in water,' the Messiah 'baptizeth in the Holy Spirit.' The fathers, both Greek and Latin, thus interpret the passage with singular unanimity." Men would have no difficulty in understanding this passage were it not that its terms apparently exclude "the pious unimmersed" from Christ's kingdom. But difficulties, however distressing, will justify no man in wresting the Scripture of God (II. Pet. iii. 16; Rom. iii. 4). Water and Spirit are joined at Matt. xxviii. 19; Acts ii. 38; xix. 1-7; Tit. iii. 5.] **6 That which is born of the flesh is flesh; and that which is born of the Spirit is spirit.** [Jesus here draws the distinction between fleshly birth and spiritual birth. He did this to prepare Nicodemus to understand that it is the *spirit* and not the flesh which undergoes the change called the new birth. Regeneration is no slight, superficial change, but a radical one, and one which we can not work for ourselves.] **7 Marvel not that I said unto thee, Ye must be born anew.** [Jesus here plainly declares that none are exempt from this gospel requirement. Man must obtain more than his fleshly nature if he would inherit eternal life.] **8 The wind bloweth where it will, and thou hearest the voice thereof, but knowest not whence it cometh, and whither it goeth: so is every one that is born of the Spirit.** [In this sentence we have the word *pneuma* translated by the *two* words "wind" and "spirit." There can be no justification in rendering *pneuma* "wind," when in the last clause of the same sentence, and three times in the immediate context, it is rendered "spirit." There can be no doubt that it means the same in both clauses of this verse, and if we render it wind in the first clause, we must say "born of the wind" in the last clause. Whatever is the meaning of this verse, it must be extracted from the rendering which the Revisers have strangely placed in the margin, viz.: "The Spirit breathes where it will, and thou hearest," etc. It teaches that a man is born of the Spirit by hearing the voice of the Spirit, breathing as he wills through inspired men. It is equivalent to Paul's maxim that faith comes by hearing the word of God.*] **9 Nicodemus answered and said unto him, How can these things be? 10 Jesus answered and said unto him, Art thou the teacher of Israel, and understandest not these things?** [The Jewish teachers or doctors of the law made very arrogant claims to knowledge, but it often happens that the professedly learned are remarkably unacquainted with the first principles of their religion. It was so with the Jewish teachers (Matt. xv. 14). Nicodemus should have understood that such a change as Jesus was speaking of would be necessary, for, 1. It was foreshadowed in the Old Testament (Deut. x. 16; I. Sam. x. 9; xvi. 13; Ps. li. 10; Ezek. xviii. 31; Jer. iv. 4). 2. John the Baptist suggested the need of some such change when he attacked the Jewish trust in their descent from Abraham.] **11 Verily, verily, I say unto thee, We** [a rhetorical plural — Mark iv. 30] **speak that which we know, and bear witness of that which we have seen** [his words were not founded upon reasonings, speculations and guesses, but were the plain testimony of an eye-witness, who was able to see and had seen things which to us are invisible]; **and ye receive not our witness.** [Ye teachers of Israel, who, above all men, should receive our guidance, are the very last to follow us. As the Jewish rulers would not receive Christ's testimony, let us not be surprised if many of our day refuse to listen to the gospel which we preach.] **12 If I told you earthly things and ye believe not, how shall ye believe if I tell you heavenly things?** [Jesus here divides religious phenomena into two divisions—earthly and heavenly. The earthly phenomena are those which have their sphere in this world. In this sense

---

*From this (Bro. McGarvey's) construction of verse 8 I dissent, and hold that the Revisers have given us the true reading in the text. The question has been fully discussed in Lard's Quarterly, Vol. III., p. 337; Benjamin Franklin's Sermons, Vol. I., p. 281; Millennial Harbinger, 1832, p. 604; 1833, p. 24; 1869, pp. 317, 478, 522, 688. I take the passage to mean that the process by which a man is regenerated by the Spirit of God is no more mysterious than other operations in the natural world, of which operations the blowing of the wind is taken as an example.—P.

regeneration is an earthly thing; for, though it has a heavenly origin, its manifestations are among the daily sights and experiences of our earthly life. Religion has also its heavenly phenomena, such as the ordering of God's celestial household; the experiences of those who pass into the divine presence; the propitiation, or the changes wrought in the attitude of God toward man by the sacrifice of Christ; the powers and limitations of Christ's priestly intercession, etc. These things have their sphere far removed from earth, and transcended the comprehension of Nicodemus. Now, if Nicodemus would not believe Jesus when he told him of things which he himself partially knew, how would he believe when Jesus spoke of that which was utterly unknown to him?] **13 And no one hath ascended into heaven, but he that descended out of heaven,** *even* **the Son of man, who is in heaven.** [Nicodemus is here informed that Christ alone can teach concerning heavenly things. Jesus can so teach, for he did not begin on earth and ascend to heaven, but he came from heaven to earth, and returned thence (afterwards) to heaven. Jesus speaks of himself as being present in heaven, because his divine nature was in constant communication with the powers of heaven. If we conceive of heaven as a locality (a proper conception), Jesus was upon the earth; but if we conceive of it as a present communion with the presence of God (also a proper conception), then Christ was in heaven as he talked with Nicodemus—John viii. 29.] **14 And as Moses lifted up the serpent in the wilderness, even so must the Son of man be lifted up; 15 that whosoever believeth may in him have eternal life.** [Jesus here indicates the prophetical and typical character of the Old Testament. The extent of Christ's indorsement of the Old Testament becomes apparent when we consider on how many occasions he revealed himself under the same symbolism which the Old Testament used to reveal him. At John ii. 19 he revealed his resurrection under the symbolism of the destroyed and restored temple. At Matt. xii. 40 the same event is revealed under the symbolism of Jonah and the whale. And

nere his crucifixion is likewise partially veiled and partially
disclosed under a symbolic reference to the brazen serpent.
The account of the brazen serpent will be found at Num. xxi.
4–9. The lesson of the brazen serpent will be found in its
main points of resemblance to the crucifixion of Christ.
When the people were bitten by fiery serpents, something
made to resemble a serpent was hung upon a pole, and the
people who looked to it in faith found through it healing and
life. Such is the epitome of Christ's gospel. When the
world was perishing because of sin, Jesus, made to resemble
sin (Rom. viii. 3; II. Cor. v. 21), was hung upon the cross, that
those who look unto him in faith (Isa. xlv. 22) may find life
through him—I. John v. 11–13.] **16 For God so loved the
world, that he gave his only begotten Son, that whosoever believeth on him should not perish, but have
eternal life.** [Luther calls this verse "the Bible in minia-
ture." It is a lesson as to God's love: 1. Its magnitude—he
gave his only begotten Son. 2. Its reach—he gave to a sinful
world (Rom. v. 8). 3. Its impartiality—he gives to whomsoever; that is, to all alike (Matt. v. 45; Rev. xxii. 17). 4. Its
beneficial richness—it blesses with life eternal. 5. Its limitations—it is nowhere said that God so loves that he will save
unbelievers. Love is the mutual and binding grace between
God and man: it may almost be said that in Christ it made
God human and man divine. John uses the word "eternal"
seventeen times in his Gospel and six times in his first Epistle.
He always applies it to life. The synoptists use it eight times,
applying it to life, and also to fire, punishment, damnation and
habitation.] **17 For God sent not the Son into the world
to judge the world; but that the world should be
saved through him.** [Christ's first mission to the world
was for salvation rather than for judgment. His second mission will be for judgment, but a judgment-hour wherein he
will be able to save those who have accepted the means of
grace which he established by his first coming. But the first
coming of Christ incidentally involved judgment (John ix. 39),
and John the Baptist emphasized the judgment of Christ.

This judgment, however, was not the principal object of Christ's coming, but was an inevitable result of it. Jesus here speaks of it as a self-executed judgment. It was a necessary result of the revealed presence of Christ (Luke ii. 35). That Christ is at present a Saviour, and not a judge, is a truth which needs to be emphasized. Catholics are taught to fear Christ and flee to the Virgin; and many ignorant Protestants are disposed to look upon him as a prosecutor rather than an advocate.] **18 He that believeth on him is not judged: he that believeth not hath been judged already, because he hath not believed on the name of the only begotten Son of God.** [The name "Jesus" means Saviour; to disbelieve this name is to reject Christ as Saviour. Verses 14 and 15 require belief in Jesus as the Son of man. This verse requires belief in him as the Son of God. Belief in this dual nature of Jesus is essential to salvation. Unbelief is the world's crowning sin; and belief is, humanly speaking, the source of its justification. The verse teaches that God's judgments are in a state of perpetually present enactment. The believer is saved now (Acts xiii. 39), and the unbeliever rests already under that condemnation which he fears the Son of God may some day pronounce against him.] **19 And this is the judgment, that the light is come into the world, and men loved the darkness rather than the light; for their works were evil. 20 For every one that doeth evil hateth the light, and cometh not to the light, lest his works should be reproved. 21 But he that doeth the truth cometh to the light, that his works may be made manifest, that they have been wrought in God.** [These verses show that when God judges a man by his faith, the judgment is not arbitrary and irrational. Men *believe* according to the secret aspirations and desires of their nature. Christ, as the example and model of life, shines out as the light of the world; those who approve and love such a life are drawn to him and constrained to believe in him. Spiritually, they abide in his presence, that they may compare their lives with his, and that they may be assured that their works are

wrought under the renewing and sanctifying influence of the
Holy Spirit, who is sent of Christ.   But one whose desires are
evil shrinks from Christ, and struggles to disbelieve in him: he
seeks to know as little of Christ as possible, because such
knowledge exposes the wickedness and depravity of his own
sinful nature.]

XXV.

FIRST MINISTRY IN JUDÆA. — JOHN'S SECOND
TESTIMONY.

(Judæa and Ænon.)

^dJOHN III. 22–36.

^d**22 After these things came Jesus and his disciples
into the land of Judaea** [That is, he left Jerusalem, the
capital of Judæa, and went into the rural districts thereof.
We find him there again in John xi. and Luke xiii.–xviii.   He
gained disciples there, but of them we know but few, such as
Mary, Martha, Lazarus, Simeon and Judas Iscariot]; **and
there he tarried with them** [it is not stated how long he
tarried, but it may have been from April to December, for the
passover was in April, and December was "yet four months"
before the harvest—John iv. 35], **and baptized.** [This baptism was not into the three names of God (John vii. 39), into
which the apostles were afterward directed to baptize (Matt.
xxviii. 19).   It was a continuation of John's baptism, preparatory to the organization of the church — a preparation for the
kingdom.   Some think that Jesus, at this time, baptized in his
own name, and afterwards gave the full baptismal formula into
the other two names—Father and Spirit.   But there is no evidence of this, and Christian baptism is a baptism into the
death of Christ (Rom. vi. 3).   Christ would hardly have
ordered baptism into his death before his crucifixion.   Such a
proceeding would have wrought confusion.] **23 And John
also was baptizing** [The fact that John also was baptizing is
a further indication that the baptism administered by Jesus was

preparatory. There would hardly be two kinds of baptism administered by divine consent at one time] **in Aenon** [This name means "springs"] **near to Salim, because there was much water there** [If one starts at Sychar, at the foot of Mount Ebal, and follows the Damascus road northward for seven miles, he comes upon the valley called Wady Farah. In this beautiful wady the stream flows eastward, having Salim three miles to its south and 'Ainun four miles to its north. For the most part the valley is narrow, and hemmed in by rocky cliffs. But if one follows the course seven miles eastward from the Damascus road, he comes upon a beautiful valley, about one mile wide and three miles broad—a place every way suitable for the gathering of multitudes to hear the preaching of John. A perennial stream, with copious springs all along its course, furnishes, even in the longest, driest summers, the "much water" required for baptism]: **and they came, and were baptized.** ["Here, then," says Lieutenant Conder, "in the wild, desert valley, beneath the red precipices, where the hawk and kite find nests in 'the stairs of the rocks,' or by the banks of the shingly stream, with its beautiful oleander blossoms shining in the dusky foliage of luxuriant shrubs, we may picture the dark figure of the Baptist, in his robe of camel's hair, with the broad leather Bedawi belt around his loins, preaching to the Judæan multitude of pale citizens—portly, gray-bearded rabbis, Roman soldiers in leathern armor and shining helmets, sharp-faced publicans, and, above all, to the great mass of oppressed peasantry, the 'beasts of the people,' uncared for, stricken with palsy, with blindness, with fever, with leprosy, but eagerly looking forward to the appearance of that Messiah who came to preach the gospel to the poor."] **24 For John was not yet cast into prison.** [John's Gospel shows that the ministry of Christ was well under way before that of the Baptist ceased: a fact which the synoptists do not reveal.] **25 There arose therefore a questioning on the part of John's disciples with a Jew about purifying.** [What this questioning was we are not told. The word "therefore" doubtless refers to

the baptisms just mentioned, so that the dispute probably
related to the necessity or purifying effects of that ordinance.
But whatever the dispute was about, it brought to notice the
fact that Jesus was baptizing more disciples than John, a fact
which some of the disciples of John quickly resented.] **26
And they came unto John, and said to him, Rabbi, he
that was with thee beyond the Jordan, to whom thou
hast borne witness, behold, the same baptizeth, and
all men come to him.** [This verse shows that John's disciples looked upon Jesus as one who owed all his position and
popularity to the Baptist's testimony, and were, therefore, surprised to find that Jesus was surpassing John. They looked
upon this conduct as a species of ingratitude on the part of
Jesus. This verse also shows us that the witness of John did
not pass unheeded. His witness was public and notorious,
and men remembered it, though they did not always profit by
it. That these friends of John felt unkindly toward Jesus
is shown by their exaggerated statement that "all men come
to him."] **27 John answered and said, A man can
receive nothing, except it have been given him from
heaven.** [Some take this to mean that Jesus could not have
had this great success unless Heaven gave it to him; but it is
more likely that John used the words with entire reference to
himself. A *man* can only take what is given him; the Son
of God takes what he chooses. The friend receives only what
hospitality extends to him, but the heir takes what he will, as
the owner of the house.] **28 Ye yourselves bear me witness, that I said** [In stating that John had borne witness
(ver. 26) John's disciples had already committed themselves to
the fact that John disclaimed to be the Messiah, and that
Jesus was the Messiah; for it was concerning these two things
that John had given his testimony], **I am not the Christ,
but, that I am sent before him. 29 He that hath the
bride is the bridegroom: but the friend of the bridegroom, that standeth and heareth him, rejoiceth greatly
because of the bridegroom's voice: this my joy therefore is made full.** [John looks upon the body of disciples as

the Lord's bride, and prophetically anticipates the very title which was subsequently applied to the church. It was the duty of "the friend of the bridegroom" to arrange the preliminaries of the wedding, and to promote the mutual interests of the bride and bridegroom. His duties and responsibilities greatly exceeded those of our "best man," for it was his place to demand the hand of the bride, and to prepare everything for the reception of the bride and bridegroom. Joy at the sound of the bridegroom's voice is part of the drapery of John's figure. Voices of bride and bridegroom are a Biblical symbol of festivity and joy (Jer. vii. 34; xxv. 10; xxxiii. 11). The Song of Solomon is the only book in the Bible which dwells upon the relationship of bride and bridegroom, and in it the voice of the bridegroom is mentioned with joy (Song ii. 8). If John meant anything more by the phrase than mere drapery, he used it to express his pleasure that the Messiah was directing his own affairs and speaking his wishes with his own voice, instead of using his friend as a mouthpiece.] **30 He must increase, but I must decrease.** [Noble words! "He must increase"—because the divine law has ordered it, and prophecy has foretold it (Isa. lii. 13), and because the very divinity of his nature absolutely requires it. "I must decrease"—in popularity, in power, in following. The Christian minister finds the increase of his work the same as the increase of Christ's kingdom; but with the Baptist the case was different. He was a Jewish prophet, and as the power of the New Dispensation, under Christ, gained headway, the Old Dispensation, of which he was a part, waxed old, and was ready to vanish away.] **31 He that cometh from above is above all: he that is of the earth is of the earth, and of the earth he speaketh: he that cometh from heaven is above all.** [Some think that the testimony of the Baptist closes with the thirtieth verse, and that the rest of the chapter is the comment of the apostle John, but there is certainly no sufficient ground for such a view.] **32 What he hath seen and heard, of that he beareth witness; and no man receiveth his witness.** [In verses 31 and 32 the Baptist draws a contrast between his testimony and that of the Messiah. The Baptist's testimony was largely of a negative character. He testified that he was not the Christ (ver. 28), and while he pointed Jesus out as the Christ, the worthy one, the spiritual baptizer, he nowhere undertook to elaborate as to the character or nature of Jesus. He looked upon Jesus as being so far above all earthly prophets that no prophet could reveal him. The task of such revelation devolved upon Jesus himself. God must be self-revealed. It was no heavy disappointment to John that his disciples had failed to grasp his testimony concerning Jesus. Jesus was himself the supreme witness concerning himself, and yet so few were persuaded by the testimony of Jesus that John hyperbolically says "no man receiveth his witness."] **33 He that hath received his witness hath set his seal to** *this,* **that God is true.** [We have here a metaphor, taken from the sealing of a document, as an expression of trust in or adherence to it. Compare John vi. 27; I. Cor. ix. 2. To receive Christ's witness was to publicly confess a conviction that God was true—true to his promise that he would send a Messiah, a Saviour (Rom. iii. 4). To believe Christ is to believe God; to make Christ a liar is to make the Father one also, for he speaks concerning Christ (I. John v. 10) and through Christ—John vii. 16; xvi. 24.] **34 For he whom God hath sent speaketh the words of God: for he giveth not the Spirit by measure.** [To give anything by measure indicates a partial, scanty bestowal (Ezek. iv. 16). The Spirit of God, even in inspired prophets, was but a partial and intermittent gift (I. Cor. vii. 25; xiii. 9; I. Pet. i. 11; Heb. i. 1), but in Jesus, the Son of God, the Spirit of God dwelt fully and uninterruptedly (Col. i. 19). The present tense, "giveth," points to a continuous communication of the Spirit. If Christ had received the Spirit "by measure," then his gift of the Spirit might be exhausted.] **35 The Father loveth the Son, and hath given all things into his hand.** [This fact was afterwards asserted by Jesus (Matt. xxviii. 18). Jesus is indeed King of kings—Ps. ii. 6-8; Matt. xi. 27; Acts ii. 33; x. 36; Eph. i.

22.]   **36 He that believeth on the Son hath eternal
life** [the New Testament represents everlasting life as a present possession obtained by belief]; **but he that obeyeth
not the Son shall not see life, but the wrath of God
abideth on him.** [In the second clause of this verse "obeyeth" stands in contrast with "believeth" in the first clause. No mental assent, however strong, is reckoned by the Scriptures as faith unless it results in obedience (Jas. ii. 20; Rom. i. 5). "Wrath of God" is a strong phrase, and is not to be lightly explained away. The unconverted sinner rests under this wrath. His study should be not only to avert a sentence to be pronounced at some future day, but to be freed from one already resting upon him. This verse shows conclusively that Christ's atoning work had its divine as well as its human side; that God had to be propitiated as truly as man had to be reconciled. The Baptist had already repeatedly warned the Jewish people of wrath to come if they rejected the Messiah, and in this, his last recorded utterance, he boldly reiterates that warning.

XXVI.

JESUS SETS OUT FROM JUDÆA FOR GALILEE.

Subdivision A.

REASONS FOR RETIRING TO GALILEE.

**ᵃMATT. IV. 12; ᵇMARK I. 14; ᶜLUKE III. 19, 20;
ᵈJOHN IV. 1-4.**

ᶜ **19 but Herod the tetrarch** [son of Herod the Great, and tetrarch, or governor, of Galilee], **being reproved by
him** [that is, by John the Baptist] **for Herodias his brother's wife, and for all the evil things which Herod had
done** [A full account of the sin of Herod and persecution of John will be found at Matt. xiv. 1-12 and Mark vi. 14-29. John had spoken the truth to Herod as fearlessly as to the Pharisees, publicans and soldiers], **20 added this also to
them all** [the sins of Herod, as a ruler, already outweighed

his virtues (comp. Dan. v. 27); but, with reckless abandon, Herod went on, adding to the weighty reasons which justified his condemnation], **that he shut up John in prison.** [In the fortress of Machærus, east of the Dead Sea, as we learn from Josephus. The duration of the ministry of John the Baptist is variously estimated at from fourteen to eighteen months.] **ᵇ14 Now after John was delivered up** [either delivered up by the people to Herod (Matt. xvii. 12), or delivered up by Herod himself to the warden of the castle of Machærus (Luke xii. 58), or by Providence to Herod himself —Acts ii. 23], **ᵃwhen he** [Jesus] **heard** [he was in Judæa when he heard it] **that John was delivered up** [and], **ᵈ1 When therefore the Lord knew that the Pharisees had heard that Jesus was making and baptizing more disciples than John** [We saw at John iii. 26 how the Baptist heard about the number of Jesus' baptisms, being informed by his jealous friends. Like jealous friends, no doubt, informed the Pharisees. Jesus may have known of this information being given by reason of his supernatural powers, but it is more likely that he heard of it in a natural way] **2 (although Jesus himself baptized not, but his disciples)** [Jesus, as divine Lawgiver, instituted baptism, and his disciples administered it. We nowhere hear of the disciples of John administering baptism. In fact, the Baptist, like the disciples of Jesus, baptized under a divine commission, and could not delegate the power to others. It was the office of Jesus to commission others to this work, not to perform it himself. Had he done so, those baptized by him might have foolishly claimed for themselves some peculiar honor by reason thereof (I. Cor. xiv. 15). Jesus was the spiritual baptizer, in which baptism the efficacy lies in the administrant; but water baptism, the efficacy of which lies rather in the spirit of the one baptized than in the virtues of the administrant, Jesus left to his disciples], **3 he left Judaea, and departed again {ᵃwithdrew ᵇcame} ᵈinto Galilee.** [We have in these verses two reasons assigned for the withdrawal of Jesus into Galilee, namely: 1. The imprisonment of the Baptist. 2.

Knowledge of the Pharisees that Jesus was baptizing more disciples than John. The first gives us the reason why he went to Galilee, the second the reason why he left Judæa. Jesus did not go into Galilee through fear of Herod, for Herod was tetrarch of Galilee. The truth is, the absence of John called for the presence of Jesus. The northern part of Palestine was the most fruitful soil for the gospel. During the last six or eight months of John's ministry we find him in this northern field, preparing it for Christ's kingdom. While we can not say definitely that John was in Galilee (Bethabara and Ænon being the only two geographical names given), yet he certainly drew his audiences largely from the towns and cities of Galilee. While John occupied the northern, Jesus worked in the southern district of Palestine; but when John was removed, then Jesus turned northward, that he might sow the seed of the kingdom in its most fruitful soil. But if there was a reason why he should *go* to Galilee, there was an equal reason why he should *depart* from Judæa. His popularity, manifesting itself in the number of his baptisms, was exciting that envy and opposition which caused the rulers of Judæa eventually to take the life of Jesus (Matt. xxvii. 18). The Pharisees loved to make proselytes themselves (Matt. xxiii. 15). They, no doubt, envied John's popularity, and much more, therefore, would they be disposed to envy Christ. The influence of the Pharisees was far greater in Judæa than in Galilee, and the Sanhedrin would readily have arrested Jesus had he remained in Judæa (John vii. 1; x. 39), and arrest at this time would have marred the work of Jesus. Therefore, since it is neither sinful nor unbecoming to avoid persecution, Jesus retired to Galilee, where he remained until his second passover. By birth a prophet of Judæa, he became, in public estimation, by this retirement, a prophet of Galilee. Though Jesus first taught in Judæa, the ministry in Galilee so far eclipsed the work in Judæa that it was spoken of as the place of beginning (Luke xxiii. 5; Acts x. 37), and prophetically designated as the scene of the divine manifestation—Matt. iv. 14.] **4 And he must needs pass through Samaria.** [The province which took its name from the city of Samaria, and wh:ch lay between Judæa and Galilee. Owing to the hatred which existed between Jews and Samaritans, many of the Jews went from Jerusalem to Galilee by turning eastward, crossing the Jordan, and passing northward through Peræa. This journey required about seven days, while the more direct route, through Samaria, only took three days. Galileans often passed through Samaria on their way to and from the Jerusalem feast (Josephus' Ant. xx. 6, 1). The arrest of John would scatter his flock of disciples (Mark xiv. 27), and Jesus, as chief shepherd (I. Pet. v. 1-4), hastened to Galilee, to gather together those which might else go astray and be lost.]

Subdivision B.

AT JACOB'S WELL, AND AT SYCHAR.

JOHN IV. 5-42.

5 So he cometh to a city of Samaria, called Sychar, near to the parcel of ground that Jacob gave to his son Joseph: 6 and Jacob's well was there. [Commentators long made the mistake of supposing that Shechem, now called Nablous, was the town here called Sychar. Sheckem lies a mile and a half west of Jacob's well, while the real Sychar, now called 'Askar, lies scarcely half a mile north of the well. It was a small town, loosely called a city, and adjoined the land which Jacob gave to Joseph (Gen. xxxiii. 19; xlviii. 22; Josh. xxiv. 32), Joseph's tomb being but about one hundred yards east of it. The mummy of Joseph, carried out of Egypt at the time of the Exodus, was buried in this parcel of ground, and there is but little doubt that it really rests in the place indicated by the tomb; and though the name Sychar may be derived from the words "liar" or "drunkard," it is more likely that it means "town of the sepulchre," referring to this tomb. The Old Testament is silent as to when or why Jacob dug this well. It lies on the southern side of the valley of Shechem, where it opens upon the plain of Moreh (now called el-Mukhnah), **about a hundred** yards south of the foot of Mt. Gerizim. It is one of the few Biblical sites about which there is no dispute, and probably the only place on earth where one can draw a circle of a few feet, and say confidently that the feet of Christ have stood within the circumference. Maundrell, who visited it in 1697, said that it was 105 feet deep, and had in it fifteen feet of water. But travelers have thrown stones into it to sound its depth, until at present it is only sixty-six feet deep, and has no water in it except in very wet winters. It is seven and a half feet in diameter, and is walled with masonry to a depth of about ten feet, below which it is cut through the solid rock. It lies 400 yards nearly due south from Joseph's tomb. As the neighborhood abounds in springs, the well would hardly have been dug save by one who wished to be independent of his neighbors—as Jacob did.] **Jesus therefore, being wearied with his journey, sat thus by the well.** [John gives us important items as to the humanity of Jesus. He tells us how he sat as a wayworn traveler, hungry and thirsty, at Jacob's well: and he alone records the words, " _ thirst," spoken on the cross (John xix. 28). The top of the well is arched over like a cistern, and a round opening is left about twenty inches in diameter. On this arch or curbing Jesus sat. We should note the perpetuity of blessings which springs from a good deed. Gutenberg did not foresee the newspaper when he invented printing; Columbus did not anticipate the land of the free when he led discoverers to our shore, nor is it likely that the prophetic eye of Jacob ever saw the wearied Christ resting upon the well-curb which he was building.] **It was about the sixth hour.** [That is, twelve o'clock, if we reckon by Jewish time, or six o'clock in the evening, if we reckon by the Roman method. We prefer the latter method.] **7 There cometh a woman of Samaria to draw water** [she was not of the city of Samaria (which was then called Sebaste—the Greek word for Augustus—in honor of Augustus Cæsar, who had given it to Herod the Great), but a woman of the province of Samaria, which lay between Judæa and Galilee, and reached from the Jordan on the east to the Mediterranean on the west, comprising the country formerly occupied by the tribe of Ephraim and the half tribe of Manasseh]: **Jesus saith unto her, Give me to drink. 8 For his disciples were gone away into the city to buy food.** [Had the disciples been present they would have bargained with the woman for the use of her rope and pitcher; but in their absence Jesus himself asked her for a drink. He met her on the ground of a common humanity, and conceded to her the power of conferring a favor. Women have been immemorially the water-carriers of the East (Gen. xxiv. 13, 14; Ex. ii. 16). Palestine is in summer a parched land, inducing intense thirst, and the people usually comply cheerfully with the request for water: it was probably so in Jesus' day (Matt. x. 42). Mohammed commanded that water should never be refused.] **9 The Samaritan woman therefore saith unto him, How is it that thou, being a Jew** [as his language and dress declared], **askest drink of me, who am a Samaritan woman? (For Jews have no dealings with Samaritans.)** [It is not likely that she meant to refuse his request, but she yielded to the temptation to banter one who she thought despised her, and whose necessities now caused him for a moment to forget his pride. The ancestors of the Samaritans were introduced into the land of Israel by the king of Assyria, after he led the ten tribes into captivity (II. Kings xvii. 24–41). When the Jews returned from their captivity in Babylon and began to rebuild their temple, the Samaritans asked permission to build with them, and when this was refused, an enmity arose between the two peoples which never died out (Ez. iv. 1–5; Neh. ii. 10, 19; iv. 1–3). We must, however, restrict the word "dealings" to social intercourse. Race antipathy did not ordinarily interfere with trade or other matters involving money, as is shown by verse 8 above. According to later tradition, a Jew accepted no hospitality from a Samaritan, and to eat his bread as a guest was as polluting as to eat swine's flesh, but such social courtesy was the very thing which Jesus here asked. There are to-day between one and two hundred Samaritans dwelling in Shechem at the foot of Mt. Gerizim, and Dr. Robinson says of them that they "neither eat, nor drink, nor marry with the Jews, but only trade with them."] **10 Jesus answered and said unto her, If thou knewest the gift of God, and who it is that saith to thee, Give me to drink; thou wouldest have asked of him, and he would have given thee living water.** [Jesus is himself the Gift of God (John iii. 16; II. Cor. ix. 15). But she knew not that God had bestowed a special Gift, and much less that the one to whom she spoke was that Gift. Had she known this she would have understood that though physically Jesus was the object of her charity, spiritually their cases were reversed, and she was the needy one, as Jesus intimates. Living water would mean literally running or spring water, as contrasted with still or cistern water (Gen. xxvi. 19; Lev. xiv. 5). Jesus here uses it in a spiritual sense. He fills us with his grace and truth (John i. 14), and grants unto us continual, untold refreshing (Rev. vii. 17). The reviving and regenerating effects of the Holy Spirit are likewise called living water (John vii. 37–39).] **11 The woman saith unto him, Sir** [the word "Sir" is elsewhere translated "Lord"], **thou hast nothing to draw with, and the well is deep: whence then hast thou that living water?** [She understood his words literally, and was puzzled by them; but, won by the courtesy which suggested an exchange of gifts, she answered respectfully, though incredulously.] **12 Art thou greater than our father Jacob, who gave us the well, and drank thereof himself, and his sons, and his cattle?** [We should note three points in this verse: 1. The greatness of Jesus. The woman had just called him "Lord." The man at Bethesda, though he knew not Jesus, afterwards did the same (John v. 7). People felt the majesty and dignity of Jesus. When he offered to give a greater blessing than that given by Jacob, the woman at once contrasted him with Jacob—Jacob with sons and cattle and wealth—and wondered if this lonely stranger could really imagine himself greater than the illustrious patriarch. 2. She claimed descent from Jacob: it was a false claim. Jesus classed the Samaritans with Gentiles (Matt. x. 5), and spoke of them as strangers or aliens (Luke xvii. 18). 3. She spoke of the well as given by Jacob. She meant that it had been given to Joseph (Gen. xlviii. 22), and that her people had inherited it as descendants of Joseph.] **13 Jesus answered and said unto her, Every one that drinketh of this water shall thirst again: 14 but whosoever drinketh of the water that I shall give him shall never thirst** [Jesus here draws a contrast between earthly and heavenly blessings. No worldly joy gives lasting satisfaction, but Jesus is the bread and water of life to his disciples (John vi. 35); their unfailing satisfaction]; **but the water that I shall give him shall become in him a well of water springing up unto eternal life.** [A beautiful figure of the joy in Christ. In heat, in cold; in drought, in shower; in prosperity, in adversity; it still springs up, cheering and refreshing the soul, and this unto all eternity—Rev. xvii. 16; xxi. 6.] **15 The woman saith unto him, Sir, give me this water, that I thirst not, neither come all the way hither to draw.** [She but dimly comprehended the nature of Christ's offer, but was persuaded of two things: 1. The wonderful water was to be desired. 2. Jesus was able and willing to give it. When she spoke of coming "to draw" her words suggested the household to which it was her duty to minister, and prepared the way for the command of Jesus to bring the head of the household.] **16 Jesus saith unto her, Go, call thy husband, and come hither.** [She had asked Jesus for the water of God's grace, but she needed to be made conscious of how much she needed it — conscious (if we follow the figure) of her dormant thirst. Jesus, therefore, gave command to call her husband, that by so doing he might reveal her life and waken her to repentance.] **17 The woman answered and said unto him, I have no husband. Jesus saith unto her, Thou saidst well, I have no husband: 18 for**

thou hast had five husbands ; and he whom thou now hast is not thy husband: this hast thou said truly. [The divine wisdom of Jesus brought to light a sad state of affairs. During the period of five marriages the woman's life had at least some outward show of respectability, but now it was professedly unclean. The number of marriages reflects somewhat upon the character of the woman, and hints that some of them may have been dissolved by her own fault, though the loose divorce law of that age permitted a man to dissolve the marriage ties on very slight provocation. Among the Jews the great Hillel is reported to have said that a man might properly divorce his wife if she burnt his dinner while cooking. It is not likely that any higher ideals of matrimony obtained among the Samaritans.] **19 The woman saith unto him, Sir, I perceive that thou art a prophet.** [She had heard of the miraculous knowledge of the Jewish prophets, and this evidence given her by Jesus persuaded her that he was one of them, as a like evidence had persuaded Nathanael (John i. 48, 49). By thus calling him a prophet she virtually confessed the truth as to all the things concerning which he had accused her.] **20 Our fathers worshipped in this mountain** [*i. e.*, Mt. Gerizim] **; and ye** [ye Jews] **say, that in Jerusalem is the place where men ought to worship.** [Though a desire to divert the conversation from her own sins may have, in some slight measure, prompted the woman to bring up this question about places of worship, yet her main motive must have been far higher. If we ourselves stood in the presence of one whom we felt assured to be fully inspired of God, how hastily would we propound to him some of the vexed questions which befog the religion of our time ! Prompted by such a feeling, this woman sought to have the great dispute between Jew and Samaritan decided. Solomon's temple in Jerusalem was soon after its erection confronted by those who denied its claims to be exclusively the place set apart for divine worship. Jeroboam, the rebellious servant of Solomon, taught the people that Bethel and Dan were as acceptable for worship as Jerusalem. But Jerusalem, as the site of the first great temple, held precedence above all rivals until its claims were discredited in popular estimation by the fact that it was destroyed by Nebuchadnezzar. When, after many years, the returning captives rebuilt its walls, it lacked the sanction of age, and it had lost many of the features of divine recognition, which contributed to the sacredness and grandeur of the first structure. Soon after its erection in the days of Nehemiah, Manasseh, son of the high priest Joiada, and brother of the high priest Jonathan (Neh. xii. 10, 11; xiii. 28), married the daughter of Sanballat, Persian governor of Samaria. Refusing to dissolve this marriage at the decree of the governor of Jerusalem, Manasseh was chased by Nehemiah from Jerusalem, and his father-in-law made him high priest of the Samaritans, and undertook to build for him the temple which afterwards crowned the summit of Mt. Gerizim. Manasseh left Jerusalem about B. C. 332. The temple built for him was destroyed by John Hyrcanus about B. C. 129, but the place where it stood was still the sacred center of Samaritan worship, as it is to this day. Mt. Gerizim, and its supporting city of Shechem, had many grounds on which to base their claims to be a sacred locality. 1, Here God appeared to Abraham for the first time after his entering Canaan (Gen. xii. 6, 7); 2, here Jacob first dwelt (Gen. xxxiii. 18); 3, here Joseph came seeking his brethren (Gen. xxxvii. 12, 13); 4, here was a city of refuge (Josh. xx. 7-9); 5, here Joshua read the blessings and cursings (Josh. viii. 33); 6, here also he gave his last address (Josh. xxiv. 1); 7, here were buried the bones of Joseph (Josh. xxiv. 32), and the neighborhood was prominent at the time of the division of the ten tribes (I. Kings xii. 1, 25). If we may consider Samaritan traditions of that day as similar to those of the present, they had added greatly to the real importance of the neighborhood, for they now contend that 1, Paradise was on the summit of Gerizim; 2, Adam was formed of the dust of Gerizim; 3, on Gerizim Adam reared his first altar; 4, Seth here reared his first altar; 5, Gerizim was the Ararat on which the Ark rested, and the only spot which the flood did not overflow ; and therefore the only place which escaped the defilement of dead bodies; 6, on it Noah reared his altar; 7, here Abraham attempted to offer Isaac ; 8, here he met Melchizedek; 9, here was the real Bethel, where Jacob slept and saw his ladder vision. Backed by such high claims, the woman deemed it possible that this prophet might decide in favor of Samaria's holy place. We should note that the Samaritans worshiped in Mt. Gerizim because they could say. " Our fathers did so." Thus many errors are perpetuated to-day because our fathers practiced them; but our fathers had no more authority to alter or amend God's word than we have. The Jews worshiped in Jerusalem because it had been prophesied that God would select a spot as the peculiar place for his worship (Deut. xii. 5–11), and because according to this prophecy God had selected Mt. Moriah in Jerusalem—I. Kings ix. 3; II. Chron. iii. 12.] **21 Jesus saith unto her, Woman, believe me, the hour cometh, when neither in this mountain, nor in Jerusalem, shall ye worship the Father.** [Jesus uses the word "hour" to indicate that the time was *near at hand* when all religious distinctions as to places would be abolished, and when every spot might be used for purposes of worship—I. Tim. ii. 8.] **22 Ye worship that which ye know not: we worship that which we know ; for salvation is from the Jews.** [Jesus here speaks as a Jew, and draws a comparison between the intelligent worship of his people and the ignorant worship of the Samaritans. Though the Samaritans possessed the Pentateuch, they were without that revelation of God which the prophets of Israel had developed, and their worship was neither authorized nor accredited by God. Moreover, it led toward nothing; for salvation was evolved from the Jewish reiigion, and not from that of Samaria. Salvation proceeded from the Jews. From them, according to the flesh, Christ came, and from them came also the prophets, apostles and inspired writers who have given us that full knowledge of salvation which we possess to-day. We must take the words of Jesus as referring rather to the two *religions* than to the two peoples. Though as a body the Jews did not know whom they worshiped, and though their teachers were blind leaders of the blind, yet the fault was in their unbelief, and not in the revelation or religion in which they refused to believe. On the contrary, if the Samaritan had believed his religion to the full, it would hardly have been sufficient to have enabled him to know what he worshiped. Samaria was, in the days of the idolatry of Israel, a chief seat of Baal worship, and in later days it was the home of magicians and sorcerers. **23 But the hour cometh, and now is** [the hour is really here, but the knowledge of it is not yet comprehended], **when the true worshippers shall worship the Father in spirit and truth: for such doth the Father seek to be his worshippers.** [Jesus draws the mind of the woman from the place of worship to the Person or Being worshiped, and from the form to the spirit of worship. God seeks for genuine, and not formal worshipers, and for those who worship him in truth; *i. e.,* those who render him the obedience of faith with a filial spirit, and not those who render him the empty service of types and shadows, ceremonies and rites, which, through disbelief, have lost their meaning.] **24 God is a Spirit** [These words contain one of the most simple, yet most profound, truths which ever fell upon mortal ear. Their truth is one of the great glories of revelation, and corrects the mistaken conclusion of human reason. They show that, 1, God is absolutely free from all limitations of space and time, and is therefore not to be localized in temples (Acts vii. 48); 2, that God is not material, as idolaters contend; 3, that he is not an abstract force, as scientists think, but a Being; 4, that he is lifted above all need of temples, sacrifices, etc., which are a benefit to man, but not to God (Acts xvii. 25). Spiritual excellence raises man above the beast, and spiritual excellence in turn raises God above man—Isa. xxxi. 3]: **and they that worship him must worship in spirit and truth.** [That is, men must offer a worship corresponding with the nature and attributes of God.] **25 The woman saith unto him, I know that Messiah cometh (he** that is called Christ): **when he is come, he will de-clare unto us all things.** [The breadth and largeness of Jesus' teaching suggested to her the great Teacher who was to come, and caused her to yearn for him who could tell, as she thought, perhaps even larger things. The Samaritans justi-fied their idea of a coming Benefactor by passages found in the Pentateuch, and got their name for him from the Jews. Relying on the prophecy found at Deut. xviii. 18, modern Samaritans regard the Messiah as a returning Moses, calling him *El-Mudy*—the Guide. They contend that his name will begin with M, and that he will live to be 120 years old. This woman's idea of the Messiah was probably also very crude, but it was in part an improvement on the general Jewish con-ception, for it regarded him as a teacher rather than a world-conquering, earthly prince.] **26 Jesus saith unto her, I that speak unto thee am** *he.* [This is the first recorded declaration of his Messiahship made by Jesus. He was not confessed to be Messiah by Simon Peter (Matt. xvi. 16) till the last year of his ministry. Jesus spoke more freely as to his office in Samaria than in Judæa or Galilee; for, 1, the Samaritans would make no effort to take him by force and make him a king (John vi. 15); 2, his short stay in Samaria justified an explicit and brief revelation.] **27 And upon this came his disciples; and they marvelled that he was speaking with a woman.** [The spirit of the Rabbis is shown by their later precept; viz.: "Let no one talk with a woman in the street, no, not with his own wife." The estate of woman was then, and had been for a long time previous, very low. Socrates thanked the gods daily that he was born neither a slave nor a woman. Roman law gave the husband absolute authority over the wife, even to put her to death; and Jewish contempt for women is made apparent by the readiness with which the Jews divorced them]; **yet no man said, What seekest thou? or, Why speakest thou with her?** [So deep was their reverence and respect that they did not question, though they did not understand.] **28 So the woman left her waterpot** [in the forgetfulness

of great joy, and as the unconscious pledge of her return],
and went away into the city [Sychar], **and saith to
the people, 29 Come, see a man, who told me all
things that** *ever* **I did** [To publish Christ is one of the first
impulses of those who feel Christ's gracious power. Her
invitation is like that given by Philip (John i. 46). On second
thought her statement is not so much of an exaggeration as it
at first appears. Her five marriages and present state covered
the whole period of her maturer life, and the way in which
Jesus had disclosed it all convinced her that every detail of
it was spread out before him]: **can this be the Christ?**
[Her question does not imply that she herself had any doubts
about the matter. She uses the interrogative form because
she does not wish to be dogmatic, but prefers to let the people
judge for themselves. Observe the woman's change of
mind concerning Jesus. She first called him "Jew" (ver. 9),
then "Sir" (ver. 11), then "prophet" (ver. 19), and now
she invites her city to come forth and see "the Christ."] **30
They went out of the city, and were coming to him.
31 In the meanwhile** [the time between the departure of
the woman and the arrival of her fellow-townsmen] **the disciples prayed him, saying, Rabbi, eat. 32 But he said
unto them, I have meat to eat that ye know not. 33
The disciples therefore said one to another, Hath any
man brought him** *aught* **to eat?** [They understood his
words literally, as a declaration that he had dined.] **34 Jesus
saith unto them, My meat is to do the will of him that
sent me, and to accomplish his work.** [His delight at
the woman's conversion, as a part of the work which his
Father had given him to do, overcame for a time his desire for
food. Food has several characteristics: 1. enjoyment; 2.
satisfaction of desire; 3. refreshment and strength. God's
work had these characteristics to Jesus, whose life fulfilled
the principle that man shall not live by bread alone.] **35
Say not ye, There are yet four months, and** *then* **cometh the harvest? behold, I say unto you, Lift up your
eyes, and look on the fields, that they are white al-**

ready unto harvest. [Jacob's well overlooked the luxuriant grainfields of the plain of Moreh. As the disciples looked abroad over its patches of varying green, they would say that it would yet be four months before these patches could be harvested. The harvests in the natural world are slow. But turning their eyes toward Sychar, the disciples could see the citizens of the town in their white garments pouring forth to see Jesus, and to be gathered by him as a harvest of disciples which had sprung up and ripened from the seeds of truth sown by the woman but a few moments before. Spiritual sowing brings speedy harvests. Some commentators look upon the words of Jesus as proverbial, but there is no proverb extant which places only four months between sowing and reaping. In Palestine this period covers six months. We must, therefore, take the words of Jesus as a plain statement as to the length of time between the date of his speaking and the date of harvest. Harvest begins about the middle of April, and counting back four months from that date we find that this visit to Sychar occurred somewhere about the middle of December.] **36 He that reapeth receiveth wages, and gathereth fruit unto life eternal; that he that soweth and he that reapeth may rejoice together.** [Harvest times were seasons of great joy (Deut. xvi. 13-15; Ps. cxxvi. 6; Isa. ix. 3). But the joy of joys shall come when God gathers his redeemed into the heavenly garner. In this present the humble teacher sows and the evangelist, or more gifted brother, reaps; but in that glad hour it shall matter little whether we have been a sower or a reaper, for we shall all rejoice together. Sower and reaper alike shall receive wages, a part of which shall be the "fruit" gathered—the souls saved. Jesus regarded gaining a brother as a large compensation, a great gain—Matt. xviii. 15.] **37 For herein is the saying true** [see Isa. lxv. 21, 22; Lev. xxvi. 16; Job xxxi. 8; Mic. vi. 15], **One soweth, and another reapeth. 38 I sent you to reap** [Christ, as Lord of the harvest, sent both sowers and reapers] **that whereon ye had not labored: others have labored, and ye are entered into**

their labor. [In earlier days many prophets and holy men had labored to prepare the people of Palestine, that they might be gathered of Christ as disciples. Later John the Baptist had wrought a mighty work toward this same end. Into a field thus sown and cultivated Jesus was now leading his apostles, that they might reap for him the ripened harvest. He bids them observe the speedy and easy reaping on this occasion as an encouraging example to them, that they may go forth with strong assurance and confidence. Even the minds of the Samaritans were prepared to receive him, and a quick harvest could be gathered among them.] **39 And from that city many of the Samaritans believed on him because of the word of the woman, who testified, He told me all things that *ever* I did.** [The Jews rejected the testimony of the prophets and holy men of God as recorded in the Scripture (John v. 46, 47); but the Samaritans accepted the testimony of this woman, and she was a sinner.] **40 So when the Samaritans came unto him, they besought him to abide with them: and he abode there two days.** ["His own" received him not, but these "strangers" welcomed him. The stay was brief, but long enough to prepare the way for a future church among the Samaritans in the neighboring city of Samaria (Acts viii. 5–8). From the nearer town of Shechem came Justin Martyr, one of the greatest Christian writers of the second century.] **41 And many more believed because of his word: 42 and they said to the woman, Now we believe, not because of thy speaking: for we have heard for ourselves, and know that this is indeed the Saviour of the world.** [Only such ready hearers could arrive at so great a truth in so short a time. Wealth of revelation and blessing had made the Jews selfish, and their conception of their Messiah was so perverted by this selfishness that they could not conceive of him as being a *world* Saviour. Thus wealth often dwarfs where it should rather enlarge the heart. The incident comprised in this section presents the expansiveness of Christianity in a threefold aspect; viz.: 1, we see it breaking down the walls of racial prejudice; 2, we observe it elevating woman, and certifying her fitness to receive the very highest spiritual instruction; 3, we behold it lifting up the degraded and sinful, and supplying them from the fountains of grace. Such is real Christianity—the Christianity of Christ.]

Subdivision C.

ARRIVAL IN GALILEE.

^cLUKE IV. 14; ^dJOHN IV. 43-45.

^d**43 And after the two days** [the two days spent among the Samaritans at Sychar] **he went forth from thence** [from Samaria] **into Galilee.** ^c**14 And Jesus returned in the power of the Spirit into Galilee** [Power of the Spirit here means its manifest *use* to perform miracles, rather than its presence, influence or direction. Jesus was always under the influence and direction of the Spirit, but did not previously perform miracles]: ^d**44 For Jesus himself testified, that a prophet hath no honor in his own country.** [Galilee was Jesus' "own country" (John i. 46; ii. 1; vii. 3, 41, 52; Luke xxiii. 5-7). In Judæa he had begun to receive so much honor as to bring him into danger at the hands of the Pharisees: he would receive less in Galilee. Verse 43 resumes the itinerary of verses 1, 2, after the interlude which tells of the woman at Sychar.] **45 So when he came into Galilee, the Galilaeans received him, having seen all the things that he did in Jerusalem at the feast: for they also went unto the feast.** [The works which Jesus had done in Jerusalem were for the most part fruitless as to its inhabitants, but they bore the fruit of faith in far-off Galilee. Of "the many who believed on him" in Jerusalem (John ii. 23), it is highly probable that a large number were Galilæan pilgrims who were then there attending the passover.

XXVII.

GENERAL ACCOUNT OF JESUS' TEACHING.

ᵃ MATT. IV. 17; ᵇ MARK I. 14, 15; ᶜ LUKE IV. 14, 15.

ᵃ **17 From that time began Jesus to preach** [The time here indicated is that of John the Baptist's imprisonment and Jesus' return to Galilee. This time marked a new period in the public ministry of Jesus. Hitherto he had taught, but he now began to preach. When the voice of his messenger, John, was silenced, the King became his own herald. Paul quoted the Greeks as saying that preaching was " foolishness," but following the example here set by Christ, he used it as the appointed means for saving souls. While Matthew gives us many of the earlier incidents of Christ's life, he enters upon the account of his *ministry* at the time when Jesus returned to Galilee. From that time forward he was probably an eye-witness of the events which he records], ᵇ **preaching the gospel of God, 15 and saying,** {ᵈ **and to say,**} **Repent ye; for** ᵇ **the time is fulfilled, and the kingdom of God** {ᵃ **of Heaven**} ᵇ **is at hand.** [Jesus preached the gospel or good news of his own advent and of the setting up of the unending kingdom which should convert the world to righteousness and save the souls of men. We should note that Jesus himself declares that the prophesied time for the setting up of his kingdom was at hand. There were many general prophecies as to this kingdom, but one which especially fixed the *time* of its coming; viz.: Dan. ix. 24–27. This prophecy tells of seventy weeks in which each day is reckoned as a year, so that the seventy weeks equal four hundred and ninety years. They are to be counted from the date of the decree which ordered the rebuilding of Jerusalem. The Messiah, or Prince, was to come at the beginning of the seventieth week, or four hundred and eighty-three years from the date of the decree. Some take the decree referred to to be that mentioned in Nehemiah ii. Jahn and Hales fix the date

of this decree in the year 444 B. C.   According to this, Jesus
would have begun his ministry in the year A. D. 39.   Others
take the decree to be mentioned in Ezra vii., which was thirteen years earlier, and which would bring the beginning of
the ministry of Jesus to the year A. D. 26.   But there is
much uncertainty about all ancient chronology.   Suffice it
to say that Daniel told in round numbers how long it would
be until Messiah should come, and that Jesus said that this
time had been fulfilled.   It would have been easy to ascertain
the correct chronology at the time when Jesus spoke, and we
have no record that any presumed to dispute his statement.
Jesus announced the coming of a new dispensation.   The
King had already come, but the kingdom in its organization
and administration was as yet only "at hand."   Until the
crucifixion of Christ and the descent of the Spirit at Pentecost the kingdom could not be fully organized, for the blood
shed upon the cross furnished the means for purification which
precedes a proper entrance into the kingdom, and the coming
of the Holy Spirit afforded that indwelling strength by which
those entering are enabled to abide therein] : **repent ye, and
believe the gospel.**   [That is, prepare for the kingdom by
repenting of sin, and by believing the glad news that the kingdom was approaching, for the King had come (John i. 49).
The preaching of Jesus at this time did not differ materially
from that of John the Baptist, for John preached repentance
and the approaching kingdom (Matt. iii. 2), and the gospel
(Luke iii. 18), and belief in the King (John i. 29, 36; iii. 36).
The fact that repentance comes before belief in this passage
is by some taken as an indication that repentance precedes
faith in the process of conversion, but it should be remembered that the preaching here is addressed to the Jewish
people, who already believed in God, and in the Scripture as
the revelation of God.   They were, therefore, required to
bring forth fruit worthy of the old faith and the old revelation
as preparatory to their reception of the new faith and the new
revelation.   Thus repentance and faith appears to be the
established order for Hebrews (Heb. vi. 1) and their prose-

lytes (Acts xx. 21), because of the spiritual standpoint or condition in which the gospel found them. But those who have no faith in God can surely have no repentance toward him, for belief precedes every call upon God, whether for mercy, pardon or any other blessing—Rom. x. 13, 14], **ᶜand a fame went out concerning him through all the region round about.** [The miracles of Jesus and the manner in which he taught caused the people to glorify his name.] **15 And he taught in their synagogues, being glorified of all.** [If we may trust later tradition (and the New Testament corroborates it), synagogues were very plentiful in that day, there being at least one in every town. In the synagogue the people met on Sabbath and feast days. The temple at Jerusalem was used for ceremonial worship, but the services in the synagogue were of far different order, the study and application of the Scripture being the principal feature.]

XXVIII.

THE SECOND MIRACLE AT CANA.

ᵈJOHN IV. 46-54.

ᵈ46 He came therefore again [that is, in consequence of the welcome which awaited him] **unto Cana of Galilee, where he made the water wine** [see page 114]. **And there was a certain nobleman** [literally, " king's man:" a word which Josephus uses to designate a soldier, courtier, or officer of the king. He was doubtless an officer of Herod Antipas, tetrarch of Galilee. That it was Chuzas (Luke viii. 3) or Manaen (Acts xii. 1) is mere conjecture], **whose son was sick at Capernaum.** [The nouns in this verse are suggestive. We have a " nobleman," yet neither riches nor office lifted him above affliction; a " son," yet approaching an untimely death before his father; and both these parties came to sorrow in " Capernaum," the city of consolation. Neither circumstance, nor age, nor situation can guarantee joy. We must still be seeking Jesus.] **47 When he heard**

that Jesus was come out of Judaea into Galilee [and was therefore within not very easy reach of his sick child's bedside], **he went unto him** [literally, "he went away unto him." The verb contains a delicate suggestion that the father was reluctant to leave the son, even to seek aid], **and besought *him* that he would come down, and heal his son: for he was at the point of death.** [Many, like this father, only seek divine aid when in the utmost extremity.] **48 Jesus therefore said unto him, Except ye see signs and wonders, ye will in no wise believe.** [Though Jesus spoke these words to the nobleman, yet he also intended them for those who stood by, for he used the plural, "ye." That the Galilæans in general deserved reproof for their lack of faith, is shown by the upbraiding words which he spoke concerning their cities (Matt. xi. 20–24). Jesus wanted men to believe in him because of his self-evidencing character and words (John x. 38; xiv. 11; xv. 22–24; xx. 29). But the people required to have their faith buttressed by miracles. There is a vast difference between believing in a man, and believing his credentials. Miracles were our Lord's credentials; his ministry among men can not be thought of without them; and when the Baptist's faith in Christ himself wavered, Jesus referred him to them (Matt. xi. 4, 5). See also John x. 37. The two words, "signs" and "wonders," indicate the two aspects of miracles. To the thoughtful they were signs or attestations that the one who performed them acted under the authority and approval of God; to all others they were mere wonders, which startled by their strangeness. Jesus was fresh from Sychar, where many required no other sign than his words.] **49 The nobleman saith unto him, Sir, come down ere my child die.** [The father felt that the case was too urgent to admit of delay for argument. It seemed to him that he raced with death. His faith differed from that of the centurion in that he felt that the *presence* of Jesus was required to perform the miracle. He also regarded the powers of Jesus as limited to the living; but we must not censure his faith as particularly weak, for in both these re-

spects it resembled that possessed by Mary and Martha—
John xi. 21, 22, 32, 39.] **50 Jesus saith unto him, Go thy
way; thy son liveth.** [Jesus enlarges the nobleman's conception of his divine power by showing him that his words take
effect without regard to distance.] **The man believed the
word that Jesus spake unto him, and he went his way.
51 And as he was now going down, his servants met
him, saying, that his son lived. 52 So he inquired of
them the hour when he began to amend.** [More correctly, "began to get better." The father expected that the
fever would depart slowly, as it usually does; but the reply of
the servants shows that he was mistaken.] **They said
therefore unto him, Yesterday at the seventh hour the
fever left him.** [Though for harmonistic reasons we are persuaded that John himself uses the Roman method of computing the hours, which would make the phrase here mean
7 P. M., yet since the phraseology here is not his, but that of
the Galilæan servants, we take it to mean 1 P. M., for they
would use the Jewish method of computing from sunset to
sunset. If both parties had started at once, they would have
met before sundown, as each had but eleven miles to traverse.
But it is more reasonable to suppose that the wearied but
now believing father sought some refreshment and a brief
rest before returning, and that the servants tarried awhile to
see if the child's recovery was permanent. This would lead
to their meeting after sundown, at which time, according to
the invariable custom, they would call the previous period of
daylight "yesterday."] **53 So the father knew that it
was at that hour in which Jesus said unto him, Thy
son liveth: and himself believed, and his whole
house.** [We note here a growth in the faith of the nobleman. He first believed in the power of Jesus' *presence*, then
in the power of Jesus' *word*, and finally he believed generally
in Jesus, and his household shared his belief. This is the first
mention of a believing household; for others see Acts xvi. 14,
15, 34; xviii. 8.] **54 This is again the second sign that
Jesus did, having come out of Judaea into Galilee.**

[One small sign and many converted in Samaria; two great miracles and one household converted in Galilee. Such is the record. Jesus doubtless had many other converts in Galilee, but it is often true that the greater labor brings the lesser harvest.]

XXIX.

JESUS' TEMPORARY RESIDENCE AT CAPERNAUM.

ª MATT. IV. 13-16.

ª **13 And leaving Nazareth** [This expression means that Jesus now ceased to make Nazareth his home. For description of Nazareth, see page 60], **he came and dwelt in Capernaum** [See page 119. Capernaum means city of Nahum, or village of consolation. Its modern name, "Tell-Hum," means hill of Nahum. The word "dwelt" means that Jesus made this town his headquarters. He owned no house there (Matt. vii. 20). He may have dwelt with some of his disciples—for instance, Simon Peter—Matt. viii. 14-16], **which is by the sea, in the borders of Zebulun and Naphtali** [Capernaum was in Naphtali, and the border of the tribe of Zebulun was three or four miles south of it. This part of the country was densely populated, and had in it many choice spirits such as Jesus chose for his apostles]: **14 that it might be fulfilled which was spoken through Isaiah the prophet** [Isa. viii. 21, 22; ix. 1, 2], **saying, 15 The land of Zebulun and the land of Naphtali, toward the sea, beyond the Jordan, Galilee of the Gentiles.** [This land or region was the first to suffer in the beginning of those wars which finally resulted in the captivity of the ten tribes. The people of this district were smitten by Benhadad (I. Kings xv. 20), and afterwards by Tiglath-pileser (II. Kings xv. 29; I. Chron. v. 26), some time before the general captivity of the ten tribes (II. Kings xvii. 6). It is called Galilee of the Gentiles, because it was, according to Strabo and others, inhabited by Egyptians, Arabians and Phœnicians, as well as by Hebrews.] **16 The people that**

sat in darkness saw a great light, And to them that
sat in the region and shadow of death, To them did
light spring up. [Those who by reason of their ignorance
and depravity suffered the torments of war, and sat as it were
under the shadow of the wing of death, were designated by
prophecies as the class among whom the light of the gospel
would spring up in all the fullness and richness of its blessing.
Jesus, the "Light of the world," fulfilled this prophecy, and
apart from him there can be no pretense of its fulfillment.
Galilee had its prophets, but the enemies of Jesus themselves
bear witness that none of them were great enough "lights"
to fulfill this prophecy—John vii. 52.]

XXX.

JESUS CALLS FOUR FISHERMEN TO
FOLLOW HIM.

(Sea of Galilee Near Capernaum.)

ᵃMATT. IV. 18–22; ᵇMARK I. 16–20; ᶜLUKE V. 1–11.

ᵃ18 And walking ᵇ16 And passing along by the
sea of Galilee [This lake is a pear-shaped body of water,
about twelve and a half miles long and about seven miles across
at its widest place. It is 682 feet below sea level; its waters
are fresh, clear and abounding in fish, and it is surrounded by
hills and mountains, which rise from 600 to 1,000 feet above it.
Its greatest depth is about 165 feet], he [Jesus] saw ᵃtwo
brethren, Simon who is called Peter, and Andrew his
brother, {ᵇthe brother of Simon} casting a net in
{ᵃinto} the sea [The New Testament speaks of three kinds
of nets, viz.: the *amphiblestron*, which is only mentioned
here; the *sagene*, mentioned only at Matt. xiii. 27; and the
dictua, which is mentioned in all other places. The *dictua*
was a casting-net; the *sagene*, a seine or dragnet; and the
amphiblestron was a drawnet, a circular bell-shaped affair,
which was thrown upon the water, so that it spread out and

caught, by sinking, whatever was below it]; **for they were fishers.** [Though Simon and Andrew had been companions of Jesus on at least one journey, they did not as yet understand that his service would require all their time. The fact that Jesus now temporarily resided at Capernaum afforded them an opportunity to return to their old occupation, which they readily embraced. Fishing was then a prosperous trade on the lake of Galilee.] **ᵇ17 And Jesus said {ᵃhe saith} ᵇunto them, Come ye after me, and I will make you to become fishers of men.** [It was an invitation to follow, that they might be instructed by hearing his teaching and beholding his work. Jesus called them from a lower to a similar but higher labor. He calls all honest tradesmen in this manner. He invites carpenters to build his temple, servants to serve the great King, physicians to heal immortal souls, merchants to invest in pearls of great price, etc. The fishermen found many points of resemblance between the old and the new calling, such as, 1, daily hardships and dangers; 2, earnest desires for the objects sought; 3, skill and wisdom in the use of means, etc. Disciples are fishers, human souls are fish, the world is the sea, the gospel is the net, and eternal life is the shore whither the catch is drawn.] **ᵃ21 And going on from thence ᵇa little further, ᵃhe saw two other brethren, James the *son* of Zebedee, and John his brother, ᵇwho also were in the boat ᵃwith Zebedee their father, mending their {ᵇthe} nets.** [They also, like Peter and Andrew, were at work when Jesus found them. God calls the busy to his business. For instances where God has called the busy, see the cases of Moses (Ex. iii. 62), Gideon (Judg. vi. 11), Saul (I. Sam. x. 1–3), David (I. Sam. xvi. 11–15), Elisha (I. Kings xix. 19–21), Matthew (Matt. ix. 9), Saul (Acts ix. 1–6). Moreover most of these were called from lowly work, for such is God's method (I. Cor. i. 26–29). We should note two reasons why God chose the lowly and unlearned: 1, their minds being free from prejudice were more ready to entertain new truth; 2, the strength of the gospel was made more apparent by the weakness of its ministers (I. Cor. ii. 3–5 ; II. Cor. iv. 7 ; Zech. iv. 6). Of these two brothers, James was the first apostolic martyr and John the last survivor of the twelve. James was beheaded about A. D. 44 (Acts xii. 1, 2) ; and John, after upwards of seventy years' Christian service, died at Ephesus about A. D. 100.] **20 And straightway he called them** [From Matthew and Mark we would suppose that Jesus was alone when he called the two sets of brothers, and that with them he immediately left the lake. But we learn from Luke that a multitude was gathering about Jesus, and that he taught and worked a miracle before leaving the lake]: **1 Now it came to pass, while the multitude pressed upon him and heard the word of God, that he was standing by the lake of Gennesaret** [This body of water bore many names. It was anciently called Chinnereth (Num. xxxiv. 11), or Chinneroth (Judg. xii. 3), from a fortified town (Josh. xix. 35) and district (I. Kings xv. 20) in Naphtali bearing that name. It is here called Gennesaret, from a plain of that name upon its northwestern shore (which may be a corruption of the old name Chinnereth). It received its name, Galilee, from the district to which it belongs, and in later times it bore the name Tiberias (John vi. 1), from the city of that name on its western shore] ; **2 and he saw two boats standing by the lake : but the fishermen had gone out of them, and were washing their nets.** [We may conceive of the fishermen, in answer to Jesus' call, drawing their boats together to the point where he stood upon the shore. Then, as Jesus stood teaching, they occupied themselves in the shallow water behind him by washing their nets while they listened to him.] **3 And he entered into one of the boats, which was Simon's, and asked him to put out a little from the land.** [He did this that he might avoid the press, and that the people might be better able both to see and to hear.] **And he sat down** [the usual attitude or posture of a teacher] **and taught the multitudes out of the boat. 4 And when he had left speaking, he said unto Simon, Put out into the deep, and let down your nets for a**

draught. ["Put out" is in the singular, being addressed to Simon alone; "let down" is plural, being addressed generally to those in the boat.] **5 And Simon answered and said, Master, we toiled all night, and took nothing: but at thy word I will let down the nets.** ["Master" is a broader word than "Rabbi"; it indicates a superior, but does not confine his superiority to matters of instruction. The words of Peter show a willingness to oblige or honor Jesus; but are devoid of hope as to the thing proposed. Night was the time for fishing (John xxi. 3); and the proper place to cast the net was near the shore; but if Jesus wished to fish by daylight in the middle of the lake, Simon was not too weary to humor the wish.] **6 And when they had done this, they inclosed a great multitude of fishes; and their nets were breaking** [that is, the nets began to snap when they tried to lift them out of the water]; **7 and they beckoned unto their partners in the other boat, that they should come and help them.** [This indicates that they were well out into the lake, where it was easier to beckon than to shout explanations. Some think the marvel wrought by Jesus made them speechless, but they were so engrossed in the magnitude and value of the catch that the full glory of the miracle had not yet come upon them.] **And they came, and filled both the boats, so that they began to sink.** [They probably ran a second net under the one which enclosed the fishes, and by thus doubling the strength of the net were able to draw the fish up between the boats. A great load being thus suddenly dumped in the side of a boat will cause it to list, dip water and threaten to sink. Such appears to have been the case here until the loads were so distributed as to right the ships.] **8 But Simon Peter, when he saw it, fell down at Jesus' knees, saying, Depart from me; for I am a sinful man, O Lord. 9 For he was amazed, and all that were with him, at the draught of the fishes which they had taken** [This miracle came home to the soul of Peter because it was wrought in his own boat, with his own nets, and concerned his own business. Relig-

ion is only powerful as it becomes personal. Peter's request
shows how deeply the miracle impressed him. It gave him
that sense of the divine presence which never fails to overwhelm the hearts of men. No man can behold God in his
glory and live (Ex. xxxiii. 20–23; Ex. xx. 18, 19); and
though there have been exceptions where men have seen God
or his representatives and lived (Ex. xxiv. 9–11; Judg. vi.
21–23; Judg. xiii. 22, 23; Isa. vi. 1–5; Dan. x. 16–19; Gen.
xxxii. 30); yet no man, not even the purest, has ever stood
in the presence of God or his ministers without feeling such a
sense of weakness and sinfulness as to almost extinguish life—
Rev. i. 17; Job xlii. 5, 6]; **10 and so were also James
and John, sons of Zebedee, who were partners with
Simon. And Jesus said unto Simon, Fear not; from
henceforth thou shalt catch men.** [Jesus here shows the
purpose for which this miracle had been wrought. It was a
prophetic type or picture which foreshadowed the triumphs of
the day of Pentecost and other seasons when the apostles had
great ingatherings of souls through the preaching of the gospel.] **11 And when they had brought their boats to
land, they ᵃ straightway ᶜ left all** [that is to say, Peter and
Andrew], **ᵃ left the nets** [but James and John], **left the
boat and their father, ᵇ Zebedee in the boat with the
hired servants, and went after him.** {ᶜ followed him}
[The four partners, boats, different kinds of nets, hired servants, etc., and the fact that Salome, the wife of Zebedee, was
one of those who ministered to Christ out of her substance
(Matt. xxvii. 55, 56; Luke viii. 3), all indicate a business of
very respectable proportions: a fact which suggests that the
church of Christ would catch more souls if all its parts were
in partnership. Evidently when the four men left the boats
and nets Zebedee took charge of them. While the four
rightly recognized that the divine call was superior to their
earthly obligations, there is nothing which leads us to imply
that their sudden departure discomfited Zebedee. The call
of Christ here marks a change in their relationship to him.
Hitherto discipleship had not materially interfered with busi-

ness, but this present call separated them from their occupation, and prepared them for the call to be apostles which came later, and which required them to be his constant companions —Mark iii. 14.]

XXXI.

HEALING A DEMONIAC IN A SYNAGOGUE.

(At Capernaum.)

ᵇMARK I. 21-28; ᶜLUKE IV. 31-37.

ᵇ **21 And they** [Jesus and the four fishermen whom he had called] **go into** {ᶜ**he came down to**} **Capernaum, a city of Galilee.** [Luke has just spoken of Nazareth, and he uses the expression, "down to Capernaum," because the latter was on the lake shore while Nazareth was up in the mountains.] **And** ᵇ**straightway on the sabbath day he entered into the synagogue and taught.** {ᶜ**was teaching them**} ᵇ **22 And they were astonished at his teaching: for he taught them as having** {ᶜ**his word was with**} ᵇ**authority, and not as the scribes.** [Mark uses the adverb "straightway" and the particle "again" (which has a similar meaning) to depict the rapid movement of Jesus. As used by him in this connection it probably indicates that this was the next Sabbath after the calling of the four fishermen. The astonishment of the people was natural. Not yet recognizing Jesus' divinity, they could not understand how one so humble could speak with such authority. They contrasted his teaching with that of the scribes. The scribes were learned men who preserved, copied and expounded the law and the tradition (Ez. vii. 6, 12; Neh. viii. 1; Matt. xv. 1–6; xxiii. 2-4; Mark xii. 35; Luke xi. 52). They were also called "lawyers" (Mark xii. 28; Matt. xxii. 35), and "doctors of the law" (Luke v. 17–21). Though the teaching of Jesus differed from the teaching of the scribes as to *matter*, the contrast here drawn is as to *manner*. They spoke on the authority of Moses or the elders, but Jesus taught by his own authority. Their way was to quote minute precedents supported by endless authorities. A passage taken from later rabbinical writings starts thus: "Rabbi Zeira says, on the authority of Rabbi Jose bar Rabbi Chanina, and Rabbi Ba or Rabbi Chija on the authority of Rabbi Jochanan," etc. Contrast with this the oft-repeated "I say unto you" of Jesus— Matt. v. 18, 20, 22, 26, 28, 34.] **23 And straightway there was in their {ᶜthe} ᵇsynagogue a man with {ᶜthat had} ᵇan unclean spirit {ᶜa spirit of an unclean demon}** [Matthew, Luke and Mark all concur in pronouncing demons unclean; that is, wicked. They thus corrected the prevailing Greek notion that some of the demons were good. The word "demon," as used in our Saviour's time by both Jews and Greeks, meant the spirits of the departed or the ghosts of dead men, and the teaching of that and prior ages was that such spirits often took possession of living men and controlled them. But whatever these demons were, the Scripture, both by its treatment of them and its words concerning them, clearly indicates that they were immaterial, intelligent beings, which are neither to be confused with maladies and diseases of the body, nor with tropes, metaphors, or other figures of speech. In proof of this we adduce the following Scriptural facts: 1, the legislation of the Old Testament proceeded upon the assumption that there was such a thing as a "familiar spirit" (Lev. xix. 31); 2, in the New Testament they are spoken of as personalities (Jas. ii. 19; Rex. xvi. 14), Jesus even founding a parable upon their habits (Luke xi. 24–26); 3, Jesus distinguished between them and diseases, and so did his disciples (Matt. x. 8; Luke x. 17–20); 4, Jesus addressed them as persons, and they answered as such (Mark v. 8; ix. 25); 5, they manifested desires and passions (Mark v. 12, 13); 6, they showed a superhuman knowledge of Jesus (Matt. viii. 29). It would be impossible to regard demon possession as a mere disease without doing violence to the language used in every instance of the expulsion of a demon. The frequency of demoniacal possession in the time of Jesus is probably due to the fact that his advent formed a great crisis in the spiritual order of things. **For** fuller treatment of the subject, see *Millennial Harbinger,* 1841, pp. 457, 580; 1842, pp. 65, 124]; ᵇ**and he cried out,** ᶜ**with a loud voice** [The man cried, the unclean spirit determined what he should cry. The silence and decorum of the synagogue made the outcry more noticeable, and the demon betrayed his excitement and alarm in speaking before he was spoken to], ᵇ**24 saying,** ᶜ**34 Ah! what have we to do with thee** [for explanation of this idiom see page 116], **Jesus thou Nazarene? art thou come to destroy us?** [Jesus came to destroy the *works* of the devil (I. John iii. 8). At his second coming the *workers* themselves shall suffer (Matt. xxv. 41). We find that they recognized that the time of this "torment" had not yet come— Matt. viii. 29.] **I know thee who thou art, the Holy One of God.** [It is impossible that fever or disease, mental or physical, could give such supernatural knowledge. The demon called Jesus the Holy One, 1, because it was one of his proper Scriptural names (Ps. xvi. 10; Acts ii. 31); 2, because holiness was that characteristic which involved the ruin of demons as unholy ones—just as light destroys darkness. We should note here the unfruitful knowledge, faith and confession of demons. They lacked neither knowledge (Matt. viii. 29) nor faith (Jas. ii. 19), nor did they withhold confession; but Jesus received them not. Repentance and **willing** obedience are as necessary as faith or confession.] **35 And Jesus rebuked him, saying, Hold thy peace, and come out of him.** [We have in this phrase two personages indicated by the personal pronoun "him"; one of whom is commanded to come out of the other; one of whom is now rebuked and hereafter to be destroyed, the other of whom is delivered. In commanding silence Jesus refused to receive the demon's testimony. We can see at least three reasons for this: 1, it was not fitting that the fate of the people should rest upon the testimony of liars; 2, because receiving such testimony might have been taken as an indication that Jesus sustained friendly relations to demons—something which the enemies of

Christ actually alleged (Matt. xii. 24); 3, the Messiahship of
Jesus was to be gradually unfolded, and the time for its public
proclamation had not yet come.] **And when the demon
{ ᵇunclean spirit} ᶜhad thrown him down in the
midst, ᵇtearing him and crying with a loud voice, ᶜhe
came out of him, having done him no hurt.** [The
demon first racked the body of the man with a convulsion,
and then, with a cry of rage, came out. All this was permitted that, 1, there might be clear evidence of demoniacal
possession; 2, the demon's malignity might be shown; 3, it
might be manifested that the spirit came not out of its own
accord, but because compelled thereto by the command of
Christ. The cry was, however, a mere impotent expression
of anger, for Luke, "the beloved physician," notes that it
did the man no hurt.] **ᵇ27 And they were all amazed,
{ᶜamazement came upon all,} ᵇinsomuch that they
questioned among themselves, ᶜand they spake together, one with another, saying, ᵇWhat is this?
ᶜWhat is this word? ᵇa new teaching! ᶜfor with
authority and power he commandeth ᵇeven the unclean spirits, ᶜand they come out. ᵇand they obey
him.** [The power to command disembodied spirits thus amazed
the people, because it was more mysterious than the power to
work physical miracles. By this miracle Jesus demonstrated his
actual possession of the authority which he had just assumed
in his teaching.] **28 And the report of him went out
straightway {ᶜ37 And there went forth a rumor concerning him} ᵇeverywhere into all {ᶜevery place of}
ᵇthe region of Galilee roundabout.** [This fame was
occasioned both by the miracle and the teaching. The
benevolence and publicity of the miracle, and its power—the
power of one mightier than Satan—would cause excitement
in any community, in any age. Though this is the first
miracle recorded by either Mark or Luke, yet neither asserts
that it was the *first* miracle Jesus wrought, so there is no
conflict with John ii. 11.]

XXXII.

HEALING PETER'S MOTHER-IN-LAW AND MANY OTHERS.

(At Capernaum.)

^aMatt. viii. 14-17; ^b Mark i. 29-34; ^c Luke iv. 38-41.

^c **38 And he rose up from the synagogue** [where he had just healed the demoniac], ^b **29 And straightway, when they were come out of the synagogue, they came {^c entered} ^b into the house of Simon and Andrew, with James and John.** [Peter and Andrew had dwelt at Bethsaida (John i. 44). They may have removed to Capernaum, or Bethsaida, being near by, may be here counted as a part, or suburb, of Capernaum. Its name does not contradict this view, for it means "house of fishing," or "fishery."] **30 Now Simon's wife's mother lay sick of {^c was holden with} a great fever.** [The Papists, who claim that Peter was the first pope, must confess that he was married at this time, and continued to be so for years afterwards (I. Cor. ix. 5). Celibacy is unauthorized by Scripture (Heb. xiii. 4). God says it is not good (Gen. ii. 18). Luke speaks as a physician; for Galen, the father of medicine, divided fevers into little and great.] ^a **14 And when Jesus was come into Peter's house, he saw his wife's mother lying sick of a fever. ^b and straightway they tell him of her: ^c and they besought him for her.** [Their interest in her shows the spirit of love and kindliness which pervaded the home.] ^b **31 and he came ^c 39 And he stood over her, and rebuked the fever** [though it was an inanimate force, it was still subject to rebuke, as were the winds and waves of Galilee —Matt. viii. 26]; ^a **15 And he touched her hand, ^b and took her by the hand, and raised her up** [thus showing that the miracle came from him, and that he felt a tender interest in the sufferer]; ^c **and it {^b the fever} ^c left her: and immediately she rose up {^a arose,} ^b and she ministered unto them. {^a him.}** [Her complete recovery emphasized the miracle. Such fevers invariably leave the patient weak,

and the period of convalescence is long and trying, and often full of danger. She showed her gratitude by her ministry.]
ᵇ**32 And at even, ᵃwhen even was come, ᶜwhen the sun was setting, {ᵇdid set,} ᶜall they that had any sick with divers diseases, brought them unto him; ᵇthey brought unto him all that were sick, and them {ᵃmany} ᵇthat were possessed with demons.** [Their delay till sundown was unquestionably caused by the traditional law of the Sabbath which forbade men to carry any burden on that day (John v. 10). The Sabbath closed at sundown (Lev. xxiii. 32). The distinction is drawn between the sick and the demon-possessed. Lightfoot gives two reasons why demoniacal possession was so common at that time, viz.: 1. the intense wickedness of the nation; 2. the addiction of the nation to magic, whereby the people invited evil spirits to be familiar with them.] ᶜ**and he laid his hands on every one of them, ᵃand he cast out the spirits with a word, and healed all ᶜthem ᵃthat were sick: 17 that it might be fulfilled which was spoken through Isaiah the prophet** [Isa. liii. 4], **saying, Himself took our infirmities, and bare our diseases.** [Isaiah's vision is progressive; he sees, first, a man of sorrows; second, a man sorrowful because he bore the sickness and sorrows of others; third, a man who also bore sin, and healed the souls of others by so doing. Such was the order of Christ's life. His early years were spent in poverty and obscurity; his days of ministry in bearing, by sympathy and compassion, the sicknesses and sorrows of others (John xi. 35; Mark xvii. 34); and in the hour of his crucifixion, he became the world's sin-bearer—John i. 29; I. Pet. ii. 24.] ᵇ**33 And all the city was gathered together at the door. 34 And he healed many that were sick with divers diseases, and cast out many demons; ᶜ41 And demons also came out from many, crying out, and saying, Thou art the Son of God. And rebuking them, he suffered them {ᵇthe demons} ᶜnot to speak, ᵇbecause they knew him. ᶜthat he was the Christ.** [Those who are disposed to frequent spiritual seances and to seek information from mediums should remember that the Son of God permitted his disciples to receive no information from such sources. He forbade demons to speak in the presence of his own, even on the most important of all topics.]

XXXIII.

JESUS MAKES A PREACHING TOUR THROUGH GALILEE.

ᵃ MATT. IV. 23–25; ᵇ MARK I. 35–39; LUKE IV. 42–44.

ᵇ **35 And in the morning, a great while before day, he rose up and went out** [*i. e.*, from the house of Simon Peter], **and departed into a desert place, and there prayed.** [Though Palestine was densely populated, its people were all gathered into towns, so that it was usually easy to find solitude outside the city limits. A ravine near Capernaum, called the Vale of Doves, would afford such solitude. Jesus taught (Matt. vi. 6) and practiced solitary prayer. We can commune with God better when alone than when in the company of even our dearest friends. It is a mistaken notion that one can pray equally well at all times and in all places. Jesus being in all things like men, except that he was sinless (Heb. ii. 17), must have found prayer a real necessity. He prayed as a human being. Several reasons for this season of prayer are suggested, from which we select two: 1. It was a safeguard against the temptation to vainglory induced by the unbounded admiration and praise of the multitude whom he had just healed. 2. It was a fitting preparation on the eve of his departure on his first missionary tour.] ᶜ **42 And when it was day, he came out and went into a desert place.** [Mark has in mind the season when Jesus sought the Father in prayer, and so he tells us that it was " a great while before day." Luke has in mind the hour when Jesus faced and spoke to the multitude, so he says, " When it was day."] ᵇ **36 And Simon** [as head of the house which Jesus had just left, Simon naturally acted as leader and guide to the party which sought Jesus] **and they that were with him** [they who were stopping in Simon's house ; viz.: Andrew, James and John] **followed after him** [literally, pursued after him. Xenophon uses this word to signify the close pursuit of an enemy in war. Simon had no hesitancy in obtruding on the retirement of the Master. This rushing after Jesus in hot haste accorded with his impulsive nature. The excited interest of the people seemed to the disciples of Jesus to offer golden opportunities, and they could not comprehend his apparent indifference to it]; **37 and they found him, and say unto him, All are seeking thee.** [The disciples saw a multitude seeking Jesus for various causes: some to hear, some for excitement, some for curiosity. To satisfy the people seemed to them to be Christ's first duty. Jesus understood his work better than they. He never encouraged those who sought through mere curiosity or admiration (John vi. 27). Capernaum accepted the benefit of his miracles, but rejected his call to repentance—Matt. xi. 23.] **38 And he saith unto them, Let us go elsewhere into the next towns** [the other villages of Galilee], **that I may preach there also; for to this end came I forth.** [*I. e.*, I came forth from the Father (John xvi. 28) to make and preach a gospel. His disciples failed to understand his mission. Afterwards preaching was with the apostles the all-important duty—Acts vi. 2; I. Cor. i.17.] c **and the multitudes sought after him, and came unto him, and would have stayed him, that he should not go from them.** [They would have selfishly kept his blessed ministries for their own exclusive enjoyment.] **43 But he said unto them, I must preach the good tidings of the kingdom of God to the other cities also: for therefore was I sent.** [Jesus sought to arouse the entire nation. That which the disciples regarded as a large work in Capernaum was consequently in his sight a very small one. Those who understand that it is God's will and wish to save every man that lives upon the earth will not be overelated by a successful revival in some small corner of the great field of labor.] b **39 And he** a **Jesus went about in all Galilee** [The extreme length of Galilee was about sixty-three miles, and its extreme width about thirty-three miles. Its average dimensions were about fifty by twenty-five miles. It contained, according to Josephus, two hundred and forty towns and villages. Its population at that time is estimated at about three millions. Lewin calculates that this circuit of Galilee must have occupied four or five months. The verses of this paragraph are, therefore, a summary of the work and influence of Jesus during the earlier part of his ministry. They are a general statement, the details of which are given in the subsequent chapters of the Gospels of Matthew, Mark and Luke— the Gospel of John dealing more particularly with the work in Judæa], b into their synagogues throughout all Galilee, a teaching in their synagogues [The word "synagogue" is compounded of the two Greek words "*sun*," together, and "*ago*," to collect. It is, therefore, equivalent to our English word "meeting-house." Tradition and the Targums say that these Jewish houses of worship existed from the earliest times. In proof of this assertion, Deut. xxxi. 11 and Ps. lxxiv. 8 are cited. But the citations are insufficient, that in Deuteronomy not being in point, and the seventy-fourth Psalm being probably written after the Babylonian captivity. It better accords with history to believe that the synagogue originated during the Babylonian captivity, and was brought into the motherland by the returning exiles. Certain it is that the synagogue only came into historic prominence after the books of the Old Testament were written. At the time of our Saviour's ministry synagogues were scattered all over Palestine, and also over all quarters of the earth whither the Jews had been dispersed. Synagogues were found in very small villages, for wherever ten "men of leisure," willing and able to devote themselves to the service of the synagogue, were found, a synagogue might be erected. In the synagogues the people met together on the Sabbaths to pray, and to listen to the reading of portions of the Old Testament, and also to hear such instruction or exhortation as might be furnished. With the permission of the president of the synagogue any one who was fitted might deliver an address. Thus the synagogues furnished Jesus (and in later times his disciples also) with a congregation and a suitable place for preaching. We find that on week days Jesus often preached in the open air. But the synagogues are thus particularly mentioned, probably, because in them were held the most important services, because they were necessary during the rainy and cold season, and because their use shows that as yet the Jewish rulers had not so prejudiced the public mind as to exclude Jesus from the houses of worship], **and preaching the gospel of the kingdom,** ᵇ **and casting out demons** [Mark singles out this kind of miracle as most striking and wonderful], ᵃ **and healing all manner of disease and all manner of sickness among the people. 24 And the report of him went forth into all Syria** [caravans passing through Galilee back and forth between the Mediterranean seaports on the west and the Persian cities on the east, and between Damascus on the north and Egypt on the south, would carry the reports concerning Jesus far and wide]: **and they brought unto him all that were sick, holden with divers diseases and torments, possessed with demons, and epileptic, and palsied; and he healed them.** [Thus, by his actions, Jesus showed that the kingdom of God had come. The wonders of Moses were mostly miracles of judgment, those of Jesus were acts of compassion. The diseases here enumerated are still among the most difficult for physicians to handle. The term "palsy" included all forms of paralysis, catalepsy and cramps.] **25 And there followed him great multitudes** [these popular demonstrations, no doubt, intensified the erroneous notion of his disciples that the kingdom of Jesus was to be one of worldly grandeur] **from Galilee and Decapolis** [Decapolis is formed from the two Greek words "*deka*," ten, and "*polis*," city. As a geographical term, Decapolis refers to that part of Syria lying east, southeast and south of the Lake of Galilee. There is some doubt as to which were the ten cities named, for there seem at times to have been fourteen of them. Those commonly reckoned are, 1. Damascus. 2. Philadelphia. 3. Raphana. 4. Scythopolis. 5. Gadara. 6. Hyppos. 7. Dion. 8. Pella. 9. Galas. 10. Kanatha. The other four are Abila and Kanata (distinct from Kanatha), Cæsarea Philippi and Gergesa. None of these were in Galilee save Scythopolis. According to Ritter, these cities were colonized principally by veterans from the army of Alexander the Great. A reminiscence of their Macedonian origin is found in the fact that there was a city named Pella in Macedonia. These cities are said to have been formed into a confederacy by Pompey the Great. In the time of Jesus they were chiefly inhabited by Greeks or heathen, and not by Jews. Josephus expressly calls Gadara and Hyppos Greek cities] **and Jerusalem and Judaea and *from* beyond the Jordan.** [The land beyond Jordan was called Peræa, which means "beyond." According to Josephus, it included territory between the cities of Pella on the north and Machærus on the south. That is to say, its northern boundary began on the Jordan opposite the southern line of Galilee, and its southern boundary was at Moab, about the middle of the east shore of the Dead Sea.] ᶜ**44 And he was preaching in the synagogues of Galilee.**

XXXIV.

JESUS HEALS A LEPER AND CREATES MUCH EXCITEMENT.

ᵃ MATT. VIII. 2–4; ᵇ MARK I. 40–45; ᶜ LUKE V. 12–16.

ᶜ**12 And it came to pass, while he was in one of the cities** [it was a city of Galilee, but as it is not named, it is idle to conjecture which city it was], **behold,** ᵇ**there cometh {ᵃcame} ᵇto him a leper** [There is much discussion as to what is here meant by leprosy. Two diseases now go by that name; viz., psoriasis and elephantiasis. There are also three varieties of psoriasis, namely, white, black and red. There are also three varieties or modifications of elephantiasis, namely, tubercular, spotted or streaked, and anæsthetic. Elephantiasis is the leprosy found in modern times in Syria, Greece, Spain, Norway and Africa. Now, since Lev. xiii., in determining

leprosy, lays great stress on a white or reddish-white depres-
sion of the skin, the hairs in which are turned white or yellow,
and since it also provides that the leper who is white all over
shall be declared clean, and since in the only two cases where
lepers are described—Num. xii. 10; II. Kings v. 27—they are
spoken of as "white as snow," scholars have been led to
think that the Biblical leprosy was the white form of psoriasis.
But the facts hardly warrant us in excluding the other forms
of psoriasis, or even elephantiasis; for, 1. Lev. xiii. also declares that any bright spot or scale shall be pronounced leprosy,
if it be found to spread abroad over the body; and this indefinite language would let in elephantiasis, cancer and many
other skin diseases. In fact, the law deals with the initial
symptoms rather than with the ultimate phases of the fully
developed disease. 2. Elephantiasis was a common disease
in our Saviour's time, and has been ever since, and would
hardly be called leprosy now, if it had not been popularly so
called then. The word "leprosy" comes from "*lepo*," which
means to peel off in scales. It is hereditary for generations,
though modern medical authorities hold that it is not contagi-
ous. However, the returning Crusaders spread it all over
Europe in the tenth and eleventh centuries, so that according
to Matthew Paris there was no less than nine thousand hospitals
set apart for its victims. The facts that the priests had to
handle and examine lepers, and that any one who was white
all over with leprosy was declared clean, led scholars to think
that the laws of Moses, which forbade any one to approach or
touch a leper, were not enacted to prevent the spread of a
contagion, but for typical and symbolic purposes. It is thought
that God chose the leprosy as the symbol of sin and its consequences, and that the Mosaic legislation was given to carry
out this conception. Being the most loathsome and incurable
of all diseases, it fitly represents in bodily form the ravages of
sin in the soul of a man. But there must also have been a
sanitary principle in God's laws, since we still deem it wise to
separate lepers, and since other people beside the Hebrews
(as the Persians) prohibited lepers from mingling with other

citizens. Elephantiasis is the most awful disease known. The body of its victim disintegrates joint by joint, until the whole frame crumbles to pieces. Psoriasis is milder, but is very distressing. Mead thus describes a case: The " skin was shining as covered with flakes of snow. And as the furfuraceous or bran-like scales were daily rubbed off, the flesh appeared quick or raw underneath." In addition to the scaly symptoms, the skin becomes hard and cracks open, and from the cracks an ichorous humor oozes. The disease spreads inwardly, and ends in consumption, dropsy, suffocation and death], ᶜ a man full of leprosy [Some have thought that Luke meant to indicate one so completely covered with leprosy as to be clean (Lev. xiii. 12–17). But the fact that Jesus sent him to the priest, shows that he was not such a clean leper. Luke meant to describe a leper in the last stages of the disease—a leper past all hope]: and when he saw Jesus, ᵇ beseeching him, and kneeling down to him, ᶜ he fell on his face, ᵃ and worshipped him, ᶜ and besought him, saying, ᵇ unto him, ᶜ Lord [The Jews, in addressing any distinguished person, usually employed the title "Lord." They were also accustomed to kneel before prophets and kings. It is not likely that the leper knew enough of Jesus to address or worship him as the Son of God. He evidently took Jesus for some great prophet; but he must have had great faith, for he was full of confidence that Jesus had power to heal him, although there was but one case of leper-cleansing in the Scriptures—II. Kings v. 1–19; Luke iv. 27], if thou wilt, thou canst make me clean. [The leper believed in the power of Jesus, but doubted his willingness to expend it on one so unworthy and so unclean. In temporal matters we can not always be as sure of God's willingness as we can be of his power. We should note that the man asked rather for the blessing of cleanness than for health. To the Jew uncleanness was more horrible than disease. It meant to be an outcast from Israel, and to be classed with swine, dogs and other odious and abhorrent creatures. The leper, therefore, prayed that the Lord would remove his shame and pollution.] ᵇ**41 And being moved with compassion, he stretched forth his hand, and touched him** [Mark habitually notes the feelings, and hence also the gestures, of Jesus. It was not an accidental, but an intentional, touch. Popular belief so confused and confounded leprosy with the uncleanness and corruption of sin, as to make the leper feel that Jesus might almost compromise his purity if he concerned himself to relieve it. The touch of Jesus, therefore, gave the leper a new conception of divine compassion. It is argued that Jesus, by this touch, was made legally unclean until the evening (Lev. xiii. 46; xi. 40). But we should note the spirit and purpose of this law. Touch was prohibited because it defiled the person touching, and aided not the person touched. In Jesus' case the reasons for the law were absent, the conditions being reversed. Touching defiled not the toucher, and healed the touched. In all things Jesus touches and shares our human state, but he so shares it that instead of his being defiled by our uncleanness, we are purified by his righteousness. Moreover, Jesus, as a priest after the order of Melchizedek (Heb. v. 6), possessed the priestly right to touch the leper without defilement—Heb. iv. 15], **and saith unto him,** {ᶜ**saying,**} **I will; be thou made clean.** [The Lord's answer is an echo of the man's prayer. The words, "I will," express the high authority of Jesus.] ᵇ**42 And straightway the** {ᵃ**his**} ᶜ**leprosy departed from him.** {ᵃ**was cleansed.**} ᵇ**and he was made clean.** ["Luke says, 'departed,' giving the merely physical view of the event. Matthew says, 'was cleansed,' using ceremonial language. Mark combines the two forms"—*Godet.*] **43 And he strictly charged him,** ᶜ**to tell no man** [The language used indicates that Jesus sternly forbade the man to tell what had been done. The man's conduct, present and future, shows that he needed severe speech. In his uncontrollable eagerness to be healed he had overstepped his privileges, for he was not legally permitted to thus enter cities and draw near to people (Num. v. 2, 3); he was to keep at a distance from them, and covering his mouth, was to cry, " *Tame,*

tame—unclean, unclean" (Lev. xiii. 45, 46; Luke xvii. 12, 13). The man evinced a like recklessness in disregarding the command of Jesus]: ᵇand straightway sent him out, ᵃ4 And Jesus saith unto him, See thou tell no man; {ᵇsay nothing to any man:} [Several reasons are suggested why the Lord thus commanded silence: 1. It may have been better for the man not to mention his cure (John ix. 34). 2. He required the decision of the priest to make him legally clean; and too much talk might so prejudice the priests as to lead them to refuse to admit his cure. 3. But the best reason is that it accorded with our Lord's general course, which was to suppress excitement, and thus prevent too great crowds from gathering about him and hindering his work. To take this view is to say that Jesus meant to prevent exactly what happened] ᶜbut go thy way, and show thyself to the priest, and offer for thy cleansing, according as Moses commanded, ᵇthe things which {ᵃthe gift that} Moses commanded, for a testimony unto them. [Though healed of his leprosy, the man was not legally clean until declared so by the priest. The priest alone could readmit him to the congregation. The local priest inspected the healed leper, and if he was found clean or cured, he was purified by the use of two birds, cedar wood, scarlet and hyssop, razor and bath. After seven days he was again inspected, and if still cured the priest repaired with him to the temple, where he offered the gift for his cleansing, which was three lambs, with flour and oil; or if the leper was poor, one lamb and two doves or pigeons, with flour and oil (Lev. xiv.). The healed leper was a testimony that Messiah, the great Physician, had come, and that he respected the law of Moses. This testimony was given both to priests and people.] ᵇ45 But he went out [from the presence of Jesus and from the city], and began to publish it much, and to spread abroad the matter, {ᶜ15 But so much the more went abroad the report concerning him:} [the leper was so elated that he could scarcely refrain from publishing his cure, and he must also have thought that this was what Jesus really wanted—that in commanding him not to publish it he did not mean what he said] **and great multitudes came together to hear, and to be healed of their infirmities.** [b] **insomuch that Jesus could no more openly enter into a city** [Not a natural or physical inability, but the inability of impropriety. Jesus could not do what he judged not best to do. The excitement caused by such an entry was injurious in several ways: 1. It gave such an emphasis to the miracles of Jesus as to make them overshadow his teaching. 2. It threatened to arouse the jealousy of the government. 3. It rendered the people incapable of calm thought. Two things constantly threatened the ministry of Jesus, namely, impatience in the multitude, and envious malice in the priests and Pharisees. Jesus wished to add to neither of these elements of opposition. Thus the disobedience of the leper interrupted Jesus, and thwarted him in his purpose to visit the villages. Disobedience, no matter how well-meaning, always hinders the work of Christ], [c] **16 But he withdrew himself in the deserts,** {[b] **was without in desert places :**} [That is, in the remote grazing-lands like that desert in which he afterwards fed the five thousand. Such was our Lord's unexampled meekness that he preferred the silent deserts to the applause of multitudes. His meekness was as high above the capacity of a merely human being as were his miracles] [c] **and prayed.** [Luke's Gospel is pre-eminently the gospel of prayer and thanksgiving] [b] **and they came to him from every quarter.**

XXXV.

JESUS HEALS A PARALYTIC AT CAPERNAUM.

[a] MATT. IX. 2–8; [b] MARK II. 1–12; [c] LUKE V. 17–26.

[c] **17 And it came to pass on one of those days,** [b] **when he entered again into Capernaum after some days,** [c] **that he was teaching;** [b] **it was noised that he was in the house.** [Luke uses the general expression

"those days," referring to the early portion of our Lord's ministry in Galilee. Mark says, "some days," which implies the lapse of a considerable interval. The healing of the leper created such excitement that for some time, probably several weeks, Jesus kept out of the cities. He now, after the excitement has subsided, quietly enters Capernaum, and probably goes to the house of Simon Peter, now looked upon as his headquarters in Capernaum (Mark i. 29). His entrance into Capernaum marks the end of his first missionary tour through Galilee.] **2 And many were gathered together, so that there was no longer room *for them,* no, not even about the door: and he spake the word unto them.** [Oriental houses are one or two storied structures, built in the form of a square, or rectangle, with an open space in the center called the court. They have one door which opens from the street into an open space called the porch, and this porch in turn opens upon the court. In this porch there is usually a stairway leading to the roof. The roofs are invariably flat, and are surrounded by a breastwork or parapet to keep those on them from falling off. Roofs or housetops are used as we use yards, only they are somewhat private. Some think that this house was a two-storied structure, and that Jesus was teaching in the upper room, or second story. If this were so, there would have been little profit to the people who clung about the street door, for they could neither see nor hear. Besides, a two-storied house would probably have been beyond the means of Simon Peter. It is more likely that Jesus was in the room opposite the porch across the court. If so, the crowd at the door might catch an occasional word, or by tiptoing obtain a momentary glance; and thus fan the hope of some ultimate satisfaction. The gospel is here called the "word," for it is the Word among words, as the Bible is the Book among books.] ᶜ **and there were Pharisees and doctors of the law sitting by** [the fact that they were sitting, shows that they were honored above the rest: Jesus did not increase their ill-will by any needless disrespect], **who were come out of every village of Galilee and Judaea and Jerusa-**

lem [It is not likely that such a gathering came together by accident. Capernaum was known to be the headquarters of Jesus, and these leaders of the people had doubtless gathered there to wait for some opportunity to see or hear Jesus. They recognized the necessity of coming to some definite judgment regarding him. We shall see in this scene the beginning of their hostility to Jesus, which developed into four objections: 1. Alleged blasphemy; 2. Intercourse with publicans and sinners; 3. Supposed neglect of ascetic duties, such as washings, fastings, etc.; 4. Alleged violation of the sabbath]: **and the power of the Lord was with him to heal.** [That is to say, the power of God the Father was then working in Jesus to perform miracles (John xiv. 10). Some take this as implying that other miracles had been wrought that day, before the arrival of the paralytic. But the words are more likely a preface for what follows; in which case the meaning is that the cold disbelief of the Pharisees did not prevent Jesus from working miracles, as disbelief usually did—Matt. xiii. 58; xvi. 1-4.] **18 And behold, men bring {ᵃthey brought ᵇthey come, bringing} unto him a man sick of the palsy, {ᶜthat was palsied:} ᵃlying on a bed: ᵇborne of four** [Palsy is an abbreviation of the word "paralysis." It is caused by a cessation of the nervous activities. See page 173. In the East bedsteads were practically unknown. An Oriental bed is a thin mattress, or pallet, just large enough for a man to lie upon; and those generally used by the poor to-day are made of sheepskin with the wool on it. Such a bed could be easily carried by four men, if each took hold of a corner.] **ᶜand they sought to bring him in** [*i. e.*, into the house], **and to lay him before him. 19 And not finding by what *way* they might bring him in because of the multitude, ᵇ4 And when they could not come nigh unto him for the crowd** [To these four who sought Jesus it seemed a case of now or never. If they waited till another season, Jesus might withdraw himself again for "some days," or the palsied man might die. "Now" is always the day of salvation], **ᶜthey went up to the**

housetop [They went up by means of the stairs in the porch, or by ascending to the roof of an adjoining house, and stepping across to the roof of Simon's house. Many commentators assert that they went up by an outside stairway, erroneously believing that such stairs are common in Palestine; but they are almost unknown there, and their presence would only expose the inmates of the house to violence and pillage], **ᵇthey uncovered the roof where he was: and when they had broken it up, they let down the bed whereon the sick of the palsy lay. ᶜand let him down through the tiles with his couch into the midst before Jesus.** [Some have thought that removing the roof merely means that they took away the awning over the court, and also that the removal of the tile merely means that they took down the parapet or wall which prevented people from falling from the roof into the court. But the language is strongly against such a construction. An awning is not a roof, and it is rolled up, not "broken up." Moreover, the man was let down "through the tiles," which seems to indicate that the remaining tiles encased an opening through which he was lowered. The tiles were plates of burnt clay, suitable for roofing rather than for building walls or parapets. We are not told in what part of the house Jesus stood, but evidently an opening was made in the flat roof above him, and the man was lowered to the floor in front of Jesus by means of short straps or pieces of rope fastened to the four corners of the bed. A stout parapet would have aided rather than have hindered, if the body had been lowered into the court.] **ᵇ5 And Jesus seeing their faith** [the four friends of the sick man showed their faith by those bold and persistent efforts which took liberties with the house of a neighbor; and the palsied man showed his faith by consenting to the extraordinary means employed in his behalf] **saith {ᵃsaid} unto the sick of the palsy, Son, {ᶜMan,} ᵃbe of good cheer; ᶜthy sins are forgiven thee.** [The affectionate address, "Son," might have ordinarily surprised the Jewish doctors, who held themselves too far removed from sinners to speak thus familiarly with them.

But the smaller surprise was swallowed up in the greater, when they heard Jesus pronounce the forgiveness of the man's sins. Since man had trod the globe sin against God had never thus been pardoned by the direct, authoritative utterance of fleshly lips. Such power resides in Jesus alone. Since then, and even in modern times, mistaken priests have presumed to speak forgiveness; but the apostles claimed no such power (Acts viii. 22). So far as the church forgives sins (John xx. 23), it does it merely as the organ of God, and must do so according to the methods and ordinances laid down by God. Those who profess to forgive sin by word of mouth, should be able to make good their claim to this boasted power by healing diseases or otherwise removing the consequences of sin. Failing to do this, they must forever rest under the justified suspicion that they are, wittingly or unwittingly, guilty of blasphemy.] ᵇ6 **But there were certain of the scribes** ᶜ**and the Pharisees** ᵇ**sitting there,** ᵃ3 **And behold,** [they] ᶜ**began to reason,** ᵇ**and reasoning in their hearts,** ᵃ**said within themselves,** ᶜ**saying,** ᵃ**This man blasphemeth.** ᵇ7 **Why doth this man thus speak?** [A scornful expression, shown by the repetition, *houtos houtoo*, which means, literally, "this one these things."] **he blasphemeth:** ᶜ**Who is this that speaketh blasphemies? Who can forgive sins,** ᵇ**but one,** *even* **God?** ᶜ**alone?** [In classic Greek to blaspheme means to speak evil of, or to slander a person, and it is used in this sense in the New Testament (Tit. iii. 2; II. Pet. ii. 2; Jude 8). Its ordinary New Testament use, however, is quite different, since it is employed to designate something which reflects evil on the character or nature of God. This use is peculiar to monotheistic writers, and was unknown to the Greeks. Such blasphemies may be divided into three general heads, thus: 1. To attribute the unworthy to God. 2. To deny the worthy to God. 3. To arrogate or claim any attribute, power, authority, etc., which belongs exclusively to God. It was under this third head that Jesus seemed to lay himself open to accusation—an accusation entirely just if he had not been the

Son of God. The Pharisees were not faulty in their logic, but were mistaken in their premises; hence Jesus does not deny their doctrine; he merely corrects their mistaken application of it to himself. As to this pronounced forgiveness of Jesus, two questions arise: 1. Why did he forgive the man's sins? The haste with which the man was brought to Jesus suggests that his condition was critical; in which case the torment of his sin would be the greater. As a searcher of hearts Jesus saw the unuttered desire of the sick man, and at once responded to it. If his words meant nothing to the conscience of the man, they were wasted; but Jesus knew what was in man. 2. Why did he pronounce the forgiveness so publicly? As the terms of pardon prescribed in the law were yet in full force, this open speech of Jesus was a surprising assertion of authority. In fact, such assertions were exceptional in his ministry; for only on three recorded occasions did he thus forgive sins (Luke vii. 48; xxiii. 43). Being the exceptional and not the established method of pardon, and being thus employed in the presence of so representative an audience, it was evidently used for a special purpose; and that purpose was to show that Jesus had such power, that men seeing this power might believe him to be the Son of God. He was vindicating an eternal law of the universe, in which all human beings throughout all generations would be interested; viz.: that humanity has a Ruler who can present it spotless before the throne of God (Jude 24). Jesus propounded this law in the presence of those most interested in exposing it if false, and most able to explode it had it not been true. Whether his words were truth or blasphemy, was the controversy between Christ and the rulers from that day to the end of his ministry—Matt. xxvi. 65.] ᵇ8 **And straightway Jesus, perceiving in his spirit that they so reasoned** {ᶜ **their reasonings,** } ᵇ **within themselves,** ᵃ4 **And Jesus knowing their thoughts** [Jesus read their thoughts by his divine insight, and not because of any recognized habit or tendency on their part to criticise him, for this is the first recorded indication of hostility on the part of the Pharisees, though it is hinted at, at John iv. 1. Such discernment of the thought was to be a characteristic mark of the expected Messiah (Isa. xi. 2, 3), and Jesus had it (John ii. 25). It also is an attribute peculiar to God—I. Chron. viii. 9; Jer. xvii. 10; Rom. viii. 27; Rev. ii. 23] **ᶜanswered and said {ᵇsaith} unto them, ᵃWherefore think ye evil in your hearts?** [Jesus could see invisible sin, and could forgive it or condemn it, as the conditions moved him. The powers of discernment, forgiveness and condemnation make him the perfect Judge.] **ᵇ Why reason ye these things in your hearts? ᵃ5 For which is easier, ᵇto say to the sick of the palsy, ᶜThy sins are forgiven thee; ᵇor to say, Arise, and take up thy bed, and walk?** [To understand this sentence we should place the emphasis upon the word "say," because the question at issue was the power or effect of his speech. The rabbis, after their first shock of surprise, thought that Jesus feared to attempt the fraud of a so-called miracle in the presence of learned men, lest he should be detected and exposed; and hence looked upon his present action as an attempt to bear himself safely off before the public, and to maintain his standing by the use of high-sounding words. They felt that he used words of unseen effect, because he dared not use those of seen effect. This was precisely the view that Jesus knew they would take, and that he wished them to take; for by showing his ability to work in the realms of sight that which is impossible; viz.: the healing of the sick man, he could place before them proof suited to their own reasoning that he had a like ability to work the impossible in the realms of the unseen; viz.: the forgiveness of the man's sins. By thus demonstrating his authority in the external and physical world, Jesus assures us of his dominion over the internal and spiritual.] **10 But that ye may know that the Son of man** [Daniel's name for the Messiah—Dan. vii. 10–13] **hath authority on earth to forgive sins** [The words "on earth" are taken by some to indicate the then existing contrast between Christ's present humiliation or ministry on earth, and his future glorification or enthronement in heaven; in which case they would mean that Jesus could grant now that which some might think could only be exercised hereafter. Others take them to mean the same as if Jesus had said, " You think that forgiveness can only be granted by the Father in heaven, but it can also be granted by the Son upon earth. That which you have heretofore sought from the Father you may now seek from me." The latter is probably the correct view. As to the test of power or authority, the miracle of Jesus was very convincing; for in the popular opinion sin was a cause of which disease was the effect. We are told, on the authority of later rabbis, that it was a maxim among the Jews that no diseased person could be healed till his sins were blotted out. We also recognize a correlation between sins and diseases, which the Saviour's use of this miracle justifies. A mere miracle, such as swallowing fire or causing iron to float, would not prove ability to forgive sins. The proof consisted in the relation which disease bears to sin, and the consequent relation which healing bears to forgiveness. The connection between disease and sin is a real and necessary one. The Jews were right in seeing this connection, but they erred in thinking that they were warranted in *personally* criminating every one whom they found afflicted, and in judging that the weight of the affliction indicated the quantity of the sin. The Book of Job should have corrected this error. Such unrighteous judgments are condemned by Christ (John ix. 3 ; Luke xiii. 2–5). Paralysis is, however, to-day looked upon as ordinarily the punishment of some personal sin, usually that of intemperance or sensuality], (ᵃ **then saith he to the sick of the palsy**), { ᶜ **(he said unto him that was palsied**),} **I say unto thee, Arise, and take up thy couch,** {ᵇ **bed,**} ᶜ **and go unto thy house.** [What command could be more pleasant than that which bade this sick man go home forgiven and healed?] **25 And immediately he rose up** {ᵃ **arose,**} ᶜ **before them,** ᵇ **and straightway took up the bed,** ᶜ **that whereon he lay** ["A sweet saying! The bed had borne the man: now the man bore the bed"—*Bengel*], ᵇ **and went forth before them all;** ᵃ **and departed to his house.** ᶜ **glorify-**

ing God. ᵇ insomuch that they were all amazed, ᵃ8 But
when the multitudes saw it, they were afraid, ᶜ 26 And
amazement took hold on all, and they glorified God
[The "all" of this passage hardly includes the scribes and
Pharisees, or, if it does, their admiration of Jesus was but a
momentary enthusiasm, which quickly passed away]; ᵃ who
had given such authority unto men. [Some take the
word "men" as the plural of category, and apply it to Christ.
Others think that they regarded Jesus as a mere man among
other men, and that they therefore looked upon his power as
a gift given to men generally, and not as something peculiar
to himself. If this latter view is correct, it is likely that they
took the words "Son of man" as referring to men generally,
and not as a reference to the Messiah, such as Jesus meant it
to be.] ᵇ saying, We never saw it on this fashion, ᶜ and
they were filled with fear, saying, We have seen
strange things to-day. [Literally, seen paradoxes: things
contrary to common thought and ordinary experience. They
had seen a threefold miracle: sins forgiven, thoughts read
and palsy healed.]

XXXVI.

THE CALL OF MATTHEW.

(At or near Capernaum.)

ᵃ MATT. IX. 9; ᵇ MARK II. 13, 14; ᶜ LUKE V. 27, 28.

ᶜ 27 And after these things [after the healing of the para-
lytic] he went forth, ᵃ again by the seaside [*i. e.*, he left
Capernaum, and sought the shore of the sea, which formed a
convenient auditorium for him, and which was hence a favorite
scene for his teaching]; and all the multitude resorted
unto him, and he taught them. 14 And as he ᵃ Jesus
passed by from thence, he saw ᶜ and beheld ᵃ a man,
ᶜ a publican, named {ᶜ called} Matthew, ᶜ Levi, ᵇ the
son of Alphaeus [It will be observed that Matthew, in his
account of his call, does not make himself prominent. All

the evangelists keep themselves in the background. Because
Mark and Luke give us the name "Levi," it has been thought
by some that they describe the call of a different person from
the one mentioned by Matthew—an opinion which seems to
have started with Origen. But the difference in name is not
an important divergence, for many in that day had two names;
as, for example, Lebbæus, who was called Thaddæus; Silas,
who was called Sylvanus; John, who was called Mark, etc.
Moreover, it was then common to change the name; as is
shown by the cases of Simon, who became Peter; Joseph,
who became Barnabas; Saul, who became Paul, etc. Therefore, as we have previously suggested (p. 111), that Nathanael
was also known as Bartholomew, so here we are satisfied that
Levi is called Matthew; for the narratives which describe the
calls are almost verbatim, and they agree chronologically,
being placed by all three Evangelists between the healing of
the paralytic and the feast where Jesus ate with publicans.
Mark involves us in another difficulty by calling Levi the son
of Alphæus; for a man named Alphæus was the father of
James the younger (Matt. x. 3). It is not likely, however,
that Matthew and James were brothers, for Alphæus was a
very common Jewish name, and brothers are usually mentioned in pairs in the apostolic lists, and these two are not so
mentioned. Pool takes the extreme view here, contending
that James, Matthew, Thaddæus and Simon Zelotes were
four brethren], **sitting at the place of toll** [Wherever it is
at all practicable, Orientals sit at their work. The place of
toil was usually a booth or small hut. Whether Matthew's
booth was by the lake, to collect duties on goods and people
ferried across; or whether it was by the roadside on the great
highway leading from Damascus to Acco, to collect taxes on
all produce brought into Capernaum, is not material. The
revenues which Rome derived from conquered nations consisted of tolls, tithes, harbor duties, taxes for use of public
pasture lands, and duties for the use of mines and salt works],
and he saith {ᶜsaid} **unto him, Follow me. 28 And
he forsook all, And he arose** {ᶜrose up} **and followed**

him. [Such obedience was not, of course, performed in ignorance; it indicates that Matthew was already a disciple, as were the four fishermen when they also received a like call. Matthew was now called to become a personal attendant of Jesus, preparatory to being chosen an apostle. Nor are we to conclude from the abruptness of his movements that he went off without settling accounts with the head of his office. Though it may be more dramatic to thus picture him as departing at once, yet the settlement of accounts was indispensable to his good name in the future, and in no way diminishes the reality and beauty of his sacrifice—a beauty which Matthew himself forbears to mention, as became him (Prov. xxvii. 2). But Matthew certainly neither delayed nor sought counsel (Gal. i. 15, 16). By thus calling a publican, Jesus reproved the religious narrowness of his times.]

PART FIVE.

FROM SECOND PASSOVER UNTIL THIRD. TIME: ONE YEAR.

XXXVII.

JESUS HEALS ON THE SABBATH DAY AND DEFENDS HIS ACT.

(A Feast-time at Jerusalem, Probably the Passover.)

ᵈ JOHN v. 1-47.

ᵈ **1 After these things there was a feast of the Jews; and Jesus went up to Jerusalem.** [Though every feast in the Jewish calendar has found some one to advocate its claim to be this unnamed feast, yet the vast majority of commentators choose either the feast of Purim, which came in March, or the Passover, which came in April. Older commentators pretty unanimously regarded it as the Passover, while the later school favor the feast of Purim. John iv. 35 locates Jesus in Samaria in December, and John vi. 4 finds him on the shores of Galilee just before a Passover. If, then, this was the feast of Purim, the Passover of John vi. 4 was the *second* in Jesus' ministry, and that ministry lasted but two years and a fraction. But if the feast here mentioned was a Passover, then the one at John vi. 4 would be the *third* Passover, and the ministry of Jesus lasted three years and a fraction. Since, then, the length of Jesus' ministry is largely to be determined by what feast this was, it becomes important for us to fix the feast, if possible. That it was not Purim the following arguments may be urged: 1. Purim was not a

Mosaic feast, but one established by human laws; hence Jesus would not be *likely* to observe it. True, we find him at the feast of Dedication, which was also of human origin, but he did not "go up" to attend it; he appears to have attended because he was already in Jerusalem (John x. 22). 2. Here the pregnant juxtaposition of "feast" and "went up" indicates that Jesus was *drawn* to Jerusalem by this feast, but Purim was celebrated by the Jews everywhere, and did not require that any one should go to Jerusalem, as did the three great festivals—Passover, Pentecost and Tabernacles. 3. It was kept in a boisterous, riotous manner, and was therefore not such a feast as Jesus would honor. 4. It came early in the year, when the weather was too rigorous and inclement for sick people to frequent porticos. 5. It did not include a Sabbath day. 6. As Purim was just a month before the Passover, Jesus would hardly have returned to Galilee before the Passover (John vi. 4) unless he intended to miss the Passover, which he would hardly do for the sake of attending Purim in Jerusalem. Those contending that it was not the Passover, present several arguments, which we note and answer as follows: 1. Since John gives the name of other Passovers, he would have named this also, had it been one. But the conclusion is inferential, and not logical; and the answer to it is twofold: first, perhaps John did give the name by prefixing the article to it, and calling it " the feast," for being the oldest —older than the law and the Sabbath—and most important of all feasts, it was rightly called by pre-eminence "the feast." Since the Sinaitic manuscript gives the article, and calls it " the feast," the manuscript authority for and against this reading is pretty evenly balanced. Second, if John did not name it, there is probably this reason for his silence. Where he names the feast elsewhere it is thought that the incidents narrated take color from, or have some reference to, the particular festal occasion which is named; but here there is no such local color, and failure to name the feast prevents mistaken attempts to find such local color. 2. Again it is objected that if this is a different Passover from John vi. 4, then John skips a year in the life of Jesus. He probably does so skip, and this is not strange when the supplemental nature of his Gospel is considered. In favor of its being the Passover we submit two points: 1. Daniel seems to forecast the ministry of the Messiah as lasting one-half of a week of years (Dan. ix. 27). 2. It fits better in the chronological arrangement, for in the next scene we find the disciples plucking grain, and the Sabbath question is still at full heat. But the harvest season opens with the Passover.] **2 Now there is** [the present tense is used, for while the city was destroyed, the pool evidently still existed] **in Jerusalem by the sheep** *gate* **a pool, which is called in Hebrew** [*i. e.*, in Aramaic, a dialect of the classic Hebrew, in which the Old Testament was written, and the language then in use in Palestine] **Bethesda, having five porches** [It had five covered porticos, probably erected for the accommodation of the sick, whence it was called Bethesda, *i. e.*, "house of mercy." Dr. Barclay thinks that this pool is buried in the rubbish of the Kedron valley. Dr. Robinson suggested that it might be the Fountain of the Virgin, which is found in a cavern under the east side of Ophel, a little north of midway between the southeast corner of the temple wall and the Pool of Siloam. Though this pool's claim has been objected to because of its inaccessibility —for it lies thirty feet below the surface of the valley and forty feet back under the mountain, and is approached by two flights of steps numbering in all twenty-six—yet it has three distinct features which make its claims exceed those of any other known pool in the temple neighborhood: 1. It is fed by an intermittent spring, whose ebbing and flowing at intervals of several hours, would cause the troubled waters called for in verse 7. 2. It has a superstition connected with it kindred to that which crept into the text at verse 4, but the Mohammedans have changed the angel into a dragon; when the dragon is awake he swallows or stops the water, but when he sleeps the waters flows! 3. The modern Jerusalem Jews believe in the special healing properties of this fountain. "Every day," says Conder, "crowds of both sexes go down to the spring, and, entering the dark archway, descend the steps, and await the fitful troubling of the waters, which rise suddenly and immerse them, fully clothed, nearly up to the neck." But Nehemiah's description of the walls seems to locate the sheep gate near the middle or northern portion of the temple area, and too far north for the Virgin's fountain to be described as near it, unless John's sheep gate differs from that of Nehemiah.] **3 In these lay a multitude of them that were sick, blind, halt, withered.** [The rest of verse 3 and all of verse 4, as given in the King James' version, were probably added as a marginal explanatory gloss early in the second century, and from thence gradually became incorporated in the text. John's failure to mention that the pool was thought to have medicinal qualities tempted transcribers to add a few marginal words in the nature of comments.] **5 And a certain man was there, who had been thirty and eight years in his infirmity.** [It is not said that he had spent all these years beside the pool, nor is it likely that he had. The time is given to mark the inveteracy of the disease, and to show the pathos of his situation. The facts that he had a bed, and that his healing was demonstrated by his walking, argue that his disease was either rheumatism, or some form of paralysis.] **6 When Jesus saw him lying, and knew** [By divine intuition, just as he also knew the lives of Nathanael and the Samaritan woman at Jacob's well] **that he had been now a long time** *in that case,* **he saith unto him, Wouldst thou be made whole?** [By this question Jesus aroused the man from the apathy of despair, awakening him to hope and effort. Moreover, Jesus only healed as men consented to his healing.] **7 The sick man answered him, Sir, I have no man, when the water is troubled, to put me into the pool: but while I am coming, another steppeth down before me.** [The man's lack of healing was not due to want of interest, but to want of means. The lower flight of ten steps leading to the Virgin's pool is only four and a half feet wide, and the pool itself is but twenty-one feet and nine inches long by nine feet in breadth at its widest part. A half-dozen selfish men rushing down this narrow passage, and filling the small space in the pool, would easily crowd out one who was friendless and more than usually helpless. **8 Jesus saith unto him, Arise, take up thy bed, and walk.** [The bed was the light mattress or pallet of the poor elsewhere noted, which could be easily rolled up and carried under the arm.] **9 And straightway the man was made whole, and took up his bed and walked.** [Christ spoke, the man obeyed, and by the obedience of faith was made whole.] **Now it was the sabbath on that day.** [There was apparently nothing urgent in the sick man's condition which made an immediate cure necessary ; but Jesus healed because it was the Sabbath, that he might thereby draw such an issue between himself and the Jewish rulers as would afford opportunity for him to present his divine claims to them in the clearest and most forceful manner. He healed on the sabbath, that he might assert divine relations to the Sabbath, and by so doing bring about a disputation which would enable him to develop before them his divine relations to the Father.] **10 So the Jews** [That is, the Jewish rulers. John frequently uses the term with this restricted meaning (John i. 19; vii. 17; ix. 22; xviii. 12, 14). The man was officially stopped and questioned] **said unto him that was cured, It is the sabbath, and it is not lawful for thee to take up thy bed.** [They would have cited in proof of their assertion Ex. xxxi. 13; Num. xv. 35; Jer. xvii. 21–23; Neh. xiii. 9. Alford and Schaff both assert that the man broke the Mosaic law; but this position is not well taken. Jesus would not have ordered the sabbath to be broken, for he came to fulfill and not to break the law. At no time did he break the sabbath or countenance its violation, as some able thinkers are erroneously led to suppose. In this case a man lying on his bed, away from home, is suddenly healed. Under such circumstances *Jewish tradition* said that he must either spend the rest of the day watching his bed, or else he must go off and leave it to be stolen. But He who rightfully interpreted the law of his own devising, and who knew that "the sabbath was made for man, and not man for the sabbath," ordered the healed one to carry his bed along home with him. The modern notions that this constituted a breach of the Mosaic sabbath doubtless arose from the nature of the accompanying justification given by Jesus, which fails to assert that the law has not been broken, but seems almost to admit that it has. Nothing, however, can be argued against Jesus on this score. A man may be able to justify an act in a dozen different ways, and may choose to rest content in justifying himself in only one way. Such is the case here. Elsewhere we shall find that Jesus was careful to show that his sabbatic actions were strictly legal; but in this case, that he might bring his divine claims plainly before the rulers, he ignored the question as to the human legality of his act that he might present without confusion its divine legality. Hence he used only one order or method of justification; viz.: an appeal to his divine rights as exhibited in the habits of his Father. It was the divine and not the human in Jesus which wrought this miracle, so Jesus causes the whole controversy to turn on the divine rights, that he may use the occasion for an elaborate discussion of his divine claims and the proofs by which they are sustained.] **11 But he answered them, He that made me whole, the same said unto me, Take up thy bed, and walk.** [The man very naturally shifts the burden of responsibility. If he was violating the sabbath, he had been ordered to do it, and that by one who had alone empowered him to do it. Of himself he would not and could not have done it.] **12 They asked him, Who is the man that said unto thee, Take up *thy bed*, and walk?** [By using the word "man" they suggest the contrast between human authority and divine law. They were more concerned about the law than about mercy.] **13 But he that was healed knew not who it was; for Jesus had conveyed himself away, a multitude being in the place.** [Jesus, not wishing to unduly excite the multitude by his presence, had passed on.] **14 Afterward Jesus findeth him in the**

temple [possibly he was there offering sacrifices in thanksgiving for his recovery, in the spirit of Ps. lxvi. 13, 14 ; but it is as likely that he was there merely enjoying the sights and privileges from which he had so long been excluded], **and said unto him, Behold, thou art made whole: sin no more, lest a worse thing befall thee.** [Many human ills are directly traceable to sin, and this one appears to have been so ; for death is the wages of sin, and sickness is partial payment. It is a solemn thought that sin can produce worse conditions than even this case, where it found its victim a youth, and left him a withered old man, bed-ridden, helpless and friendless.] **15 The man went away, and told the Jews that it was Jesus who had made him whole.** [There was evidently no unworthy motive in his action ; for, as Chrysostom observes, he did not report it that it was Jesus who made him break the sabbath to condemn Jesus; on the contrary, he said it was Jesus who made him whole, so honoring Christ. Feeling (as any Jew would have felt) that he ought to clear himself before the rulers of his people, the man, no doubt, honestly thought that the name and authority of the great Prophet of Nazareth would end all question as to the conduct of both Healer and healed. If so, he was sadly mistaken.] **16 And for this cause the Jews persecuted Jesus** [Literally, pursued, or hunted Jesus. This is John's first plain declaration of open hostility to Jesus, though he has already implied it. From this point the blood red line of conspiracy against the life of Jesus runs through this Gospel], **because he did these things on the sabbath. 17 But Jesus answered them, My Father worketh even until now, and I work.** [The dual nature of Jesus permitted both a divine and a human attitude toward the sabbath. We have shown that Jesus chose to assert his divine attitude, for in no other matter did these Jews have clearer distinction as to the difference between divine and human right than in this very matter of sabbath observance. If Jesus was mere man, their ideas of law clearly condemned him ; but if Jesus was indeed God, their knowledge of divine conduct in the whole realm of nature clearly justified him, and the miracle asserted his divine control in nature's realm. While God rested from creation on the sabbath, nothing can be clearer than that in works of sustenance, reproduction, healing and providence, God has never rested, and never made distinctions between the days of our week. In the light of the gospel we find also that his redemptive work has never ceased, and, considering the part which Jesus was even then accomplishing in this field of labor, his words, "and I work," are full of meaning.] **18 For this cause therefore the Jews sought the more to kill him, because he not only brake the sabbath** [not only violated, but denied its authority over his divine nature], **but also called God his own Father, making himself equal with God.** [They rightly interpreted Jesus as asserting relationship to God differing from that sustained by others, as expressed in some few passages in the Old Testament, where God is spoken of as a Father to the people generally; *i. e.,* their Creator. No man could claim such unity of nature as would exempt him from the obligation of the fourth commandment. Had they misunderstood Jesus in this all-important point, how quickly would he have corrected them, for he could not have been less righteous than Paul and Barnabas—Acts xiv. 11–15.] **19 Jesus therefore answered and said unto them** [His answer is a connected address, the theme being his own character, mission, authority and credentials as the Son of God. It is the Christology of Jesus, and instead of being a retraction of the claim to divinity which the Jews accused him of making, it is a complete and amplified reassertion of it, so that Luther fitly calls it "a sublime apology, which makes the matter worse." Jesus first declares his relations to the Father (vs. 19–23), which are set forth in four divisions, each of which is introduced by the word "for;" viz.: 1. Unity of action. 2. Unity of love, counsel and plan. 3. Unity in life-impartation. 4. Unity in judgment, resulting in unity of honor. This last division formed a turning-point in the discourse. Since there is this unity of honor, it is important that men should honor Jesus, and also otherwise sustain right relationships to him, and Jesus therefore, to enlighten the Jews as to their duty toward him, proceeds to set forth his relations to men (vs. 23–30), which he also gives in four divisions, closely correlative to his four statements as to the Father, thus: 1. Right to receive divine honor from men. 2. Authority to execute life and death judgment over men. 3. Power of life-impartation as to men, and that both spiritually and literally. 4. All Jesus' relationships to man to be sustained and executed according to the will and plan or mission of God. But since all these various relationships grow out of his divine nature, Jesus next submits the credentials which establish his claim to such a nature (vs. 31–39). These also are given in four divisions; namely: 1. Testimony of the Baptist. 2. Testimony of the Father. 3. Jesus' own works and ministry. 4. Testimony of Scripture. Or we may regard Jesus as asserting that the Father testifies to the Son's divinity in four different ways; that is, " God is properly the sole and original testifier, and all others are his signatures and seals." The discourse then closes with an application of its truth to the Jewish auditors (vs. 40–47). They are told that all this truth is lost on them because of their fourfold sinful condition, which is thus stated: 1. Want of will to come to Christ. 2. Want of real love towards God, or desire for his honor. 3. Love for the honor of men, rather than the honor of God. 4. Want of real faith in the Mosaic writings], **Verily, verily, I say unto you, The Son can do nothing of himself, but what he seeth the Father doing: for what things soever he doeth, these the Son also doeth in like manner.** [The Jews regarded Jesus as claiming equality with God in a vain-glorious, honor-seeking spirit ; but Jesus restates himself, so as to show that the claim is really a renunciation or abdication of all independent greatness—as having an equality exercised in absolute subservience (Isa. xlii. 1 ; Phil. iii. 6-9). They had accused him as a human being acting contrary to the law of the Father. But he declares himself to be a divine being, so united to the Father as to have no will or action apart from the Father, a condition the resultant of which is

not weakness and insufficiency, but the strength and perfection arising from an absolute and indissoluble union with the
Father—the glory of divinity. Chrysostom remarks, "Just as
when we say, it is impossible for God to do wrong, we do not
impute to him any weakness, but confess in him an unutter-
able power, so also when Christ saith, 'I can of mine own self
do nothing,' the meaning is that it is impossible—my nature
admits not—that I should do anything contrary to the Father."
Jesus asserts his equality with the Father in such a way as
not to depreciate the dignity and glory of the Father.] **20
For the Father loveth the Son, and showeth him all
things that he himself doeth: and greater works than
these will he show him, that ye may marvel.** [The
words here indicate that the love of the Father towards the
Son was the source of revelation, and that the revelation was
progressive. Love constrained the Father to reveal, and love
in turn constrained the Son to act according to the revelation.
Moreover, this unity of love would be evidenced by greater
works in the future, of which two are enumerated; namely,
resurrection and judgment, the former being at first spiritually
and afterwards literally outlined. The Father would show
these works to the Son by causing him to do them: there
would be no separate act of the Father so that the works
would be twice performed. These works would produce faith
in those of right spirit. But among such hardened hearts as
those whom Jesus addressed they would only produce wonder
and consternation. Those who withheld the tribute of faith
should pay that of amazement. Putting the statements of
verses 19 and 20 together, we find that the Son knows all that
the Father does, and likewise does all that the Father does,
and in like manner. There could be no higher assertion of
equality than this; in fact, it asserts identity rather than equality. But the equality is not the result of conquest, nor was it
one of power opposed to power, but is freely given and accorded by reason of love.] **21 For as the Father raiseth
the dead and giveth them life, even so the Son also
giveth life to whom he will.** [Since the verbs in this

verse are in the present tense, and since Jesus is not known to have raised the physically dead before this time, it is rightly taken that he here speaks only of raising the spiritually dead, our miserable existence in sin being often spoken of in Scripture as a death from which we must be revived (Eph. ii. 1, 5; Col. ii. 13; Rev. iii. 1). The use of the word "will" likewise indicates a spiritual resurrection, for Christ exercised a discrimination in such resurrections; but the final, literal resurrection is without discrimination. See the word "all" in verse 28. The meaning, therefore, is that as the Father performs physical resurrections, so the Son (for the present) performs spiritual resurrections (to be followed by physical resurrections). Jesus later gave those at Jerusalem a sign of his power to literally raise the dead by the resurrection of Lazarus. Resurrection is bestowed or withheld according to Jesus' will, but his will is not arbitrarily exercised. He visits those who receive him, and revives those who believe him. If the Son possessed right of concurrent action on these lofty planes, concurrent use of the sabbath was a small matter indeed.] **22 For neither doth the Father judge any man, but he hath given all judgment unto the Son** [That is to say, the Father does not act in judgment without the Son nor the Son without the Father, for in no work is either isolated from the other. Resurrection is nearly always associated with judgment, and in this instance it is in reviving that the judgment is manifested or executed. (See verse 29 also.) Note that judgment begins in this world—John ix. 39]; **23 that all may honor the Son, even as they honor the Father.** ["Even as" means in the same manner and in equal degrees. The prerogative of judgment was committed unto Jesus that men might behold his true majesty. If this verse does not teach us to worship Jesus as God, language can not teach it, for God gives not his glory unto another (Isa. xlvii. 2), nor could he, by reason of his very nature, arbitrarily will such honor to one whose character and nature were unworthy of it. In these words Jesus exposed the ruinous attitude assumed by the Jews in seeking to slay him.]

He that honoreth not the Son honoreth not the Father that sent him. [Honor paid to the Father pertains or belongs to his nature and character. But the Son is the manifestation of that nature and character (John xiv. 7-11; Heb. i. 3). Therefore to fail to honor the Son is to fail to honor the Father. Experience shows it to be the rule that only those who honor Jesus take pains to honor the Father.] **24 Verily, verily, I say unto you, He that heareth my word, and believeth him that sent me, hath eternal life, and cometh not into judgment, but hath passed out of death into life.** [Eternal life is a present gift, just as condemnation is a present condition (John iii. 18). To "hear" means in this case to receive and obey, so that eternal life is conditioned upon a knowledge of the revelation of the Father and Son and a right use of that knowledge. Those who have learned of and obey Jesus have already escaped or avoided the judgment—Rom. viii. 1.] **25 Verily, verily, I say unto you, The hour cometh, and now is, when the dead shall hear the voice of the Son of God; and they that hear shall live.** [The "hath passed" of verse 24 and the "now is" of this verse show that Jesus is, thus far, primarily speaking of a present and hence a spiritual resurrection, or regeneration. Christianity, or the dispensation of regeneration, was to formally begin at Pentecost, but it was already present in a preliminary form in the teaching of Jesus, for those who hearkened to it were counted as already redeemed. Yet the spiritual condition of even the apostles was at that time such that the hour of grace is spoken of as more future than present—more "coming" than "at hand."] **26 For as the Father hath life in himself, even so gave he to the Son also to have life in himself** [Not only an independdent life, such as man does not possess (Acts xxvii. 28), but a life which is a source of life to others. This regenerating power completed Jesus' official status as judge, so that wherever he awarded life he could at the same time bestow it]: **27 and he gave him authority to execute judgment, because he is a son of man.** [We can see several reasons,

humanly speaking, why the humanity of Jesus should be made
a ground for committing the judgment of the races of men to
him: 1. Jesus having experienced our infirmities and temptations, we can feel sure of his sympathy (Heb. iv. 15, 16).
2. Jesus, partaking of the nature of both God and man, is,
because of his unique nature, the only fit daysman or umpire
between them (Job ix. 33). Possibly we may regard it as a
reward of humility—Phil. ii. 8, 9.] **28 Marvel not at this**
[Jesus seems to here answer the surprised expression of their
faces by enlarging his statements]: **for the hour cometh,
in which all that are in the tombs shall hear his voice,
29 and shall come forth; they that have done good,
unto the resurrection of life; and they that have done
evil, unto the resurrection of judgment.** [We have here the
future, literal and final resurrection (Dan. xii. 2); a scene of
such stupendous grandeur as to overshadow all the marvelous in
all that Christ shall have previously done.] **30 I can of myself
do nothing: as I hear, I judge: and my judgment is
righteous; because I seek not mine own will, but the
will of him that sent me.** [Jesus here reasserts his dependence upon the Father, not as a bare repetition of his relationship to the Father, but for the purpose of developing his
relationship to men as based on or growing out of this relationship to the Father. The Jews, as they listened to him,
were conscious that he was even then judging and passing
sentence of condemnation upon them. Jesus does not deny
the correctness of this view, but shows that, because of his
relationship of dependence upon the Father, they are getting
perfect justice, for: 1. His judgment was free from all personal bias and selfish retaliation, and was, 2. Positively perfect,
being wholly inspired by the Father's will.] **31 If I bear
witness of myself, my witness is not true. 32 It is
another** [*i. e.*, the Father: for similar reference see John
viii. 50–54] **that beareth witness of me; and I know
that the witness which he witnesseth of me is true.**
[These two verses form, as noted, a transition in the discourse.
In them Jesus passes from discussing himself and the divine

and human phases of his nature and office to take up the evidences which attest him, first asserting that the truth of what he has said does not rest solely on his own veracity. There is here an indirect reference to that clause of the Jewish law which required two witnesses. See John viii. 14–18; but the saying is deeply spiritual. Since Jesus did nothing of himself, his very testimony was not his own, but was the Father's who sent him, and was therefore absolutely true in the consciousness of Jesus. If Jesus had testified independently of the Father—had it been possible—it would have been in the nature of the case contrary to that consensus of the divine will which forms the truth.] **33 Ye have sent unto John** [this shows that Jesus was addressing the rulers—John i. 19], **and he hath borne witness unto the truth.** [John had witnessed the truth concerning the Messiahship of Jesus. Some think that the pronoun " another " in verse 32 refers to John also, but by the present tense " witnesseth " of that verse, and the past tense " hath borne witness " of this verse, the ever-abiding testimony of the Father is contrasted with the finished testimony of John, who is now silenced by imprisonment.] **34 But the witness which I receive is not from man: howbeit I say these things, that ye may be saved.** [In the light of John i. 6, 7, it sounds strange to hear Jesus thus renounce the testimony of the Baptist. But the phrase, " is not from man," is the Hebrew negative, meaning *not from man alone*. Jesus therefore meant to accept it, as he in the next breath did that of Moses, as prophetic—as the testimony of the Father spoken through a human medium ; but meant to reject it as a merely human testimony, such as it was in the view of these Jews who denied in their hearts that John was a prophet. This mission of Jesus was not to be proved by uninspired testimony, for uninspired man can not testify of God from lack of full and adequate knowledge (Matt. xi. 27; xvi. 17). And yet if the Jews were willing to accept such testimony Jesus in kindness would permit it, that by any fair means they might believe and be saved.] **35 He was the lamp that burneth and shineth; and ye were willing to rejoice for a**

season in his light. [They were willing, like children, to play in John's light without stopping to seriously consider its meaning, but when he bore testimony to Christ they blasphemed him—Luke vii. 33.] **36 But the witness which I have is greater than** *that of* **John; for the works which the Father hath given me to accomplish, the very works that I do, bear witness of me, that the Father hath sent me.** [By "greater witness" Jesus means testimony which is more convincing. All divine testimony is of equal veracity, but some of it is more obviously convincing. The less the testimony savors of humanity, and the more purely divine it appears, the more convincing it is (I. John v. 9). The term "work" is not to be confined to miracles, for the word " accomplish" indicates a wider meaning. The entire Messianic mission or redemptive work which ended with our Lord's words, "It is finished" (John xvii. 4; xix. 30), and which is indicated in this very discourse in verse 20, and outlined by referring to spiritual judgment and regeneration, should be included. Christ's transforming grace still witnesses to Jew and Gentile that the Father sent him, for it manifests the love of God (John iii. 16). The Father did not send the Son to merely work miracles, but to redeem the world.] **37 And the Father that sent me, he hath borne witness of me. Ye have neither heard his voice at any time, nor seen his form. 38 And ye have not his word abiding in you: for whom he sent, him ye believe not.** [The testimony of the Father was given in three forms: 1. By direct or audible voice and the visible sending of the Spirit—as at Jesus' baptism. 2. By revelations, through the medium of prophets and angels gathered and preserved in the Old Testament Scriptures. 3. Through the Son and his works. Jesus here asserts that all testimony of the first kind had failed to reach the Jewish rulers; that the testimony of the second kind had been utterly lost upon them, for they failed to see its accordance with the testimony of the third kind which he was even then exhibiting to them, neither had it taught them to expect a personal Saviour.] **39 Ye**

search the scriptures, because ye think that in them ye have eternal life; and these are they which bear witness of me ; 40 and ye will not come to me, that ye may have life. ["Hillel used to say, More law, more life. . . . He who has gotten himself words of law has gotten himself the life of the world to come" (*Talmud*). In their zeal for the Scriptures the Jews had counted every letter of them, expecting to find life in the laws and precepts, but failed to find Him of whom the Scriptures spoke in figure, type and prophecy. In their reverence for the Book they failed to see that it was a mere means intended to acquaint them with him through whom life was to come. Hence, as Canon Cook suggests, there is deep pathos in the co-ordination, " and—and." The verses give us three points worthy of deepest reflection: 1. Protestantism may love the Book and show a martyr's loyalty to it, and yet fail utterly to render any acceptable love or loyalty toward the Being revealed in the Book. 2. Criticism, both higher and lower, may submit every text to microscopic investigation, and yet be as blind as the ancient Pharisees to its true meaning. It is profoundly true that the things of the Spirit are spiritually discerned (I. Cor. ii. 14), and that pride of literary culture, and the self-worship of intellectualism tend to spiritual blindness. It seems to come upon such as a visitation from God, as in the case of Elymas (Matt. xi. 25; Luke viii. 10; Matt. xv. 14; Eph. iv. 17, 18; Isa. v. 21). 3. Though free will is meant to be man's crowning glory, yet it may result in his shame and ruin.] 41 I receive not glory from men. [Jesus here shows that his rebuke of their disbelief does not spring from personal pique or disappointed ambition. He came seeking faith that he might save, not honor that he might be glorified, and honor paid to him is by him transferred to God (Phil. ii. 10, 11), just as honor paid to the true Christian is transferred to Christ.] 42 But I know you, that ye have not the love of God in yourselves. [He speaks as the Searcher of hearts (John i. 47-50; ii. 24, 25). Knowing them absolutely, he found them to be self-worshipers, devoid of that love Godward which begets belief, and lacking in their natures that which would enable them to understand him and his spirit, no matter what evidence was submitted to them.] **43 I am come in my Father's name, and ye receive me not: if another shall come in his own name, him ye will receive.** [Some think that this is spoken primarily of a pre-eminently great antichrist who is yet to come and deceive many of the Jews, and who, as Stier thinks, shall be such an incarnation of Satan as Jesus was of God (Rev. xiii. 1–9). But they have already received many false christs with joy. According to Schudt, as quoted by Bengel, there have been sixty-four antichrists who have misled the Jews. Among them Bar Cocheba led 24,000 to ruin, including Akiba, the President of the Sanhedrim. False christs come in their own name—for their own honor—and make no war on bosom sins, but upon earthly enemies; but Jesus came not to manifest himself, but his Father.] **44 How can ye believe, who receive glory one of another, and the glory that *cometh* from the only God ye seek not?** [The question was as to their believing Jesus to be the Messiah. Expecting one who would bring great honor to themselves by his triumphs over his foes, and seeing nothing of this kind to be expected from Jesus, they could not believe him to be the Messiah.] **45 Think not that I will accuse you to the Father: there is one that accuseth you, *even* Moses, on whom ye have set your hope.** [Jesus here assumes that the Jews gave enough credence to his words to fear that he might hereafter appear as their accuser. But Jesus designs to appear rather as Advocate than as Prosecutor (I. John ii. 1). It was their fault that he was not their Advocate.] **46 For if ye believed Moses, ye would believe me; for he wrote of me. 47 But if ye believe not his writings, how shall ye believe my words?** [In these verses Jesus explicitly endorses the Mosaic authorship and authenticity of the Pentateuch, and sets forth one purpose for which Moses wrote it. Jesus was the essential subject of the law and the prophets (Luke xxiv. 27, 44–46;

Rom. xvi. 25, 26). The emphasis is on "his writings" and
"my words." They professed to reverence Moses and to
receive his writings, while they openly despised Jesus and
repudiated his words as fast as he spoke them. The phrase
"wrote of me" is not to be restricted to Deut. xviii. 15-18.
Moses wrote symbolically of Jesus through his entire work,
as Bengel tersely puts it, "Everywhere!" The Epistle to the
Hebrews is a partial elaboration of the Christology of Moses.
But there is doubtless a depth of meaning in the Pentateuch
which has never yet been fully fathomed, for there is a fullness in Scripture greatly exceeding the popular conception.
Moreover, the Old and New Testaments are so linked together that to reject one is eventually to reject the other, or
to read it with veiled eyes—II. Cor. iii. 15.]

XXXVIII.

JESUS DEFENDS DISCIPLES WHO PLUCK GRAIN ON THE SABBATH.

(Probably while on the way from Jerusalem to Galilee.)

ᵃMATT. XII. 1-8; ᵇMARK II. 23-28; ᶜLUKE VI. 1-5.

ᵇ23 And ᶜ1 Now it came to pass ᵃ1 At that season ᵇthat he ᵃJesus went {ᵇwas going} on the {ᶜa}
ᵇsabbath day through the grainfields; ᵃand his disciples were hungry and began ᵇas they went, to pluck
the ears. ᵃand to eat. ᶜand his disciples plucked the
ears, and did eat, rubbing them in their hands. [This
lesson fits in chronological order with the last, if the Bethesda
events took place at a Passover. The paschal lamb was eaten
on the fourteenth Nisan, or about the first of April. Clark
fixes the exact date as the 29th of March, in A. D. 28, which
is the beginning of the harvest season. Barley ripens in the
Jordan valley about the 1st of April, but on the uplands it is
reaped as late as May. Wheat ripens from one to three weeks
later than barley, and upland wheat (and Palestine has many

mountain plateaus) is often harvested in June. If Scaliger is right, as most critics think he is, in fixing this sabbath as the first after the Passover, it is probable that it was barley which the disciples ate. Barley bread was and is a common food, and it is common to chew the grains of both it and wheat.] ^c 2 But {^b 24 And} ^c certain of the Pharisees ^a when they saw it, said unto him, Behold, thy disciples do that which is not lawful to do upon the sabbath. ^b why do they on the sabbath day that which is not lawful? ^c Why do ye that which is not lawful to do on the sabbath day? [The Pharisees did not object to the act of taking the grain. Such plucking of the grain was allowed by the law (Deut. xxiii. 25), and is still practiced by hungry travelers in Palestine, which is, and has always been, an unfenced land, the roads, or rather narrow paths, of which lead through the grainfields, so that the grain is in easy reach of the passerby. The Pharisees objected to the plucking of grain, because they considered it a kind of reaping, and therefore *working* on the sabbath day. The scene shows the sinlessness of Jesus in strong light. Every slightest act of his was submitted to a microscopic scrutiny. ^a 3 But {^b 25 And} ^c Jesus answering them ^a said unto them, Have ye not read {^b Did ye never read} ^c even this [There is a touch of irony here. The Pharisees prided themselves upon their knowledge of Scriptures, but they had not read (so as to understand them) even its most common incidents], what David did, ^b when he had need, and was hungry, he, and they that were with him? 26 How he entered into the house of God when Abiathar was high priest, ^c and took and ate the showbread, and gave also to them that were with him; which it is not lawful to eat {^a which it was not lawful for him to eat,} neither for them that were with him, but only {^c save} for the priests alone? [Jesus here refers to the incident recorded at I. Sam. xxi. 1. Ahimelech and Abiathar have been confused by transcribers. It should read Ahimelech. However, we are not referred to the actions of Abiathar, but to those of

David. He went with his followers to the tabernacle at Nob near Jerusalem, and being hungry, asked bread of the priests. There was no bread at hand save the showbread. This bread was called showbread, because it was "set out" or "exhibited" before Jehovah. It consisted of twelve loaves, which were baked upon the sabbath, and were placed, hot, in two rows upon the showbread-table every sabbath day. The twelve old loaves which were then removed were to be eaten by the priests and no one else (Lev. xxiv. 5–9). It was these twelve old loaves which were given to David (I. Sam. xxi. 6). Since the showbread was baked on the sabbath, the law itself ordered work on that day. The vast majority of commentators look upon this passage as teaching that necessity abrogates what they are pleased to call the ceremonial laws of God. Disregarding the so-called ceremonial laws of God is a very dangerous business, as is witnessed by the case of Uzzah (II. Sam. vi. 6, 7), and Uzziah (II. Chron. xxvi. 16–23). Christ never did it, and strenuously warned those who followed the example of the scribes and Pharisees in teaching such a doctrine (Matt. v. 17–20). The law of necessity was not urged by him as a justifiable excuse for making bread during the forty days' fast of the temptation. Life is not higher than law. "All that a man hath will he give for his life," is Satan's doctrine, not Christ's (Job ii. 4). The real meaning, as we understand it, will be developed below in our treatment of verse 7, which verse refers both to this incident and to the discussion then in progress.]   ⁵ **Or have ye not read in the law, that on the sabbath day the priests in the temple profane** [*i. e.*, degrade and, put to common use] **the sabbath, and are guiltless?** [Having cited a passage from the prophets, Jesus now turns to the law— the final authority. He also turns from a parallel argument concerning sacred food to a direct argument concerning the sacred day. The Sabbath was the busiest day in the week for the priests. They baked and changed the showbread; they performed sabbatical sacrifices (Num. xxviii. 9), and two lambs were killed on the sabbath in addition to the daily sacrifice. This involved the killing, skinning, and cleaning of the animals, and the building of the fire to consume the sacrifice. They also trimmed the gold lamps, burned incense, and performed various other duties. This profanation of the Sabbath, however, was not real, but merely apparent. Jesus cites this priestly work to prove that the Sabbath prohibition was not universal, and hence might not include what the disciples had done. The fourth commandment did not forbid labor absolutely, but labor for worldly gain. Activity in the work of God was both allowed and commanded.] **6 But I say** [asserting his own authority] **unto you, that one greater than the temple is here.** [The word "greater" is in the neuter gender, and the literal meaning is therefore "a greater thing than the temple." The contrast may be between the *service* of the temple and the service of Christ, or it may be a contrast between the divinity, sacredness cr divine atmosphere which hallowed the temple, and the divinity or Godhead of Christ. But, however we take it, the meaning is ultimately a contrast between Christ and the temple, similar to the contrast between himself and Solomon, etc. (Matt. xii. 41, 42). It was a startling saying as it fell on Jewish ears, for to them the temple at Jerusalem was the place honored by the very Shekinah of the unseen God, and the only place of effective worship and atonement. If the temple service justified the priests in working upon the Sabbath day, much more did the service of Jesus, who was not only the God of the temple, but was himself the true temple, of which the other was merely the symbol, justify these disciples in doing that which was not legally, but merely traditionally, unlawful. Jesus here indirectly anticipates the priesthood of his disciples—I. Pet. ii. 5.] **7 But if ye had known what this meaneth, I desire mercy, and not sacrifice, ye would not have condemned the guiltless.** [This passage is quoted from Hos. vi. 6, and is reiterated at Matt. ix. 13. It is an assertion of the superiority of inward life over outward form, for the form is nothing if the heart is wrong. The saying is first suggested by David himself (Ps. i. 16, 17), after which it is stated by Hosea and amplified by Paul (I. Cor. xiii. 3). The quotation has a double reference both to David and the disciples as above indicated. Having given the incident in the life of David, Jesus passes on from it without comment, that he may lay down by another example the principle which justified it. This principle we have just treated, and we may state it thus: A higher law, where it conflicts with a lower one, suspends or limits the lower one at the point of conflict. Thus the higher laws of worship in the temple suspended the lower law of sabbath observance, and thus also the higher law of mercy suspended the lower law as to the showbread when David took it and mercifully gave it to his hungry followers, and when God in mercy permitted this to be done. And thus, had they done what was otherwise unlawful, the disciples would have been justified in eating by the higher law of Christ's service. And thus also would Christ have been justified in permitting them to eat by the law of mercy, which was superior to that which rendered the seventh day to God as a sacrifice.] **8 For the Son of man is Lord of the sabbath.** ᵇ **27 And he said unto them, The sabbath was made for man, and not man for the sabbath: 28 so that the Son of man is Lord even of the sabbath.** [The expression " Son of man " is used eighty-eight times in the New Testament, and always means the Messiah, and not man generally. The Sabbath was made for man's convenience and blessing, and so Jesus, who was complete and perfect manhood, was Lord of it. But men who were incomplete and imperfect in their manhood, can not trust their fallible judgment to tamper with it. Though the day was made for man, this fact would not entitle man to use it contrary to the laws under which it was granted. As Lord of the day Jesus had right to interpret it and to apply it, and to substitute the Lord's day for it. In asserting his Lordship over it, Jesus takes the question outside the range of argument and brings it within the range of authority.

XXXIX.

JESUS DEFENDS HEALING A WITHERED HAND ON THE SABBATH.

(Probably Galilee.)

ᵃMATT. XII. 9–14; ᵇMARK III. 1–6; ᶜLUKE VI. 6–11.

ᵃ**9 And he departed thence** [The word here points to a journey as in Matt. xi. 1 and xv. 29, which are the only places where Matthew uses this expression. Greswell may be right in thinking that it indicates the return back to Galilee from the Passover, since a cognate expression used by John expresses such a journey from Galilee to Judæa. See John vii. 3], ᶜ**6 And it came to pass on another sabbath** [another sabbath than that on which the disciples plucked the grain], **that he entered** ᵇ**again** ᵃ**and went into their** {ᶜ**the**} **synagogue and taught** [The use of the pronoun "their" indicates that the synagogue in question was under the control of the same Pharisees who had caviled about plucking grain on the Sabbath. Where the synagogue was is not known. Some argue that from the presence of Herodians it was at Sepphoris, which was then the capital of Herod Antipas. But Herodians were likely to be found everywhere]: ᵃ**10 and behold,** ᵇ**there was a man there who had** {ᵃ**having**} **a** {ᵇ**his**} **hand withered.** ᶜ**and his right hand was withered.** [The hand had dried up from insufficient absorption of nutriment, until its power was gone, and there was no remedy known by which it could be restored.] ᵇ**2 And they** ᶜ**the scribes and the Pharisees watched him,** ᵇ**whether he would heal him on the sabbath day;** ᶜ**that they might find how to accuse him.** [They sought to accuse him before the local judges or officers of the synagogue; *i. e.*, before a body of which they themselves were members. Jesus gave them abundant opportunity for such accusation, for we have seven recorded instances of cures on the sabbath day; viz.: Mark i. 21 and 29; John v. 9; ix. 14; Luke xiii. 14; xiv. 2, and this case.] **ᵃAnd they asked him, saying, Is it lawful to heal on the sabbath day?** [They were afraid that Jesus might not notice the man, so they spoke about him. But, taught by their experience in the grainfield, they changed their bold assertion, "It is not lawful," and approached the subject with a guarded question, hoping to get an answer that could be used as a ground for accusation] **ᶜ8 But he knew their thoughts** [omnisciently]; **and he said to ⟨ᵇ saith unto⟩ the man that had his hand withered, ᶜRise up, and stand forth in the midst. And he arose and stood forth.** [Jesus thus placed the man openly before all the people, as though he stood on trial as to his right to be healed on the sabbath day.] **ᵃ11 And he said unto them, What man shall there be of you, that shall have one sheep, and if this fall into a pit on the sabbath day, will he not lay hold on it, and lift it out? 12 How much then is a man of more value than a sheep!** [A man who had but one sheep would set a high value upon it. But the most valuable sheep is not to be weighed in the balance against a man. The fact that Jesus used this illustration shows clearly that such an action was allowed at that time, though the rabbins forbade it afterward.] **Wherefore it is lawful to do good on the sabbath day. ᶜ9 And Jesus said ⟨ᵇ saith⟩ unto them, ᶜI ask you, Is it lawful on the sabbath ᵇ day to do good, or to do harm? to save life, or to kill? ⟨ᶜ destroy it?⟩** [The rules of the Pharisees made the Sabbath question wholly a matter of doing or of not doing. But Jesus made it a question of doing good, and his question implies that a failure to do good, when one is able, is harmful and sinful. "The ability," says Cotton Mather, "to do good imposes an obligation to do it." To refrain from healing in such an instance would have been to abstain from using a power given him for that very purpose. The Jews held it lawful to defend themselves on the Sabbath, and considered themselves justified in killing their enemies if they

attacked on that day (I. Mac. ii. 41 ; Josephus Ant. xii. vi. 2].
ᵇ **But they held their peace.** [afraid to say that Jesus was
wrong and stubbornly unwilling to admit that he was right.]
5 And when he had looked round about on them
ᶜ **all,** ᵇ **with anger, being grieved at the hardening of
their heart** [The anger of Jesus was not a spiteful, revengeful passion, but a just indignation (Eph. iv. 26). God may
love the sinner, but he is angry at sin. Anger is not sin,
but it is apt to run into it: hence it is a dangerous passion.
Righteous anger rises from the love of God and man, but that
which rises from self-love is sinful], **he saith** {ᶜ **said**} ᵃ **13
Then** ᶜ **unto him,** ᵇ **the man, Stretch forth thy hand.**
ᶜ **And he did** *so :* ᵃ **he stretched it forth ; and it** ᵇ **his
hand was restored.** ᵃ **whole, as the other.** [As Jesus
here healed without any word or action of healing, merely
ordering the man to stretch forth his hand, the Pharisees could
find no legal ground for accusation. God can not be tried by
man, because his ways are hidden from the senses of man
save as he chooses to reveal them.] ᶜ **11 But they were
filled with madness ; and communed one with another what they might do to Jesus.** ᵇ **6 And the
Pharisees went out, and straightway with the Herodians took counsel against him, how they might destroy him.** [Here the three Synoptists first tell of the
counsel to put Jesus to death, and we should note that, like
John, they described the anger of the Jewish rulers as arising
because of this Sabbath question. Their real motive was
envious hatred, but their pretext was a zeal for the law. That
it was not a genuine zeal for the law is shown by the fact that
they consulted with the Herodians or the adherents of Herod
Antipas, as they also did afterwards (Matt. xxii. 16; Mark
xii. 13). They needed the secular power of the Herodians to
secure the death of Jesus. Its efficiency for such ends had
just been shown in the imprisonment of John the Baptist.
But the Herodians were no friends of the Jewish law ; in fact,
they were real perverters of that law which Jesus merely correctly interpreted. This party and its predecessors had flatter-

ingly tried to make a Messiah of Herod the Great, and had been friends of Rome and patrons of Gentile influence. They favored the erection of temples for idolatrous ends, and pagan theaters and games, and Gentile customs generally. Unlike Jesus, the Pharisees grew angry and sinned, for it was against their conscience to consort with the Herodians.]

XL.

JESUS HEALS MULTITUDES BESIDE THE SEA OF GALILEE.

ᵃ MATT. XII. 13–21; ᵇ MARK III. 7–12.

ᵃ **15 And Jesus perceiving** *it* **withdrew** ᵇ **with his disciples** ᵃ **from thence:** ᵇ **to the sea** [This was the first withdrawal of Jesus for the avowed purpose of self-preservation. After this we find Jesus constantly retiring to avoid the plots of his enemies. The Sea of Galilee, with its boats and its shores touching different jurisdictions, formed a convenient and fairly safe retreat]: ᵃ **and many followed him;** ᵇ **and a great multitude from Galilee followed; and from Judaea, 8 and from Jerusalem, and from Idumaea, and beyond the Jordan, and about Tyre and Sidon, a great multitude, hearing what great things he did, came unto him.** [Idumæa was the land formerly inhabited by the Edomites. It is a Greek word from " Edom," which was another word for Esau (Gen. xxv. 30), and means red. This land was originally the narrow strip reaching from the Dead Sea to the Red Sea, lying between the Arabah on the west, and the desert on the east, being about one hundred miles long and fifteen or twenty broad. During the Babylo nian captivity, however, the Edomites took possession of the southern portion of Judæa, and Strabo says that they en croached as far as to the city of Hebron. They were con quered by John Hyrcanus, one of the Asmonæan princes about 120 B. C., and were by him made subservient to the law and incorporated with the Jewish people. As befoie noted, Herod the Great sprang from this people. Tyre and Sidon were Phœnician cities on the Mediterranean seacoast, westward from the Lake of Galilee.] **ᵃand he healed them all, 16 and charged them that they should not make him known: 17 that it might be fulfilled which was spoken through Isaiah the prophet** [Isa. xlii. 1-4. Partly taken from the LXX. and part an original translation], **saying, 18 Behold, my servant whom I have chosen; My beloved in whom my soul is well pleased: ı wıll put my Spirit upon him, And he shall declare judgment to the Gentiles.** [The word translated "servant" means also son, but it is rightly translated "servant" here, for the Father uses another word when he would designate Jesus as specifically his Son (Matt. iii. 17; xvii. 5). Jesus was a servant in form (Phil. ii. 1), and in obedience (Heb. x. 9). The word "judgment," as used in the Old Testament, from which it is here translated, means rule, doctrine, truth. It is usually here understood as meaning that Jesus would reveal the gospel or the full truth of the new dispensation to the Gentiles.] **19 He shall not strive, nor cry aloud; Neither shall any one hear his voice in the streets. 20 A bruised reed shall he not break, And smoking flax shall he not quench, Till he send forth judgment unto victory.** [These two verses find their fulfillment in the events of this paragraph. Jesus did not strive nor quarrel with the Pharisees, but having victoriously put them to silence, he meekly and quietly withdrew from their presence, and the healing of the multitudes which followed him as aptly fulfilled the prediction about the reed and the flax, for these two words, symbolic of weakness (Isa. xxxvi. 6) and patience-trying annoyance (Prov. x. 26), fitly represented the sick and lame and blind—sinners who, by affliction, had been made contrite and poor in spirit, remorseful and repentant, and who were brought to Jesus to be healed. If the hollow cylinder of the reed is bruised, its strength is gone, and it is no longer able to stand erect. Flax was then used where we now use cotton, as wicking for lamps. Imperfection in the fiber of it would cause it to smoke. A violent man, irritated by the fumes of the smoking wick, would put it out, and cast it from him. But the Lord's servant would patiently fan it to flames. The statement that he would not break these bruised reeds, nor quench this smoking flax, was an emphatic declaration, by contrast, that he would heal their bruises and fan their dying energies and resolutions into a flame, until he sent forth judgment unto victory; *i. e.*, until the gospel—the authoritative announcement of the divine purpose or will—shall be sent forth and advanced to its final triumph. Christ shall show patient mercy and forbearance until the gospel shall practically exclude the need of it, by triumphing over Jewish opposition and Gentile impiety so as to bring about universal righteousness.] **21 And in his name shall the Gentiles hope.** [This verse sets forth the breadth of Christ's conquest over all nations. It reaches beyond our times into a future which is yet to be. But it was partially fulfilled by the presence of Idumæans and citizens of Tyre and Sidon in the multitudes which Jesus healed—unless we say that only Jews from these quarters are meant, which is not likely.] ᵇ **9 And he spake to his disciples, that a little boat should wait on him because of the crowd, lest they should throng him: 10 for he had healed many; insomuch that as many as had plagues pressed upon him that they might touch him.** [Literally they "fell upon him;" such was their eagerness to be healed by touching him.] **11 And the unclean spirits, whensoever they beheld him, fell down before him, and cried, saying, Thou art the Son of God. 12 And he charged them much that they should not make him known.** [Because this was not the right time, nor were they the right witnesses to make him known.]

XLI.

AFTER PRAYER JESUS SELECTS TWELVE APOSTLES.

(Near Capernaum.)

ᵃMATT. X. 2–4; ᵇMARK III. 13–19; ᶜLUKE VI. 12–16.

ᶜ **12 And it came to pass in these days, that he went out into the mountain ᵇ13 And he goeth up into the mountain, ᶜto pray; and he continued all night in prayer to God.** [It was a momentous occasion. He was about to choose those to whom he was to entrust the planting, organization and early training of that church which was to be the purchase of his own blood. Jesus used such important crises, not as occasions for anxiety and worry, but as fitting times to seek and obtain the Father's grace and blessing.] **13 And when it was day, he called his disciples; ᵇand calleth unto him whom he himself would; and they went unto him. ᶜand he chose from them twelve** [We can not think that the number twelve was adopted carelessly. It unquestionably had reference to the twelve tribes of Israel, over whom the apostles were to be tribal judges or viceroys (Luke xxii. 30), and we find the tribes and apostles associated together in the structure of the New Jerusalem (Rev. xxi. 12–14). Moreover, Paul seems to regard the twelve as ministers to the twelve tribes, or to the circumcision, rather than as ministers to the Gentiles or the world in general (Gal. ii. 7–9). See also Jas. i. 1; I. Pet. i. 1. This tribal reference was doubtless preserved to indicate that the church would be God's new Israel], ᵇ**14 And he appointed twelve, that they might be with him, and that he might send them forth to preach, 15 and to have authority to cast out demons: ᶜwhom also he named apostles** [The word apostle means "one sent." Its meaning was kindred to the word ambassador (II. Cor. v.

20), the messenger whom a king sent to foreign powers, and also to our modern word missionary, which also means "one sent." Christ himself was an apostle (Heb. iii. 1), and so sent them (John xx. 21). The word apostle is translated "messenger" at II. Cor. viii. 23 and Phil. ii. 25. The apostles were to be with Jesus, that they might be taught by his words, and that they might become teachers of that word and witnesses as to the life and actions of Jesus. A necessary condition, therefore, to their apostleship was this seeing of Jesus and the consequent ability to testify as to his actions, especially as to his resurrection (Acts i. 8, 21; I. Cor. ix. 1; Acts xxii. 14, 15). They could therefore have no successors. All the apostles were from Galilee save Judas Iscariot]: ᵃ2 Now the names of the twelve apostles are these * [Mark and Luke give the names of the apostles at the time when they were chosen, but Matthew gives them at the time when they were sent out]: The first, Simon, who is called Peter, ᶜ whom he also named {ᵇ surnamed} Peter [For the surnaming of Simon see John i. 41, 42. Peter, by reason of his early prominence, is named first in the four lists. His natural gifts gave him a personal but not an ecclesiastical preeminence over his fellows. As a reward for his being first to confess Christ, he was honored by being permitted to first use the keys of the kingdom of heaven; *i. e.*, to preach the first gospel sermon both to the Jews and Gentiles. But after these two sermons the right of preaching to the Jews and Gentiles became common to all alike. That Peter had supremacy or authority over his brethren is nowhere stated by Christ, or claimed by Peter, or owned by the rest of the twelve. On

---

*NOTE.—To avoid making the text too complex and confusing, we have followed the order in which Matthew gives the names of the twelve. The names of the apostles are recorded four times in the following different arrangements and orders. Some think that Matthew divides them into groups of two, so that he may show us who went together when Jesus sent them out in pairs (Mark vi. 7). But it is idle to speculate as to the differences in arrangement. We note, however, that the twelve are divided into three quaternions, or groups of four, and that each of these has a fixed leader.

TABLE OF THE TWELVE APOSTLES.

	MATTHEW X. 2-4.	MARK III. 16-19.	LUKE VI. 14-16.	ACTS I. 13.
1	Simon, called Peter,	Simon, surnamed Peter;	Simon, named Peter,	Peter
2	and Andrew his brother ;	and James the *son* of Zebedee,	and Andrew his brother,	and John
3	James the *son* of Zebedee,	and John the brother of James;	and James	and James
4	and J h n his brother;	and Andrew,	and John,	and Andrew,
5	Philip,	and Philip,	and Philip	Philip
6	and Bartholomew ;	and Bartholomew,	and Bartholomew,	and Thomas,
7	Thomas,	and Matthew,	and Matthew	Bartholomew
8	and Matthew the publican;	and Thomas,	and Thomas,	and Matthew,
9	James the *son* of Alphæus,	and James the *son* of Alphæus,	and James the *son* of Alphæus.	James the *son* of Alphæus,
10	and Thaddæus;	and Thaddæus	and Simon called the Zealot,	and Simon the Zealot,
11	Simon the Cananæan,	and Simon the Cananæan,	and Judas the *son* of James,	and Judas the *son* of James.
12	and Judas Iscariot,	and Judas Iscariot,	and Judas Iscariot,	
	who also betrayed him.	who also betrayed him.	who became a traitor.	

the contrary, the statement of Jesus places the apostles upon a level (Matt. xxiii. 8–11). See also Matt. xviii. 18; xix. 27, 28; xx. 25–27; John xx. 21; Acts i. 8. And Peter himself claims no more than an equal position with other officers in the church (I. Pet. v. 1, 4), and the apostles in the subsequent history of the church acted with perfect independence. Paul withstood Peter to his face and (if we may judge by the order of naming which is made so much of in the apostolic lists), he ranks Peter as second in importance to James, the Lord's brother (Gal. ii. 11–14, 9). See also Acts xii. 17; xxi. 18. Again, James, in summing up the decree which was to be sent to the church at Antioch, gave no precedence to Peter, who was then present, but said, " Brethren, hearken unto me . . . my judgment is "—words which would be invaluable to those who advocate the supremacy of Peter, if only it had been Peter who spoke them. So much for the supremacy of Peter, which, even if it could be established, would still leave the papacy without a good title to its honors, for it would still have to prove that it was heir to the rights and honors of Peter, which is something it has never yet done. The papal claim rests not upon facts, but upon a threefold assumption: 1. That Peter had supreme authority. 2. That he was the first bishop of Rome. 3. That the peculiar powers and privileges of Peter (if he had any) passed at the time of his death from his own person, to which they belonged, to the chair or office which he vacated]; ᵃand Andrew his brother; James the *son* of Zebedee, and John his brother; {ᵇ the brother of James;} and them he surnamed Boanerges, which is, Sons of thunder [This selection of brothers suggests that the bonds of nature may strengthen those of grace. Why James and John were called sons of thunder is not stated, but it was probably because of their stormy and destructive temper (Luke ix. 51–56; Mark ix. 38). The vigor of the two brothers is apparent, for it marked James as a fit object for Herod's spleen (Acts xii. 2), and it sustained John to extreme old age, for Epiphanius says that he died at Ephesus at the age of ninety-four, but Jerome places his age at one hundred. No change is noted in the nature of James during the brief time which he survived his Lord. But the gracious and loving character of the aged John showed the transforming power of the Holy Spirit. But even to the last this son of thunder muttered in portentous strains against Diotrophes (John iii. 9, 10), and his denunciations of sins and sinners is very forceful, including such epithets as "liar," "antichrist," "deceiver," "children of the devil" (I. John i. 6; ii. 4, 22; iii. 15; II. John 3–11). It is also worthy of note that except in this verse in Mark, which applies the name "Son of thunder" to John, neither the word "thunder" nor any of its derivatives is found anywhere in the New Testament save in the writings of John, by whom it and its derivatives are used eleven times, a fact which causes Bengel to remark, "A son of thunder is a fit person for hearing voices of thunder"]; ᵃ3 **Philip, and Bartholomew** [as noted on page 111, Bartholomew is usually identified with the man whom John calls Nathanael, in which case his full name would be Nathanael Bar Tolmai]; **Thomas, and Matthew the publican** [Thomas is also called Didymus, the first being the Aramaic and the second the Greek word for twin. Matthew calls himself the publican. None of the others apply that term of reproach to him. Matthew doubtless assumes it in remembrance of the riches of Christ's grace toward him in loving him while he was yet a sinner. Exposing the sin of his own past life, he is silent as to the past lives of the others, not even noting that the first four were humble "fishermen"]; **James the *son* of Alphaeus, and Thaddaeus; {ᶜ Judas *the son* of James,}** [Matthew's father was also named Alphæus, but it was another Alphæus. This was a very common name. In its Hebrew form it may be pronounced Alphi or Clephi. In its Arimæan form it is Chalphai. So in the New Testament we sometimes find it Alphæus, and again Cleopas, or Clopas. The apostle James is thought by some to be our Lord's brother, and by others to be his cousin;

but he was probably neither.* This apostle was also called James the Less (Mark xv. 40); probably because he was younger than the son of Zebedee. He must not be confounded with James the Lord's brother, who, though called an apostle by Paul, was not one of the twelve apostles (nor was Barnabas—Acts xiv. 14). James the Lord's brother is mentioned at Matt. xiii. 55; I. Cor. xv. 5–7; Gal. i. 19; ii. 9, 12; Acts xv.

---

*NOTE.—To aid the reader we submit the following table of the women who watched the crucifixion of Jesus, for it is from their names and descriptions that we get our Scriptural light by which to distinguish the kindred of our Lord.

Matt. xxvii. 56.		Mary Magdalene	and Mary the mother of James and Joses,	and the mother of the sons of Zebedee.
Mark xv. 40.		Mary Magdalene	and Mary the mother of James the Less, and of Joses,	and Salome
John xix. 25.	his mother	and Mary Magdalene,	Mary the wife of Clopas,	the sister of Jesus' mother.

Matthew and Mark each name three women, whence it is thought that Salome was the name of the mother of James and John. But the solution of the problem depends on our rendering of John xix. 25, which is translated thus: "But there were standing by the cross of Jesus his mother, and his mother's sister, Mary the *wife* of Clopas, and Mary Magdalene." Now, was Mary, the wife of Clopas, named and also additionally described as sister to our Lord's mother, or was it the unnamed Salome who was her sister? Does John mention three or four women? The best modern scholarship says that there were four women, and that therefore James and John, the sons of Zebedee, were cousins of our Lord. In support of this it is urged: 1. That it is unlikely that two sisters would bear the same name, a fact which, as Meyer says, is "established by no instance." 2. John gives two pairs of women, each pair coupled by an "and." The first pair is kindred to Jesus, and is unnamed. and is paralleled by the other pair, which is not kindred and of which the names are given. Hebrew writers often used such parallelism. 3. It accords with John's custom to withhold the names of himself and all his kindred, so that in his Gospel he nowhere gives his own, his mother's or his brother's name, nor does he even give the name of our Lord's mother, who was his aunt. 4. The relationship explains in part why Jesus, when dying, left the care of his mother to John. It was not an unnatural thing to impose such a burden upon a kinsman.

6-9 and xxi. 18. He wrote the epistle which bears his name, and his brother Jude (who also must not be confounded with Judas Thaddæus, the apostle) wrote the epistle which bears his name. We do not know the James who was the father of Judas, and of Judas himself we know very little. He seems to have been known at first by his name Thaddæus, possibly to distinguish him from Iscariot, but later (for Luke and John wrote later than Matthew and Mark) by the name Judas— John xiv. 22.] **ᵃ4 Simon the Cananaean, ᶜwho was called the Zealot** [Cananæan means the same as zealot. It comes from the Hebrew kana, which means zealous. The Zealots were a sect or order of men much like our modern "Regulators," or "Black Caps." They were zealous for the Jewish law, and citing Phinehas (Num. xxv. 7, 8) and Elijah (I. Kings xviii. 40) as their examples, they took justice in their own hands and punished offenders much after the manner of our modern lynchers. It is thought that they derived their name from the dying charge of the Asmonæan Mattathias when he said, "Be ye zealous for the law, and give your lives for the covenant of your fathers" (I. Mac. ii. 50). Whatever they were at first, it is certain that their later course was marked by frightful excesses, and they are charged with having been the human instrument which brought about the destruction of Jerusalem. See Josephus, Wars IV., iii. 9; v. 1–4; vi. 3; VII., viii. 1. Simon is the least known of all the apostles, being nowhere individually mentioned outside the catalogues], **ᵃand Judas Iscariot, ᶜwho became a traitor; ᵃwho also betrayed him.** [Judas is named last in all the three lists, and the same note of infamy attaches to him in each case. He is omitted from the list in Acts, for he was then dead. As he was treasurer of the apostolic group, he was probably chosen for office because of his executive ability. He was called Iscariot from his native city Kerioth, which pertained to Judah—Josh. xv. 25.]

XLII.

THE SERMON ON THE MOUNT.

(Concerning the Privileges and Requirements of the Messianic
Reign. A Mountain Plateau not far from Capernaum.)

Subdivision A.

INTRODUCTORY STATEMENTS.

ᵃ MATT. v. 1, 2; ᶜ LUKE VI. 17–20.

ᶜ **17 and he came down with them** [the twelve apostles whom he had just chosen], **and stood on a level place**
[Harmonists who wish to make this sermon in Luke identical
with the sermon on the mount recorded by Matthew, say that
Jesus stood during the healing of the multitude, and that he
afterwards went a little way up the mountain-side and sat
down when he taught (Matt. v. 1). The "level place" is
meant by our translators to indicate a plateau on the side of
the mountain, and not the plain at its base. In this translation they were influenced somewhat by a desire to make the
two sermons one. It is more than likely that the sermons
were not identical, yet they were probably delivered about the
same time, for in each Evangelist the sermon is followed by
an account of the healing of the centurion's servant. As it is
a matter of no great importance whether there was one sermon or two, and as they contain many things in common, we
have taken the liberty of combining them to save time and
space. The sermon is an announcement of certain distinctive
features of the kingdom of heaven, which was said to be at
hand], **and a great multitude of his disciples, and a
great number of the people from all Judaea and Jerusalem, and the sea coast of Tyre and Sidon, who came
to hear him, and to be healed of their diseases; 18
and they that were troubled with unclean spirits were**

healed. 19 And all the multitude sought to touch him; for power came forth from him, and healed *them* all. [By comparing this with the foregoing section we shall find that Mark had described this same crowd; the only difference between him and Luke being that he tells about it the day before Jesus chose the twelve apostles, while Luke describes its presence on the day after that event. Thus one substantiates the other.] ᵃ1 And seeing the multitudes, he went up into the mountain: and when he had sat down, his disciples came unto him [In sitting he followed the custom of the Jewish teachers. The instruction of Jesus was at no time embellished with oratorical action. He relied upon the truth contained in his words, not upon the manner in which he uttered it]: ᶜ20 And he lifted up his eyes on his disciples [Luke notes the eloquent look of Jesus here and elsewhere (Luke xxii. 61). While spoken to all, the sermon was addressed to the disciples, revealing to them the nature of the kingdom, and contrasting with it: 1. Popular expectation; 2. The Mosaic system; 3. Pharisaic hypocrisy], ᵃ2 and he opened his mouth and taught them, ᶜand said, {ᵃsaying,} [Jesus spoke with the full-toned voice of power—with open mouth.]

Subdivision B.

BEATITUDES: PROMISES TO MESSIAH'S SUBJECTS.

ᵃ MATT. v. 3–12; ᶜ LUKE vi. 20–26.

ᵃ3 Blessed are the poor in spirit: for theirs is the kingdom of heaven. [The sayings in this subdivision are called beatitudes from the word "beati" (meaning blessed), with which they begin in the Vulgate, or Latin, Bible. According to Matthew, these beatitudes are nine in number and seven in character, for the last two, which concern persecution, do not relate to traits of character, but to certain external circumstances which lead to blessings. Luke gives us beatitudes not recorded in Matthew. Most of the beatitudes are paradoxical, being the very reverse of the world's view, but Christians who have put them to the test have learned to realize their unquestionable truth. The poor in spirit are those who feel a deep sense of spiritual destitution and comprehend their nothingness before God. The kingdom of heaven is theirs, because they seek it, and therefore find and abide in it. To this virtue is opposed the pride of the Pharisee, which caused him to thank God that he was not as other men, and to despise and reject the kingdom of heaven. There must be emptiness before there can be fullness, and so poverty of spirit precedes riches and grace in the kingdom of God.] **4 Blessed are they that mourn : for they shall be comforted.** [Isa. lxii. 2, 3 ; Luke ii. 25 ; Rom. viii. 18 ; John xvi. 20, 21. The blessing is not upon all that mourn (I. Cor. vii. 10) ; but upon those who mourn in reference to sin. They shall be comforted by the discovery and appropriation of God's pardon. But all mourning is traced directly or indirectly to sin. We may take it, therefore, that in its widest sense the beatitude covers all those who are led by mourning to a discerning of sin, and who so deplore its effects and consequences in the world as to yearn for and seek the deliverance which is in Christ. Those to whom Christ spoke the beatitude bore a double sorrow. Not only did their own sins afflict their consciences, but the hatred and opposition of other sinners added many additional sighs and tears. Joy springs from such sorrow so naturally that it is likened to harvest gathered from the seed (Ps. cxxvi. 6). But sorrows, even apart from a sense of sin, often prove blessings to us by drawing us near unto God.] **5 Blessed are the meek: for they shall inherit the earth.** [His hearers were full of hopes that, as Messiah, he would glut their martial spirit, and lead them to world-wide conquest. But the earth was not to be subjugated to him by force. Those who were meek and forbearing should receive what the arrogant and selfish grasp after and can not get. "Man the animal has hitherto possessed the globe. Man the divine is yet to take it. The struggle is going on. But in every cycle more and more does the world feel the superior authority of truth, purity, justice, kindness, love and faith. They shall yet possess the earth'' (*Beecher*). The meek shall inherit it in two ways: 1. They shall enjoy it more fully while in it. 2. They shall finally, as part of the triumphant church, possess and enjoy it. Doubtless there is also here a reference to complete possession to be fulfilled in the new earth—Dan vii. 27; Rev. iii. 21; v. 10.] **6 Blessed are they that hunger and thirst after righteousness: for they shall be filled.** [Our Lord here declares that those who feel a most intense desire for righteousness shall obtain it. Under no other religion had such a promise ever been given. Under Christianity the promise is clear and definite. Compare Rom. viii. 3, 4; Heb. vii. 11, 19, 25. This promise is realized in part by the attainment of a higher degree of righteous living, and in part by the perfect forgiveness of our sins. But the joy of this individual righteousness, blessed as it is, shall be surpassed by that of the universal righteousness of the new creation — II. Pet. iii. 13.] **7 Blessed are the merciful: for they shall obtain mercy.** [As meekness is rather a passive virtue, so mercy is an active one. The meek bear, and the merciful forbear, and for so doing they shall obtain mercy both from God and man. This beatitude, like the rest, has a subordinate, temporal application; for God rules the world in spite of its sin. This beatitude has primary reference to the forgiveness of offences. The forgiving are forgiven—Matt. vi. 14, 15.] **8 Blessed are the pure in heart: for they shall see God.** [The pure in heart are those who are free from evil desires and purposes. They have that similarity of life to the divine life which excludes all uncleanness, and which enables them to comprehend, after a sympathetic fashion, the motives and actions of God. Such see God by faith now, that is, by the spiritual vision of a regenerate heart (Eph. i. 17, 18), and shall see him face to face hereafter (I. Cor. xiii. 12; I. John iii. 2, 3). The Jews to whom Christ spoke, having their hearts defiled with carnal hopes and self-righteous pride, failed to see God, as he was then revealing himself in the person of his Son, thus forming a sad contrast to the gracious promise of the beatitude. "They only can understand God who have in themselves some moral resemblance to him; and they will enter most largely into the knowledge of him who are most in sympathy with the divine life"—*Beecher.*] **9 Blessed are the peacemakers: for they shall be called sons of God.** [The term includes all who make peace between men, whether as individuals or as communities. It includes even those who worthily endeavor to make peace, though they fail of success. They shall be called God's children, because he is the God of peace (Rom. xv. 33; xvi. 20; II. Cor. xiii. 11); whose supreme purpose is to secure peace (Luke ii. 14); and who gave his Son to be born into this world as the Prince of Peace (Isa. ix. 6). Here again Jesus varies from human ideas. In worldly kingdoms the makers of war stand highest, but in his kingdom peacemakers outrank them, for the King himself is a great Peacemaker—Col. i. 20; Eph. ii. 14.] **10 Blessed are they that have been persecuted for righteousness' sake: for theirs is the kingdom of heaven.** [Those who suffer because of their loyalty to the kingdom of heaven are blessed by being bound more closely to that kingdom for which they suffer.] c **Blessed** *are* ye poor: for yours is the kingdom of God. **21 Blessed** *are* ye that hunger now: for ye shall be filled. **Blessed** *are* ye that weep now: for ye shall laugh. [These three beatitudes given by Luke, like the two closing beatitudes of Matthew, are pronounced not upon character, but upon those in certain trying conditions. They are addressed to the disciples (Luke vi. 17), and are meant to strengthen and encourage them to continue in the life of sacrifice which discipleship demanded. For light upon the meaning of these beatitudes see such passages as these: Matt. x. 37–39; xvi. 24–36; Mark x. 28–30; Matt. x. 22–25. The service to which Jesus called meant poverty, hunger and tears, but it led to rich reward—I. Cor. xi. 23–33; xii. 1–5.] **22 Blessed are ye, when men shall hate you, and when**

232 THE FOURFOLD GOSPEL.

they shall separate you *from their company*, and reproach you, and cast out your name as evil, ᵃ and persecute you, and say all manner of evil against you
falsely, for my ᶜ the Son of man's sake. [The Master here presents the various forms of suffering which would
come upon the disciples by reason of their loyalty to him. We
shall find several like statements as we proceed with the gospel story. They would first be conscious of the coldness of
their brethren before the secret hate became outspoken and
active. Later they should find themselves excommunicated
from the synagogue (John xvi. 2). This act in turn would be
followed by bitter reproaches and blasphemy of the sacred
name by which they were called—the name Christian (Jas. ii.
7; I. Pet. iv. 4). "'Malefic' or 'execrable superstition' was
the favorite description of Christianity among Pagans (Tac.
Ann. xv. 44; Suet. *Nero* xvi.), and Christians were charged
with incendiarism, cannibalism and every infamy" (*Farrar*).
All this would finally culminate in bloody-handed persecution,
and procure the death of Christ's followers by forms of law; all
manner of false and evil accusations would be brought against
them.] 23 Rejoice in that day, ᵃ and be exceeding glad:
ᶜ and leap *for joy:* for behold, your reward is great in
heaven; for in the same manner did their fathers unto
the prophets. ᵃ for so persecuted they the prophets
that were before you. [In commanding rejoicing under
such circumstances Jesus seemed to make a heavy demand
upon his disciples, but it is a demand which very many have
responded to (Acts v. 41; xvi. 25). Anticipations of the
glorious future are a great tonic. For instances of persecution
of the prophets see I. Kings xix. 10; II. Chron. xvi. 10; I. Kings
xxii. 27; II. Chron. xxiv. 20, 21; Jer. xxvi. 23 and xxxii.
and xxxviii.; Heb. xi. 36–38.] ᶜ 24 But woe unto you that
are rich! for ye have received your consolation.
[Luke xvi. 25.] 25 Woe unto you, ye that are full now!
for ye shall hunger. Woe *unto you*, ye that laugh now!
for ye shall mourn and weep. [These three woes are
respectively the converse of the three beatitudes recorded by

Luke. This converse is to be expected, for as long as sin lasts woes stand over against beatitudes as Ebal against Gerizim. But the woe here expressed by the Saviour is more a cry of compassion than a denunciation, and may be translated, "Alas for you!" The first woe applies to those who love and trust in riches (Mark x. 24). Jesus does not clearly define the line beyond which the possession of riches becomes a danger, lest any, fancying himself to be on the safe side of the line, should lull himself to repose and be taken off his guard. Riches are *always* dangerous, and we must be ever watchful against their seduction. The second woe is kindred to the first. Righteousness is the soul's true food. Those who feast upon it shall be satisfied, but those who satiate themselves with this world shall waken some day to a sense of emptiness, since they have filled themselves with vanity (Eccl. ii. 1–11; Jas. v. 1–6). The third woe is not pronounced upon those who make merriment an occasional relief (Prov. xvii. 22; xv. 13, 15); but upon those who, through lack of earnestness, make it a constant aim. Half the world has no higher object in life than to be amused (Prov. xiii. 14; Eccl. vii. 6). Those who sow folly shall reap a harvest of tears. The truth of this saying was abundantly fulfilled in the Jewish wars, which culminated in the destruction of Jerusalem about forty years later.] **26 Woe** *unto you,* **when all men shall speak well of you! for in the same manner did their fathers to the false prophets.** [This is the converse to the beatitudes pronounced upon those who are reviled, etc. A righteous life rebukes an evil one, and the general tendency of evil is to deride that which rebukes it. This tendency caused the wicked of Christ's times to say that he had a demon, and that he cast out demons by the power of Beelzebub. If our lives draw to themselves no reproach, they can not be right in the sight of God. A good name is more to be desired than great riches; but we must not sacrifice our fidelity to Christ in order to attain it. If we adhere strictly to the virtues which Christ enjoined, we shall find that the world has an evil name for every one of them. Earnest contention for his truth is called bigotry; loyalty to his ordinances is dubbed narrowness; strict conformity to the laws of purity is named puritanism; liberality is looked upon as an effort to court praise; piety is scorned as hypocrisy, and faith is regarded as fanaticism.]

Subdivision C.

INFLUENCE AND DUTIES OF MESSIAH'S SUBJECTS.

ᵃ MATT. v. 13–16.

ᵃ **13 Ye are the salt of the earth: but if the salt have lost its savor, wherewith shall it be salted? it is thenceforth good for nothing, but to be cast out and trodden under foot of men.** [Salt has been used from time immemorial as an agent in the preservation of meats. The multitudes which heard Jesus were familiar with its use in curing fish. "The pickled fish of Galilee were known throughout the Roman world" (*G. A. Smith*). It is worthy of note that the salt of Palestine gathered from the marshes is not pure. Because of the foreign substances in it, it loses its savor and becomes insipid and useless, when exposed to the sun and air, or when permitted for any considerable time to come in contact with the ground; but pure salt does not lose its savor. The verse teaches that God's people keep the world from putrefaction and corruption. There was not salt enough in the antediluvian world to save it from the flood, in Sodom to save it from fire, nor in Canaan to preserve its people from destruction. It also teaches—as does experience—that a disciple may lose those qualities which make him salt.] **14 Ye are the light of the world. A city set on a hill cannot be hid.** [As light dispels darkness and enables a man to see his way, so the Christian, by his teaching and example, removes ignorance and prejudice, and discloses the way of life. The church, reflecting the light of Christ, is of necessity a conspicuous body, so that neither its blemishes nor its beauty can be concealed. For air and for protection cities were frequently built upon hills. Jerusalem and Samaria were both hill cities.] **15 Neither do** *men* **light a lamp, and put it under the bushel** [a common measure, found in every Jewish house, and containing about a peck], **but on the stand; and it shineth unto all that are in the house.** [Lamps were then crude affairs without chimneys, in which, for the most part, olive oil was burned. Candles were not then known. The word candle, where used in the King James version, is a mistranslation.] **16 Even so let your light shine before men; that they may see your good works, and glorify your Father who is in heaven.** [The light of the Christian is to shine not ostentatiously but naturally and unavoidably. It is to shine not only in his teaching or profession, but in such works and actions as unprejudiced men must acknowledge to be real excellencies. Moreover, it must so shine that it shall not win praise for itself, but for him who kindled it. Men do not praise the street lamps which protect them from robbery and assault, but they praise the municipal administration which furnishes the lamps.]

Subdivision D.

RELATION OF MESSIANIC TEACHING TO OLD TESTAMENT AND TRADITIONAL TEACHING.

[a] MATT. v. 17–48; [c] LUKE vi. 27–30, 32–36.

[a] **17 Think not that I came to destroy the law or the prophets: I came not to destroy, but to fulfil.** [This verse constitutes a preface to the section of the sermon which follows it. It is intended to prevent a misconstruction of what he was about to say. Destroy is here used in antithesis, not with perpetuate, but with fulfill. To destroy the law would be more than to abrogate it, for it was both a system of statutes designed for the ends of government, and a system of types foreshadowing the kingdom of Christ. To destroy it, therefore, would be both to abrogate its statutes

and prevent the fulfillment of its types. The former, Jesus
eventually did; the latter, he did not. As regards the prophets, the only way to destroy them would be to prevent the fulfillment of the predictions contained in them. Instead of
coming to destroy either the law or the prophets, Jesus came
to fulfill all the types of the former, and (eventually) all the
unfulfilled predictions of the latter. He fulfills them partly in
his own person, and partly by his administration of the affairs
of his kingdom. The latter part of the process is still going
on, and will be until the end of the world.] **18 For verily
I say unto you, Till heaven and earth pass away, one
jot or one tittle shall in no wise pass away from the
law, till all things be accomplished.** [The jot or yod
answering to our letter *i* was the smallest of the Hebrew letters. The tittle was a little stroke of the pen, by which alone
some of the Hebrew letters were distinguished from others
like them. To put it in English we distinguish the letter *c*
from the letter *e* by the tittle inside of the latter. This passage not only teaches that the law was to remain in full force
until fulfilled, but it shows the precise accuracy with which
the law was given by God.] **19 Whosoever therefore
shall break one of these least commandments, and
shall teach men so, shall be called least in the kingdom of heaven : but whosoever shall do and teach
them, he shall be called great in the kingdom of
heaven.** [Disobedience is a habit, and it is not easily laid
aside. Hence he that is unfaithful in that which is little will
also be unfaithful in that which is great. So also those who
were disobedient and reckless under the Jewish dispensation
would be inclined to act in like manner in the new, or Christian, dispensation: hence the warning. Not only shall God
call such least, but men also shall eventually do likewise.
Those who, by a false system of interpretation, or an undue
regard for the traditions of men, enervate or annul the obligations of Christ's laws or ordinances, and teach others to do
the same, shall be held in low esteem or contempt by the
church or kingdom of God as fast as it comes to a knowledge

of the truth. Greatness in the kingdom of heaven is measured by conscientiousness in reference to its least commandments. Small Christians obey the great commandments, but only the large are careful about the least.] **20 For I say unto you, that except your righteousness shall exceed** *the righteousness* **of the scribes and Pharisees, ye shall in no wise enter into the kingdom of heaven.** [Since the scribes and Pharisees were models of righteousness in their own sight and in that of the people, Jesus here laid down a very high ideal. Though one may now enter the kingdom of heaven having of himself far less righteousness than that of the Pharisees, yet he must attain to righteousness superior to theirs, or he can not abide in the kingdom. A large portion of the sermon from this point on is a development of the righteousness of the kingdom of heaven in contrast with old dispensation righteousness and Pharisaic interpretations of it. The laws of Moses regulated civil conduct, and being state laws, they could only have regard to overt acts. But the laws of the kingdom of Christ are given to the individual, and regulate his inner spiritual condition, and the very initial motives of conduct: in it the spirit-feelings are all acts—I. John iii. 15.] **21 Ye have heard** [Ex. xx. 13; Deut. v. 17. The common people, for the most part, knew the law only by its public reading, and hence the exposition of the scribes which accompanied the readings shared in their estimation the very authority of Scripture itself] **that it was said to them of old time, Thou shalt not kill; and whosoever shall kill shall be in danger of** [shall be liable to] **the judgment; 22 but I say unto you, that every one who is angry with his brother shall be in danger of the judgment; and whosoever shall say to his brother, Raca** [an expression of contempt frequently used in rabbinical writings, but of uncertain derivation, so that it may mean either "empty head" or "spit out;" *i. e.*, heretic], **shall be in danger of the council; and whosoever shall say, Thou fool** ["'thou impious wretch;' folly and impiety being equivalent with the Hebrews"—*Bloomfield*], **shall be in**

danger of the hell of fire. [We have here three degrees
of criminality or offence as to the sin of anger: 1. Silent
anger; 2. Railing speech; 3. Bitter reproach (Ps. xiv. 1).
With these there are associated respectively three different
degrees of punishment. The law of Moses provided for the
appointment of judges (Deut. xvi. 18), and Josephus informs
us that in each city there were seven judges appointed (Ant.
iv. 8, 14). This tribunal was known as the judgment, and by
it the case of the manslayer was determined. Compare Num.
xxxv. 15, 24, 25 with Josh. xx. 4. And in determining his
case this court might certify it for decision to the Sanhedrin,
or they might themselves confine the man in one of the cities
of refuge, or order him to be stoned to death. The second
punishment would be the result of a trial before the Sanhedrin or council. This chief court of the Jews sat at Jerusalem (Deut. xvii. 8-13), and common men stood in great awe
of it. The third punishment passes beyond the pale of human
jurisdiction. It is the final punishment—being cast into hell.
The Scripture word for hell is derived from the name of a
place in the neighborhood of Jerusalem, called the valley of
Hinnom. It was a deep, narrow valley, lying southeast of
Jerusalem. The Greek word Gehenna (which we translate
hell) is first found applied to it in the Septuagint translation of
Josh. xviii. 16. (For the history of the valley see the following passages of Scripture: Josh. xv. 8; II. Chron. xxviii. 3;
xxxiii. 6; Jer. vii. 31; xix. 1-5; II. Kings xxiii. 1-14; II.
Chron. xxxiv. 4, 5.) The only fire certainly known to have
been kindled there was the fire in which children were sacrificed to the god Moloch. This worship was entirely destroyed
by King Josiah, who polluted the entire valley so as to make
it an unfit place even for heathen worship. Some commentators endeavor to make this third punishment a temporal one,
and assert that fires were kept burning in the valley of Hinnom, and that as an extreme punishment the bodies of criminals were cast into these fires. But there is not the slightest
authentic evidence that any fire was kept burning there; nor
is there any evidence at all that casting a criminal into the

fire there was ever employed by the Jews as a punishment.
It was the fire of idolatrous worship in the offering of human
sacrifice which had given the valley its bad name. This
caused it to be associated in the mind of the Jews with sin
and suffering, and led to the application of its name, in the
Greek form of it, to the place of final and eternal punishment.
When the conception of such a place as hell was formed, it
was necessary to give it a name, and there was no word in
the Jewish language more appropriate for the purpose than the
name of this hideous valley. It is often used in the New
Testament, and always denotes the place of final punishment
(Matt. x. 28; xviii. 19; xxiii. 33; Mark ix. 43). We should
note that while sin has stages, God takes note of it from its
very first germination in the heart, and that a man's soul is
imperiled long before his feelings bear their fruitage of violence and murder.] **23 If therefore** [having forbidden
anger, Jesus now proceeds to lay down the course for recon-
ciliation] **thou art offering thy gift at the altar** [that
which was popularly esteemed the very highest act of wor-
ship], **and there rememberest that thy brother hath
aught against thee, 24 leave there thy gift before the
altar, and go thy way, first be reconciled to thy
brother, and then come and offer thy gift.** [Reconcilia-
tion takes precedence of all other duties, even of offerings
made to God. A very important teaching in these days, when
men, by corrupt practices, by extortionate combinations, and
by grinding the face of the poor, accumulate millions of dollars and then attempt to placate God by bestowing a little of
their pocket change upon colleges and missionary societies.
God hears and heeds the voice of their unreconciled brethren,
and the gift is bestowed upon his altar in vain. The
offering of unclean hands is an abomination. The lesson
teaches us to be reconciled with all who bear grudges against
us, and says nothing as to whether their reasons are sufficient
or insufficient, just or unjust. "It is not enough to say, I
have naught against *him*, and so justify myself"—*Stier*.]
25 Agree with thine adversary [opponent in a lawsuit]

quickly, while thou art with him in the way [on the road to the judge]; **lest haply the adversary deliver thee to the judge, and the judge deliver thee to the officer** [one answering somewhat to our sheriff], **and thou be cast into prison.** [In this brief allegory one is supposed to have an adversary at law who has just cause against him, and who will certainly gain a verdict when the case comes into court. The plaintiff himself used to apprehend the defendant" (*Bengel*). The defendant is, therefore, advised to agree with this adversary while the two are alone on the way to the judge, and thus prevent a trial. Jesus still has in his mind the preceding case of one who has given offence to his brother. Every such one is going to the final judgment, and will there be condemned unless he now becomes reconciled to his brother.] **26 Verily I say unto thee, Thou shalt by no means come out thence, till thou have paid the last farthing.** [This is the text on which the Roman Catholic Church has built its doctrine of purgatory, and one of those on which the Universalists build theirs of final restoration. But neither " prison " nor " till " necessarily points to ultimate deliverance. Compare II. Pet. ii. 4 and Jude 6. The allusion here is of course to imprisonment for debt. In such a case the debtor was held until the debt was paid, either by himself or some friend. If it were not paid at all, he remained in prison until he died. In the case which this is made to represent, the offender would have let pass all opportunity to make reparation, and no friend can make it for him; therefore the last farthing will never be paid, and he must remain a prisoner forever. So far, therefore, from being a picture of hope, it is one which sets forth the inexorable rigor of divine justice against the hardened and impenitent sinner. It is intended to teach that men can not pay their debts to God, and therefore they had better obtain his forgiveness through faith during these days of grace. It exposes the vain hope of those who think that God will only lightly exact his debts. God knows only complete forgiveness or complete exaction. This is an action founded upon the perfection of his nature. The Greek word translated "farthing" is derived from the Latin "quadrans," which equals the fourth part of a Roman *As*, a small copper or bronze coin which had become common in Palestine. The farthing was worth about one-fifth part of a cent.] **27 Ye have heard that it was said** [Ex. xx. 14; Deut. v. 18], **Thou shalt not commit adultery: 28 but I say unto you, that every one that looketh on a woman to lust after her hath committed adultery with her already in his heart.** [Here, as in reference to murder, Jesus legislates against the thought which lies back of the act. He cuts off sin at its lowest root. The essence of all vice is intention. Those who indulge in unchaste imaginations, desires and intentions are guilty before God—II. Pet. ii. 14.] **29 And if thy right eye** [the organ of reception] **causeth thee to stumble, pluck it out, and cast it from thee** [these words indicate decision and determination, and suggest the conduct of the surgeon, who, to protect the rest of the body, unflinchingly severs the gangrened members] **: for it is profitable for thee that one of thy members should perish, and not thy whole body be cast into hell. 30 And if thy right hand** [the instrument of outward action] **causeth thee to stumble, cut it off, and cast it from thee : for it is profitable for thee that one of thy members should perish, and not thy whole body go into hell.** [Jesus here emphasizes the earnestness with which men should seek a sinless life. To this the whole Scripture constrains us by the terrors of hell, and encourages us by the joys of heaven. The right eye and hand and foot were regarded as the most precious (Zech. xi. 17; Ex. xxix. 20), but it is better to lose the dearest thing in life than to lose one's self. To be deprived of all earthly advantage than to be cast into hell. Of course the Saviour does not mean that we should apply this precept literally, since bodily mutilation will not cure sin which resides in the will and not in the organ of sense or action. A literal exaction of the demands of this precept would turn the church into a hospital. We should blind ourselves by taking care not to look with evil eyes; we should maim ourselves by absolutely refusing to go to forbidden resorts, etc. "'Mortify' (Col. iii. 5) is a similar expression" —*Bengel*.]   **31 It is said also** [Deut. xxiv. 1, 3], **Whosoever shall put away his wife, let him give her a writing of divorcement: 32 but I say unto you, that every one that putteth away his wife, saving for the cause of fornication, maketh her an adulteress** [the mere fact of divorce did not make her an adulteress, but it brought her into a state of disgrace from which she invariably sought to free herself by contracting another marriage, and this other marriage to which her humiliating situation drove her made her an adulteress]: **and whosoever shall marry her when she is put away committeth adultery.** [The law of divorce will be found at Deut. xxiv. 1–4. Jesus explains that this law was given by Moses on account of the hardness of the people's heart; *i. e.*, to prevent greater evils (Matt. xix. 8). The law permitted the husband to put away the wife when he found "some unseemly thing in her." But Jesus here limits the right of divorce to cases of unchastity, and if there be a divorce on any other ground, neither the man nor the woman can marry again without committing adultery (Matt. xix. 9). Such is Jesus' modification of the Old Testament law, and in no part of the New Testament is there any relaxation as to the law here set forth. It is implied that divorce for unchastity breaks the marriage bond, and it is therefore held almost universally, both by commentators and moralists, that the innocent party to such a divorce can marry again. Of course the guilty party could not, for no one is allowed by law to reap the benefits of his own wrong. For further light on the subject see Rom. vii. 1–3; I. Cor. vii. 10–16, 39. It is much to be regretted that in many Protestant countries the civil authorities have practically set aside this law of Christ by allowing divorce and remarriage for a variety of causes. No man who respects the authority of Christ can take advantage of such legislation.] **33 Again, ye have heard that it was said to them of old time, Thou shalt not forswear thyself, but shalt perform**

unto the Lord thine oaths [Lev. xix. 12; Num. xxxii.; Deut. xxiii. 21]: **34 but I say unto you, Swear not at all; neither by the heaven, for it is the throne of God; 35 nor by the earth, for it is the footstool of his feet; nor by Jerusalem, for it is the city of the great King.** [Ps. xlviii. 2.] **36 Neither shalt thou swear by thy head, for thou canst not make one hair white or black. 37 But let your speech be, Yea, yea; Nay, nay: and whatsoever is more than these is of the evil** *one.* [It will be seen from the quotation given by Jesus that the law permitted oaths made unto the Lord. It was not the intention of Jesus to repeal this law. But the Jews, looking upon this law, construed it as giving them exemption from the binding effect of all other oaths. According to their construction no oath was binding in which the sacred name of God did not directly occur. They therefore coined many other oaths to suit their purposes, which would add weight to their statements or promises, which, however, would not leave them guilty of being forsworn if they spoke untruthfully. But Jesus showed that all oaths were ultimately referable to God, and that those who made them would be forsworn if they did not keep them. To prevent this evil practice of loose swearing Jesus lays down the prohibition, " Swear not at all;" but the universality of this prohibition is distributed by the specifications of these four forms of oaths, and is, therefore, most strictly interpreted as including only such oaths. Jesus surely did not intend to abolish now, in advance of the general abrogation of the law, those statutes of Moses which allowed, and in some instances required, the administration of an oath. See Ex. xxii. 11; Num. v. 19. What we style the judicial oaths of the law of Moses then were not included in the prohibition. This conclusion is also reached when we interpret the prohibition in the light of authoritative examples; for we find that God swore by himself (Gen. xxii. 16, 17; Heb. vi. 13; vii. 21). Jesus answered under oath before the Sanhedrin (Matt. xxvi. 63), and Paul also made oath to the Corinthian church (II. Cor. i. 23). See also Rom. i. 9; Gal. i. 20; Phil. i. 8; I.

Cor. xv. 31; Rev. x. 5, 6.   We conclude, then, that judicial oaths, and oaths taken in the name of God on occasions of solemn religious importance, are not included in the prohibition.   But as these are the only exceptions found in the Scriptures, we conclude that all other oaths are forbidden. Looking at the details of the paragraph, we find that oaths by the heaven and by the earth, by Jerusalem and by the head, are utterly meaningless save as they have reference to God.   "Swearing is a sin whereunto neither profit incites, nor pleasure allures, nor necessity compels, nor inclination of nature persuades"—*Quarles.*]   **38 Ye have heard that it was said** [Ex. xxi. 24; Lev. xxiv. 20; Deut. xix. 21], **An eye for an eye, and a tooth for a tooth: 39 but I say unto you, Resist not him that is evil** [The *lex talionis*, or law of like for like, was the best possible rule in a rude state of society. its object being not to sacrifice the second eye, but to save both, by causing a man when in a passion to realize that every injury which he inflicted upon his adversary he would in the end inflict upon himself.   From this rule the scribes drew the false inference that revenge was proper, and that a man was entitled to exercise it.   Thus a law intended to prevent revenge, was so perverted that it was used as a warrant for it.   This command which enjoins non-resistance, like most of the other precepts of this sermon, does not demand of us absolute, unqualified pacivity at all times and under all circumstances.   In fact, we may say generally of the whole sermon on the mount that it is not a code for slaves, but an assertion of principles which are to be interpreted and applied by the children of freedom.   We are to submit to evil for principle's sake and to accomplish spiritual victories, and not in an abject, servile spirit as blind followers of a harsh and exacting law.   On the contrary, taking the principle, we judge when and how to apply it as best we can.   Absolute non-resistance may so far encourage crime as to become a sin.   As in the case of the precept about swearing just above, Jesus distributes the universal prohibition by the specification of certain examples, which in this case are three in number]: **but**

whosoever smiteth thee on thy right cheek, turn to him the other also. [This first example is taken from the realm of physical violence. The example given, a slap in the face, has been regarded as a gross insult in all ages, but it is not an assault which imperils life. We find this precept illustrated by the conduct of the Master himself. He did not literally turn the other cheek to be smitten, but he breathed forth a mild and gentle reproof where he might have avenged himself by the sudden death of his adversary (John xviii. 22, 23). The example of Paul also is given, but it is not so perfect as that of the Master (Acts xxxiii. 2-5). Self-preservation is a law of God giving rights which, under most circumstances, a Christian can claim. He may resist the robber, the assassin and all men of that ilk, and may protect his person and his possessions against the assaults of the violent and lawless (Acts xvi. 35-39). But when the honor of Christ and the salvation of man demands it, he should observe this commandment even unto the very letter.] **40 And if any man would go to law with thee, and take away thy coat, let him have thy cloak also.** [This second case is one of judicial injustice, and teaches that the most annoying exactions are to be endured without revenge. The coat was the inner garment, and the cloak was the outer or more costly one. The creditor was not allowed to retain it over night, even when it was given to him as a pledge from the poor, because it was used for a bed-covering (Ex. xxii. 26, 27). The idea therefore is, "Be ready to give up even that which by law can not be taken" (*Mansel*). This case, as the one just above, is also an instance of petty persecution, and shows that the command does not forbid a righteous appeal to the law in cases where large and important interests are involved.] **41 And whosoever shall compel thee to go one mile** [the Roman mile: it was 142 yards short of the English mile], **go with him two.** [This third instance is a case of governmental oppression. It supposes a man to be impressed by government officials to go a mile. The custom alluded to is said to have originated with Cyrus, king of Persia, and it

empowered a government courier to impress both men and
horses to help him forward. For an example of governmental
impress, see Luke xxiii. 26. The exercise of this power by
the Romans was exceedingly distasteful to Jews, and this
circumstance gave a special pertinency to the Saviour's mention of it. (See Herodotus viii. 98; Xen. Cyrop. viii. 6, 7;
Jos. Ant. xiii. 2, 3.) The command, "Go with him two,"
requires a cheerful compliance with the demands of a tyran-
nical government—a doubling of the hardship or duty required rather than a resistance to the demand. But here
again the oppression is not an insupportable one. A man
might go two miles and yet not lose his whole day's labor. The
Saviour chooses these lesser evils because they bring out more
distinctly the motives of conduct. If we resist the smaller
evils of life, we thereby manifest a spirit of pride seeking
revenge; but when the larger evils come upon us, they waken
other motives. A man may strive for self-protection when
life is threatened without any spirit of revenge. He may
appeal to the law to protect his property without any bitterness toward the one who seeks to wrest it from him, and he
may set himself against the oppression of his government
from the loftiest motives of patriotism. If revenge slumbers
in our breast, little injuries will waken it as quickly as big
ones.] **42 Give to him that asketh thee, and from him
that would borrow of thee turn not thou away.** [Jesus
here turns from the negative to the positive side of life. Our
conduct, instead of being selfish and revengeful, should be
generous and liberal. A benevolent disposition casts out
revenge as light does darkness. No lending was provided for
by the law of Moses except for benevolent purposes, for no
interest was allowed, and all debts were canceled every seventh year. The giving and lending referred to, then, are
limited to cases of real want, and the amount given or loaned
is to be regulated accordingly. Giving or lending to the
encouragement of vice or indolence can not, of course, be
here included. Good actions are marred if they bear evil
fruit.] **43 Ye have heard that it was said** [Lev. xix. 18],

Thou shalt love thy neighbor, and hate thine enemy:
44 but I say unto you, ᶜ that hear, Love your enemies,
do good to them that hate you, 28 bless them that
curse you [I. Cor. iv. 12], ᵃ and pray for them that persecute you; ᶜ that despitefully use you. [The law
commanding love will be found at Lev. xix. 18, while the
sentiment "hate thine enemy" is not found in the law as a
precept. But the Jews were forbidden by law to make peace
with the Canaanites (Ex. xxxiv. 11–16; Deut. vii. 2; xxiii. 6),
and the bloody wars which were waged by God's own command
inevitably taught them to hate them. This was the feeling
of their most pious men (I. Chron. xx. 3; II. Kings xiii. 19),
and it found utterance even in their devotional hymns; *e. g.,*
Ps. cxxxvii. 8, 9; cxxxix. 21, 22. It is a true representation
of the law, therefore, in its practical working, that it taught
hatred of one's enemies. This is one of the defects of the Jewish dispensation, which, like the privilege of divorce at will,
was to endure but for a time. To love an enemy has appeared to many persons impossible, because they understand
the word *"love"* as here expressing the same feeling in all
respects which are entertained toward a friend or a near kinsman. But love has many shades and degrees. The exact
phase of it which is here enjoined is best understood in the
light of examples. The parable of the good Samaritan is
given by Jesus for the express purpose of exemplifying it
(Luke x. 35–37); his own example in praying on the cross
for those who crucified him serves the same purpose, as does
also the prayer of Stephen made in imitation of it (Luke
xxiii. 34; Acts vii. 60). The feeling which enables us to deal
with an enemy after the manner of the Samaritan, or Jesus,
or Stephen, is the love for our enemies which is here enjoined. It is by no means an impossible feeling. Prayer,
too, can always express it, for, as Hooker says, "Prayer is
that which we always have in our power to bestow, and they
never in theirs to refuse."] ᵃ 45 that ye may be sons of
your Father who is in heaven: for he maketh his sun
to rise on the evil and the good, and sendeth rain on

the just and the unjust. [Jesus here gives two reasons why we should obey this precept: 1. That we may be like God; 2. That we may be unlike publicans and sinners. Of course right action towards our enemies does not make us sons of God, but it proves us such by showing our resemblance to him. We are made children of God by regeneration. God, in his daily conduct towards the children of this earth, does not carry his discrimination to any great length. Needful blessings are bestowed lavishly upon all.] ᶜ **29 To him that smiteth thee on the *one* cheek offer also the other; and from him that taketh away thy cloak withhold not thy coat also. 30 Give to every one that asketh thee; and of him that taketh away thy goods ask them not again.** [The teaching of this passage has been explained above. It is repeated because of its difference in verbiage, and because its position here illustrates the spirit of the verses which precede it.] ᵃ **46 For** {ᶜ**32 And**} **if ye love them that love you, what thank** {ᵃ**reward**} **have ye? do not even the publicans the same?** ᶜ **for even sinners love those that love them. 33 And if ye do good to them that do good to you, what thank have ye? for even sinners do the same?** [The Roman publican proper was a wealthy man of the knightly order, who purchased from the state the privilege of collecting the taxes, but the publicans mentioned in the Scripture were their servants—the men who actually collected the taxes, and the official name for them was *portitores*. These latter were sometimes freedmen or slaves, and sometimes natives of the province in which the tax was collected. The fact that the Jews were a conquered people, paying tax to a foreign power, made the tax itself odious, and hence the men through whom it was extorted from them were equally odious. These men were regarded in the double aspect of oppressors and traitors. The odium thus attached to the office prevented men who had any regard for the good opinion of their countrymen from accepting it, and left it in the hands of those who had no self-respect and no reputation. Jesus teaches that our religion is worth little if it begets in us no higher love than that which is shown by natural, worldly men. "Christianity is more than humanity."—*M. Henry.*] **34 And if ye lend to them of whom ye hope to receive, what thank have ye? even sinners lend to sinners, to receive again as much. 35 But love your enemies, and do *them* good** [Ex. xxiii. 4; Prov. xxiv. 17; Rom. xii. 17, 19–21], **and lend, never despairing; and your reward shall be great, and ye shall be sons of the Most High: for he is kind toward the unthankful and evil.** ["To make our neighbor purchase, in any way, the assistance which we give him is to profit by his misery; and, by laying him under obligations which we expect him in some way or other to discharge, we increase his wretchedness under the pretence of relieving him."—*Clarke.*] ᵃ**47 And if ye salute your brethren only, what do ye more *than others?* do not even the Gentiles the same?** [The Jews despised the Gentiles, so that they did not usually salute them. This was especially true of the Pharisees. The morality, therefore, of this sect proved to be, in this respect, no better than that of the heathen. Salutation has always been an important feature in Eastern social life. The salutation, with all its accompaniments, recognized the one saluted as a friend.] ᶜ**36 Be ye merciful, even as your Father is merciful.** ᵃ**48 Ye therefore shall be perfect, as your heavenly Father is perfect.** [Luke emphasizes the particular characteristic of God's perfection which Jesus has been discussing; namely, mercy; but Matthew records the broader assertion which bids us resemble God's perfections in all their fullness and universality. God is our model. Everything short of that is short of what we ought to be. God can not be satisfied with that which is imperfect. This requirement keeps us in mind of our infirmities, and keeps us at work. Like Paul, we must be ever striving (Phil. iii. 12). Our standard is not the perfection of great and heroic men, but of the infinite Creator himself.

Subdivision E.

ALMSGIVING, PRAYER AND FASTING TO BE PER-
FORMED SINCERELY, NOT OSTENTATIOUSLY.

ᵃ MATT. VI. 1-18.

ᵃ 1 **Take heed that ye do not your righteousness
before men, to be seen of them: else ye have no
reward with your Father who is in heaven.** [This
verse refers back to verse 20 of the previous chapter, where
the disciple is told that his righteousness must exceed that of
the scribes and Pharisees. Matthew's fifth chapter deals with
the actions themselves, but this sixth chapter treats of the
motives and manners of our actions.] **2 When therefore
thou doest alms, sound not a trumpet before thee, as
the hypocrites do in the synagogues and in the streets,
that they may have glory of men. Verily I say unto
you, They have received their reward.** [Trumpets were
sounded as signals to large bodies. This fact gave to the
word trumpet a symbolic significance. Anything which is
noised or blazoned abroad is spoken of as being *trumpeted.*
The figure also conveys the idea of pompous self-laudation.
Hence we still speak of an egotistical man as one who "blows
his own trumpet." The hypocrites of that day did not blow
a literal trumpet to call attention to their gifts any more than
the hypocrites of this day do. But they used methods to call
attention to their generosity as those of our time do when
they publish an account of their munificence in the newspa-
pers. Almsgiving was a prominent feature of Jewish life.
Transplanted from Judaism, almsgiving became one of the
characteristic features of the early church (Acts ix. 36; x. 2;
Gal. ii. 10). Christ corrected error as to it in what he said
about the widow's mites. As these hypocrites sought the
praise of men, they had their reward when they received it.
**3 But when thou doest alms, let not thy left hand
know what thy right hand doeth: 4 that thine alms**

may be in secret: and thy Father who seeth in secret shall recompense thee. [Jesus here recommends secret and noiseless giving, by the never-to-be-forgotten metaphor of the left and right hand. Our generosity is to come so spontaneously, and with so little thought, that the liberality of one part of the body shall not be communicated to the other. The command does not forbid publicity, but that spirit which *desires* publicity. "The true Christian cares not how much men hear of his *public* charities, nor how little they hear of his *private* ones" (*Toplady*). Good deeds may be published by others to stimulate good in others; but care should be taken lest they be stimulated to give for the sake of like notoriety (Mark xii. 41–44; Acts iv. 36, 37). Salvation is a matter of favor, and not of merit. But there is, nevertheless, a recompense attendant upon it. The joys of the world come, and the blessings in this world are included in that recompense—Matt. xxv. 34–40.] **5 And when ye pray, ye shall not be as the hypocrites: for they love to stand and pray in the synagogues and in the corners of the street, that they may be seen of men. Verily I say unto you, They have received their reward.** [Jesus deals with our conduct toward God as well as toward man. However perfectly we may act toward man, our life is one-sided and imperfect if we omit or improperly perform our duties toward God. The Pharisaical habit of standing in a prayerful attitude, to be seen of men, was certainly not prayer. In their case public opinion, and not the praise of God, "was the wind that set the wind-mill a-work" (*Trapp*). As Pharisees loved the standing and not the praying, so Christians should love the praying and not the standing. Yet prayer for the edification or comfort of others is not here condemned. Prayer itself is nowhere condemned. It is the ostentatious prayer-attitude which Jesus stamps with his displeasure. Needless attitudes of private prayer in pulpit and in pew are here condemned.] **6 But thou, when thou prayest, enter into thine inner chamber, and having shut thy door pray to thy Father who is in secret,**

and thy Father who seeth in secret shall recompense thee. [The inner chamber was properly a little room in the interior of the house or on the housetop, but it is here used to indicate any place of privacy, and the shut door emphasizes the strictness of the privacy, for in all personal prayer we should strive to be alone with God. Jesus found a prayer-chamber upon the mountain-top and in the garden.] **7 And in praying use not vain repetitions, as the Gentiles do: for they think that they shall be heard for their much speaking. 8 Be not therefore like unto them: for your Father knoweth what things ye have need of, before ye ask him.** [For samples of repetition see I. Kings xviii. 26; Acts. xix. 34. Strictly speaking, Jesus does not here forbid either a long prayer, or the use of the same words in a prayer when the heart sincerely prompts their utterance. He himself prayed at great length, even continuing in prayer all night (Luke vi. 12), and in the garden he thrice repeated the same words. What he does forbid is making the number and length of prayers an object of consideration or a source of trust. This command is especially violated by the repetitions of the Roman Catholic rosary. Speech to God can not be ordered too carefully (Eccles. v. 2). In stating that God knows our desires before we ask, Jesus gives the reason against vain repetition. God does not need elaborate explanations, and prayer is not uttered to inform him, but to put ourselves in such communion with him as to make us fit to receive. Moreover, prayer is a matter of asking and receiving, and not a meritorious service, as Mohammedans and Catholics still hold, and as the Pharisees held. With them, as public prayers were to gain credit with men, so long and repeated prayers were to obtain merit before God. Christ teaches contrary to all this.] **9 After this manner therefore pray ye** [having pointed out the errors which then characterized prayer, Jesus proceeds to give a brief outline as a model in matter, arrangement and expression]: **Our Father who art in heaven** [The common Jewish invocation was, "O Lord God of our fathers." Jesus, as the brother of man, introduced this new and precious invocation, which puts us in prayer's proper attitude], **Hallowed be thy name. 10 Thy kingdom come. Thy will be done, as in heaven, so on earth.** [This is the first section of the prayer.] **11 Give us this day our daily bread.** [So long as it is "this day" we do not need to-morrow's bread.] **12 And forgive us our debts, as we also have forgiven our debtors.** [God can not forgive the temper that is unforgiving, for it can only exist in a heart blind as to the amount of its debt. Forgiveness, too, must be a completed act before we begin to pray. Our Lord lays stress on this one point in the prayer, returning to it after he has closed the form, that he may assure us that the divine procedure will, in this respect, be fashioned according to our own. Debt is a mild word for our sin, and is broader than trespass. Trespass indicates a misstep, a wrongdoing, but debt an unfulfilled obligation of any kind. We must not be hard in exacting our rights, when to do so would be oppressive.] **13 And bring us not into temptation, but deliver us from the evil *one*.** [This petition, to be effective, must be followed by an earnest effort on our part to fulfill it. We prefer to read "the evil," rather than "the evil *one*," for the neuter is more comprehensive (II. Tim. iv. 18), and includes deliverance from the evil thoughts of man's own heart, and from evils from without as well as temptations of Satan. As to the prayer generally, we note the following: It is divided into two sections, and each section is subdivided into three heads. Of these the first three are invocations for the glory of God; thus: 1. That God may be glorified in his name, so that it shall be universally reverenced; 2. That God may be glorified in his kingdom—that kingdom before which every power of evil shall eventually fall; 3. That God may be glorified in the hearts of humanity by all men becoming obedient unto his will. These petitions come first, for it is of first importance to us that God should be honored in his person, in his authority and in his desires. The three petitions represent three stages of spiritual growth in the communion and fellowship with God. We first know and revere his name as God. From that we advance to the full recognition of his royal and divine authority. And from this in turn we again advance until we know him fully as a Father, and, forgetting his authority, perform his wishes through the joyous constraint of love, as do the angels in heaven. The second three petitions are for humanity; thus: 1. *For their bodies,* that they may have sustenance. It is not a petition for milk and honey, symbols of luxury, but for bread, life's staff and necessity, and for bread in moderation—bestowed day by day, like the manna. 2. *For their souls in things concerning the past—* that past trespasses may be forgiven. This is the one thing needful to the soul in regard to the past. Since a certain soul condition is necessary (viz.: the spirit of forgiveness), as a condition precedent to obtaining this petition, that condition is plainly stated in the petition itself. 3. *For their souls as to the future,* that they may be enabled to avoid temptation, and that they may be finally delivered from evil. God does not tempt us (Jas. i. 13), but he can permit us to be led into temptation, or he can shield us from it, only permitting us to enter so far into it as to come off victorious over it (I. Cor. x. 13; II. Pet. ii. 9); so that it shall prove unto us a blessing instead of a curse (Jas. i. 12; v. 11.] **14 For if ye forgive men their trespasses, your heavenly Father will also forgive you. 15 But if ye forgive not men their trespasses, neither will your Father forgive your trespasses.** [Forgiveness may be difficult, but it is essential: we should realize that as we pray. Jesus presents this truth positively and negatively, that we may make no mistake about it. Those who are accustomed to repeat the Lord's Prayer will notice that the doxology with which it closes is omitted. It was probably inserted from some early liturgy. It is absent from the oldest manuscripts, and interrupts the connection of the thought about forgiveness. All textual editors omit it.] **16 Moreover when ye fast, be not, as the hypocrites, of a sad countenance: for they disfigure their faces** [by omitting to wash their faces and neglecting to dress or anoint their beards], **that they may**

be seen of men to fast. Verily I say unto you, They have received their reward. 17 But thou, when thou fastest, anoint thy head, and wash thy face; 18 that thou be not seen of men to fast, but of thy Father who is in secret: and thy Father, who seeth in secret, shall recompense thee. [Fasting, as an aid to meditation and prayer, is a wholesome practice, but stated fasts lead to hollow formality, and fasts which are endured for public praise are an abomination. Christ admonishes us to conceal the fast, so as to avoid the temptation to be hypocritically ostentatious, for fasting is intended for self-abasement, and not to cultivate pride. His words allude to the practice of anointing. Rich Jews were accustomed to anoint their bodies daily with olive or sweet oil. This was refreshing, and prevented many of the skin diseases which the dry, hot air of Palestine made prevalent. The custom still prevails among Eastern nations.]

Subdivision F.

SECURITY OF HEAVENLY TREASURES CONTRASTED WITH EARTHLY ANXIETIES.

ªMATT. VI. 19-34.

ª19 Lay not up for yourselves treasures upon the earth, where moth and rust consume, and where thieves break through and steal [In our Lord's time banks, such as we have, were unknown, and in order to keep money its possessor frequently buried it, thus subjecting it to rust and corrosion. The havoc caused by moths is too familiar to need comment (Jas. v. 2). Costly and ornamental apparel was reckoned among a man's chief treasures in olden times. See Josh. vii. 21; II. Kings v. 5; Luke xvi. 19. Oriental houses were frequently made of loose stone or sun-dried bricks, so that the thief found it easier to enter by digging through the wall than by opening the barred door. A too literal compliance with this negative precept would discourage thrift. The precept is not intended to discourage the possession of property in moderation, but it forbids us to hoard for selfish purposes, or to look upon our possessions as permanent and abiding. The lives of many men of our day seem to be employed to no other purpose than that of amassing an abundance of earthly treasure. But no true Christian can envy them, or follow their example]: **20 but lay up for yourselves treasures in heaven, where neither moth nor rust doth consume, and where thieves do not break through nor steal** [As the impossibility of hoarding earthly treasures is in the preceding verse urged as a reason against it, so in this verse the possibility of amassing perpetual possessions in heaven is set forth as a reason why we should do it. Thus the striking contrast between the two kinds of treasures is brought to our notice, so that it is the height of folly not to make a proper choice between them]: **21 for where thy treasure is, there will thy heart be also.** [Having contrasted the two treasures, Jesus here suggests the contrast between the two places where they are stored up. Since the heart follows the treasure, that it may dwell with the object of its love, we should place our treasures in heaven, even if the treasures there were no better than the treasures on earth; for it is better that our hearts should abide in the city of God than on this sinful earth.] **22 The lamp of the body is the eye: if therefore thine eye be single, thy whole body shall be full of light. 23 But if thine eye be evil, thy whole body shall be full of darkness. If therefore the light that is in thee be darkness, how great is the darkness!** [In these two verses there is a brief allegory, the meaning of which is to be ascertained from the context. The subject under consideration is the propriety of laying up treasures, not on earth, but in heaven, and the effect which treasures have upon the heart. Now, the heart or affection is to the soul much the same as the eye is to the body. If we do not set our affections upon spiritual things, the time quickly comes when we can not see them (I. Cor. ii. 14; John iii. 19–21). Jesus therefore represents our affections as if they were an eye. If the eye is single—*i. e.*, if it sees nothing with a double or confused vision—then the man receives through it clear views of the outside world, and his inner man is, so to speak, full of light. But if his eye is diseased or blinded, then his inner man is likewise darkened. Applying the allegory to the spiritual man, if his heart is single in its love towards God and the things of God, then he has clear views as to the relative importance and value of things temporal and eternal, things earthly and things heavenly. But if the heart looks with a double interest upon both earthly and heavenly treasure, it makes the man double-minded (Jas. i. 6–8), and so spoils his life. God does not permit a double affection any more than he does a double service, and a man who seeks to continue in it will soon be visited with great darkness as to the things of God, and will become blind in heart and conscience—Rom. i. 21–25.] **24 No man can serve two masters: for either he will hate the one, and love the other; or else he will hold to one, and despise the other. Ye cannot serve God and mammon.** [Mammon was a common Chaldee word used in the East to express material riches. It is here personified as a kind of god of this world. Jesus here assumes that we are framed to serve (Gen. ii. 15); and hence that we must choose our master, for it is impossible to serve two masters whose interests are different and conflicting. They conflict here, for it is mammon's interest to be hoarded and loved, but it is God's interest that mammon be distributed to the needy and be lightly esteemed. God claims our supreme love and our undivided service.] **25 Therefore I say unto you, Be not anxious for your life, what ye shall eat, or what ye shall drink; nor yet for your body, what ye shall put on. Is not the life more than the food, and the body than the raiment?** [The word "anxious" is derived from a word which indicates a state of doubt or double-mindedness. It therefore indicates that sense of suspense or worry which comes from a mind in doubt. Compare Luke xii. 29. Hence we may say that Jesus is here continuing the contrasts of the preceding verses, and that, having warned

against a double vision and a double service, he now warns
against a double mind as to the comparative value of the benefits to be derived from the service of God or the service of
mammon. Mammon can only supply food, but God gives
the life; mammon can only furnish clothing, but God gives
the body. By single-mindedness we can find peace, for
God is to be relied upon. By double-mindedness we fall to
worrying, for mammon may fail to supply those things
which we feel we need.] **26 Behold the birds of the
heaven, that they sow not, neither do they reap, nor
gather into barns; and your heavenly Father feedeth
them. Are ye not of much more value than they?**
[Literally, do ye not greatly excel them. The birds do not
serve mammon at all, yet God feeds them. Surely, then, man,
who excels the birds both in his intrinsic value and in his
capacity for temporal and eternal service, can expect to receive from God his sufficient food.] **27 And which of you
by being anxious can add one cubit unto the measure
of his life?** [Peace and trust characterize the service of
God. The rewards of mammon, on the contrary, are won by
anxiety. But the rewards of mammon can not lengthen life
as can God. Therefore we should not hesitate to choose
God's service.] **28 And why are ye anxious concerning
raiment? Consider the lilies of the field, how they
grow; they toil not, neither do they spin: 29 yet I say
unto you, that even Solomon in all his glory was not
arrayed like one of these.** [The magnificence of Solomon and of his court is proverbial in the East unto this day.
To the Jew he was the highest representative of earthly
grandeur, yet he was surpassed by the common lily of the
field. Which lily is here meant can not be determined. Cal-
cott thinks it was the fragrant white lily which grows profusely
all over Palestine. Smith favors the scarlet martagon; Tris-
tam, the anemone coronaria, and Thomson the Huleh lily, a
species of iris. It is likely, however, that scholars are trying
to draw distinctions where Jesus himself drew none. It is
highly probable that in popular speech many of the common

spring flowers were loosely classed together under the name lily.] **30 But if God doth so clothe the grass of the field, which to-day is, and to-morrow is cast into the oven, *shall he* not much more *clothe* you, O ye of little faith?** ["This is the only term of reproach Jesus applied to his disciples" (*Bengel*). As to the grass and oven we may say that the forests of Palestine had been cleared off centuries earlier, and the people were accustomed to use dried grass, mingled with wild flowers and weeds, for fuel. The oven was a large, round pot of earthenware, or other material, two or three feet high, and narrowing toward the top. This was first heated by fire within, after which the fire was raked out, and the dough put inside. Such is still the universal practice.] **31 Be not therefore anxious, saying, What shall we eat? or, What shall we drink? or, Wherewithal shall we be clothed?** [God's care for the grass which lasts but for a day should teach us to expect that he will show more interest in providing for those who have been fashioned for eternity.] **32 For after all these things do the Gentiles seek** [Christians having a heavenly Father to supply their wants, should not live like the Gentiles, who have no consciousness of such a Father. Of what use is all our religious knowledge if we are still as careworn and distrustful as the benighted heathen?]; **for your heavenly Father knoweth that ye have need of all these things.** [Here is the panacea for anxiety. Being God, the Supreme One knows; being a Father, he feels. Many repose with confidence upon the regularity and beneficence of his providential laws; but far sweeter is that assurance which arises from a sense of God's personal interest in our individual welfare—an interest manifested by the gift of his Son.] **33 But seek ye first his kingdom, and his righteousness; and all these things shall be added unto you.** [The kingdom of heaven is the real object of our search. It must be sought first both in point of time and of interest, and it must be kept ever first in our thoughts after it is found. That Christian faith and obedience leads to worldly prosperity is proved by countless in-

stances which are multiplied with each succeeding day. The
security of Christ's kingdom leads to that cheerfulness which
renews the strength, and to that undistracted industry which
brings success.] **34 Be not therefore anxious for the
morrow : for the morrow will be anxious for itself.
Sufficient unto the day is the evil thereof.** [Each day
has trouble enough without adding to it by borrowing somewhat from the morrow. Serve God to-day with the strength
you used to expend in carrying troubles which you borrowed
from the future, and God will order the affairs of to-morrow.]

Subdivision G.

LAW CONCERNING JUDGING.

ᵃ MATT VII. 1-6; ᶜ LUKE VI. 37-42.

ᵃ **1 Judge not, that ye be not judged.** ᶜ **37 And
judge not, and ye shall not be judged** [Here again Jesus
lays down a general principle in the form of universal prohibition. This principle is, of course, to be limited by other
Scriptural laws concerning judgment. It does not prohibit:
1. Judgment by the civil courts, which is apostolically approved (II. Pet. ii. 13-15; Heb. xiii. 17; Tit. iii. 1). 2.
Judgment of the church on those who walk disorderly; for
this also was ordered by Christ and his apostles (Matt. xviii.
16, 17; Tit. iii. 10; II. Thess. iii. 6, 14; II. John 10; I. Tim.
i. 20; vi. 5). 3. Private judgment as to wrong-doers. This
also is ordered by Christ and his apostles (Matt. vii. 15, 16;
Rom. xvi. 17; I. John iv. 1; I. Cor. v. 11). The commandment is leveled at rash, censorious and uncharitable judgments,
and that fault-finding spirit or disposition which condemns
upon surmise without examination of the charges, forgetful
that we also shall stand in the judgment and shall need mercy
(Rom. xiv. 10; Jas. ii. 13). Our judgment of Christians
must be charitable (John vii. 24; I. Cor. xiii. 5, 6), in remem-
brance of the fact that they are God's servants (Rom. xiv. 4);
and that he reserves to himself the ultimate right of judging

both them and us (Rom. xiv. 4: I. Cor. iv. 3, 4; II. Cor. v. 10]: ᵃ **2 For with what judgment ye judge, ye shall be judged: and with what measure ye mete, it shall be measured unto you. ᶜand condemn not, and ye shall not be condemned: release, and ye shall be released** [Though God shall judge us with absolute justice, yet justice often requires that we receive even in the same measure in which we have given it, so in a sense the merciful receive mercy, and the censorious receive censure (Jas. ii. 12, 13). But from men we receive judgment in the measure in which we give it. Applying the teaching here given locally, we find that Jesus, having condemned the Pharisees in their manner of praying, now turns to reprove them for their manner of judging. Their censorious judgments of Christ himself darken many pages of the gospel. But with a bitter spirit they condemned as sinners beyond the pale of mercy whole classes of their countrymen, such as publicans, Samaritans, and the like, besides their wholesale rejection of all heathen. These bitter judgments swiftly returned upon the heads of the judges and caused the victorious Roman to wipe out the Jewish leaders without mercy. It is a great moral principle of God's government that we reap as we sow. Censorious judgment and its harvest are merely one form of culture which comes under this general law]: **38 give, and it shall be given unto you; good measure, pressed down, shaken together, running over, shall they give into your bosom. For with what measure ye mete it shall be measured to you again.** [This is not necessarily a promise of the return of our gift in kind. It rather means that we shall receive an equivalent in joy and in that blessedness which Jesus meant when he said, "It is more blessed to give than to receive." The figurative language is borrowed from the market where the salesman, grateful for past kindnesses, endeavors, by pressing, shaking and piling up, to put more grain into the measure for us than it will contain. Pockets were unknown to the ancients, and what they wished to take with them was carried in the fold in the bosom of the coat, the girdle below holding it up.

Ruth thus bore a heavy burden in her mantle whi‿h, in the King James Version, is mistakenly called the veil—Ruth iii. 15.] **39 And he spake also a parable unto them, Can the blind guide the blind? shall they not both fall into a pit?** [Whoso lacks the knowledge of divine truth can not so lead others that they shall find it. They shall both fall into the pitfalls of moral error and confusion.] **40 The disciple is not above his teacher: but every one when he is perfected shall be as his teacher.** [Pupils do not surpass their teachers, or, if they do, they are self-taught, and hence do not owe to their teachers that wherein they rise superior to them. All that the scholar can hope from his teacher is that when he is perfectly instructed he shall be as his teacher. But if the teacher be a blind man floundering in a ditch, he affords but a dismal prospect for his pupils. The perfection of such teaching is certainly not desirable.] **ᵃ3 And why beholdest thou the mote** [chip or speck of wood dust] **that is in thy brother's eye, but considerest not the beam** [heavy house timber] **that is in thine own eye? 4 Or how wilt {ᶜcanst} thou say to thy brother, Brother, let me cast out the mote ᵃ out of thine eye; ᶜthat is in thine eye, when thou thyself beholdest not the beam that is in thine own eye? {ᵃand lo, the beam is in thine own eye?} 5 Thou hypocrite, cast out first the beam out of thine own eye; and then shalt thou see clearly to cast out the mote out of thy brother's eye. ᶜthat is in thy brother's eye.** [In Matthew and Luke Jesus gives slightly varying applications to this allegorical passage, by setting it in different connections. In Luke, as we see, he places it after the words which describe the disastrous effect of being blind leaders of the blind. It therefore signifies in this connection that we ourselves should first see if we would teach others to see. In Matthew he places it after the words about censorious judgment, where it means that we must judge ourselves before we can be fit judges of others. The thought is practically the same, for there is little difference between correcting others as their teachers or as their self-appointed judges. Jesus graphically and grotesquely represents a man with a log, or rafter, in his eye trying to take a chip or splinter out of his neighbor's eye. Both parties have the same trouble or fault, but the one having the greater seeks to correct the one having the less. The application is that he who would successfully teach or admonish must first be instructed or admonished himself (Gal. vi. 1). In moral movements men can not be pushed; they must be led. Hence those who would teach must lead the way. Those who have reformed their own faults can "see clearly" how to help others. But so long as we continue in sin, we are blind leaders of the blind.] **ᵃ 6 Give not that which is holy unto the dogs, neither cast your pearls before the swine, lest haply they trample them under their feet, and turn and rend you.** [The connection here is not obvious. This saying, however, appears to be a limitation of the law against judging. The Christian must not be censoriously judicial, but he should be discriminatingly judicious. He must know dogs and swine when he sees them, and must not treat them as priests and kings, the fit objects for the bestowal of holy food and goodly ornaments. Dogs and swine were unclean animals. The former were usually undomesticated and were often fierce. In the East they are still the self-appointed scavengers of the street. The latter were undomesticated among the Jews, and hence are spoken of as wild and liable to attack man. Meats connected with the sacrificial service of the altar were holy. Even unclean men were not permitted to eat of them, much less unclean brutes. What was left after the priests and clean persons had eaten was to be burned with fire (Lev. vi. 24–30; vii. 15–21). To give holy things to dogs was to profane them. We are here forbidden, then, to use any religious office, work or ordinance, in such a manner as to degrade or profane it. Saloons ought not to be opened with prayer, nor ought adulterous marriages to be performed by a man of God. To give pearls to swine is to press the claims of the gospel upon those who despise it until they persecute you for annoying them with it. When such men are known they are to be avoided. Jesus acted on this principle in refusing to answer the Pharisees, and the apostles did the same in turning to the Gentiles when their Jewish hearers would begin to contradict and blaspheme. Compare Matt. xv. 2, 3; xxi. 23–27; Acts xiii. 46; xix. 9.]

Subdivision H.

CONCERNING PRAYER.

[a] MATT. VII. 7–11.

[a] **7 Ask, and it shall be given you; seek, and ye shall find; knock, and it shall be opened unto you** [The words here are slightly climacteric. Asking is a simple use of the voice; seeking is a motion of the body, and knocking is an effort to open and pass through obstacles]: **8 for every one that asketh receiveth; and he that seeketh findeth; and to him that knocketh it shall be opened.** [Jesus here uses the universal "every one," but he means every one of a class, for the term is modified by the prescribed conditions of acceptable prayer (Matt. vi. 14, 15; Jas. i. 6, 7; iv. 3; I. John v. 14). We see also by the next verse that it means every one who is recognized by God as a son. All God's children who pray rightly are heard.] **9 Or what man is there of you, who, if his son shall ask him for a loaf, will give him a stone; 10 or if he shall ask for a fish, will give him a serpent?** [Fish and bread were the common food of the peasants of Galilee. A stone might resemble a cake, but if given it would deceive the child. A serpent might resemble an eel or a perch, but if given it would be both deceptive and injurious. We often misunderstand God's answer thus. But our sense of sonship should teach us better.] **11 If ye then, being evil, know how to give good gifts unto your children, how much more shall your Father who is in heaven give good things to them that ask him?** [Here is an argument from analogy. It is assumed that the paternal feeling which prompts us to give good

things to our children, is in a still higher degree in God with reference to his children; and hence it is argued that he will much more give good things to those who ask him. Since it is Jesus who assumes the likeness on which the argument rests, we may rely on the correctness of the reasoning; but we must be cautious how we derive arguments of our own from the analogy between God's attributes and the corresponding characteristics of man. For example, this attribute of paternal feeling has been employed to disprove the reality of the eternal punishment with which God himself threatens the sinner, because the paternal feeling in man would prevent him from so punishing his own children. The fallacy in the argument consists in assuming that the feeling in question must work the same results in every particular in God that it does in man. But Revelation teaches that such is not the case.]

Subdivision I.

THE GOLDEN RULE.

a MATT. VII. 12; c LUKE VI. 31.

a **12 All things therefore whatsoever ye would { c 31 and as ye would} that men should do to {a unto} you, even so do ye also unto { c to} them likewise.** a **for this is the law and the prophets.** [Jesus connects the Golden Rule with what precedes with the word "therefore." We are to practice the Golden Rule because God's divine judgment teaches forbearance, and his goodness teaches kindness. This precept is fitly called the Golden Rule, for it embraces in its few words the underlying and governing principle of all morality. It contains all the precepts of the law with regard to man, and all the amplifications of those precepts given by the prophets. It teaches us to put ourselves in our neighbor's place, and then direct our conduct accordingly. It assumes, of course, that when we put ourselves in our neighbor's place, we are wise enough not to make any foolish wishes, and good enough not to make any evil ones. The great sages Socrates, Buddha, Confucius and Hillel each groped after this truth, but they stated it thus: "Do not do to others what you would not have done to you;" thus making it a rule of *not* doing rather than of *doing*. But the striking difference between these teachers and Christ lies not in the statement so much as in the exemplification. Jesus *lived* the Golden Rule in his conduct toward men, and maintained perfect righteousness before God in addition thereto.]

Subdivision J.

THE TWO WAYS AND THE FALSE PROPHETS.

ᵃ MATT. VII. 13–23; ᶜ LUKE VI. 43–45.

ᵃ **13 Enter ye in by the narrow gate: for wide is the gate, and broad is the way, that leadeth to destruction, and many are they that enter in thereby. 14 For narrow is the gate, and straitened the way, that leadeth unto life, and few are they that find it.** [The Master here presents two cities before us. One has a wide gateway opening onto the broad street, and the other a narrow gate opening onto a straitened street or alley. The first city is Destruction, the second is Life.] **15 Beware of false prophets, who come to you in sheep's clothing, but inwardly are ravening wolves.** [From the two ways Jesus turns to warn his disciples against those who lead into the wrong path—the road to destruction. Prophets are those who lay claim to teach men correctly the life which God would have us live. The scribes and Pharisees were such, and Christ predicted the coming of others (Matt. xxiv. 5, 24), and so did Paul (Acts xx. 29). Their fate is shown in verses 21 and 22. By sheep's clothing we are to understand that they shall bear a gentle, meek and inoffensive outward demeanor; but they use this demeanor as a cloak to hide their real wickedness, and so effectually does it hide it that the false prophets often deceive even themselves. **16 By their fruits ye shall know them. Do *men* gather grapes of thorns, or figs of thistles? 17 Even so every good tree bringeth forth good fruit; but the corrupt tree bringeth** forth evil fruit. ᶜ43 For there is no good tree that bringeth forth corrupt fruit; nor again a corrupt tree that bringeth forth good fruit. ᵃ18 A good tree cannot bring forth evil fruit, neither can a corrupt tree bring forth good fruit. ᶜ44 For each tree is known by its own fruit. For of thorns men do not gather figs, nor of a bramble bush gather they grapes. ᵃ19 Every tree that bringeth not forth good fruit is hewn down, and cast into the fire. [It is a law of universal application that whatever is useless and evil shall eventually be swept away.] 20 Therefore by their fruits ye shall know them. ᶜ45 The good man out of the good treasure of his heart bringeth forth that which is good; and the evil *man* out of the evil *treasure* bringeth forth that which is evil: for out of the abundance of the heart his mouth speaketh. [Teachers are to be judged by their conduct as men, and also by the effect of their teaching. If either be predominantly bad, the man must be avoided. But we must not judge hastily, nor by slight and trivial actions, for some specimens of bad fruit grown on good trees. ᵃ21 Not every one that saith unto me, Lord, Lord, shall enter into the kingdom of heaven; but he that doeth the will of my Father who is in heaven. [To say, "Lord, Lord," is to call on the Lord in prayer. While it is almost impossible to overestimate the value of prayer when associated with a consistent life, it has been too common to attribute to it a virtue which it does not possess. The Pharisees were excessively devoted to prayer, and they led the people to believe that every prayerful man would be saved. The Mohammedans and Romanists are subject to the same delusion, as may be seen in their punctilious observance of the forms of prayer, while habitually neglecting many of the common rules of morality. It is here taught that prayer, unattended *by doing the will* of the Father in heaven, can not save us. Doing the will of God must be understood, not in the sense of sinless obedience, but as including a compliance with the conditions on which sins are forgiven. Whether under the

old covenant or the new, sinless obedience is an impossibility ;
but obedience to the extent of our possibility amid the weak-
nesses of the flesh, accompanied by daily compliance with the
conditions of pardon for our daily sin, has ever secured the
favor of God.] **22 Many will say to me in that day**
[the final judgment day], **Lord, Lord, did we not prophesy by thy name, and by thy name cast out demons,
and by thy name do many mighty works?** [Jesus here
prophetically forecasts those future times wherein it would be
worth while to assume to be a Christian. Times when hypocrisy would find it a source of profit and of honor to be attached to Christ's service. In these days we may well question the motives which induce us to serve Christ. High place
in the visible kingdom is no proof of one's acceptance with
God. Neither are mighty works, though successfully wrought
in his name. Judas was an apostle and miracle-worker, and
Balaam was a prophet, yet they lacked that condition of the
heart which truly allies one to God (I. Cor. xiii. 1-3). Jesus
says that the number of false teachers is large. We must not
carelessly ignore the assertion of that important fact. We
should also note that Christ will not lightly pass over their
errors on the judgment day, though they seem to have discovered them then for the first time. Such truths should
make us extremely cautious both as teachers and learners.]
23 And then will I profess [better, confess] **unto them,
I never knew you** [never approved or recognized you] **:
depart from me** [Matt. xxxv. 41], **ye that work iniquity.**
[This indicates that false teachers filled with a patronizing
spirit toward the Lord, and with a sense of power as to his
work, will be deceived by a show of success. Through life
Christ appeared to them to be accepting them and approving
their lives, but he now confesses that this appearance was not
real. It arose from a misconception on their part and on that
of others. Many works which men judge to be religious
really undermine religion. The world esteems him great
whose ministry begets Pharisees, but in Christ's eyes such a
one is a worker of iniquity.]

Subdivision K.

CONCLUSION AND APPLICATION: TWO BUILDERS.

ᵃ MATT. VII. 24–29; ᶜLUKE VI. 46–49.

46 And why call ye me, Lord, Lord, and do not the things which I say? [Why do ye give me the title, but withhold the service which should go with it?—Mal. i. 6.] ᵃ **24 Every one therefore that** ᶜ **cometh unto me, and heareth my words, {ᵃthese words of mine,} and doeth them** [John xiii. 17; Jas. i. 22], ᶜ **I will show you to whom he is like: 48 he is like {ᵃ shall be likened unto} ** ᶜ **a man building a house, who digged and went deep, and laid a foundation upon the rock:** ᵃ **a wise man, who built his house upon the rock** [The word *rock* suggests Christ himself. No life can be founded upon Christ's teaching unless it be founded also upon faith and trust in his personality. For this we must dig deep, for as St. Gregory says, "God is not to be found on the surface"]: **25 and the rain descended, and the floods came, and the winds blew, and beat upon that house;** ᶜ **and when a flood arose, the stream brake against that house, and could not shake it:** ᵃ **and it fell not:** ᶜ **because it had been well builded.** ᵃ **for it was founded upon the rock.** [The imagery of this passage would be impressive anywhere, but is especially so when used before an audience accustomed to the fierceness of an Eastern tempest. Rains, floods, etc., represent collectively the trials, the temptations and persecutions which come upon us from without. There comes a time to every life when these things throng together and test the resources of our strength.] **26 And every one {ᶜ 49 But he}** ᵃ **that heareth these words of mine, and doeth them not, shall be likened unto {ᶜ is like}** ᵃ **a foolish man, who {ᶜ that} built a {ᵃ his} house upon the sand: {ᶜ earth} without a foundation;** ᵃ **27 and the rain de-**

scended, and the floods came, and the winds blew, and smote upon that house; {^cagainst which the stream brake,} and straitway it fell in; ^aand great was the fall thereof. ^cand the ruin of that house was great. [We do not need to go to Palestine to witness the picture portrayed here. Whole towns on the Missouri and the lower Mississippi have been undermined and swept away because built upon the sand. Jesus here limits the tragedy to a single house. "A single lost soul is a great ruin in the eyes of God" (*Godet*). Jesus did not end his sermon with a strain of consolation. It is not always best to do so.] ^a28 And it came to pass, when Jesus had finished these words, the multitudes were astonished at his teaching: 29 for he taught them as *one* having authority, and not as their scribes. [See page 166.]

XLIII.

HEALING THE CENTURION'S SERVANT.

(At Capernaum.)

^aMATT. VIII. 1, 5-13; ^cLUKE VII. 1-10.

^c1 After he had ended all his sayings in the ears of the people, ^a1 And when he was come down from the mountain, great multitudes followed him. ^che entered into Capernaum. [Jesus proceeded from the mountain to Capernaum, which was now his home, or headquarters. The multitudes which are now mentioned for the third time were not wearied by his sermon, and so continued to follow him. Their presence showed the popularity of Jesus, and also emphasized the fact that the miracles which followed the sermon were wrought in the presence of vast throngs of people.] ^a5 And when he was entered into Capernaum, there came unto him a centurion [The context shows that this centurion or captain of a hundred men was a Gentile, but whether he was in the employ of Herod Antipas, tetrarch of Galilee, or an officer in the Roman army, is

not clear, neither is it very important. The army of Antipas, like that of other petty kings, was modeled after that of Rome], **c 2 And a certain centurion's servant** [slave boy], **who was dear unto him, was sick and at the point of death. 3 And when he heard concerning Jesus** [The sequel shows that he had probably heard how Jesus had healed the son of his fellow-townsman—John iv. 46–54], **he sent unto him elders of the Jews** [To reconcile Matthew and Luke, we have only to conceive of the centurion as coming to the edge of the crowd about Jesus, but modestly refraining from coming into the Lord's immediate presence], **asking him that he would come and save his servant. ª beseeching him, 6 and saying, Lord, my servant lieth in the house sick of the palsy, grievously tormented.** [Because palsy is not usually accompanied with suffering, some think that in this case it was combined with tetanus or lockjaw, a combination not infrequent in hot climates. But Sir R. Bennet, M. D., speaks thus: "In this instance we have probably a case of progressive paralysis, attended by muscular spasms, and involving the respiratory movements, where death is manifestly imminent and inevitable. In such a case there would be symptoms indicative of great distress, as well as immediate danger to life." As to palsy generally see pp. 173, 181. **c 4 And they, when they came to Jesus, besought him earnestly, saying, He is worthy that thou shouldest do this for him; 5 for he loveth our nation, and himself built us our synagogue.** [The centurion evidently believed in and worshiped God, but, influenced probably by his profession, did not become a proselyte by being circumcised and conforming entirely to the Mosaic law. He was what later Jews would have termed a Proselyte of the Gate, and not a full fledged Proselyte of Righteousness. The ruins of Capernaum show the ruins of a synagogue. It was a beautiful structure, built of white limestone, shows by its architectual features that it was built in the time of the Herods, and there is little doubt that it is the one which this pious Gentile erected, and in which Jesus taught

and healed.]   ᵃ7 **And he saith unto him** [*i. e.*, answering
him as represented by his friends], **I will come and heal
him.** ᶜ6 **And Jesus went with them.   And when he
was now not far from the house, the centurion sent
friends to him,** ᵃ8 **And the centurion answered and
said, {ᶜsaying unto him,} Lord, trouble not thyself;
for I am not worthy that thou shouldest come under
my roof** [not because his house was a poor one, for he was
evidently well to do]: **7 wherefore neither thought I myself worthy to come unto thee: ᵃbut only say the
word, and my servant shall be healed.** [The centurion,
well knowing that it was unlawful for Jews to go into the
houses of Gentiles, lest they should sully the sanctity which
they desired to maintain, wished to spare Jesus any embarrassment.   Whatever he may have thought of this custom with
regard to the Pharisees, he attributed to Jesus so high a
degree of sanctity that he accepted the doctrine as true in
reference to him.   The centurion showed his great faith partly
by believing that Jesus could heal by a word, but chiefly in
his lofty conception of Jesus as compared with himself.   The
less faith we have, the less we esteem Jesus, and the more
faith we have, the less we esteem ourselves.   As Jesus rises
we sink in the scale of our estimation.   The centurion's faith
would have been wonderful enough in an Israelite, but it was
all the more wonderful when found in the bosom of a Gentile.
The word "found" suggests that Jesus came seeking faith: he
will come seeking it again (Luke xviii. 8).   The elders, little
knowing the wideness of our Lord's vision and sympathy, supposed that Jesus would look upon the splendid synagogue
erected for the Jewish people as a sufficient motive for granting
this request.   Even the apostles were slow to learn that at
heart Jesus knew neither Jew nor Gentile.] ᶜ**8 For I also
am a man set under authority, having under myself
soldiers: and I say to this one, Go, and he goeth; and
to another, Come, and he cometh; and to my servant
** [not a soldier, but a household slave], **Do this, and he doeth
it.** [Having those over him, he knew how to obey, and hav-

ing those under him, he knew how to be obeyed. He was familiar, therefore, with all the principles of obedience. Knowing from the healing of the nobleman's son, or from other reports concerning Jesus, that the realm of nature obeyed Jesus, he judged from his knowledge of earthly obedience that Jesus had those who could come and go for him, and who could carry his messages and enforce obedience to them. He felt that the presence of Jesus was not at all necessary to the healing.] ᵃ 10 **And when Jesus heard it, {ᶜ these things,} he marvelled at him, and turned and said unto ᵃ them ᶜ the multitude that followed him, ᵃ Verily I say unto you, I have not found so great faith, no, not in Israel.** [To some it seems strange that Jesus could marvel, but he had all the actual feelings of a man. However, we should note that Jesus is never said to have marveled but twice. In this case it was because of belief, and in the other (Mark vi. 6), it was because of unbelief. Those who think that Jesus gave or gives faith should note this fact. If Jesus had given the centurion faith, he could not have been surprised to find that he had it; and, if he failed to bestow it upon the people of Nazareth, it would have been inconsistent in him to express surprise at their lack of it. It would seem, however, irreconcilable with the character and affectionate nature of Christ, to bestow faith in such profusion upon this Gentile stranger, and withhold every spark of it from his near kinsmen and fellow-townsmen. Faith is no miraculous gift. Faith means no more nor less than belief; and a man believes the Scripture facts in the same manner and by the same processes that he believes any other facts.] **11 And I say unto you, that many shall come from the east and the west, and shall sit down with Abraham, and Isaac, and Jacob, in the kingdom of heaven** [Jesus here predicts the conversion of the Gentiles, since that fact is suggested to him by the faith of this centurion. The east and the west represent the extreme points of the compass in the directions in which the world was most thickly inhabited. But Jesus refers rather to spiritual separation than to geographical distances –Mal. i. 11 ; Isa. xlix. 19 ; Jer. xvi. 19 ; Zech. viii. 22]: **12 but the sons of the kingdom** [the child of anything in Hebrew phraseology expressed the idea of special property which one has in the thing specified, as, for instance, children of disobedience (Eph. ii. 2). Jesus here means, then, the Jews, to whom the kingdom belonged by hereditary descent—Rom. ix. 4] **shall be cast forth into the outer darkness : there shall be the weeping and the gnashing of teeth.** [In this paragraph Christ's kingdom is set forth under the simile of a great feast, a familiar simile with Jesus (Matt. xxvi. 29 ; Luke xxii. 30). The Jews were accustomed to speak of the delights of the Messianic kingdom as a feast with the patriarchs (Luke xiv. 15), but lost sight of the fact that Gentiles should share in its cheer and fellowship (Isa. xxv. 6). Marriage feasts and other great feasts of the Jews were usually held in the evening. Inside, therefore, there would be joy and light and gladness, but outside there would be darkness and disappointment, tears and bitter self-reproach (Matt. xxv. 10–13). The despised outcasts should be brought in and placed at the festal board, while the long-invited guests—the natural and fleshly heirs of Abraham's invitation—would be excluded (Matt. xxi. 43). Hell is absence from spiritual light, separation from the company of the saved, lamentation and impotent rage.] **13 And Jesus said unto the centurion, Go thy way ; as thou hast believed, *so* be it done unto thee. And the servant was healed in that hour.** [In the moment when Jesus spoke, the servant was healed—not relieved, but healed.] ᶜ **10 And they that were sent, returning to the house, found the servant whole.** [The centurion, long before this when he was building the synagogue, had doubtless heard with delight concerning the wonderful works wrought by the mighty prophets in the olden time ; he little dreamed that his own eyes should see them all surpassed.]

XLIV.

JESUS RAISES THE WIDOW'S SON.

(At Nain in Galilee.)

ᶜLUKE VII. 11–17.

ᶜ **11 And it came to pass soon afterwards** [many ancient authorities read *on the next day*], **that he went to a city called Nain ; and his disciples went with him, and a great multitude.** [We find that Jesus had been thronged with multitudes pretty continuously since the choosing of his twelve apostles. Nain lies on the northern slope of the mountain, which the Crusaders called Little Hermon, between twenty and twenty-five miles south of Capernaum, and about two miles west of Endor. At present it is a small place with about a dozen mud hovels, but still bears its old name, which the Arabs have modified into Nein. It is situated on a bench in the mountain about sixty feet above the plain.] **12 Now when he drew near to the gate of the city, behold, there was carried out one that was dead, the only son of his mother, and she was a widow: and much people of the city was with her.** [Places of sepulture were outside the towns, that ceremonial pollution might be avoided. To this rule there was an exception. The kings of Judah were buried in the city of David (II. Kings xvi. 20; xxi. 18, 26). The Jews were careful to give public expression to their sympathy for those who were bereaved (John xi. 19). The death of an only child represented to them as to us the extreme of sorrow (Jer. vi. 26; Zech. xii. 10; Amos viii. 10). But in this case the sorrow was heightened by the fact that the mother was a widow, and hence evidently dependent upon her son for support. Her son had comforted her in her first loss of a husband, but now that her son was dead, there was none left to comfort.] **13 And when the Lord saw her** [some take this use of the phrase "the

Lord," as an evidence of the late date at which Luke wrote his Gospel; but the point is not well taken, for John used it even before Jesus' ascension—John xxi. 7], **he had compassion on her, and said unto her, Weep not.** [As the funeral procession came out of the gate, they met Jesus with his company coming in. Hence there were many witnesses to what followed. But the miracle in this instance was not wrought so much to attest our Lord's commission, or to show his power, as to do good. As Jesus had no other business in Nain but to do good, we may well believe that he went there for the express purpose of comforting this forlorn mother. Compare John xi. 1-15. Good blessings may come to us when reason speaks and God's wise judgment answers; but we get our best blessings when our afflictions cry unto him and his compassion replies.] **14 And he came nigh and touched the bier: and the bearers stood still.** [The word here translated " bier" may mean a bier or a coffin, and the authorities are about equally divided as to which it was. It was more likely a stretcher of boards, with the pallet or bed upon it, and the body of the young man wrapped in linen lying upon the bed. Coffins, which were common in Babylon and Egypt, were rarely used by the Jews, save in the burial of people of distinction; and, if we may trust the writing of the later rabbis, the burial of little children. When they were used, the body was placed in them, and borne without any lid to the place of sepulture. We find no coffin in the burial of either Lazarus or Jesus. Jesus was, no doubt, known to many in Nain, and it is no wonder that those who bore the bier stood still when he touched it. Though we can not say that he had raised the dead prior to this, we can say that he had healed every kind of disease known among the people, and therefore his act would beget a reasonable expectancy that he might do something even here.] **And he said, Young man, I say unto thee, Arise.** [Here, as in the other instances where Jesus revived the dead, we find that he issues a personal call to the party whose remains are before him. It suggests the sublime thought that he has as full dominion and authority over the unseen as over the seen; and that should he issue a general call, all the dead would revive again as obediently and immediately as did the single one to whom he now spoke (John v. 28, 29). The command of Jesus, moreover, is spoken with the ease and consciousness of authority known only to Divinity. Compare the dependent tone of Simon Peter—Acts iii. 6.] **15 And he that was dead sat up, and began to speak.** [Thus showing that not only life, but also health and strength, were restored.] **And he gave him to his mother.** [As the full fruitage of his compassion. The scene suggests that Christ will, with his own hands, restore kindred to kindred in the glorious morning of resurrection.] **16 And fear took hold on all** [Because the power of God had been so signally manifested among them. They recognized the presence of God's power and mercy, yet by no means apprehended the nearness of his very person]: **and they glorified God, saying, A great prophet is arisen among us: and, God hath visited his people.** [Expectation of the return of one of the prophets was at that time widely spread. See Luke ix. 8, 19. That they should esteem Jesus as no more than a prophet was no wonder, for as yet even his apostles had not confessed him as the Christ. In state and conduct Jesus appeared to them too humble to fulfill the popular ideas of Messiahship. But in wisdom and miracle he outshone all God's former messengers. The "visiting" of God refers to the long absence of the more strikingly miraculous powers of God as exercised through the prophets. None had raised the dead since the days of Elisha.] **17 And this report went forth concerning him in the whole of Judaea, and all the region round about.** [This great miracle caused the fame of Jesus to fill all Judæa as well as Galilee. It seems, from what next follows, to have reached John the Baptist in his prison on the east of the Dead Sea.]

XLV

THE BAPTIST'S INQUIRY AND JESUS' DISCOURSE SUGGESTED THEREBY.

(Galilee.)

^a MATT. XI. 2–30; ^c LUKE VII. 18–35.

^c **18 And the disciples of John told him of all these things.** ^a **2 Now when John heard in the prison the works of the Christ, he sent by his disciples** ^c **19 And John calling unto him two of his disciples sent them unto the Lord** [John had been cast into prison about December, A. D. 27, and it was now after the Passover, possibly in May or June, A. D. 28. Herod Antipas had cast John into prison because John had reproved him for taking his brother's wife. According to Josephus, the place of John's imprisonment and death was the castle of Machærus (or Makor), east of the Dead Sea (Ant. xviii.; v. 1, 2). It was built by Herod the Great, and was not very far from that part of the Jordan in which John had baptized, so that it is probable that Herod resided in this castle when he went to hear John preach. We learn elsewhere that Herod felt kindly towards John, and this fact, coupled with the statement that John called two of his disciples to him, suggests that John must have been held as an honored prisoner with liberties like those accorded to Paul at Cæsarea—Acts xxiv. 23], ^a **3 and said unto him, {** ^c **saying,} Art thou he that cometh, or look we for another ?** [The prophets spoke of the Messiah as the coming one, and John himself had done likewise—Matt. iii. 11.] **20 And when the men were come unto him, they said, John the Baptist hath sent us unto thee, saying, Art thou he that cometh, or look we for another ?** [This passage has been a puzzle to expositors from the very earliest times. Being unable to understand how the Baptist, being an inspired prophet and favored with visions of the supernatural,

could give way to skeptical doubts, they have exhausted their inventive genius to explain what John meant by his question. Among these many explanations the best is that given by Alford, viz.: that John wished to get Jesus to publicly declare himself for the sake of quieting all rumors concerning him, his fault being kindred to that of Jesus' mother when she tried to hasten Jesus' hour at the wedding at Cana (John ii. 4). But the plain, unmistakable inference of the text is that John's faith wavered. The Bible does not represent the saints as free from imperfection. It does not say that inspiration is omniscience, or that visions and miracles remove doubts. It took two miracles to persuade Gideon ; Moses harbored distrust (Ex. iii., iv.), and was guilty of unbelief (Num. xx. 12); Elijah despaired of God's power (I. Kings xix. 4–10); Jeremiah was slow of belief, and in his despondency cursed the day of his birth (Jer. xx. 7, 14–18). But the most instructive parallel is that of Simon Peter. He witnessed the transfiguration of Jesus, beheld the glory of God and heard the voice of the Father (Matt. xvii. 1–6); yet he sank below the Baptist, and denied his Lord with cursing ; and no man has ever thought it at all incredible that he should do so. The trial of John's faith, though not so clearly depicted as that of Peter, was perhaps equally searching. His wild, free life was now curbed by the irksome tedium of confinement. His expectations were not fulfilled. The unfruitful trees had not been cut down, the grain had not been winnowed, nor the chaff burned, nor could he see any visible tendency towards these results. Moreover, he held no communion with the private life of Jesus, and entered not into the sanctuary of his Lord's thought. We must remember also that his inspiration passed away with the ministry, on account of which it was bestowed, and it was only *the man John*, and not the prophet, who made the inquiry. The inquiry itself, too, should be noted. It is not, Are you what I declared you to be ? but, Being all of that, are you *the* one who should come, or must we look for *another?* John, no doubt, shared with all Jews the idea that Messiah was to set up an earthly kingdom, and seeing in Jesus none of the spirit of such a king, he seems to have questioned whether Jesus was to be the finality, or whether he was to be, like himself, a forerunner, preparing the way for the ultimate Messiah. He did not grasp the thought that Jesus was both Alpha and Omega; that Jesus, the lowly servant of humanity, by service and sacrifice is evermore preparing the way for Jesus the King.] **21 In that hour⁕he cured many of diseases and plagues and evil spirits; and on many that were blind he bestowed sight. 22 And he ᵃ Jesus answered and said unto them, Go and tell John the things which ye hear and see: {ᶜ have seen and heard;} ᵃ 5 the blind receive their sight, and the lame walk, the lepers are cleansed, and the deaf hear, and the dead are raised up, and the poor have good tidings preached to them.** [John himself, when thus questioned, had answered plainly, saying, " No " (John i. 20, 21), and he probably expected a like categorical answer from Jesus. The indirect answer of Jesus, ending with a beatitude, was well calculated to waken in John beneficial thoughtfulness, for it threw his mind back upon the prophecies of God, such as Isa. xxx. 5, 6; xlii. 7; lxi. 1–3, etc. It may be inferred that Jesus withheld answering the messengers and went on with his works of grace, that these might testify to John more potently than mere words of assertion. Jesus did not work miracles to gratify skeptical curiosity, but he did use them, as here, to strengthen wavering faith (Mark ix. 24; John xi. 15; xiv. 11); Jesus sums up his work in the form of a climax, wherein preaching the gospel to the poor stands superior even to the raising of the dead. Attention to the poor has always been a distinctive feature of Christianity. To care for the poor is above miracles. Modern Orientals are not impressed by the miracles of the New Testament as such. The sacred literature of India and China abounds in wonders, and with the people of these lands a miracle is little more than a commonplace. With them Christ's love for the lowly is above the miracles. " Wonders and miracles might be counterfeited, but a sympathy with the suffering and helpless, so tender, so laborious, so long continued, was not likely to be simulated. Such humanity was unworldly and divine "—*Beecher.*] **6 And blessed is he, whosoever shall find no occasion of stumbling in me.** [The scribes had stumbled and failed to believe in Jesus because he did not fulfill their ideal, or come up to their expectations. Jesus seeks to woo John from a like fate by the sweet persuasion of a beatitude. John must realize that it is better for the subject to fall in with the plans of the all-wise King, as he fulfills the predictions of God the Father, than for the King to turn aside and frustrate the plan of the ages to humor the passing whim of a despondent and finite mind.] ᶜ**24 And when the messengers of John were departed, {ᵃ7 And as these went their way,} ᵈ he ᵃJesus began to say unto the multitudes concerning John** [The commendation of Jesus which follows was not spoken in the presence of John's messengers. It was best that John should not hear it. We also do our work under the silent heavens and wait for the future plaudit, " Well done, good and faithful servant "], **What went ye out into the wilderness to behold? a reed shaken with the wind? 8 But what went ye out to see? ᶜa man clothed in soft raiment? ᵃBehold, they that wear soft** *raiment* ᶜ**they that are gorgeously apparelled, and live delicately, are in kings' courts. {ᵃhouses.}** [After the departure of the messengers Jesus immediately clears the character of John of unjust suspicion. John, who had testified with such confidence as to the office and character of Jesus, now comes with a question betraying a doubtful mind and wavering faith. Was John then a vacillating man? Was he guilty of that lack of steadfastness which the world looks upon as intolerable in all whom it esteems great? Was he blown about by every wind of public opinion like the tall reed (the *Arunda donax*) which skirts the Jordan, and which stands, bearing its beautiful blossoming top twelve feet high one moment, only to bow it to the earth the next, the slender stem yielding submissively to the passing breeze? Was he a voluptuary about to condescend to flatter Herod and retract

his reproof, that he might exchange his prison for a palace ?
Those who had gone to the wilderness to see John had found
no such man, and John was still the John of old.   One act
does not make a character, one doubt does not unmake it.
John was no reed, but was rather, as Lange says, " a cedar,
half uprooted by the storm."]   **9 But wherefore went ye
out?   {c 26 But what went ye out to see?} a to see a
prophet?   Yea, I say unto you, and much more than
a prophet.**   [The next verse shows us that John was a messenger as well as a prophet.   Prophets foretold the Messiah,
but John was the herald who announced him.   John was
miraculously born, and was himself the subject of prophecy.
Great as was John in popular estimation, that estimation was
insufficient.]   **10 This is he, of whom it is written, Behold, I send my messenger before thy face, Who shall
prepare thy way before thee.**   [This quotation is taken
from Mal. iii. 1, where it reads, " my messenger . . . before
me."   But Mark (Mark i. 2) concurs with Matthew and Luke
in the reading here given.   From the change in the words it
appears " that Christ is one with God the Father, and that
the coming of Christ is the coming of God "—*Hammond.*]
**11 Verily I say unto you, Among them that are born
of women there hath not arisen a greater {c there is
none greater} a than John the Baptist: yet he that
is but little in the kingdom of heaven {c of God} is
greater than he.**   [We find from this passage that all true
greatness arises from association, relation and contact with
Jesus Christ.   To be Christ's forerunner is to be above teacher
and prophet, Levite and priest, lawgiver and king, and all
else that the world estimates as great.   If all greatness be
thus measured by contact of Christ, how great must Christ
be !   But the least in the kingdom is greater than John.
"This shows: 1. That John was not in the kingdom of God.
2. That, as none greater than John had been born of women,
no one had yet entered the kingdom.   3. That, therefore, it
had not yet been set up; but as John himself, Jesus and the
twelve, under the first commission, preached, was ' at hand.'

4. All in the kingdom, even the humble, have a station superior to John's" (*Johnson*). Farrar reminds us of the old legal maxim which says, "The least of the greatest is greater than the greatest of the least," which is as much as to say that the smallest diamond is of more precious substance than the largest flint. The least born of the Holy Spirit (John i. 12, 13 and iii. 5) is greater than the greatest born of women. They are greater in station, privilege and knowledge. The dispensations rise like lofty steps, and the lowest that stand upon the New Testament dispensation are lifted above the tallest who rest upon the dispensation of Moses. This is perhaps prophetically suggested by Zechariah—Zech. xii. 8.] ᶜ **29 And all the people** [the common people, and not the rulers] **when they heard, and the publicans, justified God, being baptized with the baptism of John.** [They justified or approved the wisdom of God in sending such a prophet as John and establishing such an ordinance as baptism.] **30 But the Pharisees and the lawyers rejected for themselves the counsel of God, being not baptized of him.** [The counsel of God was that the nation should be brought to repentance by John, that it might be saved by Jesus; but the Pharisees frustrated this plan so far as they were concerned, by their proud refusal to repent. All who followed their example shared their unhappy success. It is noteworthy that Jesus emphasizes baptism as the test as to whether men justify or reject God's counsel.] ᵃ **12 And from the days of John the Baptist until now** [a period of about three years] **the kingdom of heaven suffereth violence, and men of violence take it by force.** [Jesus here pictures the kingdom of heaven as a besieged city. The city is shut up, but the enemies which surround it storm its walls and try to force an entrance—an apt illustration which many fail to comprehend. The gates of Christ's kingdom were not opened until the day of Pentecost (Acts ii.), but men hearing it was about to be opened sought to enter it prematurely, not by the gates which God would open when Simon Peter used the keys (Matt. xvi. 19), but by such breaches as they themselves sought to make

in the walls. Examples of this violence will be seen in the following instances (John vi. 15; Matt. xx. 21; Luke xix. 11, 36–38; xxii. 24–30; Acts 1–6. The people were full of preconceived ideas with regard to the kingdom, and each one sought to hasten and enjoy its pleasures as one who impatiently seizes upon a bud and seeks with his fingers to force it to bloom. The context shows that John the Baptist was even then seeking to force the kingdom.] **13 For all the prophets and the law prophesied until John. 14 And if ye are willing to receive** *it***, this is Elijah, that is to come. 15 He that hath ears to hear, let him hear.** [The Old Testament was the work of a long series of prophets, and this series was closed by John the Baptist. But John differed from all the others in the series; for they prophesied concerning the kingdom, while John turned from their course to preach that the kingdom was at hand, and thereby incidentally brought upon it the assaults of violence. As to John the Baptist being the prophetic Elijah, see p. 102.] **16 But whereunto ᶜ then shall I liken the men of this generation, and to what are they like? 32 They are {ª It is} like unto children sitting {ᶜ that sit} in the marketplace, {ª marketplaces,} ᶜ and ª who call ᶜ one to another; ª unto their fellows 17 and ᶜ who say, We piped unto you, and ye did not dance; we wailed, and ye did not weep. {ª mourn}. ᶜ 33 For John the Baptist is come {ª came} neither eating nor drinking, {ᶜ eating no bread nor drinking wine;} and ye {ª they} say, He hath a demon. 19 The Son of man came {ᶜ is come} eating and drinking; and ye {ª they} say, Behold, a gluttonous man and a winebibber, a friend of publicans and sinners! And wisdom is justified ᶜ of all her children. ª by her works.** [Oriental market-places were open squares where men transacted business and where children held their sports. Jesus here pictures two groups of little ones, one of which wishes to play, the other of which is sullen and intractable. The mirthful group first seeks to play a wedding game. They pipe and dance, but the sullen group sits unmoved. Not disheartened by failure to succeed, the mirthful ones try their hand again and hope for better luck by playing funeral. But this also fails, causing them to lift up their voices in questioning remonstrance. Singular enough, the authorities are about equally divided as to what parties this picture represents. Some say that the dancers and mourners are the Jewish rulers, and that Jesus and John refused to comply with their wishes. The grammatical construction rather favors this view, if we say that " the men of this generation " are " like children who call." But such grammatical constructions are not reliable in interpreting Oriental imagery. Jesus means that the men of this generation are like the *entire picture* presented and does not intend that they shall be taken as the subjects of the leading verbs of the sentence. A parallel instance will be found in Matt. xiii. 24–43. In the twenty-fourth verse Jesus says, " The kingdom of heaven is likened unto a man who sowed good seed," but in the thirty-seventh verse he says, " He that soweth the good seed is the Son of man," thus making the kingdom of heaven like the entire parabolic picture, and not the mere subject of its leading verb. Others say that John came mourning and Jesus came piping, and that the Jews were satisfied with neither. This was the older view, and had not expositors been confused by the grammatical difficulties above mentioned it would never have been questioned. For the context favors it, and the whole trend of Scripture demands it. It was God in his messengers—his prophets and his Son—who came to set the world right. It was these messengers who took the initiative and who demanded the changes. It was the people who sulked and refused to comply with the divine overtures. The whole tenor of Christ's teaching—the parables of the suppers, etc.—represents the Jews as being invited and refusing the invitation. It was John and Jesus who preached repentance, but there is no instance where any called on them to repent. Jerusalem never wept over an intractable Jesus, but Jesus wept over the people of Jerusalem because they " would not." Jesus and John each besought the people to prepare for the kingdom of God, but the people sneered at one as too strict and at the other as too lenient, and would be won by neither. To justify them in rejecting God's counsel they asserted that John's conduct was demoniacal and that that of Jesus was criminal, thus slandering each. But the lives or works of Jesus and John were both directed by the wisdom of God, and all those who were truly wise towards God—children of wisdom (see Luke, verse 29, above)—justified or approved of God's course in sending such messengers. We should observe that with all the cares of his great mission upon him, the great heart of our Lord took note of the sports of the children.]

20 Then began he to upbraid the cities wherein most of his mighty works were done, because they repented not. [That is to say, those cities which were especially favored. It does not mean that more miracles were worked in them than in *all* the other cities; but that more were done in *each* one of these than in *any* other.] **21 Woe** [rather "Alas for thee!" an exclamation of pity more than of anger] **unto thee, Chorazin! woe unto thee, Bethsaida! for if the mighty works had been done in Tyre and Sidon which were done in you, they would have repented long ago in sackcloth and ashes.** [Jerome says that Chorazin was two, and Eusebius (probably through the error of his transcriber) says it was twelve miles from Capernaum. Its site is identified by the Exploration Fund with the modern Kerazeh, at the northwest end of the lake, two miles from Tell Hum (Capernaum). Its site is marked by extensive ruins, including the foundations of a synagogue, columns, and walls of buildings. Bethsaida was probably a suburb of Capernaum. We have no record of a miracle wrought at Chorazin, nor of one wrought at Bethsaida either, unless the miracles wrought at Simon's house—see Sec. xxxii, page 170 —were in Bethsaida. Tyre and Sidon were neighboring Phœnician cities on the Mediterranean coast and were noted for their luxury and impiety. This comparison between the pagan cities on the seacoast and the Galilean cities by the lake no doubt sounded strange to Jesus' disciples, but in the years which followed Tyre and Sidon received the gospel

(Acts xxi. 3; xxvii. 3), and Tyre became a Christian city, while Tiberias, just south of Capernaum, became the seat of Jewish Talmudism. Sackcloth was a coarse fabric woven of goat's or camel's hair, and was worn by those who mourned. It was called sackcloth because, being strong and durable, it was used for making the large sacks in which rough articles were carried on the backs of camels. Such sacks are still so used. Ashes were put upon the head and face as additional symbols of grief. Jesus here uses these symbolic words to indicate that these cities would have repented thoroughly. **22 But I say unto you, it shall be more tolerable for Tyre and Sidon in the day of judgment, than for you. 23 And thou, Capernaum, shalt thou be exalted unto heaven? thou shalt go down unto Hades: for if the mighty works had been done in Sodom which were done in thee, it would have remained until this day. 24 But I say unto you that it shall be more tolerable for the land of Sodom in the day of judgment than for thee.** [Several great truths are taught in this paragraph. We note the following: 1. Every hearer of the gospel is left either much more blessed or much more wretched. 2. That the miracles which Jesus wrought were calculated to lead men to repentance, for they demonstrated his authority to demand that man should repent. 3. That even among those who stand condemned at the judgment there is a difference, and that it shall be more tolerable for some than for others. 4. That God takes account of our opportunities when he comes to measure our guiltiness (Matt. v. 21, 22; x. 15; Luke xii. 47, 48; John ix. 41; xv. 22-24; Rom. ii. 12). Capernaum was the most favored spot on earth, for Jesus made it his home. He therefore speaks of it figuratively as being exalted to heaven. Hades means the abode of the dead. It stands in figurative contrast to heaven and indicates that Capernaum shall be brought to utter ruin. Though Jesus was not displeased with the walls and houses, but with those who dwelt in them, yet the uncertain sites of these cities are marked only by ruins, and present to the traveler who searches among

rank weeds for their weather-worn stones the tokens of God's
displeasure against the people who once dwelt there. In less
than thirty years these three cities were destroyed. Sin destroys
cities and nations, and permanent temporal prosperity depends
upon righteousness. The history of the destruction of Sodom
in the time of Abraham is well known. As it was one of (see
Num. xiii. 22) the oldest cities of any great importance in
Palestine, this reference to its remaining is the more striking,
showing that its destruction did not come from the mere
operation of natural law, but as a divine punishment meted
upon it for its sins—a punishment which might have been
avoided by repentance (Jonah iii. 10). There is hope for the
greatest sinner if Sodom might thus escape.] **25 At that
season** [while these thoughts of judgment were in his mind]
Jesus answered [replying to the thoughts raised by this
discouraging situation—this rejection] **and said, I thank
thee, O Father, Lord of heaven and earth, that thou
didst hide these things from the wise and understanding** [the selfish and shrewd; the scribes and Pharisees, wise
in their own conceit—John ix, 40, 41], **and didst reveal
them unto babes** [the pure and childlike; the apostles and
their fellows who were free from prejudice and bigoted pre-
possession. God hid and revealed solely by his method of
presenting the truth in Christ Jesus. The proud despised
him, but the humble received him] **: 26 yea, Father, for so
it was well-pleasing in thy sight.** [This is a reiteration
of the sentiment just uttered. It means "I thank thee that
it pleases thee to do thus." The Son expresses holy acqui-
escence and adoring satisfaction in the doings of Him who, as
Lord of heaven and earth, had right to dispose of all things as
it pleased him.] **27 All things have been delivered unto
me of my Father** [John iii. 35. All things necessary to
the full execution of his office as Lord of the kingdom were
entrusted to Jesus, but for the present only potentially. The
actual investiture of authority did not take place until the
glorification of Jesus (Matt. xxviii. 18; Col. i. 16–19; Heb.
i. 8). The authority thus delivered shall be eventually returned

again—I. Cor. xv. 28] : **and no one knoweth the Son, save the Father; neither doth any know the Father, save the Son, and he to whomsoever the Son willeth to reveal** *him.* [Here again are many important truths taught: 1. While we may have personal knowledge of Jesus we can not know him completely. His nature is inscrutable. And yet, in direct opposition to our Lord's explicit assertion, creeds have been formed, defining the metaphysical nature of Christ, and enforcing their distinctions on the subject which Jesus expressly declares that no man understands, as necessary conditions of church membership in this world, and of salvation in the world to come. It would be difficult to find a more audacious and presumptuous violation of the words of Jesus than the Athanasian Creed, with its thrice repeated curses against those who do not receive its doctrines " (*Morison*). 2. We can have no correct knowledge of God except through revelation. 3. Jesus begins the revelation of the Father in this world, and completes it in the world to come. 4. By this exclusive claim as to the knowledge of the Father, Jesus asserts his own divinity. 5. Christ's exalted power comes by reason of his exalted being.] **28 Come unto me, all ye that labor and are heavy laden, and I will give you rest. 29 Take my yoke upon you, and learn of me; for I am meek and lowly in heart: and ye shall find rest unto your souls. 30 For my yoke is easy and my burden is light.** [The preceding remarks are prefatory to this invitation. The dominion which Jesus exercises, the nature which he possesses, and the knowledge which he can impart justify him in inviting men to come to him. The labor and the rest here spoken of are primarily those which affect souls. That is, the labor and the heavy burden which sin imposes, and the rest which follows the forgiveness of that sin. Incidentally, however, physical burdens are also made lighter by coming to Jesus, because the soul is made stronger to bear them. The meekness and lowliness of Jesus lend confidence to those whom he invites that no grievous exactions will be made of them. " Taking the yoke," is a symbolic expression.

It means "Submit to me and become my disciple," for the yoke is symbolic of the condition of servitude—see Jer. xxvi. 13; Isa. ix. 4; Acts xv. 10; Gal. v. 1; I. Tim. vi. 1.]

XLVI.

JESUS' FEET ANOINTED IN THE HOUSE OF A PHARISEE.

(Galilee.)

ᶜ LUKE VII. 36–50.

ᶜ **36 And one of the Pharisees desired him that he would eat with him.** [We learn from verse 40 that the Pharisee's name was Simon. Because the feast at Bethany was given in the house of Simon the leper, and because Jesus was anointed there also, some have been led to think that Luke is here describing that supper. See Matt. xxvi. 6–13; Mark xiv. 3–9; John xii. 1–8. But Simon the leper was not Simon the Pharisee. The name Simon was one of the most common among the Jewish people. It was the Greek form of the Hebrew Simeon. The New Testament mentions nine and Josephus twenty Simons, and there must have been thousands of them in Palestine at that time. The anointing at Bethany was therefore a different occasion from this.] **And he entered into the Pharisee's house, and sat down to meat.** [Literally, reclined at meat. The old Jewish method of eating was to sit cross-legged on the floor or on a divan, but the Persians, Greeks and Romans reclined on couches, and the Jews, after the exile, borrowed this custom. We are not told in plain terms why the Pharisee invited Jesus to eat with him. The envy and cunning which characterized his sect leads us to be, perhaps, unduly suspicious that his motives were evil. The narrative, however, shows that his motives were somewhat akin to those of Nicodemus. He wished to investigate the character and claims of Jesus, and was influenced more by curiosity than by hostility—for

all Pharisees were not equally bitter (John vii. 45–52). But
he desired to avoid in any way compromising himself, so he
invited Jesus to his house, but carefully omitted all the ordinary courtesies and attentions which would have been paid to
an honored guest. Jesus accepted the invitation, for it was his
custom to dine both with Pharisees and publicans, that he might
reach all classes.] **37 And behold, a woman who was
in the city, a sinner; and when she knew that he was
sitting at meat in the Pharisee's house, she brought
an alabaster cruse of ointment** [Because the definite
article " the " is used before the word "city," Meyer says it
was Capernaum, and because Nain is the last city mentioned,
Wieseler says it was Nain, but it is not certain what city it
was. Older commentators say it was Magdala, because they
hold the unwarranted mediæval tradition that the sinner was
Mary Magdalene; *i. e.,* Mary of Magdala. No trustworthy
source has ever been found for this tradition, and there are
two good reasons for saying that this was not Mary Magdalene:
1. She is introduced soon after (Luke viii. 2) as a new character and also as a woman of wealth and consequence. See
also Matt. xxvii. 55. 2. Jesus had delivered her from the
possession of seven demons. But there is no connection
between sin and demon-possession. The former implies a
disregard for the accepted rules of religious conduct, while
the latter implies no sinfulness at all. This affliction was never
spoken of as a reproach, but only as a misfortune. The cruse
which she brought with her was called " an alabaster."
Orientals are very fond of ointments and use them upon the
face and hair with profusion. They were scented with sweet-
smelling vegetable essence, especially that extracted from the
myrtle. Originally the small vases, jars or broad-mouthed
bottles, in which this ointment was stored, were carved from
alabaster, a variety of gypsum, white, semi-transparent and
costly. Afterwards other material was used, but the name
" alabaster " was still applied to such cruses. That used by
Mary of Bethany was probably the highest grade ointment in
the highest priced cruse (John xii. 3). The context here

leaves us free to suppose that both the cruse and the unguent were of a cheaper kind], **38 and standing behind at his feet, weeping, she began to wet his feet with her tears, and wiped them with the hair of her head, and kissed his feet, and anointed them with the ointment.** [To see this scene we must picture Jesus stretched upon the couch and reclining on his left elbow. The woman stood at the foot of the couch behind his feet. His feet were bare; for every guest on entering left his sandals outside the door. The woman, feeling strongly the contrast between the sinlessness of Jesus and her own stained life, could not control her emotions. " The tears," says Brom, "poured down in a flood upon his naked feet, as she bent down to kiss them; and deeming them rather fouled than washed by this, she hastened to wipe them off with the only towel she had, the long tresses of her own hair. She thus placed her glory at his feet (I. Cor. xi. 15), after which she put the ointment upon them.] **39 Now when the Pharisee that had bidden him saw it, he spake within himself, saying, This man, if he were a prophet, would have perceived who and what manner of woman this is that toucheth him, that she is a sinner.** [Public opinion said that Jesus was a prophet (Luke vii. 16), and Simon, from the Pharisee's standpoint, feared that it might be so; and therefore no doubt felt great satisfaction in obtaining this evidence which he accepted as disproving the claims of Jesus. He judged that if Jesus had been a prophet he would have both known and repelled this woman. He would have known her because discerning of spirits was part of the prophetic office—especially the Messianic office (Isa. xi. 2–4; I. Kings xiv. 6; II. Kings i. 1–3; v. 26). Comp. John ii. 25. He would have repelled her because, according to the Pharisaic tradition, her very touch would have rendered him unclean. The Pharisees, according to later Jewish writings, forbade women to stand nearer to them than four cubits, despite the warning of God (Isa. xv. 5). Thus reasoning, Simon concluded that Jesus had neither the knowledge nor the holiness which are essential to a prophet. His narrow mind did not grasp the truth that it was as wonderful condescension for Christ to sit at his board as it was to permit this sinner to touch him.] **40 And Jesus answering said unto him, Simon, I have somewhat to say unto thee. And he saith, Teacher, say on.** [Jesus heard Simon's thoughts and answered them. Simon called Jesus "Teacher," little thinking how fully Jesus was about to vindicate the justice of the title thus given him in compliment.] **41 A certain lender had two debtors: the one owed five hundred shillings and the other fifty.** [The denarius or shilling was a silver coin issued by Rome which contained nearly seventeen cents' worth of that precious metal. The two debts, therefore, represented respectively about seventy-five dollars, and seven dollars and fifty cents. But at that time a denarius was a day's wages for a laboring man (Matt. xx. 2, 4, 12, 13), so that the debt is properly translated into our language as if one owed five hundred and the other fifty days of labor.] **42 When they had not *wherewith* to pay, he forgave them both.** [In this brief parable God represents the lender, and the woman the big and Simon the little debtor. Simon was (in his own estimation) ten times better off than the woman; yet they were each in an equally hopeless case—having nothing with which to pay; and each in an equally favored case— being offered God's free forgiveness. Forgiveness is expressed in the past tense in the parable, but merely as part of the drapery and not for the purpose of declaring Simon's forgiveness. It indicates no more than that Jesus was equally *willing* to forgive both. But the Pharisee did not seek his forgiveness, and the absence of all love in him proved that he did not have it.] **Which of them therefore will love him most?** [It was Jesus' custom to thus often draw his verdicts from the very lips of the parties concerned—Luke x. 36, 37; Matt. xxi. 40, 41.] **43 Simon answered and said, He, I suppose, to whom he forgave the most.** [The "suppose" of Simon betrays a touch of supercilious irony, showing that the Pharisee thought the question very trivial.] **And he said unto him, Thou hast rightly judged.** [Simon's words were more

than an answer. They were a judgment as well. Like
Nathan with David (II. Sam. xii. 1-7), Jesus had concealed
Simon's conduct under the vestments of a parable, and had
thus led him to unwittingly pronounce sentence against himself.
Simon, the little debtor, was a debtor still; having no acts of
gratitude to plead in evidence of his acquittal. From this
point the words of Jesus take up the conduct of Simon which
we should here picture to ourselves. "We must imagine the
guests arriving; Simon receiving them with all courtesy, and
embracing each in turn; slaves ready to wash the dust of the
road from their sandaled feet, and to pour sweet olive oil over
their heads to soften the parched skin. See Gen. xviii. 4; xix.
2; xxiv. 32; Ruth iii. 3; I. Sam. xxv. 41; Ps. xxiii. 5; cxli.
5; Eccl. ix. 8; Dan. x. 3; Amos vi. 6; Matt. vi. 17. But
there is one of the guests not thus treated. He is but a poor
man, invited as an act of condescending patronage. No kiss
is offered him; no slave waits upon him; of course a mechanic
can not need the luxuries others are accustomed to!"]
**44 And turning to the woman, he said unto Simon,
Seest thou this woman?** [Simon is to look upon the
woman as the one whose actions stood in contrast to his own.]
**I entered into thy house, thou gavest me no water for
my feet: but she hath wetted my feet with her tears,
and wiped them with her hair.** [Jesus here draws the first
contrast. In the East, where the feet without stockings are
placed in sandals instead of shoes, water becomes essential to
one who would enter a house. The guest should be afforded
an opportunity to wash the dust from his feet, not only for
comfort's sake, but also that he might not be humiliated by
soiling the carpets on which he walked, and the cushions on
which he reclined. This trifling courtesy Simon had omitted;
but the woman had amply supplied his omission, bathing the
Lord's feet in what Bengel well calls "the most priceless of
waters."] **45 Thou gavest me no kiss: but she, since
the time I came in, hath not ceased to kiss my feet.**
[We have here the second contrast. A kiss was the ordinary
salutation of respect in the East. Sometimes the hand was

kissed, and sometimes the cheek (II. Sam. xv. 5, 19–29; Matt. xxvi. 49; Acts xx. 37; Rom. xvi. 16). We may note incidentally that we have no record of a kiss upon the cheek of Jesus save that given by Judas. The woman had graced the feet of Jesus with those honors which Simon had withheld from his cheek.] **46 My head with oil thou didst not anoint: but she hath anointed my feet with ointment.** [Anointing was a mark of honor which was usually bestowed upon distinguished guests (Amos vi. 6; Ps. xxiii. 5; cxli. 5). To anoint the feet was regarded as extreme luxury (Pliny *H. N.* xiii. 4). In this third case Jesus makes a double comparison. To anoint the feet was more honored than to anoint the head, and the ointment was a more valuable and worthy offering than the mere oil which ordinary courtesy would have proffered.] **47 Wherefore I say unto thee, Her sins, which are many, are forgiven; for she loved much: but to whom little is forgiven, *the same* loveth little.** [Her love was the result, and not the cause, of her forgiveness. Our sins are not forgiven because we love God, but we love God because they are forgiven (I. John iv. 19). Such is the inference of the parable, and such the teaching of the entire New Testament. We search the story in vain for any token of love on the part of Simon.] **48 And he said unto her, Thy sins are forgiven. 49 And they that sat at meat with him began to say within themselves, Who is this that even forgiveth sins?** [They were naturally surprised at this marvelous assumption of authority, but in the light of what had just been said they did not dare to express themselves. Ignorance of Christ's person and office caused them to thus question him. It is easy to stumble in the dark. We are not told that Simon joined in asking this question.] **50 And he said unto the woman, Thy faith hath saved thee; go in peace.** [Jesus did not rebuke his questioners, because the process of forgiveness was something which could not be demonstrated to their comprehension, and hence their error could not be made clear. Jesus attributed her forgiveness to her faith. " Peace " was the Hebrew and " grace " was the Greek salutation. It is here used as a farewell, and means "Go in the abiding enjoyment of peace." Several valuable lessons are taught by this incident. 1. That the sense of guiltiness may differ in degree, but nevertheless the absolute inability of man to atone for sin is common to all. 2. As sin is against Christ, to Christ belongs the right and power to forgive it. 3. That conventional respectability, having no such flagrant and open sins as are condemned by the public, is not conscious of its awful need. 4. That those who have wandered far enough to have felt the world's censure realize most fully the goodness of God in pardoning them, and hence are moved to greater expressions of gratitude than are given by the self-righteous. But we must not draw the conclusion that sin produces love, or that much sin produces much love, and that therefore much sin is a good thing. The blessing which we seek is not proportioned to the quantity of the sins; but is proportioned to the quantity of *sinful sense* which we feel. We all have sin enough to destroy our souls, but many of us fail to love God as we should, through an insufficient sense of our sinfulness.

XLVII.

FURTHER JOURNEYING ABOUT GALILEE.

ᶜLUKE VIII. 1-3.

ᶜ1 And it came to pass soon afterwards [*i. e.*, soon after his visit to the Pharisee], that he went about through cities and villages [thus making a thorough circuit of the region of Galilee], preaching and bringing the good tidings of the kingdom of God [John had preached repentance as a preparation for the kingdom; but Jesus now appears to have preached the kingdom itself, which was indeed to bring good tidings—Rom. xiv. 17], and with him the twelve [We here get a glimpse of the tireless activities of the ministry of Christ. Journeying from place to place, he was constantly preaching the gospel publicly to the people, and as ceaselessly instructing his disciples privately. The twelve

were now serving an apprenticeship in that work on which he
would soon send them forth alone. From this time forth we
can hardly look upon Capernaum as the home of Jesus. From
now to the end of his ministry his life was a wandering journey, and he and his apostles were sustained by the offerings
of friends. The circuit of Galilee here mentioned is peculiar
to Luke], **2 and certain women who had been healed
of evil spirits and infirmities: Mary that was called
Magdalene, from whom seven demons had gone out**
[what a change of service, from demoniac bondage to the
freedom of Christ!], **3 and Joanna the wife of Chuzas
Herod's steward, and Susanna, and many others, who
ministered unto them of their substance.** [As to the
vile slanders with which commentators have stained the good
name of Mary Magdalene, see p. 291. For further mention of
her, see John xix. 25; Mark xv. 47; xvi. 19; John xx. 11–18.
Mary's name indicates that she was a native of Magdala
(Hebrew, Migdol; *i. e.*, watch-tower). Of all the towns which
dotted the shores of Galilee in Christ's day, but this and Tiberias
remain. It is on the west shore of the lake, at the southeast
corner of the plain of Gennesaret, and is to-day a small collec-
tion of mud hovels. It still bears the name *el-Mejdel*, which
it probably received from the adjoining watch-tower that
guarded the entrance to the plain, the ruins of which are still
to be seen. We should note that Mary Magdalene is not
classed with restored profligates, but with those who were
healed of infirmities. Joanna is mentioned again at Luke
xxiv. 10; but of Susanna there is no other record, this being
enough to immortalize her. Of Chuzas we know nothing
more than what is stated here. There are two Greek words
for steward, *epitropos* and *oikonomos*. The first may be translated administrator, superintendent or governor. It conveys
the impression of an officer of high rank. The Jewish rabbis
called Obadiah the *epitropos* of Ahab. This was the office
held by Chuzas, and it is translated *treasurer* in the Arabic
version. The second word may be translated housekeeper,
or domestic manager. It was an office usually held by some

trusted slave as a reward for his fidelity. Chuzas was no doubt
a man of means and influence. As there was no order of
nobility in Galilee, and as such an officer might be nevertheless
styled a nobleman, this Chuzas was very likely the nobleman of John iv. 27. If so, the second miracle at Cana explains the devotion of Joanna to Jesus. Herod's capital was at
Sephoris, on an elevated tableland not far from Capernaum.
The ministration of these women shows the poverty of Christ
and his apostles, and explains how they were able to give
themselves so unremittingly to the work. Some of the apostles
also may have had means enough to contribute somewhat to
the support of the company, but in any event the support was
meager enough, for Jesus was among the poorest of earth (Luke
ix. 58 ; Matt. xvii. 24 ; II. Cor. viii. 9). His reaping of carnal
things was as scanty as his sowing of spiritual things was
abundant (I. Cor. ix. 11). We should note how Jesus began
to remove the fetters of custom which bound women, and to
bring about a condition of universal freedom (Gal. iii. 28).

XLVIII.

BLASPHEMOUS ACCUSATIONS OF THE JEWS.

(Galilee.)

^a MATT. XII. 22–37 ; ^b MARK III. 19–30 ; ^c LUKE XI. 14–23.

^b **19 And he cometh into a house.** [Whose house is not
stated.] **20 And the multitude cometh together again**
[as on a previous occasion—Mark ii. 1], **so that they could
not so much as eat bread.** [They could not sit down to a
regular meal. A wonderful picture of the intense importunity
of the people and the corresponding eagerness of Jesus, who
was as willing to do as they were to have done.] **21 And
when his friends heard it, they went out to lay hold
on him : for they said, He is beside himself.** [These
friends were his brothers and his mother, as appears from
Mark iii. 31, 32. They probably came from Nazareth. To
understand their feelings we must bear in mind their want of

faith. See John vii. 3–9. They regarded Jesus as carried away by his religious enthusiasm (Acts xxvi. 24; II. Cor. v. 13), and thought that he acted with reckless regard for his personal safety. They foresaw the conflict with the military authorities and the religious leaders into which the present course of Jesus was leading, and were satisfied that the case called for their interference. Despite her knowledge as to Jesus, Mary sympathized with her sons in this movement, and feared for the safety of Jesus.] ᵃ**22 Then was brought unto him one possessed with a demon, blind and dumb:** {ᶜ**14 And he was casting out a demon** *that was* **dumb.**} ᵃ**and he healed him, insomuch that** ᶜ**it came to pass, when the demon was gone out,** ᵃ**the dumb man spake and saw.** [The man was brought because he could not come alone. While Luke does not mention the blindness, the similarity of the narratives makes it most likely that he is describing the same circumstances which are recounted in Matthew and Mark, so we have combined the three accounts.] **23 And all the multitudes** ᶜ**marvelled.** ᵃ**were amazed, and said, Can this be the son of David?** [It was a time for amazement, for Jesus had performed a triple if not a quadruple miracle, restoring liberty, hearing and sight, and granting the power of speech. It wakened the hope that Jesus might be the Messiah, the son of David, but their hope is expressed in the most cautious manner, not only being stated as a question, but as a question which expects a negative answer. The question, however, was well calculated to arouse the envious opposition of the Pharisees.] ᶜ**15 But some of them said** [that is, some of the multitude. Who these "some" were is revealed by Matthew and Mark, thus:], ᵃ**24 But when the Pharisees heard it, they** ᵇ**22 and the scribes that came down from Jerusalem said,** ᵃ**This man doth not cast out demons, but by Beelzebub the prince of the demons.** ᵇ**He hath Beelzebub, and, By the prince of the demons casteth he out the demons.** [Beelzebub is a corruption of Baalzebub, *the god of the fly*. There was a tendency among the heathen to name their gods after the pests which they were supposed to avert. Thus Zeus was called *Apomuios* (Averter of flies), and Apollo, *Ipuktonos* (Slayer of vermin). How Beelzebub became identified with Satan in the Jewish mind is not known. In opposing the influence of Jesus and corrupting the public mind, these Pharisees showed a cunning worthy of the cultivated atmosphere, the seat of learning whence they came. Being unable to deny that a miracle was wrought (for Celsus in the second century is the first recorded person who had the temerity to do such a thing), they sought to so explain it as to reverse its potency, making it an evidence of diabolical rather than divine power. Their explanation was cleverly plausible, for there were at least two powers by which demons might be cast out, and, as both were invisible, it might appear impossible to decide whether it was done in this instance by the power of God or of Satan. It was an explanation very difficult to disprove, and Jesus himself considered it worthy of the very thorough reply which follows.]   ᶜ **16 And others, trying** *him*, **sought of him a sign from heaven.** [These probably felt that the criticisms of the Pharisees were unjust, and wished that Jesus might put them to silence by showing some great sign, such as the pillar of cloud which sanctioned the guidance of Moses, or the descending fire which vindicated Elijah.]   ᵇ **23 And he called them unto him** [thus singling out his accusers], ᵃ **25 And** {ᶜ**17 But**} ᵃ **knowing their thoughts he said unto them,** ᵇ **in parables** [We shall find that Jesus later replied to those who sought a sign. He here answers his accusers in a fourfold argument. First argument:], **How can Satan cast out Satan?** ᵃ **Every kingdom divided against itself is brought to desolation ; and every city or house** [family] **divided against itself shall not stand:** ᵇ **24 And if a kingdom be divided against itself, that kingdom cannot stand.** ᶜ **A house** *divided* **against a house falleth.** {ᵇ **25 And if a house be divided against itself, that house will not be able to stand.**} ᵃ **26 and if Satan casteth out Satan, he is divided against himself;** ᶜ **18 And if Satan also is**

divided against himself [a] **how then shall his kingdom stand?** [b] **26 And if Satan hath risen up against himself, and is divided, he cannot stand, but hath an end.** [c] **because ye say that I cast out demons by Beelzebub.** [The explanation given by the Pharisees represented Satan as divided against himself; robbing himself of his greatest achievement; namely, his triumph over the souls and bodies of men. Jesus argues, not that Satan *could* not do this, but that he *would* not, and that therefore the explanation which supposes him to do it is absurd. We should note that Jesus here definitely recognizes two important truths: 1. That the powers of evil are organized into a kingdom with a head (Matt. xiii. 29; xxv. 41; Mark iv. 15; Luke xxii. 31); 2. That division tends to destruction. His argument therefore " constitutes an incidental but strong argument against sectarianism. See I. Cor. i. 13" *(Abbott)*. Second argument:] **19 And if I by Beelzebub cast out demons, by whom do your sons cast them out? Therefore shall they be your judges.** [The sons of the Pharisees were not their children, but their disciples (II. Kings ii. 3; Acts xix. 13, 14). Josephus mentions these exorcists (Ant. viii. 2, 5, and Wars vii. 6, 3), and there is abundant mention of them in later rabbinical books. Our Lord's reference to them was merely for the purpose of presenting an *argumentum ad hominem*, and in no way implies that they exercised any *real* power over the demons; nor could they have done so in any marked degree, else the similar work of Christ would not have created such an astonishment. The argument therefore is this, I have already shown you that it is against *reason* that Satan cast out Satan; I now show you that it is against *experience*. The only instances of dispossession which you can cite are those of your own disciples. Do they act by the power of Satan? They therefore shall be your judges as to whether you have spoken rightly in saying that Satan casts out Satan. Third argument:] **20 But if I by the finger {[a] by the Spirit} of God cast out demons, then is the kingdom of God come upon you.** [The finger of God signifies the power of God (Ex. viii.

19; xxxi. 18; Ps. viii. 3). Jesus exercised this power in unison with the Spirit of God. Jesus here draws a conclusion from the two arguments presented. Since he does not cast out by Satan, he must cast out by the power of God, and therefore his actions demonstrated the potential arrival of the kingdom of God. The occasional accidental deliverance of exorcists might be evidence of the flow and ebb of a spiritual battle, but the steady, daily conquests of Christ over the powers of evil presented to the people the triumphant progress of an invading kingdom. It is an argument against the idea that there was a collusion between Christ and Satan. Fourth argument:] **ᶜ21 When the strong *man* fully armed guardeth his own court, his goods are in peace: 22 but when a stronger than he shall come upon him, and overcome him, he taketh from him his whole armor wherein he trusted, and divideth his spoils. ᵇ27 But no one can {ᵃ29 Or how can one} enter into the house of the strong *man*, and spoil his goods, except he first bind the strong *man?* and then will he spoil his house.** [Satan is the strong man, his house the body of the demoniac, and his goods the evil spirit within the man. Jesus had entered his house, and robbed him of his goods; and this proved that, instead of being in league with Satan, he had overpowered Satan. Thus Jesus put to shame the Pharisees, and caused the divinity of his miracle to stand out in clearer light than ever. The power of Jesus to dispossess the demon was one of his most convincing credentials, and its meaning now stood forth in its true light.] **30 He that is not with me is against me; and he that gathereth not with me scattereth.** [Jesus here addresses the bystanders. In the spiritual conflict between Jesus and Satan, neutrality is impossible. There are only two kingdoms, and every soul is either in one or the other, for there is no third. Hence one who fought Satan in the name of Christ was for Christ (Luke ix. 50). In the figure of gathering and scattering, the people are compared to a flock of sheep which Jesus would gather into the fold, but which Satan and all who aid him (such as the Pharisees) would scatter and destroy.] ᵇ 28 Verily ᵃ 31 Therefore I say unto you, Every sin and blasphemy {ᵇ all their sins} shall be forgiven unto the sons of men, and their blasphemies wherewith soever they shall blaspheme [Jesus here explains to the Pharisees the awful meaning of their enmity. Blasphemy is any kind of injurious speech. It is the worst form of sin, as we see by this passage. This does not declare that every man shall be forgiven all his sins, but that all kinds of sins committed by various men shall be forgiven. The forgiveness is universal as to the sin, not as to the men]: ᵃ but the blasphemy against the Spirit shall not be forgiven. 32 And whosoever shall speak a word against the Son of man, it shall be forgiven him; but whosoever shall speak {ᵇ blaspheme} against the Holy Spirit hath never forgiveness, but is guilty of an eternal sin: ᵃ it shall not be forgiven him, neither in this world, nor in that which is to come. ᵇ 30 because they said, He hath an unclean spirit. [Blasphemy against the Son may be a temporary sin, for the one who commits it may be subsequently convinced of his error by the testimony of the Holy Spirit and become a believer (I. Tim. i. 13). But blasphemy against the Holy Spirit is in its nature an eternal sin, for if one rejects the evidence given by the Holy Spirit and ascribes it to Satan, he rejects the only evidence upon which faith can be based; and without faith there is no forgiveness. The difference in the two sins is therefore in no way due to any difference in the Son and Spirit *as to their degrees of sanctity or holiness*. The punishment is naturally eternal because the sin is perpetual. The mention of the two worlds is " just an extended way of saying 'never' " *(Morison)*. Some assert that the Jews would not know what Jesus meant by the Holy Spirit, but the point is not well taken. See Ex. xxxi. 3; Num. xi. 26; I. Sam. x. 10; xix. 20; Ps. cxxxvii. 7; cxliii. 10; Isa. xlviii. 16; Ezek. xi. 24. We see by Mark's statement that blasphemy against the Spirit consisted in saying that Jesus had an unclean spirit, that his works were due to Satanic influence, and hence wrought to accomplish Satanic ends. We can not call God Satan, nor the Holy Spirit a demon, until our state of sin has passed beyond all hope of reform. One can not confound the two kingdoms of good and evil unless he does so maliciously and willfully.] a 33 **Either make the tree good, and its fruit good; or make the tree corrupt, and its fruit corrupt: for the tree is known by its fruit.** [The meaning and connection are: "Be honest for once; represent the tree as good, and its fruit as good, or the tree as evil, and its fruit as evil; either say that I am evil, and that my works are evil, or, if you admit that my works are good, admit that I am good also and not in league with Beelzebub"—*Carr.*] 34 **Ye offspring of vipers, how can ye, being evil, speak good things? for out of the abundance of the heart the mouth speaketh.** [Realizing the hopelessness of this attempt to get an honest judgment out of dishonest hearts, Jesus plainly informs them as to the condition of their hearts. Their very souls were full of poison like vipers. Their sin lay not in their words, but in a condition of heart which made such words possible. The heart being as it was, the words could not be otherwise. "What is in the well will be in the bucket"—*Trapp.*] 35 **The good man out of his good treasure bringeth forth good things: and the evil man out of his evil treasure bringeth forth evil things.** [We have here a summary of the contrast given in the two preceding verses. The good heart of Jesus brought forth its goodness, as the evil hearts of the Pharisees brought forth their evil.] 36 **And I say unto you, that every idle word that men shall speak, they shall give account thereof in the day of judgment. 37 For by thy words thou shalt be justified, and by thy words thou shalt be condemned.** [It may have seemed to some that Jesus denounced too severely a saying which the Pharisees had hastily and lightly uttered. But it is the word inconsiderately spoken which betrays the true state of the heart. The hypocrite can talk like an angel if he be put on notice that his words are heard. Jesus here makes *words* the basis of the judgment of God. Elsewhere we find it is *works* (Rom. ii. 6; II. Cor. v. 10), and **again we** find it is faith (Rom. iii. 28). There is no confusion here. The judgment in its finality must be based upon our *character.* Our faith forms our character, and our words and works are indices by which we may determine what manner of character it is.]

XLIX.

SIGN SEEKERS, AND THE ENTHUSIAST REPROVED.

(Galilee on the same day as last section.)

ᵃMATT. XII. 38–50; ᶜLUKE XI. 24–36.

ᶜ**29 And when the multitudes were gathering to-gether unto him,** ᵃ**38 Then certain of the scribes and Pharisees answered him, saying, Teacher, we would see a sign from thee.** [Having been severely rebuked by Jesus, it is likely that the scribes and Pharisees asked for a sign that they might appear to the multitude more fair-minded and open to conviction than Jesus had represented them to be. Jesus had just wrought a miracle, so that their request shows that they wanted something different. We learn from Mark (Mark viii. 11) that they wanted a sign, not coming from him, but from heaven, such a sign as other prophets and leaders had given (Ex. ix. 22–24; xvi. 4; Josh. x. 12; I. Sam. vii. 9, 10; xii. 16–18; I. Kings xviii. 36–38; II. Kings i. 10; Isa. xxxviii. 8). "In Jewish superstition it was held that demons and false gods could give signs *on earth*, but only the true God signs *from heaven*" (*Alford*). The request was the renewal of the one which had assailed him at the beginning of his ministry (John ii. 18), and re-echoed the wilderness temptation to advance himself by vulgar display rather than by the power of a life of divine holiness.] **39 But he answered and said unto them, {ᶜhe began to say,} This genera-tion is an evil generation: it seeketh after a sign;** ᵃ**An evil and adulterous generation seeketh after a sign**

[While the Jews of that generation could well be accused literally of adultery, Jesus here evidently uses it in its symbolic sense as used by the prophets. They represented Israel as being married to God and as being untrue to him—Ex. xxxiv. 15; Jer. iii. 14, 20]; **and there shall no sign be given to it** c**but the sign of Jonah.** a**the prophet** [They did not accept miracles of healing as a sign, and only one other kind of sign was given; namely, that of Jonah. Jonah was shown to be a true prophet of God, and Nineveh received him as such because he was rescued from the fish's belly, and Jesus was declared to be the Son of God by the resurrection from the dead—Rom. i. 4]: **40 for as Jonah was three days and three nights in the belly of the whale; so shall the Son of man be three days and three nights in the heart of the earth.** [Jesus was one full day, two full nights and parts of two other days in the grave. But, as the Jews reckoned a part of a day as a whole day when it occurred at the beginning or end of a series, he was correctly spoken of as being three days in the grave. The Jews had three phrases, viz.: "on the third day," "after three days," and "three days and three nights," which all meant the same thing; that is, three days, two of which might be fractional days. With them three full days and nights would be counted as four days unless the count began at sundown, the exact beginning of a day (Acts x. 1-30). For instances of Jewish computation of days see Gen. xiii. 17, 18; I. Kings xii. 5, 12; Esth. iv. 16; v. 1; Matt. xxvii. 63, 64. The Greek word here translated whale is "sea monster." It is called in Jonah "a great fish" (Jonah i. 17). Because of the supposed smallness of the whale's throat, many think it was the white shark, which is still plentiful in the Mediterranean, and which sometimes measures sixty feet in length, and is large enough to swallow a man whole. But it is now a well-established fact that whales can swallow a man, and there are many instances of such swallowing on record. The expression "heart of the earth" does not mean its center. The Jews used the word "heart" to denote the interior of anything (Ezek. xxviii. 2). The phrase is here used as one which would emphatically indicate the actual burial of Christ.] ᶜ30 **For even as Jonah became a sign unto the Ninevites, so shall also the Son of man be to this generation.** [Nineveh was the capital of the Assyrian Empire, situated on the Tigris River, and in its day the greatest city of the world. Jonah's preservation was a sign from heaven, because wrought without human instrumentality. The resurrection of Christ was such a sign to the Jews, but rejecting it they continued to seek other signs—I. Cor. i. 22.] ᵃ41 **The men of Nineveh shall stand up in the judgment with this generation, and shall condemn it: for they repented at the preaching of Jonah; and behold, a greater than Jonah is here.** [Literally, repented into the preaching of Jonah. The meaning is that they repented so that they followed the course of life which the preaching prescribed. The phrase, "stand up," refers to the Jewish and Roman custom which required the witness to stand up while testifying in a criminal case. The idea here is that the Ninevites, having improved the lesser advantage or privilege, would condemn the Jews for having neglected the greater. Nineveh's privilege may be counted thus: a sign-accredited prophet preaching without accompanying miracles, and a forty-day period for repentance. In contrast to this the Jewish privileges ran thus: the sign-accredited Son of God preaching, accompanied by miracles, in which many apostles and evangelists participated, a forty-years period in which to repent.] **42 The queen of the south shall rise up in the judgment with this generation, and shall condemn it: {ᶜwith the men of this generation, and shall condemn them:} for she came from the ends of the earth** [a Hebraism, indicating a great distance] **to hear the wisdom of Solomon; and behold, a greater than Solomon is here.** [The queen of Sheba is supposed to have been queen of Sabæa, or Arabia Felix, which lies at the southern part of the peninsula between the Red Sea and the Persian Gulf. But Josephus says she was from Ethiopia in Africa. Her testimony will also be based on compared privileges, which stand thus: notwithstanding the dangers and inconveniences of travel, she came a great distance to be taught of Solomon, but the Jews rejected the teaching of the Son of God, though he brought it to them. The teaching of Solomon related largely to this world, but Christ taught as to the world to come.] ᵃ43 **But the unclean spirit, when he is gone out of the man, passeth through waterless places** [places which are as cheerless to him as deserts are to man], **seeking rest, and findeth it not.** [Rest is the desire of every creature. Jesus here gives us a graphic description of utter wretchedness.] ᶜ**and finding none,** ᵃ44 **Then he saith, I will return into** {ᶜ**turn back unto**} **my house** [he still claimed it as his property] **whence I came out. 25 And when he is come, he findeth it** ᵃ**empty, swept, and garnished.** [It was empty, having no indwelling Spirit, swept of all righteous impressions and good influences, and garnished with things inviting to an evil spirit.] **45 Then** [seeing this inviting condition] **goeth he, and taketh with himself seven other spirits** [to reinforce and entrench himself] **more evil than himself** [while all demons are wicked they are not equally so], **and they enter in and dwell there** [take up their permanent abode there]: **and the last state of that man becometh worse than the first. Even so shall it be unto this evil generation.** [In the application of this parable, we should bear in mind that it tells of *two* states or conditions experienced by *one* man, and the comparison is between these two states or conditions and not between the condition of the man and other men. Such being the parable, the application of it is plain, for Jesus says, "Even so shall it be unto this evil generation." We are not therefore to compare that generation with any previous one, as many do; for such would be contrary to the terms of the parable. It is simply an assertion that the last state of that generation would be worse than the first. The reference is to the continually increasing wickedness of the Jews, which culminated in the dreadful scenes which preceded the destruction of Jerusalem. They were now like a man with one evil spirit; they would then be like a man with seven more demons added, each of which was worse than the original occupant.] ᶜ **27 And it came to pass, as he said these things, a certain woman out of the multitude lifted up her voice, and said unto him, Blessed is the womb that bare thee, and the breasts which thou didst suck.** [This woman is the first on record to fulfill Mary's prediction (Luke i. 48). It is the only passage in the New Testament which even suggests the idolatry of Mariolatry, but it was far enough from it, being merely a womanly way of expressing admiration for the son by pronouncing blessings upon the mother who was so fortunate as to bear him.] **28 But he said, Yea rather, blessed are they that hear the word of God, and keep it.** [Jesus does not deny the fact that Mary was blessed, but corrects any false idea with regard to her by pointing to the higher honor of being a disciple which was attainable by every one. Mary's blessing as a disciple was greater than her blessing as a mother; her moral and spiritual relation to Jesus was more precious than her maternal. Mary's blessings came through believing God's word (Luke i. 45). To know Christ after the Spirit is more blessed than to know him after the flesh—II. Cor. v. 15, 16; John xvi. 7.] **33 No man, when he hath lighted a lamp, putteth it in a cellar, neither under the bushel, but on the stand, that they which enter in may see the light. 34 The lamp of thy body is thine eye: when thine eye is single, thy whole body also is full of light; but when it is evil, thy body also is full of darkness. 35 Look therefore whether the light that is in thee be not darkness. 36 If therefore thy whole body be full of light, having no part dark, it shall be wholly full of light, as when the lamp with its bright shining doth give thee light.** [This passage given in a slightly varying form is found in the Sermon on the Mount. See page 256. It is here addressed to the Pharisees, and reproves them for not using the light (his miracles) which was given them. If they had had an eye single to goodness, Christ's light would have enlightened their souls. But their eye was double; they desired wonders and spectacular signs.]

L.

CHRIST'S TEACHING AS TO HIS MOTHER AND BRETHREN.

(Galilee, same day as last lesson.)

ᵃ MATT. XII. 46–50; ᵇ MARK III. 31–35; ᶜ LUKE VIII. 19–21.

ᵃ **46 While he was yet speaking to the multitudes, behold, his mother and his brethren stood without, seeking to speak to him.** [Jesus was in a house, probably at Capernaum—Mark iii. 19; Matt. xiii. 1.] ᶜ **19 and there came {ᵇ come} ᶜ to him his mother and ᵇ his brethren; ᶜ and they could not come at him for the crowd. ᵇ and, standing without, they sent unto him, calling him. 32 And the multitude was sitting about him** [We learn at Mark iii. 21, that they came to lay hold on him because they thought that he was beside himself. It was for this reason that they came in a body, for their numbers would enable them to control him. Jesus had four brethren (Matt. xiii. 55). Finding him teaching with the crowd about him, they passed the word in to him that they wished to see him outside. To attempt to lay hold of him in the midst of his disciples would have been rashly inexpedient. The fact that they came with Mary establishes the strong presumption that they were the children of Mary and Joseph, and hence the literal brethren of our Lord. In thus seeking to take Jesus away from his enemies Mary yielded to a natural maternal impulse which even the revelations accorded to her did not quiet. The brethren, too, acted naturally, for they were unbelieving—John vii. 5]; ᵃ **47 And one said {ᵇ they say} unto him, ᶜ 20 And it was told him, ᵃ Behold, thy mother and thy brethren ᵇ seek for thee. ᶜ stand without, desiring to see thee ᵃ seeking to speak to thee.**

[This message was at once an interruption and an interference. It assumed that their business with him was more urgent than his business with the people. It merited our Lord's rebuke, even if it had not behind it the even greater presumption of an attempt to lay hold on him.] **48 But he answered** { b **33 And he answereth**} a **and said unto him that told him,** b **and saith,** { c **and said unto them,**} a **Who is my mother? and who are my brethren?** b **34 And looking round on them that sat round about him,** a **he stretched forth his hand towards his disciples, and said,** { b **saith,**} a **Behold, my mother and my brethren!** c **My mother and my brethren are these that hear the word of God and do it.** b **35 For whosoever shall do the will of God,** a **my Father who is in heaven, he** { b **the same**} **is my brother, and sister, and mother.** [In this answer Jesus shows that he brooks no interference on the score of earthly relationships, and explodes the idea of his subserviency to his mother. To all who now call on the "Mother of God," as Mary is blasphemously styled, Jesus answers, as he did to the Jews, "Who is my mother?" Jesus was then in the full course of his ministry as Messiah, and as such he recognized only spiritual relationships. By doing the will of God we become his spiritual children, and thus we become related to Christ. Jesus admits three human relationships—"brother, sister, mother," but omits the paternal relationship, since he had no Father, save God. It is remarkable that in the only two instances in which Mary figures in the ministry of Jesus prior to his crucifixion, she stands forth reproved by him. This fact not only rebukes those who worship her, but especially corrects the doctrine of her immaculate conception.]

LI.

DINING WITH A PHARISEE, JESUS DENOUNCES THAT SECT.

ᶜ LUKE XI. 37-54.

ᶜ **37 Now as he spake, a Pharisee asketh him to dine with him: and he went in, and sat down to meat.** [The repast to which Jesus was invited was a morning meal, usually eaten between ten and eleven o'clock. The principal meal of the day was eaten in the evening. Jesus dined with all classes, with publicans and Pharisees, with friends and enemies.] **38 And when the Pharisee saw it, he marvelled that he had not first bathed himself before dinner.** [The Pharisee marveled at this because the tradition of the elders required them to wash their hands before eating, and, if they had been in a crowd where their bodies might have been touched by some unclean person, they washed their whole bodies. It was a custom which ministered to pride and self-righteousness.] **39 And the Lord said unto him** [Our Lord's speech is unsparingly denunciatory. To some it seems strange that Jesus spoke thus in a house where he was an invited guest. But our Lord never suspended the solemn work of reproof out of mere compliment. He was governed by higher laws than those of conventional politeness], **Now ye the Pharisees cleanse the outside of the cup and of the platter; but your inward part is full of extortion and wickedness. 40 Ye foolish ones, did not he that made the outside make the inside also?** [Since God made both the inner and the outer, a true reverence for him requires that both parts be alike kept clean.] **41 But give for alms those things which are within; and behold, all things are clean unto you.** [That is, give your inner life, your love, mercy, compassion, etc., to the blessing of mankind, and then your inner purity will make you proof against outward defilement—Matt. xv. 11; Tit. i. 15; Rom. xiv. 14.] **42 But woe unto you Pharisees! for ye tithe mint and rue and every herb, and pass over justice and the love of God: but these ought ye to have done, and not to leave the other undone.** [The Pharisees in paying the tenth part, or tithe, to God were so exact that they offered the tenth part of the seed even of the spearmint, rue and other small garden herbs, and many contended that the very stalks of these plants should also be tithed. Jesus commends this care about little things, but nevertheless rebukes the Pharisees because they were as careless about big things, such as justice, and the love of God, as they were careful about herb seed. Rue was a small shrub about two feet high, and is said to have been used to flavor wine, and for medicinal purposes.] **43 Woe unto you Pharisees! for ye love the chief seats in the synagogues, and the salutations in the marketplaces.** [They were vainglorious, loving the honors and attentions given by men (John v. 44). They loved on week days to be saluted in the marketplace, and on the Sabbath to sit in the semi-circular row of seats which were back of the lectern, or desk of the reader, and which faced the congregation.] **44 Woe unto you! for ye are as the tombs which appear not, and the men that walk over *them* know it not.** [According to the Mosaic law, any one who touched a grave was rendered unclean (Num. xix. 16). That they might not touch graves and be made unclean without knowing it, the Jews whitewashed their graves and tombs once a year. But Jesus likens a Pharisee to graves which defiled men unawares. Their hypocrisy concealed their true nature, so that men were injured and corrupted by their influence without being aware of it. Jesus pronounces three woes upon the Pharisees for three sins, viz.: 1. Hypocrisy, shown in pretending to be very careful when they were really extremely careless; 2. Vainglory; 3. Corruption of the public morals.] **45 And one of the lawyers answering saith unto him, Teacher, in saying this thou reproachest us also.** [Lightfoot supposes that a

scribe was one who copied the law of Moses, while a .awye.
expounded the oral law or traditions of the elders. But it is
more likely that the terms were used interchangeably. They
leaned to the Pharisee party, and hence this one felt the
rebuke which Jesus addressed to that party. The scribe
intimated that Jesus had spoken hastily, and his speech is a suggestion to Jesus to correct or modify his unguarded words. But
Jesus made no mistakes and spoke no hasty words.] **46 And
he said, Woe unto you lawyers also! for ye load men
with burdens grievous to be borne, and ye yourselves
touch not the burdens with one of your fingers.** [We
have seen in the traditions with regard to the Sabbath how
these Jewish lawyers multiplied the burdens which Moses had
placed upon the people. They were careful to lay these
burdens upon others, but equally careful not to bear them
themselves—no, not even to keep the law of Moses itself—
Matt. xxiii. 2, 3.] **47 Woe unto you! for ye build the
tombs of the prophets, and your fathers killed them.
48 So ye are witnesses and consent unto the works of
your fathers: for they killed them, and ye build *their
tombs.*** [Tombs were usually dug in the rock in the sides of
hills or cliffs. To build them therefore was to decorate or
ornament the entrance. Though their act in building the
sepulchres was a seeming honor to the prophets, God did not
accept it as such. A prophet is only truly honored when his
message is received and obeyed. The lawyers were not in
fellowship with the prophets, but with those who murdered the
prophets: hence the Saviour pictures the whole transaction
from the killing of the prophets to the building of their sepulchres as *one act* in which all concurred, and of which all were
guilty. Abbott gives the words a figurative meaning, thus:
your fathers slew the prophets by violence, and you bury them
by false teaching.] **49 Therefore also said the wisdom
of God, I will send unto them prophets and apostles;
and *some* of them they shall kill and persecute; 50 that
the blood of all the prophets, which was shed from the
foundation of the world, may be required of this gen-**

eration [The phrase " wisdom of God " has been very puzzling, for the words spoken by Jesus are not found in any Old Testament book. Among the explanations the best is that which represents Jesus as quoting the trend or tenor of several prophecies such as II. Chron. xxiv. 19–22; xxxvi. 14–16; Prov. i. 20–33. It may, however, be possible that Jesus is here publishing a new decree or conclusion of God, for the words specifically concerned that present generation. If so, Jesus assents to the decree of the Father by calling it the wisdom of God, and the language is kindred to that at Matt. xi. 25, 26]; **51 from the blood of Abel unto the blood of Zachariah, who perished between the altar and the sanctuary: yea, I say unto you, it shall be required of this generation.** [Abel is accounted a prophet because his form of sacrifice prefigured that of Christ. His murder is described at Gen. iv. 1–8, the first historical book of the Bible, while that of Zachariah is described at II. Chron. xxiv. 20–22, the last historical book of the Old Testament. From the record of one, therefore, to the record of the other embraces the entire catalogue of the Old Testament martyrs. Tradition assigns one of the four great sepulchral monuments at the foot of Olivet to Zachariah. That generation sanctioned all the sins of the past and went beyond them to the crucifixion of the Son of God. The best comment on this passage is the parable at Luke xx. 9–16. God made that generation the focus of the world's light and privilege, but the men of that time made it the focus of the world's wickedness and punishment. This punishment began about thirty-seven years later in the war with Rome, which lasted five years and culminated in the destruction of Jerusalem.] **52 Woe unto you lawyers! for ye took away the key of knowledge: ye entered not in yourselves, and them that were entering in ye hindered.** [A true knowledge of the Scriptures was a key which opened the door to the glories of Christ and his kingdom. This the lawyers had taken away by teaching not the contents of the book, but the rubbish and trifles of tradition. They did not open the door for themselves, and by their pretentious interference they confused others in their efforts to open it.] **53 And when he was come out from thence, the scribes and the Pharisees began to press upon** *him* **vehemently, and to provoke him to speak of many things ; 54 laying wait for him, to catch something out of his mouth.** [They plied him with many questions, hoping that they could irritate him into making a hot or hasty answer. For methods used to entrap Jesus see Matt. xxii.]

LII.

CONCERNING HYPOCRISY, WORLDLY ANXIETY, WATCHFULNESS AND HIS APPROACH-ING PASSION.

(Galilee.)

ᶜ LUKE XII. 1–59.

ᶜ**1 In the meantime** [that is, while these things were occurring in the Pharisee's house], **when the many thousands of the multitude were gathered together, insomuch that they trod one upon another** [in their eagerness to get near enough to Jesus to see and hear], **he began to say unto his disciples first of all** [that is, as the first or most appropriate lesson], **Beware ye of the leaven of the Pharisees, which is hypocrisy.** [This admonition is the key to the understanding of the principal part of the sermon which follows. The spirit of Phariseeism was one which sought the honor of men, and feared men rather than God. It was a spirit which yielded to public opinion, and, though seemingly very religious, was really devoid of all true loyalty to God. There were trials and persecutions ahead of Christ's followers in which no Pharisaic spirit could survive. The spirit of hypocrisy works in two ways: it causes the bad man to hide his badness for fear of the good man, and the good man to hide his goodness for fear of the bad man. It is this latter operation against which Jesus warns, and the folly of which he shows.] **2 But there is nothing covered up, that shall not be revealed; and hid, that shall not be known. 3 Wherefore whatsoever ye have said in the darkness shall be heard in the light; and what ye have spoken in the ear in the inner chambers shall be proclaimed upon the housetops.** [Many fearing the storm of persecution which was soon to come upon the disciples would attempt to conceal their faith, but the attempt would be vain, for one could not even trust his own family (verses 51–53) to keep silent about what was said even in the inner chambers of the home. Bold speech would be best. The flat tops of Eastern houses were places from whence public proclamations were made.] **4 And I say unto you my friends, Be not afraid of them that kill the body, and after that have no more that they can do. 5 But I will warn you whom ye shall fear: Fear him, who after he hath killed hath power to cast into hell; yea, I say unto you, Fear him.** [It would be a time of fear, but the fear of God must dominate the fear of man. The fear of God should cause them to speak out, though the fear of man bade them be silent—Acts iv. 18–21.] **6 Are not five sparrows sold for two pence? and not one of them is forgotten in the sight of God.** [The Roman *as* here rendered penny, was worth about four-fifths of a cent. Two sparrows were sold for a penny (Matt. x. 29). For two pennies an extra one was thrown into the bargain, yet even it, so valueless, was not forgotten of God.] **7 But the very hairs of your head are all numbered. Fear not: ye are of more value than many sparrows.** [These words assured them that whatever they might be called upon to undergo they would be at all times the objects of God's special care and providence.] **8 And I say unto you, Every one who shall confess me before men, him shall the Son of man also confess before the angels of God: 9 but he that denieth me in the presence of men shall be denied in the presence of the angels of God.** [These words were intended to strengthen those who loved honor oĭ feared disgrace. If the disgrace of being cast out of the synagogue tempted them to deny Christ, or the honors given by their fellow-men seemed too precious to be sacrificed for Christ's sake, they were to remember that the confession or denial of Jesus involved eternal honor or disgrace in the presence of the entire angelic host.] **10 And every one who shall speak a word against the Son of man, it shall be forgiven him : but unto him that blasphemeth against the Holy Spirit it shall not be forgiven.** [Persecution would urge them to blasphemy (Acts xxvi. 11). In his hour of trial a disciple must remember the tender compassion of the Master against whom he is urged to speak, and the extreme danger of passing beyond the line of forgiveness in his blasphemy. For blasphemy against the Holy Spirit see page 303.] **11 And when they bring you before the synagogues, and the rulers, and the authorities, be not anxious how or what ye shall answer, or what ye shall say : 12 for the Holy Spirit shall teach you in that very hour what ye ought to say.** [The captive disciple planning his defense would be tempted to attempt hypocritical concealment or dissimulation. To prevent this, Jesus admonishes his hearers to rely upon the Holy Spirit for their utterance at such times. How fully such reliance was honored is shown in the apology of Stephen before the Sanhedrin, in Peter's defense before that tribunal, and in Paul's justifications of his course, both before Felix and Agrippa.] **13 And one out of the multitude said unto him, Teacher, bid my brother divide the inheritance with me.** [Some one in the multitude, seeing the authority and justice of Jesus, thought it would be wise to appeal to him to assist him in getting his brother to rightly divide the inheritance.] **14 But he said unto him, Man, who made me a judge or a divider over you?** [Jesus laid down the general laws of justice and generosity, but he did not enforce these laws by any other power than love (John xiv.). If love toward Jesus did not move this brother to rightly divide the inheritance, the injured party must look to the state and not to Jesus for assistance.] **15 And he said unto them, Take heed, and keep yourselves from all covetousness** [Jesus made the incident the text for an admonition. Covetousness made one brother say "Divide," and the other one say "No, I will not;" so Jesus warned against covetousness]**: for a man's life consisteth not in the abundance of the things which he possesseth.** [A man's goods are no part of his life, and so they can not preserve it. It is lengthened or shortened, blessed or cursed, at the decree of God. Covetousness is an inordinate desire for earthly possession. Though all ages have committed it, it is the besetting sin of our time. A clear view of the limitations of the power of property quenches covetousness; and Jesus gives such a view in the following parable.] **16 And he spake a parable unto them, saying, The ground of a certain rich man brought forth plentifully** [This man's sin was not theft or extortion. His wealth came to him honestly as a blessing from God]**: 17 and he reasoned within himself, saying** [his words betray his sin—his covetousness], **What shall I do, because I have not where to bestow my fruits? 18 And he said, This will I do: I will pull down my barns, and build greater; and there will I bestow all my grain and my goods. 19 And I will say to my soul, Soul, thou hast much goods** [Prov. i. 32] **laid up for many years; take thine ease, eat, drink, be merry.** [It is a short speech, but it reveals character. The man's selfishness is shown in that he uses the pronoun "I" six times and says nothing of any one else. His covetous love of possessions is shown by the word "my," which he uses five times. Compare his words with those of Nabal at I. Sam. xxv. 11. In his speech to his soul he asserts his trust that his "abundance" is a guarantee of "many years" of happy life; but it did not guarantee one day. The Eastern barn is a pit or dry cistern built underground with an opening at the top. These the man proposed to enlarge by pulling down the walls or sides and extending them.] **20 But God said unto him** [God may be represented as saying what he does]**, Thou foolish**

one [His folly was shown in several ways: 1. He hoarded his goods instead of using them for his fellow-men; 2. Ownership of goods deceived him into thinking that he owned time also; 3. He thought to satisfy the hunger of the soul with the food of the body; 4. In commanding his soul in such a way as to show that he forgot that God could command it also], **this night is thy soul required of thee** [the man said " many years," but God said " this night "] **; and the things which thou hast prepared, whose shall they be?** [Death generally scatters possessions broadcast (Ps. xxxix. 6; Eccl. ii. 18, 19). For an echo of these words see Jas. iv. 13-15.] **21 So is he that layeth up treasure for himself, and is not rich toward God.** [To be rich in character is to be rich toward God. But we may be rich towards him by making him the repository of our hopes and expectations.] **22 And he said unto his disciples, Therefore I say unto you, Be not anxious for *your* life, what ye shall eat; nor yet for your body, what ye shall put on. 23 For the life is more than the food, and the body than the raiment. 24 Consider the ravens, that they sow not, neither reap; which have no store-chamber nor barn; and God feedeth them: of how much more value are ye than the birds! 25 And which of you by being anxious can add a cubit unto the measure of his life? 26 If then ye are not able to do even that which is least, why are ye anxious concerning the rest?** [If you can not add one little moment to your life, why should you be anxious about the smaller concerns of property?] **27 Consider the lilies, how they grow: they toil not, neither do they spin; yet I say unto you, Even Solomon in all his glory** [Song iii. 6-11] **was not arrayed like one of these. 28 But if God doth so clothe the grass in the field, which to-day is, and to-morrow is cast into the oven; how much more *shall he clothe* you, O ye of little faith? 29 And seek not ye what ye shall eat, and what ye shall drink, neither be ye of doubtful mind. 30 For all these things do the nations of the**

**world seek after: but your Father knoweth that ye
have need of these things. 31 Yet seek ye his kingdom, and these things shall be added unto you.** [This
passage from verses 22 to 31 (excepting verse 26) will be
found almost verbatim at Matt. vi. 25–33. See pages 257–259.]
**32 Fear not, little flock; for it is your Father's good
pleasure to give you the kingdom. 33 Sell that which
ye have, and give alms; make for yourselves purses
which wax not old, a treasure in the heavens that
faileth not, where no thief draweth near, neither moth
destroyeth. 34 For where your treasure is, there will
your heart be also.** [The latter part of this section will be
found at Matt. vi. 20, 21. See page 256. The original for
the words "little flock" is a double diminutive, indicating at
once the extreme smallness of the band of disciples, and also
the tenderness of the Master for them. They are exhorted
to remember that they are the heirs of the heavenly kingdom,
and that their treasures are there. They are told to sell their
possessions and give, because their official position in the
kingdom at that time required it. Compare I. Cor. vii. 36.
Purses were bound to the girdles, so that if a hole wore in
them, their contents were lost. Having discussed the folly of
amassing and trusting in earthly riches, and the wisdom of
trusting in God and amassing heavenly riches, Jesus passes to
a new theme; viz.: a watchful service and its rewards. He
may have been led into this theme by some interruption, such
as that given at verse 13 or that at verse 41, or it may have
been suggested to him by his own words about the little flock
and the kingdom. The kingdom was not to come in a day,
and the little flock must watch patiently and serve faithfully
before his coming—Luke xix. 11–13.] **35 Let your loins
be girded about** [the long Oriental robe had to be lifted up
and girded at the waist before the feet could step quickly—
I. Kings xviii. 46], **and your lamps burning** [this was
needful; for Oriental weddings take place at night]; **36 and
be ye yourselves like unto men looking for their lord,
when he shall return from the marriage feast; that,**

when he cometh and knocketh, they may straightway
open unto him. [Thus honoring him by a speedy welcome.]
37 Blessed are those servants, whom the Lord when
he cometh shall find watching: verily I say unto you,
that he shall gird himself, and make them sit down
to meat, and shall come and serve them. [The apostles
had a foretaste of this honor on the evening of the last Passover—John xiii. 4, 5.] 38 And if he shall come in the
second watch, and if in the third, and find *them* so,
blessed are those *servants*. [Originally the Jews had
three watches (Lam. ii. 19; Judg. vii. 19; I. Sam. xi. 11);
but, following the Romans, they now had four watches. The
second and third watches lasted from 9 P. M. to 3 A. M.
The first watch is not mentioned because the marriage took
place in it, and the fourth is not mentioned because in the
latter part of it the day dawns and the virtue of watching was
over—Luke xiii. 35.] 39 But know this, that if the
master of the house had known in what hour the
thief was coming, he would have watched, and not
left his house to be broken through. [Jesus here illustrates watchfulness by a second figure. To some the coming
of Jesus will be like that of a master whom they have served
more or less faithfully. To others his coming will seem like
that of a plunderer who comes in suddenly and deprives them
of all that they have. The Oriental houses were mostly made
of mud or sun-dried bricks. Hence it was so easy to dig a hole
in the wall that the thief preferred to enter that way rather than
to break open the door.] 40 Be ye also ready: for in an
hour that ye think not the Son of man cometh. [These
words of warning confront every generation.] 41 And
Peter said, Lord, speakest thou this parable unto us,
or even unto all? [Peter wished to know if the exhortation to watchfulness applied merely to the apostles or to all
who heard.] 42 And the Lord said, Who then is the
faithful and wise steward, whom his lord shall set over
his household, to give them their portion of food in
due season? 43 Blessed is that servant, whom his

lord when he cometh shall find so doing. [The answer of Jesus shows that he especially addressed the disciples, for a steward is distinct from the household. On him the whole burden and care of the domestic establishment rested. Thus Jesus showed that he meant the disciples, yet did not exclude any who heard from profiting by his discourse. Fidelity is the first requisite in a steward, and wisdom is the second. All Christians are stewards; preachers, elders, Sunday-school teachers, etc., are stewards of place and office. Rich men, fathers, etc., are stewards of influence and possession.] **44 Of a truth I say unto you, that he will set him over all that he hath.** [As Pharaoh exalted Joseph—Gen. xxxix. 4; xliv. 39–41.] **45 But if that servant shall say in his heart, My lord delayeth his coming; and shall begin to beat the menservants and the maidservants, and to eat and drink, and to be drunken; 46 the lord of that servant shall come in a day when he expecteth not, and in an hour when he knoweth not, and shall cut him asunder, and appoint his portion with the unfaithful.** [Cutting asunder was a punishment prevalent among ancient nations (II. Sam. xii. 31; Dan. ii. 5; Heb. xi. 37). The definite punishment is part of the drapery of the parable, and does not necessarily indicate the exact nature of the punishment which will be inflicted upon the wicked.] **47 And that servant, who knew his lord's will, and made not ready, nor did according to his will, shall be beaten with many** *stripes;* **48 but he that knew not, and did things worthy of stripes, shall be beaten with few** *stripes.* **And to whomsoever much is given, of him shall much be required: and to whom they commit much, of him will they ask the more.** [The greater the powers and opportunities entrusted to us, the larger the service which the Lord requires of us. Ignorance does not entirely excuse, for we are stewards, and it is a steward's duty to know his master's will. There is a guilt of ignorance as well as of transgression. The parable pointed to those who listened with delight to Jesus, but were careless about knowing his meaning. With the forty-ninth verse Jesus passes on to set forth the severe tests to which the fidelity and vigilance of his disciples would be subjected in the times upon which they were about to enter.] **49 I came to cast fire** [a firebrand] **upon the earth; and what do I desire, if it is already kindled?** [The object of Christ's coming was to rouse men to spiritual conflict, to kindle a fire in the public mind which would purify the better part and destroy the worse. But the burning of this fire would excite men and stir up their passions and cause division and discord. The opposition of the Pharisees showed that this fire was already kindled. What therefore was left for Jesus to desire? His work as a teacher was practically accomplished. But there remained for him yet his duty as priest to offer himself as a sacrifice for the world's sin. To this work, therefore, he glances briefly forward.] **50 But I have a baptism to be baptized with** [a flood of suffering; that is, the agony of the cross]; **and how am I straitened** [distressed, perplexed] **till it be accomplished!** [The language here is broken, indicating the strong emotion of him who spoke it.] **51 Think ye that I am come to give peace in the earth? I tell you, Nay; but rather division: 52 for there shall be from henceforth five in one house divided, three against two, and two against three. 53 They shall be divided, father against son, and son against father; mother against daughter, and daughter against her mother; mother in law against her daughter in law, and daughter in law against her mother in law.** [Jesus here shows the hard plight of the disciple. If he were the young son he would find his father against him, and if he were the aged father he would be persecuted by the boy whom he had raised. Jesus came to conquer a peace by overcoming evil with good; a conflict in which the good must always suffer. His warfare was not, as the people supposed, a struggle against the heathen, but against the evil within them and around them. So long as evil abounded, these unhappy divisions would last.] **54 And he said to the** multitudes also, **When ye see a cloud rising in the west** [the Mediterranean Sea lay in that quarter, and rains came from thence], **straightway ye say, There cometh a shower; and so it cometh to pass. 55 And when** *ye see* **a south wind blowing, ye say, There will be a scorching heat; and it cometh to pass.** [The south winds of Palestine blew from the equator, crossed the intervening deserts and wildernesses, and were distressingly hot.] **56 Ye hypocrites, ye know how to interpret the face of the earth and the heaven; but how is it that ye know not how to interpret this time?** [That is, this period which began with the ministry of John the Baptist. They could at once read the signs of nature so as to declare what kind of storm was coming. But with the political storm arising out of conflict with Rome impending over them, and with the spiritual storm which the teaching of Christ was bringing upon them, about to burst, they stood still in ignorant indifference, and made no provision for the times of trouble.] **57 And why even of yourselves judge ye not what is right?** [They had the warnings of both John and Jesus about matters and conditions which were so plain that they should have been able to see them without any warning whatever.] **58 For as thou art going with thine adversary before the magistrate, on the way give diligence to be quit of him; lest haply he drag thee unto the judge, and the judge shall deliver thee to the officer, and the officer shall cast thee into prison. 59 I say unto thee, Thou shalt by no means come out thence, till thou have paid the very last mite.** [A mite *(lepton)* was their smallest coin, being worth about two mills. For notes on this passage see Matt. v. 25, 26, pages 239, 240. The passage here is an appeal to the people to avert the coming disasters. The Jewish rulers looked upon Jesus as their adversary. Accepting their valuation of him, Jesus counseled them to come to terms with him before it is too late.]

LIII.

REPENTANCE ENJOINED. PARABLE OF THE BARREN FIG-TREE.

ᶜLUKE XIII. 1–9.

ᶜ **1 Now there were some present at that very season** [At the time when he preached about the signs of the times, etc. This phrase, however, is rather indefinite—Matt. xii. 1; xiv. 1] **who told him of the Galilaeans, whose blood Pilate had mingled with their sacrifices. 2 And he answered and said unto them, Think ye that these Galilaeans were sinners above all the Galilaeans, be-cause they have suffered these things? 3 I tell you, Nay: but, except ye repent, ye shall all in like manner perish.** [While Jesus spoke, certain ones came to him bear-ing the news of a barbaric act of sacrilegious cruelty committed by Pilate. It may have been told to Jesus by enemies who hoped to ensnare him by drawing from him a criticism of Pilate. But it seems more likely that it was told to him as a sample of the corruption and iniquity of the times. The Jews ascribed extraordinary misfortunes to extraordinary crimi-nality. Sacrifice was intended to cleanse guilt. How hopeless, therefore, must their guilt be who were punished at the very time when they should have been cleansed! But the Jews erred in thus interpreting the event. Quantity of individual sin can not safely be inferred from the measure of individual misfortune. It was true that the Galilæans suffered because of sin, for all suffering is the result of sin. But it was not true that the suffering was a punishment for unusual sinfulness. Our suffering is often due to the general sin of humanity—the sin of the whole associate body of which we are a part. His-tory, of course, says nothing of Pilate's act here mentioned. Pilate's rule was marked by cruelty towards the Jews, and con-tempt for their religious views and rites. **4 Or those eigh-teen, upon whom the tower in Siloam fell, and killed** them, think ye that they were offenders above all the men that dwell in Jerusalem? 5 I tell you, Nay: but, except ye repent, ye shall all likewise perish. [Of this instance, also, there is no other historic mention. It, too, was a small incident among the accidents of the day. The pool of Siloam lies near the southeast corner of Jerusalem, at the entrance of the Tyropæan valley which runs up between Mt. Zion and Moriah. The modern village of Siloam probably did not exist at that time. What tower this was is not known. As the city wall ran through the district of the fountain, it may possibly have been one of the turrets of that wall. This instance presents a striking contrast to the slaughter of which they had told him, for it was, 1. Inflicted upon the inhabitants of Jerusalem; and 2. It came upon them as an act of God. And Jesus therefore concludes that all shall likewise perish, he pronounces upon the entire people—Jew and Galilæan alike—a punishment made certain by the decree of God. It is significant that the Jewish people did, as a nation, perish and lie buried under the falling walls of their cities, and the debris of their temple, palaces and houses. But the word "likewise" is not to be pressed to cover this fact.] **6 And he spake this parable** [this parable is closely connected with verses 3 and 5 of this chapter, and verses 58 and 59 of the preceding chapter] ; **A certain man had a fig tree planted in his vineyard; and he came seeking fruit thereon, and found none. 7 And he said unto the vinedresser, Behold, these three years I come seeking fruit on this fig tree, and find none : cut it down ; why doth it also cumber the ground?** [It cumbered the ground by occupying ground which the vines should have had, and by interfering with their light by its shade, which is very dense.] **8 And he answering saith unto him, Lord, let it alone this year also, till I shall dig about it, and dung it** [a common method of treating the fig-tree to induce fruitfulness] **: 9 and if it bear fruit thenceforth, *well;* but if not, thou shalt cut it down.** [In this parable Jesus likened his hearers to a fig-tree planted in a choice place—a vineyard, the odd corners of which are still used as advantageous spots for fig-trees. There is no emphasis on the number three, and no allusion to the national history of the Jews, as some suppose. It simply means that a fig-tree's failure to bear for three years would justify its being cut down. Those to whom Jesus spoke had been called to repentance by the preaching both of John and of Jesus, and had had ample time and opportunity to bring forth the fruits of repentance, and deserved to be destroyed; but they would still be allowed further opportunity.

LIV.

THE FIRST GREAT GROUP OF PARABLES.

(Beside the Sea of Galilee.)

Subdivision A.

INTRODUCTION.

ᵃ MATT. XIII. 1-3; ᵇ MARK IV. 1, 2; ᶜ LUKE VIII. 4.

ᵃ 1 **On that day went Jesus out of the house** [It is possible that Matthew here refers to the house mentioned at Mark iii. 19. If so, the events in Sections XLVIII.–LVI. all occurred on the same day. There are several indications in the gospel narratives that this is so], **and sat by the sea side.** ᵇ 1 **And again he began to teach by the sea side.** [By the Sea of Galilee.] **And there is {ᵃwere} ᵇgathered unto him a very great multitude, {ᵃgreat multitudes,} ᵇso that he entered into a boat, and sat in the sea** [that the multitudes might be better able to see and hear him]; **and all the multitude ᵃstood on the beach. ᵇwere by the sea on the land. ᶜ4 And when a great multitude came together, and they of every city resorted unto him, he spake by a parable: ᵃ3 And he spake to them many things ᵇ2 And he taught them many things in parables, and said unto them in his teaching, {ᵃsaying,} ᵇ3 Hearken** [While Jesus had used parables before, this appears to have been the first occasion when he strung them together so as to form a discourse. Parable comes from the Greek *paraballo,* which means "I place beside" in order to compare. It is the placing of a narrative describing an ordinary event in natural life beside an implied spiritual narrative for the purpose of illustrating the spiritual.]

Subdivision B.

PARABLE OF THE SOWER.

[a] MATT. XIII. 3–23; [b] MARK IV. 3–25; [c] LUKE VIII. 5–18.

[a] **Behold,** [c] **5 The sower went forth to sow his seed** [Orientals live in cities and towns. Isolated farmhouses are practically unknown. A farmer may therefore live several miles from his field, in which case he literally "goes forth" to it]: [b] **4 and it came to pass, as he sowed, some** *seed* {[a]*seeds*} **fell by the way side,** [c] **and it was trodden under foot, and the birds of the heaven** [a] **came and** [c] **devoured it.** {[a]**them:**} [Palestine is an unfenced land, and the roads or paths lead through the fields. They are usually trodden hard by centuries of use. Grain falling on them could not take root. Its fate was either to be crushed by some foot, or to be carried off by some bird.] [b] **5 And other** {[a]**others**} **fell upon the rocky places,** [c] **on the rock;** [b] **where it** {[a]**they**} [b] **had not much earth; and straightway it** {[a]**they**} [b] **sprang up, because it** {[a]**they**} [b] **had no deepness of earth: 6 and when the sun was risen, it was** {[a]**they were**} [b] **scorched; and because it** {[a]**they**} [b] **had no root, it** {[a]**they**} **withered away.** [c] **and as soon as it grew, it withered away, because it had no moisture.** [This seed fell upon a ledge of rock covered with a very thin coating of soil. Its roots were prevented by the rock from striking down to the moisture, and so under the blazing Syrian sun it died ere it had well begun to live.] [b] **7 And other** {[a]**others**} [b] **fell among** {[a]**upon** [c]**amidst**} [b] **the thorns, and the thorns grew up,** [c] **with it,** [b] **and**

choked it, {ᵃ them:} ᵇ and it yielded no fruit. [Pales-
tine abounds in thorns. Celsius describes sixteen varieties of
thorny plants. Porter tells us that in the Plain of Gennesaret
thistles grow so tall and rank that a horse can not push through
them.] **8 And others {ᶜ other} ᵇ fell into {ᵃ upon} ᵇ the
good ground, ᶜ and grew, and brought forth a hundredfold, ᵇ and yielded fruit, growing up and increasing;
and brought forth, thirtyfold, and sixtyfold, and a
hundredfold. {ᵃ some a hundredfold, some sixty, some
thirty.}** [Thirty-fold is a good crop in Palestine, but it is
asserted that a hundred-fold has been reaped in the Plain of
Esdraelon even in recent years. These four several condi
t‘o is of soil may be readily found lying close to each other in
the Plain of Gennessaret. A sowing like this described may
have been enacted before the eyes of the people even while
Jesus was speaking.] **ᶜ As he said these things, he cried**
[a method of giving emphasis rarely employed by Jesus],
**ᵇ 9 And he said, ᵃ 9 He that {ᵇ Who} hath ears to hear,
let him hear.** [A saying often used by Jesus. He inter.ded
it to prevent the people from regarding the parable as merely
a beautiful description. It warned them of a meaning beneath
the surface, and incited them to seek for it.] **10 And when
he was alone** [that is, after he had finished speaking all the
parables. The explanation of the parable is put next to the
parable to aid us in understanding it], **ᵃ the disciples came,
ᵇ they that were about him with the twelve ᶜ 9 and
his disciples ᵇ asked him of the parables. ᶜ what this
parable might be. ᵃ and said unto him, Why speakest
thou unto them in parables?** [Their questions show that
as yet parables were unusual.] **11 And he ansv‘ered and
said unto them, Unto you it is given to know the
mysteries {ᵇ is given the mystery} ᵃ of the kingdom of
heaven, {ᵇ of God:} ᵃ but to them ᶜ the rest ᵃ it is not
given. [*save*] ᶜ in parables; ᵇ unto them that are without, all things are done in parables.** [Jesus adapted his
lessons to the condition of his pupils; hence his disciples might
know what the multitude must not yet‘know (I. Cor. ii. 6–11).

Jesus already drew a line of demarkation between disciples and unbelievers; which line became more marked and visible after the church was organized at Pentecost. The word "mystery" in current language means that which is not understood; but as used in the Scriptures it means that which is not understood because it has not been revealed, but which is plain as soon as revealed. Bible mysteries are not unraveled by science, but are unfolded by revelation—Col. i. 26; I. Tim. iii. 16; Matt. xi. 25, 26; Rev. xvii. 5; Dan. ii. 47]: ᵃ **12 For whosoever hath, to him shall be given, and he shall have abundance: but whosoever hath not, from him shall be taken away even that which he hath.** [To understand this saying, we must remember that it was the teaching of Jesus which was under discussion. In the beginning of his ministry Jesus taught plainly, and all his hearers had equal opportunity to know his doctrine and believe in him. But from now on his teaching would be largely veiled in parables. These parables would enrich the knowledge and understanding of the believers; but they would add nothing to the store of unbelievers, and their efforts to understand the parables would withdraw their minds from the truths which they had already learned, so that they would either forget them or fail to profit by them. If we improve our opportunities, they bring us to other and higher ones; but if we neglect them, even the initial opportunities are taken away.] **13 Therefore speak I to them in parables;** ᵇ **12 that seeing they may see, and not perceive; and hearing they may hear, and not understand;** {ᶜ **that seeing they may not see, and hearing they may not understand.**} ᵃ **because seeing they see not, and hearing they hear not, neither do they understand.** ᵇ **lest haply they should turn again, and it should be forgiven them.** ᵃ **14 And unto them is fulfilled the prophecy of Isaiah** [Isa. vi. 9, 10], **which saith, By hearing ye shall hear, and shall in no wise understand; And seeing ye shall see, and shall in no wise perceive: 15 For this people's heart is waxed gross, And their ears are dull of hearing,**

And their eyes they have closed; Lest haply they
should perceive with their eyes, And hear with their
ears, And understand with their heart, And should
turn again, and I should heal them. [The language
here is an elaboration of the thoughts contained in the twelfth
verse. The people saw Christ's miracles, but not in their true
light; they heard his words, but not in their true meaning.
Jesus could thus teach without hindrance, but, unfortunately
for the unbelieving, they were hearing without obtaining any
blessing. In the original passage which Matthew quotes,
Isaiah is apparently commanded to harden the hearts of the
people. If read superficially, it might seem that God desired
to harden their hearts. The true meaning is that God commanded Isaiah to teach, even though the people, by hardening
themselves against his teaching, should be made worse rather
than better by it. Thus, though rebellious, Israel might not be
blessed by Isaiah's teaching; they might, by their example,
waken a wholesome fear in their posterity, and cause it to
avoid a like sin.] **16 But blessed are your eyes, for they
see; and your ears, for they hear.** [Jesus here addresses
his disciples, who were a cheering contrast to the unbelievers.]
**17 For verily I say unto you, that many prophets and
righteous men desired to see the things which ye see,
and saw them not; and to hear the things which ye
hear, and heard them not.** [Our Lord here gives us a
glance into the very hearts of the prophets, and reveals to
us their desire to be witnesses of Messiah's ministry. But
knowing they were not to see their visions realized, they con-
tented themselves with trying to understand the full meaning
of their visions, that they might anticipate the days which
were to come—I. Pet. i. 10–12.] b **13 And he saith unto
them, Know ye not this parable? and how shall ye
know all the parables?** [This is a concession rather than
a reproof. Parables could not be understood without a key;
but a few examples of parables explained would furnish such
a key.] a **18 Hear then ye the parable of the sower.**
c **11 Now the parable is this: The seed is the word of**

God. ᵇ14 The sower soweth the word. 15 And these {ᶜthose} ᵇby the way side, where the word is sown; ᶜare they that have heard; ᵇand when they have heard, ᶜthen ᵇstraightway cometh Satan, ᶜthe devil, and taketh away the word from their heart, ᵇwhich hath been sown in them. ᶜthat they may not believe and be saved. ᵃ19 When any one heareth the word of the kingdom, and understandeth it not, *then* cometh the evil *one*, and snatcheth away that which hath been sown in his heart. This is he that was sown by the way side. [The four soils are four hearts into which truth is sown. The first heart, represented by the wayside, is one which is too hardened for the Word to make any impression. It represents several classes of people, as: 1. Those whose hearts had been made insensible by the routine of meaningless rites and lifeless formalities. 2. Those who had deadened their sensibilities by perversity and indifference. 3. Those whose hearts were hardened by the constant march and countermarch of evil thoughts. God's word lies on the surface of such hearts, and Satan can use any insignificant or innocent passing thoughts as a bird to carry out of their minds anything which they may have heard. The preacher's voice has scarcely died away until some idle criticism of him or some careless bit of gossip about a neighbor causes them to forget the sermon.] ᵇ16 And these {ᶜthose} ᵇin like manner are they that are sown upon the rocky *places*, {ᶜrock} ᵇwho, when they have heard the word, straightway receive it {ᶜthe word} with joy; ᵇ17 and they {ᶜthese} ᵇhave no root in themselves, but endure {ᶜwho believe} for a while; ᵇthen, when tribulation or persecution ariseth because of the word, straightway they stumble. ᶜand in time of temptation fall away. ᵃ20 And he that was sown upon the rocky places, this is he that heareth the word, and straightway with joy receiveth it; 21 yet hath he not root in himself, but endureth for a while; and when tribulation or persecution ariseth because

of the word, straightway he stumbleth. [This shallow, rock-covered soil represents those who are deficient in tenacity of purpose. Those who receive the word, but whose impulsive, shallow nature does not retain it, and whose enthusiasm was as short-lived as it was vigorous. Any opposition, slight or severe, makes them partial or total apostates. As sunlight strengthens the healthy plant, but withers the sickly, ill-rooted one, so tribulation establishes real faith, but destroys its counterfeit.] ᵇ **18 And others are they that are sown {ᶜwhich fell} among the thorns, these are they that have heard, ᵇ the word, ᶜand as they go on their way ᵇ the cares of the world, and the deceitfulness of riches, and the lusts of other things entering in, choke the word, and it becometh unfruitful. ᶜthey are choked with cares and riches and pleasures of *this* life, and bring no fruit to perfection. ᵃ 22 And he that was sown among the thorns, this is he that heareth the word; and the care of the world, and the deceitfulness of riches, choked the word, and he becometh unfruitful.** [This third class represents those who begin well, but afterwards permit worldly cares to gain the mastery. These to-day outnumber all other classes, and perhaps they have always done so.] ᵇ **20 And those are they that were sown upon {ᶜ15 And that in} the good ground; these are such as in an honest and good heart, having heard {ᵇhear} ᶜthe word, hold it fast, ᵇand accept it, and bear ᶜand bring forth fruit with patience. ᵇthirtyfold, and sixtyfold, and a hundredfold. ᵃ23 And he that was sown upon the good ground, this is he that heareth the word, and understandeth it; who verily beareth fruit, and bringeth forth, some a hundredfold, some sixty, some thirty.** [Christianity requires three things: a sower, good seed or a pure gospel, and an honest hearer. All hearers are not equal in fruitfulness. But we are not to take it that the diversity is limited to the three rates or proportions specified. Of the four hearts indicated, the first one hears, but heeds nothing; the second one heeds, but is checked by external influences; the third heeds, but is choked by internal influences; the fourth heeds and holds fast until the harvest. Gallio exemplifies the first (Acts xvi. 17). Peter and Mark for a time exemplified the second (Mark xiv. 66–72; Acts xii. 25; xiii. 13; xv. 57, 58). The rich ruler and Demas represent the third (Matt. xix. 22; II. Tim. iv. 10), as does also Judas Iscariot. Cornelius and the Beræans (Acts x. 33; xvii. 11) show us samples of the fourth.] ᵇ **21 And he said unto them, Is the lamp brought to be put under the bushel, or under the bed, *and* not to be put on the stand?** ᶜ **16 And no man, when he hath lighted a lamp, covereth it with a vessel, or putteth it under a bed; but putteth it on a stand, that they that enter in may see the light.** [A passage similar to this is found at Matt. v. 15. See page 235.] ᵇ **22 For there is nothing hid, save that it should be manifested;** {ᶜ **that shall not be made manifest;**} ᵇ **neither was *anything* made secret, but that it should come to light.** {ᶜ **that shall not be known and come to light.**} ᵇ **23 If any man hath ears to hear, let him hear.** [This passage is often taken to indicate the exposure of all things on the day of judgment. While all things shall be revealed at the judgment, this passage does not refer to that fact. Jesus did not come to put his light under a bushel; that is, to hide his teaching. All inner instruction and private information was but temporary. Our Lord's design was to reveal, not to conceal. What was now concealed was only kept back in order that in the end it might be more fully known. Jesus covered his light as one might shelter a candle with his hand until the flame has fully caught hold of the wick.] **24 And he said unto them,** ᶜ **Take heed therefore how** {ᵇ **what**} **ye hear: with what measure ye mete it shall be measured unto you; and more shall be given unto you.** ᶜ **for whosoever** {ᵇ **he that**} **hath, to him shall be given:** ᶜ **and whosoever** {ᵇ **he that**} **hath not, from him shall be taken away even that which he hath.** {ᶜ **which he thinketh he hath.**} [Most of this passage has been explained just above. See page 331. It warns us as to what we hear—things carnal or spiritual—and how we hear them, whether carefully or carelessly. As we measure attention unto the Lord, he measures back knowledge unto us.]

Subdivision C.

PARABLE OF THE SEED GROWING OF ITSELF.

b MARK iv. 26-29.

b **26 And he said, So is the kingdom of God, as if a man should cast seed upon the earth; 27 and should sleep and rise night and day, and the seed should spring up and grow, he knoweth not how.** [In the kingdom of grace, as well as in the kingdom of nature, we are laborers together with God. As preachers, teachers or friends we sow the seed of the kingdom and God brings it to perfection (I. Cor. iii. 6-9). The seed here spoken of, being wheat or barley, needed no cultivation, and hence the planter let it alone, and did not know how it grew, whether fast or slow, or even whether it grew at all.] **28 The earth beareth fruit of herself; first the blade, then the ear, then the full grain in the ear. 29 But when the fruit is ripe, straightway he putteth forth the sickle, because the harvest is come.** [Truth, spoken, lies hidden in the human breast, and we do not see the earliest stages of its development, but as it proceeds towards perfection it becomes step by step more visible. In both fields the sower has little to do with the field between the time of sowing and reaping. In the spiritual field, however, it is well to keep sowing until the grain shows signs of sprouting.]

Subdivision D.

THE PARABLE OF THE TARES.

a MATT. xiii. 24-30.

a **24 Another parable set he before them, saying, The kingdom of heaven is likened unto a man that**

sowed good seed in his field: **25 but while men slept**
[while they innocently rested, not while they were negligent],
his enemy came and sowed tares [darnel, which closely
resembles our cheat] **also among the wheat, and went
away.** [Though not common, there have been instances of
such malignant mischief as is here indicated.] **26 But
when the blade sprang up and brought forth fruit,
then appeared the tares also.** [The difference between
darnel and wheat does not become apparent until the two
kinds of grain are nearly ripe.] **27 And the servants of
the householder came and said unto him, Sir, didst
thou not sow good seed in thy field? whence then
hath it tares? 28 And he said unto them, An enemy
hath done this. And the servants say unto him, Wilt
thou then that we go and gather them up? 29 But
he saith, Nay; lest haply while ye gather up the tares,
ye root up the wheat with them. 30 Let both grow
together until the harvest: and in the time of the
harvest I will say to the reapers, Gather up first the
tares, and bind them in bundles to burn them; but
gather the wheat into my barn.** [The roots of wheat
and darnel so intertwine that they can not be separated without pulling up both. Jesus' explanation of this parable will
be found below in Subdivision F.]

Subdivision E.

PARABLES OF THE MUSTARD SEED AND LEAVEN.

[a] MATT. XIII. 31–35; [b] MARK IV. 30–34.

[a] **31 Another parable set he before them, saying,**
[b] **30 And he said, How shall we liken the kingdom of
God? or in what parable shall we set it forth?** [These
questions are intended to emphasize the superior excellence
of the kingdom.] **31 It** [a] **The kingdom of heaven is like
unto a grain of mustard seed, which a man took, and
sowed in his field:** [b] **a grain of mustard seed, which,**

when it is sown upon the earth, though ᵃ indeed ᵇ it be {ᵃ is} ᵇ less than all the seeds that are upon the earth [that is, the smallest of all the seeds that are sown in a garden], ᵃ but ᵇ 32 yet when it is sown, groweth up, and ᵃ when it is grown, it is {ᵇ becometh} greater than all the herbs, and putteth out great branches; ᵃ and becometh a tree [in Palestine it attains the height of ten feet], so that the birds of the heaven come and ᵇ can lodge under the shadow thereof. ᵃ in the branches thereof. [This parable sets forth the smallness of the beginning of the kingdom, and the magnitude of its growth.] 33 Another parable spake he unto them; The kingdom of heaven is like unto leaven, which a woman took, and hid in three measures of meal, till it was all leavened. [In Oriental housekeeping, yeast is not preserved in a separate form. A piece of leavened dough saved over from the last baking is added to the new dough to ferment it. Three measures contained the quantity usually taken for one baking. Leaven represents the quickness, quietness, thoroughness and sureness with which gospel truth diffuses itself through human society. A woman is named because baking was part of her household duty.] 34 All these things spake Jesus in parables unto the multitude; ᵇ 33 And with many such parables spake he the word unto them, as they were able to hear it [that is, as they had leisure or opportunity to listen]; 34 and without a parable spake he not {ᵃ nothing} unto them [that is, he used nothing but parables on that occasion, for both before and after this he taught without parables]: 35 that it might be fulfilled which was spoken through the prophet [at Ps. lxxviii. 2, which is usually attributed to Asaph, who is called a seer (II. Chron. xxix. 30). His teaching typified that of Christ], saying, I will open my mouth in parables; I will utter things hidden from the foundation of the world. [Jesus fulfilled this prophecy in a notable manner, being the only teacher in history distinguished in any marked degree by the use of parables.] ᵇ but privately to his own disciples he expounded all things.

Subdivision F.

THE PARABLE OF THE TARES EXPLAINED.

a MATT. XIII. 36–43.

a 36 Then he left the multitudes, and went into the house [probably Simon Peter's house]: and his disciples came unto him, saying, Explain unto us the parable of the tares of the field. 37 And he answered and said, He that soweth the good seed is the Son of man; 38 and the field is the world; and the good seed, these are the sons of the kingdom; and the tares are the sons of the evil *one;* 39 and the enemy that sowed them is the devil: and the harvest is the end of the world; and the reapers are angels. 40 As therefore the tares are gathered up and burned with fire; so shall it be in the end of the world. 41 The Son of man shall send forth his angels, and they shall gather out of his kingdom all things that cause stumbling, and them that do iniquity, 42 and shall cast them into the furnace of fire: there shall be the weeping and the gnashing of teeth. 43 Then shall the righteous shine forth as the sun in the kingdom of their Father. He that hath ears, let him hear. [This parable and its explanation are sometimes urged as an argument against church discipline, but such a use of them is clearly erroneous. The field is not the church, but the world, and the teaching of the parable is that we are not to attempt to exterminate evil men. Any who attempt to exterminate heretics in the name of Christ by physical force are condemned by this parable.

Subdivision G.

PARABLES OF TREASURE, PEARL AND NET.

a MATT. XIII. 44-53.

a 44 The kingdom of heaven is like unto a treasure hidden in the field; which a man found, and hid; and

in his joy he goeth and selleth all that he hath, and buyeth that field. [The three parables in this section appear to have been addressed privately to the disciples. In the absence of banks and all other trust repositories, the men of that day hid their treasures as best they could. The sudden death of the hider often resulted in the loss of all knowledge as to the whereabouts of the treasure. The parable speaks of such a lost treasure. Technically it belonged to the owner of the field, but practically it belonged to him who found it. Hence the finder conceals it again until he has made perfect his title to it by the purchase of the field. The gist of the parable does not require us to pass upon the conduct of the finder, which was certainly questionable.] **45 Again, the kingdom of heaven is like unto a man that is a merchant seeking goodly pearls: 46 and having found one pearl of great price, he went and sold all that he had, and bought it.** [In the preceding parable the treasure was found by accident; in this, the pearl was sought. Some find without seeking, as did the Samaritan woman (John iv. 28, 29); some only after diligent search, as did the eunuch—Acts viii. 27.] **47 Again, the kingdom of heaven is like unto a net, that was cast into the sea, and gathered of every kind: 48 which, when it was filled, they drew up on the beach; and they sat down, and gathered the good into vessels, but the bad they cast away. 49 So shall it be in the end of the world: the angels shall come forth, and sever the wicked from among the righteous, 50 and shall cast them into the furnace of fire: there shall be the weeping and the gnashing of teeth.** [Like the parable of the tares, this one indicates the continuance of the mixture of bad and good, and points to the final separation. The contents of a net can not be sorted while it is being drawn. The tares indicate such evils as can be seen and as tempt us to uproot them. The net shows that in the dark and turbulent waters, and in the hurry-skurry of its teeming life, there are things which can not be seen. The judgment shall be with care, as when men, in the broad light of day, on the quiet beach, sit down to sort the fish. If the parable of the tares emphasizes the waiting, the parable of the net emphasizes the careful sorting.] **51 Have ye understood all these things? They say unto him, Yea. 52 And he said unto them, Therefore every scribe who hath been made a disciple to the kingdom of heaven is like unto a man that is a householder, who bringeth forth out of his treasure things new and old.** [As a householder graces his banquet with things already in the house, and with other things which have just been provided, so a religious teacher must refresh his hearers out of both his past and his present experiences and study. Old lessons must be clothed in new garments.] **53 And it came to pass, when Jesus had finished these parables, he departed thence.** [He went from the house to the sea in the afternoon, and entering a boat a little later, he stilled the storm.]

LV.

JESUS STILLS THE STORM.

(Sea of Galilee; same day as last section.)

[a]MATT. VIII. 18–27; [b]MARK IV. 35–41; [c]LUKE VIII. 22–25.

[b]**35 And on that day {**[c]**one of those days,}** [b]**when even was come** [about sunset], [a]**when Jesus saw great multitudes about him, he gave commandment to depart unto the other side. {**[b]**he saith unto them, Let us go over unto the other side.}** [Wearied with a day of strenuous toil, Jesus sought rest from the multitude by passing to the thinly settled district on the east side of Galilee.] [a]**19 And there came a scribe** [Literally, one scribe. The number is emphatic; for, so far as the record shows, Jesus had none of this class among his disciples], **and said unto him, Teacher, I will follow thee whithersoever thou goest. 20 And Jesus saith unto him, The foxes have holes** [caves, dens], **and the birds of the heaven *have* nests; but the Son of**

man [Daniel's name for the Messiah—Dan. vii. 10-13] **hath not where to lay his head.** [This scribe had heard the wonderful parables concerning the kingdom. He, like all others, expected an earthly kingdom and sought to have a place in it. Jesus so replied as to correct his false expectations.] **21 And another of the disciples said unto him, Lord, suffer me first to go and bury my father.** [This disciple must have been one of the twelve, for these only were required to follow Jesus (Mark iii. 14). It may have been James or John, whose father, Zebedee, almost certainly died before Jesus did. He may have just heard of his father's death.*] **22 But Jesus saith unto him, Follow me; and leave the dead to bury their own dead.** [Let the spiritually dead bury the naturally dead. This was a very exceptional prohibition, intended to show not that it was ordinarily wrong to stop for burying the dead, but wrong when in conflict with a command from Jesus. God bids us recognize the claims of filial duty, but rightfully insists that our duties toward him are superior to those due our parents.] ᶜ **22 Now it came to pass that he entered into a boat, himself and his disciples;** ᵃ **23 And when he was entered into a boat, his disciples followed him.** ᶜ **and he said unto them, Let us go over unto the other side of the lake: and they launched forth.** ᵇ **36 And leaving the multitude, they take him with them, even as he was, in the boat.** [They took Jesus without any preparation for the journey. The crowd, doubtless, made it inconvenient to go ashore to get provisions.] **And other boats were with him.** [The owners of these boats had probably been using them to get near to Jesus as he preached. They are probably mentioned to show that a large number witnessed the miracle when Jesus stilled the tempest.] ᶜ **23 But as they sailed he fell asleep** [knowing his labors during the day, we can not wonder at this]: ᵇ **37 And there ariseth ᶜ and there came down ᵇ a great storm of wind, ᶜ on the lake; ᵃ 24 And behold.**

---

* I do not concur in this statement.—*P. Y. P.*

there arose a great tempest in the sea, insomuch that the boat was covered with the waves: ᵇand the waves beat into the boat, insomuch that the boat was now filling. ᶜand they were filling *with water*, and were in jeopardy. [These storms come with great suddenness. See McGarvey's "Lands of the Bible," page 519.] ᵇ38 And {ᵃbut} ᵇhe himself was in the stern, asleep on the cushion [The cushion was the seat-cover, which, as Smith remarks, was probably "a sheepskin with the fleece, which, when rolled up, served as a pillow." The stern was the most commodious place for passengers. This tossing ship has been accepted in all ages as a type of the church in seasons of peril]: ᵃ25 And they came to him, and awoke him, {ᵇthey awake him,} and say unto him, {ᵃsaying,} Save, Lord; we perish. ᶜMaster, master, we perish. ᵇTeacher, carest thou not that we perish? [There was a babble of confused voices, betraying the extreme agitation of the disciples.] 39 And he awoke, ᵃThen he arose, and rebuked the winds {ᵇwind,} ᵃand the sea; ᶜand the raging of the water: ᵇand said unto the sea, Peace, be still. ᶜand they ceased, ᵇAnd the wind ceased, and there was a great calm. [In addressing the winds and waves Jesus personified them to give emphasis to his authority over them. The calm showed the perfection of the miracle, for the waves of such a lake continue to roll long after the winds have ceased.] ᶜ25 And he said unto them, Where is your faith? ᵇWhy are ye yet fearful? have ye not yet faith? ᵃO ye of little faith? [They had little faith or they would not have been so frightened; but they had some faith, else they would not have appealed to Jesus.] ᵇ41 And they feared exceedingly, ᶜAnd being afraid they ᵃthe men marvelled, ᵇand said one to another, ᶜsaying one to another, ᵃWhat manner of man is this, that even the winds and the sea obey him? ᶜWho then is this, that he commandeth even the winds, and the water, and they obey him? [Jesus' complete lordship over the realm of nature made his disciples very certain of his divinity.]

LVI.

JESUS HEALS TWO GERGESENE DEMONIACS.

(Gergesa, now called Khersa.)

ᵃ MATT. VIII. 28–34 ; IX. 1 ; ᵇ MARK V. 1–21 ; ᶜ LUKE VIII. 26–40.

ᵇ **1 And they came to the other side of the sea** [They left in the " even," an elastic expression. If they left in the middle of the afternoon and were driven forward by the storm, they would have reached the far shore several hours before dark], ᶜ **26 And they arrived at the country of the Gerasenes, which is over against Galilee.** ᵃ **28 And when he was come into the country of the Gadarenes,** ᶜ **27 And when he was come forth** ᵇ **out of the boat,** ᶜ **upon the land** [Midway between the north and south ends of the lake, and directly east across the lake from Magdala, was the little city of Gergesa. In front and somewhat to the south of this city Jesus landed. Some sixteen miles away and to the southeast, and seven miles back from the lake, was the well-known city of Gadara. Further on to the southeast, on the borders of Arabia, and at least fifty miles from Gergesa, was the city of Gerasa. The name Gerasenes is, therefore, probably an error of transcribers for Gergesenes, as Origen suggested. The region is properly called " country of the Gadarenes," for Gadara was an important city, and the stamp of a ship on its coins suggests that its territory extended to the Lake of Galilee], ᵇ **straightway there met him out of the tombs** ᶜ **a certain man out of the city** [Gergesa], ᵇ **with an unclean spirit,** ᶜ **who had demons;** ᵇ **3 who had his dwelling in the tombs:** ᶜ **and abode not in** *any* **house, but in the tombs.** [The sides of the mountain near the ruins of Gergesa are studded with natural and artificial caves which were used as tombs.] ᵇ **and no man could any more bind him, no, not with a chain; 4 because that he had been often bound with fetters and chains, and the chains had been rent asunder by him, and the** fetters broken in pieces : and no man had strength to tame him. 5 And always, night and day, in the tombs and in the mountains, he was crying out, and cutting himself with stones. [The natural spirit of the man seeking to throw off the dominion of the demons would cry out in agony, and the demons themselves, in their own misery, would use him as a vehicle to express their own grief. It would be hard to imagine a more horrible state] ᶜ and for a long time he had worn no clothes, ᵇ6 and when he saw Jesus from afar, ᶜ he cried out, ᵇ he ran ᶜ and fell down before him, ᵇ and worshipped him ; 7 and crying out with a loud voice, he saith, {ᶜ said,} What have I to do with thee [on this phrase see page 116], Jesus, thou Son of the Most High God ? I beseech thee, ᵇ I adjure thee by God, torment me not. ᶜ29 For he was commanding the unclean spirit to come out from the man. [The demons showed the supremacy of Jesus not only by their cries to be let alone, but by the fact that they made no effort to escape from him. They ran to him, knowing that it was useless to do otherwise.] ᵇ8 For he said unto him, Come forth, thou unclean spirit, out of the man. ᶜ For oftentimes he had seized him : and he was kept under guard, and bound with chains and fetters ; and breaking the bands asunder, he was driven of the demon into the deserts. ᵇ9 And he ᶜ Jesus asked him, What is thy name ? ᵇ And he saith {ᶜ said,} ᵇ unto him, My name is Legion ; for we are many. ᶜ for many demons were entered into him. [It is likely that Jesus asked the *sufferer* his name wishing to assure him of his sympathy, but the *demons* in him had the floor and continued to do the talking. A legion was a division of the Roman army containing from four to six thousand men. If Jesus asked the demon its name, he did so that he might disclose this fact to his disciples.] ᵇ10 And he besought him much that he would not send them away out of the country. [As one mouth entreated for many, Mark uses both the singular and the plural.] ᶜ31 And they entreated him that he would not

command them to depart into the abyss. [The abyss or bottomless pit was the proper abode of the demons. It is mentioned nine times in Scripture: here and at Rom. x. 7; Rev. ix. 1, 2, 11; xi. 7; xvii. 8; xx. 1, 3. How these demons escaped from the abyss is one of the unsolved mysteries of the spirit world; but we have a parallel to it in the releasing of Satan—Rev. xx. 1–3.] ᵃ **28 And there met him two possessed with demons, coming forth out of the tombs, exceeding fierce, so that no man could pass by that way.** [Matthew tells of two, while Mark and Luke describe only one. They tell of the principal one—the one who was the fiercer. In order to tell of two, Matthew had to omit the name "legion," which belonged to one; and conversely, Mark and Luke, to give the conversation with one, do not confuse us by telling of two.] **29 And behold, they cried out, saying, What have we to do with thee, thou Son of God? art thou come hither to torment us before the time?** [The judgment-day, the time of punishment and torment—Matt. xxv. 41; II. Pet. ii. 4; Jude 6.] ᵇ **11 Now there was there** ᵃ**afar off from them** ᵇ**on the mountain side a great herd** ᵃ**of many swine feeding. 31 And the demons besought him,** ᶜ**and they entreated him that he would give them leave to enter into them.** ᵃ**saying, If thou cast us out, send us away into the herd of swine.** ᵇ**that we may enter into them. 13 And he gave them leave.** ᵃ**32 And he said unto them, Go. And they** ᵇ**the unclean spirits** ᶜ**the demons came out of the man, and entered** ᵃ**and went into the swine: and behold, the whole herd rushed down the steep into the sea, {**ᶜ**the lake,}** ᵇ*in number* **about two thousand; and they were drowned in the sea.** ᵃ**and perished in the waters.** [About a mile south of Khersa a spur of the mountain thrusts itself out toward the lake so that its foot is within forty feet of the water line. This is the only spot on that side of the lake where the mountains come near the water. The slope is so steep and the ledge at its foot so narrow that a herd rushing down could not check itself before tumbling into the water.

Skeptics have censured Jesus for permitting this loss of property. God may recognize our property rights as against each
other, but he nowhere recognizes them in the realm of nature.
What was done to the swine was done by the demons, and the
owners had no more right to complain than they would have
had if the herd had been carried off by murrain, by flood, or
by any other natural cause. All animals have a right to die,
either singly or in numbers. The demons evidently did not
intend to destroy the swine. Their desire to have live bodies to
dwell in shows that they did not. But the presence of the
demons in their bodies made the hogs crazy, as it had the
demoniac, and they ran the way their noses were pointed at
the moment. For discussion of demoniacal possession see page
167.] ᶜ **34 And when they that fed them** [there being no
fences in Palestine, herds were invariably attended by herds-
men] **saw what had come to pass, they fled, and told
it in the city and in the country.** ᵃ **and went away into
the city, and told everything, and what was befallen
to them that were possessed with demons. 34 And
behold, all the city came out to meet Jesus** [it is about
half a mile from Khersa to the seashore] : ᵇ **And they came**
{ᶜ **went out**} ᵇ **to see what it was that had come to
pass. 15 And they come** {ᶜ **came**} ᵇ **to Jesus,** ᶜ **and
found** {ᵇ **behold**} ᶜ **the man,** ᵇ **that was possessed with
demons** ᶜ **from whom the demons were gone out, sitting, clothed and in his right mind,** ʰ *even* **him that had
the legion** [a faint suggestion that there was also another] :
ᶜ **at the feet of Jesus : and they were afraid.** ᵇ **16 And
they that saw it** [the herdmen] **declared unto them how
it befell him that was possessed with demons,** ᶜ **36
And told them how he that was possessed with demons was made whole.** ᵇ **and concerning the swine.**
ᵃ **and when they saw him,** ᶜ **37 All the people of the
country of the Gerasenes round about asked him** ᵇ **17
And they began to beseech** {ᵃ **besought**} ᵇ **him** ᵃ **that he
would depart** {ᵇ **to depart**} **from their borders.** ᶜ **from
them ; for they were holden with great fear** [The loss

of the swine moved them to fear a further loss of **property.** To them the loss of swine was more important than the recovery of a man. To this day, worldly interests move men more than acts of mercy] : **and he entered into a boat,** ᵇ **18 And** {ᶜ **38 But**} ᵇ **as he was entering into the boat, he that had been possessed with demons** ᶜ **the man from whom the demons were gone out prayed him** {ᵇ **besought him**} **that he might be with him.** [As a frightened child newly wakened from a horrible dream clings to its parent, so the man clung to Christ.] ᶜ **but he sent him away,** ᵇ **19 And he suffered him not, but saith** {ᶜ **saying,**} ᵇ **unto him, Go** ᶜ **39 Return to thy house,** ᵇ **unto thy friends, and tell them** ᶜ **and declare how great things God** ᵇ **the Lord hath done for thee, and** *how* **he had mercy on thee.** [Jesus departed, but left behind him a witness whose very body was a living monument bearing testimony to Christ's compassion and power. Jesus revisited this locality some months later. See Mark vii. 31–37.] ᶜ **and he went his way, publishing throughout the whole city** [Gergesa] **how great things Jesus had done for him.** ᵇ **and began to publish in Decapolis how great things Jesus had done for him** [for the cities which constituted Decapolis, see page 173] : **and all men marvelled. 21 And when Jesus had crossed over again in the boat unto the other side, a great multitude was gathered unto him ; and he was by the sea.** ᶜ **40 And as Jesus returned, the multitude welcomed him ; for they were all waiting for him.** [They could see the sail of his boat as he started back.] ᵃ **1 And he came into his own city.** [Capernaum.]

LVII.

MATTHEW'S FEAST. DISCOURSE ON FASTING.

(Capernaum.)

^a MATT. IX. 10–17; ^b MARK II. 15–22; ^c LUKE V. 29–39.

^c **29 And Levi** [another name for the apostle Matthew] **made him a great feast in his house:** ^b **15 And it came to pass, that he was sitting** {^a **as he sat**} **at meat in the** {^b **his**} ^a **house,** ^c **and there was a great multitude of publicans** [Matthew had invited his old friends] **and of others** ^b **and** ^a **behold, many publicans and sinners came and sat down with Jesus and his disciples.** ^b **for there were many,** ^c **that were sitting at meat with them.** ^b **and they followed him.** ^c **30 And the Pharisees and their scribes** {^b **the scribes of the Pharisees,**} [that is, the scribes which were of their party or sect] **when they saw that he was eating with the sinners and publicans,** ^c **murmured against his disciples, saying,** {^a **they said**} **unto his disciples,** ^c **Why do ye eat and drink with the publicans and sinners?** ^a **Why eateth your Teacher with the publicans and sinners?** ^b *How is it* **that he eateth and drinketh with publicans and sinners?** [From their standpoint the question was natural enough. No strict Jew could eat with a Gentile (Acts xi. 3; Gal. ii. 12), and Matthew's guests were classed with the heathen.] ^a **12 But** {^b **17 And**} ^a **when he** ^b **Jesus heard it, he** ^c **answering said** {^b **saith**} **unto them, They that are whole** {^c **in health**} **have no need of a physician; but they that are sick.** ^a **13 But go ye and learn what** *this* **meaneth, I desire mercy, and not sacrifice** [For explanation of this passage, see page 212. To mercifully help sinners to repent was more precious to God than sacrifice]**: for** ^c **32 I am not come** {^a **I came not**} **to call the righteous. but sinners.** ^c **to repentance.** [Being charged with recklessly consorting

with sinners, it was necessary for Jesus to vindicate himself, else his influence would be damaged: hence he presents three arguments: 1. His office being analogous to that of a physician, required him to visit the sin-sick; 2. God himself commended such an act of mercy, and preferred it to sacrifice; 3. As he came to call sinners to repentance, he must therefore go to the sinners. These arguments do not justify us in keeping company with bad people for any other purpose than to do them good—that is, as their soul's physician. When he used the word "righteous," Jesus did not mean to admit that any were so righteous as to need no Saviour; he merely quoted the Pharisees at the value which they set upon themselves.
b 18 And John's disciples and the Pharisees were fasting: and they come {**a 14 Then come to him the disciples of John,**} **c 33 And they said** {**b say**} **unto him,** **a saying,** **c The disciples of John fast often, and make supplications** [single penitential prayers with their fasting]; **likewise also the** *disciples* **of the Pharisees; but thine eat and drink.** [As John the Baptist observed one almost continual fast, his diet being locusts and wild honey, his disciples had naturally great respect for that rite, and noted the lack of its observance by Jesus as an apparent defect in his character. They were honest inquirers, and Jesus answered them respectfully as such.] **a Why do we and the Pharisees** {**b John's disciples and the disciples of the Pharisees**} **a fast oft, but thy disciples fast not? 15 And Jesus said unto them,** **c Can ye make the sons of the bride-chamber fast,** {**a mourn,**} **as long as** {**c while**} **the bridegroom is with them?** **b as long as they have the bridgroom with them, they cannot fast.** [The bridegroom's friends were called "sons of the bride-chamber." They went with the bridegroom to the bride's house, and escorted her to her new home. Arriving at the bridegroom's house, a feast usually lasting seven days ensued (Matt. xxii. 4; Luke xiv. 8; John ii. 8, 9). Mourning and fasting would therefore ill befit such an occasion.] **c 35 But the days will come; and when the bridegroom shall**

be taken away from them, ᵇand then will they fast in that day. {ᶜthose days.} [Jesus here foretells the removal of his visible presence from his disciples by his ascension. His words predict but do not command a fast. He prescribed no stated fasts, and the apostolic church kept none. History shows that prescribed fasts become formal and tend to Phariseeism.] 36 And he spake also a parable unto them: No man rendeth a piece from a new garment and putteth it upon an old garment; else he will rend the new, and also the piece from the new will not agree with the old. ᵃ16 And no man putteth {ᵇseweth} a piece of undressed cloth on {ᵃupon} an old garment; for {ᵇelse} that which should fill it up taketh from it, {ᵃfrom the garment,} ᵇthe new from the old, and a worse rent is made. [Jesus justifies the conduct of his disciples by an appeal to the principles of the new dispensation, by which they were governed. The disciples of John looked upon Jesus as a reformer of Judaism, but he corrects their false impressions. To tear the new dispensation to pieces to renovate or embellish the old would be to injure the new and to destroy the old. By the process of fulling or dressing, new cloth was cleansed and shrunk so as to become more compact. The new cloth, therefore, had in it, so to speak, a life-element, and in its movement while shrinking it would tear the weaker fiber of the old cloth to which it was sewed, and thus enlarge the rent. The new dispensation could have rites and forms of its own, but could not conform to the rites of the Pharisees. If the conduct of his disciples had made a rent in the rabbinical traditions with regard to fasting, Jesus could not so modify the conduct of his disciples as to patch the rent without injuring the moral sense of his disciples, and without making Phariseeim a more meaningless hypocrisy than ever.] 22 And no man putteth {ᵃ17 Neither do *men* put} new wine into old wine-skins: ᶜelse the new wine will burst the skins, ᵃand the wine ᶜitself will be {ᵃis} spilled, ᵇand the wine perisheth, and the skins: ᵃburst, ᶜand the skins will perish. ᵃbut they put new wine {ᶜnew

wine must be put} ᵇ**into fresh wine-skins.** ᵃ**and both
are preserved.** [This parable is also an illustration of the
principles set forth above. Wine was then stored in casks of
skin—usually the hides of goats. Wine-skins, newly made,
were elastic, and would expand to accommodate the fermen-
tation of the new wine within. But the old wine-skins were
stiff and of little strength, and would burst if fermenting liquid
were confined within them.] ᶜ**39 And no man having
drunk old *wine* desireth new; for he saith, The old is
good.** [The thought here is that as wine should be put in
skins suited for it, and as, at an entertainment, the different
kinds of wine should be served in appropriate succession; so,
fasting should be observed on suitable occasions—not, for
instance, at a wedding.]

LVIII.

JAIRUS' DAUGHTER AND THE INVALID WOMAN.

(Capernaum, same day as last.)

ᵃ MATT. IX. 18–26; ᵇ MARK V. 22–43; ᶜ LUKE VIII. 41–56.

ᶜ**41 And** ᵃ**18 While he spake these things unto
them** [while he talked about fasting at Matthew's table],
behold, there came, {ᵇ**cometh}** ᶜ**a man named Jairus,
{**ᵇ**Jairus by name;}** ᶜ**and he was a ruler {**ᵇ**one of the
rulers} of the synagogue** [He was one of the board of
elders which governed the synagogue at Capernaum. These
elders were not necessarily old men—Matt. xix. 19; Luke
xviii. 8], **and seeing him,** ᶜ**he fell {**ᵇ**falleth}** ᶜ**down at
Jesus' feet,** ᵃ**and worshipped him** [It was a very lowly
act for the ruler of a synagogue thus to bow before the Man
of Nazareth. But the ruler was in trouble, and his needs
were stronger than his pride], ᶜ**and besought him to come
into his house; 42 for he had an only daughter, about
twelve years of age, and she was dying.** ᵇ**23 and be-
seecheth him much, saying, My little daughter is at
the point of death:** ᵃ**is even now dead** [he left her dying,

and so stated his fears in the very strongest way]: **but** ᵇ*I pray thee*, **that thou come and lay thy hands on** {ᵃhand upon} **her,** ᵇ**that she may be made whole, and live.** ᵃ**and she shall live. 19 And Jesus arose** [From Matthew's table. Jesus did not fast for form's sake, but he was ever ready to leave a feast that he might confer a favor], **and followed him, and** *so did* **his disciples.** ᵇ**24 And he went with him; and a great multitude followed him** [The ruler, of highest social rank in the city, found Jesus among the lowliest, and they were naturally curious to see what Jesus would do for this grandee], **and they** {ᶜ**But as he went the multitudes**} **thronged him.** ᵃ**20 And behold, a woman, who had** {ᶜhaving} **an issue of blood twelve years,** ᵇ**26 and had suffered many things of many physicians, and** ᶜ**who had spent** ᵇ**all that she had,** ᶜ**all her living upon physicians,** ᵇ**and was nothing bettered, but rather grew worse,** ᶜ**and could not be healed of any** [Medicine was not a science in that day. Diseases were not cured by medicine, but were exorcised by charms. The physician of Galilee in that age did not differ very widely from the medicine-man of the North American Indians. One in easy circumstances could readily spend all during twelve years of doctoring with such leeches], ᵇ**27 having heard the things concerning Jesus** [her faith rested on hearing rather than on sight], **came in the crowd behind,** ᶜ**him, and touched the border of his garment:** ᵃ**21 for she said within herself, If I do but touch his garment,** {ᵇgarments,} **I shall be made whole.** [The nature of her disease made her unclean (Lev. xv. 26). Her consciousness of this made her, therefore, timidly approach Jesus from behind.] **29 And straightway** {ᶜimmediately} ᵇ**the fountain of her blood was dried up;** ᶜ**the issue of her blood stanched.** ᵇ**and she felt in her body that she was healed of her plague.** [The feeble pulse of sickness gave way to the glow and thrill of health.] **30 And straightway Jesus, perceiving in himself that the power** *proceeding* **from him had gone forth, turned him about in the**

crowd, and said, Who touched my garments? ᶜWho
is it that touched me? And when all denied, Peter
and they ᵇhis disciples ᶜthat were with him, ᵇsaid
unto him, ᶜMaster, the multitudes press thee and
crush *thee*. ᵇThou seest the multitude thronging thee,
and sayest thou, Who touched me? ᶜ46 But Jesus
said, Some one did touch me; for I perceived that
power had gone forth from me. ᵇ32 And he looked
round about to see her that had done this thing. ᶜ47
And {ᵇ33 But} ᶜwhen the woman saw that she was
not hid, she came ᵇfearing and trembling [because being
unclean, any rabbi would have rebuked her severely for touching him], knowing what had been done to her, and fell
{ᶜfalling} down before him ᵇand told him all the truth.
ᶜdeclared in the presence of all the people for what
cause she touched him, and how she was healed immediately. [To have permitted the woman to depart without
this exposure would have confirmed her in the mistaken notion
that Jesus healed rather by his *nature* than by his *will*. Hence
he questions her, not that he may obtain information, but rather
as a means of imparting it. By his questions he reveals to her
that no work of his is wrought without his consciousness, and
that it was himself and not his garment which had blessed her.]
ᵃ22 But Jesus turning and seeing her said, ᶜunto her,
ᵃDaughter, be of good cheer [Faith gets a sweet welcome];
thy faith hath made thee whole. ᶜgo in peace. ᵇand be
whole of thy plague. [Be permanently whole: an assurance
that relief was not temporal, but final.] ᵃAnd the woman was
made whole from that hour. [Faith healed her by causing her to so act as to obtain healing. Faith thus saves: not
of itself, but by that which it causes us to do. It causes us to
so run that we obtain.] ᵇ35 While he yet spake, they
come from {ᶜthere cometh one from} the ruler of the
synagogue's *house*, saying, Thy daughter is dead;
ᵇwhy troublest thou the Teacher any further? ᶜtrou-
ble not the Teacher. [The delay caused by healing this
woman must have sorely tried the ruler's patience, and the sad

news which followed it must have severely tested his faith; but we hear no word of murmuring or bitterness from him.] **50 But Jesus hearing it, ᵇnot heeding the words spoken** [not succumbing to the situation], **ᶜanswered him, {ᵇsaith unto the ruler of the synagogue,} Fear not, only believe. ᶜand she shall be made whole.** [Thus, with words of confidence and cheer, Jesus revived the ruler's failing faith.] **ᵇ37 And he suffered no man to follow with him** [into the house with him], **save Peter, and James, and John the brother of James.** [These three were honored above their fellows by special privileges on several occasions, because their natures better fitted them to understand the work of Christ.] **ᶜ51 And when he came to the house, he suffered not any man to enter in with him, save Peter and John, and James, and the father of the maiden and her mother. ᵇ38 And they come to the house of the ruler of the synagogue; ᵃ23 And when Jesus came into the ruler's house, ᵇhe beholdeth a tumult, and** *many* **weeping and wailing greatly. ᵃand saw the flute-players, and the crowd making a tumult, 24 he said, Give place** [Mourning began at the moment of death, and continued without intermission until the burial, which usually took place on the day of the death. Even to this day Oriental funerals are characterized by noisy uproar and frantic demonstrations of sorrow, made by real and hired mourners. Flute-players, then as now, mingle the plaintive strains of their instruments with the piercing cries of those females who make mourning a profession]: **ᶜ52 And all were weeping, and bewailing her: but he said, {ᵇsaith} unto them, Why make ye a tumult, and weep? ᶜWeep not; for she ᵇthe child ᵃthe damsel is not dead, but sleepeth.** [Jesus used this figurative language with regard to Lazarus, and explained that by it he meant death—John xi. 14.] **And they laughed him to scorn. ᶜknowing that she was dead.** [His words formed a criticism as to their judgment and experience as to death, and threatened to interrupt them in earning their funeral dues.] ᵃ25 But when the crowd was put forth, ᵇhe, having put them all forth [because their tumult was unsuited to the solemnity and sublimity of a resurrection. They were in an outer room—not in the room where the dead child lay], taketh the father of the child and her mother and them [the three] that were with him, and goeth in {ᵃ he entered in,} ᵇwhere the child was. [Jesus took with him but five witnesses, because in the small space of the room few could see distinctly what happened, and those not seeing distinctly might circulate inaccurate reports and confused statements as to what occurred. Besides, Jesus worked his miracles as privately as possible in order to suppress undue excitement.] ᵃand took {ᵇtaking} the child {ᶜher} by the hand, called, saying, {ᵇsaith} unto her, Talitha cumi; which is, being interpreted, Damsel, {ᶜMaiden,} ᵇI say unto thee, Arise. [Mark gives the Aramaic words which Jesus used. They were the simple words with which any one would waken a child in the morning.] ᶜ55 And her spirit returned, ᵇ42 And straightway the damsel rose up, {ᵃarose.} ᶜshe rose up immediately: ᵇand walked [her restoration was complete]; for she was twelve years old. ᶜand he commanded that *something* ᵇshould be given her to eat. [Her frame, emaciated by sickness, was to be invigorated by natural means.] ᶜ56 And her parents were amazed: ᵇthey were amazed straightway with a great amazement. [Faith in God's great promises is seldom so strong that fulfillment fails to waken astonishment.] 43 And {ᶜbut} ᵇhe charged them much ᶜto tell no man what had been done. ᵇthat no man should know this [A command given to keep down popular excitement. Moreover, Jesus did not wish to be importuned to raise the dead. He never was so importuned]: ᵃ26 And the fame hereof went forth into all that land.

LIX.

HEALING BLIND MEN AND A DUMB DEMONIAC.

(Probably Capernaum.)

ᵃ MATT. IX. 27–34.

ᵃ **27 And as Jesus passed by from thence** [If construed strictly, this phrase means, as he departed from Jairus' house. But the phrase is indefinite], **two blind men followed him, crying out, and saying, Have mercy on us, thou son of David.** [This, among the Jews, was a common and thoroughly recognized name for the expected Messiah.] **28 And when he was come into the house** [possibly Peter's. But the place is not important. The house is mentioned to show that the blind men persistently followed Jesus until he stopped], **the blind men came to him: and Jesus saith unto them, Believe ye that I am able to do this? They say unto him, Yea, Lord.** [In the earlier stages of his ministry Jesus had worked his miracles with little or no solicitation; but now, as the evidences of his power were multiplied, Jesus demanded a fuller expression of faith; for faith was the fruitage for which the miracles were wrought.] **29 Then touched he their eyes, saying, According to your faith be it done unto you. 30 And their eyes were opened. And Jesus strictly** [sternly] **charged them, saying, See that no man know it. 31 But they went forth, and spread abroad his fame in all that land.** [Jesus might well speak severely when charging his beneficiaries to be silent, for apparently no one of them ever obeyed him.] **32 And as they went forth, behold, there was brought to him a dumb man possessed with a demon. 33 And when the demon was cast out, the dumb man spake: and the multitudes marvelled, saying, It was never so seen in Israel.** [Some regard this demoniac as being the victim of combined physical and spiritual maladies, but it is more likely that the dumbness was caused by the demon, since in some instances they deprived men of reason (Mark v. 15), and in others they threw men into convulsions or distortions—Mark ix. 18; Luke xiii. 11, 16.] **34 But the Pharisees said, By the prince of the demons casteth he out demons.** [If we are correct in our chronology, Jesus had already fully answered this charge. See pages 300-302. If he repeated any part of this answer at this time, Matthew is silent as to it.]

LX.

JESUS VISITS NAZARETH AND IS REJECTED.

a MATT. XIII. 54–58; b MARK VI. 1–6; c LUKE IV. 16–31.

b **1 And he went out from thence** [from Capernaum]; **and he cometh** {a **And coming**} b **into his own country; and his disciples follow him.** c **16 And he came to Nazareth, where he had been brought up** [As to this city, see pages 14 and 55. As to the early years of Jesus at Nazareth, see page 60]: b **2 And when the sabbath was come,** c **he entered, as his custom was, into the synagogue on the sabbath day, and stood up to read.** [This does not mean that it had been the custom of Jesus when he was a young man in Nazareth to read in the synagogue. It means that after he entered his public ministry it was his custom to use the synagogue as his place of teaching on the sabbath day (Mark i. 39; iii. 1, 2). For comment on this usage of the synagogue see pages 172 and 173.] **17 And there was delivered unto him the book of the prophet Isaiah. And he opened the book, and found the place** [Isa. lxi. 1, 2; but the quotation embraces other lines from Isaiah] **where it was written, 18 The Spirit of the Lord is upon me, Because he anointed me to preach good tidings to the poor** [Anointing was the method by which prophets, priests and kings were consecrated or set apart to their several offices. This prophecy says that the Holy Spirit came upon Jesus because he was appointed to do a work of divine helpfulness]: **He hath sent me to proclaim release to the captives, And recovering of sight to the blind, To set at liberty them that are bruised, 19 To proclaim the acceptable year of the Lord.** [The prophecy set forth in physical terms what Jesus should perform in both the physical and spiritual realms. The prophecy closes with a reference to the jubilee year, which, being a time of liberation, forgiveness, and fresh starts, was a type of Christ's ministry and kingdom.] **20 And he closed the book, and gave it back to the attendant** [This officer corresponded to our sexton. Part of his duty was to take charge of the synagogue rolls], **and sat down** [Reader and congregation both stood during the reading; then, usually, both sat down to hear the passage explained. They stood out of reverence for God's word]: **and the eyes of all in the synagogue were fastened on him.** [They had heard of his miracles, and were curious to see what he would say and do.] **21 And he began to say unto them, To-day hath this scripture been fulfilled in your ears. 22 And all bare him witness, and wondered at the words of grace which proceeded out of his mouth** [The word grace refers rather to the manner than to the matter. The speech of Jesus flowed easily, and gracefully]: ª**54 And he taught** {ᵇ**began to teach**} ª**them in their** {ᵇ**the synagogue**}: ª**insomuch that** ᵇ**many hearing him were astonished,** ª**and said,** {ᵇ**saying,**} **Whence hath this man these things?** ª**this wisdom, and these mighty works?** ᵇ**and, What is the wisdom that is given unto this man, and *what mean such mighty works wrought by his hands?*** [They admitted his marvelous teaching and miraculous works, but were at a loss to account for them because their extreme familiarity with his humanity made it hard for them to believe in his divinity, by which alone his actions could be rightly explained. Twice in the early part of his ministry Jesus had been at Cana, within a few miles of Nazareth, and turning away from it had gone down to Capernaum. He did not call upon his townsmen to believe in him or his divine mission until

the evidences were so full that they could not deny them.]
**3 Is not this the carpenter, ᶜ Joseph's son? ᵃ the car-
penter's son? ᵇ the son of Mary, and brother of James,
and Joses, and Judas, and Simon? ᵃ is not his mother
called Mary? and his brethren, James, and Joseph, and
Simon, and Judas? 56 And his sisters, are they not
all ᵇ here with us?** [They brought forth every item of trade
and relationship by which they could confirm themselves in
their conviction that he was simply a human being like themselves. The question as to his identity, however, suggests that
he may have been absent from Nazareth some little time. As
to Jesus' kindred, see pages 224–226.] ᵃ **Whence then hath
this man all these things? 57 And they were offended
in him.** [His claims were too high for them to admit, and
too well accredited for them to despise, so they sought refuge
from their perplexity by getting angry at Jesus.] ᶜ **23 And
he said unto them, Doubtless ye will say unto me this
parable, Physician, heal thyself: whatsoever we have
heard done at Capernaum, do also here in thine own
country.** [Jesus quoted a familiar proverb, the meaning of
which is this: he was part of Nazareth, and hence the claims
of Nazareth upon him were superior to those of Capernaum,
and therefore Nazareth should have been blessed by his healing. But the expression was evidently used contemptuously,
as if they said, "You can do big things at Capernaum, but
you can not do them here. You can not deceive us; we know
you."] ᵃ **But {ᵇ 4 And} Jesus said unto them, ᶜ Verily
I say unto you, ᵇ a prophet is not without honor, save
in his own country, and among his own kin, and in
his own house. ᶜ No prophet is acceptable in his own
country.** [Jealousy forbids the countrymen of a prophet to
honor him. Base as this passion is, it is a very common one,
and is not easily subdued, even by the best of men. In Nazareth Jesus was no more than the son of a carpenter, and the
brother of certain very common young men and girls, while
abroad he was hailed as the prophet of Galilee, mighty in word
and deed.] **25 But of a truth I say unto you** [Jesus

now proceeds to make two close applications of the proverb], **There were many widows in Israel in the days of Elijah, when the heaven was shut up three years and six months, when there came a great famine over all the land; 26 and unto none of them was Elijah sent, but only to Zaraphath, in the land of Sidon, unto a woman** [a Gentile] **that was a widow. 27 And there were many lepers in Israel in the time of Elisha the prophet; and none of them was cleansed, but only Naaman the Syrian.** [Naaman was also a Gentile. The first instance cited by Jesus will be found at I. Kings xvii. 8–16, and the second at II. Kings v. 1–14. Palestine was filled with poor people even in times of plenty, so there must have been large numbers of hungry people during that long-continued period of famine. Then, too, there has always been a large number of lepers in the land, and surely if any disease ought to prompt a man to lay aside his prejudices that he might obtain healing it was leprosy; but as Nazareth was now reject-ing Jesus, so their ancesters had despised the two mighty proph-ets. Not one of all the hungry would have received bread from Elijah by an act of faith, nor did one of all the lepers ask healing from Elisha.] **28 And they were all filled with wrath in the synagogue, as they heard these things** [The Nazarenes were jealous enough of the claims of Jesus when put in their most modest dress; but when Jesus placed himself alongside Elijah and Elisha, and likened his hearers to widows for want, and lepers for uncleanness, they were ready to dash him to pieces]; **29 and they rose up, and cast him forth out of the city, and led him** [they evidently had hold of him] **unto the brow of the hill whereon their city was built, that they might throw him down head-long.** [Near the eastern end of Nazareth there is a cavern in the rock which forms a precipice down which, if a man were hurled, he would be killed. At the western end there is a per-pendicular cliff about forty feet high, with a naked floor of rock at the bottom. To which place they led Jesus we can not decide.] **30 But he passing through the midst of them** went his way. [A simple statement of a marvelous fact. Miracles are not explained in the Bible.] ᵇ5 And he could there do no mighty work, ᵃ58 And he did not many mighty works there, because of their unbelief. ᵇsave that he laid his hand upon a few sick folk, and healed them. 6 And he marvelled because of their unbelief. [As to this statement that Jesus felt surprised, see page 273. " It should also be borne in mind," says Canon Cook, " that surprise at the obtuseness and unreasonableness of sin is constantly attributed to God by the prophets." The statement, therefore, is perfectly consonant with the divinity of Jesus.] ᶜ31 And he came down to Capernaum, a city of Galilee. [We have followed the chronology of Mark, according to which Jesus had already been living at Capernaum for some time. Luke tells of the rejection of Jesus early in his narrative, and adds this line to show that from the earlier days of his ministry Jesus made Capernaum his headquarters.]

LXI.

THIRD CIRCUIT OF GALILEE.   THE TWELVE INSTRUCTED AND SENT FORTH.

ᵃ MATT. ix. 35-38; x. 1, 5-42; xi. 1; ᵇMARK vi. 6-13; ᶜLUKE ix. 1-6.

ᵇ And he ᵃJesus ᵇwent round about ᵃall the cities and the villages, teaching in their synagogues, and preaching the gospel of the kingdom, and healing all manner of disease and all manner of sickness. [In the first circuit of Galilee some of the twelve accompanied Jesus as disciples (see Section XXXIII.); in the second the twelve were with him as apostles; in the third they, too, are sent forth as evangelists to supplement his work.] 36 But when he saw the multitudes, he was moved with compassion for them, because they were distressed and scattered, as sheep not having a shepherd. 37 Then saith he unto his disciples, The harvest indeed is plenteous, but the

**laborers are few. 38 Pray ye therefore the Lord of
the harvest, that he send forth laborers into his harvest.** [These verses contain the reason why Jesus separated
his apostles from himself, and scattered them among the people.
The masses of the people in Galilee had been deeply stirred by
the teaching and miracles of Jesus, but they knew not as yet
what direction was to be given to this popular movement. They
were in a bewildered state, like shepherdless sheep, scattered
over the hills and faint from running. The twelve were to
assist him as undershepherds in gathering these sheep. In
the second figure Jesus likens the people to a ripened harvest,
and he sends the apostles among them as reapers who shall
garner them.] **1 And he called {ᵇcalleth} ᶜtogether
ᵃunto him his {ᵇthe} ᵃtwelve disciples, ᵇand he gave
them ᶜpower and authority over all demons, ᵃover the
unclean spirits, to cast them out, and to heal all manner of disease {ᶜto cure diseases.} ᵃand all manner of
sickness.** [At this point Matthew gives the names of the
apostles, a complete list of which will be found at page 222.]
**5 These twelve Jesus sent forth, ᵇand he began to
send them forth by two and two** [He sent them in pairs
because, 1. Under the law it required two witnesses to establish the truth. 2. They could supplement each other's work.
Different men reach different minds, and where one fails
another may succeed. 3. They would encourage one another.
When one grew despondent the zeal and enthusiasm of the
other would quicken his activities]; **ᶜ2 And he sent them
forth to preach the kingdom of God, and to heal the
sick. ᵇ8 and he charged them that they should take
nothing for *their* journey, save a staff only; no bread,
no wallet, no money in their purse; 9 but *to go* shod
with sandals: and, *said he*, put not on two coats. ᵃand
charged them, saying, Go not into *any* way of the
Gentiles, and enter not into any city of the Samaritans: 6 but go rather to the lost sheep of the house of
Israel.** [This first commission *restricted* Christ's messengers
to the Jewish people, and the parts of Palestine which they

inhabited, but his second commission *impelled* them to go everywhere and to preach to every creature (Mark xvi. 15). As Jesus himself was sent only to the Jews, so during his days on earth he sent his disciples only to them.] **7 And as ye go, preach, saying, The kingdom of heaven is at hand.** [It was set up about a year later, on the day of Pentecost, under the direction of the Holy Spirit—Acts ii.] **8 Heal the sick, raise the dead, cleanse the lepers, cast out demons: freely ye received, freely give.** [Here is the true rule of giving. Paul repeats it at I. Cor. xvi. 2. If we would obey this rule, we would make this a happy world.] ᶜ **3 And he said unto them, Take nothing for your journey, ᵃ 9 Get you no gold, nor silver, ᶜ nor money; ᵃ nor brass in your purses; ᶜ neither staff, nor wallet, ᵃ for *your* journey, ᶜ nor bread, neither have two coats. ᵃ nor shoes, nor staff: for the laborer is worthy of his food.** [The prohibition is against securing these things before starting, and at their own expense. It is not that they would have no need for the articles mentioned, but that "the laborer is worthy of his food," and they were to depend on the people for whose benefit they labored, to furnish what they might need. This passage is alluded to by Paul (I. Cor. ix. 14). To rightly understand this prohibition we must remember that the apostles were to make but a brief tour of a few weeks, and that it was among their own countrymen, among a people habitually given to hospitality; moreover, that the apostles were imbued with powers which would win for them the respect of the religious and the gratitude of the well-to-do. This special and temporary commission was, therefore, never intended as an rule under which we are to act in preaching the gospel in other ages and in other lands. ᵇ **10 And he said unto them, ᵃ 11 And into whatsoever city or village ye shall enter, search out who in it is worthy; and there abide till ye go forth.** [The customs of the East gave rise to this rule. The ceremonies and forms with which a guest was received were tedious and time-consuming vanities, while the mission of the apostles required haste.] **12 And as ye enter** into the house, salute it. 13 And if the house be worthy, let your peace come upon it: but if it be not worthy, let your peace return to you. [The form of salutation on entering a house was, "Peace to this house." The apostles are told to salute each house, and are assured that the peace prayed for shall return to them if the house is not worthy; that is, they shall receive, in this case, the blessing they pronounced on the house.] ᵇ**Wheresoever ye enter into a house, there abide till ye depart thence.** {ᶜ**4 And into whatsoever house ye enter, there abide, and thence depart.**} ᵇ**11 And whatsoever place shall not receive you, and they hear you not** [Jesus here warns them that their experience would not always be pleasant], ᵃ**14 And whosoever** ᶜ**as many as** ᵃ**shall** ᶜ**receive you not,** ᵃ**nor hear your words,** ᵇ**as ye go forth thence,** ᵃ**out of that house or that city** [The word "house" indicates a partial and the word "city" a complete rejection], {ᶜ**when you depart from that city,**} ᵇ**shake off the dust that is under your feet** {ᵃ**of your feet.**} ᶜ**from your feet** ᵇ**for a testimony unto them.** ᶜ**against them.** [The dust of heathen lands as compared with the land of Israel was regarded as polluted and unholy (Amos vii. 7; Ezek. xiv. 1). The Jew, therefore, considered himself defiled by such dust. For the apostles, therefore, to shake off the dust of any city of Israel from their clothes or feet was to place that city on a level with the cities of the heathen, and to renounce all further intercourse with it.] ᵃ**15 Verily I say unto you, It shall be more tolerable for the land of Sodom and Gomorrah in the day of judgment, than for that city.** [For comment on similar remarks, see page 287. God judges all men with reference to their opportunities.] **16 Behold, I send you forth as sheep in the midst of wolves: be ye therefore wise as serpents, and harmless as doves.** [At this point Jesus passes from the first, or temporary, to the second, or final, commission of the apostles; for all the persecutions enumerated were encountered under the latter.] **17 But beware of men: for they will deliver you up to** councils, and in their synagogues they will scourge you [Councils and synagogues were both Jewish powers], 18 yea and before governors and kings shall ye be brought for my sake, for a testimony to them and to the Gentiles. [The phrase "governors and kings" indicates Gentile powers, for most all governors and kings were then appointed by Rome.] 19 But when they deliver you up, be not anxious how or what ye shall speak: for it shall be given you in that hour what ye shall speak. 20 For it is not ye that speak, but the Spirit of your Father that speaketh in you. [For comment on similar words, see page 318.] 21 And brother shall deliver up brother to death, and the father his child: and children shall rise up against parents, and cause them to be put to death. [Jesus here foretells the intense religious bigotry with which his ministers should be opposed. Having foretold persecution, he here predicts actual martyrdom.] 22 And ye shall be hated of all men for my name's sake [The term "all" is used in its general and not in its absolute sense. The apostles had some few friends among the unbelievers. Jesus gives the exact cause of the hatred. It would not be because of any personal faults or peculiarities, but simply because of adherence to Christ]: but he that endureth to the end, the same shall be saved. [Since the persecution was unto death, the endurance which should meet it must be to the end of life.] 23 But when they persecute you in this city, flee into the next: for verily I say unto you, Ye shall not have gone through the cities of Israel, till the Son of man be come. [The apostles were not to meet obduracy with obduracy. Moving as swiftly as they could along the line of least resistance, they would not be able to evangelize all the Jewish cities before the time set for their desolation— before the Son of man should come in the demonstration of his judicial power and destroy the Jewish nationality.] 24 A disciple is not above his teacher, nor a servant above his lord. 25 It is enough for the disciple that he be as his teacher, and the servant as his lord. [Jesus applied similar words to the Jewish teachers. See page 262.] **If they have called the master of the house Beelzebub, how much more them of his household!** [Jesus here warns the apostles that they can not expect better treatment than he himself received—no, not so good. Nor should they ask exemption from what he himself suffered.] **26 Fear them not therefore: for there is nothing covered, that shall not be revealed; and hid, that shall not be known. 27 What I tell you in the darkness, speak ye in the light; and what ye hear in the ear, proclaim upon the house-tops. 28 And be not afraid of them that kill the body, but are not able to kill the soul: but rather fear him who is able to destroy both soul and body in hell. 29 Are not two sparrows sold for a penny? and not one of them shall fall on the ground without your Father: 30 but the very hairs of your head are all numbered. 31 Fear not therefore: ye are of more value than many sparrows. 32 Every one therefore who shall confess me before men, him will I also confess before my Father who is in heaven. 33 But whosoever shall deny me before men, him will I also deny before my Father who is in heaven.** [For comment on similar remarks see page 317.] **34 Think not that I came to send peace on the earth: I came not to send peace, but a sword. 35 For I came to set a man at variance against his father, and the daughter against her mother, and the daughter in law against her mother in law: 36 and a man's foes *shall be* they of his own household.** [For comment on similar language see page 324.] **37 He that loveth father or mother more than me is not worthy of me; and he that loveth son or daughter more than me is not worthy of me.** [Love for the old religion would make the members of Jewish and pagan families persecute those who apostatized from it to give their hearts to Christ. But if the Jew and the pagan thus held *their* religions at a higher value than the ties of kindred, much more should the Christian value his religion above these ties.]

38 And he that doth not take his cross and follow after me, is not worthy of me. [This is doubtless an allusion to the manner of his death, and being the first of the kind it must have been very puzzling to his disciples, unless explained by prior words of Jesus, of which we have no record. As such allusion its full meaning is this: " If I bear for each the vicarious cross and suffer for each the full measure of the divine displeasure, then each should be willing cheerfully to follow me that he may obtain the benefits of my sacrifice, and if the light cross of human displeasure deter him from this, he is not worthy of me."] **39 He that findeth his life shall lose it; and he that loseth his life for my sake shall find it.** [Jesus declares that all self-seeking is self-losing. He that makes his own life the chief object of his endeavor really fails the more he seems to succeed. He who saves and husbands his powers to expend them on those lower carnal joys which a sinner calls "life" shall lose those higher spiritual joys which God calls "life," and *vice versa*.] **40 He that receiveth you receiveth me, and he that receiveth me receiveth him that sent me.** [Having depicted in all their darkness the persecutions which awaited the apostles, Jesus here, by an easy transition, proceeds to declare the honor of their apostleship in that they were representatives directly of Christ, and indirectly of the Father.] **41 He that receiveth a prophet in the name of** [that is, because he is] **a prophet shall receive a prophet's reward: and he that receiveth a righteous man in the name of a righteous man shall receive a righteous man's reward. 42 And whosoever shall give to drink unto one of these little ones a cup of cold water only, in the name of a disciple, verily I say unto you he shall in no wise lose his reward.** [Whoever honors a prophet, a righteous man or a disciple, as such recognizes that person's relation to God as the ground of the act; and to that extent honors God in the act, just as he who performs a similar act in the name of a friend thereby honors that friend. A prophet's reward is not synonymous, however, with final salvation, for salvation is a matter of grace and not of reward.] ᶜ6 And they departed, ᵇ12 And they went out, ᶜand went throughout the villages, ᵇand preached that *men* should repent. ᶜpreaching the gospel, ᵇ13 And they cast out many demons, and anointed with oil many that were sick, and healed them. ᶜhealing everywhere. ᵃ1 And it came to pass when Jesus had finished commanding his twelve disciples, he departed thence to teach and preach in their cities. [Oil was not used as a medicine. The Jews anointed their hair and their faces every day, especially when about to depart from the house to move among their fellows. This anointing was omitted when they were sick and when they fasted (II. Sam. xii. 20; Matt. vi. 16, 17). When an apostle stood over a sick man to heal him by a touch or a word, he was about to send him out of his sick chamber, and just before the word was spoken, the oil was applied. It was, therefore, no more than a token or symbol that the man was restored to his liberty, and was from that moment to be confined to his chamber no longer. Comp. Jas. v. 14. This practice bears about the same relation to the Romish practice of extreme unction as the Lord's Supper does to the mass, or as a true baptism does to the sprinkling of an infant.]

LXII.

HEROD ANTIPAS SUPPOSES JESUS TO BE JOHN.

ᵃMATT. XIV. 1–12; ᵇMARK VI. 14–29; ᶜLUKE IX. 7–9.

ᵇ14 And ᶜ7 Now ᵃ1 At that season ᵇking Herod [Herod Antipas, son of Herod the Great. See page 63] ᶜthe tetrarch heard of all that was done: ᵃheard the report concerning Jesus, ᵇfor his name had become known: ᶜand he was much perplexed, because that it was said by some, that John was risen from the dead; 8 and by some, that Elijah had appeared; and by others, that one of the old prophets was risen again. [The work of Jesus impressed the people as prophetic rather than Messianic, for they associated the Messiah in their thoughts with an earthly kingdom of great pomp and grandeur. Jesus, therefore, did not appear to them to be the Messiah, but rather the prophet who should usher in the Messiah. Their Scriptures taught them that Elijah would be that prophet. But the Apocrypha indicated that it might be Isaiah and Jeremiah (I. Macc. xiv. 41). Hence the many opinions as to which of the prophets Jesus was. If he was Elijah, he could not be properly spoken of as risen from the dead, for Elijah had been translated.] **9 And Herod said, ᵃunto his servants, ᶜJohn I beheaded** [For the imprisonment of John see pages 138, 139. The mission of the twelve probably lasted several weeks, and the beheading of John the Baptist appears to have taken place about the time of their return. See page 374]: **but who is this, about whom I hear such things? ᵃ This is John the Baptist; {ᵇthe Baptizer} ᵃhe is risen from the dead; and therefore do these powers work in him.** [John had wrought no miracle while living (Matt. x. 41), but there was a prevalent idea among the ancients that departed spirits were endowed with superhuman powers, and Herod therefore supposed that the risen John had brought these powers with him from the spirit world.] **ᶜAnd he sought to see him.** [Jesus purposely kept out of the reach of Herod, knowing the treacherous cunning of his nature (Luke xiii. 32), and Herod's curiosity was not gratified until the day of Christ's crucifixion (Luke xxiii. 8–12), and then its gratification was without satisfaction.] **ᵇ15 But others said, It is Elijah. And others said, *It is* a prophet, *even* as one of the prophets. 16 But Herod, when he heard *thereof*, said, John, whom I beheaded, he is risen.** [Some thought that Elijah might have returned, as the Scripture declared, or that Jesus might be a prophet just like the great prophets of old. Matthew, by introducing what follows with the word "for," gives us the reason why Herod clung to his singular opinion concerning Jesus. He did so because this opinion was begotten by the morbid musings of a conscience stained with the blood of John.] **17 For Herod himself had sent forth**

**and laid hold upon John, ᵃand bound him, and put him
in prison for the sake of Herodias, his brother Philip's
wife. ᵇfor he had married her.** [Herodias was the daughter of Aristobulus, who was the half-brother of Herod Philip
I. and Herod Antipas, and these two last were in turn half-
brothers to each other. Herodias, therefore, had married her
uncle Herod Philip I., who was disinherited by Herod the
Great, and who lived as a private citizen in Rome. When
Herod Antipas went to Rome about the affairs of his tetrarchy,
he became the guest of his brother Herod Philip I., and repaid
the hospitality which he received by carrying off the wife of
his host.] **18 For John said unto Herod, It is not lawful for thee to have thy brother's wife.** [The marriage
was unlawful for three reasons: 1. The husband of Herodias
was still living; 2. The lawful wife of Antipas (the daughter
of Aretas, king or emir of Arabia) was still living; 3. Antipas
and Herodias, being nephew and niece, were related to each
other within the forbidden degrees of consanguinity.] **19 And
Herodias set herself against him, and desired to kill
him; and she could not; 20 for Herod feared John,
knowing that he was a righteous and holy man, and
kept him safe. And when he heard him, he was much
perplexed; and he heard him gladly. ᵃ5 And when he
would have put him to death, he feared the multitude,
because they counted him as a prophet.** [Herod feared
both John and his influence. His fear of the man as a prophet
caused him to shelter John against any attempts which his
angry wife might make to put him to death, and led him to
listen to John with enough respect to become perplexed as to
whether it were better to continue in his course or repent. At
other times, when the influence of Herodias moved him most
strongly, and he forgot his personal fear of John, he was yet
restrained by fear of John's influence over the people.] **6 But
when Herod's birthday came, ᵇ21 And when a convenient day was come** [A day suited to the purposes of Herodias.
The phrase refers to verse 19], **that Herod on his birthday
made a supper to his lords, and the high captains, and**

the chief men of Galilee; 22 and when the daughter
of Herodias herself [the language seems to indicate that
others had first come in and danced] came in and danced,
ᵃ in the midst, ᵇ she pleased Herod and them that sat
at meat with him [This dancer was Salome, daughter of
Herod Philip and niece of Herod Antipas. The dancing of
the East was then, as now, voluptuous and indecent, and nothing but utter shamelessness or inveterate malice could have
induced a princess to thus make a public show of herself at
such a carousal]; ᵃ 7 Whereupon he promised with an
oath to give her whatsoever she should ask. ᵇ and the
king said unto the damsel, Ask of me whatsoever thou
wilt, and I will give it thee. 23 And he sware unto
her, Whatsoever thou shalt ask of me, I will give it
thee, unto the half of my kingdom. [The rashness of the
king's promise is characteristic of the folly of sin. Riches,
honors, kingdoms, souls are given for a bauble in the devil's
market.] 24 And she went out, and said unto her
mother, What shall I ask? [She may have known beforehand what to ask. If so, she retired and asked her mother
that the brunt of the king's displeasure might fall upon her
mother.] And she said, The head of John the Baptist.
ᵃ 8 And she, being put forward by her mother, ᵇ came
in straightway with haste unto the king [she wished to
make her request known before the king had time to put limitations upon her asking], and asked, saying, {ᵃ saith,} ᵇ I
will that thou forthwith give me ᵃ here on a platter the
head of John the Baptist. [She asked for the prophet's
head that she and her mother might have the witness of their
own eyes to the fact that he was dead, and that they might
not be deceived about it.] 9 And the king was grieved;
ᵇ was exceeding sorry [because the deed went against his
conscience and his sense of policy as above stated]; but for
the sake of his oaths, and of them that {ᵃ which} sat
at meat with him, ᵇ he would not reject her. ᵃ he commanded it to be given [The oath alone would not have
constrained Herod to grant Salome's request, for if left alone

he would rightly have construed the request as not coming within the scope of the oath. The terms of his oath looked to and anticipated a pecuniary present, and not the commission of a crime. But Herod's companions, being evil men, joined with the evil women against the man of God, and shamed Herod into an act which committed him forever to a course of guilt. Thus, a bad man's good impulses are constantly broken down by his evil companions]; ᵇ **27 And straightway the king sent forth a soldier of his guard, ᵃ and beheaded John in the prison. ᵇ and commanded to bring his head: and he went and beheaded him in the prison, 28 and brought his head {ᵃ his head was brought} ᵇ on a platter, and gave it {ᵃ and given} ᵇ to the damsel; and the damsel ᵃ brought it ᵇ gave it to her mother.** [To the anxious, unrestful soul of Herodias this seemed a great gift, since it assured her that the voice of her most dangerous enemy was now silent. But as Herod was soon filled with superstitious fears that John had risen in the person of Christ, her sense of security was very short-lived. The crime stamped Herod and Herodias with greater infamy than that for which John had rebuked them.] **29 And when his disciples heard *thereof*, they came and took up his {ᵃ the} corpse, ᵇ and laid it in a tomb. ᵃ and buried him; and went and told Jesus.** [Herod had feared that the death of John would bring about a popular uprising, and his fears were not mistaken. As soon as they had decently buried the body of the great preacher, John's disciples go to Jesus, expecting to find in him a leader to redress the Baptist's wrongs. They knew the friendship of John for Jesus, and. knowing that the latter intended to set up a kingdom, they believed that this would involve the overthrow of Herod's power. They were ready now to revolt and make Jesus a king. See Matt. xii. 13; John vi. 1, 2, 15. But Jesus would not aid them to seek the bitter fruits of revenge, nor did he intend to set up such a kingdom as they imagined.]

LXIII.

FIRST WITHDRAWAL FROM HEROD'S TERRITORY AND RETURN.

(Spring, A. D. 29.)

Subdivision A.

RETURN OF THE TWELVE AND RETIREMENT TO THE EAST SHORE OF GALILEE.

[a] MATT. XIV. 13; [b] MARK VI. 30–32; [c] LUKE IX. 10; [d] JOHN VI. 1.

[b] **30 And the apostles gather themselves together unto Jesus;** [c] **when they were returned,** [b] **and they told {** [c] **declared unto}** [b] **him all things, whatsoever they had done, and whatsoever they had taught.** [They had fulfilled the mission on which Jesus had sent them, and on returning each pair made to him a full report of their work.] **31 And he saith unto them, Come ye yourselves apart into a desert place** [an uninhabited place], **and rest a while. For there were many coming and going, and they had no leisure so much as to eat.** [Need of rest was one reason for retiring to the thinly settled shores east of the lake. Matthew proceeds to give us another reason for his retiring.] [a] **13 Now** [d] **1 After these things** [a] **when Jesus heard** *it* [Heard about John's death. The excitement caused by this event, and the efforts to use Jesus as a leader in revolt, as indicated at the close of the last section, constituted another reason why Jesus should withdraw from the multitude], [c] **he took them** [the apostles], **and withdrew** [a] **thence** [c] **apart** [b] **32 And they went away in the {** [a] **a} boat,** [d] **to the other side of the sea of Galilee, which is** *the sea* **of Tiberias.** [c] **to a city called Bethsaida.** [b] **to a desert place apart.** [They sailed to the northeastern shore of the lake to a plain lying near the city of Bethsaida Julius.]

Subdivision B.

FEEDING THE FIVE THOUSAND.

^a MATT. XIV. 13–21 ; ^b MARK VI. 33–44; ^c LUKE IX. 11–17 ;
^d JOHN VI. 2–14.

^c 11 But {^a and} when the multitudes heard *thereof*
[heard of Jesus and his disciples crossing the lake], ^b 33 And
they saw them going, and ^c perceiving it, ^b many knew
them, ^d 2 And a great multitude followed him, because
they beheld the signs which he did on them that were
sick. ^b and they ran together there on foot from all the
cities, and outwent them. ^a 14 And he came forth,
and saw a great multitude, and he had compassion on
them, ^b because they were as sheep not having a shepherd: ^c and he welcomed them, ^b and he began to teach
them many things. ^c and spake to them of the kingdom
of God, ^a and healed their sick. ^c and them that had
need of healing he cured. [Jesus probably set sail from
near Capernaum, and from thence across the lake to the
narrow, secluded plain of El Batihah where he landed is less
than five miles. Seeing him start, the people followed him by
running along the northern shore, and, though having a little
farther to go, they traveled faster than the sailboat, and were
waiting for him on the shore when he arrived.] ^d 3 And
Jesus went up into the mountain, and there he sat
with his disciples. [The level plain did not afford a good
platform from which to address the people.] 4 Now the
passover, the feast of the Jews, was at hand. [This
passover is computed to have been held on April 16, A. D. 29.
This statement as to the time of year prepares us for his further
statement that there was much grass in the plain. It also explains in part the gathering of a multitude in this secluded
region. Pilgrims on their way to the passover would gladly
go several miles out of their way to see the great Prophet perform a miracle. The excitement, due to the mission of the
twelve and the death of the Baptist, also tended to swell the

crowd.] ᶜ 12 And the day began to wear away; ᵇ 35 And when the day was now far spent, ᵃ 15 And when even was come, ᵇ his disciples ᶜ the twelve ᵇ came unto him, ᶜ and said unto him, {ᵃ saying,} ᵇ The place is desert, and the day is now far spent; ᵃ and the time is already past [the time to seek lodging and provisions had gone by, and therefore the multitude must act quickly]; ᵇ 36 send them ᵃ the multitudes {ᶜ multitude} away, that they may go into the villages and country round about, and lodge, and get provisions: ᵃ and buy themselves food. ᵇ somewhat to eat. ᶜ for we are here in a desert place. [The apostles were the first to think of eating, and naturally enough, for they had started on empty stomachs, and their own discomfort made them anticipate the sad plight in which the multitude would soon find itself.] ᵃ 16 But Jesus said unto them, They have no need to go away; ᵈ 5 Jesus therefore lifting up his eyes, and seeing that a great multitude cometh to him, saith unto Philip, Whence are we to buy bread, that these may eat? 6 And this he said to prove him: for he himself knew what he would do. 7 Philip answered him, Two hundred shillings' worth of bread is not sufficient for them, that every one may take a little. [Jesus tested Philip to see which way he would turn in his weakness. Jesus asked where the bread might be bought, knowing that power to feed the multitude resided in himself (Isa. lv. 1), but Philip wondered where the money was to be had with which to buy it.] ᵇ 37 But he answered and said unto them, Give ye them to eat. And they say unto him, Shall we go and buy two hundred shillings' worth of bread, and give them to eat? [The word translated shilling is the Roman denarius, worth about seventeen cents. The sum was not large, as we reckon money, but, considering the purchasing power of money in those days, it was an imposing sum, and it is to be doubted if the treasury-bag of Judas ever contained the fourth part of it. For a denarius was the regular price for a day's labor.] 38 And he saith unto them, How many loaves have ye? go *and* see. ᵈ8 One of his disciples, Andrew, Simon Peter's brother, saith unto him, 9 There is a lad here, who hath five barley loaves, and two fishes: but what are these among so many? ᵇ And when they knew, they say, Five, and two fishes. ᵃ 17 And they say unto him, {ᶜ said,} ᵃWe have here but ᶜ no more than five loaves and two fishes; except we should go and buy food for all this people. 14 For they were about five thousand men. [When sent to see what was in their larder, it appears that they had nothing at all. Andrew reports the finding of the boy's lunch while it was as yet the boy's property. Some of the others, having secured it from the boy, report it now at the disposal of Jesus, but comment on its insufficiency. Eastern loaves were thin and small, like good-sized crackers, and, around the sea of Galilee, the salting and preserving of small fish was an especial industry. These fish, therefore, were about the size of sardines. The whole supply, therefore, was no more than enough for one hungry boy. But each loaf had to be divided between a thousand, and each fish between twenty-five hundred men.] ᵃ 18 And he said, Bring them hither to me. 19 And he commanded the multitudes to sit down ᵇ that all should sit down by companies upon the green grass. ᶜ And ᵈ 10 Jesus said, ᶜ unto his disciples, Make them ᵈ the people sit down. ᶜ in companies, about fifty each. 15 And they did so, and made them all sit down. ᵇ 40 And they sat down in ranks, by hundreds, and by fifties. ᵈ Now there was much grass in the place. So the men sat down, in number about five thousand. [By thus arranging them in orderly companies, Jesus accomplished several things. He saved his apostles much time and labor in distributing the food. He insured that each one should be fed, and that the reality of the miracle could not be questioned, and he ascertained definitely how many men were fed.] ᶜ 16 And ᵈ 11 Jesus therefore took ᵃ the five loaves, and the two fishes, and looking up to heaven, ᶜ he blessed and brake them, ᵇ and brake the loaves; ᵈ and having given thanks, he distributed to them that were set down; ᵃand gave the loaves to the disciples, and the disciples to the multitudes. {ᶜand gave to the disciples to set before the multitude.} ᵈlikewise also of the fishes as much as they would. ᵇand the two fishes divided he among them all. **42** And they all ate, ᶜand were all filled [He blessed the loaves and fishes by returning thanks for them. This and similar acts of Jesus are our precedents for giving thanks, or, "asking the blessing," at our tables]: ᵈ**12** And when they were filled, he saith unto his disciples, Gather up the broken pieces which remain over, that nothing be lost. [Christ is the economist of the universe. This command was in keeping with his laws which permit nothing to suffer annihilation. Ruin and destruction have no other effect than merely to change the form of things. Every atom of the material world which was here at the beginning of creation is here to-day, though it may have changed its form a million times in the progress of events.] So they gathered them up, ᶜand there was taken {ᵃthey took} ᶜup that which remained over to them of ᵃthe broken pieces, ᵈand filled ᵃtwelve baskets full. {ᵇbasketfuls,} ᵈwith broken pieces from the five barley loaves, which remained over unto them that had eaten. ᵇand also of the fishes. ᵃ**21** And they that did eat {ᵇate} the loaves were ᵃabout five thousand men, besides women and children. [Considering the distance from any town, the women and children would not likely be numerous. They form no part of the count, for Eastern usage did not permit the women to sit with the men. They, with the little ones, would stand apart.] ᵈ**14** When therefore the people saw the sign which he did, they said, This is of a truth the prophet that cometh into the world. [That is to say, this is the Messiah, the prophet promised at Deut. xviii. 15. Their desire to avenge the death of John made them feverishly anxious for the appearance of the Messiah, but this faith was inconstant.

Subdivision C.

THE TWELVE TRY TO ROW BACK. JESUS WALKS UPON THE WATER.

ᵃMATT. XIV. 22–36; ᵇMARK VI. 45–56; ᵈJOHN VI. 15–21.

ᵈ15 Jesus therefore perceiving that they were about to come and take him by force, to make him king, withdrew again into the mountain himself alone. [Jesus had descended to the plain to feed the multitude, but, perceiving this mistaken desire of the people, he frustrated it by dismissing his disciples and retiring by himself into the mountain.] ᵃ22 And straightway he constrained the {ᵇhis} ᵃdisciples to enter into the boat, and to go before him unto the other side, ᵇto Bethsaida [the suburb of Capernaum], ᵃtill he should send the multitudes {ᵇwhile he himself sendeth the multitude} away. [The obedience of the disciples in leaving him helped to persuade the multitude to do likewise.] 46 And after he had taken leave of them, ᵃ23 And after he had sent the multitudes away, he went up {ᵇdeparted} ᵃinto the mountain apart to pray: and when even was come, he was there alone. [The news of John's assassination was calculated to exasperate him in the highest degree, and also to deeply distress him. He needed the benefits of prayer to keep down resentment, and to prevent despondency. For this he started away as soon as he heard the news, but the people prevented him till night.] ᵈ16 And when evening came, his disciples went down unto the sea; 17 and they entered into a boat, and were going over the sea unto Capernaum. ᵇ47 And when even was come, the boat was in the midst of the sea, and he alone on the land. ᵈand it was now dark, and Jesus had not yet come to them. [They evidently expected that he would follow. Possibly they skirted the shore, hoping that he would hail them and come on board.] 18 And the sea was rising by reason of a great wind that blew. ᵃ24 But the boat was now in the midst of the sea, distressed by the waves; for the wind was contrary. [That is, it blew from the west, the direction toward which the disciples were rowing.] ᵇ48 And seeing them distressed in rowing, for the wind was contrary unto them, about {ᵃin} ᵇthe fourth watch of the night [from 3 to 6 A. M.] he cometh {ᵃcame} ᵇunto them, ᵃwalking upon the sea. [The disciples of Jesus can rest assured that the eyes of the Lord will behold their distresses, and that sooner or later the Lord himself will arise and draw near for their deliverance.] ᵈ19 When therefore they had rowed about five and twenty or thirty furlongs [that is, about three and a half miles, or about half way across the sea], they behold Jesus walking on the sea, and drawing nigh unto the boat: ᵇand he would have passed by them: ᵃ26 And {ᵇ49 but} ᵃwhen the disciples saw him walking on the sea, they were troubled, ᵈand they were afraid. ᵇthey supposed that it was a ghost, and cried out; ᵃsaying, It is a ghost; and they cried out for fear. ᵇ50 for they all saw him, and were troubled. [Their fears would probably have been greater if Jesus had approached the boat, for they were severe enough to make them cry out, even when he was seen to be passing by them.] ᵃ27 But straightway Jesus spake unto {ᵇwith} them, and saith unto them, {ᵃsaying,} Be of good cheer; it is I; be not afraid. [There was no mistaking that voice. If Isaac knew the voice of Jacob (Gen. xxvii. 22), Saul the voice of David (I. Sam. xxvi. 17), and Rhoda the voice of Peter (Acts xii. 17), much more did the apostles know the voice of the great Master.] ᵈ21 They were willing therefore to receive him into the boat [Superstitious fears are not always so soon allayed. His voice brought great assurance]: ᵃ28 And Peter answered him and said, Lord, if it be thou, bid me come unto thee upon the waters. 29 And he said, Come. And Peter went down from the boat, and walked upon the waters to come to Jesus. [The scene comports with the character of Peter, who had always a rash willingness ᴊᴏ go into danger, and a lack of steadfastness to hold out through it.] **30 But when he saw the wind, he was afraid; and beginning to sink, he cried out, saying, Lord, save me.** [So long as the attention of Peter was fixed upon the Lord's command he succeeded in his venture; but so soon as he let the power of the tempest distract his thoughts, his faith failed and he began to sink.] **31 And immediately Jesus stretched forth his hand, and took hold of him, and saith unto him, O thou of little faith, wherefore didst thou doubt?** [Fear is a source of doubt and an enemy of faith. Those who would achieve the victories of faith must overcome their fears.] ᵇ**51 And he went up unto them into the boat;** ᵃ**32 And when they were gone up into the boat, the wind ceased.** ᵇ**and they were sore amazed in themselves; 52 for they understood not concerning the loaves, but their heart was hardened,** ᵈ**and straightway the boat was at the land whither they were going.** ᵃ**33 And they that were in the boat worshipped him, saying, Of a truth thou art the Son of God.** [The disciples showed the hardness of their hearts in that the working of one miracle did not prepare them either to expect or to comprehend any other miracle which followed. They ought to have worshipped Jesus as the Son of God when they saw the five thousand fed, but they did not. But when he had done that, and had walked upon the water, and quieted the wind, and transported the boat to the land, they were overcome by the iteration of his miraculous power, and confessed his divinity.] **34 And when they had crossed over, they came to the land, unto Genessaret.** ᵇ**and moored to the shore.** [The land of Genessaret was a plain at the western side of the lake of Galilee. Josephus describes it as about thirty furlongs in length by about twenty in average width, and bounded on the west by a semicircular line of hills.] **54 And when they were come out of the boat, straightway** *the people* **knew him,** ᵃ**35 And when the men of that place knew him, they sent into** ᵇ**and ran round about that whole region, and began to carry about on**

their beds those that were sick, where they heard he
was. ᵃand brought unto him all that were sick; ᵇ56
And wheresoever he entered, into villages, or into
cities, or into the country, they laid the sick in the
marketplaces, ᵃ36 and they besought him that they
might only touch ᵇif it were but the border of his garment: and as many as touched him were made whole.
[Though the apostles had started their boat toward Capernaum, the storm appears to have deflected their course, and
the language of the text suggests that they probably came to
land at the south end of the plain, somewhere near Magdala,
and made a circuit of the cities in the plain of Genessaret on
their way to Capernaum. As he did not stop in these cities,
the sick were laid in the street that they might touch him in
passing through. Moreover, as they knew the course that he
was taking, by running ahead they could anticipate his arrivals
and have the sick gathered to take advantage of his presence.
The story of the woman who touched the hem of his garment
had evidently spread far and wide, and deeply impressed the
popular mind.]

LXIV.

DISCOURSE ON SPIRITUAL FOOD AND TRUE
DISCIPLESHIP. PETER'S CONFESSION.

(At the synagogue in Capernaum.)

ᵈJOHN VI. 22-71.

ᵈ22 On the morrow [the morrow after Jesus fed the five
thousand] the multitude that stood on the other side of
the sea [on the east side, opposite Capernaum] saw that
there was no other boat there, save one, and that Jesus
entered not with his disciples into the boat, but *that*
his disciples went away alone 23 (howbeit there came
boats from Tiberias nigh unto the place where they ate
the bread after the Lord had given thanks): 24 when

the multitude therefore saw that Jesus was not there, neither his disciples, they themselves got into the boats, and came to Capernaum, seeking Jesus. [This sentence is a complicated one, because it contains much in a condensed form. On the evening of the miracle the multitude had seen that there was but one boat, and that the disciples had gone away in it, leaving Jesus in the mountain. Jesus had dispersed the multitude, but many of them had not gone very far. On the morrow they came again to the scene of the miracle, and were perplexed at not finding Jesus. After some time they became convinced that he was not there, because if if he had been his disciples would have returned to seek him. In the meantime the keen-eyed boatmen about Tiberias, then the largest city on the lake, seeing the multitude on the farther shore, saw in their presence there an opportunity to earn a ferry fee, so they soon crossed the lake to accommodate the people. As Capernaum was the well-known headquarters of Jesus, the boatmen were directed to proceed thither that the multitude might find him.] **25 And when they found him on the other side of the sea, they said unto him, Rabbi, when camest thou hither?** [They found him at Capernaum in the synagogue, having but lately arrived from the land of Genessaret. Though their question relates only to the time when Jesus crossed, it implies and includes a desire to know the manner also.] **26 Jesus answered them and said, Verily, verily** [his answer was as serious as their question was flippant], **I say unto you, Ye seek me, not because ye saw signs** [Jesus includes the healing of the sick as well as the feeding of the multitude], **but because ye ate of the loaves, and were filled.** [They did not seek Jesus because they saw in him a divine Friend who could satisfy the deep needs of the soul, but as a wonder-worker who could fill their bodies with food when occasion required.] **27 Work not for the food which perisheth** [bodily food], **but for the food which abideth unto eternal life** [spiritual food], **which the Son of man shall give unto you: for him the Father, *even* God, hath sealed.** [In our land a man consents to and makes a written instrument his own—an expression of his will—by signing it; but in the East he did this by affixing his seal to it (I. Kings xxi. 8; Esth. iii. 12; viii. 10; Jer. xxxii. 10). The meaning of Jesus' words, therefore, is that God the Father had commissioned him as Messiah, and had authenticated his mission as such by the works which he had given him to do—John xxxv. 6.] **28 They said therefore unto him, What must we do, that we may work the works of God?** [They wished to know what to do in order to earn the abiding food; that is, by what works they might so please God as to obtain it. Humanity, in seeking to answer this question, has invented pilgrimages, penances, fasts, mutilations and many other methods of self-punishment; not heeding the plain and decisive answer of Jesus.] **29 Jesus answered and said unto them, This is the work of God, that ye believe on him whom he hath sent.** [Belief in Jesus as the Son of God is the one all-comprehensive work which pleases God (Heb. xi. 6). Jesus reiterates this important truth several times in this discourse: see verses 35, 36, 40, 47, etc., and the doctrine contained in it is elaborated in the epistles of Paul.] **30 They said therefore unto him, What then doest thou for a sign, that we may see, and believe thee? what workest thou? 31 Our fathers ate the manna in the wilderness; as it is written, He gave them bread out of heaven to eat.** [The trend of the questions and answers in this discourse forms a close parallel to that at John iv., but with a different conclusion. There Jesus discoursed of life under the figure of water, and here under the figure of bread. There the woman vacillated between her good and evil impulses until her better nature triumphed. Here there was a like vacillation, terminating in an opposite result. There the woman compared Jesus with Jacob, the well-digger (John iv. 12); here the people compare him with Moses, the manna-giver—each comparing him unfavorably.] **32 Jesus therefore said unto them, Verily, verily, I say unto you, It was not Moses that gave you the bread out of heaven; but**

my Father giveth you the true bread out of heaven.
**33 For the bread of God is that which cometh down
out of heaven, and giveth life unto the world.** [In test-
ing the claims of Jesus the Jews proceeded upon the hypothesis that the Messiah must be greater than all the prophets,
and that this greatness must be authenticated or sealed by
greater signs than those wrought by others. Proceeding under
this method, they compared the miracle just wrought by Jesus
with the fall of manna in the days of Moses and drew con-
clusions unfavorable to Jesus. They reasoned thus: "Moses
fed many million for forty years with bread from heaven, but
Moses was less than the Messiah. This man fed but five
thousand for only one day and gave them barley bread. This
man is even less than Moses, and consequently far less than
the Messiah.] **34 They said therefore unto him, Lord,
evermore give us this bread.** [They readily recognized
the insufficiency of manna and the possibility of God sending
a better bread, and in a vague, wondering, half-credulous
mood they asked for it just as the woman asked for the water
(John iv. 15). In answer to each set of questions Jesus proceeded to reveal himself, and to show that the blessings sought
were not external to himself, but were in himself and were
obtained by belief in him. When Jesus stood thus self-
revealed the Samaritan woman believed in him and was satisfied; but these Jews at Capernaum disbelieved and murmured.
**35 Jesus said unto them, I am the bread of life: he
that cometh to me shall not hunger, and he that believeth on me shall never thirst.** [Compare John iv. 10,
13, 14.] **36 But I said unto you, that ye have seen me,
and yet believe not.** [The personality of Jesus was the
great proof of his divinity, but the Jews, though familiar with
that personality, refused to consider it, and kept clamoring for
a sign. Hence Jesus states the hopelessness of the situation.
If one refuses to believe in the sun when he sees its light,
feels its heat and witnesses its life-giving power, by what sign
will you demonstrate to him the existence of the sun?] **37 All
that which the Father giveth me shall come unto me;**

and him that cometh to me I will in no wise cast out.
[These words of Christ arise naturally out of the situation.
The Jews, having wavered between belief and disbelief, had
settled in a proud disbelief which was about to be expressed in
murmuring and scorn. They were complacently self-satisfied,
and felt that they had displayed great wisdom in arriving at
this decision. But Jesus strikes at their pride by informing
them that they are not his because God has rejected them as
unworthy to be given to him. There is no suggestion or hint
that the Father acts arbitrarily in selecting whom he shall give
to Christ. The Son of God *followed a prescribed course* in
the winning of men. If this did not win them, it was the
Father's decree that they were not his. If this course did
win them, Jesus in nowise rejected them, no matter how
lowly their station or how vile their past record.] **38 For I
am come down from heaven, not to do mine own will,
but the will of him that sent me. 39 And this is the
will of him that sent me, that of all that which he hath
given me I should lose nothing, but should raise it up
at the last day. 40 For this is the will of my Father,
that every one that beholdeth the Son, and believeth
on him, should have eternal life; and I will raise him
up at the last day.** [It was the purpose of God the Father
to offer to the sons of men an eternal life through the life-
giving power of Jesus Christ. The power which was to work
in men a fitness for this exalted honor was a belief in the Son.
How could signs and wonders be wrought contrary to the
Father's will? They ought to have believed for the signs and
wonders he had already wrought, instead of pretending that
he had wrought none that were conclusive of his claims.]
**41 The Jews therefore murmured concerning him,
because he said, I am the bread which came down out
of heaven. 42 And they said, Is not this Jesus, the
son of Joseph, whose father and mother we know?
how doth he now say, I am come down out of heav-
en?** [The Jews had entered with Christ upon a discussion
as to whether he was a greater prophet than Moses, and as

they denied even this fact, it is not to be wondered that they murmured at the turn which the discussion had taken. In asserting that he came down from heaven, etc., he ascribed to himself a participation in the divine glory which entitled him to an absolute superiority over all men, prophets or others. This claim was to them insufferable, and they thought they had a sufficient answer to it in that they supposed themselves to be acquainted with his birth and parentage.] **43 Jesus answered and said unto them, Murmur not among yourselves. 44 No man can come to me, except the Father that sent me draw him: and I will raise him up in the last day. 45 It is written in the prophets** [Isa. liv. 13; Jer. xxxi. 33, 34; Joel iii. 16, 17], **And they shall all be taught of God. Every one that hath heard from the Father, and hath learned, cometh unto me.** [Jesus rebukes their murmuring as out of place. They thought themselves offended by what they believed to be an intolerable assumption on his part. But they were really offended in him for an entirely different cause, viz.: because they were not drawn to him by the Father. The Father had given the law as a tutor to draw to Christ (Gal. iii. 24), and he had also sent forth his prophets for the same purpose. Those who had availed themselves of this instruction, and had learned the Father's lesson, were ready to come to Christ. The sense of misery and desire of redemption begotten by the law drove one to Christ, and all the yearnings and aspirations inspired by the prophets attracted him thither. The Father had taught, but the people had not learned, just as their fathers had not learned; and Jesus accuses them in language kindred to the accusation of Moses when he says, "But Jehovah hath not given you a heart to know, and eyes to see, and ears to hear, unto this day" (Deut. xxix. 4). In each case the people were to blame.] **46 Not that any man hath seen the Father, save he that is from God, he hath seen the Father.** [The Jews might have construed the words of Jesus as indicating an immediate relation to the Father and of obtaining instruction directly from him. Such a doctrine would strike at the mediation of Christ. Jesus therefore guards against this false apprehension by denying humanity's direct access to God the Father, and claiming it as his own exclusive right. The teaching of the Father which he spoke of was obtained through the Scriptures and (in earlier times) the prophets, who were the authors of the Scriptures.] **47 Verily, verily, I say unto you, He that believeth hath eternal life. 48 I am the bread of life.** [Jesus here reasserts the proposition to which the Jews had objected. Having paused to speak of the cause of their objections, he now asserts the main propositions, that he may enlarge upon them.] **49 Your fathers ate the manna in the wilderness, and they died.** [Manna did not stay death. During the forty years' sojourn in the wilderness all the grown men who started from Egypt died save two.] **50 This is the bread which cometh down out of heaven, that a man may eat thereof, and not die.** [He quietly condescends to contrast the two breads. Manna simply sustained the body like any other natural food; it did no more. Jesus is supernatural food; he sustains the spirit unto eternal life.] **51 I am the living bread which came down out of heaven: if any man eat of this bread, he shall live for ever: yea and the bread which I will give is my flesh, for the life of the world.** [He had declared himself to be the bread of life, but bread must be assimilated. The assimilation of natural bread requires eating, but Jesus, the spiritual bread, is assimilated by believing on him. But he was not then perfected as the bread of life. It was necessary that he should sacrifice himself for our sins before sins could be forgiven, and it was necessary for sins to be forgiven before men could have life with God. By his sacrifice on the cross he opened the fountain of forgiveness. By raising his humanity from the dead and by taking it with him in his ascension into heaven, he showed the results which men may expect to accrue to them by his death upon the cross.] **52 The Jews therefore strove one with another, saying, How can this man give us his flesh to eat?** [They were not all of one mind with regard to Christ, and they discussed from opposite sides the problem raised by these mysterious words.] **53 Jesus therefore said unto them, Verily, verily, I say unto you, Except ye eat the flesh of the Son of man and drink his blood, ye have not life in yourselves.** [He here expressed in words what he afterward expressed in symbols, when he gave the Lord's supper. The vital force of a disciple is proportioned to his belief in, remembrance of, and desire to assimilate the Christ.] **54 He that eateth my flesh and drinketh my blood hath eternal life; and I will raise him up at the last day. 55 For my flesh is meat indeed, and my blood is drink indeed.** [The flesh to be eaten must be broken, and the blood, if it is to be drunk, must be poured out. Christ speaks of himself as the sacrifice given for the saving of the world, and one must appropriate to himself by faith this expiation and find in it reconciliation with God if he would live; but the next verse enlarges the thought, and shows that it includes more than the idea of expiation.] **56 He that eateth my flesh and drinketh my blood abideth in me, and I in him.** [The thought of drinking blood was startling to the Jew, for he was forbidden to taste even the blood of animals, and the reason assigned was very pertinent—because the blood was the life of the animal (Gen. ix. 4; Lev. xvii. 10–14). By insisting, therefore, on the drinking of his blood, Jesus has insisted that his very life be absorbed and assimilated. To be disciples of other teachers it is only necessary that we accept and follow their doctrine. But to be a disciple of Christ is to do more than this. His divinity permits us to have a spiritual communion and fellowship with him, an abiding in his presence, an indwelling of his Spirit and a veritable assimilation of life from him. Were it otherwise he could not be food for the spirit—bread of life. He had started to show to the Jews that he was to the spirit what bread was to the body. It was difficult to bring home to their carnal minds so spiritual a thought, and therefore Jesus clothed it in carnal metaphors and made it as plain as possible. Christians to-day, being more spiritually minded, and more used to spiritual language, are somewhat confused by the carnal dress in which Jesus clothed his thought.] **57 As the living Father sent me, and I live because of the Father; so he that eateth me, he also shall live because of me.** [The result of our union or abiding with Christ is a perfect life. The life of the Father enters the soul of the disciple through the mediatorship of the Son. The Father, who is the fountain of life, sent forth the Son that he might bestow it upon all who believe in him and abide in him.] **58 This is the bread which came down out of heaven: not as the fathers ate and died; he that eateth this bread shall live for ever.** [Thus Jesus sums up the comparison which the Jews had thrust upon him between himself and the manna.] **59 These things said he in the synagogue, as he taught in Capernaum.** [It was in the synagogue built by the centurion, which we have before mentioned. Pots of manna appear to have been engraved upon its walls, possibly upon the frieze, for Colonel Wilson says of it: "It was not without a certain strange feeling that, on turning over one of the blocks (in the ruins), we found the pot of manna engraved on its face, and remembered the words, 'I am that bread of life. Your fathers did eat manna in the wilderness, and are dead.'"] **60 Many therefore of his disciples, when they heard *this*, said, This is a hard saying; who can hear it? 61 But Jesus knowing in himself that his disciples murmured at this, said unto them, Doth this cause you to stumble? 62 *What* then if ye should behold the Son of man ascending where he was before?** [If the prophecy of his sacrifice disturbed their dreams of a temporal kingdom, what would be the effect of his ascension on those dreams? The Book of Acts answers our Lord's question. In the very hour of the ascension the very apostles were still expecting the revival of the kingdom of David, with Jerusalem for its capital. But ten days later, at Pentecost, they had abandoned the earthly idea and looked upon Jesus as enthroned at the right hand of God—Acts i. 6; ii. 32–36.] **63 It is the spirit that giveth life; the flesh profiteth nothing: the words that I**

have spoken unto you are spirit, and are life. [Jesus here tells them plainly that his words relate to the spiritual realm, and to life in that realm. It is his Spirit in our spirit which gives eternal life. His flesh in our flesh would profit nothing, even were a priest able, by his blessing, to perform the miracle of transubstantiation. The life-principle of Jesus lay in his divinity, and his divinity lay in his Spirit, and not in his flesh. We would not come in contact with his divinity by eating that which represented his humanity.] **64 But there are some of you that believe not. For Jesus knew from the beginning who they were that believed not, and who it was that should betray him. 65 And he said, For this cause have I said unto you, that no man can come unto me, except it be given unto him of the Father.** [Jesus here distinguishes between those who were drawn to him by divine influences, and who were therefore ready to follow him as he really was, and those who were drawn to him by mistaken notions concerning him, and who would desert him as soon as they discovered that their conceptions of him were incorrect. He knew the reason which prompted each to become his disciple.] **66 Upon this many of his disciples went back, and walked no more with him.** [He had sifted them, for their false following could be of no benefit either to them or to his kingdom.] **67 Jesus said therefore unto the twelve, Would ye also go away?** [Jesus had sifted the outer circle of his disciples, and the loss, though prophetically anticipated, was not without its pang. In this sixty-seventh verse he proceeds to sift the innermost circle, and his words are full of pathos. By giving them an opportunity to depart he called forth from them an expression of loyalty which bound them more closely to him.] **68 Simon Peter answered him, Lord, to whom shall we go? thou hast the words of eternal life. 69 And we have believed and know that thou art the Holy One of God. 70 Jesus answered them, Did not I choose you the twelve, and one of you is a devil? 71 Now he spake of Judas *the son* of Simon Iscariot,**

for he it was that should betray him, *being* **one of the twelve.** [We have seen from verse 64 that Jesus has already had the betrayer in his mind. Here he speaks of him openly. In a discourse which forecasted his passion it was natural that he should allude to his betrayer, especially when his presence enforced remembrance. But there was another reason to mention him at this time. He was an illustration of the truth that no man could be a real follower of Jesus unless he became such by the drawing of the Father.]

Note.—On the following page will be found a foot-note indicating a disagreement as to chronology. In the preparation of this work the senior editor preferred to let the junior editor be responsible for the harmonistic and chronological features of it, and hence his corrections as to these particulars are obliged to appear as foot-notes, since it is now impossible to readjust the work to suit them.—P. Y. P.

PART SIX.

FROM THE THIRD PASSOVER UNTIL OUR LORD'S ARRIVAL AT BETHANY.

(Time: One Year Less One Week.)

LXV.

JESUS FAILS TO ATTEND THE THIRD PASS-OVER.

Scribes Reproach Him for Disregarding Tradition.

(Galilee, probably Capernaum, Spring, A. D. 29.)

ᵃ MATT. xv. 1-20; ᵇ MARK vii. 1-23; ᵈ JOHN vii. 1.

ᵈ 1 **And after these things Jesus walked in Galilee: for he would not walk in Judaea, because the Jews sought to kill him.** [John told us in his last chapter that the passover was near at hand. He here makes a general statement which shows that Jesus did not attend this passover. The reason for his absence is given at John v. 18.] ᵃ 1 **Then there came to Jesus from Jerusalem** ᵇ 1 **And there are gathered together unto him the Pharisees, and certain of the scribes, who had come from Jerusalem, 2 and had seen that some of his disciples ate their bread with defiled, that is, unwashen, hands.** [Evidently several days intervened between the address of John vi. and the events here recorded, for the Pharisees and scribes would not be likely to leave Jerusalem until after the passover.*] **3 (For the Pharisees, and all the Jews, except they wash their hands diligently, eat not, holding the tradition of the elders; 4 and** *when they come* **from the market-**

---

* It was a whole year.—J. W. McG.

place, except they bathe themselves, they eat not; **and
many other things there are, which they have received
to hold, washings of cups, and pots, and brasen vessels.) 5 And the Pharisees and the scribes ask him,**
ᵃ **saying,** ᵇ **Why walk not thy disciples according to the
tradition of the elders, but eat their bread with defiled
hands?** ᵃ**2 Why do thy disciples transgress the tradition of the elders? for they wash not their hands
when they eat bread.** [For former comment on the custom
of washing or dipping see page 312. Belief in the tradition of
the elders was the fundamental peculiarity of the Pharisaic
system. They held that these traditions, or oral expositions
of and additions to the law, were revealed to Moses along
with the law, and were communicated by him orally to the
elders of the people, by whose successors they had been
handed down through each successive generation. They regarded these traditions as equal in authority with the written
word. Various uncleannesses are specified in the Mosaic law.
Traditions extended the idea of uncleanness so as to hold the
man as probably unclean who had been in the marketplace,
where he might have touched an unclean person, and to hold
certain cups, pots and brazen vessels as ceremonially unclean
when neither the laws of Moses nor the laws of hygiene declared them to be so. Since the law of Moses ordered the
unclean to dip himself in a bath for his cleansing, the tradition of the elders required a like dipping in these cases of uncleanness which they had invented. When we remember that
bathing was a daily practice among the Pharisees, we are less
surprised at this observance. As to the theory that the tradition of the elders was derived from Moses, Jesus here flatly
contradicts it. There is no trustworthy evidence to show that
it is of higher antiquity than the time of the return from the
Babylonian captivity.] **3 And he answered and said
unto them, Why do ye also transgress the commandment of God, because of your tradition? 7 Ye hypocrites,** ᵇ **Well did Isaiah prophesy of you hypocrites**
[Isa. xxix. 13], ᵃ **saying,** ᵇ **as it is written, This people**

honoreth me with their lips, But their heart is far from me. 7 But in vain do they worship me, Teaching *as their* doctrines the precepts of men. 8 Ye leave the commandment of God, and hold fast the tradition of men. 9 And he said unto them, Full well do ye reject the commandment of God, that ye may keep your tradition. [These Pharisees coming from Jerusalem could find nothing wherein Jesus or his disciples transgressed the law, so they eagerly grasped this transgression of the tradition as affording ground for an accusation. Jesus does not deny their charge, but justifies his disciples by attacking the whole traditional system, basing his attack upon a pointed prophecy which condemns it. It is hard for us to learn and apply the distinction between serving God as God wishes to be served, and serving him according to our own wishes and notions.] ᵃ4 For God {ᵇMoses} said [that is, God said it through Moses], Honor thy father and thy mother; and, He that speaketh evil of father or mother, let him die the death [see Ex. xx. 12; Deut. v. 16; Ex. xxi. 17; Lev. xx. 9]: 11 but ye say, If a man {ᵃWhosoever} shall say to his father or his mother, That wherewith thou mightest have been profited by me ᵇis Corban, that is to say, Given *to God*; ᵃ6 he shall not honor his father. ᵇ12 ye no longer suffer him to do ought for his father or his mother; ᵃAnd ye have made {ᵇ13 making} void the word of God by {ᵃbecause of} your tradition. ᵇwhich ye have delivered: and many such like things ye do. [Leaving for a moment the main question concerning uncleanness and washing, Jesus makes good his indictment against their tradition by giving an example of the mischievous way in which it set aside God's command-ments. The law required the honoring of parents, and for any one to cast off his parents in their old age, thus subjecting them to beggary or starvation, was to do more than to speak evil of them. Such conduct was practically to curse them, and to incur the death penalty for so doing. But at this point the Pharisees interfered with their tradition, which taught that a son could say of that part of his estate by which his **parents** might be profited, It is a gift; that is, a gift to God, and by thus dedicating that part to God, he would free himself from his obligation to his parents. Thus tradition undid the law. God's law leads to pure and acceptable worship, while human additions and amendments make worship vain, if not abominable. There is probably not one such addition or amendment which does not to a greater or less degree make some commandment void.] **14 And he called to him the multitude again, and said unto them** [Having been accused by the scribes and Pharisees of a breach of their tradition, Jesus points out to *them* generally the iniquity of tradition, for it lay within their power as leaders to remedy the whole system of things. Having done this, he turns to the *multitude* and answers before them as to the offense with which he is specifically charged. Thus he gives to the leaders general principles, and to the common people the single instance], **Hear me all of you, and understand: ᵃ 11 Not that which entereth into the mouth defileth the man ; but that which proceedeth out of the mouth, this defileth the man. ᵇ 15 there is nothing from without the man, that going into him can defile him; but the things which proceed out of the man are those that defile the man. 17 And when he was entered into the house from the multitude, ᵃ 12 Then came the disciples, and said unto him, Knowest thou that the Pharisees were offended, when they heard this saying?** [The entire speech offended them. He charged them with hypocrisy. He showed that their tradition, which they reverenced as a revelation from God, led them into sin, and he disturbed their self-complacency by showing that the ceremonial cleanness, which was founded on tradition, and in which they prided themselves, was worthless in comparison with the moral cleanness required by God's law, which they had ignored. It grieved the disciples to see Jesus offend these reverend gentlemen from Jerusalem. Like many modern disciples their respect for men counteracted their zeal for truth.] **13 But he answered and said, Every**

plant which my heavenly Father planted not, shall be rooted up. [God had planted the law with its doctrine: he had planted the Hebrew religion as given by Moses. He had not planted the tradition of the elders; so it, and the religion founded upon it, was doomed to be rooted up.] **14 Let them alone: they are blind guides. And if the blind guide the blind, both shall fall into a pit.** [This proverbial expression is found in the Sermon on the Mount. See page 262. There it taught that the disciple could expect to attain no higher felicity than his teacher. Here it teaches the lesson of patience, and is akin to the words of David which begin, "Fret not thyself because of evil-doers" (Ps. xxxvii. 1, 2). The words of Jesus are full of encouragement to those who adhere to the simple teachings of God; for they show that God guarantees that every error shall be uprooted, and that every teacher of error or false religion shall participate in the judgment which uproots, and shall fall into the pit of ruin; and his disciples, no matter how numerous, shall share his fate. In this particular instance, the destruction of Jerusalem was the pit. The Jewish leaders led their disciples into it, and God uprooted their system of tradition, that the pure gospel might be sowed in the room which they occupied.] **15 And Peter answered and said unto him, Declare unto us the parable.** [The word "parable" is here used in its looser sense to indicate an obscure saying.] ᵇ **his disciples asked him of the parable.** [They asked him what he meant by the words contained in the eleventh verse.] **18 And he saith {ᵃsaid,} ᵇ unto them, ᵃAre ye even yet ᵇ so without understanding also?** [It was to be expected that the multitude, swayed by the teaching of the Pharisees, would be slow to grasp what Jesus said about uncleanness; but the disciples, having been so long taught of him, and having felt free to eat with unwashed hands, should have been more quick of understanding.] **Perceive ye not, that whatsoever from without goeth into the man, *it* cannot defile him; 19 because it goeth not into his heart, but ᵃpasseth into the {ᵇhis} belly, and goeth out into {ᵃand is cast out into} the**

draught? ᵇ *This he said,* making all meats clean. 20
And he said, ᵃ 18 But the things which proceed out of
the mouth come forth out of the heart; and they defile
the man. ᵇ That which proceedeth out of the man, that
defileth the man.   21 For from within, out of the
heart of men, ᵃ come forth {ᵇ proceed,} ᵃ evil thoughts,
ᵇ fornications, thefts, murders, adulteries, 22 covet-
ings, wickednesses, deceit, lasciviousness, an evil
eye [an envious eye], ᵃ false witness, railings: {ᵇ railing,} pride, foolishness: 23 all these evil things proceed from within, and ᵃ 20 these are the things which
defile the man; but to eat with unwashen hands, defileth not the man.   [Thus Jesus sets forth the simple doctrine that a man's moral and spiritual state is not dependent upon
the symbolic cleanness of his physical diet, much less is it dependent on ceremonial observances in regard to things eaten,
or the dishes from which they are eaten. Of course, Jesus
did not mean at this time to abrogate the Mosaic law of legal
uncleannesses.   These uncleannesses worked no *spiritual* defilement, but were merely typical of such; for the food in no
way touched or affected the mind or soul, the fountains of
spiritual life, but only the corporeal organs, which have no
moral susceptibility.   The Pharisees had erred in confusing
legal and spiritual defilement, and had added error to error
by multiplying the causes of defilement in their tradition.   By
thus showing that legal defilement was merely symbolic, Jesus
classed it with all the other symbolism which was to be done
away with when the gospel reality was fully ushered in (Col.
ii. 16, 17).   In saying, therefore, that Jesus made all meats
clean, Mark does not mean that Jesus then and there repealed
the law.   The declaration of such repeal came later (Acts x.
14, 15).   He means that he there drew those distinctions and
laid down those principles which supplanted the Mosaic law
when the kingdom of God was ushered in on the day of Pentecost.   Here was the fountain whence Paul drew all his
teaching concerning things clean and unclean.]

LXVI.

SECOND WITHDRAWAL FROM HEROD'S TERRITORY.

ᵃ MATT. XV. 21; ᵇ MARK VII. 24.

ᵇ **24 And from thence** ᵃ **Jesus** ᵇ **arose, and went** ᵃ **out** ᵇ **away** ᵃ **and withdrew into the parts {**ᵇ **borders} of Tyre and Sidon.** [The journey here is indicated in marked terms because it differs from any previously recorded, for it was the first time that Jesus ever entered a foreign or heathen country. Some commentators contend from the use of the word "borders" by Mark that Jesus did not cross over the boundary, but the point is not well taken, for Mark vii. 31 shows that the journey led through Sidon. For location of Tyre and Sidon, see page 286. Jesus withdrew to escape the opposition of his enemies and the mistaken movements of his friends. As he was not on a missionary tour it was perfectly proper for him to enter heathen territory.]

LXVII.

HEALING A PHŒNICIAN WOMAN'S DAUGHTER.

(Region of Tyre and Sidon.)

ᵃ MATT. XV. 22–28; ᵇ MARK VII. 25–30.

ᵇ **And he entered into a house, and would have no man know it** [Jesus sought concealment for the purposes noted in the last section. He also, no doubt, desired an opportunity to impart private instruction to the twelve]; **and he could not be hid.** [The fame of Jesus had spread far and wide, and he and his disciples were too well known to escape the notice of any who had seen them or heard them described.] **25 But {**ᵃ **22 And} behold,** ᵇ **straightway** ᵃ **a Canaanitish woman** ᵇ **whose little daughter** [the word for daughter **is** a diminutive, such as is often used to indicate affection] **had** an unclean spirit, having heard of him [having formerly heard of his power and having recently heard of his arrival in her neighborhood], ᵃcame out from those borders [this does not mean, as some construe it, that she crossed over into Galilee from Phœnicia: it means that she came out of the very region *where Jesus then was*], and cried, saying, Have mercy on me, O Lord, thou son of David [Sympathy so identified her with her daughter that she asked mercy for herself. The title "son of David" shows that the Jewish hopes had spread to surrounding nations and that some, like this woman and the one at Jacob's well, expected to share in the Messianic blessings]; my daughter is grievously vexed with a demon. 23 But he answered her not a word. [God's unanswering silence is a severe test of our faith.] ᵇ26 Now the woman was a Greek, a Syrophoenician by race. [The Macedonian conquest had diffused Greek civilization throughout western Asia till the word Greek among the Jews had become synonymous with Gentile. The term Canaanite was narrower and indicated an inhabitant of Canaan—that is, a non-Jewish inhabitant of Palestine. The term *Syrophœnician* was narrower still. It meant a Syrian of Phœnicia, and distinguished the Phœnicians from the other Syrians. Phœnicia was a narrow strip near the northeast corner of the Mediterranean Sea. It was some twenty-eight miles long with an average width of about one mile. Canaan means lowland, Phœnicia means palmland. The Canaanites founded Sidon (Gen. x. 19), and the Phœnicians were their descendants.] And she besought him that he would cast forth the demon out of her daughter. ᵃAnd his disciples came and besought him, saying, Send her away; for she crieth after us. [The woman by her loud entreaties was drawing to Jesus that very attention which he sought to avoid. The disciples therefore counseled him to grant her request for his own sake—not for mercy or compassion, but merely to be rid of her.] 24 But he answered [answered the disciples, not the woman] and said, I was not sent but unto the lost sheep of the house of Israel. [Jesus had not forborne

answering her prayer through lack of feeling, but from principle. It was part of the divine plan that his *personal* ministry should be confined to the Jewish people. Divine wisdom
approved of this course as best, not only for the Jews, but for
the Gentiles as well. Variations from this plan were to be few
and were to be granted only as rewards to those of exceptional
faith.] **25 But she came ᵇand fell down at his feet.
ᵃand worshipped him, saying, Lord, help me.** [The
narrative indicates that Jesus had left the house and was
moving on, and that the woman obtruded herself upon his
notice by falling in front of him and obstructing his way.]
**26 And he answered and said, ᵇunto her, Let the
children first be filled: for it is not meet** [suitable, be-
coming] **to take the children's bread and cast it to the
dogs.** [By the use of the word "first" Jesus suggested that
there would come a time of mercy for the Gentiles. He uses
the diminutive for the word dog, thus indicating a tame pet,
and suggesting rather the dependence and subordinate position than the uncleanness of the dog. By so doing he gave
the woman an argumentative handle which she was not slow
to grasp.] **28 But she answered and saith {ᵃsaid,}
ᵇunto him, Yea, Lord; ᵃfor even the dogs ᵇunder the
table eat of the children's crumbs. ᵃwhich fall from
their masters' table.** [Jesus had suggested that domestic
order by which dogs are required to wait until the meal is
over before they receive their portion; but with a wit made
keen by her necessity, she replies by alluding to the well-
known fact that dogs under the table are permitted to eat
the crumbs *even while the meal is in progress;* intimating
thereby her hope to receive aid before all the needs of Israel
had first been satisfied. By using the word dogs Jesus did
not mean to convey the impression that he shared the Jewish
prejudices against the Gentiles; a construction which would
be contrary to Luke iv. 25, 26, and Matt. viii. 10–12.] **28
Then Jesus answered and said unto her, O woman,
great is thy faith: ᵇFor this saying go thy way; ᵃbe
it done unto thee even as thou wilt. ᵇthe demon is**

gone out of thy daughter. [Thus by its ending this little incident illustrates the doctrine that men should pray and not faint (Luke xviii. 1–8). The woman's experience has been often repeated by other parents who have prayed for children which, if not demon-possessed, were certainly swayed by diabolical influences. The woman's faith is shown in many ways: 1. She persisted when he was silent. 2. She reasoned when he spoke. 3. She regarded this miracle, though a priceless gift to her, as a mere crumb from the table of his abundant powers. It is noteworthy that the two most notable for faith—this woman and the centurion—were both Gentiles.] ᵃ**And her daughter was healed from that hour.** ᵇ **30 And she went away unto her house, and found the child laid upon the bed, and the demon gone out.** [The posture of the daughter indicated that physical exhaustion which would naturally succeed the intense nervous strain of demoniacal possession—especially the last paroxysms produced by the departing demon.

LXVIII.

ANOTHER AVOIDING OF HEROD'S TERRITORY.

ᵃ MATT. XV. 29; ᵇ MARK VII. 31.

ᵇ **31 And** ᵃ**Jesus** ᵇ**again went out** ᵃ**And departed thence,** ᵇ **from the borders of Tyre, and came through Sidon** ᵃ**and came nigh unto the sea of Galilee;** ᵇ**through the midst of the borders of Decapolis.** ᵃ**and he went up into the mountain, and sat there.** [From Tyre Jesus proceeded northward to Sidon and thence eastward across the mountains and the headwaters of the Jordan to the neighborhood of Damascus. Here he turned southward and approached the sea of Galilee on its eastern side. Somewhere amid the mountains on the eastern side he sat down; *i. e.,* he ceased his journeying for some days.

LXIX.

THE DEAF STAMMERER HEALED AND FOUR THOUSAND FED.

ᵃ MATT. XV. 30–38; ᵇ MARK VII. 32–VIII. 9.

ᵇ 32 And they bring unto him one that was deaf, and had an impediment in his speech [The man had evidently learned to speak before he lost his hearing. Some think that defective hearing had caused the impediment in his speech, but verse 35 also suggests that he was tongue-tied]; and they beseech him to lay his hand upon him. 33 And he took him aside from the multitude privately, and put his fingers into his ears, and he spat, and touched his tongue [He separated him from the crowd to avoid publicity (see verse 36, below), and by signs indicating an intention to heal, he gives him the assurance which in other cases he is accustomed to give by words. He evidently induced the man by signs to stick out his tongue. He then placed one finger of each hand in the man's ears, after which he spat. Where he spit is not said. He then touched with one or both his thumbs the man's tongue, and, speaking the healing word, the cure was accomplished]; 34 and looking up to heaven, he sighed, and saith unto him, Ephphatha, that is, Be opened. [Jesus here, as in the healing of Jairus' daughter, spoke the Aramaic. Why he sighed is not said. It was doubtless an expression of sympathy, though Farrar thinks he did so because he thought of the millions there were of deaf and dumb who in this world would never hear and never speak.] 35 And his ears were opened, and the bond of his tongue was loosed, and he spake plain. [He was evidently not deaf from his birth, or he would not have known how to speak at all.] 36 And he charged them that they should tell no man: but the more he charged them, so much the more a great deal they published it. [Jesus was still seeking to suppress excitement. A very little encouragement from him would have brought together a multitude, the very thing which he was journeying to avoid. He therefore cautioned the people to be silent, but by a common freak of human nature, his desire to avoid publicity made him more wonderful in the eyes of the people, and thereby inspired a greater eagerness on their part to tell about him.] **37 And they were beyond measure astonished** [Mark here coins a double superlative to express the boundlessness of their amazement], **saying, He hath done all things well** [commendation upon the workman which had originally been bestowed upon his work—Gen. i. 31] **; he maketh even the deaf to hear, and the dumb to speak.** [These were the people who had asked Jesus to depart from their coast on account of the loss of their swine. A complete change in their feelings had taken place since that day.] ᵃ**30 And there came unto him great multitudes, having with them the lame, blind, dumb, maimed, and many others, and they cast them down at his feet; and he healed them** [We have here an instance of the common difference between the narratives of Matthew and Mark. Where Matthew is wont to mention the healing of multitudes, Mark picks out one of the most remarkable cases and describes it minutely. The hasty action of those who brought in the sick and returned to bring in others is indicated by the way in which they cast down their burdens at Jesus' feet] **: 31 insomuch that the multitude wondered, when they saw the dumb speaking, the maimed whole, and the lame walking, and the blind seeing: and they glorified the God of Israel** [The people whom Jesus healed were Jews, but daily intercourse with the heathen of Decapolis had tended to cool their religious ardor. The works of Jesus revived this ardor and caused them to praise the God whose prophet they esteemed Jesus to be.] ᵃ**32 And** ᵇ**1 In those days** [*i. e.,* while Christ was in Decapolis], **when there was again a great multitude, and they had nothing to eat,** ᵃ**Jesus called unto him his disciples. and said, {**ᵇ**saith} unto**

them, 2 I have compassion on the multitude, because
they continue with me now three days, and have
nothing to eat: ᵃ And I would not send them away
fasting, lest haply they faint on the way. ᵇ 3 and if I
send them away fasting to their home, they will faint
on the way; and some of them are come from far.
[When the five thousand had been caught in similar circumstances, the apostles had come with suggestions to Jesus,
but now, being taught by experience, they keep silence and
let Jesus manage as he will. The multitude had not been
three days without food, but it had been with Jesus three
days and was *now* without food.] 4 And his {ᵃ the} disciples say unto {ᵇ answered} him, Whence shall one
be able to fill these men with bread here in a desert
place? ᵃ Whence should we have so many loaves in
a desert place as to fill so great a multitude? [It seems
strange that the apostles should ask such a question after having assisted in feeding the five thousand. But the failure to
expect a miracle, despite previous experience, was a common
occurrence in the history of Israel and of the twelve (Num.
xi. 21–23; Ps. lxxviii. 19, 20). In this case the failure of
the apostles to expect miraculous relief suggests that they
had probably often been hungry and had long since ceased
to look for supernatural relief in such cases. Their disbelief
here is so similar to their disbelief in the first instance that
it, with a few other minor details, has led rationalistic commentators to confound this miracle with the feeding of the
five thousand. But the words of Jesus forbid this—Matt. xvi.
9, 10; Mark viii. 19, 20.] 34 And Jesus said unto them,
ᵇ 5 And he asked them, How many loaves have ye?
And they said, Seven. ᵃ and a few small fishes. 35
And he commanded {ᵇ commandeth} the multitude to
sit down on the ground [they were on the bleak mountain, and not in the grassy plain of Butaiha]: and he took
the seven loaves ᵃ and the fishes; and he gave thanks
ᵇ and having given thanks, he brake, and gave to his
{ᵃ the} disciples, and the disciples to the multitudes.

{ᵇto set before them; and they set them before the multitude.} 7 And they had a few small fishes: and having blessed them, he commanded to set these also before them. ᵃ37 And they all ate, and were filled: and they took up that which remained over of the broken pieces, seven baskets full. 38 And they that did eat were ᵇabout ᵃfour thousand men, besides women and children. 39 And he sent away the multitudes.

LXX.

THIRD WITHDRAWAL FROM HEROD'S TERRITORY.

Subdivision A.

PHARISAIC LEAVEN. A BLIND MAN HEALED.

(Magadan and Bethsaida. Probably Summer, A. D. 29.)

ᵃ MATT. XV. 39–XVI. 12; ᵇ MARK VIII. 10–26.

ᵇ And straightway he entered into the boat with his disciples, ᵃand came into the borders of Magadan. ᵇinto the parts of Dalmanutha. [It appears from the context that he crossed the lake to the west shore. Commentators, therefore, pretty generally think that Magadan is another form of the name Magdala, and that Dalmanutha was either another name for Magdala, or else a village near it.] ᵃ1 And the Pharisees and Sadducees ᵇcame forth, and began to question with him, seeking of him a sign ᵃand trying him [testing the strength of his miraculous power] asked him to show them a sign from heaven. [They rejected his miracles as signs of his Messiahship, the Pharisees holding that such signs could be wrought by Beelzebub. They therefore asked for a sign from heaven such as only God could give, and such as he had accorded to Moses, Joshua, Samuel and Elijah, or such as Joel foretold (Joel ii. 31). It is generally thought that the

Herodians were the Sadducees of Galilee. If so, we note the beginning of their hostility recorded at Mark iii. 6, page 216.] ᵇ**12 And he sighed deeply in his spirit** [being grieved deeply at the sinful obduracy which demanded signs in the midst of overwhelming demonstrations of divine power], ᵃ**2 But he answered and said** {ᵇ**saith,**} ᵃ**unto them,** ᵇ**Why doth this generation seek a sign?** ᵃ**When it is evening, ye say,** *It will be* **fair weather: for the heaven is red. 3 And in the morning,** *It will be* **foul weather to-day: for the heaven is red and lowering. Ye know how to discern the face of the heaven; but ye cannot** *discern* **the signs of the times.** [For comment on similar language see page 325. The signs of the times being fulfillments of prophecies, were better evidence of the period and presence of Messiah than heavenly portents. It is useless to bestow new signs upon those who are blind as to the signs already existing. Jews continued to require a sign—I. Cor. i. 22.] **4 An evil and adulterous generation seeketh after a sign; and** ᵇ**verily I say unto you, There shall no sign be given unto this generation.** [*i. e.*, none such as was demanded] ᵃ**but the sign of Jonah.** [For comment on similar language see pages 305–306. The resurrection or Jonah sign was a sign from heaven in the sense in which they used the words; that is, it was wrought directly by God, and not through man.] **And he left them,** ᵇ**And again entering into** *the boat* **departed to the other side.** [*I. e.*, from Magdala back again to the east shore, or rather, toward Bethsaida Julias, on the northeast shore.] ᵃ**5 And the disciples came to the other side and forgot to take bread.** ᵇ**and they had not in the boat with them more than one loaf.** [This loaf was probably left over from the previous supply.] ᵃ**6 And Jesus said unto them,** ᵇ**15 And he charged them, saying,** ᵃ**Take heed and beware of the leaven of the Pharisees and Sadducees.** ᵇ**and the leaven of Herod.** [Leaven, which answered to our modern yeast, was a symbol of a secret, penetrating, pervasive influence, usually of a corrupting nature. The influence of the Pharisees was that of formalism, hypocritical ostentation and traditionalism; that of the Sadducees was sneering rationalistic unbelief, free thought and cunning worldliness, manifesting itself among the Herodians in political corruption.] **16 And they reasoned one with another, ᵃ among themselves, saying, We took {ᵇ have} no bread.** [They thought that Jesus reproved them for their carelessness in forgetting to take bread, *since* that carelessness might lead them to be without bread on their journey. So his rebuke below indicates.] **ᵃ 8 And Jesus perceiving it said, {ᵇ saith} unto them, ᵃ O ye of little faith, why reason ye among yourselves, because ye have no bread? 9 Do ye not yet perceive, ᵇ neither understand? ᵃ neither remember the five loaves of the five thousand, and how many baskets** [*cophini*, probably traveling baskets] **ye took up? 10 Neither the seven loaves of the four thousand, and how many baskets** [*spurides*, probably grain baskets or hampers] **ye took up? 11 How is it that ye do not perceive that I spake not to you concerning bread? ᵇ have ye your hearts hardened? 18 Having eyes, see ye not? and having ears, hear ye not? and do ye not remember? 19 When I brake the five loaves among the five thousand, how many baskets** [*cophini*] **full of broken pieces took ye up? They say unto him, Twelve. 20 And when the seven among the four thousand, how many basketfuls** [*spurides*] **of broken pieces took ye up? And they say unto him, Seven. 21 And he said unto them, Do ye not yet understand? ᵃ But beware of the leaven of the Pharisees and Sadducees. 12 Then understood they that he bade them not beware of the leaven of bread, but of the teach'ng of the Pharisees and Sadducees.** [Jesus had resorted to metaphor because the word leaven better expressed his idea than did the word teaching. The formulated dogmas of the Pharisees were not so bad, but the subtle influence of their spirit and example corrupted without warning, like a concealed grave. There are those to-day like them who are too skillful to be openly convicted of heterodox statements, but whose teaching, nevertheless, in its very essence and spirit, tends to infidelity.] ᵇ **22 And they come unto Bethsaida.** [Not the suburb of Capernaum, but Bethsaida Julias, a town on the east side of the Jordan, near where it flows into the sea of Galilee. Jesus was proceeding northward toward Cæsarea Philippi.] **And they bring to him a blind man, and beseech him to touch him. 23 And he took hold of the blind man by the hand, and brought him out of the village** [Jesus increased the sympathy between himself and the man by separating him from the crowd. Our greatest blessings can only come to us after we have been alone with God] ; **and when he had spit on his eyes, and laid his hands upon him, he asked him, Seest thou aught? 24 And he looked up, and said, I see men; for I behold** *them* **as trees, walking. 25 Then again he laid his hands upon his eyes; and he looked steadfastly, and was restored, and saw all things clearly.** [The man's eyes were probably sore and Jesus made use of saliva to soften and soothe them. But it was our Lord's custom to give variety to the manifestation of his power, sometimes using one apparent auxiliary means, and sometimes another; and also healing instantly or progressively, as he chose, that the people might see that the healing was altogether a matter of his will. The man had evidently not been born blind, else he would not have been able to recognize men or trees by sight, for those not used to employ sight can not by it tell a circle from a square.] **26 And he sent him away to his home, saying, Do not even enter into the village.** [The man, of course, lived in the village, and to send him home was to send him thither, but he was to go directly home and not spread the news through the town, for if he did the population would be at once drawn to Jesus, thus breaking up the privacy which he sought to maintain.]

Subdivision B.

THE GREAT CONFESSION MADE BY PETER.

(Near Cæsarea Philippi.)

Summer, A. D. 29.

ᵃ MATT. XVI. 13–20; ᵇ MARK VIII. 27–30; ᶜ LUKE IX. 18–21.

ᵇ **27 And Jesus went forth, and his disciples, into the villages of Caesarea Philippi** [The city of Paneas was enlarged by Herod Philip I., and named in honor of Tiberias Cæsar. It also bore the name Philippi because of the name of its builder, and to distinguish it from Cæsarea Palestinæ or Cæsarea Stratonis, a city on the Mediterranean coast. Paneas, the original name, still pertains to the village, though now corrupted to Banias. It is situated under the shadow of Mt. Hermon at the eastern of the two principal sources of the Jordan, and is the most northern city of the Holy Land visited by Jesus, and, save Sidon, the most northern point of his travels]: ᵃ **13 Now when Jesus came into the parts of Caesarea Philippi,** ᶜ **it came to pass,** ᵇ **on the way** ᶜ **as he was praying apart, the disciples were with him: and he asked** ᵇ **his disciples, saying unto them,** ᵃ **Who do men say that the Son of man is?** ᵇ **Who do men {** ᶜ **the multitudes} say that I am?** [Jesus asks them to state the popular opinion concerning himself as contrasted with the opinion of the rulers, Pharisees, etc.] **19 And they answering** ᵇ **told him, saying, {** ᶜ **said,}** ᵃ **Some** *say* **John the Baptist;** ᶜ **but {** ᵇ **and}** ᵃ **some,** ᵇ **others, Elijah; but {** ᶜ **and} others,** ᵃ **Jeremiah, or** ᶜ **that one of the old prophets is risen again.** [For comment on similar language see page 370 (Section LXII.). It should be noted that popular opinion did not honor him as Messiah, but since it accepted him as a prophet, the people were therefore inexcusable in not receiving the statements which he made in regard to himself, and admitting the Messianic claims which he set forth.] **20 And he said {** ᵃ **saith} unto them,** ᵇ **29 And he**

asked them, But who say ye that I am? [Jesus here first asks the disciples this question, having given them abundant time and opportunity in which to form a correct judgment. The proper answer of the heart to this question forms the starting-point of the true Christian life.] ᵃ**16 And Simon Peter answered and said,** {ᶜ**answering** ᵇ**answereth and saith**} **unto him, Thou art the Christ.** ᶜ**of God.** ᵃ**the Son of the living God.** [Peter asserts this as an assured fact and not as a mere opinion. This confession embraces two propositions: 1. The office of Jesus—the Christ; 2. The divinity of Jesus—the Son of God. The Christhood of Jesus implies his humanity, for as such he was to be the son of David. It also identifies him as the hero or subject of prophecy, the long-expected deliverer. In declaring Jesus to be the Son of God, Peter rose above the popular theories as to the personality of Messiah, for the Jews generally did not expect him to be divine. The term "living God" was used by prophets to express the contrast between dead idols and the supreme Being who is possessed of vitality, reason and feeling.] **17 And Jesus answered and said unto him, Blessed art thou, Simon Bar-Jonah** [Jesus gives the full name to make his saying more personally emphatic]: **for flesh and blood** [The common words of contrast by which humanity was distinguished from divinity. See also Gal. i. 16] **hath not revealed it unto thee, but my Father who is in heaven.** [Peter was blessed by having a revelation from God by which facts were made known that could not be discovered by the unaided human reason. God had revealed the truth to him in the words and works of Jesus, and this revealed truth was to him a source of happiness both temporal and eternal. Like confessions as to this truth had been made before (Matt. xiv. 33; John i. 49), but they had been made under the pressure of miraculous display and strong emotion. Hence they were rather exclamatory guesses at the truth, and differed from this now made by Peter which was the calm expression of a settled conviction produced both by the character and by the miracles of Jesus.] **18 And I also say unto**

thee, that thou art Peter [*petros*, a noun masculine], **and upon this rock** [*petra*, a noun feminine] **I will build my church** [The tense here is future. Christ had followers, but they were not yet organized, and hence had no such structural form as to suggest a similitude to a building]; **and the gates of Hades** [Hades was the name for the abode of the dead. Its gates symbolized its power because the military forces of an ancient city always sallied forth from its gates] **shall not prevail against it.** [Death shall neither destroy the organic church which is in the world, nor the members thereof which go down into the grave (I. Thess. iv. 15 ; I. Cor. xv. 54–56). No passage in the word of God has called forth more discussion than this and the succeeding verse, the first point in dispute being as to what is meant by the rock; *i. e.*, whether Christ or Peter or Peter's confession is the foundation of the church; the second point being as to the extent of the power and authority bestowed on Peter by the symbol of the keys. To aid us in reaching a correct conclusion we must note that Jesus speaks in metaphorical language. He represents: 1. His kingdom as a city about to be built upon a rock. 2. Himself as a builder of this city. 3. Simon Peter as the one who holds the keys to the gates by which egress and regress is had to the city. 4. The gates or powers of the opposing city of Hades are not able to prevail against this kingdom city. Now, since Jesus himself occupies the position of builder in the metaphor, and Simon Peter the position of key-bearer, neither of them can properly be regarded as the foundation. The foundation must therefore be the confession which Peter has just spoken, since it is all that remains that is liable to such application. The case would present no difficulty at all were it not for the unmistakable allusion to Peter (*petros*, a loose stone) as in some way associated with *petra*, the bedrock or foundation. But in the light of other Scriptures this allusion presents no difficulty; for all the apostles were such stones, and were closely allied to the foundation (Eph. ii. 19–22 ; Gal. ii. 9). Compare also I. Pet. ii. 3-8. The Christian religion in **all** its redemptive completeness rests and can rest on no other foundation than Christ (I. Cor. iii. 11). But the church or kingdom of Christ among men rests organically and constitutionally upon a foundation of apostolic authority, for the apostles were the mouthpieces of the Holy Spirit; but in this apostolic foundation the other apostles had equal rights, each one of them becoming a living foundation stone as soon as his faith led him to make a like confession with Simon Peter. Hence we find the apostle Paul asserting the superior authority of the apostles to all other Christian teachers and workers (I. Cor. xii. 28), and times without number asserting his apostolic office and authority (I. Cor. ix. 1, 2; II. Cor. xii. 12; xiii. 1-4; Gal. i. 1, 8; Eph. iii. 1-6; Phil. 8, 9). **19 I will give unto thee the keys of the kingdom of heaven: and whatsoever thou shalt bind on earth shall be bound in heaven; and whatsoever thou shalt loose on earth shall be loosed in heaven.** [Continuing his metaphorical language, Jesus promised to Peter the keys; *i. e.*, the authority to lay down the rules or laws (under the guidance of the Holy Spirit, however) for admission to or exclusion from the kingdom or church. This office was of course given to Peter in a secondary sense, since it must ever belong to Christ in a primary sense (Rev. iii. 7). The figure of key-bearer is taken from Isa. xxii. 22. Peter used the keys on the day of Pentecost to open the church to the Jews, and about seven years afterward, at Cæsarea Palestinæ, he used them again to admit the Gentiles. In fixing the terms of admission he also fixed the terms of exclusion, for all who are not admitted are excluded. The keys as used by Peter have never been changed; that is to say, the terms of admission abide forever. Plurality of keys is merely part of the parabolic drapery, since cities were accustomed to have several gates, thus requiring a plurality of keys. The kingdom was not opened to Jews and Gentiles by different keys, since both were admitted on the same terms. The words "bind" and "loose" were commonly used among the Jews in the sense of forbid and allow. Abundant instances of this usage have been collected by Lightfoot. They relate to the binding and annulling of laws and rules.

In this sense the word for loose is used very many times in the New Testament, but it is translated by the word break or broken (Matt. v. 19; John vii. 23; x. 35). The power here given to Peter was soon after extended to the rest of the apostles (Matt. xviii. 18). The apostles were to lay down, as they afterward did, the organic law of the new kingdom, defining what things were prohibited and what permitted. Their actions in this behalf would of course be ratified in heaven, because they were none other than the acts of the Holy Spirit expressed through the apostles.] ᵇ **30 And** ᵃ **20 Then** {ᶜ **21 But**} ᵃ **charged he the disciples** ᶜ **and commanded** *them* **to tell this to no man ;** ᵇ **that they should tell no man of him.** ᵃ **that he was the Christ.** [The people were not ready to receive this truth, nor were the apostles sufficiently instructed to rightly proclaim it. Their heads were full of wrong ideas with regard to Christ's work and office, and had they been permitted to teach about him, they would have said that which it would have been necessary for them to subsequently correct, thus producing confusion.]

Subdivision C.

PASSION FORETOLD. PETER REBUKED.

ᵃ MATT. XVI. 21–28; ᵇ MARK VIII. 31–39; IX. 1; ᶜ LUKE IX. 22–27.

ᵃ **21 From that time** [*i. e.*, the time of Peter's confession, and about three-quarters of a year before the crucifixion] **began Jesus to show unto his disciples,** ᵇ **31 And to teach them, that the Son of man must suffer many things** [Since the apostles, by the mouth of Peter, had just confessed Jesus as Christ, it was necessary that their crude Messianic conceptions should be corrected and that the true Christhood—the Christhood of the atonement and the resurrection—should be revealed to them. In discourse and parable Jesus had explained the principles and the nature of the kingdom, and now, from this time forth, he taught the apostles about himself, the priestly King], ᵃthat he must go up to Jerusalem, ᵇand be rejected by ᵃand suffer many things of the elders and ᵇthe chief priests, and the scribes [The Jewish Sanhedrin was generally designated by thus naming its three constituent parts. See page 45], and be killed, ᵃand the third day be raised up. {ᵇand after three days rise again.} [For comment on these variant phrases see page 306.] 32 And he spake the saying openly. ᶜ22 saying, The Son of man must suffer many things, and be rejected of the elders and chief priests and scribes, and be killed, and the third day be raised up. [Very early in his ministry Jesus had given obscure intimations concerning his death (John ii. 19–22; iii. 14; Matt. xii. 38–40), but these had not been understood by either friend or foe. Now that he thus spoke plainly, we may see by Peter's conduct that they comprehended and were deeply moved by the dark and more sorrowful portion of his revelation, and failed to grasp the accompanying promise of a resurrection.] ᵃ22 And Peter took him, and began to rebuke him, saying, Be it far from thee, Lord: this shall never be unto thee. [Evidently Peter regarded Jesus as overcome by a fit of despondency, and felt that such talk would utterly dishearten the disciples if it were persisted in. His love, therefore, prompted him to lead Jesus to one side and deal plainly with him. In so doing, Peter overstepped the laws of discipleship and assumed that he knew better than the Master what course to pursue. In his feelings he was the forerunner of those modern wiseacres who confess themselves constrained to reject the doctrine of a suffering Messiah.] ᵇ33 But he turning about, and seeing his disciples, ᵃturned, ᵇrebuked Peter, and saith, {ᵃsaid} unto Peter, Get thee behind me, Satan: thou art a stumbling-block unto me: for thou mindest not the things of God, but the things of men. [Jesus withdrew from Peter and turned back to his disciples. By the confession of the truth Simon had just won his promised name of Peter, which allied him to Christ, the foundation. But when he now turned aside to speak the language of the tempter he receives the name Satan, as if he were the very devil himself. Peter presented the same temptation with which the devil once called forth a similar rebuke from Christ (Matt. iv. 10). He was unconsciously trying to dissuade Jesus from the death on which the salvation of the world depended, and this was working into Satan's hand. Peter did not mind or think about the Messiah's kingdom as divinely conceived and revealed in the Scriptures. **ᵇ34 And he called unto him the multitude with his disciples, ª24 Then said Jesus unto his disciples, ᶜ23 And he said unto all** [despite the efforts of Jesus to seek privacy, the people were still near enough at hand to be called and addressed], **If any man would come after me, let him deny himself, and take up his cross daily** [comp. Rom. viii. 36; I. Cor. xv. 31], **and follow me.** [For comment, see page 368. The disciple must learn to say "no" to many of the strongest cravings of his earthly nature. The cross is a symbol for duty which is to be performed daily, at any cost, even that of the most most painful death. The disciple must follow Jesus, both as to his teaching and example.] **24 For whosoever would save his life shall lose it; ªand {ᶜbut} whosoever shall lose his life for my sake, ᵇand the gospel's ᶜthe same shall ªfind it. ᶜsave it.** [Jesus here plays upon the two meanings of the word life, one being of temporal and the other of eternal duration. For comment on a similar expression see page 368.] **ᵇ36 For what doth it profit a man, {ᶜis a man ªshall a man be profited,} if he shall gain {ᵇto gain} the whole world, ᶜand lose or forfeit his own self? ªhis life? or {ᵇ37 For} ªwhat shall {ᵇshould} a man give in exchange for his life?** [Peter and the rest of the apostles had been thinking about a worldly Messianic kingdom, with its profits and rewards. Jesus shows the worthlessness even of the whole world in comparison with the rewards of the true kingdom. It is the comparison between the things which are external, and which perish, and the life which is internal, and which endures. External losses may be repaired, but a lost life can never be regained, for with what shall a man buy it back?] **38 For whosoever shall be ashamed of me and of my words** [comp. Luke ii. 9; II. Tim. i. 8, 12; ii. 12] **in this adulterous and sinful generation** [see pp. 305, 306], **the Son of man also shall be ashamed of him, ᶜwhen he cometh in his own glory, and** *the glory* **of the {ᵇhis} ᶜFather, and of {ᵇwith} the holy angels.** [Peter had just been ashamed of the words in which Christ pictured himself as undergoing his humiliation. Jesus warns him and all others of the dangers of such shame.] **ᵃ27 For the Son of man shall come in the glory of his Father, with his angels; and then shall he render unto every man according to his deeds.** [The Father's glory, the angels and the rendering of universal judgment form a threefold indication that Jesus here speaks of his final coming to judge the world.] **ᵇ1 And he said unto them, Verily I say unto you, ᶜ27 But I tell you of a truth, ᵃThere are some of them that stand here, who shall in no wise taste of death, till they see the Son of man coming in his kingdom. ᶜtill they see the kingdom of God. ᵇcome with power.** [The mention of his final coming suggested one nearer at hand which was to be accomplished during the life of most of those present, since none but Jesus himself and Judas were to die previous to that time. The kingdom was to come and likewise the King. The former coming was literal, the latter spiritual. Those who refer this expression to the transfiguration certainly err, for no visible kingdom was established at that time. The expression refers to the kingdom which was organized and set in motion on the Pentecost which followed the resurrection of Jesus. It was set up with power, because three thousand souls were converted the first day, and many other gospel triumphs speedily followed.]

Subdivision D.

THE TRANSFIGURATION. CONCERNING ELIJAH.

(A Spur of Hermon, near Cæsarea Philippi.)

ᵃMATT. XVII. 1–13; ᵇMARK IX. 2–13; ᶜLUKE IX. 28–36.

ᶜ**28 And it came to pass about eight days {ᵃsix days}** ᶜ**after these sayings** [Mark agrees with Matthew in saying six days. Luke qualifies his estimate of time by saying "about." But if we regard him as including the day of the "sayings" and also the day of transfiguration, and the other two as excluding these days, then the three statements tally exactly. The "sayings" referred to were the words of Jesus with regard to his suffering at Jerusalem], **that** ᵃ**Jesus taketh {ᶜtook} ᵃwith him Peter, and James, and John his brother** [These three, as leaders among the apostles, needed the special encouragement which was about to be given. For further comment see page 355], **and bringeth them {ᶜwent} ᵃup into a {ᶜthe} ᵇhigh mountain apart by themselves: ᶜto pray.** [A tradition dating from the fourth century fixes upon Mt. Tabor as the site of the transfiguration, but this is unquestionably a mistake. Mt. Tabor is in Galilee, while Jesus was still in the region of Cæsarea Philippi (Mark ix. 30). Moreover there is little doubt that at that time and for centuries previous there was an inhabited fortress upon Mt. Tabor (Josh. xix. 12; Jos. *B. J.* i. 8, 7; *Vit.* 37). Moreover, Tabor is not a high mountain, its elevation above the sea being but 1,748 feet. Hermon, on the contrary, is the highest mountain in Palestine, its elevation, according to Reclus, being 9,400 feet. It was Jesus' custom to withdraw for prayer by night (Matt. xiv. 23, 24; Luke vi. 12; xxi. 37; xxii. 39), and the transfiguration took place at night.] **29 And as he was praying, the fashion of his countenance was altered, and his raiment *became* white *and* dazzling. ᵃ2 and he was transfigured** [*i. e.*, transformed; the description shows to what extent] **before** them; and his face did shine as the sun, and his garments became white as the light. ᵇglistering, exceeding white, so as no fuller on earth can whiten them. [We may conceive of the body of Jesus becoming luminous and imparting its light to his garments. The Christian looks forward to beholding such a transfiguration and also to participating in it—I. John iii. 2.] ᵃ3 And behold, there appeared unto them ᶜtwo men, who were Moses and {ᵇwith} ᶜElijah; ᵇand they were talking with Jesus. [The three apostles could identify Moses and Elijah by the course of this conversation, though it is possible that miraculous knowledge may have accompanied miraculous sight.] ᶜ31 who [*i. e.*, Moses and Elijah] appeared in glory, and spake of his decease which he was about to accomplish at Jerusalem. [The word for decease is " exodus," an unusual word for death. It means a departure and is, as Bengel says, a very weighty word, since it includes the passion, crucifixion, death, burial, resurrection and ascension.] 32 Now Peter and they that were with him were heavy with sleep [it being night]: but when they were fully awake, they saw his glory, and the two men that stood with him. 33 And it came to pass, as they were parting from him, ᵃPeter answered, and said {ᵇanswereth and saith} ᵃunto Jesus, ᵇRabbi, ᶜMaster, ᵃLord, it is good for us to be here: ᵇand let us make three tabernacles; ᵃif thou wilt, I will make here three tabernacles; one for thee, and one for Moses, and one for Elijah. ᶜnot knowing what he said. ᵇ6 For he knew not what to answer; for they became sore afraid. [Peter's fears overcame his discretion, but did not silence his tongue. Though he trembled at the fellowship of Moses and Elijah, he also realized the blessedness of it and could not let them depart without an effort to detain them, though the best inducement that he could offer was to build three booths, or arbors, made of the branches of trees, for their and Christ's accommodation. By thus speaking he placed Jesus upon the same level with Moses and Elijah—all three being alike worthy of a booth.] ᶜ**34 And while he said these things, ˣ5 While he was yet speaking, behold,** ᵇ**there came** ˣ**a bright cloud** ᵇ**overshadowing them:** {ᶜ**and overshadowed them:**} **and they feared as they entered into the cloud.** [Clouds often roll against the sides of Mt. Hermon, but the brightness of this cloud and the fear which it produced suggests that it was the Shechinah, or cloud of glory, which was the symbol of God's peculiar presence—Ex. xiii. 21, 22; xix. 9, 18; xxiv. 16; xl. 34, 35; I. Kings viii. 10.] ˣ**and behold,** ᵇ**there came a voice out of the cloud,** ˣ**saying, This is my beloved Son,** ᶜ**my chosen:** ˣ**in whom I am well pleased; hear ye him.** [This command contains the chief significance of the entire scene. Spoken in the presence of Moses and Elijah, it gave Jesus that pre-eminence which a son has over servants. He is to be heard. His words have pre-eminence over those of the lawgiver and the prophet (Heb. i. 1, 2.) Peter recognized Jesus as thus honored by this voice—II. Pet. i. 16–18.] **6 And when the disciples heard it, they fell on their face, and were sore afraid.** [As every man is who hears the voice of God.] **7 And Jesus came and touched them and said, Arise, and be not afraid.** [As mediator between man and God, Jesus removes fear.] ᵇ**8 And suddenly looking round about,** ˣ**8 And lifting up their eyes,** ᵇ**they saw no one any more, save Jesus only with themselves.** ᶜ**36 And when the voice came, Jesus was found alone.** [Leaders and prophets depart, but Christ abides—Heb. iii. 5, 6.] ᵇ**9 And as they were coming down from the mountain, he charged them that they should tell no man what things they had seen, save when the Son of man should have risen again from the dead.** ˣ**9 And Jesus commanded them, saying, Tell the vision to no man, until the Son of man be risen from the dead.** [The people were not ready for the publication of such an event. To have told it now would only have been to raise doubts as to their veracity.] ᵇ**10 And they kept the saying, ques-**

tioning among themselves what the rising again from the dead should mean. [Jesus spake so often in parables and made so frequent use of metaphors that the apostles did not take his words concerning his resurrection in a literal sense. They regarded his language as figurative, and sought to interpret the figure.] ᶜAnd they held their peace, and told no man in those days any of the things which they had seen. ᵃ10 And his disciples asked him, saying, Why then say the scribes that Elijah must first come? ᵇ*How is it* that the scribes say that Elijah must first come? [They were puzzled by the disappearance of Elijah. They looked upon him as having come to fulfill the prophecy of Malachi (Mal. iv. 5, 6), but they marveled that, having come, he should so soon withdraw, and that they should be forbidden to tell that they had seen him, since the sight of him would be some sign of Jesus' Messiahship.] ᵃ11 And he answered and ᵇsaid unto them, Elijah indeed cometh first, and restoreth {ᵃshall restore} all things [this sentence leads some to think that Elijah will appear again before the second coming of our Lord, but the words are to be interpreted in connection with the rest of the passage]: ᵇand how is it written of the Son of man, that he should suffer many things and be set at naught? [If the writings concerning Elijah perplexed the apostles, those concerning the Messiah perplexed them also. From one set of prophecies they might learn something about the other. Elijah came, but the Scriptures concerning him were so little understood that he was put to death. The Messiah also came, and the prophecies concerning him were so little understood that he, too, would be set at naught.] 13 But I say unto you, that Elijah is come, ᵃalready, and they knew him not, but did {ᵇand they have also done} unto him whatsoever they would. Even as it is written of him. ᵃEven so shall the Son of man also suffer of them. 13 Then understood the disciples that he spake unto them of John the Baptist. [Malachi used the name of Elijah figuratively to represent John the Baptist. See pp.

102, 284. That there shall be a second coming of Elijah in fulfillment of this prophecy is hardly possible, for the office of Elijah is prophetically outlined as that of the restorer. But Elijah could not restore Judaism, for that dispensation had been done away in Christ. He could hardly be chosen to restore Christianity, for even if it should need such a restoration, a Jewish prophet would be ill suited to such an office. One of the apostles would be vastly preferable.]

Subdivision E.

HEALING THE DEMONIAC BOY.

(Region of Cæsarea Philippi.)

ᵃMATT. XVII. 14–20; ᵇMARK IX. 14–29; ᶜLUKE IX. 37–43.

ᶜ**37 And it came to pass, on the next day, when they were come down from the mountain, ᵇ14 And when they came to the disciples** [the nine apostles which had been left behind], **they saw a great multitude about them** [We last heard of the multitude at Mark viii. 34. See page 416. It had no doubt been with Jesus until he ascended the mount and had remained with his apostles until he came down], **and scribes questioning with them.** [These scribes had caught the apostles in one and perhaps the only case where they had failed to cure, and they were making full use of this advantageous opportunity to discredit Christ and his apostles before the people by asking sneering and sarcastic questions.] **15 And straightway all the multitude, when they saw him, were greatly amazed, and running to him ᶜa great multitude met him. ᵇsaluted him.** [Why were the multitude amazed? Most commentators answer that it was because the face of Jesus shone with remaining traces of the transfiguration glory, as did that of Moses (Ex. xxxiv. 29), but this can hardly have been so, for it would have been at variance with the secrecy which Jesus enjoined as to his transfiguration. Moreover, so important a feature could hardly have escaped from the narratives of all three evangelists. Undoubtedly the amazement was caused by the sudden and opportune return of Jesus. Those who urge that this was not enough to produce amazement show themselves to be poor students of human nature. The multitude had been listening to and no doubt enjoying the questions of the scribes. The unexpected appearance of Jesus therefore impressed them with that sudden sense of having been detected in wrong-doing which invariably leads to amazement. Moreover, those who remained loyal to Jesus would be equally amazed by his approach, since they could not but feel that an exciting crisis was at hand.] ᵃ **14 And when they were come to the multitude** [*i. e.*, when Jesus and the multitude met], ᵇ **he asked them, What question ye with them?** [He surprised the scribes by this demand and they saw at once that he knew all and they felt rebuked for their unwarranted exultation, and so kept silent.] ᶜ **38 And behold,** ᵃ **there came to him a man,** ᵇ **one of** {ᶜ **from**} **the multitude** ᵃ **kneeling to him,** ᵇ **answered him,** ᶜ **cried, saying,** ᵇ **Teacher,** ᵃ **15 Lord,** ᵇ **I brought unto thee my son, who hath a dumb spirit;** ᵃ **have mercy on my son: for he is epileptic, and suffereth grievously;** ᶜ **I beseech thee look upon my son; for he is mine only child: 39 and behold, a spirit taketh him, and he suddenly crieth out;** ᵇ **18 and wheresoever it taketh him, it dasheth him down:** ᶜ **and it teareth him that he foameth,** ᵇ **and grindeth his teeth, and pineth away:** ᶜ **and it hardly departeth from him, bruising him sorely.** [When the scribes did not answer, the father of the demoniac boy broke the embarrassing silence by telling Jesus about the matter in question. His child was deaf, dumb and epileptic, but all these physical ailments were no doubt produced by the demon or evil spirit which possessed him. The phrase "hardly departeth from him" rather suggests the continual unrest in which the demon kept his victim than that the demon ever really relinquished his possession of him. Pauses in the delirium of agony were regarded as departures of the

demon.] ᵃ **16 And I brought him to thy disciples,** ᵇ **and
I spake to thy disciples that they should cast it out;**
ᶜ **40 And I besought thy disciples to cast it out; and
they could not.** ᵇ **they were not able.** ᵃ **they could not
cure him. 17 And Jesus answered and said,** {ᵇ **answereth them and saith,**} ᵃ **O faithless and perverse
generation, how long shall I be with you? how long
shall I bear with you?** ᶜ **bring hither thy son.** ᵇ **unto
me.** [As there was no reason to accuse the apostles of perversity, it is evident that the rebuke of Jesus is addressed
generally to all and not particularly to the disciples. The
perverse faithlessness and infidelity of the scribes had operated
upon the multitude, and the doubts of the multitude had in turn
influenced the apostles, and thus, with the blind leading the
blind, all had fallen into the ditch of impotent disbelief. The
disbelief of the people was a constant grief to Jesus, but it must
have been especially so in this case, for it fostered and perpetuated this scene of weakness, mean-spiritedness, misery
and suffering which stood out in such sharp contrast with
the peace, blessedness and glory from which he had just
come.] **20 And they brought him unto him:** ᶜ **42 And
as he was yet a coming,** ᵇ **when he saw him** [saw
Jesus], **straightway** ᶜ **the demon dashed him down,
and** ᵇ **the spirit tare him grievously; and he fell on the
ground, and wallowed foaming. 21 And he asked his
father, How long time is it since this hath come unto
him? And he said, From a child. 22 And oft-times
it hath cast him both into the fire and into the waters,
to destroy him:** {ᵃ **he falleth into the fire, and oft-
times into the water.**} [By causing the long-standing
nature of the case and the malignity of it to be fully revealed,
Jesus emphasized the power of the cure] ᵇ **but if thou canst
do anything, have compassion on us, and help us. 23
And Jesus said unto him, If thou canst! All things
are possible to him that believeth.** [Jesus echoed back
the "if thou canst" which the man had uttered. If Jesus
marveled at the faith of a Gentile which trusted the fullness

of his divine power, he also marveled at the disbelief of this Jew which thus coolly and presumptuously questions the sufficiency of that power. In the remainder of his answer Jesus shows that the lack of power is not in him, but in those who would be recipients of the blessings of his power, for those blessings are obtained by faith.] **24 Straightway the father of the child cried out, and said, I believe; help thou mine unbelief.** [He confessed his faith, but desired so ardently to have the child healed that he feared lest he should not have faith enough to accomplish that desire, and therefore asked for more faith.] **25 And when Jesus saw that a multitude came running together, he rebuked the unclean spirit, saying unto him, Thou dumb and deaf spirit, I command thee, come out of him, and enter no more into him.** [Jesus had found the multitude when he came down from the mountain, but the excitement in this multitude was evidently drawing men from every quarter, so that the crowd was momentarily growing greater. A longer conversation with the man might have been beneficial, but to prevent the gathering of any larger company Jesus acted at once and spoke the words of command. Since the demon was manifestly of a most daring, impudent and audacious nature, Jesus took the precaution to forbid its attempting to re-enter its victim, a precaution which the conduct of the demon abundantly justified.] **26 And having cried out, and torn him much, he came out: and *the boy* became as one dead; insomuch that the more part said, He is dead.** [The malicious effrontery and obstinacy displayed by this demon stands in marked contrast to the cowed, supplicating spirit shown by the Gergesene legion. See pp. 345, 346.] **27 But Jesus took him by the hand, and raised him up; and he arose.** ᶜ**But Jesus healed the boy, and gave him back to his father.** [For comment on similar conduct see page 277.] ᵃ**and the demon went out of him: and the boy was cured from that hour.** ᶜ**43 And they were all astonished at the majesty of God.** [The failure of the disciples had only emphasized the power of the Master.] ᵇ28 And when he was come into the house, ᵃ19 Then came the disciples to Jesus apart, and said, ᵇasked him privately, *How is it* that we could not cast it out? ᵃWhy could not we cast it out? 20 And he saith unto them, Because of your little faith [The failure of the disciples was not because of any insufficiency of power in Jesus, but was due to their own failure to appropriate that power by faith. The relation of belief and unbelief to miraculous power is fully illustrated in Peter's attempt to walk upon the waters. See page 380]: for verily I say unto you, If ye have faith as a grain of mustard seed, ye shall say unto this mountain [Mount Hermon], Remove hence to yonder place; and it shall remove; and nothing shall be impossible unto you. [The mustard seed was the proverbial type for the infinitely little (Matt. xiii. 32). Faith has such power with God that even little faith becomes well-nigh omnipotent in an age of miracles.] ᵇ29 And he said unto them, This kind can come out by nothing, save by prayer. [Prayer was the means of increasing faith. Demons, like spirits in the flesh, have different degrees of will force, some being easier to subdue than others, and this one, being particularly willful and obstinate, required more faith to expel it.]

LXXI.

RETURN TO GALILEE. THE PASSION FORETOLD.

ᵃMATT. XVII. 22, 23; ᵇMARK IX. 30–32; ᶜLUKE IX. 43–45.

ᵇ30 And they went forth from thence [from the region of Cæsarea Philippi], and passed through Galilee [on his way to Capernaum]; and he would not that any man should know it. [He was still seeking that retirement which began on the journey to Tyre. See page 399. This is the last definite mention of that retirement, but we find it referred to again at John vii. 3, 4. See page 439]

31 For he taught his disciples [the reason for his retirement is here given: he wished to prepare his disciples for his passion], **and said unto them, The Son of man is delivered up** [the present tense is used for the future to express the nearness and certainty of the event] **into the hands of men,** ᵃ**22 And** {ᶜ**But**} ᵃ**while they abode in Galilee,** ᶜ**while all were marvelling at all the things which he did,** ᵃ**Jesus** ᶜ**said unto his disciples, 44 Let these words sink into your ears: for the Son of man shall be delivered up into the hands of men.** [We have here two notes of time during which Jesus spoke of his passion. It was all the while he was in Galilee, between his return from Cæsarea and his departure into Judæa, for which see page 439. The length of time suggests that the sad lesson was oft repeated, but was at a time when the marvels of his works strengthened the faith of the disciples so as to enable them to bear the instruction] ᵇ**and they shall kill him; and when he is killed, after three days he shall rise again.** {ᵃ**and the third day he shall be raised up.**} [For comment on similar language see page 306.] **And they were exceeding sorry.** [Peter's experience taught them not to attempt to correct Jesus while thus speaking, so there was nothing left for them but to grieve at his words.] ᶜ**45 But they understood not this** {ᵇ**the**} **saying,** ᶜ**and it was concealed from them, that they should not perceive it** [What was told to them was not for their present but their future benefit, and therefore they were left to puzzle over the words of Jesus]; **and they were afraid to ask him about this saying.** [Not so much from any awe with which they regarded him, as from the delicacy of the subject itself, and their own sorrow, which shrank from knowing it more fully.]

LXXII.

JESUS PAYS THE TRIBUTE MONEY.

(Capernaum, Autumn, A. D. 29.)

ᵃMATT. XVII. 24-27.

ᵃ**24 And when they were come to Capernaum, they that received the half-shekel came to Peter, and said, Doth not your teacher pay the half-shekel?** [The law of Moses required from every male of twenty years and upward the payment of a tax of half a shekel for the support of the temple (Ex. xxx. 12-16; II. Chron. xxiv. 5, 6). This tax was collected annually. We are told that a dispute existed between the Pharisees and Sadducees as to whether the payment of this tribute was voluntary or compulsory. The collectors of it may have thought that Jesus regarded its payment as voluntary, or they may have thought that Jesus considered himself exempt from it because he was so great a rabbi. Though this temple tax was usually collected in March, Lightfoot informs us that the payment of it was so irregular that its receivers kept two chests; in one of which was placed the tax for the current year, and in the other that for the year past. The demand was made upon Jesus at Capernaum because that was his residence, and it was not made sooner because of the wandering life which he led. It appears that since the first of April he had been in Capernaum only once for a brief period, probably no longer than a Sabbath day (John xi. 22-24). The Jewish shekel answered to the Greek stater, which has been variously estimated as worth from fifty to seventy-five cents. The stater contained four drachmæ, and a drachm was about equivalent to a Roman denarius, or seventeen cents.] **25 He saith, Yea.** [Peter answered with his usual impulsive presumption. Probably he had known the tribute to be paid before out of the general fund held by Judas; or he may have assumed that Jesus would fulfill this as one of God's requirements.] **And when he came into the house, Jesus spake first to him** [without waiting for him to tell what he had said], **saying, What thinkest thou, Simon? the kings of the earth, from whom do they receive toll or tribute? from their sons, or from strangers? 26 And when he said, From strangers, Jesus said unto him, Therefore the sons are free.** [The argument is this: If the sons of kings are free from the payment of tribute, I, the Son of God, am free from God's tribute. The half-shekel was regarded as given to God—Jos. *Ant.* xviii. 9. 1.] **27 But, lest we cause them to stumble** [lest we be totally misunderstood, and be thought to teach that men should not pay this tribute to God], **go thou to the sea** [of Galilee], **and cast a hook, and take up the fish that first cometh up; and when thou hast opened his mouth, thou shalt find a shekel: that take, and give unto them for me and thee.** [Jesus paid the tribute in such a manner as to show that the whole realm of nature was tributary to him, and that he was indeed the Son of the great King. Some have thought that our Lord's beneficence, in paying Peter's tax also, was an evidence that Peter, too, was exempt from tribute. But the conclusion is not well drawn. Had this been intended, Jesus would have said "for us," and would not have used the words "for me and thee," which distinguished between the exempted Son and the unexempted subject. Though afterward Peter might possibly have claimed exemption as a child of God by adoption, he was not yet free from his duty to pay this tax —John iv. 21.]

LXXIII.

FALSE AMBITION VERSUS CHILDLIKENESS.

(Capernaum, Autumn, A. D. 29.)

ᵃ MATT. XVIII. 1–14; ᵇ MARK IX. 33–50; ᶜ LUKE IX. 46–50.

ᶜ**46 And there arose a reasoning among them,
which of them was the greatest.** ᵇ**33 And they came
to Capernaum:** ᶜ**47 But when Jesus saw the reasoning of their heart,** ᵇ**and when he was in the house**
[probably Simon Peter's house] **he asked them, What
were ye reasoning on the way? 34 But they held their
peace: for they had disputed one with another on the
way, who *was* the greatest.** [The Lord with his disciples
was now on his way back to Galilee from Cæsarea Philippi,
where, some ten days before, he had promised the keys of
the kingdom to Peter, and where he had honored Peter and
the sons of Zebedee by a mysterious withdrawal into the
mount. These facts, therefore, no doubt started the dispute
as to which should hold the highest office in the kingdom.
The fires of envy thus set burning were not easily quenched.
We find them bursting forth again from time to time down
to the very verge of Christ's exit from the world—Matt. xx.
20–24; Luke xxii. 24.] **35 And he sat down, and called
the twelve; and he said unto them, If any man would
be first, he shall be last of all, and servant of all.** [The
spirit which proudly seeks to be first in place thereby consents to make itself last in character, for it reverses the graces
of the soul, turning love into envy, humility into pride, generosity into selfishness, etc.] ᵃ**1 In that hour came the
disciples unto Jesus, saying, Who then is greatest in
the kingdom of heaven?** [Not comprehending our Lord's
answer and wishing to have him definitely point out the honored person, they now come asking this question. Had Jesus
wished to teach the primacy of Peter, no better opportunity

could have been found.]] **2 And he called to him a little child,** ᵇ**36 And he took a little child,** ᶜ**and set him by his side,** ᵇ**and set him in the midst of them : and taking him in his arms, he said unto them,** ᵃ**Verily I say unto you, Except ye turn, and become as little children, ye shall in no wise enter into the kingdom of heaven. 4 Whosoever therefore shall humble himself as this little child, the same is the greatest in the kingdom of heaven.** [Jesus told them plainly that they must turn from their sin of personal ambition or they could not be his disciples—part of his kingdom—and he pointed them to a little child as the model life in this particular, because the humble spirit in which a child looks up to its parents stood out in sharp contrast to their self-seeking, self-exalting ambition.] **5 And** ᵇ**37 Whosoever shall receive one of such little children {**ᶜ**this little child} in my name receiveth me : and whosoever shall receive {**ᵇ**receiveth} me, receiveth not me, but** ᶜ**receiveth him that sent me : for he that is least among you all, the same is great.** [Greatness does not consist in place. Disciples who receive those of a childlike spirit and disposition that they may thereby honor the name of Christ are honored of Christ as the greatest. The words "in my name" probably suggested to John the incident which follows.] **49 And John answered and said, Master,** ᵇ**Teacher, we saw one casting out demons in thy name ; and we forbade him,** ᶜ**because he followeth {**ᵇ**followed}** ᶜ**not with us.** [Was not one of our immediate company. This man's action had excited the jealousy of John. Jealousy as to official prerogative is very common. His zeal for Jesus reminds us of the friends of Moses (Num. xi. 27-29). But Jesus shows that one who knows enough of him to use his power is not apt to dishonor him.] **50 But Jesus said unto him,** ᵇ**Forbid him not : for there is no man who shall do a mighty work in my name, and be able quickly to speak evil of me. 40 For he that is not against us is for us.** ᶜ**for he that is not against**

you is for you. [The converse of this statement is found at Matt. xii. 30. The two statements taken together declare the impossibility of neutrality. If a man is in no sense against Christ, then he is for him; and if he is not for Christ, he is against him.] ᵇ**41 For whosoever shall give you a cup of water to drink, because ye are Christ's, verily I say unto you, he shall in no wise lose his reward.** [Jesus here returns to the discussion of greatness, and reasserts the doctrine that the smallest act of righteousness, if performed for the sake of the King, shall be honored in the kingdom. For comment, see page 368.] **42 And {ᵃ6 but} ᵇ whosoever shall cause one of these little ones that believe on me to stumble, it were better for him if {ᵃit is profitable for him that} ᵇa great millstone** [the word indicates a large millstone which was turned by an ass] **were {ᵃshould be} ᵇhanged about his neck, and he were {ᵃ*that* he should be} ᵇcast into the sea. ᵃsunk in the depth of the sea.** [Character depends upon small things. If a small act of goodness receives its reward, an act of evil, made apparently small by the trifling insignificance of the person against whom it is committed, receives just as inevitably its punishment. In short, there is no smallness in good and evil that men may rely upon, for heavy penalties may be meted out for what the world judges to be light sins. Those who cause the weak to lapse into unbelief through their ecclesiastical arrogance have a heavy reckoning for which to answer. Greeks, Romans and Egyptians were punished by such millstone drowning. But the fate of one who, by striving for place, causes others to sin, will be worse than that. From offenses caused by a proud spirit Jesus now passes to discuss offences or sins caused by any spirit of evil.] **7 Woe unto the world because of occasions of stumbling! for it must needs be that the occasions come; but woe to that man through whom the occasion cometh!** [The depravity of man makes sin inevitable, but nevertheless it does not remove or reduce the personal responsibility of him who tempts to or causes to sin.] ᵇ**43 And if thy hand cause thee to stumble, cut it off: it is good for thee to enter into life maimed, rather than having thy two hands to go into hell, into the unquenchable fire. 45 And if thy foot cause thee to stumble, cut it off: it is good for thee to enter into life halt, rather than having thy two feet to be cast into hell. {ᵃthe eternal fire.}** [We see from this that "hell" and "eternal fire" are interchangeable terms, and stand in contrast to eternal life.] **9 And if thine eye causeth {ᵇcause} ᵃthee to stumble, pluck it out, and cast it from thee: it is good for thee to enter into life {ᵇthe kingdom of God} with one eye, rather than having two eyes to be cast ᵃinto the hell of fire. ᵇ48 where their worm dieth not, and the fire is not quenched.** [It is better to deny ourselves all unlawful pleasures, even if the denial be as painful and distressing as the loss of a member. The image of the worm is taken from Isa. lxvi. 24, and refers to those worms which feed upon the carcasses of men. The fire and worm can hardly be taken literally, for the two figures are incompatible—worms do not frequent fires. The two figures depict hell as a state of decay which is never completed and of burning which does not consume. Some regard the worm as a symbol of the gnawings of remorse, and the fire as a symbol of actual punishment.] **49 For every one shall be salted with fire.** [At this point many ancient authorities add, "and every sacrifice shall be salted with salt."] **50 Salt is good: but if the salt have lost its saltness, wherewith will ye season it? Have salt in yourselves, and be at peace one with another.** [We have here one of the most difficult passages in the Bible. If the word "fire" were found in an isolated text it might be taken as a symbol either of purification or of punishment. But the context here determines its meaning, for it has just been taken twice as a symbol for punishment. Salt is a symbol of that which preserves from decay. Now, Jesus has just been talking about the future state, with its two conditions or states of bliss and punishment. In both of these states the souls of men are salted or preserved. Every one of the wicked is preserved by a negative or false salt—a worm which feeds but does not die, and a fire which consumes but refuses to go out. Though this state is a condition of life, it is such a negative and false condition that it is elsewhere termed a second death. It is therefore rightly called a "salted" or preserved condition, yet it contradicts the symbolic idea of saltness. As we understand it, the difficulty of the passage lies in this contradictory sense in which the term "salt" is used—a contradiction in which the term "eternal life" also shares, for eternal life is the constant contrast to life in hell, though that life also is spoken of as eternal. The true Christian—the man who offers his body as "a living sacrifice, holy, acceptable to God"—is preserved by the true salt or element of preservation, which is a divinely begotten life of righteousness within him. This is the good state of preservation which a man is counseled to obtain, and not to lose, since it will not be restored to him. The passage summarizes and contrasts the two states of future preservation, one being the salt of eternal life which preserves a man to enjoy the love of God in heaven, and the other being the salt of fire which preserves him in hell to endure the just punishment of God. The "every one" in verse 49 refers to the sufferers mentioned in verse 48.] **10 See that ye despise not one of these little ones: for I say unto you, that in heaven their angels do always behold the face of my Father who is in heaven.** [Jesus here resumes his warning against that pride which exalts itself and despises the humble; disclosing the fact that the ministration of angels is not only general but special, certain angels being entrusted with the care of certain individuals, and all of them supplementing their own wisdom and power by direct access to the presence of God.] **12 How think ye? if any man have a hundred sheep, and one of them be gone astray, doth he not leave the ninety and nine, and go unto the mountains, and seek that which goeth astray? 13 And if so be that he find it, verily I say unto you,** he rejoiceth over it more than over the ninety and nine which have not gone astray.   14 Even so it is not the will of your Father who is in heaven, that one of these little ones should perish.   [Those who have led highly moral lives have a tendency to despise those who have been defiled by gross sin.   This truth is abundantly illustrated by the conduct of the Pharisees, but that such little ones should not be despised Jesus speaks this warning parable.   Though the sheep in the fold and the one that is lost have, as individuals, the same intrinsic value, yet this even balance of value is somewhat modified by the sentiments and emotions incident to loss and recovery.   Moreover, the anxiety and trouble caused by the sheep's wandering do not *depreciate* but rather *enhance* the value of that sheep, because the heart of the Shepherd is so replete with goodness that the misbehavior of the sheep prompts him to feel pity and compassion, rather than to cherish resentment and revenge. Sin does not add to a man's intrinsic value in God's sight— nay, it detracts from it; but it excites in the heart of God pity, compassion and other tender emotions which make it extremely dangerous for those who hinder his reformation and imperil his soul by despising him.]

LXXIV.

SIN AND FORGIVENESS BETWEEN BRETHREN.

(Autumn, A. D. 29.)

[a]MATT. XVIII. 15-35.

[a]15 And if thy brother sin against thee, go, show him his fault between thee and him alone: if he hear thee, thou hast gained thy brother.   [Having warned against giving offense, Jesus now shows how to act when offense is received.   The fault is to be pointed out to the offender, but for the purpose of gaining him—not from a desire to humiliate him.   The offended is to seek the offender,

and the offender is likewise to seek the offended (Matt. xv. 23, 24), and neither is to wait for the other.] **16 But if he hear *thee* not, take with thee one or two more, that at the mouth of two witnesses or three every word may be established.** [Reconciliation is still to be sought, but witnesses are now to be called in preparatory to the next step, which is the hearing before the church, wherein their testimony will be needed.] **17 And if he refuse to hear them, tell it unto the church: and if he refuse to hear the church also, let him be unto thee as the Gentile and the publican.** [As the Saviour was giving preparatory instruction, he was compelled to thus speak of the church by anticipation before it actually existed. The word "church" means assembly, and the apostles knew that there would be some form of assembly in the kingdom about to be set up. When Matthew wrote his Gospel, churches were already in existence. One who will not hear the church is to be regarded as an outsider. This implies that such a one is to be excluded from the church.] **18 Verily I say unto you, What things soever ye shall bind on earth shall be bound in heaven; and what things soever ye shall loose on earth shall be loosed in heaven.** [The binding and loosing here mentioned is limited by the context or the subject of which Jesus now treats. Binding represents exclusion from membership. Loosing, the restoration to fellowship in cases of repentance. The church's act in thus binding or loosing will be recognized in heaven if performed according to apostolic precept or precedent. Hence it is a most august and fearful prerogative.] **19 Again I say unto you, that if two of you shall agree on earth as touching anything that they shall ask, it shall be done for them of my Father who is in heaven. 20 For where two or three are gathered together in my name, there am I in the midst of them.** [These two verses illustrate the sublime power of the church which has just been suggested by its right of excommunication. A small church of two or three can prevail with God in prayer (in matters not wholly at variance with his will) and can be honored by the very presence of the Christ.] **21 Then came Peter and said to him, Lord, how oft shall my brother sin against me, and I forgive him? until seven times?** [Peter, seeing that the language of Jesus called for large forbearance, asked the Lord to fix the bounds. If we accept the Talmud as probably representing the ideals of forgiveness which pertained among the Jews of that age, we find that Peter was striving to be liberal, for the Talmud limits forgiveness to three times.] **22 Jesus saith unto him, I say not unto thee, Until seven times; but, Until seventy times seven.** [Jesus here plays upon the words so as to show that there is no numerical limitation. To keep track of four hundred and ninety offenses one would have to open a set of books with his neighbor, which would be ridiculous. Forgiveness, prayer and charity know no arithmetic. Peter's question brings to mind the forgiveness of God and calls forth the following parable.] **23 Therefore is the kingdom of heaven likened unto a certain king, who would make a reckoning with his servants. 24 And when he had begun to reckon, one was brought unto him, that owed him ten thousand talents.** [Assuming that the silver talent is meant ($1,600), the debt was $16,-000,000, which would render the debtor hopeless enough. If it was a gold talent, it would be nearly twenty times as much.] **25 But forasmuch as he had not** *wherewith* **to pay, his lord commanded him to be sold, and his wife, and children, and all that he had, and payment to be made.** [The law of Moses allowed such a sale—Lev. xxv. 39–47; II. Kings iv. 1.] **26 The servant therefore fell down and worshipped him, saying, Lord, have patience with me, and I will pay thee all. 27 And the lord of that servant, being moved with compassion, released him, and forgave him the debt.** [Seeing the man's apparent willingness to pay, and knowing the hopelessness of his offer to do so, the lord compassionately forbore to sell him and forgave him the whole debt.] **28 But that**

servant went out, and found one of his fellow-servants, who owed him a hundred shillings [The denarius
or shilling was worth about seventeen cents. The debt was,
therefore, about $100]: **and he laid hold on him, and
took** *him* **by the throat, saying, Pay what thou owest.**
[This frenzy to collect might have been somewhat pardona-
ble had the lord still been demanding his debt, but, that debt
being forgiven, such harsh conduct was inexcusable.] **29
So his fellow-servant fell down and besought him,
saying, Have patience with me, and I will pay thee.**
[Compare this conduct with that depicted in verse 26 above.]
**30 And he would not: but went and cast him into
prison, till he should pay that which was due.** [Prison
life was far worse than slavery. The Roman law permitted
such a punishment, and it was practised in this country until
after the beginning of the last century.] **31 So when his
fellow-servants saw what was done, they were exceeding sorry, and came and told unto their lord all
that was done.** [They were sorry for the sin of the one
and the suffering of the other. Human nature rarely grows
so wicked that it fails to resent sin in others.] **32 Then his
lord called him unto him, and saith to him, Thou
wicked servant, I forgave thee all that debt, because
thou besoughtest me: 33 shouldest not thou also have
had mercy on thy fellow-servant, even as I had mercy
on thee?** [God's forgiveness places us under obligation to
be forgiving. The lord does not call the servant wicked
because he had contracted a debt which he could not pay,
but because of the merciless, unforgiving spirit which he had
manifested toward his fellow-servant. Thus God freely forgives sin against himself, but the sin of refusing to forgive
our fellow-man is with him an unforgivable sin. No doctrine
of the Bible is more plainly taught than this.] **34 And his
lord was wroth, and delivered him to the tormentors,
till he should pay all that was due.** [The picture is to
be interpreted by the usages of the East, where even at the
present day torture is used to compel debtors to confess the

possession of property which they are suspected of hiding. Thus the man had escaped being sold into slavery only to receive sentence of death by torture.] **35 So shall also my heavenly Father do unto you, if ye forgive not every one his brother from your hearts.** [Jesus reminds us that God is a Father unto him whom we have refused to forgive. The key to the parable is introduced by the words, " So shall also." God will so deliver to the tormentors the unforgiving. Incidentally the parable draws comparisons between the forgiving spirit of God and the revengeful spirit of man, and the magnitude of our debt to him and the insignificance of our debts to each other. The retraction of forgiveness is merely a part of the parabolic drapery, but it is nevertheless true that those who are delivered from sin come to a worse state than ever if they return to it—II. Pet. ii. 20–22.]

LXXV.

JESUS' BROTHERS ADVISE HIM TO GO TO JUDÆA.

(Galilee, probably Capernaum.)

ᵈ JOHN VII. 2–9.

ᵈ**2 Now the feast of the Jews, the feast of tabernacles, was at hand.** [The first verse of this chapter tells us that Jesus kept away from Judæa because the Jews sought his life. See page 393. This keeping away or seclusion began at the Passover season, and led Jesus not only to keep away from Judæa, but even to hover upon the outskirts of Galilee itself. This seclusion is described in Sections LXV.– LXXI. We now turn back to take up with John the narrative which tells how, after his six months' retirement, Jesus prepared to appear once more in Judæa. The Feast of Tabernacles began on the 15th day of the month Tisri, which answers to our September—October. and consequently came six months after and six months before the Passover. It was the most joyous of the two great feasts, and not only commemorated the time when Israel dwelt in the wilderness in tents, but also celebrated the harvest home. It was, therefore, a thanksgiving both for permanent abodes and for the year's crops. As the people dwelt in booths, the feast partook much of the form and merriment of a picnic.] **3 His brethren therefore said unto him, Depart hence, and go into Judaea, that thy disciples also may behold thy works which thou doest. 4 For no man doeth anything in secret, and himself seeketh to be known openly. If thou doest these things, manifest thyself to the world.** [When we consider how Jesus had withdrawn into the regions of Tyre, Sidon, Decapolis and Cæsarea Philippi, and with what assiduity he had avoided crowds and concealed miracles, these words become very plain. The twelve had been instructed sufficiently to confess his Messiahship, but thousands of his disciples had not seen a miracle for six months. To his brothers such secrecy seemed foolish on the part of one who was ostensibly seeking to be known. They were not disposed to credit the miracles of Jesus, but insisted that if he could work them he ought to do so openly.] **5 For even his brethren did not believe on him.** [This verse explodes the idea that the parties known in the New Testament as our Lord's brothers were sons of Alphæus and cousins to Jesus. The sons of Alphæus had long since been numbered among the apostles, while our Lord's brothers were still unbelievers. As to his brothers, see pp. 224–226, 360.] **6 Jesus therefore saith unto them, My time is not yet come; but your time is always ready.** [Jesus is answering a request that he manifest himself. The great manifestation of his cross and resurrection could not properly take place before the Passover, which was still six months distant. But his brothers, having no message and no manifestation, could show themselves at Jerusalem any time.] **7 The world cannot hate you; but me it hateth, because I testify of it, that its works are evil.** [The world can not hate you because you are in mind and heart a part of it, and it can not hate itself. It hates those who are not of it, and who rebuke its sins and oppose its ways.] **8 Go ye up unto the feast: I go not up unto this feast; because my time is not yet fulfilled. 9 And having said these things unto them, he abode** *still* **in Galilee.** [He did go to the feast, but he did not go up to manifest himself, as his brothers asked, and hence, in the sense in which they made the request, he did not go up. Six months later, at the Passover, he manifested himself by the triumphal entry somewhat as his brothers wished.]

LXXVI.

THE PRIVATE JOURNEY TO JERUSALEM.

(Through Samaria. Probably September, A. D. 29.)

ᶜLUKE IX. 51–56; ᵈJOHN VII. 10.

ᵈ**10 But when his brethren were gone up unto the feast, then went he also up, not publicly, but as it were in secret.** [This section follows immediately after the preceding. The secrecy of this journey consists in the fact that Jesus did not join the caravans or pilgrim bands, and that he did not follow the usual Peræan route, but went directly through Samaria.] ᶜ**51 And it came to pass, when the days were well-nigh come that he should be received up, he stedfastly set his face to go to Jerusalem, and sent messengers before his face: 52 and they went, and entered into a village of the Samaritans, to make ready for him.** [Taken in its strictest sense, the expression "taken up" refers to our Lord's ascension, but it is here used to embrace his entire passion. Though our Lord's death was still six months distant, his going to Jerusalem is described as attended with a special effort, because from that time forth Jerusalem was to occupy the position of headquarters, as Capernaum had done, and his withdrawals and returns would be with regard to it. The presence of the twelve alone is sufficient to account for the messengers. He did not wish to overtax the fickle hospitality of the Samaritans by coming unannounced.] **53 And they did not receive him, because his face was** *as though he were* **going to Jerusalem.** [Had Jesus come among them on a missionary tour he would doubtless have been received. But when he came as a Jew passing through to Jerusalem, and using their highways as a convenience, they rejected him.] **54 And when his disciples James and John saw** *this***, they said, Lord, wilt thou that we bid fire to come down from heaven, and consume them? 55 But he turned, and rebuked them. 56 And they went to another village.** [Refusing to receive a religious teacher was considered a rejection of his claim. This rejection roused the ire of the two sons of thunder and prompted them to suggest that the example of Elijah be followed (II. Kings i. 9–12), but Jesus was a Saviour and not a destroyer, so he passed on to another village. The conduct of John in after years contrasts sharply with the wish which he here expressed—Acts viii. 14–25.]

LXXVII.

AS TO SACRIFICE FOR CHRIST'S SERVICE.

(Samaria. Probably September, A. D. 29.)

ᶜLUKE IX. 57–62.

ᶜ**57 And as they went on the way** [the way through Samaria to Jerusalem], **a certain man said unto him, I will follow thee whithersoever thou goest. 58 And Jesus said unto him, The foxes have holes, and the birds of the heaven** *have* **nests; but the Son of man hath not where to lay his head. 59 And he said unto another, Follow me. But he said, Lord, suffer me first to go and bury my father. 60 But he said unto** him, Leave the dead to bury their own dead; but go thou and publish abroad the kingdom of God. [For comment upon similar language see pp. 341, 342.] **61 And another also said, I will follow thee, Lord; but first suffer me to bid farewell to them that are at my house. 62 But Jesus said unto him, No man, having put his hand to the plow, and looking back, is fit for the kingdom of God.** [Comparing Luke with Matthew, as indicated above, we find that Matthew gives two and Luke three proposals to follow him, and that they differ widely as to the time. It is likely that the first instance occurred where Matthew places it, and that the last two occurred where Luke places them, and that each Evangelist borrowed an item from another period and joined it to his incident because of the similarity of the subject. But as such proffers of discipleship may have been very common, the incidents may be entirely different. The teaching of the last incident is that at a command of Christ all conflicting obligations must be set aside.]

LXXVIII.

IN THE TEMPLE AT THE FEAST OF TABERNACLES.

(October, A. D. 29.)

d JOHN VII. 11–52.

d **11 The Jews therefore sought him at the feast, and said, Where is he?** [It was now eighteen months since Jesus had visited Jerusalem, at which time he had healed the impotent man at Bethesda. His fame and prolonged obscurity made his enemies anxious for him to again expose himself in their midst. John here uses the word *"Jews"* as a designation for the Jerusalemites, who, as enemies of Christ, were to be distinguished from the multitudes who were in doubt about him, and who are mentioned in the next verse.] **12 And there was much murmuring** among the multitudes concerning him: some said, He is a good man; others said, Not so, but he leadeth the multitude astray. [The use of the plural, "multitudes," suggests that the vast crowd disputed as groups rather than as individuals. The inhabitants of some towns were disposed to unite in his defense, while those from other towns would concur in condemning him.] 13 Yet no man spake openly of him for fear of the Jews. [They would not commit themselves upon a question so important until the Sanhedrin had given its decision.] 14 But when it was now the midst of the feast Jesus went up into the temple, and taught. [As the feast lasted eight days, the middle of it would be from the third to the fifth day. Though Jesus had come up quietly to prevent public demonstrations in his favor, he now taught boldly and openly in the very stronghold of his enemies. His sudden appearance suggests the fulfillment of Mal. iii. 1.] 15 The Jews therefore marvelled, saying, How knoweth this man letters, having never learned? [The enemies of Christ were content to know but little about him, and now when they heard him they could not restrain their astonishment at his wisdom. By letters was meant the written law and unwritten traditions which were taught in the great theological schools at Jerusalem. The same word is translated "learning" at Acts xxvi. 24. No one was expected to teach without having passed through such a course. Skeptics of our day assert that Jesus derived his knowledge from the schools, but the schoolteachers who are supposed to have taught him complained of him that he was not their scholar, and surely they ought to have known.] 16 Jesus therefore answered them, and said, My teaching is not mine, but his that sent me. [Seeing the Jews inquiring as to the source of his wisdom, Jesus explains that it was given him of God, and was therefore not derived from any school.] 17 If any man willeth to do his will, he shall know of the teaching, whether it is of God, or *whether* I speak from myself. [Those who would test the divinity of the doctrine of Christ can not do so by rendering a mere mechanical obedience to his teaching. A willing, heart-felt obedience is essential to a true knowledge of his doctrine. Such a disposition makes a good and honest heart in which the seeds of the kingdom must inevitably grow. But a spirit of disobedience is the general source of all skepticism.] **18 He that speaketh from himself seeketh his own glory: but he that seeketh the glory of him that sent him, the same is true, and no unrighteousness is in him.** [Those who bear their own message seek their own glory. Those who bear God's message seek God's glory, and such seeking destroys egotism.] **19 Did not Moses give you the law, and *yet* none of you doeth the law? Why seek ye to kill me?** [The point he makes here is, that their seeking to kill him was proof that they were not keeping the law.] **20 The multitude answered, Thou hast a demon: who seeketh to kill thee?** [The multitude had sought to kill him at his last visit, and it now affects to deny it. Wild notions and extraordinary conduct indicated insanity, and insanity was usually attributed to demoniacal possession. Comp. Matt xi. 18. Their meaning therefore was that the words of Jesus were insanely preposterous, and their words therefore savored more of roughness and irreverence than of malignant unkindness.] **21 Jesus answered and said unto them, I did one work, and ye all marvel because thereof.** [Jesus forbears to speak further as to the plot to murder him, knowing that time would reveal it; but refers to the miracle performed on the Sabbath day at Bethesda eighteen months before, which gave rise to the plot to murder him. A reference to the excitement at that time would recall to the thoughtful the evidence and bitter hostility which the Jerusalemites had then manifested.] **22 Moses hath given you circumcision (not that it is of Moses, but of the fathers); and on the sabbath ye circumcise a man. 23 If a man receiveth circumcision on the sabbath, that the law of Moses may not be broken; are ye wroth with me, because I made a man every whit whole on the sabbath? 24 Judge not**

according to appearance, but judge righteous judgment. [The law which said that no work must be done on the Sabbath day was in conflict with the law which said that a child must be circumcised on the eighth day, whenever that eighth day happened to fall on the Sabbath. It was a case of a specific command making *exception* to a general law. Circumcision was great because it purified legally a portion of the body. But the healing worked by Jesus was greater, for it renewed the whole man. If the act of Christ in healing a man were judged as a mere act, it might be considered a breach of the Sabbath. But if the nature of the act be taken into account and all the laws relative to it be considered—in short, if it be judged righteously in all its bearings—it would be amply justified.] **25 Some therefore of them of Jerusalem said, Is not this he whom they seek to kill? 26 And lo, he speaketh openly, and they say nothing unto him. Can it be that the rulers indeed know that this is the Christ?** [Thus, by referring to the miracle at Bethesda, Jesus not only brought to mind the former opposition of the Jewish rulers, but he started the people of Jerusalem (who were acquainted with the present temper of the hierarchy) to talking about the intention to kill him, thus warning the people beforehand that they would be called upon to assist in his crucifixion. The men of Jerusalem spoke more freely because the present boldness of Jesus led them to think that maybe the rulers were changing their attitude toward him.] **27 Howbeit we know this man whence he is: but when the Christ cometh, no one knoweth whence he is.** [Jerusalem shared the prejudice of its rulers: its citizens felt sure that the rulers could not accept Jesus as Christ because his manner of coming did not comply with accepted theories. Prophecy fixed upon Bethlehem as the birthplace and the line of David as the family of the Christ, but the Jews, probably influenced by Isa. liii. 8, appear to have held that there would be a mystery attached to the immediate and actual parentage of the Messiah. Surely there could have been no greater mystery than the real origin of Jesus as he here outlines it to them, and as they might have fully known it to be had they chosen to investigate the meaning of his words.] **28 Jesus therefore cried in the temple, teaching and saying, Ye both know me, and know whence I am; and I am not come of myself, but he that sent me is true, whom ye know not. 29 I know him; because I am from him, and he sent me.** [Our Lord here asserts their ignorance as to his divine origin. Since he came from God, and they did not know God, they consequently did not know whence he came. As they expected a Messiah who would be supernaturally sent, they ought to have been satisfied with Jesus. But they had no eyes with which to discern the supernatural.] **30 They sought therefore to take him** [because they understood his language as referring to God and were incensed that he should so openly declare them ignorant of God]: **and no man laid his hand on him, because his hour was not yet come.** [Because it was not the will of God that he should be arrested at this time.] **31 But of the multitude many believed on him; and they said, When the Christ shall come, will he do more signs than those which this man hath done?** [Their question was an argument in favor of the Messiahship of Jesus.] **32 The Pharisees heard the multitude murmuring these things concerning him; and the chief priests and the Pharisees** [that is, the Sanhedrin, described by its constituent classes] **sent officers to take him.** [When the Sanhedrin heard the people expressing their faith in Jesus they felt that it was time to take action.] **33 Jesus therefore said, Yet a little while am I with you, and I go unto him that sent me.** [Knowing their attempt to arrest him, Jesus tells them that it is not quite time for them to accomplish this purpose.] **34 Ye shall seek me, and shall not find me: and where I am, ye cannot come.** [They would soon destroy Jesus; after which they would seek him in vain. Their violence would result in his return to his Father. In the dark days which were about to come the Jews would long for a Messiah, for the Christ whom they had failed to recognize in Jesus. They, too, would desire the heavenly rest and security of the better world, but their lack of faith would debar them from entering it.] **35 The Jews therefore said among themselves, Whither will this man go that we shall not find him? Will he go unto the Dispersion among the Greeks, and teach the Greeks? 36 What is this word that he said, Ye shall seek me, and shall not find me; and where I am, ye cannot come?** [The *words* of Jesus were plain enough, but the assertion that he would return to God, and that such a return would be denied to them was, in their ears, too preposterous to be entertained. They therefore made light of it by construing it nonsensically. They asked if he would go among the Jews who had been dispersed or scattered by the captivity and who had never returned to Palestine, and if, when so doing, he would teach the heathen among whom these dispersed were scattered, assuming that such teaching would certainly frustrate and render absurd his claims to be a Jewish Messiah. They little suspected that Jesus, through his apostles, would do this very thing and thereby vindicate his claim as the true Messiah of God.] **37 Now on the last day** [the eighth day], **the great** *day* **of the feast, Jesus stood and cried, saying, If any man thirst, let him come unto me and drink.** [If we may trust the later Jewish accounts, it was the custom during the first seven days for the priests and people in joyful procession to go to the pool of Siloam with a golden pitcher and bring water thence to pour out before the altar, in commemoration of the water which Moses brought from the rock and which typified the Christ (I. Cor. x. 4). If this is so, it is likely that the words of Jesus have some reference to this libation, and are designed to draw a contrast between the earthly water which ceases and the spiritual water which abides, similar to the contrast which he presented to the Samaritan woman at Jacob's well.] **38 He that believeth on me, as the scripture hath said** [in such passages as Isa. lviii. 11; Zech. xiv.

8, etc.], **from within him shall flow rivers of living water.** [For comment on similar expressions see page 145.] **39 But this spake he of the Spirit, which they that believed on him were to receive: for the Spirit was not yet** *given;* **because Jesus was not yet glorified.** [The first and second chapters of the Book of Acts is the best comment upon this passage. When Jesus ascended to the right hand of the Father and was glorified, he sent forth the Spirit upon his apostles on the day of Pentecost, and the apostles in turn promised the gift of the Spirit to all who would believe, repent and be baptized.] **40** *Some* **of the multitude therefore, when they heard these words, said, This is of a truth the prophet. 41 Others said, This is the Christ. But some said, What, doth the Christ come out of Galilee? 42 Hath not the scripture said that the Christ cometh of the seed of David, and from Bethlehem, the village where David was? 43 So there arose a division in the multitude because of him.** [Some of the well disposed toward Jesus, seeing the boldness with which he proclaimed himself, asserted that he was the prophet spoken of by Moses (Deut. xviii. 15), which prophet was thought by some to be the Messiah himself, and by others to be no more than Messiah's forerunner. Still others of the multitude went further and asserted that he was the Christ. These latter were confronted by those who contended that Jesus was not born in the right place nor of the right family. These did not know that he had satisfied the very objections which they named.] **44 And some of them would have taken him; but no man laid hands on him.** [We note here that the enmity of the rulers which had been taken up by the men of Jerusalem (see verse 30) had now reached a faction even of the multitude, so that it desired his arrest, but was restrained from acting.] **45 The officers therefore came to the chief priests and Pharisees** [*i. e.,* to those that sent them]; **and they said unto them, Why did ye not bring him?** [These officers were temple police or Levites, under direction of the chief priests. The words suggest that the Sanhedrin was assembled and waiting for the return of the officers. An extraordinary proceeding for so great a day, but no more extraordinary than that assembly at the feast of the Passover which met and condemned Jesus six months later.] **46 The officers answered, Never man so spake.** [Their report has passed into a saying, which is as true now as when first spoken.] **47 The Pharisees therefore answered them, Are ye also led astray? 48 Hath any of the rulers believed on him, or of the Pharisees? 49 But this multitude that knoweth not the law are accursed.** [This rebuke to the officers may be paraphrased thus: You are to respect the authority of the officers and the judgment of the Pharisees, but you have permitted yourselves to be influenced by a multitude which rests under a curse because of its ignorance.] **50 Nicodemus said unto them (he that came to him before, being one of them)** [therefore able to speak from a position of equality], **51 Doth our law judge a man, except it first hear from himself and know what he doeth?** [Nicodemus bids these proud rulers note that they were breaking the very law which they extolled—Deut. i. 16; Ex. xxiii. 1.] **52 They answered and said unto him, Art thou also of Galilee? Search, and see that out of Galilee ariseth no prophet.** [They laid the lash to the pride of Nicodemus by classing him with the Galilæans who formed the main body of Jesus' disciples, thus separating him from the true Jews. There is no clear evidence that any of the prophets save Jonah was from the district at this time called Galilee, and this fact would justify the hasty demand of the objectors, who were not very scrupulous as to accuracy.]

LXXIX.

THE STORY OF THE ADULTERESS.

(Jerusalem.)

^d JOHN VII. 53–VIII. II.

This section is wanting in nearly all older manuscripts, but Jerome (A. D. 346–420) says that in his time it was contained "in many Greek and Latin manuscripts," and these must have been as good or better than the best manuscripts we now possess. But whether we regard it as part of John's narrative or not, scholars very generally accept it as a genuine piece of history. ^d **53 And they went every man unto his own house** [confused by the question of Nicodemus, the assembly broke up and each man went home]: **1 but Jesus went unto the mount of Olives.** [Probably crossing the mountain to the house of Lazarus and sisters.] **2 And early in the morning he came again into the temple, and all the people came unto him, and he sat down** [as an authoritative teacher did—Matt. v. 1], **and taught them. 3 And the scribes and the Pharisees bring a woman taken in adultery; and having set her in the midst, 4 they say unto him, Teacher, this woman hath been taken in adultery, in the very act.** [The woman had probably been brought to the rulers for trial, and they had seen in her case what appeared to be a promising means of entrapping Jesus. In the presence of the woman and the form of their accusation we see their coarse brutality. The case could have been presented to Jesus without the presence of the woman, and without a detailed accusation.] **5 Now in the law Moses commanded us to stone such** [It was a case under verse 22 of Deut. xxii. Stoning was the legal method of capital punishment]: **what then sayest thou of her? 6 And this they said, trying him, that they might have *whereof* to accuse him.** [They were placing Jesus in a dilemma. They reasoned that he could not set aside the law of Moses and clear the woman without so losing the confidence and favor of the people as to frustrate his claim to be Messiah. They thought he would therefore be compelled to condemn the woman. But if he ordered her to be put to death, he would be assuming authority which belonged only to the Roman rulers, and could therefore be accused and condemned as a usurper.] **But Jesus stooped down, and with his finger wrote on the ground.** [His act was intended to make them vehement, and to give his answer greater effect. What he wrote is unimportant and immaterial, and hence was not told.] **7 But when they continued asking him** [they insisted on an answer, hoping that he would so explain away the seventh commandment as to encourage them in breaking the sixth], **he lifted up himself, and said unto them, He that is without sin among you, let him first cast a stone at her.** [Under the law (Deut. xvii. 7), the witnesses were to cast the first stone. Jesus maintained and vindicated the law, but imposed a condition which they had overlooked. The one who executed the law must be free from the same crime, lest by stoning the woman he condemn himself as worthy of a like death. There is no doubt that the words of Jesus impressed upon them the truth that freedom from the outward act did not imply inward purity or sinlessness—Matt. v. 27, 28.] **8 And again he stooped down, and with his finger wrote on the ground.** [Thus giving them the opportunity to retire without the embarrassment of being watched.] **9 And they, when they heard it, went out one by one, beginning from the eldest, *even* unto the last** [the oldest was first to be convicted of his conscience, because his experience of life's sinfulness was necessarily the fullest]: **and Jesus was left alone, and the woman, where she was, in the midst.** [*I. e.*, in the midst of the court, where the crowd had been.] **10 And Jesus lifted up himself, and said unto her, Woman, where are they? did no man condemn thee?** [This question is asked to pave the way for the dismissal of the woman.] **11 And she said, No man, Lord.** ["Lord" is ambiguous; it may mean "Master" or simply "sir."] **And Jesus said, Neither do I condemn thee: go thy way; from henceforth sin no more.** [The woman did not ask forgiveness, so no words of pardon are spoken. Compare this case with Luke xii. 14. Jesus did not come as an earthly judge; neither did he come to condemn, but to save. The narrative shows how Jesus could deal with malice and impurity in a manner so full of delicacy and dignity as to demonstrate the divine wisdom which dwelt within him.]

LXXX.

MESSIANIC CLAIMS MET BY ATTEMPT TO STONE JESUS.

(Jerusalem. October, A. D. 29.)

[d] JOHN VIII. 12-59.

[d] **12 Again therefore Jesus spake unto them, saying, I am the light of the world: he that followeth me shall not walk in the darkness, but shall have the light of life.** [The metaphor of light was common, and signified knowledge and life; darkness is opposed to light, being the symbol of ignorance and death.] **13 The Pharisees therefore said unto him, Thou bearest witness of thyself; thy witness is not true.** [They perhaps recalled the words of Jesus at John v. 31.] **14 Jesus answered and said unto them, Even if I bear witness of myself, my witness is true; for I know whence I came, and whither I go; but ye know not whence I come, or whither I go.** [No man can bear testimony of his own nature, for he knows neither its origin nor its end. The Jews could not judge as to Christ's nature—that he was the source of light and life, because of their ignorance as to him. But Jesus, having complete knowledge as to his eternal existence, was qualified to testify. There are truths about Deity to which Deity alone can testify, and as to the truth of which

Deity alone is fully competent to judge.]   **15 Ye judge after the flesh** [*i. e.*, carnally, superficially, according to appearances. Carnal tests are not suited to spiritual truth]; **I judge no man. 16 Yea and if I judge, my judgment is true; for I am not alone, but I and the Father that sent me.** [He contrasts his spirit with theirs. They came upon him eager to condemn, but he had come not to condemn, but to save (John iii. 17). As an exception to his general course he might at intervals condemn a sinner; but should he do so the sentence would be just, for it would be the judgment of the Father, and hence devoid of any personal resentment or other biasing, perverting influence; the Father being lifted above and removed from the heats of argument in which the Son engaged.] **17 Yea and in your law it is written, that the witness of two men is true. 18 I am he that beareth witness of myself, and the Father that sent me beareth witness of me.** [Jesus here returns to the point raised in verse 13. He cites the law as to two witnesses, found at Deut. xix. 15, and calls the law *their* law because they had arrogantly claimed possession of it (John vii. 49). The Father had borne witness to the Son by the prophets, including John the Baptist, by his voice at the baptism and the transfiguration, by the works wrought by Jesus, and by the very nature of the life manifested by our Lord throughout his entire ministry. If the witness of two *men* establishes truth, much more the witness of the two divine voices—that of the Father and of the Son.]   **19 They said therefore unto him, Where is thy Father?** [They evidently thought that Jesus referred to the testimony of some earthly parent (see verse 27), and appeal to him to produce this absent, unseen witness. It was according to their carnal or fleshly judgment to thus think.] **Jesus answered, Ye know neither me, nor my Father: if ye knew me, ye would know my Father also.** [If they had really known the Son they would have recognized in him the Father, and *vice versa*—John xiv. 6, 8.]   **20 These words spake he in the treasury, as** he taught in the temple: and no man took him; because his hour was not yet come. [The treasury, or place where the chests for offerings were placed, was in the court of the women, the most public part of the Jewish temple. It was near the hall Gazith, where the Sanhedrin met. Though he taught in a place so suited to his arrest, he was not taken. There is evidently a pause after verse 20, but probably not a very long one.] **21 He said therefore again unto them, I go away, and ye shall seek me, and shall die in your sin: whither I go, ye cannot come.** [See comment on page 447. Seeking their Messiah as an earthly and not as a spiritual deliverer, they would not find him, and hence would die unforgiven, and therefore could not come to the land whither Jesus went, since the unforgiven cannot enter there.] **22 The Jews therefore said, Will he kill himself, that he saith, Whither I go, ye cannot come? 23 And he said unto them, Ye are from beneath; I am from above: ye are of this world; I am not of this world. 24 I said therefore unto you, that ye shall die in your sins: for except ye believe that I am** *he***, ye shall die in your sins.** [Jesus had made *their* sins the ground of separation between him and them, but they assumed that they could go wherever he went, unless he went *some place* for self-murder. Thus they adroitly attempt to make *his sin* the cause of the separation. To this Jesus replies that they are even now separated from him by their origin and nature, and that theirs is a sinful nature, and that they shall die in it unless delivered from it through faith in him.] **25 They said therefore unto him, Who art thou? Jesus said unto them, Even that which I have also spoken unto you from the beginning.** [His bold call to them to believe in him leads them to make a counter demand that he confess himself to them, but Jesus had all along confessed himself to them as the Son of the Father, the bread and water of life, the light of the world, etc., and had no new confession to make.] **26 I have many things to speak and to judge concerning you: howbeit he** that sent me is true; and the things which I heard from him, these speak I unto the world. [Up to this point Jesus had sought to reveal himself; from this point on he would reveal his enemies also, and though the revelation would be displeasing, it was from the Father, and hence would be spoken.] **27 They perceived not that he spake to them of the Father. 28 Jesus therefore said, When ye have lifted up the Son of man, then shall ye know that I am** *he*, **and** *that* **I do nothing of myself, but as the Father taught me, I speak these things. 29 And he that sent me is with me; he hath not left me alone; for I do always the things that are pleasing to him.** [The words which he was about to speak would seem to them to be prompted by personal malevolence. Misconstruing his words as spoken in this spirit, the Jews would crucify him; but when their rage had accomplished his death and spent itself, they would look back upon his life—especially the closing scenes of it—and see that his soul contained no bitterness toward them, that what he had said was true, and was spoken at the dictation of his Father. At the day of Pentecost and the season which followed it, the repentance of the Jews amply fulfilled this prophecy.] **30 As he spake these things, many believed on him.** [The tender manner in which Jesus spoke these words convinced many that he was filled with the spirit of loving good will, and they believed him. Among these converts were some of the Jewish hierarchy, which had been but even now opposing him. The succeeding verses show how Jesus tried to correct their false views of his Messiahship, and to raise their faith te a higher level, and how their faith utterly broke down under the test.] **31 Jesus therefore said to those Jews** [those of the hierarchy] **that had believed him** [the words indicate a less faith than the "believed on him" of the previous verse], **If ye abide in my word,** *then* **are ye truly my disciples** [Discipleship is an abiding condition—a life, not an act. The prejudices and preconceived notions of these Jews would prevent them from believing on him]; **32 and ye shall**

know the truth, and the truth shall make you free.
[Freedom consists in conformity to that which, in the realm
of intellect, is called truth, and in the realm of morality, law.
The only way in which we know truth is to obey it, and
God's truth gives freedom from sin and death.] **33 They
answered unto him, We are Abraham's seed, ard
have never yet been in bondage to any man. how
sayest thou, Ye shall be made free? 34 Jesus answered them, Verily, verily, I say unto you, Every
one that committeth sin is the bondservant of sin.**
[Jesus here shows that the freedom of which he spoke was
spiritual—a relief from the distress mentioned in verses 21,
24.] **35 And the bondservant abideth not in the house
for ever: the son abideth for ever. 36 If therefore
the Son shall make you free, ye shall be free indeed.**
[For light on this passage read Gal. iv. 19–21. Slaves have
no permanent relationship to a house, and may be changed
at will. God was about to dismiss the Jews as unfaithful
slaves (Luke xx. 16–19). Sons, on the contrary, have a
permanent relationship to the house, and if a son take one
into fraternal adoption, he communicates to such a one his
own perpetuity—Rom. viii. 2.] **37 I know that ye are
Abraham's seed; yet ye seek to kill me, because my
word hath not free course in you.** [Outwardly and carnally ye are Abraham's seed, but ye are not so inwardly and
spiritually, for he was the friend of God (Jas. ii. 23), but ye
are the enemies of God's Son, even seeking to kill him because ye are so corrupt that his words are distasteful to you,
and ye resist them.] **38 I speak the things which I have
seen with *my* Father: and ye also do the things which
ye heard from *your* father.** [An introductory statement
leading up to verse 44. In the discourse which follows,
Jesus discloses two households, two sets of children and two
styles of language or thought—one divine, the other diabolic.]
**39 They answered and said unto him, Our father is
Abraham.** [Seeing that he was distinguishing between his
parentage and their parentage, they reassert for themselves

the fatherhood of Abraham, leaving him to find a better one if he could.] **Jesus saith unto them, If ye were Abraham's children, ye would do the works of Abraham. 40 But now ye seek to kill me, a man that hath told you the truth, which I heard from God: this did not Abraham.** [Jesus here asserts that true descent is spiritual —a common nature manifesting itself in a similarity of works. According to this standard, the works of the Jews disproved their claim to be derived from Abraham.] **41 Ye do the works of your father.** [This refers back to verse 38, and shows that in distinguishing between his and their parentage Jesus had not allotted them the parentage of Abraham which they so glibly claimed.] **They said unto him, We were not born of fornication; we have one Father, *even* God.** [Perceiving that he spoke of spiritual parentage, and recognizing the fact that he had shattered their claim of spiritual derivation from Abraham, they fell back upon the citadel of Jewish confidence and pride—spiritually they were begotten of God, they were not begotten of an idolatrous but of a godly stock. Fornication is here used as the common symbol for idolatry—Ex. xxxiv. 15, 16; Hos. i. 2; ii. 4.] **42 Jesus said unto them, If God were your Father, ye would love me: for I came forth and am come from God; for neither have I come of myself, but he sent me.** [If ye were God's children, ye would recognize me as of the same household, and love me accordingly, for I am both God-derived and God-sent. Thus their hatred destroyed this claim also.] **43 Why do ye not understand my speech?** *Even* **because ye cannot hear my word.** [By "speech" here Jesus means the outward form or expression of an idea; by "word" he means the inner thought or substance—the idea itself. Throughout this whole dialogue the Jews had failed to understand the verbiage of Jesus, because his thoughts were so utterly unfamiliar that no words could make them plain. Minds filled with ideas of the devil find it difficult to comprehend the thoughts of God, no matter how plainly expressed.] **44 Ye are of *your* father the devil,**

and the lusts [wishes, desires] **of your father it is your will to do. He was a murderer from the beginning, and standeth not in the truth, because there is no truth in him. When he speaketh a lie, he speaketh of his own: for he is a liar, and the father thereof.** [By your hatred of the truth and your desire to commit murder, which are notable lusts of the devil, you show that you are spiritually derived from him. He was a murderer in the very beginning, for he brought sin into the world, which caused death (Rom. v. 12), and he shrinks from the truth as you do, because it meets with no response in his heart. When he speaks a lie he speaks of his own offspring, for he is a liar and the father of lying.] **45 But because I say the truth, ye believe me not.** [As children of Satan they were used to his flattering speech; hence they rejected the word of Jesus because it was the bitter truth, and convicted them of sin.] **46 Which of you convicteth me of sin? If I say truth, why do ye not believe me?** [If you can not convict me of sin, then what I say must be true. Why, then, do you not believe me?] **47 He that is of God heareth the words of God: for this cause ye hear** *them* **not, because ye are not of God.** [The word "hear" is used in the sense of receive. Children of God love the honesty of God, but children of the devil prefer to be deceived. The saying is akin to John iii. 20, 21.] **48 The Jews** [the same mentioned in verse 31] **answered and said unto him, Say we not well that thou art a Samaritan, and hast a demon?** [They present this piece of scorn as though it were a current saying; but it was probably suggested by the distinction in parentage which Jesus had just made. See verse 38. He had shown they were no true sons of either Abraham or God, and they retaliate by calling him a Samaritan, swayed by diabolical influences. Jesus had visited Samaria (John iv.), and had just come through Samaria to this feast; these things, coupled with his bitter charges against the sons of Abraham, were sufficient to suggest the slanderous accusation.] **49 Jesus answered, I have not a demon; but**

I honor my Father, and ye dishonor me. [He did not deny the charge of being a Samaritan, not choosing to recognize the difference which they attached to race—John iv. 39–42; Luke x. 33; xvii. 16.] **50 But I seek not mine own glory: there is one that seeketh and judgeth.** [I do not mind your abuse, for I do not seek my own glory. My Father seeks it, and judges those in whom he finds it not —John v. 23.] **51 Verily, verily, I say unto you, If a man keep my word, he shall never see death.** [Jesus here re-states the thought in verses 31, 32. "To keep" here means to cherish and obey. Sin is bondage, and its wages is death. The fleshly body of the Christian dies, but the spirit within him does not. His eternal life begins in this world—John v. 24.] **52 The Jews said unto him, Now we know that thou hast a demon.** [They thus construed his words as a confirmation of their former accusation.] **Abraham died, and the prophets; and thou sayest, If a man keep my word, he shall never taste of death. 53 Art thou greater than our father Abraham, who died? and the prophets died: whom makest thou thyself?** [The argument is this: God's word spoken to Abraham and the prophets had not preserved their lives, yet you claim power of life for your words greater than God's, yet surely you will not claim even to be as great as Abraham. Such wild talk is mere raving. They expected Jesus to disclaim the high position to which he seemed to have exalted himself.] **54 Jesus answered, If I glorify myself, my glory is nothing** [he prefaces his answer by showing that his words are not spoken in a spirit of self-exaltation, but in accordance to the will of his Father]: **it is my Father that glorifieth me; of whom ye say, that he is your God; 55 and ye have not known him: but I know him; and if I should say, I know him not, I shall be like unto you, a liar** [referring back to verse 44]: **but I know him, and keep his word.** [Jesus here makes plain as sunlight his entire discourse by showing that he has used the word Father where they would have used the word God.

There is a distinction, too, between the "known" and the "know" used by Jesus. The first represents knowledge which is acquired. The Jews had not acquired a knowledge of God from their Scriptures. The second, "know," indicates that which is grasped intuitively, by direct personal cognition.] **56 Your father Abraham rejoiced to see my day; and he saw it, and was glad.** ["My day" means the mediatorial manifestation of Messiah. Abraham saw it by faith in the promised seed.] **57 The Jews therefore said unto him, Thou art not yet fifty years old, and hast thou seen Abraham?** [They continue to persist in a literal interpretation, and even wrest the words of Jesus; for Abraham might well have seen him as the seed of promise, without his fleshly eyes ever seeing Abraham. Fifty years indicated the prime of life. It had been two thousand years since the time of Abraham, and Jesus was not yet a mature man as estimated by years.] **58 Jesus said unto them, Verily, verily, I say unto you, Before Abraham was born, I am.** ["I was" would simply have expressed priority, but "I am" marks timeless existence. It draws the contrast between the created and the uncreated, the temporal and the eternal. Compare Ex. iii. 14.] **59 They took up stones therefore to cast at him** [judging him to be a blasphemer]: **but Jesus hid himself, and went out of the temple.** [He doubtless drew back into the crowd and was concealed by his friends.]

LXXXI.

CONTENTION OVER THE MAN BORN BLIND.

(Jerusalem.)

d JOHN IX. 1-41.

[Some look upon the events of this and the next section as occurring at the Feast of Tabernacles in October, others think they occurred at the Feast of Dedication in December, deriving their point of time from John x. 22.] **d1 And as**

he passed by, he saw a man blind from his birth.
[The man probably sought to waken compassion by repeatedly stating this fact to passers-by.] **2 And his disciples
asked him, saying, Rabbi, who sinned, this man, or
his parents, that he should be born blind?** [They assumed that all suffering was retributive, and asked for whose
sins this man suffered, regarding it as a case of extreme hardship, for to be born blind is uncommon, even in the East.
Their question had reference to the doctrine of transmigra-
tion of souls, the man being regarded as possibly having sinned
in some pre-existing state.] **3 Jesus answered, Neither
did this man sin, nor his parents: but that the works
of God should be made manifest in him.** [Jesus found
a third alternative to their dilemma. The man's parents were
sinners, but neither their sin nor the beggar's own sin had
caused this calamity. It had come upon him as part of God's
plan for his life; it was part of the providential arrangement
by which God governs the world.] **4 We must work the
works of him that sent me, while it is day: the night
cometh, when no man can work.** [As to the duration of
his earthly works, Jesus classifies himself with his disciples, for
his humanity, like ours, had its season of activity, or day, which
was practically terminated by the night of death. After his resurrection, Jesus performed no miracles of healing.] **5 When
I am in the world, I am the light of the world.** [In
the spiritual sense Christ is ever the light of the world, but
while he lived among men, even the privileges of physical light
were imparted by him.] **6 When he had thus spoken,
he spat on the ground, and made clay of the spittle,
and anointed his eyes with the clay, 7 and said unto
him, Go, wash in the pool of Siloam (which is by
interpretation, Sent).** [Jesus probably used the clay to aid
the man's faith. His so doing gave the Pharisees a chance
to cavil at Jesus for breaking the Sabbath. If later rabbis
report correctly the traditions of that day, clay might be put
on thees ey for pleasure on the Sabbath, but not for medicine,
nor might the eyes be anointed with spittle on that day. As

to the pool of Siloam, see page 327. It was probably called
Sent because its waters are sent to it from the Virgin's Fountain through a tunnel cut through the hill Ophel. For the
Virgin's Fountain, see page 194.] **He went away therefore, and washed, and came seeing.** [He did not come
back to Jesus, but came to his own home.] **8 The neighbors therefore, and they that saw him aforetime, that
he was a beggar, said, Is not this he that sat and
begged? 9 Others said, It is he: others said, No,
but he is like him.** [The confusion of the neighbors is
very natural. Such a cure would slightly change his appearance, but in any event the impossibility of the cure would
raise doubts as to the identity of the cured.] **He said, I
am *he*. 10 They said therefore unto him, How then
were thine eyes opened?** [They question him as to the
manner, not as to the fact.] **11 He answered, The man
that is called Jesus made clay, and anointed mine
eyes, and said unto me, Go to Siloam, and wash: so
I went away and washed, and I received sight.** [He
speaks of Jesus as of one well known. He had learned who
sent him before he went to Siloam. We shall note how opposition enlarges the faith and the confession of this man.]
**12 And they said unto him, Where is he? He saith,
I know not. 13 They bring to the Pharisees him that
aforetime was blind.** [They wanted to see how the Pharisees would deal with his miracles. See McGarvey's "Credibility," page 112 *f.*] **14 Now it was the sabbath on the
day when Jesus made the clay, and opened his eyes.**
[Such conduct on the Sabbath raised legal questions of which
the Pharisees were also the recognized judges.] **15 Again
therefore the Pharisees also asked him how he received his sight. And he said unto them, He put clay
upon mine eyes, and I washed, and I see.** [The Pharisees ascertained no more than the neighbors had learned.]
**16 Some therefore of the Pharisees said, This man
is not from God, because he keepeth not the sabbath.
But others said, How can a man that is a sinner do**

such signs? And there was a division among them. [The cause for division is apparent. One party laid stress upon the Jewish tradition and judged Jesus a sinner because he had violated them. The other party laid stress upon the sign or miracle and argued that one who could do such things could not be a violator of God's laws.] **17 They** [both parties] **say therefore unto the blind man again, What sayest thou of him, in that he opened thine eyes?** [Each party asked the opinion of the blind man, hoping to get something to aid their side of the argument—one party trusting to the man's gratitude, and the other to his fear of the rulers.] **And he said, He is a prophet.** [A far more pronounced confession than that which he gave in verse 11.] **18 The Jews therefore did not believe concerning him, that he had been blind, and had received his sight, until they called the parents of him that had received his sight, 19 and asked them, saying, Is this your son, who ye say was born blind? how then doth he now see?** [The man's advocacy of Jesus as a prophet suggested to these cunning diplomats that there was collusion between Jesus and the man, and that the cure was fraudulent. They therefore denied the cure and sent for the parents, to whom they put the threefold question as to sonship, blindness and cure.] **20 His parents answered and said, We know that this is our son, and that he was born blind** [thus they answer clearly as to the first two points]: **21 but how he now seeth, we know not; or who opened his eyes, we know not: ask him; he is of age; he shall speak for himself.** [The emphasis in this verse lies in the pronouns. Thus the parents timidly declined to answer the third point, alleging that their son is old enough to answer for himself.] **22 These things said his parents, because they feared the Jews: for the Jews had agreed** [informally] **already, that if any man should confess him** *to be* **Christ, he should be put out of the synagogue.** [The parents, having heard the unrestrained, freely spoken account given by their son as to his healing, had no doubt in their own minds as to who effected that healing. They therefore declined to speak because of fear, and not through lack of knowledge.] **23 Therefore said his parents, He is of age; ask him. 24 So** [following the suggestion of the parents, and because a miracle could not now be denied] **they called a second time the man that was blind, and said unto him, Give glory to God: we know that this man is a sinner.** [Taken in their English sense, these words would mean, "praise God and not Jesus for what has been done," but the phrase, "give glory to God," is, in Hebrew usage, an adjuration to a criminal to confess his guilt (Josh. vii. 9; I. Sam. vi. 5). The idea may then be paraphrased thus: confess that you and Jesus have conspired to work a pretended miracle. It is your best course, since we know all about the frauds of Jesus and will soon unearth this one.] **25 He therefore answered, Whether he is a sinner, I know not: one thing I know, that, whereas I was blind, now I see.** [As to the doings of Jesus, whether fraudulent or not, he could not answer, but he could say that there was no sham or deception about his eyesight.] **26 They said therefore unto him, What did he to thee? how opened he thine eyes? 27 He answered them, I told you even now, and ye did not hear; wherefore would ye hear it again? would ye also become his disciples?** [Perceiving that their boasted knowledge as to the frauds of Jesus was untrue, and that they were even then questioning him to obtain material to be used against Jesus, he declines to repeat his statement and shows them that he understands their sinister motive in questioning him by ironically asking them if they wished to become disciples of Jesus.] **28 And they reviled him, and said, Thou art his disciple; but we are disciples of Moses. 29 We know that God hath spoken unto Moses: but as for this man, we know not whence he is.** [In Jewish estimation, Moses stood next to God. To forsake Moses for another prophet was to be an apostate. Such reviling was a severe test, but the man stood it.] **30 The man answered and**

said unto them, Why, herein is the marvel, that ye
know not whence he is, and *yet* he opened mine eyes.
[The man answers contempt with contempt; with biting irony
he declares that the miracle of his healing is no wonder at
all when compared with the fact that such wonderfully learned
men should be totally ignorant of so great a miracle-worker
as Jesus. Thus he scorned their superlative claim to infallible
knowledge, expressed in verses 24 and 29.] **31 We know**
[he takes up their style of speech] **that God heareth not
sinners: but if any man be a worshipper of God, and
do his will, him he heareth.** [Such was the teaching of
the Old Testament—Prov. xv. 29; Isa. i. 15; Mic. iii. 4; Jas.
v. 16, 17.] **32 Since the world began it was never
heard that any one opened the eyes of a man born
blind.** [The Old Testament contains no record of such a
miracle: the case stood alone as a marvel of power.] **33 If
this man were not from God, he could do nothing.**
[He draws the same conclusion which the better element of
the Pharisees had drawn. See verse 16.] **34 They answered and said unto him, Thou wast altogether born
in sins, and dost thou teach us?** [They give here the
Jewish answer to the question asked in verse 2. Do you, so
stamped as a sinner from birth, presume to teach us, the heads
of Israel? They had been denying that he had been blind;
they now inconsistently taunt him with blindness as an evidence of his sin.] **And they cast him out.** [The vast
majority of commentators take this as an immediate act, and
hence allege that the language refers to his being cast out of
the hall or place where they were assembled, and not to his
being excommunicated. Their reason for this is found in
the fact that the man could not be excommunicated without
a formal meeting of the Sanhedrin. But there is nothing to
show that the act was not a deliberate one, including a formal
meeting, etc. We agree with DeWette that his expulsion
from a hall " would not be important enough to occasion verse
35."] **35 Jesus heard that they had cast him out** [His
was a sad plight, indeed. To be put out of the synagogue

was to be put on a level with the heathen, and to be left without a country or a religious fellowship]; **and finding him, he said, Dost thou believe on the Son of God?** [Being cut off from all that came through Moses, Jesus was leading him into all that came through the Son of God.] **36 He answered and said, And who is he, Lord, that I may believe on him?** [The form of the man's question showed that he regarded a knowledge of the Son of God as a privilege beyond all hope or expectation, and the reply of Jesus is suited to this idea.] **37 Jesus said unto him, Thou hast both seen him, and he it is that speaketh with thee.** [Thus the unhoped for had been actually and sensually realized. To the outcast of the synagogue here and to the outcast of the nation at Jacob's well (John iv. 26), how fully Jesus revealed himself!] **38 And he said, Lord, I believe. And he worshipped him. 39 And Jesus said** [not addressing any one in particular, but rather as summing up the whole incident], **For judgment came I into this world, that they that see not may see; and that they that see may become blind.** [The life course of Jesus attracted the needy and repelled the self-satisfied, and was, therefore, a continuous judgment. Those conscious of their deficiencies and ready to ask for light received it (verses 36–38), while those satisfied with their own opinion became daily more blinded by their bigotry. See verses 24 and 34, and Matt. xi. 25.] **40 Those of the Pharisees who were with him** [not as disciples, but for curiosity's sake] **heard these things, and said unto him, Are we also blind? 41 Jesus said unto them, If ye were blind, ye would have no sin: but now ye say, We see: your sin remaineth.** [If you were conscious of your spiritual darkness, and sought light, you would either find it or not be blamed for your failure to do so. They could see if they would, and were responsible for their blindness.]

LXXXII.

DISCOURSE ON THE GOOD SHEPHERD.

(Jerusalem, December, A. D. 29.)

^d JOHN X. 1-21.

^d1 **Verily, verily, I say unto you** [unto the parties whom he was addressing in the last section], **He that entereth not by the door into the fold of the sheep, but climbeth up some other way, the same is a thief and a robber.** [In this section Jesus proceeds to contrast his own care for humanity with that manifested by the Pharisees, who had just cast out the beggar. Old Testament prophecies were full of declarations that false shepherds would arise to the injury of God's flock (Ezek. xxxiv. 1-6; Jer. xxxiii. 1-6; Zech. xi. 4-11). But other prophecies spoke of the true shepherding of God and his Messiah (Ps. xxiii.; lxxvii. 20; Ps. lxxx. 1; xcv. 7; Jer. xxxi. 10; Ezek. xxxiv. 31; Mic. vii. 14; Isa. xliii. 11). The Pharisees were fulfilling the first line of prophecies, and Jesus was fulfilling the second. The sheepfolds of the East are roofless enclosures, made of loose stone, or surrounded by thornbushes. They have but one door. Jesus, the true shepherd, came in the proper and appointed way (and was the proper and appointed Way), thus indicating his office as shepherd. A thief steals by cunning in one's absence; a robber takes by violence from one's person. The Pharisees were both. They stole the sheep in Messiah's absence, and they slew Messiah when he came. They did not come in the ways ordained of God.] **2 But he that entereth in by the door is the shepherd of the sheep. 3 To him the porter openeth; and the sheep hear his voice: and he calleth his own sheep by name, and leadeth them out.** [Several small flocks were sometimes kept in one fold. The door was fastened from the inside with sticks or bars by the porter, who remained with the sheep during the night, and opened for the shepherds in the morning. The fold is the church, Christ is the door, the sheep

are the disciples, and the shepherd is Christ. The porter is probably part of the drapery of the parable. If he represents anybody, it is God, who decides who shall enter through the door.] **4 When he hath put forth all his own, he goeth before them, and the sheep follow him: for they know his voice.** [In the East, sheep are not driven, but led, and each sheep has and knows its name. Disciples also are led. There is no rough road or thorny path which the feet of Jesus have not first trod. The Pharisees had put forth the beggar to be rid of him; the true shepherd puts forth to feed.] **5 And a stranger will they not follow, but will flee from him: for they know not the voice of strangers.** [The mingled flocks are separated by the calling voices of the several shepherds. The control of the Pharisees was not of this order. The authority of the synagogues had passed into their hands, and their rule was about the same as when thieves and robbers gained possession of the sheepfold. The people were disposed to flee from them—Matt. ix. 36.] **6 This parable spake Jesus unto them: but they understood not what things they were which he spake unto them.** [The idea of loving care was so foreign to the nature of the Pharisees that they could not comprehend the figures which clothed such a thought. The word here translated "parable" is not the word *"parabole,"* which John never uses, but the word *"paroimia,"* which the synoptists never use. *Paroimia* means, literally, "beside the way," *i. e.,* a speech not of the common or direct form, *i. e.,* a similitude or allegory.] **7 Jesus therefore said unto them again, Verily, verily, I say unto you, I am the door of the sheep.** [Seeing that they did not understand the allegory, Jesus gives a twofold explanation of it found in verses 7–10 and 11–16.] **8 All that came before me are thieves and robbers: but the sheep did not hear them.** [He speaks of the past, and refers to false Messiahs.] **9 I am the door; by me if any man enter in, he shall be saved, and shall go in and go out, and shall find pasture.** [The door is here spoken of with reference to the *sheep*, and hence becomes the symbol of **entrance** into protection and shelter, or exit to liberty and plenty.] **10 The thief cometh not, but that he may steal, and kill, and destroy: I came that they may have life, and may have *it* abundantly.** [Through the life of Jesus, as through a heavenly portal, men have entered upon true civilization, with its schools, colleges, railroads, telegraph, telephone and innumerable privileges and liberties.] **11 I am the good shepherd** [The relations of Christ to his people are so abounding and complex as to overburden any parable which seeks to carry them. He is not only the passive doorway to life, but also the active, energizing force which leads his people through that doorway into life]: **the good shepherd layeth down his life for the sheep.** [Verses 11–14 set forth the perfect self-sacrifice through which the blessings of Christ have been obtained for us. The world-ruling spirit blesses itself through the sacrifice of the people; the Christ-spirit blesses the people through the sacrifice of self.] **12 He that is a hireling, and not a shepherd, whose own the sheep are not** [shepherds were not, as a rule, owners of the sheep, but they were expected to love and care for them by reason of their office of shepherds], **beholdeth the wolf coming, and leaveth the sheep, and fleeth, and the wolf snatcheth them, and scattereth *them*** [the perils of the Oriental shepherd accord with the picture here given —Gen. xiii. 5; xiv. 12; xxxi. 39, 40; xxxii. 7, 8; xxxvii. 33; Job i. 7; I. Sam. xvii. 34, 35]: **13 *he fleeth* because he is a hireling, and careth not for the sheep.** [He flees because he loves his wages rather than the flock.] **14 I am the good shepherd; and I know mine own, and mine own know me, 15 even as the Father knoweth me, and I know the Father** [Our Lord's relationship to his flock is one of mutual knowledge and affection, and is far removed from the spirit of hire. The knowledge existing between disciple and Master springs from mutual acquaintanceship and love. Thus it is the same *kind* of knowledge which exists between Father and Son, though it is not of the same *quality*, being infinitely less full and perfect]; **and I lay down my life for the sheep.** [The sacrifice of the good shepherd to shield his sheep has never been in vain.] **16 And other sheep I have, which are not of this fold: them also I must bring, and they shall hear my voice; and they shall become one flock, one shepherd.** [Jesus was speaking to the Jews, who had been frequently spoken of in Scripture as God's flock. The other sheep were Gentiles. They are spoken of as scattered sheep, and not as flocks, because with them there was no unity. Here, as everywhere, the truth breaks through, revealing Christ as the world's Redeemer, who would break down the middle wall of partition between Jew and Gentile, and cause all true worshipers to have a common relationship to one Master.] **17 Therefore doth the Father love me, because I lay down my life, that I may take it again.** [Jesus did not permit his life to be sacrificed so as to become cast away, but to be raised again as an earnest of the resurrection of all flesh.] **18 No one taketh it away from me, but I lay it down of myself. I have power to lay it down, and I have power to take it again. This commandment received I from my Father.** [This shows that his death was voluntary, and with the resurrection which followed, it was in full and perfect accordance with his original commission or commandment from the Father.] **19 There arose a division again among the Jews because of these words.** [The word "again" refers to John vii. 43, and ix. 16.] **20 And many of them said, He hath a demon, and is mad; why hear ye him?** [The theory that demons could produce supernatural effects (Matt. xii. 24) formed a handy device for explaining away the miracles of Christ.] **21 Others said, These are not the sayings of one possessed with a demon. Can a demon open the eyes of the blind?** These defenders refer to the well-remembered cure of the man born blind, and argue, as he did, that a demoniac could not work such a miracle. They fail, however, to make a positive confession of faith in Jesus.]

LXXXIII.

MISSION AND RETURN OF THE SEVENTY.

(Probably in Judæa, October, A. D. 29.)

^cLUKE X. 1–24.

^c1 Now after these things the Lord appointed sev‑ enty others [*i. e.*, other messengers in addition to the twelve apostles], and sent them two and two before his face into every city and place, whither he himself was about to come. [Luke has told us of the journey through Samaria to Jerusalem, and John has told us what occurred at the Feast of Tabernacles in Jerusalem. We learn from John also that Jesus was at the Feast of Dedication (John x. 22). The first feast was in October and the latter in December. Jesus evidently spent the time between these feasts in Judæa, making a tour of that province and sending the seventy before him, thus thoroughly evangelizing it as he had Galilee, by sending out the twelve.] 2 And he said unto them, The harvest indeed is plenteous, but the laborers are few: pray ye therefore the Lord of the harvest, that he send forth laborers into his harvest. 3 Go your ways; behold, I send you forth as lambs in the midst of wolves. 4 Carry no purse, no wallet, no shoes; and salute no man on the way. [This last was probably a common direction in cases of haste (II. Kings iv. 29). East‑ ern salutations were tedious and overburdened with ceremony. Those in haste were excused from them.] 5 And into whatsoever house ye shall enter, first say, Peace *be* to this house. 6 And if a son of peace be there, your peace shall rest upon him: but if not, it shall turn to you again. 7 And in that same house remain, eating and drinking such things as they give [they were not to give trouble and waste time by asking for better food]: for the laborer is worthy of his hire. Go not from house to house. 8 And into whatsoever city ye enter, and

they receive you, eat such things as are set before you: 9 and heal the sick that are therein, and say unto them, The kingdom of God is come nigh unto you. 10 But into whatsoever city ye shall enter, and they receive you not, go out into the streets thereof and say, 11 Even the dust from your city, that cleaveth to our feet, we wipe off against you: nevertheless know this, that the kingdom of God is come nigh. 12 I say unto you, It shall be more tolerable in that day for Sodom, than for that city. [For comment, see pp. 262–265.] 13 Woe unto thee, Chorazin! woe unto thee, Bethsaida! for if the mighty works had been done in Tyre and Sidon, which were done in you, they would have repented long ago, sitting in sackcloth and ashes. 14 But it shall be more tolerable for Tyre and Sidon in the judgment, than for you. 15 And thou, Capernaum, shalt thou be exalted unto heaven? thou shalt be brought down unto Hades. [For comment on a similar passage, see pp. 286, 287.] **16 He that heareth you heareth me; and he that rejecteth you rejecteth me; and he that rejecteth me rejecteth him that sent me.** [For comment, see page 368.] **17 And the seventy returned with joy, saying, Lord, even the demons are subject unto us in thy name.** [The report of the seventy is more joyful than that of the twelve, for the sayings of the latter on their return were overshadowed by the news of John the Baptist's death.] **18 And he said unto them, I beheld Satan fallen as lightning from heaven.** [This may be translated "I was beholding Satan fallen as lightning falls from heaven." The sense indicates that the words refer to the victories over the unclean spirits just reported by the seventy. In their successes Jesus saw Satan falling from lofty heights with the swiftness of lightning. The overthrow of Satan was then in progress— John xvi. 11; xii. 31.] **19 Behold, I have given you authority to tread upon serpents and scorpions, and over all the power of the enemy: and nothing shall**

in any wise hurt you. [While the messengers of Christ were, no doubt, literally protected from the poisons of reptiles, etc. (Acts xxviii. 3–6), serpents and scorpions are here to be taken as emblematic of the powers of evil.] **20 Nevertheless in this rejoice not, that the spirits are subject unto you; but rejoice that your names are written in heaven.** [Your joy in visible and temporal success, and in the subjection to you of the powers of evil, is not to be compared to the joy that you have the prospect of heaven.] **21 In that same hour he rejoiced in the Holy Spirit, and said, I thank thee, O Father, Lord of heaven and earth, that thou didst hide these things from the wise and understanding, and didst reveal them unto babes: yea, Father; for so it was well-pleasing in thy sight. 22 All things have been delivered unto me of my Father: and no one knoweth who the Son is, save the Father; and who the Father is, save the Son, and he to whomsoever the Son willeth to reveal** *him.* [For comment, see pp. 288, 289.] **23 And turning to the disciples, he said privately, Blessed** *are* **the eyes which see the things that ye see: 24 for I say unto you, that many prophets and kings desired to see the things which ye see, and saw them not; and to hear the things which ye hear, and heard them not.** [For comment, see p. 332.]

LXXXIV.

PARABLE OF THE GOOD SAMARITAN.

(Probably Judæa.)

ᶜLUKE X. 25-37.

ᶜ**25 And behold, a certain lawyer stood up and made trial of him, saying, Teacher, what shall I do to inherit eternal life?** [For the term lawyer see pp. 313, 314. The lawyer wished to make trial of the skill of Jesus in solving the intricate and difficult question as to how to obtain salvation. Jesus was probably teaching in some house or courtyard, and his habit of giving local color to his parables suggests that he was probably in or near Bethany, through which the road from Jerusalem to Jericho passes. The lawyer stood up to attract attention to himself, and thus give emphasis to his question and its answer.] **26 And he said unto him, What is written in the law? how readest thou?** [Looking upon Jesus as a sabbath-breaker and a despiser of tradition, the lawyer no doubt expected that Jesus would lay down some new rule for obtaining salvation. If so, he was surprised to be thus referred to the law of Moses for his answer.] **27 And he answering said, Thou shalt love the Lord thy God with all thy heart, and with all thy soul, and with all thy strength, and with all thy mind; and thy neighbor as thyself.** [Deut. vi. 4, 5; Lev. xix. 18. Having made himself conspicuous by standing up, the lawyer had to give the best answer he knew or sully his own reputation for knowledge. He therefore gives the two great laws which comprise all other laws.] **28 And he said unto him, Thou hast answered right: this do, and thou shalt live.** [The lawyer had asked his question simply as a test. With him the law was simply matter for speculation and theory, and the word "do" was very startling. It showed the difference between his and the Master's views of the law He had hoped by a question to expose Jesus as one who set aside the law, but

Jesus had exposed the lawyer as one who merely theorized about the law, and himself as one who advocated the doing of the law.] **29 But he, desiring to justify himself, said unto Jesus, And who is my neighbor?** [He could justify his conduct if permitted to define the word "neighbor." He asked his question, therefore, in the expectation of securing such a definition of the word as would enable him to maintain his public standing and quiet his conscience.] **30 Jesus made answer and said, A certain man** [evidently a Jew, for otherwise the nationality would have been specified] **was going down from Jerusalem to Jericho; and he fell among robbers, who both stripped him and beat him, and departed, leaving him half dead.** [The road from Jerusalem to Jericho is eighteen miles long, and descends about 3,500 feet. About two miles from Jerusalem it passes through the village of Bethany, and for the rest of the eighteen miles it passes through desolate mountain ravines without any habitation save the inn, the ruins of which are still seen about half way to Jericho. This district from that time till the present has been noted for robberies, and Jerome tells that the road was called the " bloody way."] **31 And by chance a certain priest was going down that way** [a very natural thing for a priest to do, for there was a very large priestly settlement at Jericho]**: and when he saw him, he passed by on the other side.** [He did this although the law commanded mercy and help to a neighbor —Ex. xxiii. 4, 5; Deut. xxiii. 1-4.] **32 And in like manner a Levite also** [A temple minister. The tribe of Levi had been set apart by God for his service], **when he came to the place, and saw him, passed by on the other side.** [In the priest and Levite the lawyer saw the picture of his own life, for he saw in them those who knew the law, but did not practice it. There may have been many excuses for this neglect of the wounded man: danger, haste, dread of defilement, expense, but Jesus does not consider any of them as worth mentioning.] **33 But a certain Samaritan** [the hereditary enemy of the Jew—John iv. 9], **as he journeyed, came** where he was : and when he saw him, he was moved with compassion, 34 and came to him, and bound up his wounds, pouring on *them* oil and wine [the ordinary remedies for wounds—Isa. i. 6]; and he set him on his own beast, and brought him to an inn, and took care of him. 35 And on the morrow he took out two shillings [the shilling or denarius was worth about seventeen cents, but it represented the price of a day's labor], and gave them to the host [the inn-keeper], and said, Take care of him; and whatsoever thou spendest more, I, when I come back again, will repay thee. [The compassion of the Samaritan bore full fruitage. However heterodox he was, he was after all a worshiper of Jehovah and more orthodox at heart than either the priest or the Levite. Though it was not customary for an inn-keeper to furnish food either for man or beast, he could do so if he chose out of his own stores. The scant cash left by the Samaritan indicates a poverty which made his charity the more praiseworthy. His eye and heart and hand and foot and purse were all subservient to the law of God.] 36 Which of these three, thinkest thou, proved neighbor unto him that fell among the robbers? [Instead of answering didactically, "Everybody is your neighbor," Jesus had incarnated the law of neighborliness in the good Samaritan, and had made it so beautiful that the lawyer could not but commend it even when found in a representative of this apostate race. He showed, too, that the law was not for casuistry but for practice.] 37 And he said, He that showed mercy on him. [The lawyer avoided the name Samaritan as distasteful to his lips. Jesus gave countenance to no such racial prejudice, even though the Samaritans had rejected him but a few weeks before this—Luke ix. 53.] And Jesus said unto him, Go, and do thou likewise. [All the laws and teachings of God are to be generously interpreted (Matt. v. 43, 44), and are to be embodied in the life—Matt. vii. 24-27.]

LXXXV.

JESUS THE GUEST OF MARTHA AND MARY.

(Bethany, near Jerusalem.)

c LUKE x. 38–42.

c 38 Now as they went on their way [he was journeying through Judæa, attended by the twelve], he entered
into a certain village [it was the village of Bethany (John
xi. 1), which was on the eastern slope of the Mount of Olives,
less than two miles from Jerusalem]: and a certain woman
named Martha received him into her house. 39 And
she had a sister called Mary, who also sat at the
Lord's feet, and heard his word. [Sitting at the feet
was the ancient posture of pupils (Acts xxii. 3). Martha honored Christ as a *Guest*, but Mary honored him as a Teacher.]
40 But Martha was cumbered about much serving
[she was evidently preparing an elaborate repast, and was
experiencing the worry and distraction which usually accompanies such effort]; and she came up to him, and
said, Lord, dost thou not care that my sister did leave
me to serve alone? bid her therefore that she help
me. [Martha so forms her appeal to Christ as to make it a
covert insinuation that Mary would not listen to *her* requests.]
41 But the Lord answered and said unto her, Martha,
Martha, thou art anxious and troubled about many
things [By thus repeating the name, Jesus tempered the
rebuke. See also Luke xxii. 31; Acts ix. 4]: 42 but one
thing is needful [*I. e.*, one duty or privilege is pre-eminent.
Bread for the body may be important, but food for the soul
is, after all, the one thing needful]: for Mary hath chosen
the good part, which shall not be taken away from
her. [The expression "good part" is an allusion to the
portion of honor sent to the principal guest at a banquet. Its
use shows that Jesus had food in mind when he used the ex-

pression "one thing is needful," and that he was contrasting spiritual nourishment with physical. The description of the two sisters here tallies with that given at John xii. 2, 3, for there Martha serves and Mary expresses personal devotion. Our Lord's rebuke is not aimed at hospitality, nor at a life full of energy and business. It is intended to reprove that fussy fretfulness which attempts many unneeded things, and ends in worry and faultfinding. It does not set a life of religious contemplation above a life of true religious activity, for contemplation is here contrasted with activity put forth with a faulty spirit. The trend of New Testament teaching shows that a man must be a *doer* as well as a *hearer* of the Word.

LXXXVI.

PRAYER TAUGHT AND ENCOURAGED.

(Probably Judæa.)

ʿLUKE XI. 1-13.

1 And it came to pass, as he was praying in a certain place, that when he ceased, one of his disciples said unto him, Lord, teach us to pray, even as John also taught his disciples. [Jesus had already taught his disciples how to pray in the Sermon on the Mount. This disciple probably thought that the prayer already taught was too brief to be sufficient, especially as Jesus often prayed so long. It was customary for the rabbis to give their disciples forms of prayer, and the Baptist seems to have followed this practice, though the prayer taught by him appears soon to have been forgotten.] **2 And he said unto them, When ye pray, say, Father, Hallowed be thy name. Thy kingdom come. 3 Give us day by day our daily bread. 4 And forgive us our sins; for we ourselves also forgive every one that is indebted to us. And bring us not into temptation.** [The form given by Matthew is fuller than this. See pp. 252–254. The variation of the two prayers is an evidence of the independence of the two Gospels. In the prayer as usually publicly repeated the word "trespasses" is often used in place of the word "debts." This is a remnant of Tyndale's translation (A. D. 1526) which has been preserved and handed down in the Episcopal Liturgies. Tyndale renders Matthew as follows: "And forgive us our treaspases even as we forgive them which treaspas vs." **5 And he said unto them, Which of you shall have a friend, and shall go unto him at midnight** [a most unseasonable hour], **and say unto him, Friend, lend me three loaves; 6 for a friend of mine is come to me from a journey, and I have nothing to set before him** [In the summer Orientals often travel by night to avoid the heat of the day, and the customs of the land then made hospitality so obligatory that the greatest inconvenience and deepest poverty did not excuse one from practicing it. The occasion here described would call for three loaves, that the host and the guest might each have one, and that there might be one in reserve as an evidence of liberality]; **7 and he from within shall answer and say, Trouble me not: the door is now shut, and my children are with me in bed; I cannot rise and give thee?** [The man within does not use the word "friend." His answer is blunt and discouraging. In the house of a laboring man the family all sleep in one room. The pallets, or thin mattresses, are spread upon the divan, or raised platform, which passes around the room next to the wall. Where there was no divan they were spread upon the floor. For a father to rise and grope about in the dark that he might unbolt the door and find the required bread was indeed no slight trouble. He would be apt to step upon, or otherwise disturb, the sleeping children.] **8 I say unto you, Though he will not rise and give him because he is his friend, yet because of his importunity he will arise and give him as many as he needeth.** [Friendship should have prompted the man to supply his friend. It failed, however; yet the bread was given to get rid of a noisy beggar, to be rid of whom all the bread in the house would be willingly sacrificed if necessary. If a selfish man can be thus won by importunity, much more can a generous God, whose reluctance is never without reason, and whose ever-present desire is to bless. Idle repetition of prayers is forbidden; but persistence and importunity are encouraged. See Isa. xlii. 6; Gen. xviii. 23–33; Matt. xv. 27, 28.] **9 And I say unto you, Ask, and it shall be given you; seek, and ye shall find; knock, and it shall be opened unto you. 10 For every one that asketh receiveth; and he that seeketh findeth; and to him that knocketh it shall be opened. 11 And of which of you that is a father shall his son ask a loaf, and he give him a stone? or a fish, and he for a fish give him a serpent? 12 Or *if* he shall ask an egg, will he give him a scorpion? 13 If ye then, being evil, know how to give good gifts unto your children, how much more shall *your* heavenly Father give the Holy Spirit to them that ask him?** [The substance of this passage is recorded by Matthew as a portion of the Sermon on the Mount. See pp. 264, 265. Verse 12 is peculiar to Luke, and in verse 13 Matthew has "good things" where Luke has "Holy Spirit." The Holy Spirit is the best of all gifts, being as necessary to the soul as food to the body. The scorpion is an insect somewhat similar to a small lobster. It is two or three inches long, and has a sting at the end of its tail which is about as severe as that of a wasp. The old commentators tell us that the white scorpion, when rolled up, closely resembled an egg.]

LXXXVII.

SABBATH HEALING. MUSTARD SEED AND LEAVEN.

(Probably Peræa.)

^cLUKE XIII. 10–21.

^c**10 And he was teaching in one of the synagogues on the sabbath day.** [Our Lord's habit of teaching in the synagogue, which had been for some time interrupted by his retirement, had probably been revived during the mission of the seventy.] **11 And behold, a woman that had a spirit of infirmity eighteen years; and she was bowed together, and could in no wise lift herself up.** [The use of the word "spirit" in this verse indicates that the curvature of the spine which afflicted this woman was attributed to demoniacal agency.] **12 And when Jesus saw her, he called her, and said to her, Woman, thou art loosed from thine infirmity. 13 And he laid his hands upon her: and immediately she was made straight, and glorified God. 14 And the ruler of the synagogue, being moved with indignation because Jesus had healed on the sabbath, answered and said to the multitude, There are six days** [quite enough] **in which men ought to work: in them therefore come and be healed, and not on the day of the sabbath.** [There is no evidence that the woman came with any intention of being healed, nor was the ruler angry at her, but at Jesus. Too cowardly to openly rebuke Jesus, the ruler fell to reprimanding the people, and thus indirectly censuring the Lord.] **15 But the Lord answered him, and said, Ye hypocrites, doth not each one of you on the sabbath loose his ox or his ass from the stall, and lead him away to water him?** [The word "hypocrite" was among the strongest ever used by our Lord. He here applies it to the whole class

to whom the ruler belonged and for whom he was the spokesman—the class who are mentioned as "adversaries" in verse 17. Their hypocrisy appears in two ways: 1. They were disguising their hatred toward Christ under a pretended zeal for the Sabbath. 2. Their zeal for the Sabbath was at no time sincere, for they favored indulgence where their own interests were involved, but applied their Sabbath rules sharply where others were concerned. It was their tradition and not the Sabbath which Jesus had broken, and he here attempts no other justification of himself than to show that he is guiltless under a fair application of their own precedents.] **16 And ought not this woman, being a daughter of Abraham, whom Satan had bound, lo, *these* eighteen years, to have been loosed from this bond on the day of the sabbath?** [Taking their own conduct on the Sabbath day as the basis for his justification, Jesus presents three contrasts, each of which made his action better than theirs: 1. He had blessed the woman instead of an ox. 2. He had loosed from a disease instead of from a comfortable stall. 3. He had relieved a waiting of eighteen years' standing instead of one of some few hours' duration—the brief time since the watering of the morning. He mentions the woman's descent from Abraham because, according to their ideas, it made her worthy of every consideration. In attributing the infirmity to Satan he acknowledges the action of the demon as Satan's agent. Diseases were not infrequently ascribed to Satan and the demons—Acts x. 38; II. Cor. xii. 7.] **17 And as he said these things, all his adversaries were put to shame: and all the multitude rejoiced for all the glorious things that were done by him.** [The people rejoiced not only in the miracle, but in that wisdom which silenced the narrow-minded rulers. This triumph which they rejoiced in was but a slight foretaste of the victories to come, and to point out the nature of those victories the Lord spoke the two parables which follow.] **18 He said therefore, Unto what is the kingdom of God like? and whereunto shall I liken it? 19 It is like unto a grain of** mustard seed, which a man took, and cast into his own garden; and it grew, and became a tree; and the birds of the heaven lodged in the branches thereof. 20 And again he said, Whereunto shall I liken the kingdom of God? 21 It is like unto leaven, which a woman took and hid in three measures of meal, till it was all leavened. [For comment, see pp. 337, 338.]

LXXXVIII.

FEAST OF DEDICATION. THE JEWS ATTEMPT TO STONE JESUS AND HE RETIRES TO PERÆA.

(Jerusalem and beyond Jordan.)

d JOHN X. 22–42.

d 22 And it was the feast of the dedication at Jerusalem: 23 it was winter; and Jesus was walking in the temple in Solomon's porch. [The feast of dedication was one of eight days' duration and began upon the 25th Chisleu, which, according to the calculation of M. Chevannes, fell upon the nineteenth or twentieth of December, A. D. 29. The feast was kept in honor of the renovation and purification of the temple in the year B. C. 164, after it had been desecrated by the Syrians under Antiochus Epiphanes (II. Macc. i. 20–60; iv. 36–59; II. Macc. x. 1–8; Jos. Ant. xii. 7. 6, 7). As this feast was commemorative of national deliverance, the rulers considered it an opportune time to tempt Jesus to declare himself to be the Messiah, or coming Deliverer from the present Roman oppression. We are told that it was winter, that we may understand why Jesus walked under cover in Solomon's porch. This was a colonnade on the east side of the temple court, the name probably being derived from the wall against which it was built, which Josephus tells us was the work of Solomon—Jos. Ant. xx. 9. 7.] 24 The Jews therefore came round

about him [as if to detain him until he answered], **and said unto him, How long dost thou hold us in suspense? If thou art the Christ, tell us plainly.** [The previous conduct and temper of the questioners, together with the context (which includes an attempt to stone, followed by an effort to arrest), shows that this question was asked for the purpose of committing Jesus to an open declaration which might be used as an accusation against him.] **25 Jesus answered them, I told you, and ye believe not: the works that I do in my Father's name, these bear witness of me.** [Jesus was the Christ of the Old Testament, but not the Christ of Pharisaic hopes. Had he assumed to himself in their presence the *title* of Christ, it would have led them to false expectations. By his declarations and works Jesus had repeatedly published and proved to all his claims to be the true Messiah. He had, at the feast of tabernacles, set himself forth as the Good Shepherd, and on other occasions as the Son of God, etc. (John v. 19; viii. 36, 56). Had they understood or received the Old Testament ideal of the Messiah, they could not have failed to understand his claims.] **26 But ye believe not, because ye are not of my sheep.** [Failure to be Christ's sheep was not the cause, but the evidence, of their unbelief.] **27 My sheep hear my voice, and I know them, and they follow me: 28 and I give unto them eternal life; and they shall never perish, and no one shall snatch them out of my hand.** [The thought here is similar to that set forth on pp. 469, 470.] **29 My Father, who hath given *them* unto me, is greater than all; and no one is able to snatch *them* out of the Father's hand.** [This passage is taken by Calvinists as asserting the doctrine of the impossibility of apostacy. It is certainly a strong assurance that the Christian may expect to succeed in fighting the good fight. It may be taken in connection with Rom. viii. 38, 39; but both passages must be interpreted in the light of Heb. vi. 4–8. We can not be taken from God against our will; but our will, being free, we may choose to leave him. We can not be protected against ourselves in spite of ourselves. If that were so, no one could be lost.] **30 I and the Father are one.** [This assertion as to the unity of power residing in the hand brings forward the idea of the general unity which subsists between the Father and the Son. This unity Jesus asserts fully, without limitation or restriction; the unity of interest, design and essence are all included. It is the advance from an assertion of special unity to an assertion of general unity.] **31 The Jews took up stones again to stone him.** [They prepared to act on Lev. xxiv. 14–16, and a precedent as to it found at I. Kings xxi. 10; though the right to stone for blasphemy was now abrogated by the Roman dominion. The repairs and enlargements then going on in the temple no doubt supplied an abundance of missiles. The word "again" refers back to John viii. 59.] **32 Jesus answered them, Many good works have I showed you from the Father; for which of those works do ye stone me? 33 The Jews answered him, For a good work we stone thee not, but for blasphemy; and because that thou, being a man, makest thyself God.** [Jesus, conscious that he was living the divine life, endeavored to arouse the Jews to a consciousness of that life by asking them to point out what part of it offended them. It was a demand that his claim to be divine be tested and judged by his *life*. But the Jews insisted upon judging him by his *words* without in any way taking his life into account. Jesus urged that a divine claim was made good by a divine life, but they replied that a divine claim issuing from a human body was blasphemy. **34 Jesus answered them, Is it not written in your law** [Ps. lxxxii. 6. The whole Old Testament not infrequently is thus designated as the "law"], **I said, Ye are gods? 35 If he called them gods, unto whom the word of God came (and the scripture cannot be broken), 36 say ye of him, whom the Father sanctified and sent into the world, Thou blasphemest; because I said, I am *the* Son of God?** [Since the civil rulers of a land are ordained of God (Rom. xiii. 1–7; I. Sam.

xxiv. 6, 7), they were regarded as God's delegates or ministers, and as such the inspired Psalmist addresses them, calling them gods. Compare also Ex. xxii. 28. If it was not blasphemy to call those gods who so remotely represented the Deity, how much less did Christ blaspheme in taking unto himself a title to which he had a better right than they, even in the subordinate sense of being a mere messenger. The expression "word of God" is equivalent to "commission from God." Compare Luke iii. 2, where John was commissioned. The Jews regarded the Scripture as final authority. Jesus asserted this view by stating that the Scripture could not be broken; that is, could not be undone or set aside. We may regard Jesus as here ratifying their view, since he elsewhere concurred in it—see Matt. v. 19.] **37 If I do not the works of my Father, believe me not. 38 But if I do them, though ye believe not me, believe the works: that ye may know and understand that the Father is in me, and I in the Father.** [Having set aside their false judgment which was based upon his mere words, Jesus again bids them to consider his works or manner of life.] **39 They sought again to take him: and he went forth out of their hand.** [The calm reasoning of Jesus cooled their violence, and so far changed their evil designs that they now sought to arrest him that they might bring him before the Sanhedrin. The word "again" refers back to John vii. 30, 32, 44.] **40 And he went away again beyond the Jordan into the place where John was at the first baptizing; and there he abode.** [The word "again" either refers to John i. 28, or else it refers to some former escape beyond the Jordan not recorded by John, but by one of the other evangelists. The supplementary nature of John's Gospel makes this latter view somewhat plausible. **41 And many came unto him; and they said, John indeed did no sign: but all things whatsoever John spake of this man were true.** [John at first baptized "in the wilderness of Judæa," and afterwards at Bethany and Ænon. The presence of Jesus in this place recalled to the minds of the people the work of the Baptist and his testimony concerning Jesus. They had held John to be a prophet, yet when they searched for his credentials as a prophet, they found them inextricably intertwined with the claims of Jesus. John had failed to prove himself a prophet by miracles and signs—the accustomed credentials. But he had done so by his predictions which had come true, and all of these predictions related to Jesus.] **42 And many believed on him there.** [The word "there" stands in contrast to Jerusalem, which rejected Jesus.]

LXXXIX.

THE STRAIT GATE.   WARNED AGAINST HEROD.

(Paræa.)

ᶜLUKE XIII. 22–35.

ᶜ**22 And he went on his way through cities and villages, teaching, and journeying on unto Jerusalem.** [This verse probably refers back to verse 10, and indicates that Jesus resumed his journey after the brief rest on the Sabbath day when he healed the woman with the curvature of the spine.] **23 And one said unto him, Lord, are they few that are saved?** [It is likely that this question was asked by a Jew, and that the two parables illustrating the smallness of the kingdom's beginning suggested it to him. The Jews extended their exclusive spirit even to their ideals of a world to come, so that they believed none but the chosen race would behold its glories. The circumstances attending the conversion of Cornelius, recorded in the Book of Acts, show how this exclusiveness survived even among Jewish Christians. The questioner wished Jesus to commit himself to this narrow Jewish spirit, or else to take a position which would subject him to the charge of being unpatriotic.] **And he said unto them, 24 Strive** [literally, agonize] **to enter in by the narrow door: for many, I say unto**

you, shall seek to enter in, and shall not be able. [Jesus answers that *many* shall be excluded from the kingdom, and that the questioner, and all others who hear, need to exercise themselves and give the matter their own personal attention lest they be among that many. The passage should be compared with that in Matthew, p. 266. There one enters by a narrow gate upon a narrow road, indicating the strictness of the Christian life. Here one enters by a narrow door upon a season of festivity, indicating the joyous privileges of a Christian life.] **25 When once the master of the house is risen up, and hath shut to the door, and ye begin to stand without, and to knock at the door, saying, Lord, open to us; and he shall answer and say to you, I know you not whence ye are** [This verse gives the reason why one should strive to enter in. The *time* for entrance is limited, and he must get in before it expires; for when the limited time has passed he can not enter, no matter how earnestly he may seek or strive. Our Lord pictures a householder who refuses to receive any guest that has shown contempt for his feast by coming late. This strict spirit of the Lord in giving his invitation is indicated by the phrase "narrow door," but the phrase includes more than this, for those who would strive must not only be prompt to act, but must be painstaking so as to act intelligently, and of obedient spirit so as to act acceptably]; **26 then shall ye begin to say** [in answer to the Lord's statement that he does not know them], **We did eat and drink in thy presence, and thou didst teach in our streets** [Thus they idly urged their privileges to him who was condemning them for having neglected to make a proper use of those privileges. Had these privileges been valued and improved, the clamoring outcasts would have been inside and not outside the door]; **27 and he shall say, I tell you, I know not whence ye are; depart from me, all ye workers of iniquity.** [Thus pleading avails not. The door would not be narrow if it opened to excuses.] **28 There shall be the weeping and the gnashing of teeth, when ye shall see Abraham, and**

**Isaac, and Jacob, and all the prophets, in the kingdom
of God, and yourselves cast forth without.** [See pp.
273 and 274.] **29 And they shall come from the east
and west, and from the north and south, and shall sit
down in the kingdom of God.** [See p. 273.] **30 And
behold** [little as you may think it], **there are last who
shall be first, and there are first who shall be last.**
[A familiar proverb of Christ's (Matt. xix. 30; xx. 16), to be
interpreted by such passages as Matt. xxi. 31 and Rom. ix.
30, 31. The Jew who thought the Gentile had no hope at
all, and that he himself was sure of salvation, would be surprised to find that his opinion was the very reverse of the real
fact as time developed it.] **31 In that very hour there
came certain Pharisees, saying to him, Get thee out,
and go hence: for Herod would fain kill thee.** [This
shows that Jesus was in the territory of Herod Antipas, and
hence probably in Peræa. The Pharisees, no doubt, wished
to scare Jesus, that they might exult over his fright. We
might suppose, too, that their words were untrue, were it not
that Jesus sends a reply to Herod. Herod long desired to see
Jesus (Luke ix. 9; xxiii. 8), but it is not likely that he desired to put him to death. He was, doubtless, glad enough
to get Jesus out of his territory, lest he might foment an uprising, and to this end he employed this strategy of sending
messengers to warn Jesus under the guise of friendship.] **32
And he said unto them, Go and say to that fox** [*i. e.*,
say to that crafty, sly fellow. The fox is a type of craftiness
and treachery. We have no other instance where Jesus used
such a contemptuous expression; but Herod richly merited
it. An Idumæan by his father, a Samaritan by his mother,
a Jew by profession, and a heathen by practice, he had need
to be foxy by nature. And he was even now playing the
fox in sending these messengers], **Behold, I cast out demons and perform cures to-day and to-morrow, and
the third** *day* **I am perfected. 33 Nevertheless** [al-
though I know what lies before me] **I must go on my
way to-day and to-morrow and the** *day* **following: for**

it cannot be that a prophet perish out of Jerusalem.
[Wieseler, Meyer, Alford and other able commentators think
that the days mentioned in this difficult passage are literal
days. If the language is to be thus construed, the saying
amounts to a promise to leave Herod's territory in three days.
Such construction, however, is not consistent with the elevation of the sentiment and the solemnity of its repetition.
Three days are thus sometimes used proverbially to designate
a short time (Hos. vi. 2), and they are unquestionably so used
here. The meaning then is this: "For a little while I lib-
erate and heal and abide in your territory to disturb your
peace. But in a few days I shall be perfected in my office
as a liberator and healer, after which I shall be seen no more
in your territory. And though I understand these plots against
me, I must fill up my time and go on my course till I suffer
martyrdom at Jerusalem, which has the gruesome honor of
being the prophet-slaying city." The word "perfected" in
this passage finds its complement in the "It is finished" of
John xix. 30. Both the verbs are derived from the Greek
word *telos*, which means end or completion. Ccmpare also
II. Cor. xii. 9; Phil. iii. 12; Heb. ii. 10; v. 8, 9; xi. 40.
John the Baptist having perished at Machærus in Peræa is
regarded as an exception to this rule that prophets die at
Jerusalem. The exception does not disprove the rule, if it
be a true exception; which may be questioned, since John
died at the hands of Herod and Herodias, neither of whom
were, properly speaking, Jews. John, therefore, died as a
prophet to foreigners rather than as a prophet to the Jewish
people.] **34 O Jerusalem, Jerusalem, that killeth the
prophets, and stoneth them that are sent unto her!
how often would I have gathered thy children** [inhab-
itants] **together, even as a hen *gathereth* her own brood
under her wings, and ye would not!** [Jesus repeated
these words again as recorded at Matt. xxiii. 37-39. With
such beautiful imagery does Jesus set forth his tender love
for the people of that city which he knew would soon compass
his death.] **35 Behold, your house** [temple] **is left unto**

you *desolate* [he was about to withdraw from the temple,
which for centuries to come was to be visited by no heavenly
messenger whatever] : **and I say unto you, Ye shall not
see me, until ye shall say, Blessed *is* he that cometh
in the name of the Lord.** [It is hardly possible that these
words can refer to the triumphal entry for their fulfillment
(Matt. xxi. 9). The use of them on that occasion may have
had no reference to his prediction. They undoubtedly refer
to the Parousia, or second coming of the Lord in his glory, before which time the Jews must turn and believe (Rom. xi. 25–
27). Not until they were thus prepared would they again see
him whom they were now rejecting.]

XC.

DINING WITH A PHARISEE. SABBATH HEALING
AND THREE LESSONS SUGGESTED BY
THE EVENT.

(Probably Paræa.)

c LUKE XIV. 1–24.

c **1 And it came to pass, when he went into the
house of one of the rulers of the Pharisees on a sabbath to eat bread, that they were watching him.** [The
Pharisees were an unorganized party, hence their rulers were
such not by *office*, but by influence. Those who were members of the Sanhedrin, or who were distinguished among the
rabbis, might fitly be spoken of as rulers among them. The
context favors the idea that Jesus was invited for the purpose
of being watched—a carrying out of the Pharisaic purpose
declared at Luke xi. 53, 54. Bountiful feasts on the Sabbath day were common among the Jews; the food, however,
was cooked the previous day in obedience to the precept at
Ex. xvi. 23.] **2 And behold, there was before him a
certain man that had the dropsy.** [The phrase " let him
go " of verse 4 shows that the man was not a guest, but

rather one who seems to have taken advantage of the freedom of an Oriental house to stand among the lookers-on.
He may have been there purely from his own choice, but the
evil intention with which Jesus was invited makes it highly
probable that the man's presence was no accident, but part of
a deep-laid plot to entrap Jesus.] **3 And Jesus answering**
[replying to their unspoken thoughts, in which they were
assuming that he would heal the sick man] **spake unto the
lawyers and Pharisees, saying, Is it lawful to heal
on the sabbath, or not? 4 But they held their peace.**
[They evidently expected Jesus to act on the impulse, and
were confused by his calm, deliberate question. If they declared it lawful, they defeated their plot, and if they said
otherwise, they involved themselves in an argument with him
in which, as experience taught them, they would be humiliated before the people. Hence they kept silence, but their
silence only justified him, since it was the duty of every lawyer to pronounce this act unlawful if it had been so.] **And
he took him, and healed him, and let him go. 5 And
he said unto them, Which of you shall have an ass
or an ox fallen into a well, and will not straightway
draw him up on a sabbath day? 6 And they could
not answer again unto these things.** [Here Jesus
again asserts that the Sabbath law did not forbid acts
of mercy. See pp. 212, 213, 215. Though silenced, the
Pharisees relented not, either as to their bigotry or their
hatred.] **7 And he spake a parable unto those that
were bidden, when he marked how they chose out
the chief seats** [The *triclinia*, or Grecian table, then in
use had three sections which were placed together so as to
form a flat-bottomed letter U. The space enclosed by the
table was not occupied. It was left vacant that the servants
might enter it and attend to the wants of the guests who
reclined around the outer margin of the table. The central
seat of each of these three sections was deemed a place of
honor. This struggle for precedence was a small ambition,
but many of the ambitions of our day are equally small];

saying unto them, 8 When thou art bidden of any
man to a marriage feast [Jesus mentions another kind of
feast than the one in progress, that he may not be needlessly
personal], sit not down in the chief seat; lest haply a
more honorable man [Phil. ii. 3] than thou be bidden
of him, 9 and he that bade thee and him shall come
and say to thee, Give this man place; and then thou
shalt begin with shame to take the lowest place. [Be-
cause when ousted from the top he would find every place
full except the bottom.] 10 But when thou art bidden,
go and sit down in the lowest place; that when he
that hath bidden thee cometh, he may say to thee,
Friend, go up higher: then shalt thou have glory in
the presence of all that sit at meat with thee. [The
words here used by our Lord teach how to avoid earthly
shame and to obtain worldly honor. But they form a parable which is intended to teach the great spiritual truth that
true humility leads to exaltation.] 11 For every one that
exalteth himself shall be humbled; and he that humbleth himself shall be exalted. [This is one of our Lord's
favorite maxims (Luke xviii. 14; Matt. xxiii. 12). Both man
and God look upon humiliation as the just punishment of
pride; but it is a pleasure to every right-minded spirit to give
joy to the humble by showing him respect and honor.] 12
And he said to him also that had bidden him, When
thou makest a dinner or a supper, call not thy friends,
nor thy brethren, nor thy kinsmen, nor rich neighbors; lest haply they also bid thee again, and a recompense be made thee. 13 But when thou makest a
feast, bid the poor, the maimed, the lame, the blind:
14 and thou shalt be blessed; because they have not
wherewith to recompense thee: for thou shalt be rec-
ompensed in the resurrection of the just. [According
to the Oriental mode of speech Jesus here emphatically commands one course of action by prohibiting a contrary course.
But his prohibition is not to be construed strictly. He does
not forbid the exercise of social hospitality, but disconte-

nances that interested form of it which seeks a return. His teaching is positive rather than negative, and should constrain us to live more for charity and less for sociability. Some think that the fourteenth verse teaches that there shall be two resurrections, but the contrast is not between two *times*, but rather between two *parties* or divisions of one resurrection. If one has part in the resurrection of the just he may expect recompense for his most trivial act. But if he be resurrected among the unjust he need expect no reward, even for the most meritorious deeds of his whole life. **15 And when one of them that sat at meat with him heard these things, he said unto him, Blessed is he that shall eat bread in the kingdom of God.** [The language of Christ implied that God himself would feast those who feasted the poor, and this implication accorded with the Jewish notion that the kingdom of God would be ushered in with a great festival. Inspired by this thought, and feeling confident that he should have part in the festivities, this guest exclaimed upon the anticipated blessedness.] **16 But he said unto him, A certain man made a great supper; and he bade many: 17 and he sent forth his servant at supper time to say to them that were bidden, Come; for *all* things are now ready.** [The custom of sending a second invitation at the supper hour is a very old one (Esth. v. 8; vi. 14), and is still observed.] **18 And they all with one *consent* began to make excuse. The first said unto him, I have bought a field, and I must needs go out and see it; I pray thee have me excused. 19 And another said, I have bought five yoke of oxen, and I go to prove them; I pray thee have me excused. 20 And another said, I have married a wife, and therefore I cannot come.]** These three excuses show: 1. That the guests had made their engagements, either for business or pleasure, without the least regard for the hour of the banquet; 2. That they set little value upon either the friendship or the feast of the one who had invited them. Moreover, the excuses progress in disrespect, for the first excuse is on the ground of necessity, the second simply offers a reason, and the third is almost impudent in its bluntness. Viewing the excuses spiritually, we note that each one contains an element of *newness*—new field, new oxen, new wife. Thus the things of earth seem new and sweet in comparison with the gospel invitation. Again, all the excuses are trifling, for the parable is intended to teach that men forego their rights to heaven for trifles. Again, the "sacred hate" of Luke xiv. 25, 26 would have eliminated all these excuses. Possibly Paul had this parable in mind when he wrote I. Cor. vii. 29–33. The three excuses warn us not to be hindered by 1. The love of possessions; 2. The affairs of business; 3. Our social ties.] **21 And the servant came, and told his lord these things. Then the master of the house being angry said to his servant, Go out quickly into the streets and lanes of the city, and bring in hither the poor and maimed and blind and lame. 22 And the servant said, Lord, what thou didst command is done, and yet there is room. 23 And the lord said to the servant, Go out into the highways and hedges, and constrain *them* to come in, that my house may be filled. 24 For I say unto you, that none of those men that were bidden shall taste of my supper.** [We have here a preliminary or general invitation followed by three special invitations. We may regard the general invitation as given by Moses and the prophets in the ages before the feast was prepared. Then the first special one would be given by John the Baptist and Christ to the Jewish nation in the first stages of Christ's ministry. The second special invitation was given by Christ, the twelve and the seventy, and came more especially to the poor and outcast, the publicans and sinners, because the leading men of the nation spurned the invitation. The third invitation was begun by the apostles after the Lord's ascension and is still borne forward by those who have come after them and includes all nations. The three conditions of Jew, outcast and Gentile are indicated by the three orders of guests, 1. The honorable citizens of the city; 2. Those who frequent the streets and lanes, but are still in and of the city; 3. Those who live without the city and are found upon the highways and in the hedgepaths of the vineyards and gardens. The second and third classes are depicted as needing to be constrained. This would be so, because they would hold themselves unworthy of the invitation. But they were to be constrained by moral and not by physical means (Matt. xiv. 22; II. Cor. xii. 11; Gal. ii. 14). Physical constraint would have been contrary to all custom, as well as impossible to one servant. Incidentally the parable shows the roominess of heaven and the largeness of divine hospitality, so that Bengel aptly observes, "Grace, no less than nature, abhors a vacuum."]

XCI.

COST OF DISCIPLESHIP MUST BE COUNTED.

(Probably Peræa.)

ᶜLUKE XIV. 25-35.

ᶜ**25 Now there went with him great multitudes** [he had hitherto spent but little time in Peræa, and the people were availing themselves of this opportunity to see and hear him]: **and he turned, and said unto them, 26 If any man cometh unto me, and hateth not his own father, and mother, and wife, and children, and brethren, and sisters, yea, and his own life also, he cannot be my disciple.** ["Hateth," as used here, is an example of phenomenal speech, or speaking from appearances. In the cases supposed the person would *appear* to hate those whom he abandoned for Christ. It is like repent, anger, etc., when spoken of God. To construe the passage literally as enjoining hatred would be contrary to the fifth commandment as re-enacted at Eph. vi. 1-3 and Col. iii. 20; and also contrary to our Lord's own example (John ix. 25-27). Seeing the number of loose adherents which now surrounded him, Jesus made use of this striking statement that he might startle each hearer, and impress upon him the wide difference between a mere outward attendance upon him and a real, disciple-like adhesion to him. The latter requires that we be ready to sacrifice all, even our animal life, in so far as it tends to separate from Christ—Rom. xii. 11; Acts xx. 24.] **27 Whosoever doth not bear his own cross, and come after me, cannot be my disciple.** [Christ must be followed and imitated even to the extremity of suffering. This costliness of discipleship is illustrated in the two brief parables which follow.] **28 For which of you, desiring to build a tower, doth not first sit down and count the cost, whether he have *wherewith* to complete it? 29 Lest haply, when he hath laid a foundation, and is not able to finish, all that behold begin to mock him, 30 saying, This man began to build, and was not able to finish.** [Discipleship is character-building, and shame awaits him who attempts to be a Christian and fails to live up to his profession. Unless his tower rises to the heavenly heights to which it aspired, it is but a Babel at last. The parable is not intended to discourage any one from attempting to be a disciple. It is meant to warn us against attempting so great an undertaking with that frivolity of spirit and want of determination which insure failure.] **31 Or what king, as he goeth to encounter another king in war, will not sit down first and take counsel whether he is able with ten thousand to meet him that cometh against him with twenty thousand? 32 Or else, while the other is yet a great way off, he sendeth an ambassage, and asketh conditions of peace.** [Is the adversary here God or the devil? As warring against God is no part of discipleship, it might seem that the conflict was with Satan. But the case supposed is that of a man who, after counting the cost, is about to decline taking up his cross—about to rebel against the claims of God. But while in this rebellious state he sees a superior force coming against him. This superior force can not be the devil's, for Jesus could not counsel any to make peace with him, as the parable advises. The superior force, then, is God's, and the lesson is, that however fearful the task of being a disciple may be, it is not so dreadful as to fight against God. As soon as the hesitating man takes in this thought, he will immediately take up the cross which he was about to refuse.] **33 So therefore whosoever he be of you that renounceth not all that he hath, he cannot be my disciple.** [The tower can not be built by him who spends his time or squanders his money on other enterprises, nor can the peace be maintained by one who does not fully renounce his rebellion.] **34 Salt therefore is good: but if even the salt have lost its savor, wherewith shall it be seasoned? 35 It is fit neither for the land nor for the dunghill:** *men* **cast it out.** [Our Lord twice before used such language. See pp. 234, 433. Salt is here used as a symbol of perseverance. The condition of those who begin the Christian life and fail to persevere is dangerous in the extreme—Heb. vi. 4–12; x. 26–39.] **He that hath ears to hear, let him hear.** [See p. 330.]

XCII.

SECOND GREAT GROUP OF PARABLES.

(Probably in Peræa.)

Subdivision A.

INTRODUCTION.

c LUKE xv. 1, 2.

c **1 Now all the publicans and sinners were drawing near unto him to hear him. 2 And both the Pharisees and the scribes murmured, saying, This man receiveth sinners, and eateth with them.** [For publicans see p. 76, and for eating with them see p. 349. The Pharisees classed as "sinners" all who failed to observe the traditions of the elders, and especially their traditional rules of purification. It was not so much the wickedness of this class as their legal uncleanness that made it wrong to eat with them. Compare Gal. ii. 12, 13. In answer to their murmuring, Jesus spoke three parables, in which he set forth the yearnings of redemptive love. Having thus replied to the Pharisees, Jesus continued his discourse, adding two other parables concerning the right employment of worldly goods, and ending with some teaching concerning offenses, etc. We defer comparing the parables until we have discussed them.]

Subdivision B.

PARABLE OF THE LOST SHEEP.

^c LUKE XV. 3-7.

^c 3 **And he spake unto them this parable** [Jesus has spoken this parable before. See pp. 434, 435], **saying, 4 What man of you** [man is emphatic; it is made so to convey the meaning that if man would so act, how much more would God so act], **having a hundred sheep** [a large flock], **and having lost one of them, doth not leave the ninety and nine in the wilderness** [the place of pasture, and hence the proper place to leave them], **and go after that which is lost, until he find it?** [The ninety-nine represent Jewish respectability, and the lost sheep stands for a soul which has departed from that respectability.] **5 And when he hath found it, he layeth it on his shoulders, rejoicing.** [A touch suggesting the weakness of the sheep and the willing affection of the shepherd.] **6 And when he cometh home, he calleth together his friends and his neighbors, saying unto them, Rejoice with me** [Heb. xii. 2], **for I have found my sheep which was lost.** [The call implies that the loss was known to the neighbors, and that they felt concerned about it. Had the Pharisees been neighbors to the spirit of Christ they would have sympathized with him in his joy; but they were false undershepherds—Ezek. xxxiv.] **7 I say unto you, that even so there shall be joy in heaven over one sinner that repenteth,** *more* **than over ninety and nine righteous persons, who need no repentance.** [How little Jesus thought of external morality may be seen by his words at

Luke xviii. 9, but he here quoted the Pharisees at their own valuation to show that even when so doing God's love for the sinner was the paramount love.]

Subdivision C.

PARABLE OF THE LOST COIN.

ᶜ Luke xv. 8–10.

ᶜ8 Or what woman having ten pieces of silver, if she lose one piece, doth not light a lamp [because oriental houses are commonly without windows, and therefore dark], and sweep the house, and seek diligently until she find it? 9 And when she hath found it, she calleth together her friends and neighbors, saying, Rejoice with me, for I have found the piece which I had lost. [The *drachma*, or piece of silver, corresponded to the Latin *denarius*, and was worth about seventeen cents. The woman, having only ten of them, was evidently poor. Such small coin have been for centuries worn by oriental women as a sort of ornamental fringe around the forehead. The phrase "till she find it," which is practically repeated in both parables, is a sweet source of hope; but it is not to be pressed so as to contradict other Scripture. 10 Even so, I say unto you, there is joy [Ezek. xxxiii. 11] in the presence of the angels of God over one sinner that repenteth. [By thus reaffirming the heavenly joy, Jesus sought to shame the Pharisees out of their cold-blooded murmuring.]

Subdivision D.

PARABLE OF THE LOST SON.

ᶜ Luke xv. 11–32.

ᶜ11 And he said, A certain man had two sons [These two sons represent the professedly religious (the elder) and the openly irreligious (the younger). They have special reference to the two parties found in the first two verses of this chapter—the Pharisees, the publicans and sinners]:

12 and the younger of them [the more childish and easily deceived] **said to his father, Father, give me the portion of** *thy* **substance that falleth to me.** [Since the elder brother received a double portion, the younger brother's part would be only one-third of the property—Deut. xxi. 17.] **And he divided unto them his living.** [Abraham so divided his estate in his lifetime (Gen. xxv. 1–6); but the custom does not appear to have been general among the Jews. God, however, gives gifts and talents to us all, so the parable fits the facts of life—Ps. cxlv. 9; Matt. v. 45; Acts x. 34.] **13 And not many days after** [with all haste], **the younger son gathered all together and took his journey into a far country** [He yearned for the spurious liberty of a land where he would be wholly independent of his father. Thus the sinful soul seeks to escape from the authority of God]; **and there he wasted his substance with riotous living.** [Sin now indulges itself with unbridled license, and the parable depicts the sinner's course: his season of indulgence (vs. 12, 13); his misery (vs. 14–16); his repentance (vs. 17–20); his forgiveness (vs. 20–24). **14 And when he had spent all, there arose a mighty famine in that country; and he began to be in want.** [Sooner or later sinful practices fail to satisfy, and the sense of famine and want mark the crises in our lives as they did in the life of the prodigal. The direst famine is that of the word of God—Amos viii. 11–13; Jer. ii. 13.] **15 And he went and joined** [literally, glued] **himself to one of the citizens of that country; and he sent him into his fields to feed** [literally, to pasture or tend] **swine.** [This was, to the Jew, the bottom of degradation's pit. They so abhorred swine that they refused to name them. They spoke of a pig as *dabhar acheer; i. e.,* "the other thing." **16 And he would fain have filled his belly with the husks that the swine did eat: and no man gave unto him.** [The master upon whom he had forced himself did not deem his services worthy of enough food to sustain life; so that he would gladly have eaten the husks or pods of the carob bean, which are very similar to our

honey-locust pods, if they would have satisfied his hunger.]
17 But when he came to himself [his previous state had
been one of delusion and semi-madness (Eccl. ix. 3); in it
his chief desire had been to get away from home, but returning reason begets a longing to return thither] **he said, How
many hired servants of my father's have bread enough
and to spare, and I perish here with hunger! 18 I
will arise and go to my father, and will say unto him,
Father, I have sinned against heaven, and in thy sight:
19 I am no more worthy to be called thy son: make
me as one of thy hired servants.** [The humility of his
confession indicates that the term "riotous living" means
more than merely a reckless expenditure of money. But vile
as he was he trusted that his father's love was sufficient to
do something for him.] **20 And he arose, and came to
his father.** [Repentance is here pictured as a journey. It
is more than a mere emotion or impulse.] **But while he
was yet afar off, his father saw him** [being evidently
on the lookout for him], **and was moved with compassion** [seeing his ragged, pitiable condition], **and ran, and
fell on his neck, and kissed him.** [Giving him as warm
a welcome as if he had been a model son.] **21 And the
son said unto him, Father, I have sinned against
heaven, and in thy sight: I am no more worthy to
be called thy son.** [The son shows a manly spirit in ad-
hering to his purpose to make a confession, notwithstanding
the warmth of the father's welcome; in grieving for what he
had done, and not for what he had lost; and in blaming no
one but himself.] **22 But the father said to his servants** [interrupting the son in his confession], **Bring forth
quickly the best robe, and put it on him; and put a
ring on his hand, and shoes on his feet** [none but
servants went barefooted]: **23 and bring the fatted calf**
[which, according to Eastern custom, was held in readiness
for some great occasion (Gen. xviii. 7; I. Sam. xvi. 28;
xxviii. 24; II. Sam. vi. 13), and which custom still exists],
and **kill it, and let us eat, and make merry** [the robe,

ring, etc., are merely part of the parabolic drapery, and are so many sweet assurances of full restoration and forgiveness, and are not to be pressed beyond this]: **24 for this my son was dead, and is alive again; he was lost, and is found.** [The condition of the impenitent sinner is frequently expressed in the Bible under the metaphor of death —Rom. vi. 13; Eph. ii. 1; v. 14; Rev. iii. 1.] **And they began to be merry.** [Having thus finished his account of the openly irreligious, Jesus now turns to portray that of the professedly religious; *i. e.*, he turns from the publican to the Pharisee. He paints both parties as alike children of God, as both faulty and sinful in his sight, and each as being loved despite his faultiness. But while the story of the elder son had a present and local application to the Pharisees, it is to be taken comprehensively as describing all the self-righteous who murmur at and refuse to take part in the conversion of sinners.] **25 Now his elder son was in the field** [at work]: **and as he came and drew nigh to the house, he heard music and dancing.** [He heard evidences of joy, a joy answering to that mentioned at verses 7 and 10; the joy of angels in seeing the publicans and sinners repenting and being received by Jesus—the joy at which the Pharisees had murmured.] **26 And he called to him one of the servants, and inquired what these things might be. 27 And he said unto him, Thy brother is come; and thy father hath killed the fatted calf, because he hath received him safe and sound. 28 But he was angry, and would not go in** [he refused to be a party to such a proceeding]: **and his father came out, and entreated him.** [In the entreating father Jesus pictures the desire and effort of God then and long afterwards put forth to win the proud, exclusive, self-righteous spirits which filled the Pharisees and other Jews—Luke xiii. 34; Acts xiii. 44–46; xxviii. 22–28.] **29 But he answered and said to his father, Lo, these many years do I serve thee** [literally, I am thy slave], **and I never transgressed a commandment of thine** [He speaks with the true Pharisaic spirit

(Luke xviii. 11, 12; Rom. iii. 9). His justification was as proud as the prodigal's confession was humble]; **and *yet* thou never gavest me a kid** [much less a calf], **that I might make merry with my friends** [he reckons as a slave, so much pay for so much work, and his complaint suggests that he might have been as self-indulgent as his brother had he not been restrained by prudence]: **30 but when this thy son** [he thus openly disclaims him as a brother] **came, who hath devoured thy living with harlots** [and not decent friends such as mine], **thou killedst for him the fatted calf. 31 And he said unto him, Son, thou art ever with me** [a privilege which the elder brother had counted as naught, or rather as slavery], **and all that is mine is thine.** [See Rom. ix. 4, 5. The younger brother had the shoes, etc., but the elder still had the inheritanc. **32 But it was meet to make merry and be glad** [Acts xi. 18]: **for this thy brother was dead, and is alive *again*; a:.d *was* lost, and is found.** [Here the story ends. We a.e not told how the elder brother acted, but we may read hi. history in that of the Jews who refused to rejoice with Jesus in the salvation of sinners. At the next Passover they carried their resentment against him to the point of murder, and some forty years later the inheritance was taken from them. Thus we see that the elder brother was not pacified by the father. He continued to rebel against the father's will till he himself became the lost son. A comparison of the three preceding parables brings out many suggestive points, thus: The first parable illustrates Christ's compassion. A sentient, suffering creature is lost, and it was bad for *it* that it should be so. Hence it must be sought, though its value is only one out of a hundred. Man's lost condition makes him wretched. The second parable shows us how God values a soul. A lifeless piece of metal is lost, and while it could not be pitied, it could be valued, and since its value was one out of ten, it was bad for the *owner* that it should be lost. God looks upon man's loss as his impoverishment. The first two parables depict the efforts of Christ in the salvation of man, or that side of conversion more apparent, so to speak, to God; while the third sets forth the responsive efforts put forth by man to avail himself of God's salvation—the side of conversion more apparent to us. Moreover, as the parabolic figures become more nearly literal, as we pass from sheep and coin to son, the values also rise, and instead of one from a hundred, or one from ten, we have one out of two!]

Subdivision E.

PARABLE OF THE UNRIGHTEOUS STEWARD.

^cLUKE XVI. 1–18.

^c1 **And he said also unto the disciples** [If we remember that many publicans were now taking their stand among Jesus' disciples, we will more readily understand why Jesus addressed to them a parable about an unjust man. They would be more readily affected by such a story], **There was a certain rich man, who had a steward; and the same was accused unto him that he was wasting his goods.** ["Wasting" of this verse and "wasted" of Luke xv. 13 are parts of the same verb. The attitude of the two brethren to their father's estate, as set forth in the previous parable, introduced thoughts as to the proper relation which a man bears to his possessions, and these relations Jesus discusses in this parable. While no parable has been so diversely explained, yet the trend of interpretation has been in the main satisfactory. In verse 8 the Lord himself gives the key to the parable, which is that the children of light, in the conduct of their affairs, should emulate the wisdom and prudence of the children of the world in the conduct of their affairs. The difficulty of the parable is more apparent than real. The whole parabolic machinery is borrowed from worldly and irreligious life, where dishonest cunning and rascality are freely tolerated. The child of light is to be equally shrewd and wise in the management of his affairs; *using, however, only those means and methods which are permissible in his sphere of action.* God's word, of course, nowhere teaches the absurdity

that sinful methods are permitted to him whom it calls to lead a sinless life. While the steward's conduct teaches valuable lessons, the steward himself is condemned as an "unrighteous" man in verse 8.] **2 And he called him, and said unto him, What is this that I hear of thee?** [an indignant expression of surprise arising from abused confidence] **render the account of thy stewardship; for thou canst be no longer steward.** [Ordinarily the stewards were slaves; but this was evidently a free man, for he was neither punished nor sold, but discharged.] **3 And the steward said within himself, What shall I do, seeing that my lord taketh away the stewardship from me? I have not strength to dig** [Being too weak in body because of my luxurious living. Digging refers generally to agricultural labor]; **to beg I am ashamed.** [Being too strong in pride because of my exalted manner of life.] **4 I am resolved what to do** [a way of escape comes to him in a sudden flash of discovery], **that, when I am put out of the stewardship, they** [my lord's debtors] **may receive me into their houses. 5 And calling to him each one of his lord's debtors, he said to the first, How much owest thou unto my lord? 6 And he said, A hundred measures of oil.** [The measure mentioned here is the Hebrew *bath*, which corresponded roughly to a firkin or nine gallons.] **And he said unto him, Take thy bond** [literally, writings], **and sit down quickly and write fifty.** [The amount remitted here—450 gallons of olive oil—represented a large sum of money. Such a reduction would put the debtor under great obligation to the steward.] **7 Then said he to another, And how much owest thou? And he said, A hundred measures of wheat.** [The measure here is the Hebrew *cor*, which contains ten baths, or ephahs, or, more exactly, eighty-six and seven-tenths gallons.] **He saith unto him, Take thy bond, and write fourscore.** [The amount remitted was about 267 bushels, and the debtor himself altered the writing, that he might be in no uncertainty about it. Scholars disagree as to whether these debtors were tenants or traders; *i. e.*, purchasers of produce who had given their bonds or notes for the same. Meyer, Trench, Godet and others favor this latter view, but the language used and the customs of the land rather indicate that the former is correct. In the East rents are in proportion to the crop, and hence they vary as it varies. It was natural, therefore, that the steward should ask the amount of the rent; and also natural, since rents were thus payable in kind, that the tenant should answer as to the very thing owed. A trader would have been held, not for the *purchase*, but for the *price*, and would rather have specified the money due than the quantity or thing bought. Since the price of produce varies, it has been the immemorial custom everywhere to fix the amount to be paid for it at the very time it is purchased, and this amount becomes the debt.] **8 And his lord commended the unrighteous steward because he had done wisely** [shrewdly]: **for the sons of this world are for their own generation** [their own clan or class] **wiser than the sons of the light.** [That is to say, the steward, a worldly-minded rascal, knew better how to deal with a worldly-minded master above him and dishonest tenants beneath him, than a son of light knows how to deal with the God over him and his needy brethren about him. The verse contrasts the sons of two households; the children of the worldly household exercise more forethought and prudence in gaining among their brethren friends for the day of need, and in expending money to that end, than do the children of the light. The "devil's martyrs," in their skillful prudence, often shame the saints. If the latter showed a wisdom in their affairs analogous to that which the unjust steward employed in his affairs, God would commend them as the lord commended the steward.] **9 And I say unto you, Make to yourselves friends by means of the mammon of unrighteousness** [see p. 257]; **that, when it shall fail, they may receive you into the eternal tabernacles.** [Worldly possessions are the Christian's stewardship. If he has been wasting them in self-indulgence, he must take warning from the parable and so employ them in deeds of usefulness and mercy that, when the stewardship is taken from him, he may have obtained for himself a refuge for the future. But how can those whom the Christian has befriended receive him into heaven? The key to the difficulty is found at Matt. xxv. 35–40, where our Lord altogether identifies himself with his poor and unfortunate disciples, and returns on their behalf a heavenly recompense for any kindness which has been shown them on the earth. Only in this secondary and subordinate sense can those whom the Christian has benefited receive him into heaven. Nor does the passage teach that there is any *merit* in almsgiving, since the thing given is already the property of another (verse 12). Almsgiving is only a phase of the fidelity required of a steward, and the reward of a steward is not of merit but of grace—Luke xvii. 7–10; Matt. xxv. 21.] **10 He that is faithful in a very little is faithful also in much: and he that is unrighteous in a very little is unrighteous also in much.** [God does not judge by the magnitude of the act, but by the spiritual principles and motives which lie back of the act. A small action may discover and lay bare these principles quite as well as a large one. In the administration of the small properties entrusted to us on the earth we reveal our disposition and temper as stewards quite as well as if we owned half the universe.] **11 If therefore ye have not been faithful in the unrighteous mammon, who will commit to your trust the true** *riches?* [The word "unrighteous" is here used to mean deceitful, as opposed to true. Worldly riches deceive us by being temporal and transitory, while the true riches are eternal—II. Cor. iv. 18.] **12 And if ye have not been faithful in that which is another's, who will give you that which is your own?** [We are all God's stewards, and the perishing possessions of earth are not our own (I. Chron. xxix. 14), but that which is given us *forever* is *our own*—I. Cor. iii. 22.] **13 No servant can serve two masters** [Gal. i. 10; Jas. iv. 4]: **for either he will hate the one, and love the other; or else he will hold to one, and despise the other. Ye cannot serve God and** mammon. [See p. 257.] **14 And the Pharisees, who were lovers of money, heard all these things; and they scoffed at him.** [They derided him with open insolence (Luke xxiii. 35). This was a new phase of their opposition, and showed that they no longer feared Jesus as formerly, being assured that he aimed at no earthly dominion. Because of his poverty they may have regarded him as prejudiced against wealth. At any rate, they regarded themselves as living contradictions of this to them ridiculous statement that a man could not be rich and yet religious.] **15 And he said unto them, Ye are they that justify yourselves in the sight of men; but God knoweth your hearts: for that which is exalted among men is an abomination in the sight of God.** [The Pharisees lived in such outward contrast to the publicans and made such pretensions and claims that men esteemed them righteous, but they were none the less abominable in God's sight. God approves righteousness when *inward*, but despises the mere outward show of it.] **16 The law and the prophets *were* until John: from that time the gospel of the kingdom of God is preached, and every man entereth violently into it.** [See p. 283.] **17 But it is easier for heaven and earth to pass away, than for one tittle of the law to fall.** [See page 236. The law and the prophets had been used of God to set up the old dispensation, and it had been so perverted and abused that in it the Pharisees could pass for righteous men, though abominable according to its true standard. Since the days of John the old dispensation has been merging into the new, and this also has been subjected to violence. But despite all the changes made, approved and justified by men, the God-given law had never changed. Its smallest letter could no more be eliminated than the universe could be obliterated. But of course the Lawgiver could with notice modify his law.] **18 Every one that putteth away his wife, and marrieth another, committeth adultery: and he that marrieth one that is put away from a husband committeth adultery.** [See page 242. This precept is inserted here as an illustration of a flagrant violation of the law of God both countenanced and practiced by these Pharisees.]

Subdivision F.

PARABLE OF THE RICH MAN AND LAZARUS.

ᶜ LUKE XVI. 19-31.

[The parable which we are about to study is a direct advance upon the thoughts in the previous section. We may say generally that if the parable of the unjust steward teaches how riches are to be used, this parable sets forth the terrible consequences of a failure to so use them. Each point of the previous discourse is covered in detail, as will be shown by references in the discussion of the parable.] ᶜ **19 Now there was a certain rich man, and he was clothed in purple and fine linen, faring sumptuously every day** [For convenience' sake this rich man has been commonly called Dives, which is simply the Latin for *rich man*, and is therefore not truly a name, for it is not fitting to name him whom the Lord left nameless. Along the coast of Tyre there was found a rare shell-fish (*Murex purpurarius*) from which a costly purple dye was obtained, each little animal yielding about one drop of it. Woolen garments dyed with it were worn by kings and nobles, and idol images were sometimes arrayed in them. This purple robe formed the outer, and the linen the inner garment. The *byssus*, or fine linen of Egypt, was produced from flax which grew on the banks of the Nile. It was dazzlingly white, and worth twice its weight in gold (Gen. xli. 42; Ex. xxvi. 31-33; xxviii. 5; I. Chron. xv. 27; Ezek. xxvii. 7). The mention of these garments and a continual banqueting indicates a life of extreme luxury] **: 20 and a certain beggar** [literally, one who crouches. It is used thirty-four times in the New Testament, and is everywhere translated "poor" save here and at Gal. iv. 9. In the last stages of life Lazarus had become an object of charity, but there is nothing to indicate that he had been an habitual beggar] **named Lazarus** [This is the only name which occurs in our Lord's parables. It is derived from Eleazar, which means, God a help. The name is symbolic of destitution, and many words indicative of beggary are derived from it] **was laid at his gate** [in the East the gates of the rich are still the resorts of the poor], **full of sores, 21 and desiring to be fed with the *crumbs* that fell from the rich man's table; yea, even the dogs came and licked his sores.** [The contrast here is sharp. Lazarus is naked and clothed with sores instead of royal apparel, and desires crumbs instead of a banquet. That he limited his desire to crumbs suggests a freedom from both worldly lust and envy. Whether he got the crumbs is not stated. His sufferings may have been as unmitigated on earth as those of the rich man were in Hades (verse 24), and it is certain that even if he received the crumbs they did not count as a gift, being mere refuse, utterly worthless in the sight of the rich man. The very point of the parable is that the rich man *gave* him nothing. The dogs also suggest a contrast. The rich man is surrounded by loyal brethren and attentive servants, while Lazarus is the companion of dogs, the scavengers of the streets, who treat him with a rude compassion as one of their number, soothing his sores with their saliva.] **22 And it came to pass, that the beggar died, and that he was carried away by the angels into Abraham's bosom** [it is the office of angels to minister to the heirs of salvation—Matt. xxiv. 31; Mark xiii. 27; Heb. i. 14]: **and the rich man also died, and was buried.** [In death as well as in life the two men stand in contrast. The rich man passes from view with the pomp and pageantry of a burial (II. Chron. xvi. 13, 14), an earthly honor suited to a worldly life. But Lazarus passes hence with the angels, a spiritual triumph suited to one accepted of God.] **23 And in Hades he lifted up his eyes, being in torments, and seeth** [Rev. xiv. 10] **Abraham afar off, and Lazarus in his bosom.** [Hades (Greek), or Sheol (Hebrew), was the name given to the abode of the dead between death and the resurrection. In it the souls of the wicked are in torment, and those of the righteous enjoy a paradise (Luke xxiii. 43). The joys of Paradise were conceived of as those of a feast, and the expression "Abraham's bosom " is taken from the custom of reclining on couches at feasts. As a guest leaned upon his left arm, his neighbor on his left might easily lean upon his bosom. Such a position with respect to the master of the house was one of special honor, and indicated great intimacy (John i. 18 ; xiii. 23). What higher honor or joy could the Jew conceive of than such a condition of intimacy and fellowship with Abraham, the great founder of their race ?—Matt. viii. 11.] **24 And he cried** [in earnest entreaty] **and said, Father Abraham** [the claim of kindred is not denied, but it is unavailing —Luke iii. 8], **have mercy on me, and send Lazarus, that he may dip the tip of his finger in water, and cool my tongue; for I am in anguish in this flame.** [The smallness of the favor asked indicates the greatness of the distress, as it does in verse 21, where crumbs were desired. There is a reciprocity also between the desired *crumbs* and the prayed-for *drop* which contains a covert reference to verses 4 and 5. Had the rich man given more he might now have asked for more. The friendship of Lazarus might have been easily won, and now the rich man needed that friendship, but he had neglected the principle set forth in verse 9, and had abused his stewardship by wasting his substance upon himself, Again the former condition of each party is sharply reversed. Lazarus feasts at a better banquet, and the rich man begs because of a more dire and insatiable craving. Thus the life despised of men was honored of God, and (verse 15) the man who was exalted among men is found to have been abominable unto God.] **25 But Abraham said, Son** [a tender word— Josh vii. 19], **remember** [Prov. v. 11–14] **that thou in thy lifetime receivedst thy good things, and Lazarus in like manner evil things : but now here** [where a different order pertains from that of the earth] **he is comforted, and thou art in anguish.** [The woes received by Lazarus are not spoken of as *his*. He neither earned nor deserved them (Rev. vii. 13–17). His was the stewardship of suffering (I.

Cor. iv. 9; II. Cor. iv. 17), and in its small details he had shown great faithfulness. The rich man had the stewardship of wealth, with its accompanying obligation of generosity. This obligation he had esteemed as too contemptibly small to deserve his notice; but in neglecting it he had inadvertently been unfaithful in much. See verse 10. This had been the sin of omission on the part of the rich man, and his sin of commission answered as a complement to it, for he had been guilty of that money-loving self-indulgence which was condemned by Jesus and justified by the Pharisees (verses 14, 15). No other crime is charged against the rich man, yet he is found in torment. But the rich man during his lifetime had been so deceived by his wealth that he had failed to detect his sin. Moreover, as he indicates in verse 28, a like deception was now being practiced upon his brethren. Thus the parable justifies the term "unrighteous" which Jesus had given to mammon at verses 9, 11.] **26 And besides all this, between us and you there is a great gulf fixed, that they that would pass from hence to you may not be able, and that none may cross over from thence to us.** [We have here a clear statement of the separation which parts the good from the evil in the future state. But it has been urged that the coloring and phraseology of this parable is derived from rabbinical teaching, that our Lord made use of a current but erroneous Jewish notion to teach a valuable lesson, and that therefore it is not safe to draw any inferences from the narrative relative to the future state. But it should be observed that the parables of Jesus never introduce fictitious conditions, nor do they anywhere violate the order and course of nature. It is hardly possible that he could have made this an exception to his rule, especially since it is in a field where all the wisdom of the world is insufficient to make the slightest correction. Moreover, it is certainly impossible that he could exaggerate the differences between the states of the lost and saved in the hereafter. Nor can the teaching of the parable be set aside on the ground that it represents merely the intermediate and not the final condition of things. If the intermediate condition of things is fixed and established, the final condition must, *a fortiori*, be more so. Moreover, the teaching here differs from that of the rabbis, for, according to Lightfoot, a wall and not a gulf separated between the just and the unjust, and they were not "afar off" from each other, the distance being but a handbreadth. The passage therefore confirms the doctrine that the righteous are neither homeless nor unconscious during the period between death and the resurrection (Phil. i. 23), and refutes the doctrine of Universalism, for the gulf is, 1, fixed; and, 2, it can not be passed or bridged. The gulf of pride and caste between the rich man and Lazarus while on earth was easy to cross.] **27 And he said, I pray thee therefore, father, that thou wouldest send him to my father's house** [The double attempt of Dives to use Lazarus as his servant shows how hard it was for him to adjust himself to his new condition]; **28 for I have five brethren** [there is no typical significance in the nnmber]; **that he may testify unto them, lest they also come into this place of torment.** [Deceived by his wealth, the rich man looked upon his earthly possessions as real and substantial, and, like rich sinners of to-day, had simply disregarded the affairs of the future life. Aroused by the sudden experience of the awful realities of the future state, he desires to make it as real to his brethren as it had now become to him. In endeavoring to carry out this desire he proceeds on the theory that the testimony of the dead in reference to the realities of the future state are more trustworthy and influential than the revelations of God himself, given through his inspired spokesmen. This dishonoring of God and his law was to be expected from one who had made mammon his real master, even though professing (as the context suggests) to serve God. The singleness of his service is shown in that he, though practically discharged by one master—mammon, can not even now speak respectfully of God. Some commentators make much of the so-called repentance of the rich man, manifested in this concern for his brethren; but the Lord did not count kindness shown to kindred as evidence of goodness,

516 THE FOURFOLD GOSPEL.

much less of repentance (Luke vi. 32-35, pp. 248, 249). Besides the natural feeling for his brothers, he knew that their presence in torment would add to his own. His concern for his brethren is not told to indicate repentance. It is mentioned to bring out the point that the revealed will of God of itself and without more makes it inexcusable for a man to lead a selfish life.] **29 But Abraham saith, They have Moses and the prophets** [*i. e.*, the entire Old Testament]; **let them hear them.** [John i. 45; v. 39-46; Luke xxiv. 27. The Scriptures are a sufficient guide to godliness—II. Tim. iii. 16, 17, and a failure to live rightly when possessing them is due to lack of will, and not to lack of knowledge.] **30 And he said, Nay, father Abraham: but if one go to them from the dead, they will repent.** [With the spirit of a true Pharisee he sought a sign for his brothers. See page 305. But the guidance of Scripture is better than any sign.] **31 And he said unto him, If they hear not Moses and the prophets, neither will they be persuaded, if one rise from the dead.** [These words might sound like an overstatement of the obduracy of unbelief were they not amply verified by the literal facts. Jesus had already raised at least two from the dead as witnesses to his divine power, and he was about to raise a third, who, with startling suggestiveness, would bear this very name of Lazarus. But despite all these witnesses the majority of the Jews disbelieved and continued to disbelieve in him; nay, they even went so far as to seek the death of Lazarus that they might be rid of his testimony (John xii. 10). This is also a reference to Jesus' own resurrection. It is true that he did not appear in person to those who disbelieved in him, but they had clear knowledge of his resurrection (Matt. xxviii. 11-15), and it was considered as proved to all men (Acts xvii. 31).

Subdivision G.

CONCERNING OFFENSES, FAITH AND SERVICE.

ᶜ LUKE XVII. 1–10.

ᶜ 1 **And he said unto his disciples** [Jesus here ceases to speak to the Pharisees, and begins a new series of sayings addressed to the disciples, which sayings are, however, pertinent to the occasion, and not wholly disconnected with what he has just been saying], **It is impossible** [in a world where Pharisees abound, etc.—I. Cor. xi. 19] **but that occasions of stumbling should come ; but woe unto him, through whom they come !** [See page 432.] **2 It were well for him if a millstone** [not the large millstone mentioned by Matthew and Mark, but the small one which was turned by hand] **were hanged about his neck, and he were thrown into the sea, rather than that he should cause one of these little ones** [beginners in the faith, or weaklings—Rom. xiv. 1] **to stumble.** [See page 432.] **3 Take heed to yourselves** [our dangers are not overpassed when we avoid giving offenses, for it is also required of us that we should forgive the evils which we receive]: **if thy brother sin, rebuke him ; and if he repent, forgive him.** [Righteousness has its obligation to rebuke as well as love has to forgive.] **4 And if he sin against thee seven times in the day** [a general expression indicating a great number of times], **and seven times turn again to thee, saying, I repent ; thou shalt forgive him.** [See p. 437. But the passage differs from that in Matthew in that the repentance of the sinner is required as a condition precedent to forgiveness.] **5 And the apostles said unto the Lord, Increase our faith.** [The apostles asked for faith that they might be able to fulfill the great moral requirements which Jesus has just revealed. Our Lord sanctions the wisdom of their prayer by showing the greatness of faith.] **6 And the Lord said, If ye had faith as a grain of mustard seed, ye would say unto this sycamine tree, Be thou rooted up, and be thou**

planted in the sea; and it would obey you. [See pp. 424, 426. "The only real power of the universe," says Godet, "is the divine will. The human will, which has discovered the secret of blending with this force of forces, is raised, in virtue of this union, to omnipotence." But our distance from omnipotence measures how far we are from attaining that desired union of will. The sycamine is the well-known black mulberry-tree, which belongs to the same natural order as the fig-tree, and is a tree distinguished for being deeply rooted.]
7 **But who is there of you, having a servant plowing or keeping sheep, that will say unto him, when he is come in from the field, Come straightway and sit down to meat; 8 and will not rather say unto him, Make ready wherewith I may sup, and gird thyself, and serve me, till I have eaten and drunken; and afterward thou shalt eat and drink? 9 Doth he thank the servant because he did the things that were commanded? 10 Even so ye also, when ye shall have done all the things that are commanded you, say, We are unprofitable servants; we have done that which it was our duty to do.** [In this passage, which is in the nature of a parable, Jesus teaches that duty is coextensive with ability, and explodes the doctrine that it is possible for a man to do "works of supererogation." Since in God's sight no man can even do his full duty (Ps. cxliii. 2), it is impossible that he can do *more* than his duty. We may be rewarded for the discharge of our duty, but the reward is of grace and not of merit. Compare Luke xii. 3-48. The theme is no doubt suggested by verse 6. When one's faith endows him with great gifts he need not consider himself as an unusually profitable servant for he can do no more than it is his duty to do. Godet denies this connection with verse 6, contending that miracles are not among "the things that are commanded" in the terms of verse 10; but miracles were commanded, and for those who could bestow it, a gift of healing was as much an obligation as a gift of alms (Matt. x. 8; Acts iii. 1-6). The paragraph is a fitting close to a discourse so much of which relates to Phariseeism.]

XCIII.

PERÆA TO BETHANY. RAISING OF LAZARUS.

ᵈ JOHN XI. 1-46.

ᵈ **1 Now a certain man was sick, Lazarus of Bethany, of the village of Mary and her sister Martha.** [For Bethany and the sisters, see p. 478.] **2 And it was that Mary who anointed the Lord with ointment, and wiped his feet with her hair** [John xii. 3], **whose brother Lazarus was sick.** [This anointing had not yet taken place, as John himself shows. For a similar anticipation see Matt. x. 4. There are five prominent Marys in the New Testament: those of Nazareth, Magdala and Bethany; the mother of Mark, and the wife of Clopas.] **3 The sisters therefore sent unto him, saying, Lord, behold, he whom thou lovest is sick.** [The message and its form both indicate the close intimacy between this family and Christ. They make no request, trusting that Jesus' love will bring him to Bethany.] **4 But when Jesus heard it, he said, This sickness is not unto death, but for the glory of God, that the Son of God may be glorified thereby.** [The sickness of Lazarus was for the purpose or design of a resurrection, so that death was a mere preceding incident. By this resurrection the Son of God would be glorified by manifesting more clearly than ever before that death came under his Messianic dominion, and by gathering believers from amongst his enemies. In all this the Father would also be glorified in the Son.] **5 Now Jesus loved Martha, and her sister, and Lazarus.** [In this passage we have two Greek words for love. In verses 3 and 36 we have *philein*, which expresses natural affection such as a parent feels for a child. In this verse we have *agapan*, an affection resulting from moral choice, loftier and less impulsive. We are told of the Lord's love that we may understand that his delay was not due to indifference.] **6 When therefore he heard that he was sick, he abode at that time two**

days in the place where he was. [It is urged that the exigencies of his ministry delayed Jesus in Peræa. But the import of the text is that he kept away because of his love for the household of Lazarus and his desire to bless his disciples. He delayed that he might discipline and perfect the faith of the sisters and the disciples. He withheld his blessing that he might enlarge it. Strauss pronounces it immoral in Christ to let his friend die in order to glorify himself by a miracle. In the vocabulary of Strauss glorification means the gratification of personal vanity, but in the language of Christ it means the revelation of himself as the divine Saviour, that men may believe and receive the blessing of salvation.] **7 Then after this he saith to the disciples, Let us go into Judaea again.** [The word "again" refers back to John x. 40. Jesus does not propose to them to return to Bethany, where he had friends, but to go back to Judæa, the land of hostility. In so doing he caused them to think of his death, of which he had for some time been seeking to accustom them to think.] **8 The disciples say unto him, Rabbi, the Jews were but now seeking to stone thee** [John x. 31]; **and goest thou thither again? 9 Jesus answered, Are there not twelve hours in the day? If a man walk in the day, he stumbleth not, because he seeth the light of this world. 10 But if a man walk in the night, he stumbleth, because the light is not in him.** [This parabolic expression resembles that at John ix. 4. See p. 462. In this passage, day represents the allotted season of life which was to be terminated by what Jesus called "his hour." Until this "hour" came, Jesus felt no fear. He did not thrust himself into danger, thus tempting God; but he feared not to go whither his duty and the Spirit led him. As yet it was still day, but the evening shadows were falling, and the powers of darkness were soon to prevail (Luke xxii. 53), and then the further prosecution of the work would lead to death, for death was part of the work, and had its allotted time and place.] **11 These things spake he: and after this he saith unto them, Our friend Lazarus is fallen asleep; but I go,**

that I may awake him out of sleep. **12 The disciples therefore said unto him, Lord, if he is fallen asleep, he will recover. 13 Now Jesus had spoken of his death: but they thought that he spake of taking rest in sleep.** [Jesus had before this spoken of death under the figure of sleep (Luke viii. 52, p. 355), and the disciples might have understood him to mean death in this case had they not misunderstood his promise given at verse 4. As it was, they looked upon the mentioned sleep as marking the crisis of the disease, as it so often does in cases of fever. They were glad to urge it as an evidence of complete recovery, and thus remove one of the causes of the dreaded journey into Judæa.] **14 Then Jesus therefore said unto them plainly, Lazarus is dead. 15 And I am glad for your sakes that I was not there, to the intent ye may believe; nevertheless let us go unto him.** [Had Jesus been present during the sickness of Lazarus he would have felt constrained to heal him, and so would have lost the opportunity of presenting to his disciples a more striking proof of his divine power, a proof which has been the joy of each succeeding age. The disciples were soon to learn by sad experience how little belief they really had— Mark xiv. 50; xvi. 11; Luke xxiv. 11, 21, 25.] **16 Thomas therefore, who is called Didymus** [see p. 224], **said unto his fellow-disciples, Let us also go, that we may die with him.** [*I. e.*, die with Christ, see verse 8. They could not die with Lazarus, as some have foolishly supposed, for he was already dead. This mention of Thomas is closely connected with the thought in verse 15. Jesus was about to work a miracle for the express purpose of inducing his disciples to believe in him, especially as to his power over death. In this despairing speech Thomas shows how little faith he had in Christ's ability to cope with death. Thomas sadly needed to witness this miracle of the resurrection of Lazarus, and even after seeing it, it proved insufficient to sustain his faith in the ordeal through which he was about to pass—John xx. 25-29.] **17 So when Jesus came, he found that he had been in the tomb four days already.** [If Lazarus was buried on the day he died, as is the custom in the East, and in hot climates generally (Acts v. 6, 10), he probably died on the day that the messengers brought word to Jesus about his sickness. If so, Jesus set forth for Bethany on the third day and arrived there on the fourth. The resurrections wrought by Jesus are progressional manifestations of power. Jairus' daughter was raised immediately after death, the young man at Nain was being carried to his grave, and Lazarus had been buried four days. All these were preparatory to that last and greatest manifestation of resurrectional power—the raising of his own body.] **18 Now Bethany was nigh unto Jerusalem, about fifteen furlongs off** [the furlong, or stadium, was six hundred feet, so that the distance here was one and seven-eighth miles]; **19 and many of the Jews had come to Martha and Mary to console them concerning their brother.** [These Jews were present four days after the death because Jewish custom prolonged the season of mourning (Gen. i. 3, 10; Num. xx. 29; Deut. xxxiv. 8; I. Sam. xxviii. 13). The Mishna prescribed seven days for near relatives, and the rules as laid down by rabbis, required seven days' public and thirty days' private mourning for distinguished or important personages.] **20 Martha therefore, when she heard that Jesus was coming, went and met him: but Mary still sat in the house.** [Jesus evidently paused on the outskirts of the town. He probably wished to avoid the noisy conventional wailing, the hypocrisy of which was distasteful to him (Mark v. 40). It comports with the businesslike character of Martha as depicted by Luke to have heard of our Lord's arrival before Mary. She was probably discharging her duty towards the guests and new arrivals, as was her wont. See p. 478.] **21 Martha therefore said unto Jesus, Lord, if thou hadst been here, my brother had not died. 22 And even now I know that, whatsoever thou shalt ask of God, God will give thee.** [We might take it that Martha confidently expected the Lord to raise Lazarus, were it not for the subsequent conversation, and especially verse 39. We must therefore look upon her hope as more vague than her words would indicate. Such vague and illusive hopes are common where a great expectation, such as she had before indulged, has but lately departed.] **23 Jesus saith unto her, Thy brother shall rise again. 24 Martha saith unto him, I know that he shall rise again in the resurrection at the last day. 25 Jesus said unto her, I am the resurrection, and the life: he that believeth on me, though he die, yet shall he live ; 26 and whosoever liveth and believeth on me shall never die. Believest thou this?** [Instead of saying "I will raise Lazarus," Jesus uses the wholly impersonal phrase "thy brother shall rise again," for it was this very impersonal feature of faith which he wished to correct. Martha assents to it at once. The doctrine of a resurrection was commonly held by all the Jews except the Sadducees. It was in their view, however, a remote, impersonal affair, a very far distant event powerless to comfort in bereavement. From this comparatively cheerless hope Jesus would draw Martha to look upon *himself* as both resurrection and life. Where he is there is life and there also is resurrection at his word without limitation. No mere man, if sane, could have uttered such words. They mean that Jesus is the power which raises the dead and bestows eternal life—John vi. 39-54; x. 28.] **27 She saith unto him, Yea, Lord: I have believed that thou art the Christ, the Son of God, *even* he that cometh into the world.** [She could not say she believed it, for Lazarus had believed in Jesus and yet he had died. So, evading the question, she confessed her faith in him. Believing him, she accepted whatever he might say. She responds in the words of that apostolic creed which, in its ultimate application, embraces all that is true and discards all that is false (Matt. xvi. 16; John vi. 68, 69; xx. 31; I. John v. 1-5). See p. 411.] **28 And when she had said this, she went away, and called Mary her sister secretly, saying, The Teacher is here and calleth thee.** [She called Mary secretly, for she wished that Mary might have a private word with Jesus such as she had just had.] **29 And she, when she heard it, arose quickly** [moved by ardent feeling], **and went unto him. 30 (Now Jesus was not yet come into the village, but was still in the place where Martha met him.) 31 The Jews then who were with her in the house, and were consoling her, when they saw Mary, that she rose up quickly and went out, followed her, supposing that she was going unto the tomb to weep there.** [Rather to wail (Matt. ii. 18; Mark v. 38). According to Eastern custom, the Jews followed her as friends, to assist in the demonstration of mourning. This frustrated the effort of Martha to keep secret the Lord's coming, and caused the miracle to be wrought in the presence of a mixed body of spectators.] **32 Mary therefore, when she came where Jesus was, and saw him, fell down at his feet** [in grief and dependence; but with less self-control than Martha], **saying unto him, Lord, if thou hadst been here, my brother had not died.** [That both sisters used this phrase, shows that it is an echo of the past feelings and conversations of the sisters. It is clear that they felt hurt at his not coming sooner, as he could have done.] **33 When Jesus therefore saw her weeping, and the Jews *also* weeping who came with her, he groaned in the spirit, and was troubled** [The verb translated "groaned" carries in it the idea of indignation. But the fact that sin had brought such misery to those he loved was enough to account for the feeling.] **34 and said, Where have ye laid him?** [This question was designed to bring all parties to the tomb: it was not asked for information. See pp. 353, 354, 376.] **They** [the sisters] **say unto him, Lord, come and see. 35 Jesus wept.** [This is not the verb for wailing, but for shedding tears. On another occasion, when Jesus saw with prophetic eye a vast city, the center of God's chosen nation, sweeping on to destruction, he lamented aloud (Luke xix. 41), but here, as a friend, he mingled his quiet tears with the two broken-hearted sisters, thus assuring us of his sympathy with the individual grief of each lowly disciple (Rom. xii. 15). Nor did the nearness of comfort prevent his tears. They were tears of sympathy. "A sympathetic physician," says Neander, "in the midst of a family drowned in grief,—will not his tears flow with theirs, though he knows that he has the power of giving immediate relief?"] **36 The Jews therefore said, Behold how he loved him! 37 But some of them said, Could not this man, who opened the eyes of him that was blind, have caused that this man also should not die?** [Knowing the miracle which he had performed upon a blind man (John ix. 1-13), they could therefore see no reason why he should not have performed one here.] **38 Jesus therefore again groaning in himself cometh to the tomb. Now it was a cave, and a stone lay against it.** [These stones were frequently in the shape of large grindstones resting in a groove, so that they could be rolled in front of the door of the tomb. Tombs had to be closed securely to keep out jackals and other ravenous beasts.] **39 Jesus saith, Take ye away the stone.** [Miracles only begin where human power ends.] **Martha, the sister of him that was dead, saith unto him, Lord, by this time the body decayeth; for he hath been *dead* four days.** [She evidently thought that Jesus wished to see the remains of his friend, and her sisterly feeling prompted her to conceal the humiliating ravages of death. Her words show how little expectation of a resurrection she had.] **40 Jesus saith unto her, Said I not unto thee, that, if thou believedst, thou shouldest see the glory of God?** [Jesus reminds her of his words which are recorded in verses 25 and 26, and of the message which he sent, found in verse 4, thus removing her objections.] **41 So they took away the stone. And Jesus lifted up his eyes, and said, Father, I thank thee that thou heardest me. 42 And I knew that thou hearest me always: but because of the multitude that standeth around I said it, that they may believe that thou didst send me.** [Jesus, dwelling in constant communion with the Father, knew that the Father concurred in his wish to raise Lazarus. He therefore makes public acknowledgment, and offers a prayer of thanksgiving, for the Father's gracious answer to this and all his petitions. He states, too, that the prayer is publicly made that it may induce faith in the bystanders. He wishes all present to know that the miracle about to be wrought is not the work of some independent wonder-worker, but is performed by him as one commissioned and sent of God. In other words, the miracle was wrought to prove the concord between the Son and the Father, the very fact which the Jews refused to believe. Rationalists criticize this prayer as a violation of the principle at Matt. vi. 5, 6, and Weisse called it "prayer for show." But it shows on its face that it is not uttered by Jesus to draw admiration to himself as a praying man, but to induce faith unto salvation in those who heard.] **43 And when he had thus spoken, he cried with a loud voice, Lazarus, come forth.** [The loud cry emphasized the fact that the miracle was wrought by personal authority, and not by charms, incantations or other questionable means. His voice was as it were an earnest of that final calling which all shall hear (Rev. i. 5; John v. 28, 29; I. Thess. iv. 16). It has been happily said that he called Lazarus by name, lest all the dead should rise.] **44 He that was dead came forth, bound hand and foot with grave-clothes; and his face was bound about with a napkin. Jesus saith unto them, Loose him, and let him go.** [It is thought by some that Lazarus walked forth from the tomb, and the fact that the Egyptians sometimes swathed their mummies so as to keep the limbs and even the fingers separate is cited to show that Lazarus was not so bound as to prevent motion. But the grave-clothes were like a modern shroud, wrapped around arms and legs, and mummies also were thus wrapped after their limbs were swathed. It was part of the miracle that Lazarus came out bound hand and foot, and John puts emphasis upon it.] **45 Many therefore of the Jews, who came to Mary and beheld that which he did, believed on him. 46 But some of them** [some of the class mentioned in verse 37] **went away to the Pharisees, and told them the things which Jesus had done.** [By the miracle Jesus had won many from the ranks of his enemies, but others, alarmed at this deflection, rush off to tell the Pharisees about this new

cause for alarm. Farrar argues that these may have gone to
the Pharisees with good intentions toward Jesus, but surely no
friend of Jesus could have been so hasty to communicate with
his enemies. But the way in which the Evangelist separates
these from the believers of verse 45, stamps their action as unquestionably hostile.]

XCIV.

RETIRING BEFORE THE SANHEDRIN'S DECREE.

(Jerusalem and Ephraim in Judæa.)

ᵈ JOHN XI. 47–54.

**ᵈ 47 The chief priests therefore and the Pharisees
gathered a council** [called a meeting of the Sanhedrin],
and said, What do we? [Thus they reproach one another
for having done nothing in a present and urgent crisis. As
two of their number (Nicodemus and Joseph of Arimathæa)
were afterwards in communication with Christians, it was easy
for the disciples to find out what occurred on this notable occa-
sion] **for this man doeth many signs.** [They did not deny
the miracles, therefore their conduct was the more inexcusable.] **48 If we let him thus alone, all men will believe on him** [they found that despite the threat of excommunication, Jesus was still winning disciples under the very
shadow of Jerusalem]: **and the Romans will come and
take away both our place and our nation.** [The course
of Jesus seemed to them to undermine Judaism, and to leave
it a prey to the innovations of Rome. It is uncertain what is
meant by the noun "place." Meyer says it refers to Jerusalem; Luecke to the temple, while Bengel says that place and
nation are a proverbial expression, meaning "our all;" but
the Greek language furnishes no example of such proverbial
use. It is more likely that place refers to their seats in the
Sanhedrin, which they would be likely to lose if the influence
of Jesus became, as they feared, the dominant power. They

feared then that the Romans would, by removing them, take away the last vestige of civil and ecclesiastical authority, and then eventually obliterate the national life.] **49 But a certain one of them, Caiaphas, being high priest that year** [that notable, fatal year; he was high priest from A. D. 18 to A. D. 36], **said unto them, Ye know nothing at all, 50 nor do ye take account that it is expedient for you that one man should die for the people, and that the whole nation perish not.** [His words are a stinging rebuke, which may be paraphrased thus: "If you had any sense you would not sit there asking, 'What do we?' when there is but one thing you can do; viz.: Let Jesus die and save the people. Expediency, not justice, is his law.] **51 Now this he said not of himself: but being high priest that year, he prophesied that Jesus should die for the nation; 52 and not for the nation only, but that he might also gather together into one** [Gal. iii. 28; Col. iii. 11] **the children of God that are scattered abroad.** [The expression "not of himself" is a very common Hebrew idiom for "not of himself *only*." God had a meaning in his words different from his own. In earlier, better days the high priest had represented the divine headship of the nation, and through him, by means of the Urim and Thummim, the inspired oracles and decisions had been wont to come. This exalted honor had been lost through unworthiness. But now, according to the will of God, the high priest prophesies in spite of himself, as did Balaam and Saul, performing the office without the honor.] **53 So from that day forth they took counsel that they might put him to death.** [Thus, acting on the advice of Caiaphas the Sanhedrin condemned Jesus without a hearing, and sought means to carry their condemnation to execution. Quieting their consciences by professing to see such political dangers as made it necessary to kill Jesus for the public welfare, they departed utterly from justice, and took the course which brought upon them the very evils which they were professedly seeking to avoid.] **54 Jesus therefore walked no more openly among the Jews, but departed** thence into the country near to the wilderness, into a city called **Ephraim**; and there he tarried with the disciples. [Ephraim is supposed to be the city called Ophrah at Josh. xviii. 23, and Ephraim at II. Chron. xiii. 19. Dr. Robinson and others identify it with the village now called et Taiyibeh, which is situated on a conical-shaped hill about sixteen miles northeast of Jerusalem, and five miles east of Bethel. It is on the borders of a wilderness, and commands an extensive view of the Jordan valley. Here Jesus remained till shortly before his last passover.]

XCV.

JOURNEY TO JERUSALEM. TEN LEPERS. CONCERNING THE KINGDOM.

(Borders of Samaria and Galilee.)

c LUKE XVII. 11-37.

c 11 **And it came to pass, as they were on the way to Jerusalem, that he was passing along the borders of Samaria and Galilee.** [If our chronology is correct, Jesus passed northward from Ephraim about forty miles, crossing Samaria (here mentioned first) and coming to the border of Galilee. He then turned eastward along that border down the wady Bethshean which separates the two provinces, and crossed the Jordan into Peræa, where we soon find him moving on toward Jericho in the midst of the caravan of pilgrims on the way to the passover.] 12 **And as he entered into a certain village, there met him ten men that were lepers, who stood afar off** [One may still meet such groups of lepers outside the villages. They do not stand directly in the road so as to make an actual meeting, but are off to one side and near enough to beg. The law required lepers to keep away from the rest of the people (Lev. xiii. 45, 46). The rabbis are said to have prescribed a fixed distance at which lepers must keep, but authority varies as to this distance, some giving it as low as a rod, and others as high as a hundred paces]: **13 and they lifted up their voices** [such as they had, for the leper's bronchial tubes are dry, and the voice is harsh and squeaky], **saying, Jesus, Master, have mercy on us.** [Considering their condition, their prayer was definite enough.] **14 And when he saw them** [the disciples about him probably at first obstructed the Lord's view], **he said unto them, Go and show yourselves unto the priests.** [See p. 108.] **And it came to pass, as they went, they were cleansed.** [They received the blessing when they showed their faith by their obedience.] **15 And one of them, when he saw that he was healed, turned back** [like Naaman— II. Kings v. 15], **with a loud voice** [made strong by health and gratitude] **glorifying God; 16 and he fell upon his face at his feet, giving him thanks: and he was a Samaritan.** [On his way to the priests at Mt. Gerizim the Samaritan turned back to express his thanks. Apparently nine of the lepers were Jews. A Samaritan was among them because they were along the border of his country, and because the fellowship of affliction and disease obliterated the distinctions of race as it does to this day. In the leper-houses at Jerusalem Mohammedans and Jews now live together despite the rancor existing between the healthy representatives of these two religions.] **17 And Jesus answering said, Were not the ten cleansed? but where are the nine?** [The Lord publicly noted the indifference and ingratitude of the nine and the thanksgiving of the tenth. As we look around to-day and see how many are ungrateful for the blessings which they receive, the words ring like an echo in our ears.] **18 Were there none found that returned to give glory to God, save this stranger?** [It sometimes happens that we receive most where we expect least. Though the Samaritan's religion was partly Jewish, yet by blood he was a foreigner, as the word "stranger" means.] **19 And he said unto him, Arise, and go thy way: thy faith hath made thee whole.** [Thus Jesus emphasized the fact that the blessing came through faith, encouraging the man to seek higher blessings by the same means.] **20 And being asked by the Pharisees, when the kingdom of God cometh, he answered them and said, The kingdom of God cometh not with observation : 21 neither shall they say, Lo, here ! or, There ! for lo, the kingdom of God is within you.** [Rom. xiv. 17. The question of the Pharisees was doubtless a covert criticism. More than three years before this Jesus had begun to say that the kingdom of heaven was at hand; and they thought that after all this preparation it was high time that the kingdom should commence. They were looking for some manifestation of the sovereignty of God in the realm of the civil and the external, which would raise the Jewish nation to conspicuous supremacy, but they are told that the work of the kingdom is internal and spiritual (John iii. 8; xviii. 36; Rom. x. 8; Col. i. 27), and that its effects are not such as can be located in space. They were seeking honors and joys, and would find contempt and sorrow (Amos v. 18-20). Some have thought it strange that Jesus should say "within you" when addressing the Pharisees, but the word "you" is used generally and indefinitely.] **22 And he said unto the disciples** [giving them instructions suggested by the question of the Pharisees], **The days will come, when ye shall desire to see one of the days of the Son of man, and ye shall not see it. 23 And they shall say to you, Lo, there ! Lo, here ! go not away, nor follow after** *them :* **24 for as the lightning, when it lighteneth out of the one part under the heaven, shineth unto the other part under heaven; so shall the Son of man be in his day.** [Acts xxvi. 13; II. Thess. xi. 8. If the Pharisees looked eagerly for a sensuous external Messianic kingdom, so also would the disciples be tempted in the days to come to cherish a somewhat similar yearning. Knowing that Jesus was to come again to rule in power and in great glory, they would, under the stress of persecution, hunger to see one of the days of his rule. This longing for the coming of the Christ is frequently expressed (Phil. iv. 5; Tit. ii. 13; Jas v. 7-9; Rev. xxii. 20). In their restless eagerness the unwary disciples would be tempted to follow the false Messiahs who excited widespread admiration and attention. Against all this Jesus warns them, telling them that when the kingdom of heaven does at last assume a visible shape in the manifestation of its King, that manifestation will be so glorious, universal and pronounced as to be absolutely unmistakable.] **25 But first must he suffer many things and be rejected of this generation** [Thus when he speaks of his glory Jesus is careful to mention the humiliation and suffering which precedes it, that the faith of his disciples may not be weakened by false expectations and misunderstandings. The day of glory was not for that generation, since it would reject him.] **26 And as it came to pass in the days of Noah** [Gen. vii. 11-23], **even so shall it be also in the days of the Son of man. 27 They ate, they drank, they married, they were given in marriage, until the day that Noah entered into the ark, and the flood came, and destroyed them all. 28 Likewise even as it came to pass in the days of Lot** [Gen. xix. 15-28; Ezek. xvi. 46-56; Jude 7]; **they ate, they drank, they bought, they sold, they planted, they builded; 29 but in the day that Lot went out from Sodom it rained fire and brimstone from heaven, and destroyed them all: 30 after the same manner shall it be in the day that the Son of man is revealed.** [Our Lord here gives us two historical incidents of the false security of the ungodly, and in doing so he endorses them as real history. The antediluvians and the citizens of Sodom discharged the business of the day and laid their plans for to-morrow and had no thought of evil or anticipation of trouble down to the very moment that the bowls of wrath were poured upon them. Despite all warnings, they were taken by surprise when completely off their guard. The coming of Christ shall be a like surprise to the people of the last day (Matt. xxiv. 44; Luke xii. 39; I. Thess. v. 2; II. Pet. iii. 10; Rev. iii. 3; xvi. 15), and it shall be a day of like punishment—II. Thess. i. 6-10.] **31 In that day, he that shall be on the housetop** [the flat roofs of Oriental houses are used much the same as we use porches], **and his goods in the house, let him not go down to take them away: and let him that is in the field likewise not return back. 32 Remember Lot's wife.** [Gen. xix. 26; Luke ix. 62.] **33 Whosoever shall seek to gain his life shall lose it: but whosoever shall lose *his life* shall preserve it.** [See p. 416. It seems strange that the terrors of the last day should be accompanied by any thought or concern for property, but such is the plain intimation of the text. If our hope has been centered upon earthly things we will be found seeking them even in that hour, just as the face of Lot's wife was turned toward Sodom despite the glare of the penal fires. Our earthly characters become fixed, and great catastrophes do not change them (Rev. xxii. 10-12). If in that hour we be found seeking to save our carnal treasures, it will be a sign that we have lost the spiritual from our lives and have no heavenly treasures.] **34 I say unto you, In that night there shall be two men on one bed; the one shall be taken, and the other shall be left. 35 There shall be two women grinding together** [making meal or flour with the little stone hand-mills, as they still do in the East]**; the one shall be taken, and the other shall be left.** [Day and night exist simultaneously upon the earth, and the Lord's coming will be at noon to some and at midnight to others. His saints will be found mingled with the rest of the people and engaged in the duties befitting the hour. But the Lord will receive them to himself as his own (John xiv. 3; I. Thess. iv. 17), and they will be ready to be detached from their worldly ties that they may go to meet and welcome the bridegroom at his coming—Matt. xxv. 6, 7.] **37 And they answering say unto him, Where, Lord? And he said unto them, Where the body *is*, thither will the eagles also be gathered together.** [The disciples desired to know where this manifestation and division would take place, looking upon it as a local prediction. Jesus gave a proverbial answer, the meaning of which is that sin courts and draws to itself punishment and destruction just as a carcass draws winged

scavengers. Applying his words, we may say that as the corruption of the antediluvians drew upon them the devastation of
the flood, and as the crimes of the Sodomites called down
upon them the fires from heaven, and as the unbelief of the
Jews of Christ's day caused the destruction of Jerusalem and
the death of the nation, so the wickedness of the men of the
last times will result in the ending of the world. The word
translated eagles is generic, and included the vultures also
(Pliny Nat. Hist. ix. 3). It is likely that the Revision Committee retained the word "eagles" instead of vultures because
of the mistaken notion of Lightfoot and others that our Lord
here made a covert allusion to the eagles which were borne
upon the Roman standards. A passage similar to the latter
part of this section will be found at Matt. xxiv. 17-41.

XCVI.

PARABLE OF THE IMPORTUNATE WIDOW.

^c LUKE XVIII. 1-8.

 ^c 1 And he spake a parable unto them to the end that
they ought always to pray, and not to faint; 2 saying,
There was in a city a judge, who feared not God, and
regarded not man [an utterly abandoned character]: 3
and there was a widow in that city; and she came oft
unto him, saying, Avenge me of [rather, Do justice by me
as to] mine adversary. [In Scripture language widowhood is
symbolic of defenselessness (Ex. xxii. 22-24; Deut. x. 18;
xxvii. 19; Mal. iii. 5; Mark xii. 40), and the early church
concerned itself much about the welfare of widows—Acts
vi. 1; ix. 41; Jas. i. 27; I. Tim. v. 3.] 4 And he would
not for a while: but afterward he said within himself,
Though I fear not God, nor regard man; 5 yet because
this widow troubleth me, I will avenge her, lest she
wear me out by her continual coming. [The point of
this soliloquy is this: Though the high motives such as account-
ability to God for my office and my good name and respect

among men do not lead me to do this woman justice, yet will I do it simply to be rid of her importunity.] **6 And the Lord said** [this expression indicates that the Lord paused for a moment, that the parable might be fully grasped before he made the application], **Hear what the unrighteous judge saith. 7 And shall not God avenge his elect, that cry to him day and night** [The application is an argument *a fortiori*, and presents a triple antithesis: 1. In the petitioned—a just God and an unrighteous judge. 2. In the petitioners—a despised widow and the beloved elect. 3. The petition—the frequent visits of the one, and the continual cries of the many], **and *yet* he is longsuffering over them? 8 I say unto you, that he will avenge them speedily. Nevertheless, when the Son of man cometh, shall he find faith on the earth?** [Though a beloved people cry continually unto a just God, yet will he in mercy be longsuffering to their enemies, and because of this longsuffering he will seem to delay his answer, but the delay will not be extended a moment longer than is necessary. When the season of repentance is past, and the measure of iniquity is full (Gen. xv. 16), then the Lord's answer will be speedy, immediate. But despite this admonition to pray without discouragement, and this promise to answer with all speed, God's patience with the wicked, and his consequent delays in answering the prayers of the just, will prove such a trial to his people as to leave it questionable whether any of them will have faith enough to pray until the coming of the Lord. We find an echo of this passage at II. Pet. iii. 1-13. Compare also Matt. xxiv. 12, 13. The parable resembles that of the friend who came at midnight (Luke xi. 5), see p. 480, but there the petitioner asked a gift, and here the request is for justice and deliverance. And this parable also teaches that the saints must be patient in prayer until the Lord's return.]

XCVII.

PARABLE OF THE PHARISEE AND PUBLICAN.

^c LUKE XVIII. 9-14.

^c **9 And he spake also this parable unto certain who trusted in themselves that they were righteous, and set all others at nought** [It is commonly said that this parable teaches humility in prayer, but the preface and conclusion (see verse 14) show that it is intended to set forth generally the difference between self-righteousness and humility, and that an occasion of prayer is chosen because it best illustrates the point which the Lord desired to teach. The parable shows that the righteousness in which these parties trusted was devoid of that true charity or heart-love toward God and man without which our characters are worthless in the sight of God—Prov. xxx. 12, 13; Isa. lxv. 5; I. Cor. xiii. 1-3]: **10 Two men went up into the temple to pray** [The temple was the appointed place for Jewish prayer. To it the Jew went if near at hand, and towards it he prayed if afar off. The stated hours of prayer were 9 A. M. and 3 P. M., but men went there to pray whenever they felt like it]; **the one a Pharisee, and the other a publican.** [The two represent the extremes of Jewish social and religious life—see pp. 71 and 76.] **11 The Pharisee stood and prayed thus with himself** [This may mean that he stood alone, withdrawing from the contamination of others, but it seems rather to mean that he prayed having himself, rather than God, uppermost in his thoughts], **God, I thank thee, that I am not as the rest of men, extortioners, unjust, adulterers, or even as this publican.** [His prayer is more a boast as to himself than an expression of worship toward God (Rev. iii. 17, 18), and he makes the sinful record of the publican a dark background on which to display the bright contrast of his own character—a character for which he was thankful, and apparently with reason.] **12 I fast twice in the week** [the law appointed one fast in the year,

viz.: on the day of Atonement (Lev. xvi. 29, 30), but the Pharisees fasted on Mondays and Thursdays of each week]; **I give tithes of all that I get.** [I give the tenth part of my income. The law required that tithes be given from the corn, wine, oil and cattle (Deut. xiv. 22, 23), but the Pharisees took account of the humblest herbs of the garden, and gave a tenth of their mint, anise, and cummin (Matt. xxiii. 23). Thus he confessed his virtues rather than his sins.] **13 But the publican, standing afar off** [remote from the Holy Place], **would not lift up so much as his eyes unto heaven** [Ps. cxxiii. 1, 2; xl. 12; Ez. ix. 6], **but smote his breast** [as if to remind himself of the stroke of God which he so richly deserved (Nah. ii. 7; Luke xxiii. 48], **saying, God, be thou merciful to me a sinner.** [He makes full confession of his sin without excuse or justification, and without offset of righteousness. Moreover, he petitions for no temporal blessings, but simply asks for mercy—I. Tim. i. 15.] **14 I say unto you, This man went down to his house justified rather than the other** [we are taught here, as in the parable of the prodigal son, that the penitent unrighteous are more acceptable to God than the righteous who make no confession of their sins]: **for every one that exalteth himself shall be humbled; but he that humbleth himself shall be exalted.** [Luke xiv. 11, see p. 494. The Pharisee was an example of the first, and the publican of the second.]

XCVIII.

JOURNEY TO JERUSALEM. CONCERNING DIVORCE.

ᵃ MATT. XIX. 1-12; ᵇ MARK X. 1-12.

ᵃ **1 And it came to pass when Jesus had finished these words** [the words contained in Matt. xviii., which are the last teachings in Galilee recorded by any of the Evangelists, p. 435 and p. 439], **he departed from Galilee** [Having come into the borders of it again from Ephraim. It seems likely that

Matthew takes in at one view both departures from Galilee, viz.: that mentioned on p. 441 and that at Sec. XCV., for Matthew records none of the intervening events and Jesus spent no time in Galilee between the two journeys, merely returning to the border of the land and making a second journey thence to Jerusalem. He now left Galilee to return thither no more until after the resurrection—Matt. xxviii. 16, 17; John xxi. 1], ᵇ1 **And he arose from thence, and cometh** {ᵃ **came**} ᵇ **into the borders of Judaea and beyond the Jordan** [The land beyond the Jordan was called Peræa. See p. 176. It was no part of Judæa, but belonged to the tetrarchy of Herod. It and the river Jordan bordered Judæa on the east]: ᵃ2 **and great multitudes** ᵇ **come together unto him again;** ᵃ **followed him;** ᵇ **and, as he was wont, he taught them again.** [The teachings of this journey will be found in Sections XCVIII–CI.] ᵃ **and he healed them there.** [No doubt bands of pilgrims on their way to the passover helped to swell the multitudes which now surrounded the Lord.] ᵇ2 **And there came unto him Pharisees, and asked him, ** ᵃ **saying,** ᵇ **Is it lawful for a man** ᵃ **to put away his wife for every cause?** [*I. e.*, every cause satisfactory to the husband.] ᵇ **trying him.** [Knowing that Jesus had modified the law of Moses, the Pharisees asked this question seeking to entrap him. If he reaffirmed his teaching in the Sermon on the Mount (Matt. v. 32), they hoped to make it appear that he despised the authority of Moses. But if he ratified the law of Moses, then they would show that he was contradicting his former teaching, and hence too inconsistent to be worthy of credit. For the Lord's teaching concerning divorce see p. 242.] 3 **And he answered and said unto them, What did Moses command you? 4 And they said, Moses suffered to write a bill of divorcement, and to put her away.** ᵃ4 **And he answered and said, Have ye not read, that he who made** *them* **from the beginning made them male and female, 5 and said, For this cause shall a man leave his father and mother, and shall cleave to his wife; and the two shall become one flesh? 6 So**

**that they are no more two, but one flesh. What there-
fore God hath joined together, let not man put asunder.**
[Jesus went back to the original law propounded by God and
recorded by Moses, and shows from it: 1. That marriage is a
fundamental principle of social order, God having it in view
from the creation, and hence making male and female. 2. That
the relation of marriage is superior even to the parental relation. 3. That by it the pair become one flesh, so that a man is
as much joined to his wife as he is to his own body. Now, since
a man can only be separated from his parental relations or from
his own body by death, which is an act of God, so it follows
that the superior or similar relation of marriage can only be
dissolved by the act of God. Thus Jesus draws the conclusion
that no man or body of men, whether acting in private, civil
or ecclesiastical capacity, can dissolve marriage otherwise than
according to the decrees of God.] **7 They say unto him,
Why then did Moses command to give a bill of divorcement, and to put *her* away?** [Seeing that Jesus reaffirmed his former teaching, the Jews proceed to show that he
is in conflict with the law of Moses, apparently failing to note
that Jesus has merely cited Scripture, and that therefore the
issue is really Moses against Moses.] ᵇ**5 But Jesus said
{ᵃ saith} unto them, Moses for your hardness of heart
ᵇ wrote you this commandment. ᵃ suffered you to put
away your wives: but from the beginning it hath not
been so. ᵇ6 But from the beginning of the creation,
Male and female made he them.** [Thus Jesus replies that
Moses did not *command*, but *suffered* or permitted (the word
"commandment" used by Mark having reference not to the
matter but to the manner; *i. e.*, commanding it to be done by
giving a writing) men to put away their wives because at the
time when the law was given the wickedness of men made such
a concession beneficial. Had the law propounded at creation
been re-enacted by Moses, many would have refused to marry
at all, preferring an illicit life to the hazard of matrimony under
a stringent law, and others finding themselves unhappily married would have secretly murdered their wives to gain their

liberty. As a choice of two evils God therefore temporarily modified the law out of compassion for the women. It was expected that as the hearts of men softened they would recognize the wisdom, justice and wholesomeness of the original law, and cease to take advantage of their permission to evade it. But men had not done this, and Christ himself had brought this concession to an end, and since then it has been the most daring interference with the divine prerogative, for men to venture on a continuance of the same concession, as though they were possessed of divine authority.] **10 And in the house the disciples asked him again of this matter. 11 And he saith unto them, ᵃ9 And I say unto you, Whosoever shall put away his wife, except for fornication, and shall marry another, committeth adultery: ᵇ against her: ᵃ and he that marrieth her when she is put away committeth adultery. ᵇ 12 and if she herself shall put away her husband, and marry another, she committeth adultery.** [Thus Jesus reaffirms the teaching at Matt. v. 32.] **ᵃ 10 The disciples say unto him, If the case of the man is so with his wife, it is not expedient to marry.** [The disciples illustrate not only the hardness of heart of which Jesus spoke, but also the wisdom of allowing divorce under the law of Moses.] **11 But he said unto them, Not all men can receive this saying, but they to whom it is given. 12 For there are eunuchs, that were so born from their mother's womb: and there are eunuchs, that were made eunuchs by men: and there are eunuchs, that made themselves eunuchs for the kingdom of heaven's sake. He that is able to receive it, let him receive it.** ["This saying" is the saying which Jesus himself had just uttered concerning divorce: and his teaching is that the prohibition of divorce does not apply to eunuchs. If a woman finds herself married to a eunuch, she is not bound to him. So with a man if married to a hermaphrodite.*]

---

*NOTE.—I dissent from the above interpretation for many reasons: If the cases be confined to the two instances given, the rule presents

XCIX.

BLESSING CHILDREN. CONCERNING CHILD-LIKENESS.

(In Peræa.)

ᵃ MATT. XIX. 13-15; ᵇ MARK X. 13-16; ᶜ LUKE XVIII. 15-17.

ᵃ 13 Then were there brought ᵇ 13 And they were bringing ᵃ unto him little children, {ᶜalso their babes,} that he should touch them: ᵃthat he should lay his hands on them, and pray [According to Buxtorf, children were often brought to the presidents of the synagogue in order that they might pray over them. The prayers of a good man in our behalf have always been regarded as a blessing: no wonder, then, that the mothers of these children desired the prayers of Jesus in behalf of their little ones. It was customary to put the hand upon the person prayed for, probably following the patriarchal precedent (Gen. xlviii. 14, 15). Compare Acts vi. 6]: ᶜbut {ᵃand} ᶜwhen the disciples saw it, they re-

nothing but what every man and woman would gladly receive, which is contrary to what Jesus says about the saying. But, if the cases be extended to cover those who make themselves eunuchs for the kingdom of heaven's sake, and it be contended that evangelists and others who sacrifice their home ties for the good of the cause thereby give to their wives a right of divorce, the saying becomes on the other hand too hard for any to receive. My understanding of the passage is this: The disciples, startled by the Lord's declaration as to the indissolubility of marriage, declared that marriage was inexpedient. Jesus accepts their sayings as a logical deduction from his teaching; but a difficult saying, because applicable to but three cases. Jesus is therefore speaking with regard to *celibacy* and not *divorce*. He says that eunuchs are unfit for marriage, whether made so by nature or by the violence of man. The two first—the *physical* eunuchs—are introduced to illustrate the last or *spiritual* eunuch—the man whose intense interest in the affairs of the kingdom of heaven makes him prefer the celibate state. The saying with regard to him is indeed hard to receive, for it borders on the abnormal and unnatural, and hence it is no command save to those who, being in that abnormal and almost buked them. ᵇ14 But when Jesus saw it, he was moved with indignation, and ᶜcalled them unto him, saying, {ᵇsaid} unto them, ᶜSuffer the little children to come unto me, and forbid them not: ᵃfor to such belongeth the kingdom of heaven. {ᵇof God.} [The disciples wished to protect Jesus from what appeared to them to be an unseemly intrusion and annoyance, and possibly, as the context suggests, they thought it was beneath the dignity of the Messiah to turn aside from the affairs of the kingdom of heaven (Matt. xix. 12) to pay attention to children. But Jesus was indignant at their officious interference, and directed that the children be brought to him, declaring at the same time that the kingdom of heaven is composed, not of little children, but of such as are childlike in their nature.] ᶜ17 Verily I say unto you, Whosoever shall not receive the kingdom of God as a little child, he shall in no wise enter therein. [See p. 431.] ᵇ16 And he took them in his arms, ᵃ15 And he laid {ᵇlaying} ᵃhis hands on {ᵇupon} ᵃthem, ᵇand blessed them, ᵃand departed thence. [They were

unnatural condition, are in a shape to receive it. Marriage is the normal condition of man, and celibacy is abnormal, but to some extent Biblically countenanced. The trend of Scripture shows that Jesus here speaks about celibacy and not about divorce, for it has much to say about the celibate principle involved here—those who prefer to be eunuchs for the kingdom of heaven's sake, and nothing to say about women obtaining divorces because of their husbands' sacrifices for the kingdom of heaven. The Scripture everywhere treats of celibacy as a difficult problem, and the teaching is this: When any in the kingdom of heaven feel called to such extreme labors therein as render marriage impracticable (Acts xiii. 2; I. Cor. ix. 4, 5), they are permitted to abstain from marriage; and when seasons of persecution seriously interfere with the regular order and course of life among Christians, they may find it expedient to live as eunuchs (I. Cor. vii. 25-34). But in no case must celibacy be practiced unless it can be done so without the sin of incontinency (I. Cor. vii. 1-9). The Bible nowhere countenances any celibate vow, for it teaches that celibacy is to be continued only so long as it is expedient. Much less does it give countenance to the doctrine that a church can pass laws enforcing celibacy on the whole class of clergy, without any regard for their natural constitution, their spiritual powers, or their faithful continuance.—P. Y. P.

brought that he might lay his hands on them and bless them, and that is what he did for them.   The command therefore that they be suffered to come to him should not be perverted into a precept directing that they be brought for other purposes. Those who have construed this as commanding or even permitting either infant baptism or an infant church membership, have abused the text.   They are indebted for these ideas, not to the Bible, but to their creeds.   The incident told in this section is a fitting sequel to the discourse on divorce.   The little children, the offspring of happy wedlock, and a source of constant joy and pleasure to faithful husbands and wives, serve by their presence to correct false impressions as to supposed inconvenience of an indissoluble marriage bond.   The sight of them in the arms of Jesus could not fail to leave a good impression with reference to married life.]

C

THE RICH RULER. PERIL OF RICHES. REWARD OF SACRIFICE.   PARABLE OF THE LABORERS IN THE VINEYARD.

(In Peræa.)

ᵃMATT. XIX. 16–XX. 16; ᵇ MARK X. 17-31; ᶜLUKE XVIII. 18-30.

ᵇ 17 And as he was going forth into the way, ᵃ behold, ᵇ there ran {ᵃ came} ᵇ one ᶜ a certain ruler ᵇ to him, and kneeled to him, and asked him, ᵃ and said, {ᶜ saying,} ᵇ Good Teacher, ᵃ what good thing shall I do, that I may have {ᵇ may inherit ᶜ to inherit} eternal life? [The action of this young man in running and kneeling shows that he was deeply anxious to receive an answer to his question, and also that he had great reverence for Jesus.   He seemed to think, however, that heaven could be gained by performing some one meritorious act.   He made the mistake of thinking that eternal life is a reward for *doing* rather than for *being*, a mistake from which the Roman Catholic Church developed the doctrine of "works of supererogation."] **19 And Jesus said unto him Why callest thou me good? none is good save ne, *even* God. ª Why askest thou me concerning that which is good? One there is who is good** [To the *address* of the young man, viz.: "Good Master," Jesus replies, "Why callest," etc., and to his *question*, "What good thing," etc. Jesus replies "Why askest," etc. The ruler using the inconsiderate, conventional language of the thoughtless, had taken an unwarrantable freedom with the word "good." Jesus shows that if his language had been used sincerely it would have committed him to a declaration of great faith, for he had addressed Jesus by a title which belongs only to God, and he had asked Jesus the question concerning that of which God alone was fitted to speak. As the ruler had not used this language sincerely Jesus challenged his words. The challenge showed the ruler that he has unwittingly confessed the divinity of Jesus, and thus startled him into a consideration of the marvelous fact which his own mouth had stated. This is done because the young man would need to believe in the divinity of Jesus to endure the test to which he was about to be subjected—I. John v. 5]: **but if thou wouldest enter into life, keep the commandments.** [By referring the ruler to the commandments, Jesus not only answered the question as to obtaining life, but he emphasized the confession of his divinity contained in the question, "Why askest," etc. God, who knows what is good, had revealed that good in the commandments which he had given. Yet the ruler had asked Jesus to be wise above God's revelation, and to propound a law or rule of goodness in addition to that already given, and of such a nature as to more fully insure the attainment of life by obeying it. The ruler's question reveals that common weakness in man which prompts him to look to his fellow-men for religious and moral instruction; forgetting that only God can propound the absolute standards of goodness. We should note, too, that the young man, being under the law given through Moses, was bidden to attain life by keeping that law. After the death of Christ a new law was

given. Had the man waited until that time, he would have
been directed to this new law, and obedience to it would
have been required. Compare Acts ii. 37, 38; II. Thess. i. 8,
et al.] **18 He saith unto him, Which? And Jesus said,**
ᶜ**20 Thou knowest the commandments, Do {ᵃThou
shalt}** ᶜ**not commit adultery, Do {ᵃThou shalt}** ᶜ**not
kill, Do {ᵃThou shalt}** ᶜ**not steal, Do {ᵃThou shalt}**
ᶜ**not bear false witness,** ᵇ**Do not defraud,** ᵃ**19 Honor
thy father and thy mother; and, Thou shalt love
thy neighbor as thyself.** [The ruler still sought for
some prominent commandment, but was referred to the
last six of the Decalogue, these being at that time more
frequently violated than the first four. For the last commandment, "Thou shalt not covet," Jesus substitutes its
equivalents "Do not defraud," and "Thou shalt love thy
neighbor as thyself," the last being a summary of all the six
—Rom. xiii. 9.] ᵇ**20 And he** ᵃ**20 The young man saith
{**ᵇ**said} unto him, Teacher,** ᶜ**All these things have I
observed from my youth up.** ᵃ**what lack I yet?** [He
had kept these commandments as far as he knew his heart and
as far as he understood their import.] ᵇ**21 And Jesus**
ᶜ**when he heard it,** ᵇ**looking upon him** [gazing earnestly
and searchingly at him] **loved him** ["*agapan.*" See p. 519.]**,
and said unto him,** ᶜ**One thing thou lackest yet** [a direct
answer to the direct question "What lack," etc.]: ᵃ**If thou
wouldest be perfect** [*i. e.*, in keeping the commandments
and in securing eternal life—Jas. ii. 10], **go, sell that which
thou hast,** ᶜ**sell all** ᵇ**whatsoever thou hast,** ᶜ**and dis-
tribute {**ᵇ**give}** ᶜ**unto {**ᵃ**to} the poor, and thou shalt
have treasure in heaven: and come, follow me.** [The
command to sell all is not a general one, but a special precept
needed in this case, 1. To dispel the ruler's self-deception. On
the negative side his character was good, but on the positive
it was deficient. He had done his neighbor no harm, but he
had also done him very little good. 2. To show impartiality.
The invitation of Jesus shows that the ruler desired to be in
some manner a disciple, and hence he is subjected to the same

test which the other disciples had accepted, and of which Peter soon after speaks. Paul also was rich in self-righteousness like this man, but cheerfully sacrificed all, that he might follow Christ (Phil. iii. 6-9). Moreover, the reference to treasure in heaven and the invitation to follow Christ tested the ruler's obedience to the first four commandments of the Decalogue as condensed in the great summary or first commandment. (Matt. xxii. 37, 38.) Though the ruler perhaps did not fully realize it, those who heard the conversation must afterwards have been impressed with the great truth that the ruler was called upon to make his choice whether he would love Christ or the world, whether he would serve God or mammon. The whole scene forms an illustration of the doctrine expressed by Paul, that by the law can no flesh be justified (Rom. iii. 20), for perfection is required of those who approach God along that pathway; those therefore, who have done all, still need a Christ to lead them.] ᵃ **22 But when the young man heard the saying, {ᶜ these things,} ᵇ his countenance fell at the saying, ᶜ he became exceeding sorrowful; ᵇ and he went away sorrowful: ᶜ for he was very rich. ᵇ he was one that had great possessions.** [He was not offended at the extravagance of Jesus' demands, for he was not one of the most hardened of the rich. He belonged to that class which hold Christ and their wealth in nearly an even balance. The narrative shows us how uncompromisingly Jesus held to principle. Though the ruler was sorry to turn away, and though Jesus loved him, yet the Lord did not modify his demand by a hair's-breadth to gain an influential disciple.] ᶜ **24 And Jesus seeing him ᵇ looked round about, and saith {ᵃ said} unto his disciples, ᵇ How hardly shall they that have riches enter into the kingdom of God! ᵃ Verily I say unto you, It is hard for a rich man to enter into the kingdom of heaven.** [I. Tim. vi. 9, 10, 17-19. It should be remembered that Judas heard these words only a few days before he sold his Lord.] ᵇ **24 And the disciples were amazed at his words. But Jesus answereth again, and saith unto them, Children, how hard is it for them that trust in**

riches to enter into the kingdom of God! [The possession and use of riches is permitted to the Christian, but their possession becomes a sin when the one who owns them comes to trust in them or in any way suffers them to interfere with his duties toward or relations to God.] ᵃ**24 And again I say unto you,** ᶜ**25 For it is easier for a camel to enter in {ᵇto go} through a needle's eye, than for a rich man to enter into the kingdom of God.** [The needle's eye here is that of the literal needle, and the expression was a proverbial one to indicate that which was absolutely impossible. Lord George Nugent (1845-6) introduced the explanation that Jesus referred to the two gates of a city, the large one for beast of burden, and the small one for foot-passengers. This smaller one is now called "The Needle's Eye," but there is no evidence whatever that it was so called in our Saviour's time. In fact, as Canon Farrar observes, we have every reason to believe that this smaller gate received its name in late years because of the efforts of those who were endeavoring to soften this saying of Jesus.] ᵃ**25 And when the disciples heard it, they were astonished exceedingly,** ᶜ**26 And they that heard it said, {ᵇsaying} unto him,** ᵃ**Who then {ᵇThen who} can be saved?** ᵃ**26 And Jesus** ᵇ**looking upon them saith, {ᶜ27 But he said,}** ᵇ**With men it is impossible, but not with God: for all things are possible with God.** ᶜ**The things which are impossible with men are possible with God.** [The Jews were accustomed to look upon the possession of riches as an evidence of divine favor, and the heads of the apostles were filled with visions of the riches and honors which they would enjoy when Jesus set up his kingdom. No wonder, then, that they were amazed to find that it was impossible for a rich man to enter that kingdom, and that, moreover and worse than all, riches appeared to exclude from salvation itself: that even this virtuous rich man, this paragon of excellence, could not have eternal life because he clung to his riches. But they were comforted by the assurance of Jesus that though the salvation of some men might present more difficulties than the salvation of others

—might, as it were, require a miracle where others only required simple means, yet the gracious, mighty God might still be trusted to overcome the obstacles. It is impossible for any man to save himself, so that in every case of salvation God is called upon to assist man in accomplishing the impossible. God can so work upon the rich man's heart as to make him a dispenser of blessings.] ᵃ**27 Then answered Peter** ᶜ**28 And** ᵇ**began to say unto him,** {ᵃ**and said unto him,**} ᵇ**Lo, we have left all,** {ᶜ**our own,**} ᵇ**and have followed thee.** ᵃ**what then shall we have?** [The negative conduct of the rich man reminded the disciples of their own positive conduct when confronted with a similar crisis (Luke v. 11), and the "all" which they had left was by no means contemptible, though perhaps none of them could have been said to have held great possessions. The mention of treasure in heaven, therefore, set Peter to wondering what manner of return would be made to them to compensate them for their sacrifice.] **28 And Jesus said unto them, Verily I say unto you, that ye who have followed me, in the regeneration when the Son of man shall sit on the throne of his glory, ye also shall sit upon twelve thrones, judging the twelve tribes of Israel.** [By the term "regeneration" Jesus in this case means the period in which the process of regenerating men would be in progress; *i. e.*, the period of the mediatorial reign. After his ascension Jesus sat upon his throne (Acts ii. 33-35; Heb. i. 13; Matt. xxv. 31; I. Cor. xxv. 24-28). And on the day of Pentecost next following he began this process of regeneration. Having enthroned himself, Jesus enthroned the apostles also, not as kings but as judges, having jurisdiction over all questions of faith and practice in the earthly kingdom. During their personal ministry, they judged in person; and since then they judge through their writings. True, we have written communications from only a part of them, but judgments pronounced by one of a bench of judges with the known approval of all, are the judgments of the entire bench. Moreover, the passage must be construed metaphorically, for the apostles are judges in the church of Christ—the true Israel—and not over the literal twelve tribes of Jacob. And again, the twelve who then heard Jesus speak were not all enthroned, Judas having fallen from his position before the day of enthronement, and Matthias and Paul were afterwards added to the group. Jesus here causes the number of the judges to correspond to the number of the tribes, to indicate that there will be a sufficiency of judgment commensurate to the need.] **29 And every one {ᵇ There is no man that} ᵃhath left houses, {ᵇ house,} ᶜ or wife, or brethren, ᵇ or sisters, or mother, or father, ᶜ or parents, ᵇ or children, or lands, for my sake, {ᵃ my name's sake,} ᵇ and for the gospel's sake, ᶜ for the kingdom of God's sake, 30 who shall not receive manifold more in this time, and in the world to come eternal life. ᵇ30 but he shall receive a hundredfold now in this time, houses, and brethren, and sisters, and mothers, and children, and lands, with persecutions; and in the world to come ᵃ shall inherit eternal life.** [The rewards of Christian self-denial are here divided into two parts—the temporal and the eternal. The earthly joys—the rewards "in this time"—shall outweigh the sacrifices made for the kingdom. The return, of course, will not be in kind, houses for house, and fathers for father, etc., but spiritual relationships and blessings which compensate abundantly for whatever has been resigned (Matt. xii. 49; I. Tim. iv. 8). But these joys shall be mingled with the bitterness of persecution, for no pleasure is perfected in this world, but only in the inheritance which lies beyond—I. Pet. i. 4.] **30 But many shall be last *that are* first; and first *that are* last. ᵇ 31 But many *that are* first shall be last; and the last first.** [The promise of large recompense which Jesus had just given was apt to tempt some to labor not for love, but for the rewards which might be reaped thereby. Jesus corrects this spirit by this statement, and the parable that follows which illustrates it, and which ends with the same sentiment. See verse 16 below.] **ᵃ1 For the kingdom of heaven is like unto a man that was a householder,** who went out early in the morning to hire laborers into his vineyard. [He rose early, because the working day began with the rising of the sun.] 2 And when he had agreed with the laborers for a shilling a day [see p. 376], he sent them into his vineyard. 3 And he went out about the third hour [The Jews divided the time between sunrise and sunset into twelve hours, so that the first hour would be about six o'clock, the third about nine, the sixth noon, the ninth about three, and the twelfth about six. As the length of the days differed, the lengths of the hours differed. The longest day in Palestine is fourteen hours and twelve minutes; the shortest, nine hours and forty-eight minutes; so it would follow that an hour on the longest day would be seventy-one minutes; and on the shortest it would be only forty-nine minutes. None of the hours, therefore, would correspond exactly to ours except the sixth or noon hour], and saw others standing in the marketplace idle; 4 and to them he said, Go ye also into the vineyard, and whatsoever is right I will give you. And they went their way. 5 Again he went out about the sixth and the ninth hour, and did likewise. 6 And about the eleventh *hour* he went out, and found others standing; and he saith unto them, Why stand ye here all the day idle? 7 They say unto him, Because no man hath hired us. He saith unto them, Go ye also into the vineyard. 8 And when even was come [the time of settlement—Lev. xix. 13; Deut. xxiv. 15], the lord of the vineyard saith unto his steward [his overseer], Call the laborers, and pay them their hire, beginning from the last unto the first. [Thus following the order indicated by verse 30 above. The lord paid the last first that he might make conspicuous the fact that these received as much wages as those who had labored all day. 9 And when they came that *were hired* about the eleventh hour, they received every man a shilling. 10 And when the first came, they supposed that they would receive more [seeing the lord's liberality to those who had worked only one hour, they expected that they would be recipients of a like liberality proportioned to their hours of service]; **and they likewise received every man a shilling. 11 And when they received it, they mur-murmured against the householder, 12 saying, These last have spent** *but* **one hour, and thou hast made them equal unto us, who have borne the burden of the day and the scorching heat. 13 But he answered and said to one of them** [the answer given to one is taken as an example of what he said to them all], **Friend, I do thee no wrong: didst not thou agree with me for a shilling? 14 Take up that which is thine, and go thy way** [do not stop to argue] **; it is my will to give unto this last, even as unto thee. 15 Is it not lawful for me to do what I will with mine own? or is thine eye evil, because I am good?** [The evil eye is a synonom for jealousy. It originated with the malicious leer with which jealousy regards its object (Mark vii. 22; I. Sam. xviii. 9; Prov. xxiii. 6-8; xxviii. 22; Deut. xv. 9). The lord had done no wrong to those who had labored longest, for he had paid them what they had bargained for and earned. If he chose to be generous with those whose misfortune had prevented them from being hired earlier in the day, no one had any just cause to murmur.] **16 So the last shall be first, and the first last.** [The meaning of this parable has often been misunderstood by those who fail to note the maxim with which Jesus begins and ends it. This maxim acts as a safeguard in the interpretation of it; and the parable also in turn guards against misunderstanding the maxim. The maxim can not be applied to Judas; for, though he then stood high in honor and afterwards fell into disgrace, yet he stands outside the pale of the maxim as interpreted by the parable, for in the parable both the first and the last were received and rewarded of their master, while Judas was rejected of Christ and received no reward. The term "last," therefore, must be applied to those who were included among the accepted laborers, and not to those who were excluded from that class. In the parable the *denarius* or shilling stands for the gift of eternal life. The vineyard represents the Lord's field of work in the world. The evening is the close of the Christian dispensation, and the coming of Christ to judgment. The parable as it unfolds and develops suggests that in no case was the reward earned by the inherent merits and toil of the laborers, but was rather bestowed because of a desire on the part of the householder to that effect, just as eternal life is bestowed, not by merit, but by covenant grace (Rom. ii. 6, 7; iv. 3-5; v. 16-21). The main object of the parable is to show that longer labor does not necessarily, as the apostles and others might think, establish a claim to higher reward. Degrees of difference there no doubt will be, but they form no account in the general covenant of grace in which the one great gift is offered to us all. As the gift can be *no less than eternal life*, there must of necessity be a difference in the ratio of service which is rendered for it, since it will be bestowed on the octogenarian and the child, upon Paul who made good the confession of his faith through years of toil, and the dying thief who passed to his reward while his voice of confession was, as it were, still ringing in the ears of those who heard it (I. Cor. xv. 8-11; II. Tim. iv. 6-9). The murmuring and envy of those who had labored longest is merely part of the parabolic drapery, introduced to bring out the answer of the householder, and to make plain the point to be illustrated. There will be no envy among those who inherit eternal life. By thus speaking of the envy, however, and showing how ineffectual it was, Jesus warns us to be prepared not to cherish it. The parable is not intended to teach that the characters of men will be exactly similar in the world to come. Paul will not be Peter, nor will Martin Luther be identical with Hugh Latimer and John Knox. God may award eternal life to the character which we are forming, but we should be careful what kind of character we bring to receive the gift. The lesson is that works are valued *qualitatively* and not *quantitatively*. Nor may the parable be rightly used to encourage hope in death-bed repentance. It certainly does teach, that however little the labor which a man does in the Lord's vineyard, he will receive the final reward if only he be really in the vineyard; that is, if he be really a child of God. But whether a man who repents on his death-bed actually becomes a child of God, is a different question, and is not touched by the parable. Certainly the eleventh-hour laborer who had stood idle all day only because no man had hired him, and who came into the vineyard as soon as he was called, can not represent the man who has been called by the gospel every hour of his life, but has rejected every call until his sun has sunk so low that he knows he can do but little work when he comes. In order to represent this class of sinners, the eleventh-hour men should have been invited early in the morning, and should have replied, "No, it is too early; we will not go now." Then they should have been invited at the third, the sixth, and the ninth hours, and should have made some equally frivolous excuse each time, then, finally, at the eleventh hour, they should have said, "Well, as you pay a man just the same for an hour's work as for a day's work, and as we are very anxious to get your money, we believe we will now go." Had they acted thus, it is not likely that they would have found the vineyard gates open to them at all. Yet such is the sharp practice which some men attempt in dealing with God.

CI.

FORETELLING HIS PASSION. REBUKING AMBITION.

(Peræa, or Judæa, near the Jordan.)

[a] MATT. xx. 17-28; [b] MARK x. 32-45; [c] LUKE xviii. 31-34.

[b] **32 And they were on the way, going up to Jerusalem** [Dean Mansel sees in these words an evidence that Jesus had just crossed the Jordan and was beginning the actual ascent up to Jerusalem. If so, he was in Judæa. But such a construction strains the language. Jesus had been going up to Jerusalem ever since he started in Galilee, and he may now have still been in Peræa. The parable of the vineyard which

closed the preceding section was likely to have been spoken before he crossed the Jordan, for Peræa abounded in vineyards]; **and Jesus was going before them: and they were amazed; and they that followed were afraid.** [When Jesus turned his face toward Jerusalem his disciples dropped behind and hung back. The outer circle of his disciples knew enough to be fearful of the consequences, and the inner circle, fully acquainted with the dangers, were amazed that he should dare to go thither. A short while before this they had despaired of his life when he had proposed to go even into Judæa (John xi. 7-16), and his going at that time had not bettered the situation, but had, on the contrary, greatly increased the enmity and danger (John xi. 47-57). Notwithstanding all this, Jesus was now on his way to Jerusalem itself, and was speaking no reassuring word as he formerly had done—John xi. 9, 10.] ᵃ **17 And as Jesus was going up to Jerusalem, he took** ᵇ **again** ᶜ **unto him** ᵃ **the twelve disciples apart** [He separated them from the throng of pilgrims on the way to the Passover, and from the outer circle of the disciples, for it was not expedient that these should hear what he was about to reveal concerning his death. Such a revelation might have spurred his Galilæan friends to resist his arrest, and might have resulted in riot and bloodshed], ᵇ **and began to tell them the things that were to happen unto him,** ᵃ **and on the way he said unto them, 18 Behold, we go up to Jerusalem; and the Son of man shall be delivered unto the chief priests and** ᵇ **the** ᵃ **scribes; and they shall condemn him to death, 19 and shall deliver him unto the Gentiles to mock, and to scourge, and to crucify:** ᵇ **34 and they shall mock him, and shall spit upon him, and shall scourge him, and shall kill him; and after three days he shall rise again.** {ᵃ **and the third day he shall be raised up.**} ᶜ **and all the things that are written through the prophets shall be accomplished unto the Son of man. 32 For he shall be delivered up unto the Gentiles, and shall be mocked, and shamefully treated, and spit upon: 33 and they shall scourge and kill him:**

and the third day he shall rise again. [This was the third and by far the clearest and most circumstantial prophecy concerning his death. For the other two see pp. 415 and 427. The details are minute even to that complicated arrangement by which the Jewish authorities pronounced sentence (Matt. xxvi. 66) and forced Pilate to confirm their sentence (Luke xxiii. 24). Since the evangelists honestly record an actual prediction, we may well pause to note how remarkable it is in that it gives seven details as follows: 1. Delivery or betrayal by Judas. 2. Condemnation. 3. Delivery to the Gentiles. 4. Mocking, and the manner of it. 5. Scourging. 6. Death by crucifixion. 7. Resurrection on the third day. The announcement of these sufferings was made for the purpose of checking any materialistic hopes which the apostles might entertain as to the glories, honors and offices of the Messianic reign. That such hopes were present is shown by the ambitious request which immediately follows. Moreover, to prepare them that they might not be crushed either by the announcement or the accomplishment of his death he gives them the clear promise of his resurrection.] **34 And they understood none of these things; and this saying was hid from them, and they perceived not the things that were said.** [So fixed and ineradicable was their false conception of the Messianic reign that they could not believe that what Jesus said could be literally true (Matt. xvi. 22). Only later did the full significance of his saying dawn upon them—John xii. 16–xiv. 26.] ᵇ**35 And there** ᵃ**20 Then came {**ᵇ**come} near unto him** ᵃ**the mother of the sons of Zebedee with her sons,** ᵇ**James and John,** ᵃ**worshipping** *him* [giving him homage as a coming ruler, not worshipping him as a divine being]**, and asking a certain thing of him.** ᵇ**saying unto him, Teacher, we would that thou shouldest do for us whatsoever we shall ask of thee.** [Zebedee's wife was named Salome. See note on p. 225. They were ashamed of the selfish ambition of their request, and betrayed that fact by desiring Christ to grant it without hearing it. For a similar petition see I. Kings ii. 19, 20. They asked through their mother, thinking that Jesus would be more likely to favor her than themselves.] ᵃ**21 And he said unto her,** {ᵇ**them,**} ᵃ**What wouldest thou?** ᵇ**What would ye that I should do for you?** [Though Jesus knew what they wished, he required them to state it plainly and specifically, that their self-seeking might be clearly exposed and properly rebuked.] ᵃ**She saith unto him, Command that these my two sons may sit, one on thy right hand, and one on thy left hand, in thy kingdom.** ᵇ**37 And they said unto him, Grant unto us that we may sit, one on thy right hand, and one on *thy* left hand, in thy glory.** [In the previous section Jesus had spoken about the thrones to be occupied by the apostles. The sons of Zebedee, presuming on their high standing among the apostles, and their near relationship to Jesus, were emboldened to ask for special seats of honor among these promised thrones—the seats to the right and left of the sovereign being next to his in dignity and consideration; thus Josephus represents Saul as seated with Jonathan on his right hand and Abner on his left. The terms "kingdom" and "glory" are here used synonymously. Despite the fact that Jesus was now telling them plainly of his death, these apostles could not rid their minds of the delusion that he was about to ascend the earthly throne of David.] ᵃ**22 But Jesus answered and said,** ᵇ**unto them, Ye know not what ye ask. Are ye able to drink the cup that I drink?** {ᵃ**that I am about to drink?**} ᵇ**or to be baptized with the baptism that I am baptized with?** [The word "cup" among the Hebrews meant *a portion assigned* (Ps. xvi. 5 ; xxiii. 5), whether of pleasure or of sorrow. But the idea of sorrow usually predominated (Matt. xxvi. 39, 42 ; Rev. xiv. 10; xvi. 19; xviii. 6; Ps. lxxv. 8; Isa. li. 17; Jer. xxv. 15). To be baptized with suffering means to be overwhelmed with it, a metaphorical use of the word arising from the fact that it means an immersion. This metaphorical use of baptism aids us to understand the meaning of that word, for neither sprinkling nor pouring could have suggested the overpowering force which the metaphor implies. Alford distinguishes between cup and baptism, making the former refer to inward spiritual suffering, and the latter to outer persecution and trial.] **39 And they said {ᵃ say} unto him, We are able.** ᵇ**And Jesus said {ᵃ saith} unto them, My {ᵇ The} cup that I drink ᵃ indeed ye shall drink : ᵇ and with the baptism that I am baptized withal shall ye be baptized** [They probably thought that Jesus referred to some battle or conflict which would attend the ushering in of the kingdom, and as they were not wanting in physical courage, they were ready enough to pledge themselves to endure it. They spoke with unwarranted self-confidence, but Jesus rebuked them very gently, as he foreknew what suffering they would indeed endure. James was the first apostolic martyr (Acts xii. 2), and John's spirit was sorely troubled with the conflict of error, as his epistles show, and his last days were darkened by the shadow of persecution—Rev. i. 5]: **40 but to sit on my right hand or {ᵃ and} on *my* left hand, is not mine to give; ᵇ but *it is for them* for whom it hath been prepared. ᵃ of my Father.** [Future rewards are indeed meted out by the hand of Christ (II. Tim. iv. 8; Rev. ii. 10, 17, 26, 28; iii. 12, 21, *et al.*), but they are not distributed according to caprice or favoritism, but according to the will of the Father and the rules which he has established. Jesus proceeds to set forth the principles by which places of honor are obtained in his kingdom.] **24 And when the ten heard it, they were {ᵇ began to be} ᵃ moved with indignation concerning the two brethren. ᵇ James and John. 42 And {ᵃ but} Jesus called them unto him, and said {ᵇ saith} unto them, Ye know that they who are accounted to rule over {ᵃ the rulers of} the Gentiles lord it over them, and their great ones exercise authority over them. 26 Not so shall it be {ᵇ 43 But it is not so} among you : but whosoever would become great among you, shall be your minister ; 44 and whosoever would be first among you, ᵃ shall be your servant : ᵇ shall be servant of all.** [The ten, sharing the same ambition as the two, jealously resented their efforts to take an unfair advantage of

the Lord's known affection for them. To restore peace among
them, and to correct their false views, he draws the distinction
between the worldly greatness to which they aspired, and the
spiritual greatness which they ought to have sought.   In an
earthly kingdom honor and authority measure greatness, but
in Christ's kingdom it is measured by humility and service.
Jesus added power to his rebuke by showing them that their
spirit was not even Jewish, but altogether heathenish.]   **45
For {ᵃ 28 even as} ᵇ the Son of man also came not to
be ministered unto, but to minister, and to give his
life a ransom for many.**   [He enforces this lesson by his
own example in that he came to serve men and not to have
them serve him.   Jesus could ever refer to himself as the best
example of the virtues which he taught.   Since honor consists in being like the King, the highest honor consists in being
most like him.   The closing words state the vicarious nature
of Christ's suffering as plainly as language can express it.
The ransom is offered for all (I. Tim. ii. 6), and will be effica-
cious for as many as accept it.   The words are nearly a reproduction of the words of Isaiah—Isa. liii. 12.]

CII.

BARTIMÆUS AND HIS COMPANION HEALED.

(At Jericho.)

ᵃ MATT. xx. 29-34;   ᵇ MARK x. 46-52;   ᶜ LUKE xviii. 35-43.

ᶜ **35 And it came to pass, as he drew nigh unto
Jericho, a certain blind man sat by the way side beg-
ging: 36 and hearing a multitude going by, he inquired
what this meant.   37 And they told him, that Jesus of
Nazareth passeth by.**   [Jesus came from the Jordan, and
was entering Jericho by its eastern gate.   As the crowd following Jesus passed by, Bartimaeus asked its meaning and learned
of the presence of Jesus.   Jesus on this last journey went in
advance of the crowd, and hence he had already entered
Jericho before the sounds of the following multitude roused

the beggar to question its meaning. Knowing that Jesus was on the way to Jerusalem, he resolved to avail himself of the opportunity to be healed by him before he left the neighborhood. Not knowing how long Jesus would remain in Jericho, and not being sure of his ability to find him if he entered the city, he appears to have passed around the wall till he came to the southern gate, by which Jesus would depart on his way to Jerusalem. Here he stationed himself and waited patiently for the coming of Jesus. The persistency with which he cried when Jesus again appeared goes far to corroborate this determined preparation and fixed expectation of the beggar. While he waited at the southern gate the events narrated in Sec. CIII. occurred. But to avoid confusion we omit them for the present, that we may finish the story of Bartimæus.] ᵇ **46 And they come to Jericho: and as he {ᵃthey} ᵇ went out from Jericho, with his disciples and a great multitude, ᵃ a great multitude followed him.** [Being so near the Passover season, great crowds would be on their way to Jerusalem, and all the multitudes coming from Galilee and from Peræa would pass through Jericho on their way thither. Jesus, as we have just seen, entered the city with a multitude, and as he spent some little time there, he would leave with even a larger crowd, for it would be augmented by those who had arrived at Jericho during his stay there and citizens of Jericho itself. Few would leave Jericho alone while they might have the pleasure and excitement of going with the crowd.] ᵇ **The son of Timaeus, Bartimaeus** [Bar is the Aramaic for son. It is likely that both Timæus and Bartimæus were well known in apostolic days, but all memory of them is now lost save that contained in this passage], **a blind beggar** [blindness and beggary form an awful combination, and when coupled with the general poverty then prevailing in Palestine, they suggest a fullness of suffering], **was sitting by the way side. ᵃ 30 And behold, two blind men sitting by the way side** [Here Matthew tells of two, while Mark and Luke tell only of one —the principal one. They vary here as in the account of the two demoniacs, and for similar reasons. See page 346], **when** they {ᵇhe} ᵃheard ᵇthat it was Jesus the Nazarene, ᵃthat Jesus was passing by {ᵇ he} began to cry {ᵃcried} out, ᵇand say, {ᵃsaying,} Lord, ᵇJesus, thou son of David, ᵃhave mercy on us, {ᶜme.} [The title " son of David" was the popular Jewish designation for the Messiah, and Bartimæus thus confessed his faith in the Messiahship of Jesus. Blind as he was, he saw more than those who spoke of the Lord as Jesus of Nazareth, thus making Jesus differ from other men merely in the matter of his residence.] **39 And they that went before** [they that came out of the city just ahead of Jesus] {ᵇmany ᵃthe multitude} **rebuked them,** {ᶜhim,} ᵃthat they {ᵇhe} ᵃshould hold their {ᵇhis} **peace:** ᵃbut they {ᶜhe} **cried out the more a great deal,** ᵃsaying, Lord, have mercy on us, {ᵇme.} ᵃthou son of David. [Various motives influenced the multitude to silence the beggar's cries. Some regarded his clamor as indecorous, distracting the thoughts and interrupting conversation. Others did not like to hear Jesus thus confessed as Messiah. Others still, believing that Jesus was about to be crowned king, thought that it was high time that he should cease paying so much attention to beggars, and to begin to assume the dignities of royalty. But Bartimæus was filled with the spirit of Jacob. The more resistance he met, the more strenuously he wrestled to obtain the blessing.] **32 And Jesus stood still, and called them,** ᶜand **commanded him to be brought unto him:** ᵇand **said, Call ye him. And they call the blind man, saying unto him, Be of good cheer: rise, he calleth thee.** [The multitude had rebuked the cry, but Jesus stood still to hear and answer it. He is no respecter of persons. Rich rulers and blind beggars received his attention and care without respect of station. He died for every man.] **50 And he, casting away his garment, sprang up, and came to Jesus.** [He cast off his outer garment or *pallium*, which was like a large shawl thrown over the shoulders, and is elsewhere called a cloak (see p. 245). It probably represented more than half the beggar's wealth, but he valued his eyesight more than it, and cast it aside because it hindered him in reaching Jesus through the crowd. Many to-day would come to Jesus, but their steps are impeded by some trifling obstacle (Isa. lxiv. 6). In the race to win the presence of Christ on high, Christians are advised to lay aside every weight—Heb. xii. 1, 2.] ᶜand when he was come near, ᵇJesus answered him, ᶜasked him, ᵇand said, ªWhat will ye {ᶜwilt thou} ªthat I should do unto you? {ᵇthee?} ª33 They say {ᵇAnd the blind man said} ªunto him, Lord, that our eyes may be opened. ᶜLord, ᵇRabboni, that I may receive my sight. [Bartimæus had cried for mercy without specifying what mercy, and he had asked this mercy of Christ as the Messiah. The Lord therefore in his royal majesty asked Bartimæus to name the mercy, thus suggesting to him the fullness of the treasury of power and grace to which he came. He was not to blame for this.] ª34 And Jesus, being moved with compassion, touched their eyes; ᵇ52 And Jesus said unto him, Go thy way; ᶜReceive thy sight: thy faith hath made thee whole. [We can see in this instance what faith really is. It caused Bartimæus to cry out, to come to Jesus and to ask for sight. Thus we see that faith saves by leading to proper actions.] 43 And immediately ªstraight-way they {ᶜhe} ªreceived their {ᵇhis} sight, ªand followed him. ᵇin the way. ᶜglorifying God: and all the people, when they saw it, gave praise unto God. [Being a beggar, it would have been natural for him to hunt first for means of livelihood, but faith and gratitude prompted him to follow Jesus.]

CIII.

ZACCHÆUS, PARABLE OF THE POUNDS, JOURNEY TO JERUSALEM.

(Jericho.)

^cLUKE XIX. 1-28.

^c**And he entered and was passing through Jericho.** [This was about one week before the crucifixion. Jericho is about seven miles from the Jordan and about seventeen and a half from Jerusalem.] **2 And behold, a man called by name Zacchaeus; and he was a chief publican, and he was rich.** [See p. 76. It is probable that Zacchæus was a sub-contractor under some Roman knight who had bought the privilege of collecting taxes at Jericho, or perhaps the privilege of all Judæa. As the Jordan separated between the provinces of Judæa and Peræa, and as Jericho was the border city between these two provinces, the custom duties of the place were apt to be considerable. The famous balm of Gilead was cultivated in Peræa, and probably added considerably to the trade which passed through Jericho. Herod the Great had raised Jericho to opulence, and to be rich in such a city was no small matter. Zacchæus had not consented to become a social outcast without reaping his reward.] **3 And he sought to see Jesus who he was; and could not for the crowd, because he was little of stature.** [Jericho had been filled with reports about Jesus, and great excitement existed among the people. Zacchæus shared this excitement.] **4 And he ran on before, and climbed up into a sycamore tree to see him: for he was to pass that way.** [This tree differs from the sycamine, and grows only in those parts of Palestine where the climate is warmest. It is the wild fig, and because of its low trunk and spreading branches it is very easy to climb. The sycamore which grows along our streams is the "buttonwood," and is in no way related to the fig family.] **5 And when Jesus came to the**

place, he looked up, and said unto him, Zacchaeus, make haste, and come down ; for to-day I must abide at thy house. [This is the only instance where Jesus invited himself to be any man's guest. He knew the feeling of Zacchæus toward him as well as he knew his name, and hence had no doubt as to his welcome. Jesus says " I must." Love constrained him to pause in Jericho that he might save the house of Zacchæus.] **6 And he made haste, and came down, and received him joyfully.** [Glad that he had obtained not only the wished-for sight of Jesus, but a favor which he had not dared to hope for. To be thus honored of the Messiah was balm indeed to the outcast's heart.] **7 And when they saw it, they all murmured, saying, He is gone in to lodge with a man that is a sinner.** [See pp. 349 and 499. The "all" in this case does not include Jesus' disciples. Jesus was a constant disappointment to those who were seeking to make him an earthly king and who therefore desired him to manifest a kingly pride.] **8 And Zacchaeus stood, and said unto the Lord, Behold, Lord, the half of my goods I give to the poor ; and if I have wrongfully exacted aught of any man, I restore fourfold.** [Zacchæus stood to give emphasis and publicity to his words. He does not mean that he is in the habit of giving half his goods to the poor, but that he does so now, immediately, on the spot, without delay. He does not merely promise to do so hereafter, or to make such a provision in his will. The laws of restoration in cases of theft or fraud will be found at Ex. xxii. 1-4; Num. v. 7. The proposition of Zacchæus to restore fourfold suggests that the bulk of his wealth had not been gained in dishonest ways, for if so he would not have been able to make such a restitution.] **9 And Jesus said unto him, To-day is salvation come to this house, forasmuch as he also is a son of Abraham. 10 For the Son of man came to seek and to save that which was lost.** [The visit of Jesus had converted Zacchæus and brought salvation to his house. Though as yet Jesus was sent only to the lost sheep of the house of Israel (Matt. xv. 24), and was not proclaiming

salvation to the Gentiles, yet he could consistently receive
Zacchæus, for, though an outcast publican, he had not so for-
feited his sonship in Abraham as to bar him from this right.
He was one of the "lost sheep," the very class to which Jesus
was sent.] **11 And as they heard these things, he added
and spake a parable, because he was nigh to Jerusalem,
and *because* they supposed that the kingdom of God
was immediately to appear.** [The opening words show
that the parable which follows was spoken in the house of
Zacchæus. So far as the record shows, this was the first time
in his ministry that Jesus ever approached Jerusalem with a
crowd. By thus approaching it with a multitude it seemed to
the people that Jesus was consenting to be crowned. And
they were filled with those dreams and expectations which a
few days later resulted in the triumphal entry. All things
pointed to a crisis, and the people were eagerly looking for
honors and rewards under the new ruler. Jesus corrected
these false hopes by a parable which showed that there must
be patient waiting and faithful work before there could be any
season of reward.] **12 He said therefore, A certain nobleman went into a far country, to receive for himself a
kingdom, and to return.** [Those present were looking for the
crowning of Jesus at Jerusalem, but he was to ascend into that
far country called heaven and was there to receive the kingdom
of the earth (Acts ii. 32, 33; Matt. xxviii. 18) and his return
in kingly majesty is yet to take place—I. Cor. xi. 26.] **13
And he called ten servants of his, and gave them ten
pounds, and said unto them, Trade ye *herewith* till I
come.** [To each of the servants he gave a crown, which was
equal to about seventeen dollars of our money. It was a paltry
sum for a nobleman and suggests a state of poverty and humiliation such as would give small incentive to any to remain faithful to his service.] **14 But his citizens hated him, and
sent an ambassage after him, saying, We will not that
this man reign over us.** [In addition to the servants, this
nobleman had citizens, or subjects who owed him respect and
reverence pending the confirmation of his kingdom, and hom-

age and obedience after that confirmation. But their hatred of
him led them to oppose his confirmation, saying, "We will
not," etc. These citizens represented the Jews, and Theophy-
lact well observes how near the Jews came to repeating these
very words of rejection when they said to Pilate, "We have no
king but Cæsar. . . . Write not the King of the Jews."] **15
And it came to pass, when he was come back again,
having received the kingdom, that he commanded these
servants, unto whom he had given the money, to be
called to him, that he might know what they had gained
by trading. 16 And the first came before him, saying,
Lord, thy pound hath made ten pounds more.** [Thus
Jesus shall call us to account for our stewardship (II. Cor. v.
10), and some, despite the long absence of their Lord, and the
rebellion of the citizens, will be found to have been faithful.
As to this servant's answer Grotius says (comparing it with I.
Cor. xv. 10), "He modestly attributes this to his lord's money,
and not to his own work."] **17 And he said unto him,
Well done, thou good servant: because thou wast
found faithful in a very little, have thou authority over
ten cities.** [Thus by small faithfulness are we proved worthy
of great trust (II. Cor. iv. 17). We should note that while
the bounty is royal, yet it is proportionate. It suggests
the difference in estate between the nobleman who departed
and the king who returned.] **18 And the second came,
saying, Thy pound, Lord, hath made five pounds. 19
And he said unto him also, Be thou also over five cities.**
[The faithful servants are promoted to be rulers (II. Tim. ii.
12). The nobleman, having been of low estate himself, could
sympathize with his servants and delight in promoting them—
Phil. ii. 7.] **20 And another came, saying, Lord, behold,
here is thy pound, which I kept laid up in a napkin**
[Having no banks in which to store money, such as we have, the
men of Palestine usually concealed it. At the present time the
people of that land are accustomed to bury their money in the
ground within their houses]: **21 for I feared thee, because
thou art an austere man: thou takest up that which**

thou layedst not down, and reapest that which thou didst not sow. [He impudently criticizes his lord, saying that he was one hard to please and one who expected others to do all the work and let him reap all the gain. The injustice of his criticism had just been exposed beforehand by the king's treatment of the two preceding servants. This servant represents those who make the labors and difficulties of the Christian life an excuse for doing nothing.] **22 He saith unto him, Out of thine own mouth will I judge thee, thou wicked servant. Thou knewest that I am an austere man, taking up that which I laid not down, and reaping that which I did not sow; 23 then wherefore gavest thou not my money into the bank, and I at my coming should have required it with interest?** [The king patiently grants for argument's sake all that is urged, but shows that even so, the conduct of this servant could not be justified. Thus no argument can justify the sinner who contends against God. The word here translated "bank" means the table of the money-changer and is so translated at Matt. xxi. 12; Mark xi. 15, and John ii. 15. It would appear from this passage that the money-changers were willing to borrow and pay some rate of interest. The bank, therefore, was not a thing incorporated and watched by the government, but merely an individual with whom money might be secure or not, according to his personal honesty. Our present banking system has been the slow growth of many centuries. The lesson taught is that we should work with others if we have not self-confidence enough to work alone.] **24 And he said unto them that stood by, Take away from him the pound, and give it unto him that hath the ten pounds. 25 And they said unto him, Lord, he hath ten pounds. 26 I say unto you, that unto every one that hath shall be given; but from him that hath not, even that which he hath shall be taken away from him.** [See p. 331. The meaning here is that every one who makes use of what he has shall increase his powers, a rule which applies to all the affairs of life.] **27 But these mine enemies, that would not that I should reign over them,**

bring hither, and slay them before me. [A reference in the first instance to the Jews who were citizens of Christ's kingdom and who were justly destroyed for rejecting him when he ascended his throne. A reference in the second instance to all the inhabitants of the globe who are all in his kingdom and who shall be destroyed at his coming if they have rejected him. It is a fearful thing to contemplate the destruction of sinners, but it is more fearful to think of sin, rebellion and uncleanness being tolerated forever.] **28 And when he had thus spoken, he went on before, going up to Jerusalem.** [The crowd had paused, waiting for Jesus, and he now leads on toward Jerusalem.]

PART SEVEN.

LAST WEEK OF OUR LORD'S MINISTRY, THE FOURTH PASSOVER, THE CRUCIFIXION.

CIV.

JESUS ARRIVES AND IS FEASTED AT BETHANY

(From Friday Afternoon till Saturday Night, March 31 and April' 1, A. D. 30.)

ᵈJOHN XI. 55-57; xii. 1-11; ªMatt. xxvi. 6-13; ᵇMark xiv. 3-9.

ᵈ**55 Now the passover of the Jews was at hand: and many went up to Jerusalem out of the country before the passover, to purify themselves.** [These Jews went up before the passover that they might have time to purify themselves from ceremonial uncleanness before the feast. They were expected to purify before any important event (Ex. xix. 10, 11), and did so before the passover (II. Chron. xxx. 13-20), for those who were ceremonially unclean were excluded from it—John xviii. 28.] **56 They sought therefore for Jesus, and spake one with another, as they stood in the temple, What think ye? That he will not come to the feast? 57 Now the chief priests and the Pharisees had given commandment, that, if any man knew where he was, he should show it, that they might take him.** [The decree of the Sanhedrin ordering the arrest of Jesus led the people to question as to whether he would dare to approach the city. But this mention of it and the stir and question which it created have a dark significance. It shows that the Jews generally were forewarned of the evil purpose of the Sanhedrin, and the dangers which surrounded Jesus. They were not taken unawares when their rulers told them to raise the cry "Crucify him!" And they raised it after they had due notice and time for deliberation.] ᵈ1 **Jesus therefore six days before the passover came to Bethany, where Lazarus was, whom Jesus raised from the dead.** [The word "therefore" refers to the decree and the consequent dangers just mentioned. Because his "hour" had come Jesus went to face these dangers. We are told that he came to the house of Lazarus and that he kept near Lazarus because these facts emphasized the great miracle which roused the hatred of the Jews, and caused them more earnestly to seek the death of Christ. Jesus appears to have arrived in Bethany Friday afternoon, March 31, A. D. 30. It is likely that he spent the Sabbath day at that place, and that the supper mentioned below was given him after sunset on Saturday, which, according to Jewish reckoning, would be the beginning of Sunday. This supper is mentioned later by Matthew and Mark, but without any note of time to show that it belongs specifically where they put it. But John does give us a note of time. The twelfth verse of this chapter shows that it was the night before the triumphal entry, and therefore we follow the chronology of John.] **2 So ᵃ6 Now when Jesus was in Bethany, ᵈthey made him a supper there: ᵃin the house of Simon the leper, ᵈand Martha served; but Lazarus was one of them that sat at meat with him.** [Who Simon the leper was is not known. It is not unlikely that he was one whom Jesus had healed, and that he united with the household of Lazarus in a joint effort to show gratitude unto the Lord for his goodness to this group of his friends.] ᵇ**3 And while he was** [there] **as he sat at meat, there came ᵃunto him a woman** {ᵈ3 **Mary**} ᵃ**having an alabaster cruse of exceeding precious ointment, ᵇof pure nard very costly;** ᵈ**3 Mary therefore took a pound** [a *litra*, a Greek weight containing nearly twelve ounces avoirdupois] **of ointment of pure nard, very precious** [Nard was a liquid perfume distilled from some odorous plant or plants and mingled with oil. It was sealed in flasks or alabaster boxes and imported from the far East], ᵇ*and* **she brake the cruse, and poured it over** {ᵃ **upon**} ᵇ**his head. ᵃas he sat at meat. ᵈand anointed**

the feet of Jesus, and wiped his feet with her hair [The
cruse seems to have been a long-necked flask sealed with wax
so tightly as to necessitate it being broken to extract the nard.
These flasks were tasteful and costly objects such as women
delight to possess. Many of them were so delicate that Pliny
compares them to closed rosebuds, and the same writer, speaking of nard, reckons it as an instance of excessive luxury to
anoint the feet or ankles with it] : **and the house was
filled with the odor of the ointment.** [Thus the liberality
of Mary contributed to the pleasure of all the guests. The
odor of a good deed is generally diffusive.] **4 But Judas
Iscariot, one of the disciples, that should betray him,
saith, 5 Why was not this ointment sold for three
hundred shillings, and given to the poor? 6 Now this
he said, not because he cared for the poor; but because
he was a thief, and having the bag took away what
was put therein.** ᵃ**8 But when the disciples saw it,
they {**ᵇ**there were some that} had indignation among
themselves,** ᵃ**saying, To what purpose is this waste?**
ᵇ**To what purpose hath this waste of the ointment
been made? 5 For this ointment might have been
sold** ᵃ**for much,** ᵇ**for above three hundred shillings,
and given to the poor. And they murmured against
her.** [It seems very likely that this murmuring was started
by Judas Iscariot, for the murmurers fall in with his notions
that the price of the ointment should be deposited in the poor
fund. It is a singular thing that Jesus permitted a thief to
occupy the office of treasurer. It is probable that Judas was
honest when he was called to serve, but that the same management and spirit of economy which made him fit for the place
ruined him when he got it. Thus our strong points are often
our weakest. The price of the pound of nard would be about
fifty-one dollars of our money, but the purchasing power of
money was then nearly ten times as great as it is now. The
price here named agrees almost exactly with the figures at
which Pliny rates the most costly nard.] ᵃ**10 But Jesus
perceiving it** ᵈ**therefore said,** ᵃ**unto them,** ᵇ**Let her**

alone; ᵃ Why trouble ye the woman? for she hath
wrought a good work upon me.   ᵈ Suffer her to keep it
against the day of my burying.   ᵃ 12 For in that she
poured this ointment upon my body, she did it to prepare me for burial.   ᵇ 8 She hath done what she could;
she hath anointed my body beforehand for the burying.
[The expression " Suffer," etc., used by John, is taken by
some as implying that all the ointment was not poured out,
and that some of the apostles were endeavoring to persuade
Mary to keep and sell what was left, and that Jesus ordered it
kept to finish the embalming of his body which Mary had already begun.   But there is nothing in the language to require
such an interpretation.   Jesus meant, "Let her use it rightly,"
using the word "keep" as in the expression, "keep the feast;"
i. e., observe the ceremony.   The words of Jesus about the
ointment taken as a whole may be construed thus : " The sorrows of my coming passion oppress me (Matt. xxvi. 38), and
Mary, conscious of that sorrow, wishes to cheer me with the
evidence of her love and gratitude.   She sympathizes with me
as I approach the shadow of death, and anoints me beforehand
for the burial.   You do not begrudge what is given to the
dead.   You do not censure as extravagant what is spent for
the embalming of a dear one.   You yourselves would be ready
enough to anoint me in this same manner after I am dead.   So
do not censure her because in the fullness of her sympathy she
has anticipated the coming catastrophe and has anointed me
beforehand."]   ᵈ 8 For the poor ye have always with
you [Deut. xv. 11] ; ᵇ and whensoever ye will ye can do
them good : but me ye have not always.   [There would
be plenty of opportunities in which to do good to the poor, but
the time for conferring a personal benefit upon Christ in the
flesh was now limited to seven days.   Thereafter gifts could
only be given to Christ by bestowing them upon the poor.]   9
And verily I say unto you, Wheresoever the {ᵃ this}
gospel shall be preached in {ᵇ throughout} the whole
world, that also which this woman hath done shall be
spoken of for a memorial of her.   [Jesus here makes

prominent the different estimates which God and man place upon the same acts. That which the disciples had censured as a waste and that which they had regarded as worthy of rebuke was in his sight an action fit to be kept in everlasting remembrance as a model for the conduct of future generations throughout the whole earth, and he accordingly decreed that it be so kept in mind.] **ᵈ9 The common people therefore of the Jews learned that he was there** [in Simon's house]: **and they came, not for Jesus' sake only, but that they might see Lazarus also, whom he had raised from the dead. 10 But the chief priests took counsel that they might put Lazarus also to death; 11 because that by reason of him many of the Jews went away** [withdrew from the party headed by the Jewish rulers], **and believed on Jesus.** [The presence of the resurrected man and the Christ who had resurrected him both at one table greatly excited the curiosity of the multitudes who had come up to Jerusalem to attend the passover. When word of this supper spread among the people it was natural that they should slip out to Bethany to see the sight, and it was equally natural that seeing it they should believe in Jesus. This deflection of the common people gave a keener venom to the hatred of the rulers.

CV.

JESUS' TRIUMPHAL ENTRY INTO JERUSALEM.

FROM BETHANY TO JERUSALEM AND BACK.

(Sunday, April 2, A. D. 30.)

ᵃ MATT. XXI. 1-12, 14-17; ᵇ MARK XI. 1-11; ᶜ LUKE XIX. 29-44; ᵈ JOHN XII. 12-19.

ᶜ **29 And** ᵈ **12 On the morrow** [after the feast in the house of Simon the leper] ᶜ **it came to pass, when he drew nigh unto Bethphage and Bethany, at the mount that is called Olivet,** ᵃ **1 And when they drew nigh unto Jeru-**

salem, and came unto Bethphage, unto{ ᵇ at}ᵃ the mount
of Olives [The name, Bethphage, is said to mean *house of
figs*, but the derivation is disputed. Canon Cook and others
think that the region on the eastern slope of Olivet was called
Bethphage, and that Bethany was located in it. If it was a village, all trace of it has long since vanished, and it is not worth
while to give the guesses and surmises of commentators as to
its location. But it was evidently near Bethany], then Jesus
sent { ᵇ sendeth} two of his { ᶜ the} disciples, ᵇ 2 and
saith { ᵃ 2 saying} unto them, ᶜ Go your way into the
village [probably Bethphage, for Jesus started from Bethany]
ᵃ that is over against you, ᵇ and straightway as ye enter
into it, ᵃ ye shall find an ass tied, and a colt ᵇ tied,
ᵃ with her : ᵇ whereon no man ever yet sat ; loose him,
{ ᵃ *them*,} ᵇ and bring him. { ᵃ *them*} unto me. [Numerous
Scripture references show that the ass was held in high estimation in the East. The sons of the judges used them, and
David's mule was used at the coronation of Solomon (Judg.
x. 4 ; I. Kings i. 33). It is specifically stated that no man had
ever sat upon this colt, for if the colt had been used by men it
would have been unfit for sacred purposes—Num. xix. 2 ;
Deut. xxi. 3 ; I. Sam. vi. 7.] 3 And if any one say aught
unto you, ᶜ 31 And if any one ask you, { ᵇ say unto
you,} Why do ye this ? ᶜ Why do ye loose him ? thus
shall ye say, The Lord hath need of him. { ᵃ them ;}
ᵇ and straightway he will send him { ᵃ them.} ᵇ back
hither. [The owner of the ass was no doubt a disciple or
well-wisher of Jesus, and therefore readily consented to re-
spond to the Master's need. Such a well-wisher might readily be found in a multitude ready to lay their garments in the
road to honor Christ. The words "send him back" are
usually construed to be a promise on the part of Christ that he
would return the colt when through with him. But such a
promise seems rather out of keeping with the dignity of the occasion. We prefer to construe the words as referring to the
movements of Christ's two messengers from the neighborhood
of Bethany to Bethphage and back again, or to a backward

movement along the caravan's line of march.] ᵃ4 **Now this is come to pass, that it might be fulfilled which was spoken through the prophet, saying, 5 Tell ye the daughter of Zion** [the poetical name for the city of Jerusalem], **Behold, thy King cometh unto thee, Meek, and riding upon an ass, And upon a colt the foal of an ass.** [The prophecy is a combination of Isa. lxii. 11 and Zech. ix. 9. This is the only instance given in which Jesus rode. He entered in meekness, for the ass was a symbol of peace as the horse was of war (Job xxxix. 19-25), but there was nothing degrading about riding such a beast. The Eastern ass is smaller, but livelier, and better framed than the specimens found in our country. They constituted a chief asset in the property of the wealthy—Gen. xii. 16; xxx. 43; Job xlii. 12; I. Chron. xxvii. 30; I. Kings i. 38.] **6 And the disciples** {ᶜthey} **that were sent went away,** ᵃ**and did even as Jesus appointed them,** ᶜ**and found even as he had said unto them.** ᵇ**a colt tied at the door without in the open street** [the streets being narrow, one would very seldom see an ass tied in one]; **and they loose him.** ᶜ**33 And as they were loosing the colt,** ᵇ**certain of them that stood there** ᶜ**the owners thereof said unto them, Why loose ye the colt?** ᵇ **What do ye, loosing the colt? 6 And they said unto them even as Jesus had said: and they let them go. 7 And they bring** {ᵃbrought} **the ass, and the colt,** {ᶜhim} ᵇ **unto Jesus,** ᵃ**and put on them their garments** [The garments were the loose cloaks worn over the tunics or shirts. This cloak survives in the abba or hyke of the modern Arab. The unbroken colt would of course have no saddle, and these loyal disciples lent their cloaks to supply the deficiency, and to do Jesus royal honor. Compare the enthronement of Jehu (II. Kings ix. 12). They prepared both beasts, not knowing which he would choose to ride]; ᶜ**and they threw** {ᵇcast} ᶜ**their garments upon the colt, and set Jesus thereon.** ᵃ**and he sat thereon.** {ᵇ**upon him.**} ᵈ**a great multitude that had come to the feast, when they heard that Jesus was coming to Je-**

rusalem, **13 took the branches of the palm trees, and
went forth to meet him** [Palm-trees were never abundant
in Palestine, but there were many around Jericho, through
which city these Galilean pilgrims had so recently come.
They were date palms, the leaves of which were often ten feet
in length. They are now comparatively rare, but are found in
the plains of Philistia. The palm branch is emblematic of
triumph and victory—Lev. xxiii. 40; Rev. vii. 9; I. Macc.
xiii. 51; II. Macc. x. 7], **and cried out, Hosanna:
Blessed** *is* **he that cometh in the name of the Lord, even
the King of Israel.** [The shouting appears to have been
started by those who came out from Jerusalem; it is evident,
therefore, that the apostles who were approaching the city with
Jesus had nothing to do with inciting this praise.] **14 And
Jesus having found a young ass, sat thereon; as it is
written, 15 Fear not, daughter of Zion: behold, thy
King cometh, sitting on an ass's colt. 16 These
things understood not his disciples at the first: but
when Jesus was glorified, then remembered they that
these things were written of him, and that they had
done these things unto him.** [The apostles were not conscious that the prophecies were being fulfilled nor did they understand that Jesus was approaching a heavenly rather than an
earthly coronation. But after Jesus was glorified, their under-
standings were spiritually illuminated (John xvi. 13). They not
only remembered the prophecy, but saw in what sense it was
that Jesus was king, and how badly mistaken they had been
when they expected him to antagonize the Romans. The
greatness of her king would have removed all cause for fear if
Jerusalem had but accepted him.] **17 The multitude therefore that was with him when he called Lazarus out of
the tomb, and raised him from the dead, bare witness.**
[The two parts of the miracle—the calling and the raising—
are both mentioned as alike impressive, sublime and wonderful.] **18 For this cause also the multitude went and
met him, for that they heard that he had done this
sign.** [It is evident from this that the testimony of those **who**

witnessed the raising of Lazarus had enthused the pilgrims in Jerusalem and had sent a large band of them forth charged with that ardent admiration which produced the shouting of the triumphant entry.] **19 The Pharisees therefore said among themselves, Behold how ye prevail nothing; lo, the world is gone after him.** [Again, as at John xi. 47-49, we notice the self-confessed impotency of the Pharisees, but the Sadducees, under the determined and more resolute leadership of Caiaphas, did not participate in this despair. The Pharisees speak of the world as if its acquisition by Jesus was their loss.] **ᶜ36 And as he went, ᵃ the most part of the multitude {ᵇ many}** [Matthew would have us know that the demonstration was no small affair, but was well-nigh universal. Josephus estimates that the number present at one passover was three million, or about one-half the population of Judæa and Galilee. The language of the Pharisees in verse 19 above—"the world"—shows that there must have been indeed an immense multitude. The people had always been ready to acknowledge Jesus as king, and, seeing that he had now an evident disposition to accept their homage, they hastened to render it] **spread their garments upon {ᵃ in} ᵇ the way; and others ᵃ spread ᵇ branches, ᵃ in the way. ᵇ which they {ᵃ cut} ᵇ had cut from the fields. {ᵃ trees,}** [It has been the custom of all lands to bestrew in some manner the pathway of those who are thought worthy of the highest honor. When Lafayette visited our fathers after the Revolution the roads over which he approached our cities were strewn with flowers. Thus over flowers Alexander entered Babylon, and Xerxes crossed the bridge of the Hellespont over a myrtle-strewn pathway. Monier tells of a Persian ruler who in modern times made his honored progress over a road covered for three miles with roses. But it is more natural to contrast the entry of Jesus with the Roman triumphs so popular in that day. The wealth of conquered kingdoms was expended to insure their magnificence. We find none of that tinsel and specious glitter in the triumph of Christ. No hired multitudes applaud him; no gold-broidered banners wave in his honor. There is nothing here but the lusty, honest shout of the common people, and the swaying of the God-made banners of the royal palms. The rich in purse, the learned in schoolcraft and the high in office were, as usual, not there—I. Cor. i. 26.] ᶜ **37 And as he was now drawing nigh,** *even* **at the descent of the mount of Olives, the whole multitude of the disciples began to rejoice and praise God with a loud voice for all the mighty works which they had seen** [John has shown us just above that the raising of Lazarus was most prominent in their thoughts]; ᵃ **9 And the multitudes that went before him, and that followed** [Jesus approached the city leading a multitude of pilgrims, and we have seen from John's account above that another multitude came out of the city to meet him: Jesus approached the city between two great multitudes], **cried, saying,** ᵇ **Hosanna** [This is the Greek form or spelling of the two Hebrew words, Hoshiah-na, which means, Save now, or, Save, I pray, na being a particle of entreaty added to imperatives. The two words are taken from Ps. cxviii. 25, which was recognized as the Messianic Psalm. The shout " Hosanna" was customarily used at the feast of the tabernacles and the other festivals. It was a shout of exultation about equivalent to " Salvation "]; ᵃ **Hosanna to the son of David** [see p. 357]: **blessed** *is* **he that cometh in the name of the Lord** [Ps. cxviii. 26]; ᶜ **blessed** *is* **the King that cometh in the name of the Lord:** ᵇ **10 blessed** *is* **the kingdom that cometh, the** *kingdom* **of our father David:** ᶜ **peace in heaven, and glory in the highest.** ᵃ **Hosanna in the highest.** [This phrase is taken to mean in the highest degree or highest strains or in the highest heavens. It is likely that they were calling upon heaven to participate in glorifying and to ratify their shouts of salvation. The Evangelists give us the various cries of the multitude, for they did not all cry one thing. The cries, if seriously construed, were a fore-recognition of the Messiahship of Jesus, but popular cries are soon caught up and are as fickle as the impulses which beget them. But this public recognition of the Messiahship of Jesus gave

578 THE FOURFOLD GOSPEL.

weight to the accusation made by Simon Peter on the day of
Pentecost that they had slain the Messiah—Acts ii. 36. Comp.
Acts iii. 14, 15.] ^c**39 And some of the Pharisees from
the multitude** [not a committee sent from Jerusalem for
that purpose] **said unto him, Teacher, rebuke thy disciples.** [It is possible that these may have been moved with an
honest fear that the enthusiasm of the people would call down
the vengeance of the Romans (John xi. 48), but it is more likely
that they were prompted solely by envy.] **40 And he answered and said, I tell you that, if these shall hold their
peace, the stones will cry out.** [The expression is probably
proverbial (Hab. ii. 11). The meaning is that the occasion of
the great King's visit to his city (Matt. v. 35) was so momentous
that, if man withheld his praise, inanimate nature would lend
its acclamations.] **41 And when he drew nigh, he saw
the city and wept over it, 42 saying, If thou hadst
known in this day, even thou, the things which belong
unto peace! but now they are hid from thine eyes.**
[The summit of Olivet is two hundred feet higher than the
nearest part of the city of Jerusalem and a hundred feet higher
than its farthest part, so that the Lord looked upon the
whole of it as one looks upon an open book. As he looked upon
it he realized the difference between what his coming might
mean to it and what it did mean to it; between the love and
gratitude which his coming should have incited and the hatred
and violence which it did incite; between the forgiveness,
blessing and peace which he desired to bring it and the judgment, wrath and destruction which were coming upon it. The
vision of it all excited strong emotion, and the verb used does
not indicate silent tears, but audible sobbing and lamentation.
The day then passing was among the last before the crucifixion, which would present to the Jews a strong motive for repentance. Had Jerusalem hearkened unto Jesus then, he would
have saved her from that self-exaltation which proved her ruin.
But bigotry and prejudice blinded her eyes.] **43 For the
days shall come upon thee, when thine enemies shall
cast up a bank about thee, and compass thee round,**

and keep thee in on every side [from where Jesus then stood he could see the houses which were to be thrown down, he could locate the embankments which would be built, and he could trace almost every foot of the line of the wall by which Titus in his anger girdled the city when his embankments were burned—Jos. Wars V. 6. 2, 11. 4-6, 12. 1, 2], **44 and shall dash thee to the ground, and thy children within thee** [the city is figuratively spoken of as a mother, and her citizens as her children]; **and they shall not leave in thee one stone upon another; because thou knewest not the time of thy visitation.** [The term "visitation" usually refers to a season of judgment, but here, as elsewhere also (Ex. iv. 31), it means a season of grace. To not leave one stone upon another is a proverbial expression descriptive of a complete demolition, but in the overthrow of Jerusalem it was well-nigh literally fulfilled. Thus, while the people rejoiced in the present triumph, the prophetic eye and ear of our Lord beheld the judgments which were coming upon the city, heard the bitter cry of the starved defenders during the siege, the screams of the crucified left to perish upon their crosses after its capture, all ending in the final silence of desolation when not one stone was left upon another.] [b] **11 And he entered into Jerusalem** [his route led him down the steep face of Olivet, past Gethsemane, across the stone bridge which spans the Kedron, and up the slope of Moriah to the eastern gate of the city], [a] **10 And when he was come into Jerusalem, all the city was stirred, saying, Who is this? 11 And the multitudes said, This is the prophet, Jesus, from Nazareth of Galilee. 12 And Jesus entered into the temple of God** [here Matthew tells of the cleansing of the temple which evidently occurred the next day], **14 And the blind and the lame came to him in the temple; and he healed them. 15 But when the chief priests and the scribes saw the wonderful things that he did, and the children that were crying in the temple and saying, Hosanna to the son of David; they were moved with indignation, 16 and said unto him, Hearest thou what**

these are saying? And Jesus saith unto them, Yea:
did ye never read [Ps. viii. 2 as rendered by the LXX.],
Out of the mouth of babes and sucklings thou hast
perfected praise? [Matthew mingles this scene with events
which apparently occurred on Monday, but the enthusiasm and
the Hosanna cry evidently belonged to the triumphant Sunday.* The presence of our Lord in the temple should, indeed,
have been heralded with joy, for as that was the day in which
the paschal lamb was presented and set apart, it was fitting
that Christ our passover should thus be presented there amidst
rejoicing.] ᵇ and when he had looked round about upon all
things, it being now eventide [a general expression covering the period both before and after sunset], ᵃ he left them,
and went forth out of the city ᵇ unto Bethany with
the twelve. ᵃ and lodged there. [Having inspected the
temple as his Father's house, Jesus withdrew from it, for in
the present state of rancor which fermented within his enemies
it was not safe for him to spend the night within Jerusalem.]

CVI.

BARREN FIG-TREE. TEMPLE CLEANSED.

(Road from Bethany and Jerusalem. Monday.)

ᵃ MATT. XXI. 18, 19, 12, 13 ; ᵇ MARK XI. 12-18;
ᶜ LUKE XIX. 45-48.

ᵇ 12 And ᵃ 18 Now ᵇ on the morrow [on the Monday
after the triumphal entry], ᵃ in the morning ᵇ when they
were come out from Bethany, ᵃ as he returned to the
city [Jerusalem], he hungered. [Breakfast with the Jews
came late in the forenoon, and these closing days of our Lord's
ministry were so full of activity that he did not have time to
tarry at Bethany for it. Our Lord's hunger implies that of the
disciples also.] 19 And seeing a fig tree by the way side,
ᵇ afar off having leaves, ᵃ he came to it, ᵇ if haply he
might find anything thereon: and when he came to it,

he ᵃ found nothing thereon, but leaves only; ᵇ for it was not the season of figs. [Two varieties of figs are common in Palestine, the bicura or boccore, an early fig with large green leaves and with fruit which ripens in May or June, and sometimes earlier near Jerusalem. Thomson found ripe fruit of this variety as early as May in the mountains of Lebanon, one hundred and fifty miles north of Jerusalem, and Professor Post, of Beyrut, states that fig-trees there have fruit formed as early as February, which is fully ripe in April. The second variety is the summer fig or kermus. This ripens its main crop in August, but its later fruitage often hangs on all winter when the weather is mild, dropping off when the new spring leaves come. As the fruit usually appears before the leaves, the leaves were a promise that fruit might be found, and the fruit, though not perfectly ripe, is considered edible when the leaves are developed. Though it was too early for fruit, it was also too early for leaves. The tree evidently had an unusually favorable position. It seemed to vaunt itself by being in advance of the other trees, and to challenge the wayfarer to come and refresh himself.] **14 And he answered and said {ᵃ saith} unto it, Let there be no fruit from thee henceforward for ever. ᵇ No man eat fruit from thee henceforward for ever. And his disciples heard it. ᵃ And immediately the fig tree withered away.** [The disciples did not pause to watch the effect of Christ's words upon the tree. But from the degree to which it had shriveled when they saw it next day it became evident to them that it had begun to wither as soon as Christ had finished uttering its sentence. Our Lord here performed a miracle of judgment unlike any other of his wonderful works. The reader can hardly fail to note how perfectly this fig-tree, in its separation from the other trees, its showy pretensions, its barrenness of results and its judgment typifies the Jewish people. In fact, Christ's treatment of it appears in some respects to be a visible and practical application of the principles which he had formerly set forth in a parable (Luke xiii. 6-9). But we must not too confidently make such an application of the parable since Jesus himself gave no hint that he intended us so to apply it.] ᵇ15 **And they come to Jerusalem: and he entered into the temple, and began to cast out** ᵃ**all them that sold** ᵇ**and them that bought in the temple, and overthrew the tables of the moneychangers, and the seats of them that sold the doves** [three years before, Jesus had thus cleansed the temple at the first passover of his ministry, for an account of which see pp. 121-125]; **16 and he would not suffer that any man should carry a vessel through the temple.** [The temple space being level and roomy tempted the people of Jerusalem to use it as a thoroughfare, or short-cut from one part of the city to another, but Jesus did not permit them to carry any sack, bag, jug, pail, basket, parcel or such like thing through the sacred enclosure. The Greek word *skeuos* which is here translated "vessel" embraces all kinds of household furniture. It is translated "goods" at Matt. xii. 29, and Luke xvii. 31. The LXX. uses it as equivalent to "instruments of war" at Deut. i. 41, and to "vestments" at Deut. xxii. 5.] **17 And he taught, and said** {ᵃ**saith**} ᶜ**46 saying unto them, It is written** [the prophecy cited is a combination of Isa. lvi. 7, and Jer. vii. 11], {ᵇ **Is it not written,** } ᶜ **And my house shall be** {ᵇ **shall be called**} **a house of prayer for all the nations? but ye have made** {ᵃ**ye make**} **it a den of robbers.** [The caves in certain sections of Palestine have been immemorially infested with robbers, and Jesus, because of the injustice of extortion practiced by the merchants, likens the polluted temple to such a den. The dickering and chafing and market talk were probably not unlike the grumbling and quarreling of thieves as they divide the booty.] ᵇ**18 And the chief priests and the scribes heard it, and sought how they might destroy him: for they feared him,** ᶜ**47 And he was teaching daily in the temple. But the chief priests and the scribes and the principal men of the people sought to destroy him: 48 and they could not find what they might do; for the people all hung upon him, listening.** ᵇ**for all the multitude was astonished at his teaching.** [Overawed by the magnitude of the popular demonstration made on Sunday, the Jewish rulers feared to attempt any violent measures in dealing with Jesus. But they neglected no opportunity by appeals to Jesus himself, by treacherous questions, etc., to divert the popular favor from the Lord that they might put him to death.]

CVII.

FINDING THE FIG-TREE WITHERED.

(Road from Bethany to Jerusalem. Tuesday.)

ᵃ MATT. XXI. 20-22; ᵇ MARK XI. 19-25; ᶜ LUKE XXI. 37, 38.

ᶜ **37 And every day he was teaching in the temple** [he was there Sunday, Monday and Tuesday, but he seems to have spent Wednesday and Thursday in Bethany]; **and every night** {ᵇ **evening**} **he went forth out of the city.** ᶜ **and lodged in the mount that is called Olivet.** [As Bethany was on the Mount of Olives, this statement leaves us free to suppose that he spent his nights there, but it is not likely that he retired to any one house or place continuously, for had he done so the rulers could easily have ascertained his whereabouts and arrested him.] **38 And all the people came early in the morning to him in the temple, to hear him.** [The enthusiasm of the triumphal entry did not die out in a day: Jesus was still the center of observation.] ᵇ **20 And as they passed by in the morning, they saw the fig tree withered away from the roots.** [It was completely withered —dead root and branch. We have observed before, p. 578, that one coming into Jerusalem from Bethany is apt to come down the steep side of Olivet, and that one returning to Bethany is apt to take the easier grade, though longer way, around the south end of the mountain. The fig-tree was apparently on this short road, and was sentenced Monday morning. The disciples, returning by the other or longer road to Bethany or its vicinity, did not see the tree Monday evening, but they saw it Tuesday morning, when they again came back by the short road. From these facts argue a method of coming and going, from which it may be fairly inferred that Jesus, on the day of his triumphal entry, approached Jerusalem by the short road, though Stanley, Edersheim, and many others, think he came in over the long road.] ᵃ **20 And when the disciples saw it, they marvelled, saying, How did the fig tree immediately wither away?** [Jesus had simply condemned it to fruitlessness, but his condemnation involved it in an evil which it justly deserved. The judgment of God reveals; and that which is dead in fact is by it made dead in appearance also.] ᵇ **21 And Peter calling to remembrance saith unto him, Rabbi, behold, the fig tree which thou cursedst** [devotedst to death] **is withered away.** [Peter is surprised both at the suddenness and at the fullness of the judgment. Since the miracles of Jesus, heretofore, had been only those of mercy, Peter boldly invited the Lord to discuss this miracle, hoping for more light on its meaning.] **22 And Jesus answering saith** {ᵃ answered and said} **unto them, ᵇ Have faith in God. 23 Verily I say unto you, ᵃ If ye have faith, and doubt not, ye shall not only do what is done to the fig tree, but even if ye** {ᵇ whosoever} **shall say unto this mountain** [Olivet], **Be thou taken up and cast into the sea ; and shall not doubt in his heart, but shall believe that what he saith cometh to pass ; he shall have it. ᵃ it shall be done. 22 And ᵇ 24 Therefore I say unto you, All things whatsoever ye pray and ask for,** {ᵃ ye shall ask in prayer,} ᵇ **believe that ye receive them, and ye shall have them.** {ᵃ believing, ye shall receive.** } [Jesus here lays down the broad general rule in the application of which we must be guided by other Scriptures. The rule is, indeed, liberal and gracious, and the limitations are just and reasonable. We must not expect to obtain that which it is unlawful for us to desire (Jas. iv. 2, 3), or which it is unwise for us to seek (II. Cor. xii. 7-9), nor must we selfishly run counter to the will of God (Luke xxii. 42; I. John v. 14, 15), nor must we expect that God shall perform a miracle for us, for miracles have ceased—in short, we

must pray to God in full remembrance of the relationship between us, we must consider that he is the Ruler and we his
subjects, and are not to think for one moment that by faith we
can alter this eternal, unchangeable relation.   The disciples
whom Jesus addressed were very soon to enter upon a task which
would seem to them as difficult as the removal of mountains.
The license and immorality of paganism, and the bigotry and
prejudice of Judaism, would seem insurmountable obstacles in
their pathway to success.   They needed to be assured that the
power of faith was superior to all these adverse forces, and
that the judgments of God could accomplish in a moment
changes which apparently could not be wrought out in the
tedious course of years.   As we to-day look back upon this
promise of Christ we can see that the mountains then standing
have, indeed, been removed ; and that which seemed vigorous
and flourishing has been blasted in a day.]   ᵇ **25 And whensoever ye stand** [a customary attitude—Luke xviii. 13] **praying, forgive, if ye have aught against any one; that
your Father also who is in heaven may forgive you
your trespasses.** [Forgiveness has already been enjoined
(see pp. 253, 254).   Here our Lord emphasizes the need of
forgiveness because he had just performed a miracle of judgment, and he wished his disciples to understand that they must
not exercise their miraculous gifts with a vengeful, unforgiving
spirit.   They must suffer evil and not retaliate with miracles
of judgment.]

CVIII.

IN REPLY TO THE QUESTIONS AS TO HIS AUTHORITY, JESUS GIVES THE THIRD GREAT GROUP OF PARABLES.

(In the Court of the Temple. Tuesday.)

Subdivision A.

INTRODUCTION.

^a MATT. XXI. 23-27; ^b MARK XI. 27-33; ^c LUKE XX. 1-8.

^c **1 And it came to pass, on one of the days,** ^b **they** [Jesus and the disciples] **come again to Jerusalem:** ^a **23 And when he was come into the temple,** ^b **and as he was walking in the temple** [The large outer court of the temple, known as the court of the Gentiles, was thronged during the feasts, and was no doubt the part selected by Jesus and his apostles when they taught or preached in the temple. We thrice find them on that side of it where Solomon's porch was located—John x. 23; Acts iii. 11; v. 23], ^c **as he was teaching the people and preaching the gospel** [viz.: "the time is fulfilled, and the kingdom of God is at hand: repent ye"— Mark i. 15], **there came upon him** {^b **come** ^a **unto him**} ^b **the chief priests, and the scribes, and** {^c **with**} **the elders;** {^a **of the people**} [the Sanhedrin (see p. 415). This committee of that august tribunal came in formal state and with a great show of authority, hoping to make it apparent to the people that Jesus was an unauthorized, self-appointed meddler in matters over which they had exclusive control.] ^c **2 and they spake,** ^b **28 and they said** {^c **saying**} **unto him Tell us: By what authority doest thou these things?** ^a **and** {^c **or**} **who is he that gave thee this authority?** ^b **to do these things?** [To regulate and control the affairs of the temple belonged unquestionably and exclusively to the priests and Levites. Knowing that Jesus had no authority from

any priest or from any scribe, they boldly challenged his right to cleanse the temple or to teach in it, feeling sure that to defend himself he would be forced to publicly declare himself as the Messiah and thus give them the matter for accusation which they had long scught—John x. 24.] ᵃ**24 And Jesus answered and said unto them,** ᶜ**I also will ask you a** {ᵃ **one**} **question, which if ye tell me,** ᵇ **and answer me,** ᵃ **I likewise will tell you by what authority I do these things. 25 The baptism of John, whence was it?** ᵇ **Was it from heaven, or from men? answer me.** [The question which Jesus asked was intimately and inseparably connected with the question which they had asked. Jesus, of course, did not derive his authority from John the Baptist, but John had testified plainly to the Messiahship of Jesus, and had, in no uncertain terms, designated Jesus as immeasurably greater than himself. Now, if the Pharisees admitted that John was a heaven-sent messenger or witness (of which fact his baptism was propounded as a test, since it was a religious ordinance introduced on his authority), then John had already answered the Sanhedrin that Jesus derived his authority from his Messiahship, and hence, all that the Sanhedrin had to do to satisfy their minds was simply to *believe* John. But if, on the other hand, the Pharisees rejected John's pretensions and claims as a heaven-sent messenger in the face of the almost universal popular conviction, then what use was there for Jesus to present his claims to so blind, bigoted and unreasoning a body?] **31 And they reasoned with themselves, saying, If we shall say, From heaven; he will say,** ᵃ **unto us, Why then did ye not believe him?** [When he testified to the Messiahship of Jesus (John i. 7, 15, 34; iii. 26-36; x. 40-42). The Sanhedrin could not admit that the messenger was heaven-sent and yet deny his testimony.] **26 But if we shall** {ᵇ **should we**} **say, From men—**ᶜ **all the people will stone us:** ᵃ **we fear the multitude; for all hold John as a prophet.** ᶜ **for they are persuaded that John was a prophet.** ᵇ **they feared the people: for all verily held John to be a prophet. 33 And they answered**

Jesus ^c that they knew not whence *it was.* ^a and said,
{^b say,} We know not. [It should be noted that in their
consultation there was no effort either to ascertain or to speak
the truth. The question as to whether John really was or was
not a prophet was in no sense the subject of their investigation. They were merely deciding what to say. They
were seeking for the most expedient answer, and as neither
truthful answer was expedient, they resolved to falsely deny
any knowledge of the case. Men of such brazen dishonesty
could not be dealt with openly and fairly as could sincere
seekers after truth.] And Jesus ^a also said {^b saith} unto
them, Neither tell I you by what authority I do these
things. [Their spoken lie was, "We know not," but their
inward and true answer was, "We will not tell," and Jesus answered the suppressed truth saying, "Neither tell I." How
readily the subtle minds of the Jewish people would justify
Jesus in thus declining to submit the question of his authority
to judges who at that very moment publicly confessed their inability to even hazard an opinion, much less render a decision,
as to the authority of John the Baptist, whose claims were in
popular estimation so obvious. It was plain that however
well these men might judge human credentials, the divine
testimonials of a prophet or of the Messiah were above their
carnal sphere. Thus Jesus put his enemies to confusion in
the first of the many conflicts of that perilous Tuesday. But
we may well imagine that they were rendered more bitter by
this evidence of a wisdom so much beyond any which they
possessed.]

Subdivision B.

PARABLE OF THE TWO SONS.

^a MATT. XXI. 28-32.

^a 28 But what think ye ? [By these words Jesus put
them on notice that he was about to propound something
which would require an answer, and therefore demanding the

strictest attention.] **A man had two sons** [the two sons
stand for the Jewish rulers and the Jewish common people]**;
and he came to the first, and said, Son, go work to-day
in the vineyard. 29 And he answered and said, I will
not : but afterward he repented himself, and went.** [The
common people made no special pretension to religious excellence, and the rulers regarded them as very careless about
the will or law of their Father, God, and made disparaging
contrasts between their own conduct and that of the people
(John vii. 48, 49). But this very same common people repented and did the will of God when they heard the preaching
of John the Baptist—Matt. iii. 5, 6.] **30 And he came to
the second** [the rulers], **and said likewise. And he answered and said, I *go*, sir : and went not.** [The rulers,
though all the while professing to be very zealous for the will
of God, utterly refused to enter the kingdom or to work therein
as God bade them to by the voice of John the Baptist—Matt.
iii. 7-9.] **31 Which of the two did the will of his
father? They say, The first.** [They gave the true answer and did not perceive that in so doing they confirmed a
parable which condemned themselves.] **Jesus saith unto
them, Verily I say unto you, that the publicans and
the harlots** [the very worst representatives of the common
people] **go into the kingdom of God before you.** [Rather
than you.] **32 For John came unto you in the way of
righteousness** [The term "righteousness," as Plumptre observes, seems used in a half-technical sense, as expressing the
aspect of righteousness which the Pharisees themselves recognized (Matt. vi. 1), and which includes, as its three great elements, the almsgiving, fasting, and prayer that were so conspicuous both in the life and the teaching of the Baptist. Surely
they could have had no true preacher of righteousness who
could have presented its demands in a form more acceptable to
the Jewish rulers], **and ye believed him not ; but the publicans and the harlots believed him : and ye, when ye
saw it, did not even repent yourselves afterward, that
ye might believe him.** [The parable of this subdivision is

the outgrowth of the preceding subdivision. These rulers had demanded that Jesus show his authority for his assumption of right as teacher, prophet, etc. The parable is an indirect response to this demand, as if Jesus said, "It is in vain for me to tell you that I act under the authority of the Father, for despite all your great profession to the contrary, you really and actually, in your persistent rejection of another (the Baptist), who also acted under it, repudiate utterly his authority; though in so doing you see yourselves condemned by the conduct of even the publicans and harlots, who have felt the force of the Father's authority, and have repentantly obeyed it." The situation must have given great force to the parable; for the rulers in their private conversation had just admitted to each other that the people recognized and obeyed the divine authority of John, while they, though rulers, rejected it.]

Subdivision C.

PARABLE OF THE WICKED HUSBANDMEN.

ᵃ MATT. XXI. 33-46; ᵇ MARK XII. 1-12; ᶜ LUKE XX. 9-19.

ᵇ **1 And he began to speak unto them** ᶜ **the people** [not the rulers] ᵇ **in parables.** {ᶜ **this parable:**} ᵃ **33 Hear another parable: There was a man that was a householder** [this party represents God], **who planted a vineyard** [this represents the Hebrew nationality], **and set a hedge about it, and digged a** ᵇ **pit for the** ᵃ **winepress in it** [The winepress consisted of two tub-shaped cavities dug in the rock at different levels, the upper being connected with the lower by an orifice cut through from its bottom. Grapes were placed in the upper cavity, or trough, and were trodden by foot. The juice thus squeezed from them ran through the orifice to the trough below, from which it was taken and stored in leather bottles until it fermented and formed wine], **and built a tower** [a place where watchmen could be stationed to protect the vineyard from thieves as the grapes ripened for the vintage], **and let it out to husbandmen** [the rulers are here represented; and the rental was, as usual, a part of the fruits], **and went into another country.** ᶜ **for a long time.** [Jesus frequently refers to this withdrawal of the visible presence of God from the world, always bringing out the point that the withdrawal tests faithfulness. God had come down upon Mt. Sinai, given the law and established the Hebrew nation, after which he had withdrawn. That had indeed been a long time ago; and for four hundred years before the appearance of John the Baptist, God had not even sent a messenger to demand fruit. Some think the hedge refers to the manner in which Palestine was protected by sea and desert and mountain, but the hedge and the winepress and the tower are mere parabolic drapery, for every man who planted a vineyard did all three.] ᵃ **34 And when** {ᶜ **at**} **the season** ᵃ **of the fruits drew near,** ᶜ **he sent unto the husbandmen a servant,** {ᵃ **his servants**} [*i. e.*, the prophets] ᶜ **that they should give him** {ᵇ **that he might receive** ᵃ **to receive from the husbandmen**} **of the** {ᵃ **his**} ᵇ **fruits of the vineyard.** [Luke iii. 8—He expected the children of Israel to bring forth joy, love, peace and all the other goodly fruits of a godly life. And he looked to those in authority to bring forth such results, and the prophets were sent to the rulers to encourage them to do this.] **3 And** {ᶜ **but**} **the husbandmen** ᵇ **took him, and beat him, and sent him away empty. 4 And again he sent unto them** ᶜ **yet another servant: and him also they beat,** ᵇ **wounded in the head, and handled shamefully.** ᶜ **and sent him away empty.** ᵇ **5 And he sent** ᶜ **yet** ᵇ **another;** ᶜ **a third: and him also they wounded,** ᵇ **and him they killed:** ᶜ **and cast him forth.** ᵇ **and many others; beating some, and killing some.** ᵃ **35 And the husbandmen took his servants, and beat one, and killed another, and stoned another. 36 Again, he sent other servants more than the first: and they did unto them in like manner.** [For the treatment of the prophets see such passages as I. Kings xviii. 13; xxii. 24-27; II. Kings vi. 31; II. Chron. xxiv. 19-22; xxxvi. 15. For a summary of the treatment of the prophets or messengers of God see Heb. xi. 35-38.] **37 But** [b]**6 He had yet one, a be-loved son:** [a]**afterward** [b]**he sent him last unto them,** [c]**13 And the lord of the vineyard said,** {[b]**saying,**} [c]**What shall I do?** [Isa. v. 4.] **I will send my beloved son; it may be they will reverence him.** [b]**They will reverence my son.** [The lord of the vineyard was thoroughly perplexed. The conduct of his husbandmen was outrageous beyond all expectation. He had no better servants to send them unless his only son should take upon him the form of a servant and visit them (Phil. ii. 5-8). Being tender and forgiving, and unwilling to resort to extreme measures, the lord of the vineyard resolved to thus send his son, feeling sure that the son would represent the person, authority and rights of the father so much better than any other messenger (Heb. i. 1-5; ii. 1-3), that it would be well-nigh impossible for the husbandmen to fail of reverence towards him. In striking contrast, however, with this expectation of the Father, the rulers, or the husbandmen, had just now harshly demanded of the Son that he tell by what authority he did anything in the vineyard.] [a]**38 But the** {[b]**those**} [a]**husbandmen, when they saw** {[c]**him**} [a]**the son,** [c]**they reasoned one with another,** [a]**said among themselves,** {[c]**saying,**} [a]**This is the heir; come, let us kill him, and take his inheritance.** [c]**that the inheritance may be ours.** [b]**and the inheritance shall be ours.** [In thus bringing the story down to the immediate present, and stating a counsel which his enemies had just spoken privately in each others' ears, Jesus must have startled them greatly. He showed them, too, that those things which made them deem it necessary to kill him were the very things which proved his heirship. They regarded the Jewish nation as their property, and they were plotting to kill Jesus that they might withhold it from him (John xii. 19; xi. 47-50). That men might hope by such high-handed lawlessness to obtain a title to a vineyard seems incredible to us who have always been familiar with the even-balanced justice of constitutional government; but in the East the looseness of the governments, the selfish apathy and lack of public spirit among the people, and the corrupt bribe-receiving habits of the judges make our Lord's picture even to this day, though rather exceptional, still true to life. At this point Jesus turns from history to prophecy.] **8 And they took him,** ᶜ **15 And they cast him forth out of the vineyard, and killed him.** [After two intervening days the Jews would fulfill this detail by thrusting Jesus outside the walls of Jerusalem and crucifying him there.] ᵃ **40 When therefore the lord of the vineyard shall come, what will he do unto those husbandmen? 41 They say unto him, He will miserably destroy those miserable men, and will let out the vineyard unto other husbandmen, who shall render him the fruits in their seasons.** ᶜ **16** [Jesus said] **He will come and destroy these {**ᵇ**the} husbandmen, and will give the vineyard unto others.** ᶜ **And when they heard it, they said, God forbid.** [Part of the multitude, hearing only the story, pronounced unhesitatingly the judgment which ought to be inflicted upon such evil-doers, and Jesus confirmed their judgment. But others, perceiving the meaning underlying the parable, shrank from accepting what would otherwise have been to them a very proper ending, and said, *Mee genoito*, which means literally, Be it not so, and which might properly be paraphrased by our emphatic "Never!" but which the revisers in translating have, with small warrant, seen fit to paraphrase by using the semi-profane expression, "God forbid." There are fourteen such mistranslations in the epistles of Paul according to the King James version, and only one of them (Gal. vi. 14) is corrected in the Revised version. In defense of these translations it is asserted that the phrase is an idiomatic invocation to the Deity, but the case can not be made out, since the Deity is not addressed.] **17 But he looked upon them** [Thus emphasizing the fact that they had repudiated a most just decree. His look, doubtless, resembled that of a parent surprised at the outspoken rebellion of his children], **and** ᵃ **42 Jesus saith {**ᶜ **said,} ** ᵃ **unto them,** ᶜ **What then is this that is written,** ᵇ **10 Have ye not read even this scripture:** ᵃ **Did ye never**

read in the scriptures, ᶜThe stone which the builders
rejected, The same was made the head of the corner?
ᵃThis was from the Lord, And it is marvellous in our
eyes? [The quotation is from Ps. cxviii. 22, 23, which is
here by Jesus applied as a prophecy to the Pharisees, who, in
their treatment of him, were like unskilled builders who reject
the very corner-stone of the building which they seek·to erect.
The Pharisees were eager enough in their desire to set up a
Messianic kingdom, but were so blindly foolish that they did
not see that this kingdom could not be set up unless it rested
upon Christ Jesus, its corner-stone. They blundered in con-
structing their theory of the coming kingdom, and could find no
room for one such as Jesus in it.] **43 Therefore I say unto
you, The kingdom of God shall be taken away from you,
and shall be given to a nation bringing forth the fruits
thereof. 44 And he** {ᶜ **18 Every one**} ᵃ**that falleth on
this** {ᶜ**that**} ᵃ**stone shall be broken to pieces : but on
whomsoever it shall fall, it will scatter him as dust.**
[The stone, of course, represents Jesus, and the two fallings
set forth his passive and active state. In the day when he pas-
sively submitted to be judged, those who condemned him were
broken (Matt. xxvii. 3-5 ; Luke xxiii. 48 ; Acts ii. 3ɣ) ; but in
the great day when he himself becomes the acting party and
calls his enemies to judgment, they shall prefer, and pray.
that a mountain fall upon them—Rev. vi. 15-17.] **45 And
when the chief priests and the Pharisees,** ᶜ **19 And the
scribes** ᵃ**heard his parables, they** ᶜ **sought to lay hands
on him in that very hour ,** ᵇ**for they perceived that he**
ᵃ**spake of them.** ᵇ spake the {ᶜ**this**} **parable against
them.** ᵃ**46 And when they sought to lay hold on him,**
ᶜ**they feared the people :** {ᵇ **multitude ;** ᵃ **multitudes,**}
because they took him for a prophet. ᵇ**and they left
him, and went away.** [Despite the warning which Jesus
gave them that they were killing the Son and would reap the
consequences, and despite the fact that he showed that the
Psalm which the people had used so recently with regard to
him foretold a great rejection which would prove to be a mis-

take, yet the rulers persisted in their evil intention to take his life, and were only restrained by fear of the people, many of whom were Galilæans, men of rugged courage, ready to draw swords on Jesus' behalf. Since they could neither arrest nor answer him, they withdrew as a committee, but returned again in the person of their spies.]

Subdivision D.

PARABLE OF THE MARRIAGE OF THE KING'S SON.

ᵃ MATT. XXII. 1-14.

ᵃ 1 And Jesus answered and spake again in parables unto them, saying, 2 The kingdom of heaven is likened unto a certain king, who made a marriage feast for his son, 3 and sent forth his servants to call them that were bidden to the marriage feast: and they would not come. 4 Again he sent forth other servants, saying, Tell them that are bidden, behold, I have made ready my dinner; my oxen and my fatlings are killed, and all things are ready: come to the marriage feast. 5 But they made light of it, and went their ways, one to his own farm, another to his merchandise; 6 and the rest laid hold on his servants, and treated them shamefully, and killed them. 7 But the king was wroth; and he sent his armies, and destroyed those murderers, and burned their city. 8 Then said he to his servants, The wedding is ready, but they that were bidden were not worthy. 9 Go ye therefore unto the partings of the highways, and as many as ye shall find, bid to the marriage feast. 10 And those servants went out into the highways, and gathered together all as many as they found, both bad and good: and the wedding was filled with guests. [This parable is very

much like the one given in Luke xiv. 16-24—see pp. 495-97.*]
**11 But when the king came in to behold the guests, he
saw there a man** [this one man is taken as a type of many—see
verse 14] **who had not on a wedding-garment: 12 and
he saith unto him, Friend, how camest thou in hither
not having a wedding-garment? And he was speechless.** [We are of the opinion that the king furnished upper
garments to his guests. But the antiquity of this custom is
disputed. See Meyer, Lange and Trench, etc., *in loco*. However, the fact is immaterial, for the man was speechless—without excuse—which shows that he could have had a garment
from some source had he chosen to wear it.] **13 Then the
king said to the servants, Bind him hand and foot** [the
phrase suggests the impossibility of escaping from divine judg-
ment], **and cast him out into the outer darkness** [the
outdoor darkness: wedding feasts were usually held at night];
**there shall be the weeping and the gnashing of teeth. 14
For many are called, but few chosen.** [Many guests are
invited, but few are accepted; because some neglect and despise the invitation, and others cast dishonor upon the one who
invites, by the self-willed and irreverent way in which they accept his invitation. In this parable the first parties invited represent the Jews; the city of the murderers is Jerusalem; the
persons called from the highways are the Gentiles; the entrance
of the king is the coming of the Lord to final judgment; and

---

*Note.—I regard this parable as a remodeling of the parable given
by Luke, the changes being made to suit the changed relation between Jesus and his auditors. In the parable in Luke, God is represented as one who invites us as a friend, and whose invitation is simply
disregarded. Since the speaking of that parable the situation had become more tense and the relations more strained, and hence the parable
takes on a more severe form. The host is not to be disregarded, for he
is a king, and the supper is not to be despised, for it is a marriage supper. The invitation, therefore, savors of commandment, and while
some still continue to treat it with indifference, others feel the constraint of the invitation and reject it in a spirit of rebellion which
manifests itself in violence toward the king's servants. The king, in
turn, is moved by this to retaliate, and visits upon the offenders an
overwhelming judgment.—P. Y. P.

the man without the wedding-garment is any one who will be found in the church without a suitable character. The character of Christ is our wedding-garment, and all the regenerated must wear it—Eph. iv. 24; Col. iii. 10; Gal. iii. 27; John iii. 5; Rev. xix. 8, 9.]

CIX.

JEWISH RULERS SEEK TO ENSNARE JESUS.

(Court of the Temple. Tuesday.)

Subdivision A.

PHARISEES AND HERODIANS ASK ABOUT TRIBUTE.

[a] MATT. XXII. 15-22; [b] MARK XII. 13-17; [c] LUKE XX. 20-26.

[a] 15 Then went the Pharisees, and took counsel how they might ensnare him in *his* talk. [c] 20 And they watched him, and sent forth {[b] send unto him} [a] their disciples, [b] certain of the Pharisees and of {[a] with} [b] the Herodians, that they might catch him in talk. [Perceiving that Jesus, when on his guard, was too wise for them, the Pharisees thought it best to speak their cunning through the mouths of their young disciples, whose youth and apparent desire to know the truth would, according to their calculation, take Jesus off his guard. Having no ancient statement giving us the tenets or principles of the Herodians, we are left to judge them solely by their name, which shows that they were partisans of Herod Antipas. Whether they were out-and-out supporters of the Roman government, or whether they clung to Herod as one whose intervening sovereignty saved them from the worse fate of being directly under a Roman procurator (as Judæa and Samaria then were), would not, as some suppose, affect their views as to the payment of tribute. If they accepted Herod merely for policy's sake, policy would also compel them to favor the tribute, for Antipas, being appointed

by Rome, would have to favor the tribute, and could coun;
none as his adherents who opposed it] ᶜ **spies, who feigned
themselves to be righteous** [sincere seekers after truth],
**that they might take hold of his speech, so as to deliver
him up to the rule and to the authority of the governor.**
[Pontius Pilate was the governor. We are not surprised at
the destruction of Jerusalem when we see the religious teachers of the nation employing their young disciples in such a
work as this. To play detective and entrap a rogue in his
speech and thus become a man-hunter is debasing enough;
but to seek thus to entrap a righteous man is simply diabolical.] ᵇ **14 And when they were come, they say unto
him, {ᶜ saying,} Teacher, we know that thou sayest
and teachest rightly, ᵇ we know that thou art true, and
carest not for any one; for thou regardest not the person of men, ᶜ and acceptest not the person *of any*, but
of a truth teachest the way of God: ᵃ in truth** [The
meaning of their preface is this: " We see that neither fear
nor respect for the Pharisees or the rulers prevents you from
speaking the plain, disagreeable truth; and we are persuaded
that your courage and love of truth will lead you to speak the
same way in political matters, and that you will not be deterred therefrom by any fear or reverence for Cæsar." Fearless
loyalty to truth is indeed one of the noblest attributes of man.
But instead of honoring this most admirable quality in Jesus,
these hardened reprobates were endeavoring to employ it as
an instrument for his destruction], **17 Tell us therefore,
What thinkest thou? ᶜ 22 Is it lawful for us to give
tribute unto Caesar, or not? ᵇ 15 Shall we give, or shall
we not give?** [The Jews were required to pay annually a
large sum of money to the Roman government as an acknowledgment of their subjection. About twenty years before this
Judas of Galilee had stirred up the people to resist this tribute,
and the mass of the Jews was bitterly opposed to it. To decide in favor of this tribute was therefore to alienate the affection and confidence of the throng in the temple who stood
listening to him—an end most desirable to the Pharisees. **If,**

on the other hand, Jesus said that the tribute should not be paid, the Herodians were present to hear it, and would be witnesses sanctioned by Herod, and therefore such as Pilate would be compelled to respect. What but divine wisdom could escape from so cunningly devised a dilemma !] ᵃ **18 But Jesus perceived their wickedness,** ᶜ **craftiness,** ᵇ **knowing their hypocrisy, said unto them, {ᵃand said} Why make ye trial of me, ye hypocrites?** [Thus, before answering, Jesus exposes the meanness and hypocrisy in their question, thereby emphasizing the important fact that he did not dodge, but answered it.] **19 Show me the tribute money.** ᶜ **24 Show me a denarius.** ᵇ **bring me a denarius, that I may see it.** [Religious dues and tributes had been paid in shekels or old Jewish coin, but the tribute to Rome was paid in Roman coin of which the denarius was a sample.] ᵃ **And they brought unto him a denarius.** [See p. 376.] **20 And he saith unto them, Whose is this image and superscription?** ᶜ **Whose i m a g e and superscription hath it?** [The little silver coin had the head of the emperor stamped upon it, and the superscription TICAESARDIVIAVGFAVGVSTVS, which stands for the words *Tiberias Cæsar, Divi Augusti filius Augustus; i. e.,* Tiberias Cæsar, the August son of the Divine Augustus.] **And they said, {ᵃsay} unto him, Caesar's.** ᵇ **17 And** ᵃ **Then** ᵇ **Jesus said {ᵃsaith}** ᵇ **unto them,** ᶜ **Then render** ᵃ **therefore unto Caesar the things that are Caesar's; and unto God the things that are God's.** [Each nation uses its own coin. Had the Jews not been under the Roman sovereignty they would not have been using Roman money; but the coin which they brought to Jesus bore witness against them that the Roman sovereignty was established in their land, and that tribute to it was therefore justly due ; for whoso uses Cæsar's coin must pay Cæsar's tribute. This part of the answer satisfied the Herodians; and the last part " and unto God," etc., satisfied the people, for it asserted, in a manner which carried conviction with it, that the payment of enforced tribute was not inconsistent with maintaining complete allegiance to God.

God was no longer, as of old, the civil ruler of his people, and hence the payment of tribute to a temporal sovereign is in no sense incompatible with his service, but is enjoined as a Christian duty—Rom. xiii. 1, 7.] ^c26 And they were not able to take hold of the saying before the people: ^a22 And when they heard it, they marvelled, ^bgreatly at him. ^cat his answer, and held their peace. ^aand left him, and went away. [They were amazed to find how far his wisdom transcended that of the teachers in whom they had such supreme confidence.]

Subdivision B.

SADDUCEES ASK ABOUT THE RESURRECTION.

^aMATT. XXII. 23-33; ^bMARK XII. 18-27; ^cLUKE XX. 27-39.

^a23 On that day there came {^bcome} unto him ^ccertain of the Sadducees, they that {^bwho} say that there is no resurrection [As to the Sadducees, see p. 71. We may regard their attitude toward Christ as expressed by their leader Caiaphas, see p. 528]; and they asked him, saying, 19 Teacher, Moses wrote unto us [See Deut. xxv. 5, 6. The object of this law was to preserve families. But the custom was older than the law—Gen. xxxviii. 6-11], ^cthat ^bIf a man's brother die, ^chaving a wife, and he be childless, {^band leave a wife behind him, and leave no child,} that his brother should take his {^cthe} wife, and raise up seed unto his brother. ^aMoses said, If a man die, having no children, his brother shall marry his wife, and raise up seed unto his brother. 25 Now there were ^ctherefore ^awith us seven brethren: and the first ^ctook a wife, ^amarried and deceased, ^band dying left no seed; {^cand died childless;} ^aand having no seed left his wife unto his brother; ^b21 And ^a26 In like manner the second also, ^btook her, and died, leaving no seed behind him; and the third likewise: ^ctook her; ^aunto the seventh. ^cand likewise the seven also left no children, {^bleft no seed.} ^cand died. 32 Afterward

ᵇ Last of all ᵃ 27 And after them all, ᵇ the woman also died. ᵃ 28 In the resurrection therefore whose wife shall she be of the seven? {ᵇ of them?} for the seven ᵃ all had her. ᵇ to wife. [This was evidently a favorite Sadducean argument against the resurrection. On the assumption that the marital state is continued after the resurrection it makes the doctrine of a resurrection appear ridiculous, because, seemingly, it involves difficulties which even brothers could hardly settle amicably, and which even God would have in a sense to settle arbitrarily.] ᶜ 34 And {ᵃ 29 But} Jesus answered and said unto them, Ye do err, not knowing the scriptures, nor the power of God. ᵇ Is it not for this cause that ye err, that ye know not the scriptures, nor the power of God? [The relevancy of these statements will be discussed in the treatment of verse 38 below.] ᵃ 30 For ᶜ the sons of this world marry, and are given in marriage: 35 but they that are accounted worthy to attain to that world, and the resurrection from the dead, neither marry, nor are given in marriage: ᵇ 25 For when they shall rise from the dead, ᵃ in the resurrection they neither marry, nor are given in marriage, but are as angels in heaven. ᶜ 36 for neither can they die any more: for they are equal unto the angels; and are sons of God, being sons of the resurrection. [This favorite argument of the Sadducees could not be successfully answered by the Pharisees because they could not refute the assumption that marriage is continued in the future world. But Jesus does refute it on his own authority.] ᵃ 31 But as touching the resurrection of the dead, ᶜ that the dead are raised, even Moses showed, in *the place concerning* the Bush, when he calleth the Lord the God of Abraham, and the God of Isaac, and the God of Jacob. ᵇ have ye not read in the book of Moses, ᵃ that which was spoken unto you by God, ᵇ how God spake unto him, saying, I *am* the God of Abraham, and the God of Isaac, and the God of Jacob? ᶜ 38 Now ᵃ God is not ᶜ the God of the dead, but of the living: for all live unto him. ᵇ ye do

greatly err. [The disbelief of the Sadducees manifested itself in a triple form, for they denied the resurrection and the existence of angels and spirits (Acts xxiii. 8), but the basal principle of their infidelity was the denial of spirits. It was, as it were, the tree trunk from which their other errors sprang as branches. If there were such things as spirits, it was not worth while to deny that there was an order of them known as angels. If man had a spirit which could survive his body, it was reasonable to believe that God, having so fashioned him that a body is essential to his activity and happiness, would in some manner restore a body to him. Jesus therefore does not pursue the argument until he has *proved a resurrection ;* but rests when he has proved that man has a spirit. Jesus proves that man has a spirit by a reference from the Pentateuch, that part of Scripture which the Sadducees accepted as derived from God through Moses. The reference shows that God was spoken of and spoke of himself as the God of those who were, humanly speaking, long since dead. But the Sadducees held that a dead man had ceased to exist, that he had vanished to nothingness. According to their view, therefore, God had styled himself the God of nothing, which is absurd. The Sadducees could not thus have erred had they known or understood the significance of this Scripture, and they could not have doubted the resurrection had they known the absolute power with which God deals with material such as that of which the body is formed. See verses 24 and 39 *supra*.] ᵃ **33 And when the multitudes heard it, they were astonished at his teaching.** ᶜ **39 And certain of the scribes answering said, Teacher, thou hast well said.** [Some of the scribes of less bitter spirit could not refrain from expressing their admiration at the ease with which Jesus answered an argument which their own wisdom could not refute.]

Subdivision C.

A LAWYER ASKS ABOUT THE GREAT COMMANDMENT.

ᵃ MATT. XXII. 34-40; ᵇ MARK XII. 28-34; ᶜ LUKE XX. 40.

ᵃ **34 But the Pharisees, when they heard that he had put the Sadducees to silence, gathered themselves together. 35 And one of them, a lawyer,** ᵇ **one of the scribes came, and heard them questioning together, and knowing that he had answered them well,** ᵃ **asked him a question, trying him** [he was evidently deputed by those who counseled to ask this question]: **36 Teacher, which is the great commandment in the law?** ᵇ **What commandment is the first of all?** [According to the statement of Jewish writers, there had been an old and interminable dispute among the rabbis as to which was the greatest commandment. Some held that it was the law which commanded sacrifices; others, that which commanded the wearing of phylacteries; others contended for those about purification; others, for those about the great feasts. But as they reckoned the commandments of Moses as numbering over six hundred, there was plenty of room for argument. On this memorable day the answers of Jesus had hitherto been of such a nature as to put his questioners to silence. Therefore, in asking this question, they hoped to get an answer about which they could at least find room to wrangle, and thus discredit the wisdom of Jesus.] **29 Jesus answered,** ᵃ **37 And said unto him,** ᵇ **The first is, Hear, O Israel; The Lord our God, the Lord is one: 30 and** ᵃ **Thou shalt love the Lord thy God with all thy heart, and with all thy soul, and with all thy mind.** ᵇ **and with all thy strength.** ᵃ **38 This is the great and first commandment.** [Deut. vi. 4-9. This command is first, because it is the foundation of the entire law of God. It is greatest, because, in a sense, it includes all the other laws. Polytheism, atheism, idolatry and all sins against God are forbidden by it. All sins against man are likewise, in a sense, prohibited by it; for sin against man is sin against God's image, and against the objects of God's love. Those who truly love God can not consistently sin against man (I. John iv. 20). The curious may make metaphysical distinctions in the analysis of this required fourfold love, but the sum of it is that we are to love God with our whole being.] **39 And a {ᵇ 31 The} second** ᵃlike *unto it* ᵇis this, **Thou shalt love thy neighbor as thyself.** [Love is the cure for sin, for we can not sin against those whom we truly love. Where we love we desire to bless. But sin always carries with it a willingness to injure or to curse.] **There is none other commandment greater than these.** ᵃ**40 On these two commandments the whole law hangeth, and the prophets.** [The generic nature of the law of love is also noted by Paul (Rom. xiii. 8-10); but love without law is not sufficient. Love begets a desire to bless, but the law guides to the accomplishment of that desire. Perfect righteousness is the result of wisdom as well as affection. Love without law is power without direction, and law without love is machinery without a motor—I. Cor. xiii. 1-3.] ᵇ**32 And the scribes said unto him, Of a truth, Teacher, thou hast well said that he is one; and there is none other but he: 33 and to love him with all the heart, and with all the understanding, and with all the strength, and to love his neighbor as himself, is much more than all whole burnt-offerings and sacrifices.** [Here, as in the preceding subdivision, the answer of Jesus was so clearly right that it enforced admiration.] **34 And when Jesus saw that he answered discreetly, he said unto him, Thou art not far from the kingdom of God.** [Prejudice is the great obstacle to entering the kingdom. In proportion as we overcome it we draw near to God.] **And no man after that durst {ᶜ 40 For they durst not any more} ask him any question.** [They found it expedient to keep silence when their questions only exposed their own shallowness, and made more conspicuous the supreme wisdom of Jesus.]

Subdivision D.

JESUS' QUESTION WHICH NONE COULD ANSWER.

ᵃ MATT. XXII. 41-46; ᵇ MARK XII. 35-37; ᶜ LUKE XX. 41-44.

ᵃ 41 Now while the Pharisees were gathered together, ᵇ as he taught in the temple, ᵃ Jesus asked them a question [They had questioned him seeking to expose his lack of wisdom, but the question of Jesus was devoid of retaliation. It was asked to teach a most important lesson], ᵇ 35 And Jesus answered and said, {ᵃ 42 saying,} ᶜ unto them, ᵃ What think ye of the Christ? whose son is he? They say unto him, *The son* of David. [The answer was true, but it was not *all* the truth as the Scriptures themselves showed. And this additional truth was what the opposers of Jesus needed to learn.] 43 He saith unto them, ᵇ How say {ᶜ they} ᵇ the scribes that the Christ is the son of David? {ᶜ David's son?} ᵃ How then doth David in the Spirit call him Lord, ᶜ 42 For David himself saith {ᵇ said} in the Holy Spirit, ᶜ in the book of Psalms, {ᵃ saying,} ᵇ The Lord said unto my Lord, Sit thou on my right hand, Till I make thine enemies the footstool of thy feet. {ᵃ Till I put thine enemies underneath thy feet?} 45 If ᵇ 37 David himself therefore ᵃ then calleth him Lord, how ᵇ and whence is he his son ? [The quotation is from Psalm cx. The context here shows that the rabbis of that day accepted this Psalm as written by David, and as Messianic in meaning. Since then the Jews have denied that the Psalm is Messianic, and that it was written by David ; some saying that Abraham, and others that Hezekiah, wrote it. This Psalm speaks of the Messiah as the Lord of David, and other Scriptures call him David's son. So also the Scriptures describe Christ as conquering yet suffering, as divine yet human, as dying yet living, as judged yet judging, etc. The Jewish rulers seem able to grasp only one side of the character of Christ as revealed either in his life or in the Scriptures, and hence they stumbled.] ᵃ **46 And no one was able to answer him a word, neither durst any man from that day forth ask him any more questions.** ᵇ **And the common people heard him gladly.** [By all their questioning, the Jews had not been able to weaken public confidence in Christ.]

CX.

JESUS' LAST PUBLIC DISCOURSE. DENUNCIATION OF SCRIBES AND PHARISEES.

(In the Courts of the Temple. Tuesday.)

ᵃ MATT. XXIII. 1-39; ᵇ MARK XII. 38-40; ᶜ LUKE XX. **45-47.**

ᵃ **1 Then spake Jesus** ᵇ **38 And in his teaching** ᶜ **in the hearing of all the people he said unto** ᵃ **the multitudes, and to his disciples** [he spoke in the most public manner], **2 saying,** ᶜ **46 Beware of the scribes,** ᵃ **The scribes and the Pharisees sit on Moses' seat: 3 all things therefore whatsoever they bid you,** *these* **do and observe: but do not ye after their works; for they say, and do not.** [As teachers of the law of Moses the scribes and Pharisees were the only religious guides whom the people had, so they were obliged to follow them as expounders of that law, but they were by no means to look to them as living exemplifications of that law.] **4 Yea, they bind heavy burdens and grievous to be borne, and lay them on men's shoulders; but they themselves will not move them with their finger.** [The law itself was a heavy yoke (Acts xv. 10), but these teachers added to the burden of it a vast volume of traditions, but they themselves did not keep these traditions, excusing themselves by inventing subtle distinc. tions like those in reference to the Corban (Matt. xv. 4-6) and to oaths (Matt. xv. 16-22). See p. 314.] **5 But all their works they do to be seen of men** [what laws and traditions they did keep were not kept privately and sincerely, but publicly that they might secure to themselves a reputation for sanctity]: **for they make broad their phylacteries** [Literally, *preservatives* or *remembrances*. They were probably so called because designed to aid the wearer in remembering his obligations to the law. They were strips of parchment on which were written four passages of the law; viz.: Ex. xiii. 3-10; 11-16; Deut. vi. 4-9; xi. 13-21. These were enclosed in a leather case and were fastened to the forehead and left arm. The authority for wearing them was purely traditional, and the practice seems to have arisen from a literal interpretation of Ex. xiii. 9, 16; Deut. vi. 8; xi. 18. The Pharisees made the leather case large, that their righteousness might be more conspicuous], **and enlarge the borders** *of their garments* [These were the fringes mentioned in Num. xv. 38, 39. But **the** Pharisees offended again, even in their obedience, by **wearing** broader fringes than other people that they might appear more religious], ᶜ **who desire to walk in long robes** [This robe was a professional dress, as marked as that worn by priests and kings. It showed that its wearer was professionally religious], ᵃ **6 and love the chief places at feasts** [see p. 493], **and the chief seats in the synagogues, 7 and** ᶜ **love** ᵃ **the salutations in the marketplaces** [see p. 313], **and to be called of men, Rabbi.** [The term "Rabbi" means master, or teacher.] ᶜ **47 who {** ᵇ **40 they that} devour widows' houses, and for a pretense make long prayers; these shall receive greater condemnation.** [It is doubtful in what way the Pharisees devoured widows' houses, or property. Godet suggests that they extorted presents under pretense of interceding for them in their prayers, and Lightfoot thinks that they got the goods of widows "by subtle attractives," and by the management of their estates as judges, and as men acquainted with the law and therefore fit to administer estates. According to the later rabbinical teaching it is urged that a rabbi should pray one hour, and that he should meditate for an hour before and an hour after prayer. On days when they carried out this rule and the other rule which required three seasons of prayer a day, they would spend nine hours in prayer. But this was no doubt one of the cases where they said and did not. For thus making their religion a cloak for their vices they would be more severely punished. As to the peculiar blackness of the crime of robbing widows, see Ex. xxii. 22-24; Deut. xxvii. 19.] ª**8 But be not ye called Rabbi: for one is your teacher** [Christ], **and all ye are brethren. 9 And call no man your father on the earth: for one is your Father,** *even* **he who is in heaven. 10 Neither be ye called masters: for one is your master,** *even* **the Christ. 11 But he that is greatest among you shall be your servant.** [See pp. 557, 558.] **12 And whosoever shall exalt himself shall be humbled; and whosoever shall humble himself shall be exalted.** [See pp. 431, 494, 537. Thus Jesus reproves those who make religion a matter of praise-seeking ostentation, whether they do so by seeking position, or by peculiarity of dress, or by assuming or accepting titles of honor or distinction. This sin of ostentation was the first enumerated sin of the Pharisees.] **13 But woe unto you, scribes and Pharisees, hypocrites! because ye shut the kingdom of heaven against men: for ye enter not in yourselves, neither suffer ye them that are entering in to enter.** [Our Lord's language is figurative and presents the kingdom of God as a house around the door of which the Pharisees have gathered, not entering in themselves, and blocking the way against those who would enter. This they did by their opposition to Jesus. For a similar charge see p. 315.] **15 Woe unto you, scribes and Pharisees, hypocrites! for ye compass sea and land to make one proselyte; and when he is become so, ye make him twofold more a son of hell than yourselves.** [Proselytes here meant are not those converted from heathenism to worship God, but Jews converted to Phariseeism. These become worse than their instructors, because each generation drifted further from the law and became more zealously and completely devoted to the traditions.] **16 Woe unto you, ye blind guides** [Jesus above denounced them for their hypocrisy, but this woe is pronounced upon them for their ignorance and folly], that say, Whosoever shall swear by the temple, it is nothing; but whosoever shall swear by the gold of the temple, he is a debtor. [The word "debtor" is here meant to describe one who owes it to himself and to God to keep his oath. The Pharisees graduated oaths according to their own foolish conceptions of the sanctity of the object invoked, so that if the object by which a man swore was not sacred enough, he was not forsworn if he did not keep his oath. Esteeming the gold of the temple more sacred than the temple itself, they held that an oath by the former was binding while an oath by the latter was not. The gold meant is probably the golden ornaments on the temple.] **17 Ye fools and blind: for which is greater, the gold, or the temple that hath sanctified the gold? 18 And, Whosoever shall swear by the altar, it is nothing; but whosoever shall swear by the gift that is upon it, he is a debtor. 19 Ye blind: for which is greater, the gift or the altar that sanctifieth the gift? 20 He therefore that sweareth by the altar, sweareth by it, and by all things thereon. 21 And he that sweareth by the temple, sweareth** by **it, and by him that dwelleth therein. 22 And he that sweareth by the heaven, sweareth by the throne of God, and by him that sitteth thereon.** [Our Lord designed to teach that all oaths were binding. See p. 243.] **23 Woe unto you, scribes and Pharisees, hypocrites! for ye tithe mint and anise and cummin, and have left undone the weightier matters of the law, justice, and mercy, and faith: but these ye ought to have done, and not to have left the other undone.** [See p. 313. The anise was used for medical purposes and also for culinary seasoning, so that Pliny says "the kitchen can not be without it." Cummin also was a condiment and a medicine, the bruised seed mixed with wine being used as a styptic, especially after circumcision. It was also used as an ingredient for salves or plasters such as were applied to the ulcers of cattle produced from the bites, grubs, etc., of insects.] **24 Ye blind guides, that strain out the gnat, and swal-**

low the camel! [A proverbial expression, indicating care
for little faults and a corresponding unconcern for big ones.]
**25 Woe unto you, scribes and Pharisees, hypocrites!
for ye cleanse the outside of the cup and of the platter,
but within they are full from extortion and excess.**
[Jesus here compares the Pharisees to a woman who washes
the outside of her dishes and leaves the inside unclean.   But
in describing that inner uncleanness he passes from the figure
to the reality, and specifies that it consists of extortion and
self-indulgence.   They made their outside clean by tradition-
ary ablutions.   See pp. 393, 394.]   **26 Thou blind Pharisee,
cleanse first the inside of the cup and of the platter,
that the outside thereof may become clean also.** [Here
again the literal peeps through the figurative : a pure inner
life makes clean outward conduct.]   **27 Woe unto you,
scribes and Pharisees, hypocrites! for ye are like unto
whited sepulchres, which outwardly appear beautiful,
but inwardly are full of dead men's bones, and of all
uncleanness.   28 Even so ye also outwardly appear
righteous unto men, but inwardly ye are full of hypocrisy and iniquity.** [Luke records Jesus as having taught
this lesson by an exactly opposite figure.   See p. 313.   There
men were contaminated by the touch of a grave because there
was nothing outside to notify them of its presence.   Here men
are contaminated by the same thing because the outside is rendered so white and beautiful that men are deceived into thinking that the inside is harmless.]   **29 Woe unto you, scribes
and Pharisees, hypocrites! for ye build the sepulchres
of the prophets, and garnish the tombs of the righteous, 30 and say, If we had been in the days of our
fathers, we should not have been partakers with them
in the blood of the prophets.   31 Wherefore ye witness to yourselves, that ye are sons of them that slew
the prophets.   32 Fill ye up then the measure of your
fathers.** [See p. 314.]   **33 Ye serpents, ye offspring of
vipers, how shall ye escape the judgment of hell?** [See
p. 73.]   **34 Therefore, behold, I send unto you proph-**

ets, and wise men, and scribes: some of them shall
ye kill and crucify; and some of them shall ye scourge
in your synagogues, and persecute from city to city:
35 that upon you may come all the righteous blood
shed on the earth, from the blood of Abel the righteous unto the blood of Zachariah son of Barachiah,
whom ye slew between the sanctuary and the altar.
36 Verily I say unto you, All these things shall come
upon this generation. [See pp. 314, 315.] 37 O Jerusalem, Jerusalem, that killeth the prophets, and stoneth them that are sent unto her! how often would
I have gathered thy children together, even as a hen
gathereth her chickens under her wings, and ye would
not! 38 Behold, your house is left unto you desolate.
39 For I say unto you, ye shall not see me henceforth,
till ye shall say, Blessed *is* he that cometh in the name
of the Lord. [See pp. 491, 492.]

CXI.

OBSERVING THE OFFERINGS AND WIDOW'S MITES.

(In the Temple Treasury. Tuesday.)

ᵇ MARK XII. 41-44; ᶜ LUKE XXI. 1-4.

ᵇ 41 And he sat down over against the treasury
[It is said that in the court of the women there were
cloisters or porticos, and under the shelter of these were
placed thirteen chests with trumpet-shaped mouths into which
offerings might be dropped. The money cast in was for the
benefit of the temple. An inscription on each chest showed
to which one of the thirteen special items of cost or expenditure the contents would be devoted; as, for the purchase of
wood, or gold, or frankincense, etc.], and beheld how the
multitude cast money into the treasury [We should
remember this calm inspection of our Lord when we are about

to make an offering to his work. He is by no means indifferent as to our actions]: **and many that were rich cast in much.** ᶜ**1 And he looked up, and saw the rich men that were casting their gifts into the treasury.** ᵇ**42 And there came** ᶜ**2 And he saw a certain poor widow casting in thither** ᵇ**and she cast in two mites, which make a farthing.** [The *lepton* or mite was worth one-fifth of a cent. It was a Greek coin, and the *kodrantes* or farthing was a Roman coin. It is suggested that she might have retained one of the coins, since she had two.] **43 And he called unto him his disciples** [he had found an object-lesson which he wished them to see], **and said unto them, Verily** ᶜ**Of a truth I say unto you,** ᵇ**This poor widow cast in more than all they that are casting into the treasury: 44 for they {**ᶜ**these}** ᵇ**all did cast in of their superfluity;** ᶜ**unto the gifts;** ᵇ**but she of her want did cast in all that she had,** *even* ᶜ**all the living that she had. {**ᵇ**all her living.}** [We are disposed to measure the value of actions quantitatively rather than qualitatively. Moreover, we are better judges of actions than of motives, and can see the outward conduct much clearer then the inward character. God, therefore, in his word, constantly teaches us that he looks rather upon the inward than the outward. In this case the value of the woman's gift was measured, not by quantity, but by its quality; in quantity it was two mites, in quality it was the gift of all she had. From considering the corrupt characters of the Pharisees, Jesus must have turned with pleasure to look upon the beautiful heart of this devout widow.]

CXII.

GREEKS SEEK JESUS. HE FORETELLS THAT HE SHALL DRAW ALL MEN UNTO HIM.

(In the Temple. Jerusalem. Tuesday.)

^d JOHN XII. 20-50.

^d **20 Now there were certain Greeks among those that went up to worship at the feast** [The language indicates that they were Greek converts to Judaism, such as were called proselytes of the gate. It is to be noted that as Gentiles came from the east at the beginning of Jesus' life, so they also came from the west at the close of his ministry]: **21 these therefore came to Philip, who was of Bethsaida of Galilee** [See p. 111. They were possibly drawn to Philip by his Greek name], **and asked him, saying, Sir** [the dignity of the master elevates the disciple], **we would see Jesus.** [Jesus was evidently still in the court of the women, where the treasury was, and this court, being part of the sanctuary, no Gentile was permitted to enter it.] **22 Philip cometh and telleth Andrew** [Philip wished another to share the responsibility of the situation]: **Andrew cometh, and Philip, and they tell Jesus. 23 And Jesus answereth them, saying, The hour is come, that the Son of man should be glorified.** [The humble seeking of these Gentiles formed a striking contrast to the persistent rejection of the Jews. And the occasion forcibly suggested that the gospel invitation, which had hitherto been confined to the lost sheep of the house of Israel, should be extended to the vast throng of waiting Gentiles. But, according to the counsel of God, this extension was not to take place until Jesus had been glorified by his death, resurrection and enthronement. The demand for extension, therefore, suggested the advisability of a speedy glorification, which accorded with the plans of God.] **24 Verily, verily** [with these emphatic words Jesus prepares them for a hard saying], **I say unto you, Except a grain of**

wheat fall into the earth and die, it abideth by itself alone ; but if it die, it beareth much fruit. [As the germ of life in the grain of wheat can only pass into other grains by departing from the original grain and leaving it dead, so the life which was in Christ Jesus could only pass into his disciples by his death.] **25 He that loveth his life loseth it ; and he that hateth his life in this world shall keep it unto life eternal.** [Though Jesus had his own death in view, yet he shows himself governed by a principle which he had already declared to be of universal application. See p. 368. If a grain of wheat saves itself, it remains but one grain until it rots ; but if it yields up its life-germ as a sacrifice to the law of growth, it multiplies itself thirty, sixty or a hundred fold and continues its multiplication through an innumerable pos⁻ terity.] **26 If any man serve me, let him follow me ; and where I am, there shall also my servant be : if any man serve me, him will the Father honor.** [Jesus here recommends to his disciples that they follow him in fruit-bearing self-sacrifice, promising them the joy of being with him and the honor of the Father. The joy of being with Christ is the chief expectation of the Christian—II. Cor. v. 8; Phil. i. 23; Rev. xxi. 3; xxii. 20.] **27 Now is my soul troubled** [Thus Jesus admits that it was difficult for him to live up to the principle of sacrifice which he had just enunciated. Had it not been thus difficult for him, he would hardly have been a fitting example for his disciples; for certainly it is and has always been difficult for them] **; and what shall I say ?** [In his trouble Jesus raises the question as to what prayer he shall offer to the Father.] **Father, save me from this hour. But for this cause** [for this purpose of imparting life through a sacrificial death] **came I unto this hour.** [Thus Jesus proposes a prayer for deliverance, but repudiates it as contrary to the very purpose of his life.] **28 Father, glorify thy name.** [Having refused to ask for deliverance, Jesus prays that he may glorify the Father by suffering according to his original statement contained in verses 23 and 24. The two prayers are counterparts to the two offered in Gethsemane

(Luke xxii. 42). The prayer here is the climax of the thought begun at verse 23. We are first shown that nature is glorified by sacrifice (verse 24). Then that discipleship is so glorified (verses 25, 26) and this prayer shows that our Lord himself is glorified by the same rule.] **There came therefore a voice out of heaven,** *saying,* **I have both glorified it, and will glorify it again.** [The Father had glorified his name in the Son. By words of commendation at his baptism (Matt. iii. 17) and at his transfiguration (Matt. xvii. 5), and by the performance of miracles (John xi. 40), and he would glorify it again by the preaching of the universal gospel, and by making Jesus head over all to the church and the final judge of all men.] **29 The multitude therefore, that stood by, and heard it, said that it had thundered: others said, An angel hath spoken to him.** [Those who thought it thundered were nervous persons who were so startled as not to distinguish the words.*] **30 Jesus answered and said, This voice hath not come for my sake, but for your sakes.** [The voice was not spoken to encourage Jesus in his hour of suffering, but to aid the Jews to believe on him, and to warn them of the coming judgment which would follow their disbelief, and make them partakers in the condemnation of Satan.] **31 Now is the judgment of this world: now shall the prince of this world be cast out.** [The Greek word for judgment survives in our English word "crisis," but conveys much more meaning, since it embraces also the idea of final settlement and adjudication. The crucifixion of Jesus was the crisis in the contest between Satan and

---

*NOTE —I dissent here, as in the case of a similar passage found on page 85, and for like reasons. The apprehension of the divine voice depends upon the soul's capacity for hearing it, as appears from Saul's conversion (Acts ix 7; xxii. 9; xxvi. 13 f.). To the mass, therefore, the voice was mere sound; to others the utterance was articulate though incomprehensible, while to John, and perhaps to all the disciples, the voice communicated a thought. "Thus," says Godet, "the wild beast perceives only a *sound* in the human voice; the trained animal discovers a *meaning*; a command, for example, which it immediately obeys: man alone discerns therein a *thought.*" (P. Y. P.)

God. See Gen. iii. 15. "The meaning of it," says Barnes,
"may be thus expressed: Now is approaching the decisive
scene, the eventful period—*the crisis*—when it shall be determined who shall rule this world." In the long conflict which
had hitherto been carried on, Satan had earned for himself the
name "prince of this world," and it was no empty title (Matt.
iv. 8, 9; II. Cor. iv. 4; Eph. vi. 12); but by his approaching
death Jesus would break down the power of Satan, and cast
him out, not suddenly, but by the advancing power of a superior kingdom. The kingdom of darkness recedes before the
kingdom of light as the night withdraws before the rising sun.]
**32 And I, if I be lifted up from the earth, will draw all
men unto myself. 33 But this he said, signifying by
what manner of death he should die.** [Jesus thrice
speaks of his death as a lifting up, a euphemism for being crucified (John viii. 28). While the distinctions between the
three statements are not to be insisted upon, yet they suggest
that the first is as a saving sacrifice, a priestly work (John iii.
14); the second is mentioned as the convincing credential that
he is the prophet sent from God, speaking the message of God
(John viii. 26-28); and in the passage before us he is evidently
the king who shall wrest his kingdom from the usurping
Satan.] **34 The multitude therefore answered him,
We have heard out of the law that the Christ abideth for
ever: and how sayest thou, The Son of man must be
lifted up? who is this Son of man?** [The term "law" is
used loosely for the whole of the Old Testament Scriptures (John
x. 34). The people were persuaded by certain passages such as
Isa. ix. 6, 7; Ps. lxxxix. 36; cx. 4; Dan. vii. 13, 14; Ezek.
xxxvii. 25, etc., that the Messiah was to abide forever. They
knew that Jesus in his triumphal entry had received honors
which they thought belonged to the Messiah, but when they
heard him use words indicating that he should die, and thus
(as they construed it) *not* abide forever, they felt that he was
openly disavowing all claim to Messiahship. Having heard
him style himself the Son of man (verse 23), they now catch
at it as if Jesus had used it to distinguish himself from the true

Messiah, and ask with more or less contempt, "Who is this Son of man?" Thus blinded by their preconceived opinions and misconstructions of Scripture, the people wavered in their loyalty to Jesus, and Watkins well says, "This question came midway between the 'Hosanna' of the entry into Jerusalem and the 'Crucify him' of the trial."] **35 Jesus therefore said unto them, Yet a little while is the light among you.** [The phrase "little while" stands in contrast with "abideth for ever."] **Walk while ye have the light, that darkness overtake you not: and he that walketh in the darkness knoweth not whither he goeth. 36 While ye have the light, believe on the light, that ye may become sons of light.** [Jesus did not reply to their question, because it was asked contemptuously and not seriously, and because any effort to make their carnal mind grasp the idea that he could be lifted up, and yet still abide, would have resulted in more contempt. He therefore speaks a solemn warning to them, counseling them to make use of his presence while they had it, even if his fleshly abiding with them was but brief; and promises that a proper use of the light then given them would make them sons of light.] **These things spake Jesus, and he departed and hid himself from them.** [This was his last public appeal to the people. He now retired, probably to Bethany, and they saw him no more until he was a prisoner in the hands of his enemies.] **37 But though he had done so many signs before them, yet they believed not on him** [the multitude had long oscillated between belief and unbelief, but, despite all his past miracles and the marvelous wisdom shown on this the day of hard questions, they settled down in unbelief] : **38 that the word of Isaiah the prophet** [Isa. liii. 1] **might be fulfilled, which he spake, Lord, who hath believed our report? And to whom hath the arm of the Lord been revealed? 39 For this cause they could not believe, for that Isaiah said again** [Isa. vi. 10], **40 He hath blinded their eyes, and he hardened their heart; Lest they should see with their eyes, and perceive with their heart, And should turn, And**

I should heal them. [See p. 332. The quotation from Isaiah is not exact, for there God enjoins on the prophet the duty of hardening the people's hearts, while here it is spoken of as God's own act. Had God, however, hardened their hearts by a direct act and without any reference to their moral or spiritual condition, they could not have been held morally responsible for their disbelief. But this God did not do. He hardened their hearts and blinded their eyes by the manner in which he approached them through the person of his Son, Christ Jesus. Jesus so came, so lived, and so taught that those who hunger for godliness are drawn to him and enlightened by him, while those who despise the grace and love of God are repelled and blinded. John here recognizes that the type (Isaiah) should be fulfilled in the antitype (Christ). If Isaiah was to so preach that the wicked would be blinded, then Christ in his ministry should likewise so teach and preach as to produce similar results.] **41 These things said Isaiah, because he saw his glory; and he spake of him. 42 Nevertheless even of the rulers many believed on him; but because of the Pharisees they did not confess *it*, lest they should be put out of the synagogue: 43 for they loved the glory *that is* of men more than the glory *that is* of God.** [These members of the Sanhedrin believed with the head rather than with the heart (Rom. x. 10); their hearts already being occupied with the love of praise or man-glory. Their disbelief accorded with the words of Jesus (John v. 44). As to expulsion from the synagogue, see John ix. 22.] **44 And Jesus cried and said** [These words were of course spoken before the departure mentioned in verse 36. They are placed here to bring out in stronger light the final unbelief of the Jews and the patient, persistent effort which Jesus had made to win those who were the better inclined], **He that believeth on me, believeth not on me, but on him that sent me. 45 And he that beholdeth me beholdeth him that sent me. 46 I am come a light into the world, that whosoever believeth on me may not abide in the darkness. 47 And if any man hear my sayings, and keep**

them not, I judge him not: for I came not to judge the
world, but to save the world. [See pp. 131 and 454.]   **48**
**He that rejecteth me, and receiveth not my sayings,
hath one that judgeth him: the word that I spake, the
same shall judge him in the last day.   49 For I spake
not from myself; but the Father that sent me, he hath
given me a commandment, what I should say, and
what I should speak.   50 And I know that his commandment is life eternal; the things therefore which
I speak, even as the Father hath said unto me, so I
speak.** [The Father had sent the Son into the world to bring
life and immortality to light in the gospel.   Jesus therefore
here declared that men will be tried by the gospel law and
that some will be saved and some condemned by it.]

CXIII.

DESTRUCTION OF JERUSALEM FORETOLD.

ᵃ MATT. XXIV. 1-28;   ᵇ MARK XIII. 1-23;   ᶜ LUKE XXI. 5-24.

ᵃ **1 And Jesus went out from the temple** [leaving it to
return no more], **and was going on his way; and his disciples came unto him** ᵇ **as he went forth** ᵃ **to show him
the buildings of the temple.** ᵇ **one of his disciples
saith unto him, Teacher, behold, what manner of
st**ᵃ**nes, and what manner of buildings!** ᶜ **5 And as
some spake of the temple, how it was adorned with
goodly stones and offerings, he said** [The strength and
wealth of the temple roused the admiration of the Galilæans.
The great stones in its fortifications promised safety from its
enemies, and the goodly offerings bespoke the zeal of its
friends.   According to Josephus, some of the stones were
nearly seventy feet in length, twelve feet in height, and eighteen feet in breadth.   The same historian tells us of the gifts
or offerings which adorned it: crowns, shields, goblets, chain of
gold presented by Agrippa, and a golden vine with its vast
clusters which was the gift of Herod.   The temple was built of

white limestone, and its beauty and strength made it admired of all nations. It took forty-six years to finish it, and ten thousand skilled workmen are said to have been employed in its construction], {ª 2 But ᵇ Jesus ª answered and said unto them, ᵇ him,} Seest thou these great buildings? ª See ye not all these things? ᶜ 6 As for these things which ye behold, ª verily I say unto you, ᶜ the days will come, in which there shall not be left here one stone upon another, that {ᵇ which} shall not be thrown down. [In the very hour when the disciples exulted in the apparent permanency of their glorious temple, Jesus startled them by foretelling its utter destruction, which, within forty years, was fulfilled to the letter. The emperor Vespasian, and his son Titus, after a three years' siege, took Jerusalem and destroyed its temple A. D. 70. Of the temple proper not a vestige was left standing, but the vast platform upon which it stood, composed partly of natural rock and partly of immense masonry, was for the most part left standing. The destruction of the city and temple, however, was so complete that those who visited it could hardly believe that it had ever been inhabited (Jos. Wars vii. 1.] **3 And as he sat on the mount of Olives, over against the temple** [he was in the middle portion of the mountain, for that is the part which is opposite the temple], ª **the disciples** ᵇ **Peter and James and John and Andrew** [on this occasion Andrew was in company with the chosen three when they were honored by a special revelation, but he is put last as being the least conspicuous of the four] ª **came unto him privately,** ᵇ **asked him privately,** ª **saying,** ᶜ **Teacher,** ᵇ **4 Tell us, when** ᶜ **therefore shall these things be? and what** *shall be* **the sign when these things are about to come to pass?** {ᵇ **to be accomplished?**} ª **and what** *shall be* **the sign of thy coming, and of the end of the world?** [Dismayed by the brief words which Jesus had spoken as he was leaving the temple, these four disciples asked for fuller details. Their question is fourfold. 1. When shall the temple be destroyed? 2. What shall be the signs which precede its destruction? 3.

What shall be the sign of Christ's coming? 4. What shall be the sign of the end of the world? Jesus had said nothing of his coming nor of the end of the world; but to these four disciples the destruction of the temple seemed an event of such magnitude that they could not but associate it with the end of all things. Jesus deals with the first two questions in this section, and with the two remaining questions in Section CXIV.] **4 And Jesus answered and said {ᵇbegan to say} unto them, Take heed that no man lead you {ᶜthat ye be not led} astray: for many shall come in my name** [claiming my name], **saying, I am *he*; ªI am the Christ; ᶜand, The time is at hand: ᵇand shall lead many astray. ᶜgo ye not after them.** [The first sign of the approaching destruction would be the appearance of false Christs. These would boldly claim the title, and assert that the time for the setting up of the eternal kingdom had arrived. We have no direct history of the appearance of such persons, the nearest approach to it being the parties mentioned by Josephus (Ant. xx. 5. 1; 8. 6, 10; Wars ii. 13. 4, 5.) But as these men left no institutions or followers, it is quite natural that they should be overlooked or dropped by historians. Nothing is more natural, however, than that the excitement attendant upon the ministry of Jesus should encourage many to attempt to become such a Christ as the people wanted. The Gospels show so widespread a desire for a political Christ that the law of demand and supply would be sure to make many such.] **ª6 And ᵇwhen ªye shall hear of wars ᶜand tumults, ªand rumors of wars; see that ye ᵇbe not troubled: ᶜbe not terrified: for these things must needs come to pass first; ªbut the end** [the destruction of the temple] **is not yet. {ᶜimmediately.} 10 Then said he unto them, ᵇ8 For ᶜNation shall rise against nation, and kingdom against kingdom** [Wars and rumors of wars would be the second sign, but Christians in Jerusalem could rest there in safety until a more definite token bid them depart. Of course the wars here mentioned were only such as threatened particularly to affect the Jews, for the trouble coming upon the Jews was the subject of discourse. Alford, in commenting on this paragraph, takes the pains to enumerate three threats of war made against the Jews by as many Roman emperors, and three uprisings of Gentiles against Jews in which many thousands of the latter perished] ; **11 and there shall be great earthquakes, ᵇ in divers places ; ᶜ and in divers places ᵇ there shall be ᶜ famines and pestilences ; and there shall be terrors and great signs from heaven.** [Great natural disturbances would constitute the third sign. That these preceded the destruction of Jerusalem there is abundant historic evidence. Alford enumerates the earthquakes as follows : 1. A great earthquake in Crete, A. D. 46 or 47. 2. One at Rome on the day when Nero assumed the manly toga, A. D. 51. 3. One at Apamæa in Phrygia, mentioned by Tacitus, A. D. 53. 4. One at Laodicea in Phrygia, A. D. 60. 5. One in Campania, A. D. 62 or 63. There were an indefinite number of famines referred to by Roman writers, and at least one pestilence during which thirty thousand perished in Rome alone. All these signs are mentioned by unbelieving writers such as Josephus, Tacitus, Suetonius, Philostratus and Seneca, who speak of them because of their importance and not with any reference to the prophecy of Christ.] ᵃ **8 But all these things are the beginning of travail.** ᶜ **12 But before all these things, they shall lay their hands on you, and shall persecute you, delivering you up to the synagogues and prisons, bringing you before kings and governors for my name's sake.** ᵇ **9 But take ye heed to yourselves : for** ᵃ **9 Then shall they deliver you up** ᵇ **to councils ;** ᵃ **unto tribulation, and shall kill you :** ᵇ **and in synagogues shall ye be beaten ;** ᵃ **and ye shall be hated of all the nations for my name's sake.** ᵇ **and before governors and kings shall ye stand for my sake, for a testimony unto them.** ᶜ **13 It shall turn out unto you for a testimony.** [A fourth sign which they needed to heed particularly would be an outbreak of persecution. The Book of Acts furnishes an abundant evidence of the fulfillment of these details. The civil and ecclesiastical authorities (syna-

gogues and kings) united to oppress the church. See Acts iv.
3; v. 18, 40; vii. 59; viii. 3; xii. 1, 2; xiv. 19; xvi. 19-24;
xxii. 30; xxiv. 1; xxv. 2, 3. Peter, James the elder and
James the younger, and Paul, and doubtless many more of the
apostles, suffered martyrdom before the destruction of the
temple. Tacitus bears testimony to the hatred and blind bigotry of the age when he speaks of Christians as "a class of
men hated on account of their crimes" (Annals xv. 44). See
also Suetonius on Nero 16, and Pliny (Ep. x. 97). For comment on a similar passage see pp. 365, 366.] ᵇ **10 And the
gospel must first be preached unto all the nations.**
[Paul says that this was done (Col. i. 23). Of course the lan_
guage of both Jesus and Paul must be understood with reference to the geography of the earth as then known. Paul's
declaration was written about the year A. D. 63, or seven
years before the destruction of Jerusalem. His meaning is not
that every creature had actually heard the gospel, but that each
had been given an opportunity to hear because the gospel had
been so universally preached.] **11 And when they lead
you *to judgment,* and deliver you up, be not anxious
beforehand what ye shall speak:** ᶜ **14 Settle it therefore in your hearts, not to meditate beforehand how to
answer: 15 for I will give you a mouth and wisdom,
which all your adversaries shall not be able to withstand or to gainsay.** ᵇ **but whatsoever shall be given
you in that hour, that speak ye; for it is not ye that
speak, but the Holy Spirit.** [See p. 318. This is the
third time Jesus has given this promise. See p. 366.] ᵃ **10
And then shall many stumble** [persecution always causes a
deflection of the faint-hearted, see pp. 333, 334], **and shall
deliver up one another, and shall hate one another.**
[Apostates have ever been among the most bitter enemies of
the church.] **11 And many false prophets shall arise,
and shall lead many astray.** [This refers to the false
teachers which arose in the church. The apostles bear abundant testimony to their appearance—II. Cor. xi. 13-15; Gal.
ii. 1-4; I. Tim. i. 3-7, 19, 20; II. Tim. iii. 8, 9; Tit. i. 10, 11;

II. Pet. ii. ; Jude.] **12 And because iniquity shall be multiplied, the love of the many shall wax cold.** [The prevalence of sin tempts and encourages the feeble to commit it.] ᶜ **16 But ye shall be delivered up even by parents, and brethren, and kinsfolk, and friends;** ᵇ **12 And brother shall deliver up brother to death, and the father his child; and children shall rise up against parents, and cause them to be put to death.** ᶜ **and** *some* **of you shall they cause to be put to death.** [Hatred against Christianity would prove stronger than all family ties.] **17 And ye shall be hated of all men for my name's sake.** [See p. 366.] **18 And not a hair of your head shall perish.** [The previous verses show that this promise is spiritual. The destruction of a saint's body would work no real injury to him.] ᵇ **but he that endureth to the end** [*i. e.*, to his death]**, the same shall be saved.** [See p. 366.] ᶜ **19 In your patience ye shall win your souls.** [The Christian's battle is won by endurance and not by violence, and he that can patiently hold out unto the end can, by the grace of God, save his soul.] ᵃ **14 And this gospel of the kingdom shall be preached in the whole world for a testimony unto all the nations; and then shall the end come.** [See the tenth verse of Mark's Gospel given above. Jerusalem, the seat of the old dispensation, was not removed until the new dispensation was sown throughout the then known world.] ᶜ **20 But when ye see Jerusalem compassed with armies, then know that her desolation is at hand.** ᵇ **14 But** ᵃ **15 When therefore ye see the abomination of desolation, which was spoken of through Daniel the prophet** [Dan. xi. 31]**, standing in the holy place** ᵇ **where he ought not** [for comment, see end of the paragraph, page 626] **(let him that readeth understand)** [Matthew also gives a similar parenthesis. If the words in the parentheses were spoken by our Lord, they would constitute an exhortation to understand the prophecy of Daniel, and would be unnecessary, since our Lord's application of the prophecy explains it. The words are, therefore, exhortations by the Evangelists Matthew and Mark, bidding their readers take heed to this part of the prophecy (which constituted the last sign, and, therefore, the final warning) that they might not share in the bitter fate impending over Jerusalem and Judæa if they chanced to be in either in the hour of judgment], **then let them that are in Judaea flee unto the mountains: ᶜand let them that are in the midst of her** [Jerusalem] **depart out; and let not them that are in the country enter therein. ᵇ15 and let him that is on the housetop not go down, nor enter in, ᵃto take out the things that are in {ᵇto take anything out of} his house** [see pp. 532, 533]: **16 and let him that is in the field not return back to take his cloak. ᶜ22 For** [this word introduces the reason for such hot haste] **these are days of vengeance, that all things which are written may be fulfilled.** [Deut. xxviii. 49-57; Dan. ix. 26, 27; xii. 1, 11; Joel ii. 2.] **ᵇ17 But woe unto them that are with child and to them that give suck in those days!** [because their condition would impede their flight] **ᶜfor there shall be great distress upon the land, and wrath unto this people.** [The city of Jerusalem was divinely sentenced to punishment for her sins.] **24 And they shall fall by the edge of the sword, and shall be led captive into all the nations** [According to Josephus, one million one hundred thousand perished during the siege, and ninety-seven thousand were taken captive. Of these latter, many were tortured and slain, being crucified, as he tells us, till " room was wanted for the crosses, and crosses wanted for the bodies"]: **and Jerusalem shall be trodden down of the Gentiles, until the times of the Gentiles be fulfilled.** [By comparing this passage with Romans xi., we find that the times of the Gentiles signify that period wherein the church is made up of Gentiles to the almost utter exclusion of the Jews. The same chapter shows that this period is to be followed by one wherein the Jew and the Gentile unite together in proclaiming the gospel. This prophecy, therefore, declares that until this union of the Jew and the Gentile takes place, the city of Jerusalem shall not only be controlled by the Gentiles, but shall be trodden under foot—*i. e.*, oppressed—by them. The history of Jerusalem, to this day, is a striking fulfillment of this prophecy.]   **ᵇ18 And pray ye that it ᵃ your flight ᵇ be not in the winter.** [Because the flight will be so precipitate that it would necessitate much exposure to the weather, sleeping under the open heaven, etc.] **ᵃneither on the sabbath** [Jewish tradition limited travel on the Sabbath day to a distance of seven furlongs.   The early training of many Christians led them to have scruples about breaking the Sabbath.   It is possible that Jesus had these scruples in view, but by no means conclusive, for in fleeing they would need the support and friendship of their Jewish brethren, who would be apt, not only to hinder, but even, in those troublous and turbulent days, to show violence to any who openly disregarded the Sabbath. For it must be remembered that the Jews, not being guided by the admonitions of Christ, would regard the sudden flight of the Christians as unnecessarily hasty]: **21 for then {ᵇthose days} ᵃshall be great tribulation, ᵇ such as there hath not been the like from the beginning of the creation {ᵃthe world} ᵇ which God created until now, and never, {ᵃno, nor ever} shall be.** [These words spoken before the event are strikingly verified by the statements of Josephus written after it. "No other city," says he, "ever suffered such miseries, nor did any age, from the beginning of the world, ever breed a generation more fruitful in wickedness than this was." And again: "If the miseries of all mankind from the creation were compared with those which the Jews then suffered, they would appear inferior." The promise that there shall be no days like it of course excludes the terrors and miseries of the judgment day, since it belongs to celestial rather than terrestrial history. Having now the whole paragraph before us, we are ready to discuss the phrase "abomination of desolation" mentioned in Matt. xxiv. 15 (p. 624). Taking it in connection with the entire paragraph, we can readily see, 1. That it was a sign practically simultaneous with the compassing of Jerusalem by the Roman army. 2. That it was a clearly marked sign which was to be followed by im-

mediate flight, even if the day of its appearing should chance
to be the Sabbath—a flight so sudden that a man must not
stop to enter his house, or to get his coat. Now, some translate the phrase "abomination of desolation" (or abomination
that causeth desolation, for it may be so translated) as referring to the crimes of the zealots, a faction in Jerusalem,
who took possession of the temple and profaned its sanctuary by using it as a fort, thus making themselves an
abomination in the eyes of the Jews by polluting God's house
and entering where they had no right to enter. But a long
interval intervened between this evil deed of theirs and the
coming of the Romans, during any day of which a Christian
might have taken his departure after the most leisurely manner. Others take the phrase as referring to the entrance of the
triumphant Roman army upon the temple courts; but as this
was one of the last scenes of the prolonged siege it could not
properly be coupled with the encompassing of the Roman army.
Meyer, aware of this difficulty, takes the position that there
were *two* flights prescribed by Jesus, one from *Jerusalem* at
the time when the Romans appeared, and the other from
Judæa at the time when the temple fell. But the language
used by Luke (Luke xxi. 20, 21) forbids us to make the flight
from Judæa subsequent to the flight from Jerusalem, for both
flights were to begin when the Romans appeared. Again it
should be noted that the phrase "the holy place" is apt to mis-
lead, especially when coupled with Mark's "where he ought
not." These words when seen in English cause us to think of
some person or thing polluting the sanctuary of the temple by
standing in its holy place. But it is evident that the words do
not refer to the temple at all. When the New Testament
speaks of the holy place in the temple it styles it *en too
hagioo* (in the holy), while the words here are *en topoo
hagioo* (in a place holy). Moreover, after a careful perusal of the
LXX. we are persuaded that they used those two terms to distinguish between the holy place in the sanctuary and other
holy places, a distinction which the Revised Version recognizes (Lev. vi. 16, 26, 27, etc.). As none but priests could enter

the holy place, it is evident that another place is meant at Ps. xxiv. 3 ; but in this place the Septuagint gives us *en topoo hagioo*. We, therefore, conclude that in this place Matthew uses the term "holy place" to designate the holy territory round about the Holy City, and that the combined expression of Matthew and Mark signifies the investiture of the city by the Roman armies and is equivalent to the plainer statement made by Luke. The Roman armies were fittingly called the abomination of desolation, because, being heathen armies, they were an abomination to the Jews, and because they brought desolation upon the country. The sight of them, therefore, became the appointed signal for Christians to quit the city.]   **22 And except those days had been shortened, ᵇ 20 And except the Lord had shortened the days, no flesh would have been saved** [since the Lord is speaking of the Jews, this means that if God had not shortened the siege and restrained the Romans, they would have exterminated the Jewish race] ; **but for the elect's sake, whom he chose, he shortened the days. ᵃ those days shall be shortened.** [Since the term "elect" in verses 24 and 31 evidently means *Christians*, it doubtless means that here, though it may mean that God spared a remnant of the Jewish people because he had covenanted with the patriarchs that they should be his *chosen* people, for the Jews also are God's elect (Rom. xi. 28, 29). Moreover, it should be noted that there were few, if any, Christians remaining in the city, and that those who were spared were spared as Jews without discrimination.]   ᵇ **21 And then if any man shall say unto you, Lo, here is the Christ; ᵃ or, Here; ᵇ or, Lo, there; believe *it* not: 22 for there shall arise false Christs and false prophets, and shall show ᵃ great signs and wonders; so as to {ᵇ that they may} lead astray, if possible, ᵃ even the elect.** [For accounts of these lying prophets who appeared before and during the siege, see Josephus, Wars iv., v., vi. Christ warns his followers: 1. Not to be deceived by spurious Christs. 2. Not to believe that he himself has again appeared. This latter warning is further enforced in what follows.]   ᵇ **23 But take**

ye heed: behold, I have told you all things beforehand.
ᵃ 26 If therefore they shall say unto you, Behold, he is
in the wilderness ; go not forth : Behold, he is in the
inner chambers ; believe *it* **not. 27 For as the light-**
ning cometh forth from the east, and is seen even
unto the west; so shall be the coming of the Son of
man. [The coming of Christ would be an event needing no
herald ; every man would see it for himself. See p. 531.] **28**
Wheresoever the carcass is, there will the eagles be
gathered together. [See pp. 533, 534.]

CXIV.

THE SECOND COMING OF CHRIST.

ᵃ MATT. XXIV. 29-51 ; ᵇ MARK XIII. 24-37 ; ᶜ LUKE XXI. 25-37.

ᵇ **24 But in those days, ᵃimmediately after the**
{ᵇ that} ᵃ tribulation of those days [Since the coming of
Christ did not follow close upon the destruction of Jerusalem,
the word "immediately" used by Matthew is somewhat puzzling. There are, however, three ways in which it may be
explained: 1. That Jesus reckons the time after his own
divine, and not after our human, fashion. Viewing the word
in this light, the passage at II. Pet. iii. 4-9 may almost be
regarded as an inspired comment with reference to this passage. 2. The terrible judgment upon Jerusalem and the corresponding terror of the judgment day have between them no
intervening season of judgment in any way worthy to be compared to either of them. The two periods, therefore, stand
with regard to each other in immediate connection. 3. The
tribulation which came upon the Jewish people merely began
with the destruction of Jerusalem, other woes followed *at*
once, and, coming down through all the centuries of wandering
and dispersion, they were yet unfulfilled and incomplete. See
Deut. xxviii. 58-68] **the sun shall be darkened, and the**
moon shall not give her light, and the stars shall fall
{ᵇ shall be falling} from heaven, ᵃ and the powers of

{^b that are in} **the heavens shall be shaken.** [The language is that of the ancient prophets. See Amos viii. 9; Joel ii. 30, 31; Ezek. xxxii. 7, 8. Compare also Rev. vi. 12-14. Some regard the language as metaphorical, indicating the eclipse of nation and the downfall of rulers, but there are many similar passages of Scripture which constrain us to regard the language here as literal rather than figurative. See II. Pet. iii. 10; Heb. i. 12; Rev. xx. 11.] ^c **25 And there shall be signs in sun and moon and stars; and upon the earth distress of nations, in perplexity for the roaring of the sea and the billows** [We can conceive of nothing which would produce greater mental distress or perplexity than changes in the position or condition of the heavenly bodies. Such changes will be followed by corresponding commotions on our planet, as, for instance, great tidal waves and vast agitation in the ocean]; **26 men fainting for fear, and for expectation of the things which are coming on the world: for the powers of the heavens shall be shaken.** ^a **30 and then shall appear the sign of the Son of man in heaven** [The coming and the sign are the same thing. The word " sign " is used in connection with the coming of Christ to indicate that the nature of the coming (that is, the manner of its manifestation) will be fully commensurate with the importance of the event. His first coming in the manger was not so]: **and then shall all of the tribes of the earth mourn** [The coming will occasion universal mourning in the unprepared, and apparently the majority of people will be in that condition. The term " all " is not, however, to be construed as including all individuals—I. Thess. iv. 15-17], ^b **26 And then shall they see the Son of man coming in** {^a on the} **clouds** {^c in a cloud} ^a **of heaven** ^b **with great power** ^a **and great glory.** ^b **27 And then shall he send forth the** {^a his} **angels with a great sound of a trumpet, and they shall gather together his elect from the four winds, from one end of heaven to the other.** ^b **from the uttermost part of the earth to the uttermost part of heaven.** [To the Jew the trumpet would naturally be associated with the assembling of the people, for silver trumpets were used to call Israel together (Num. x. 1-4; Ex. xix. 13, 16, 19; Ps. lxxxi. 3-5). We are not told why angels are used on this occasion, but they appear to be employed in all the great operations of Providence (Matt. xiii. 41). The phrases "four winds," etc., indicate that the angelic search shall extend over the entire globe. The language is that which was then used when one desired to indicate the whole earth. It is based upon the idea which then prevailed that the earth is flat, and that it extends outward in one vast plain until it meets and is circumscribed by the overarching heavens.] ᶜ **28 But when these things begin to come to pass, look up, and lift up your heads; because your redemption draweth nigh.** [The preliminary death-throes of this present physical universe, which will strike terror to the souls of those who have limited themselves to material hopes, will be to the Christian a reassuring sign, since he looks for a new heaven and a new earth.] **29 And he spake to them a parable:** ᵃ **32 Now from the fig tree learn her parable: when her branch is now become tender, and putteth forth its leaves, ye know that the summer is nigh;** ᶜ **Behold the fig tree, and all the trees: 30 when they now shoot forth, ye see it and know of your own selves that the summer is now nigh. 31 Even so ye also, when ye see** ᵃ **all** ᶜ **these things coming to pass, know ye that the kingdom of God is nigh.** ᵃ **know ye that he is nigh,** *even* **at the doors.** [As the change of the season in the natural world has its preliminary signs, so the change of conditions in the spiritual realm has its premonitory symptoms. When men see the symptoms which Jesus has described, they will recognize that changes are coming as to the nature of which they can only guess. But the Christian is informed that these changes indicate the coming of the Son of God—a change from a worse to a better season.] **34 Verily I say unto you, This generation shall not pass away,** ᵇ **until all things be accomplished.** [Commentators differ widely as to the import of these words. Godet is so perplexed by them that he thinks they refer to the destruction of Jerusalem, and have been misplaced by the Evangelist. Cook straddles the difficulty by giving a dual significance to all that our Lord has said concerning his coming, so that our Lord in one narrative speaks *figuratively* of a coming in the power of his kingdom before, during, and right after the destruction of Jerusalem, and *literally* of his final coming at the end of the world. But this perplexing expression under this theory refers exclusively to the figurative and not to the literal sense of the passage. The simplest solution of the matter is to take the word "generation" to mean the Jewish family or race—and the word does mean race or family—Luke xvi. 8. Thus interpreted, the passage becomes a prophecy that the Jewish people shall be preserved as such until the coming of Christ. The marvelous and almost miraculous preservation of the racial individuality of the Jews, though dispersed among all nations, might well become the subject of prophecy, especially when Jesus had just spoken of an event which threatened their very extermination.] **31 Heaven and earth shall pass away: but my word shall not pass away.** [The disciples had regarded the temple as so permanent that they found it hard to conceive that Christ's words could be fulfilled with regard to it; but he assures them that his predictions and prophecies are the stable and imperishable things. That even the more permanent structure of the heavens is not so abiding as his utterances.] ᵃ**36 But of that day and {ᵇ or that} hour knoweth no one, not even the angels in {ᵃ of} heaven, neither the Son, ᵇ but the Father.** ᵃ **only.** [These words indicate the profound secrecy in which God has concealed the hour of judgment. It is concealed from all people, that each generation may live in expectation of its fulfillment, and we are to watch for the signs, though we may not fully know the times. They also indicate that either by reason of his assumption of our human nature, or by a voluntary act on his part, the knowledge of Jesus became in some respects circumscribed. They also suggest that it is not only idle, but also presumptuous, for men to strive to find out by mathematical calculation and expositions of prophecy that which the Son of God did not know.] **37 And as** *were* **the days of Noah, so shall be the coming of the Son of man.** 38 For as in those days which were before the flood they were eating and drinking, marrying and giving in marriage, until the day that Noah entered into the ark, 39 and they knew not until the flood came, and took them all away; so shall be the coming of the Son of man. [See p. 532.] **40 Then** shall two men be in the field; one is taken, and one is left: **41** two women *shall be* grinding at the mill; one is taken, and one is left. [See p. 533.] **42** Watch therefore: for ye know not on what day your Lord cometh. **43** But know this, that if the master of the house had known in what watch the thief was coming, he would have watched, and would not have suffered his house to be broken through. **44** Therefore be ye also ready; for in an hour that ye think not the Son of man cometh. [See p. 322.] ᶜ**34** But take heed to yourselves, lest haply your hearts be overcharged with surfeiting and drunkenness, and cares of this life, and that day come on you suddenly as a snare: **35** for *so* shall it come upon all them that dwell on the face of all the earth. [The image of a snare is that of a net which suddenly encloses a covey of birds as they feed in seeming safety. The warnings here given are applicable to our appearing before Christ whether he comes to meet us, or we depart from this life to meet him. The result is the same, *whether he comes and finds us unprepared or whether we go hence without preparation.*] ᵃ**45 Who then is the faithful and wise servant,** whom his lord hath set over his household, to give them their food in due season? **46** Blessed is that servant, whom his lord when he cometh shall find so doing. **47** Verily I say unto you, that he will set him over all that he hath. **48** But if that evil servant shall say in his heart, My lord tarrieth; **49** and shall begin to beat his fellow-servants, and shall eat and drink with the drunken; **50** the lord of that servant shall come in a day when he expecteth not, and in an hour when he knoweth not, 51 and shall cut him asunder, and appoint his portion with the hypocrites: there shall be the weeping and the gnashing of teeth. [See p. 323.] ᶜ 36 But watch ye at every season, making supplication, that ye may prevail to escape all these things that shall come to pass, and to stand before the Son of man. [The revealed presence of God is represented as such an overpowering event that sinners are crushed to the earth by it. Only the godly are able to stand in his presence—Ps. i. 5; Mal. iii. 2.] ᵇ 33 Take ye heed, watch and pray: for ye know not when the time is. 34 *It is* as *when* a man, sojourning in another country, having left his house, and given authority to his servants, to each one his work, commanded also the porter to watch. [Under the figure of the householder and the thief, Jesus appealed to the sense of danger. Under the figure of the servant he appealed to the sense of duty, and under this figure of the porter he appealed to the sense of loyalty. The porter's desire to honor his lord was to make him so vigilant that he would open the door at once upon his lord's appearing.] 35 Watch therefore: for ye know not when the lord of the house cometh, whether at even, or at midnight, or at cockcrowing, or in the morning [The night was then divided into four watches. See p. 322. Jesus may here refer either to the duration of the world or to the life of the individual. He divides either period into four sections, in accordance with the night watches which were so fully associated with watchfulness]; 36 lest coming suddenly he find you sleeping. 37 And what I say unto you I say unto all, Watch. [This warning message was not for the apostles alone, but for all disciples.]

CXV.

CONCLUSION OF OUR LORD'S DISCOURSE. PAR-
ABLES OF VIRGINS AND TALENTS.
THE FINAL JUDGMENT.

(Mount of Olives. Tuesday.)

ª MATT. xxv. 1-46.

ª **1 Then** [*i. e.*, at the time of the Lord's coming. Jesus is
still emphasizing the lesson of watchfulness, and proceeds to enforce it by two parables] **shall the kingdom of heaven be
likened unto ten** [probably the usual number on such oc-
casions] **virgins, who took their lamps** [small earthenware vessels, with flax wicks, and without glass chimneys],
and went forth to meet the bridegroom. [The Oriental
wedding began with a feast in the house of the bride's father.
After this the bridegroom led the bride to his own home, and
it was the duty of his servants and household (of whom the ten
virgins in this case were part) to honor him and the bride with
an enthusiastic welcome.] **2 And five of them were foolish, and five were wise. 3 For the foolish, when they
took their lamps, took no oil with them: 4 but the
wise took oil in their vessels with their lamps.** [The
foolish showed their folly in failing to provide for their lord's
delay. The oil in their lamps would only burn till about midnight. But the wise had provided an additional supply to burn
from then till daylight.] **5 Now while the bridegroom
tarried, they all slumbered and slept.** [Rather, "nodded
and slept." They did not lie down to regular slumber, but
took such innocent rest as their office permitted. Others
were on the lookout, and would give the warning; so these
were permitted to sleep, but only in such a posture that they
would be ready to arise and go at once when apprised of their
lord's approach.] **6 But at midnight there is a cry, Behold, the bridegroom! Come ye forth to meet him. 7
Then all those virgins arose, and trimmed their lamps.**

8 And the foolish said unto the wise, Give us of your oil; for our lamps are going out. [The signal-call roused all ten, and each group of five prepared by trimming the lamps, etc. But then became apparent the difference between them. All had made some preparation, but that of the foolish five had been insufficient. Their glory began to depart, and their light waned into darkness at the approach of the bridegroom.] 9 But the wise answered, saying, Peradventure there will not be enough for us and you: go ye rather to them that sell, and buy for yourselves. [There will be no borrowed righteousness on the day of the Lord's coming, for no one shall have any to spare. The Roman Catholic confidence in saints, and the trust of some Protestants in pious parents, are alike unavailing: each soul must see to its own lamp. Those who had the oil to sell are merely part of the drapery of the parable, put in to bring out the point that it was then *too late* to secure any oil. The oil of God's grace is given without money and without price, but in the hour of the Lord's appearing it will be too late to seek for it.] 10 And while they went away to buy, the bridegroom came; and they that were ready went in with him to the marriage feast: and the door was shut. [The feast in the bridegroom's house was considered the most important part of the marriage, and certainly for those of the lord's own household it was the only feast. To be shut out from it was to be deprived of all participation in the marriage joy. All the wisdom and shrewdness of Universalism can never open this shut door.] 11 Afterward came also the other virgins, saying, Lord, Lord, open to us. 12 But he answered and said, Verily I say unto you, I know you not. [The verb "know" is here used, according to the Jewish idiom, for favorable knowledge (Matt. vii. 23). It signified that these virgins, on account of their remissness, were no longer counted even as acquaintances, much less as part of the household.] 13 Watch therefore, for ye know not the day nor the hour. [Thus Jesus makes his own application of the parable.] 14 For *it is* as *when* a man, going into an-

other country, called his own servants, and delivered unto them his goods. 15 And unto one he gave five talents, to another two, to another one; to each according to his several ability; and he went on his journey. 16 Straightway he that received the five talents went and traded with them, and made other five talents. [The parable of the virgins represented watchfulness displaying itself in *waiting* for the Lord, while it is here displayed in *working* for him. There it was inward spiritual life, here it is external activity.] 17 In like manner he also that *received* the two gained other two. 18 But he that received the one went away and digged in the earth, and hid his lord's money. 19 Now after a long time the lord of those servants cometh, and maketh a reckoning with them. [We have here one of the Lord's intimations that the day of judgment would not come at once. The word for servants is *douloi*, which means slaves. They were the property of the master and he might dispose of them as he pleased. The reckoning is as sure as the trust; judgment is as sure as life. A man who had entrusted a talent (from $1,600 to $1,800) would surely not forget to ask a settlement, nor will God fail to demand an accounting from all those to whom he had entrusted the riches and privileges of this wonderful human life which he has given us, though many of us may lightly esteem it.] 20 And he that received the five talents came and brought other five talents, saying, Lord, thou deliveredst unto me five talents: lo, I have gained other five talents. 21 His lord said unto him, Well done, good and faithful servant: thou hast been faithful over a few things, I will set thee over many things ; enter thou into the joy of thy lord. [The joy of the lord was doubtless some festival in celebration of his return, and it stands for the joy of Christ in the Father's house.] 22 And he also that *received* the two talents came and said, Lord, thou deliveredst unto me two talents: lo, I have gained other two talents. 23 His lord said unto him, Well done, good and faithful servant: thou hast been faithful over a few things, I will set thee over many things; enter thou into the joy of thy lord. [The second servant, having done as well proportionately as the first, received the like precious commendation.] **24 And he also that had received the one talent came and said, Lord, I knew thee that thou art a hard man, reaping where thou didst not sow, and gathering where thou didst not scatter; 25 and I was afraid, and went away and hid thy talent in the earth: lo, thou hast thine own. 26 But his lord answered and said unto him, Thou wicked and slothful servant, thou knewest that I reap where I sowed not, and gather where I did not scatter; 27 thou oughtest therefore to have put my money to the bankers, and at my coming I should have received back mine own with interest. 28 Take ye away therefore the talent from him, and give it unto him that hath the ten talents. 29 For unto every one that hath shall be given, and he shall have abundance: but from him that hath not, even that which he hath shall be taken away. 30 And cast ye out the unprofitable servant into the outer darkness: there shall be the weeping and the gnashing of teeth.** [See pp. 565, 566. This parable is much like that of the pounds, but differs in several particulars. There the *same amount* was entrusted to each one, but the returns were *different*, and the rewards were different. Here *different* amounts were entrusted, the returns were in proportion to the trust, and the rewards were the same.] **31 But when the Son of man shall come in his glory, and all the angels with him, then shall he sit on the throne of his glory** [Christ's judgment throne is called his throne of glory because in the day that he sits upon it his glory will be exhibited to men more brightly than ever before; for in the decisions of that hour his mercy, justice and righteousness will most fully appear, and all the obscure things in the past administration of his government will be made clear]: **32 and before him shall be gathered all the nations: and he**

shall separate them [not the nations, but the individuals which compose them] **one from another, as the shepherd separateth the sheep from the goats** [It was the custom for the shepherd to let the sheep and goats feed together during the day and to separate them at night. This custom is placed in the parable because it is analogous to the present commingling and final separation of men. Goats are here employed to represent the evil class of men, because goats have to be *driven* while sheep follow the shepherd] **; 33 and he shall set the sheep on his right hand, but the goats on the left.** [The right hand is always represented as the place of honor and preferment. The Jews in their traditions say that when criminals were tried by the Sanhedrin those who were acquitted were placed on the right hand, and those who were condemned on the left.] **34 Then shall the King say unto them on his right hand, Come, ye blessed of my Father, inherit** [take possession of as rightful heirs] **the kingdom prepared for you from the foundation of the world** [God's purpose designed such a kingdom from the beginning (Eph. i. 9-14), and we may conceive of it as in process of preparation ever since—John xiv. 2]: **35 for I was hungry, and ye gave me to eat; I was thirsty, and ye gave me drink; I was a stranger, and ye took me in; 36 naked, and ye clothed me; I was sick, and ye visited me; I was in prison, and ye came unto me.** [The acts here enumerated indicate more than a mere outlay of money. They are not such as are the offspring of impulse, but such as call for the sacrifice of time, strength, sympathy, etc., and clearly demonstrate the fullness of the Christian life. Moreover, Jesus does not mean to teach that mere works of benevolence are a sufficient ground for salvation. The meaning is that none can be saved *without* these fruits of faith and love. The passage must be construed in the light of other Scriptures which teach the further necessity of forgiveness on the part of God and of obedience on the part of man.] **37 Then shall the righteous answer him, saying, Lord, when saw we thee hungry, and fed thee? or athirst, and gave thee**

drink? 38 And when saw we thee a stranger, and took thee in? or naked, and clothed thee? 39 And when saw we thee sick, or in prison, and came unto thee? 40 And the King shall answer and say unto them, Verily I say unto you, Inasmuch as ye did it unto one of these my brethren, *even* these least, ye did it unto me. [This conversation is the drapery of the narrative. Such words will not be actually spoken at the judgment, but they are introduced for the twofold purpose of illustrating the beautiful unconsciousness of merit which characterizes the noblest of deeds and the more important fact that anything done for his sake is the same as if done to his person—Matt. x. 42; Mark ix. 41.] 41 Then shall he say also unto them on the left hand, Depart from me, ye cursed, into the eternal fire which is prepared for the devil and his angels [The two preparations stand in contrast. God prepared a kingdom of joy and designed that man should be with him in it. He also prepared a place of punishment for Satan and his angels, and man can cast his lot there and share that punishment if he wills to do so]: 42 for I was hungry, and ye did not give me to eat; I was thirsty, and ye gave me no drink; 43 I was a stranger, and ye took me not in; naked, and ye clothed me not; sick, and in prison, and ye visited me not. 44 Then shall they also answer, saying, Lord, when saw we thee hungry, or athirst, or a stranger, or naked, or sick, or in prison, and did not minister unto thee? 45 Then shall he answer them, saying, Verily I say unto you, Inasmuch as ye did it not unto one of these least, ye did it not unto me. [The neglect or abuse of Christ's disciples is a direct affront to his person—Acts ix. 4.] 46 And these shall go away into eternal punishment: but the righteous into eternal life. [This verse contains two important truths: 1. That the doom of the wicked is as durable as the reward of the righteous. 2. That the doom of the wicked is a punishment. The word "punishment" expresses misery and suffering purposely inflicted.]

CXVI.

JESUS PREDICTS, THE RULERS PLOT FOR AND JUDAS BARGAINS FOR HIS DEATH.

(Mount of Olives, Bethany and Jerusalem. Tuesday after sunset, which Jews regarded as the beginning of Wednesday.)

ᵃ MATT. XXVI. 1-5, 14-16; ᵇ MARK XIV. 1, 2, 10, 11; ᶜ LUKE XXII. 1-6.

ᶜ 1 Now the feast of unleavened bread drew nigh, which is called the Passover. {ᵇ 1 Now after two days was *the feast of* the passover and the unleavened bread:} ᵃ 1 And it came to pass, when Jesus had finished all these words, he said unto his disciples, 2 Ye know that after two days the passover cometh, and the Son of man is delivered up to be crucified. [We may regard Jesus as having entered the temple Tuesday morning, and as having taught there until the evening.* He then retired to the slopes of Olivet and delivered the discourse which occupies Sections CXIII.-CXV. The discourse finished, it is likely that he arose about or a little after sunset (which the Jews reckoned as Wednesday) and proceeded on his way to Bethany, where he remained until late Thursday afternoon. On his way to Bethany he spoke the words of this section. The two days mentioned are Wednesday and Thursday. The passover was eaten Thursday night after sunset, which the Jews reckoned as Friday. For a full discussion of the time when the passover was eaten, see Andrews' "Life of Christ," pp. 423-460.] 3 Then were gathered together the chief priests, ᵇ and the scribes ᵃ and the elders of the people, unto the court of the high priest, who was called Caiaphas; 4 and they took counsel together ᶜ 2 And

---

*NOTE.—If this had been Tuesday, he would have said "after three days," as in the case of the resurrection. In all such expressions the remaining part of the present day was counted as one.—J. W. McG.

sought ᵇ how ᵃ that they might take Jesus by subtlety, and ᶜ how they might put him to death ; {ᵃ kill him.} [This council may have begun on the evening of Tuesday and continued until the beginning of Wednesday, Jewish time. It seems to have been a formal rather than an informal conference. The court where they met was the open space enclosed by the palace of the high priest. Caiaphas had been appointed high priest in A. D. 26 by the Procurator, Valerius Gratus, and was deposed A. D. 38. Ishmael, Eleazar and Simon held the office between the deposition of Annas and the appointment of Caiaphas (Jos. Ant. xviii. 2. 2). See also p. 64.] 5 But {ᵇ 2 for} they said, Not during the feast, lest haply there shall be a tumult ᵃ arise among {ᵇ of} the people. ᶜ for they feared the people. [They knew that there were many at the feast from Galilee, and other sections of the country where Jesus ministered ; and, judging by the demonstration made at the triumphal entry, they felt that there were plenty to take arms in Jesus' behalf. The sense of their council, therefore, seemed to be that if Jesus could be taken by subtlety—*i. e.*, arrested privately—he might be taken during the feast. But if he had to be arrested publicly, then it was better to postpone his apprehension until after the feast. The treachery of Judas caused them to adopt the former course. At this place Matthew and Mark insert the account of the supper given to Jesus in the house of Simon the leper. They do this because the treacherous determination of Judas was formed at it and dates from it. The rebuke of the Lord then administered, or the desire to reimburse himself for the price of the ointment, which Mary expended, and which he felt that he ought to have had, or some other reasons, evidently induced him at that time to decide upon our Lord's betrayal. Since then he had been seeking opportunity to betray the Master.] 3 And Satan entered into Judas who was called Iscariot, being of the number of the twelve. {ᵇ he that was one of the twelve,} [See pp. 226, 391, 392.] ᵃ 14 Then one of the twelve, who was called Judas Iscariot, ᵇ went away unto the chief priests, that

he might deliver him unto them. ᶜand communed
with the chief priests and captains, how he might deliver him unto them. ª15 and said, What are ye willing to give me, and I will deliver him unto you? [It is
probable that the proposal to sell his Master was made by
Judas to individual members of the Sanhedrin, and that this
proposal was one of the moving causes leading to the assembling of the council. The language implies that Judas appeared
before the council and bargained openly with it.] ᵇ11 And
they, when they heard it, were glad, and promised
ᶜand covenanted to give him money. ªAnd they
weighed unto him thirty pieces of silver. [There had
been coined shekels since the time of Simeon, or 143 B. C.,
before that money was weighed. It is likely that the term
"weighed" survived the practice and became a synonym or
equivalent for "paid." The amount paid him was about fifteen dollars of our money. It was indeed a low price for so
base a deed, but from the language used it may be fairly
implied that it was but the earnest money of a larger sum.
But Judas evidently hardened himself, and shut out all thought
as to anything save the *actual labor involved.* Viewed thus,
his task was neither difficult nor dangerous.] ᶜ6 And he
consented, ª16 And from that time he sought opportunity to deliver him ᵇhow he might conveniently
deliver him *unto them.* ᶜin the absence of the multitude. [He soon found his opportunity. He bargained on
Tuesday night and fulfilled his contract on Thursday night.
Or, as the Jews reckoned time, he agreed in the beginning of
Wednesday and fulfilled his covenant on the beginning of
Friday.]

CXVII.

PREPARATION FOR PASSOVER. DISCIPLES CONTEND FOR PRECEDENCE.

(Bethany to Jerusalem. Thursday afternoon and (after sunset) beginning of Friday.)

^a MATT. XXVI. 17-20; ^b MARK XIV. 12-17; ^c LUKE XXII. 7-18, 24-30.

^c 7 **And the day of unleavened bread came, on which the passover must be sacrificed.** [See p. 57. Leaven was to the Jew a symbol of corruption and impurity, because it causes bread to become stale. The feast of unleavened bread began properly on the fifteenth of Nisan, and lasted seven days, but this was the fourteenth Nisan, the day on which the paschal lamb was slain. However, it was common to blend the slaying of the passover, the passover feast and the feast of unleavened bread, and to look upon all three as one great festival, and to use the names passover and unleavened bread interchangeably to describe the entire eight days. This appears from the writings of Josephus, who sometimes reckons the feast as beginning on the fifteenth (Ant. iii. 10. 5), and again as beginning on the fourteenth (Wars v. 3. 1). He also sometimes reckons the feast as lasting seven days (Ant. iii. 10. 5), and again he reckons it as lasting eight days (Ant. ii. 15. 1). The Rabbinists say that all the leaven was carefully removed from the houses on the evening before the fourteenth Nisan. To the present day leaven is removed from the houses of the Jews on the night between the thirteenth and fourteenth. Hence the day could be very fittingly called "the first day of unleavened bread.'] ^b 12 **And** ^a 17 **Now** ^b **on the first day of unleavened bread, when they sacrificed the passover, his {^a the} disciples came to Jesus [as** the head of the household], **saying {^b say} unto him, Where wilt thou that we go and make ready** ^a **for thee to eat {^b that thou mayest eat} the passover?** [It re-

quired considerable preparation. The lamb must be slain in tne temple, and roasted, and unleavened loaves, wine, and bitter herbs, etc., must be provided (Ex. xii. 8), and a room for the feast must be secured.] **13 And he sendeth {ᶜ sent}** **Peter and John, ᵇ two of his disciples, ᶜ saying, Go and** **make ready for us the passover, that we may eat. 9** **And they said unto him, Where wilt thou that we** **make ready? 10 And he said {ᵇ saith} unto them, Go** **into the city, and ᶜ Behold, when ye are entered into** **the city, there shall meet you a man bearing a pitcher** **of water; follow him into the house whereinto he goeth.** **ᵇ 14 and wheresoever he shall enter in, say to {ᶜ 11** **And ye shall say unto} the master of the house,{ᵃ Go** **into the city to such a man, and say unto him,} ᶜ The** **Teacher saith unto thee, ᵃ My time is at hand; I keep** **the passover at thy house with my disciples. ᶜ Where** **is the {ᵇ my} guest-chamber, where I shall eat the** **passover with my disciples?** [It was customary for the residents of Jerusalem to open their houses for guests during this feast, and therefore Jesus might have presumed on the hospitality of almost any one; but the probability is that the man to whom he sent this message was an acquaintance and a friend. It is not improbable that Jesus let Peter and John thus find the place that Judas might not know its whereabouts in time to bring the officers of the Sanhedrin so as to interrupt the feasts which meant so much to him and to his church.] **15 And he will himself show you a large upper room** **furnished *and* ready: and there make ready for us. 16** **And the disciples went forth, and came into the city,** **and found as he had said unto them: ᵃ 19 And the dis-** **ciples did as Jesus appointed them; and they made** **ready the passover. ᵇ 17 And ᵃ 20 Now when even** **was come, {ᵇ when it was evening} he cometh with** **the twelve.** [The law required that the paschal lamb should be slain "between the evenings." The Jews reckoned the two evenings as from three o'clock to sunset, and from sunset to nine o'clock, which was the end of the first watch. But

Josephus tells us that the lambs were killed from the ninth to
the eleventh hours, or between the hours of three and five.   It
would take some time to dress the lamb and to roast it, so that
it must have been about sundown or shortly afterward when
Jesus and his disciples sat down to the feast.]   ᶜ **14 And
when the hour was come, he sat down, and the apostles with him.   15 And** ᵃ **he was sitting at meat with
the twelve disciples ; 21 and** ᶜ **he said unto them, With
desire I have desired to eat this passover with you
before I suffer: 16 for I say unto you, I shall not eat
it, until it be fulfilled in the kingdom of God.** [Jesus
had desired to keep with his disciples this last type which
stood so close to the thing typified.   It was a feast commemo-
rating a great deliverance from death through the sacrifice of a
lamb, and the real sacrifice and deliverance of which it was
typical were about to be fulfilled in the unfolding of the kingdom of God.]   **17 And he received a cup, and when he
had given thanks, he said, Take this, and divide it
among yourselves: 18 for I say unto you, I shall not
drink from henceforth of the fruit of the vine, until the
kingdom of God shall come.** [Luke brings out the parallelism between the passover and the Lord's supper.   Each
consisted in eating followed by drinking, and the closeness of
the parallel is emphasized by the use of almost the same words
with regard to the cup.   The passover was typical of the Lord's
suffering *before* the event, and the Lord's supper is typical of
the same thing *after* the event.]   **24 And there arose also a
contention among them, which of them was accounted
to be greatest.   25 And he said unto them, The kings
of the Gentiles have lordship over them ; and they that
have authority over them are called Benefactors.   26
But ye** *shall* **not** *be* **so : but he that is the greater among
you, let him become as the younger ; and he that is
chief, as he that doth serve.   27 For which is greater,
he that sitteth at meat, or he that serveth? is not he
that sitteth at meat? but I am in the midst of you as
he that serveth.** [In sending to secure the room in which

the paschal supper was being eaten, Jesus had said, "My time is at hand." Such expressions were falsely construed by the apostles. They thought that Jesus was about to set up his kingdom, and began at once to contend for the chief places. Jesus rebuked this false ambition in much the same manner as he had previously. See pp. 430, 557, 558.] **28 But ye are they that have continued with me in my temptations; 29 and I appoint unto you a kingdom, even as my Father appointed unto me, 30 that ye may eat and drink at my table in my kingdom; and ye shall sit on thrones judging the twelve tribes of Israel.** [The word "temptations" is here used to mean trials (Jas. i. 2, 3). For the rest of the passage compare the remarks on pp. 548, 549. The words concerning eating and drinking at the Lord's table refer to the ancient custom of thus bestowing honor and distinction (II. Sam. ix. 7; xix. 28), and indicate that the apostles, being about to participate in the Lord's condemnation and suffering, should in the end share his exaltation and its attendant joys.]

CXVIII.

THE PASCHAL MEAL. JESUS WASHES THE DISCIPLES' FEET.

(Thursday evening or the beginning of Friday.)

ᵈ JOHN XIII. 1-20.

ᵈ **1 Now before the feast of the passover, Jesus knowing that his hour was come that he should depart out of this world unto the Father, having loved his own that were in the world, he loved them unto the end.** [Since the second century a great dispute has been carried on as to an apparent discrepancy between John and the synoptists in their statements concerning the passover. The synoptists, as we have seen in the previous section, clearly represent Jesus as having eaten the passover at the proper time, and as having been arrested on that same night, while John

here and elsewhere (ch. xiii. 29; xviii. 28; xix. 14, 31, compared with xviii. 1-14), seems to represent Jesus as being arrested *before* the passover. Our space does not permit us to
enter upon a discussion of this difficulty. The reader is
referred to a thorough rehearsal of the arguments found in
Tholuck *in loco* (or, after the seventh edition, in his introduc-
tion to John's Gospel). The simplest solution of the difficulty
is to attribute the apparent discrepancy to that loose way of
speaking of the feast which we mentioned in the last section.
When the synoptists speak of the passover they refer to the
actual paschal supper; when John speaks of the feast of the
passover, or the passover, he refers to the *seven days' feast of
unleavened bread* which followed the actual paschal supper.
Jesus was put to death on the first day of this latter feast, and
therefore John here uses the festival to designate the time of
the Lord's suffering and death. The meaning, then, is that
Jesus, having loved his disciples prior to this great trial or
crisis of his life, was not deterred from loving them by its
approach, but continued to give the most precious and unmistakable evidences of his love down to the very hour of its
arrival, being neither driven from such a course by the terrors
of his coming hour nor wooed from it by the glorious prospects
of returning to his Father. These words form a preface to the
remainder of John's Gospel in which John enumerates the
tokens and evidences of that love which manifested itself
throughout the entire passion, and continued until the hour of
ascension; and which, by so doing, gave sweet assurance that
it continues still.] **2 And during supper** [This was the
paschal supper proper. It accords with the supplementary
nature of John's Gospel to thus mention it as a meal thoroughly
familiar to his readers], **the devil having already put into
the heart of Judas Iscariot, Simon's** *son*, **to betray him**
[see p. 642], **3** *Jesus*, **knowing that the Father had
given all things into his hands, and that he came forth
from God, and goeth unto God** [Being about to narrate an
act of loving humility, John prefaces it by stating that it was
done in full knowledge of his threefold glory; viz.: 1. That all

authority was committed to him (Matt. xviii. 28).   2. That by
nature he was divine (John i. 1, 14), and, 3. That he was
about to return to the divine exaltation which for our sakes he
had laid aside—Phil. ii. 5-11], **4 riseth from supper, and
layeth aside his garments ; and he took a towel, and
girded himself. 5 Then he poureth water into the
bason, and began to wash the disciples' feet, and to
wipe them with the towel wherewith he was girded.**
[John narrates in detail each of these acts : to him they seem
as so many successive steps leading down to the depth of
humility.   The whole formed a striking but wholesome contrast to the self-seeking and ambitious spirit which the disciples
had just manifested.]   **6 So he cometh to Simon Peter.
He saith unto him, Lord, dost thou wash my feet?**
[The others were awed into silence by the strange conduct of
their Master; but it accorded with the bold impulsiveness of
Peter to challenge the act.]   **7 Jesus answered and said
unto him, What I do thou knowest not now ; but thou
shalt understand hereafter.** [It was no mere feet-washing;
or Jesus would not have so spoken.   It was at once an example of humility and a symbol of the purification which the
Lord accomplished for us by reason of his humiliation.   The
full meaning of the act was afterward revealed to them by the
Holy Spirit.]   **8 Peter saith unto him, Thou shalt never
wash my feet.   Jesus answered him, If I wash thee
not, thou hast no part with me.   9 Simon Peter saith
unto him, Lord, not my feet only, but also my hands
and my head.** [Since Jesus spoke of the act as in some
sense a license or token of permission to have "part" with
him, Peter desired that his head and hands also might be
included, that he might in his entire man have part with
Christ.]   **10 Jesus saith to him, He that is bathed needeth not save to wash his feet, but is clean every whit :
and ye are clean, but not all.   11 For he knew him
that should betray him ; therefore said he, Ye are not
all clean.** [The language implies that the disciples had
bathed before leaving Bethany, and that only their feet, soiled

by the journey to Jerusalem, needed to be rewashed. The saying is spiritually true as well, for one who has once been washed thoroughly by baptism needs not to be re-baptized. After that general cleansing the particular sins are removed by confession (I. John i. 7-9). But there is no efficacy in any ordinance when the heart and will do not accord with the purposes for which it is administered. Hence it was that Judas, though he had done all that the others had done, was still as foul as ever.] **12 So when he had washed their feet, and taken his garments, and sat down again, he said unto them, Know ye what I have done to you? 13 Ye call me, Teacher, and, Lord: and ye say well; for so I am. 14 If I then, the Lord and the Teacher, have washed your feet, ye also ought to wash one another's feet. 15 For I have given you an example, that ye also should do as I have done to you. 16 Verily, verily, I say unto you, A servant is not greater than his lord; neither one that is sent greater than he that sent him. 17 If ye know these things, blessed are ye if ye do them.** [Since a servant is not greater than his lord he should not be ashamed to do what his lord does. It is well known that many, by a literal construction of this passage, have esteemed it to be their duty to wash each other's feet in their churches. But it should be noted that in the entire New Testament there is no command for this, nor is there any passage which recognizes any such church ordinance or practice. Jesus did not *institute* feet-washing; he found it already a *familiar* custom of the land, and merely used it as a most appropriate way of showing the proper spirit of humble service. Hence he does not say "Do *what* I have done," but "Do *as* I have done," which requires us to do something *similar* to that which Christ had done, but not necessarily the very *same* thing. The washing of feet as an act of courtesy or hospitality was never a custom among Western people, and to adopt it because of these words of Christ is to entirely miss his meaning. What he did was a natural daily act of hospitality. But what we would do if we followed his words literally would be to introduce a strange, outlandish practice, which would put a guest to great embarrassment and inconvenience.] **18 I speak not of you all : I know whom I have chosen : but that the scripture may be fulfilled, He that eateth my bread lifted up his heel against me.** [Ps. xli. 9.] **19 From henceforth I tell you before it come to pass, that, when it is come to pass, ye may believe that I am** *he.* **20 Verily, verily, I say unto you, He that receiveth whomsoever I send receiveth me ; and he that receiveth me receiveth him that sent me.** [The meaning of the above passage may perhaps be brought out more easily if we paraphrase it as follows : "I do not speak of blessing to you all, for there is one who shall never be blessed. His conduct does not deceive or surprise me, for I know those whom I have chosen whether they be good or bad. His choosing is in accordance with the prophecy contained in the Book of Psalms. Hitherto I have held my peace about him, but henceforth I shall point out his course, that my foreknowledge of his actions may strengthen your faith in my Messiahship, and not leave you in that condition of hopelessness and despair in which the consequences of his actions would place you if you thought those consequences had come upon me unawares. Do not let his treachery shake your confidence in me, for verily I say unto you that in being my messengers ye are indeed the messengers of the Most High."]

CXIX.

JUDAS' BETRAYAL AND PETER'S DENIAL FORETOLD.

(Jerusalem. Evening before the crucifixion.)

ᵃMATT. XXVI. 21-25, 31-35 ; ᵇMARK XIV. 18-21, 27-31 ; ᶜLUKE XXII. 21-23, 31-38 ; ᵈJOHN XIII. 21-38.

ᵇ **18 And** ᵈ **21 When Jesus had thus said,** ᵇ **as they sat and were eating,** ᵈ **he was troubled in the spirit, and** ᵇ **Jesus** ᵈ **testified, and said, Verily, verily, I say**

unto you, that one of you shall betray me.   ᵇ *even* **he**
that eateth with me.   ᶜ 21 But behold, the hand **of**
him that betrayeth me is with me on the table.   [The
foreknowledge of Judas' crime did not relieve the Lord from
the sting of it.   By the use of the word "betray" Jesus
revealed to Judas that he had perfect knowledge of the peculiar crime which he was about to commit.   To induce repentance the enormity of the crime is pointed out in two ways: 1.
It was the act of one, an act in which no other could be found
willing to have a part.   2. It was the act of one whose hand
rested on the table, who was admitted to the closest intercourse and fellowship.]   ᵈ 22 **The disciples looked one on**
another [in startled amazement], **doubting of whom he**
spake.   ᵃ 22 **And they** ᵇ **began to be** {ᵃ **were**} **exceeding**
sorrowful [that the Lord should be betrayed was sorrow
enough, but that one of the twelve should do the deed was an
added grief], ᶜ 23 **And they began to question among**
themselves, which of them it was that should do this
thing. ᵇ **and** ᵃ **began** ᵇ **to say unto him one by one,**
ᵃ **every one, Is it I, Lord?** [The form of the question in
the Greek indicates that it expects "No" for an answer, so
that it may be rendered, "Surely it is not I?"] **23 And he**
answered and said, ᵇ **unto them,** *It is* **one of the twelve,**
ᵃ **He that dipped** {ᵇ **dippeth**} ᵃ **his hand with me in the**
dish, the same shall betray me. [According to Oriental
custom, knives and forks were not used.   One dish served to
hold the sop for several people, that they might dip their bread
into it.   In so large a company two or three bowls would be
used for convenience' sake.   The words of Jesus, therefore,
limited the circle of accused ones from twelve to four or five,
and also further emphasized the tender and close intimacy
between the traitor and the Master.] ᵇ 21 **For the Son of**
man goeth, ᶜ **as it hath been determined:** ᵇ **even as it is**
written of him: but woe unto that man through whom
the Son of man is betrayed! good were it for that man
if he had not been born. [Jesus was following with unfalter-
ing step the path of suffering marked out by the prophets.

But this fact in no way exculpated the authors of his death. The prophecies referred to are many. As examples see Ps. xxii., Isa. liii. The woe pronounced upon Judas was no vindictive or vengeful wish; it is the solemn announcement of the divine judgment. The words of Jesus stop the mouths of the apologists for Judas. When the judge thus speaks in condemnation, who shall presume to argue in extenuation?] ᵈ**23 There was at the table reclining in Jesus' bosom one of his disciples, whom Jesus loved.** [John thus speaks of himself. His couch was in front of that of the Lord, so that when he laid his head back it rested upon Jesus' bosom. See p. 513.] **24 Simon Peter therefore beckoneth to him, and saith unto him, Tell** *us* **who it is of whom he speaketh. 25 He leaning back, as he was, on Jesus' breast saith unto him, Lord, who is it? 26 Jesus therefore answereth, He it is, for whom I shall dip the sop, and give it him.** [It was a mark of special respect and courtesy to thus dip a sop and hand it to a guest.] **So when he had dipped the sop, he taketh and giveth it to Judas,** *the son* **of Simon Iscariot.** [Thus Jesus advanced in his disclosure from twelve to three or four, and from three or four to one, and that one a friend most highly honored. But Judas was neither to be warned nor wooed from his purpose.] ª**25 And Judas, who betrayed him, answered and said, Is it I, Rabbi? He saith unto him, Thou hast said.** [It seems strange that the disciples showed no resentment toward Judas, and made no effort to interfere with this course, but their conduct is plain if we regard them as viewing the predictions of Jesus as referring to the indefinite future, and not the immediate present.] ᵈ**27 And after the sop, then entered Satan into him.** [Exposure only hardened Judas and made him resign himself more fully to the influence of the devil.] **Jesus therefore saith unto him, What thou doest, do quickly.** [Jesus does not command the deed, but since it has already been determined upon, he dismisses Judas from his presence with words which fix the manner in which the deed shall be done. Judas was still under divine command in a limited sense, for Satan himself is not beyond divine authority.] **28 Now no man at the table knew for what intent he spake this unto him.** [Jesus had not fully and openly revealed Judas as the traitor. To have done so in the presence of these fiery Galilæans might have resulted in violence to the person of the betrayer.] **29 For some thought, because Judas had the bag, that Jesus said unto him, Buy what things we have need of for the feast** [the feast on the evening of the first day of the festival of unleavened bread appears to have been both joyful and very bountiful] **; or, that he should give something to the poor.** [Probably to aid them in preparing for this feast.] **30 He then having received the sop went out straightway : and it was night.** [Though this expression, "it was night," is merely one which marks the time of day, nearly all commentators feel the weird force of it (Luke xxii. 53). Alford says, "I feel, with Meyer, that there is something awful in this termination—'it was night.'"] **31 When therefore he was gone out, Jesus saith, Now is the Son of man glorified, and God is glorified in him; 32 and God shall glorify him in himself, and straightway shall he glorify him.** [The departure of Judas was the first step in the progress of the Lord's Passion, and in this moment of its beginning Jesus exults in the prospect of its end. Having just condemned the false pride and glory of men by washing his disciples' feet, Jesus rejoices that the true glory of God is about to be immediately manifested in himself—the glory of humility, charity, service, and self-sacrifice, which was realized to the utmost in the person of Jesus.] **33 Little children, yet a little while I am with you. Ye shall seek me : and as I said unto the Jews** [see pp. 447, 448], **Whither I go, ye cannot come ; so now I say unto you. 34 A new commandment I give unto you, that ye love one another ; even as I have loved you, that ye also love one another. 35 By this shall all men know that ye are my disciples, if ye have love one to another.** [In the term of tenderness "my little children," with which

Jesus opens this paragraph, we see one of the marks of love referred to by John (John xiii. 1). It is found nowhere else in the Gospels. In the light of his near separation Jesus looked upon his apostles as about to be made orphan children. As to the new commandment, love had been commanded before (Lev. xix. 18), but the Christian love here commanded is different from that which the Jew was bade to feel for the Jew, just as the affection of a loving family differs from the mere broad and kindly spirit of neighborliness. A love which had Christ's heart as the standard would of necessity be new, and would distinguish those who possessed it from all men.] ᵇ**27 And** ᵃ**31 Then saith Jesus unto them, All ye shall be offended in me this night: for it is written** [Zech. xiii. 7], **I will smite the shepherd, and the sheep of the flock shall be scattered abroad. 32 But** ᵇ**28 Howbeit, after I am raised up, I will go before you into Galilee.** [The scattering would take place after the return of the apostles to Galilee, and there after his resurrection Jesus would gather them together as their shepherd.] ᵈ**36 Simon Peter saith unto him, Lord, whither goest thou? Jesus answered, Whither I go, thou canst not follow me now; but thou shalt follow afterwards. 37 Peter saith unto him, Lord, Why cannot I follow thee even now? I will lay down my life for thee.** [Peter, grieved at the prospect of separation, can see no reason why he should not follow, since he is willing to pass even through the portal of the grave that he may do so. Though perhaps prevented by no moral inability, he was prevented by the plan of life which God had designed for him. It was not in accordance with the divine will that he should die at this time.] **38 Jesus answereth, Wilt thou lay down thy life for me?** ᶜ**31 Simon, Simon, behold, Satan asked to have you, that he might sift you as wheat: 32 I made supplication for thee, that thy faith fail not** [The language here suggests a repetition, in some degree, of Satan's conduct in the case of Job. See Job i., ii. Jesus, having insight into what was going on in the spirit world, made supplication that Peter might be enabled to endure the trial]; **and do thou, when once thou hast turned again, establish thy brethren.** [The language sadly intimates that Satan's test would leave him in need of repentance. As the one who perhaps exercised the strongest influence over the ten other apostles, Peter is exhorted to use his own bitter experience for their benefit and strengthening.] **33 And he said unto him, Lord, with thee I am ready to go both to prison and to death** ª **33 But Peter answered and said unto him,** ᵇ**Although,** {ª**If**} **all shall be offended in thee,** ᵇ**yet will not I.** ª**I will never be offended.** [Thus Peter repudiates the idea that he could not stand the test.] ᵇ**30 And Jesus saith** {ª**said**} **unto him, Verily I say unto thee,** ᶜ**I tell thee, Peter,** ᵇ**that thou to-day,** *even* **this night, before the cock crow twice,** ᶜ**thou shalt thrice deny that thou knowest me.** ᵈ**Verily, verily, I say unto thee, The cock shall not crow,** ᶜ**this day,** ᵈ**till** {ᶜ**until**} ᵈ**thou hast denied me thrice.** [Mark speaks of two cock-crowings and shows that the denial of Peter occurred between them (Mark xiv. 68-72). But John and Luke speak of but *one* cock-crowing, and place the denial of Jesus before it. The discrepancy is not an important one. Luke and John look upon the night in its entirety and speak of the cock-crowing at three in the morning, the signal of the dawning day. Mark looks at the night in its details, and shows that the denials of Peter began at midnight, the time of the first cock-crowing, and were finished before the last, or about three in the morning. Peter appears to have been thunderstruck at this prediction, which showed the nature, the details, and the nearness of his sin. He lapsed into silence, and we hear no more from him during the discourses which followed. But he did not yield without one final protest, as the sequel shows.] ᵇ**31 But** ª**Peter** ᵇ**spake exceeding vehemently,** ª**saith unto him, Even** ᵇ**If I must die with thee, I will not deny thee. And in like manner** {ª**Likewise**} **also said all the disciples.** [According to Matthew's account these accusations of our Lord and protestations of Peter were taken up again after

Jesus left the upper room and was on his way to Gethsemane. The reader may therefore conceive of them as occurring again in the opening lines of Section CXXIII.] ᶜ **35 And he said unto them, When I sent you forth without purse, and wallet, and shoes, lacked ye anything?** [See pp. 363, 364.] **And they said, Nothing. 36 And he said unto them, But now, he that hath a purse, let him take it, and likewise a wallet; and he that hath none, let him sell his cloak, and buy a sword. 37 For I say unto you, that this which is written** [Isa. liii. 12] **must be fulfilled in me, And he was reckoned with transgressors: for that which concerneth me hath fulfilment. 38 And they said, Lord, behold, here are two swords. And he said unto them, It is enough.** [In this passage our Lord draws a contrast between the favor with which his messengers had been received on their *former* mission and the trials and persecutions which awaited them in their *future* course. If they had prepared then to be received with joy, they were to prepare now to be opposed with bitterness; for the utter rejection of the Master would be followed by the violent persecution of the servants. The apostles took the words of Jesus literally, and showed two swords, and the Lord, for their future enlightenment, said, " It is enough, " thus intimating that he did not mean a literal arming with carnal weapons, for, had he done so, two swords would not have sufficed for twelve men.]

CXX.

THE LORD'S SUPPER INSTITUTED.

(Jerusalem. Evening before the crucifixion.)

ᵃ MATT. XXVI. 26-29; ᵇ MARK XIV. 22-25; ᶜ LUKE XXII. 19, 20;
ᶠ I. COR. XI. 23-26.

ᵃ **26 And as they were eating,** ᶠ **the Lord Jesus in the night in which he was betrayed took bread; and when he had given thanks,** {ᵇ **blessed,**} ᶠ **he brake it,** ᵃ **and he**

gave to the disciples, and said, ᵇ Take ye : ª Take, eat ;
this is my body. ᶠ which is ᶜ given ᶠ for you : this do
in remembrance of me. [As only unleavened bread was
eaten during the paschal supper, that kind of bread must have
been used by our Lord, and it is fitting that it should still be
used by us in keeping the Lord's Supper, not only for propriety's
sake, but because that bread which is emblematic of purity is
most suitable to represent the body of the sinless Christ.   The
Catholics and some few others take our Lord's words literally
when he says, "This is my body."   On this they found the
doctrine of transubstantiation ; *i. e.*, that the bread and the
wine become literal body and blood when blessed by the priest.
There are many weighty arguments *against* such a doctrine,
but the main one *for* it is found in these words of our Lord.
But Jesus could not have meant them literally, for his body
was untouched and his blood unshed on this occasion when
he spoke them.   Moreover, in the twenty-fifth verse of Mark
given below, Jesus calls the wine "the fruit of the vine,"
when, according to the theory of transubstantiation, it had
been turned into blood and hence was not wine at all.]   ᵇ **23
And he took a {ᶜ the} cup in like manner ꜰ also ᶜ after
supper** [Luke distinguishes between the cup taken during
(see p. 646) and that taken after supper.   The first belonged
to the passover, this to the Lord's Supper.   Wine, mingled
with water, was drunk during the paschal supper.   Jesus took
a cup of this for his new institution.   But the word "wine" is
nowhere used in any of the accounts of the Lord's Supper, the
terms "cup" and "fruit of the vine" being employed in its
stead.   Those, therefore, who choose to use unfermented
grape juice are guilty of no irregularity], ª **and gave thanks,
and** ᵇ **when he had given thanks, he gave to them : 24
And he said {ª saying} ᵇ unto them,** ª **Drink ye all of it**
["All" refers to the persons and not to the wine.   It was important that all the disciples participate in the cup, but not that
all the wine should be used]; **28 for this is my blood of
the covenant,** ᶜ **This cup is the new covenant in my
blood** [Jer. xxxi. 31-34.   It was the practice of Eastern

peoples to use blood in making any pact or covenant (Ex. xxiv. 6-8). Christ represents himself as the victim from whence the blood was to be taken to ratify or seal the new covenant, and he makes the cup the symbol of that blood. A full discussion of the old and new covenants will be found in the Book of Hebrews. We may, however, sum them up by saying that the old covenant promised the land of Canaan and Christ in the flesh to the Israelites, while the new covenant promises heaven and Christ in glory to the Christian], ᵇ **which is poured out for many.** [It is explicitly stated elsewhere that Christ died for *all* (Heb. ii. 9; II. Cor. v. 14, 15), and the word "many" is used, not to contradict, but to emphasize that fact. When the persons included are contemplated individually, the term *many* is employed on account of the vast number of them; for no man can number the individuals for whom Christ died. But when they are contemplated under the feebler conception of the whole, the term *all* is employed.] ª **unto remission of sins.** ᶜ *even* **that which is poured out for you.** [The prime object of Christ's death is here declared. It was to accomplish the forgiveness of sins. All other purposes which it served are subordinate to this, and all other blessings which it secures are consequent upon this—John i. 29; Eph. v. 2; Heb. vii. 27; I. John ii. 2; iv. 10; Isa. liii. 10; Rom. viii. 2; I. Cor. v. 15.] ᶠ **this do, as often as ye drink** *it,* **in remembrance of me.** [The word "remembrance" comes as a refrain after both the loaf and the cup. The central purpose of the supper is to bring the sacrifice of Christ and all its blessed results vividly to mind.] **26 For as often as ye eat this bread, and drink the cup, ye proclaim the Lord's death till he come.** [This verse is a comment of Paul's upon the nature of the supper. In keeping the Lord's Supper we proclaim to our own souls and to the world our trust in the death of Christ, and our hope that he will return and fulfill the expectations begotten in us by it.] ª **29 But** ᵇ **25 Verily I say unto you, I shall no more drink** {ª **shall not drink henceforth**} ᵇ **of the** {ª **this**} **fruit of the vine, until that day when I drink it new with you in** ᵇ **the kingdom of**

God. ᵃ **my Father's kingdom.** ᵇ **and they all drank of it.** [In speaking of this future drinking of the fruit of the vine Jesus does not mean literal wine, for he does not drink literal wine with his disciples in the kingdom as it now is, nor will he do so in the eternal kingdom. The term "drink," therefore, is used figuratively for that communion which Jesus has with his disciples while they are drinking the wine of the Lord's Supper. The term *new* is most naturally understood as modifying *wine*, but as the wine of the supper is not necessarily *new* wine, we think it rather indicates the *new method* of drinking wine just described.]

CXXI.

FAREWELL DISCOURSE TO DISCIPLES.

(Jerusalem.   Evening before the crucifixion.)

ᵈ JOHN XIV.-XVI.

ᵈ **1 Let not your heart be troubled: believe in God, believe also in me.** [That one should betray him and one should deny him, that all should be offended, and that the Lord should depart, raised anxieties which Jesus here seeks to quiet. That they should go out as homeless wanderers without the presence of their Lord and be subjected to persecution, was also in their thoughts. But Jesus sustains their spirits by appealing to them to trust in the unseen Father, and his yet present self. As to the two verbs "believe," both may be either indicatives or imperatives.] **2 In my Father's house are many mansions** [Many abiding places or homes. They were not to be homeless always]; **if it were not so, I would have told you** [That is to say, if heaven had been of such limited capacity that there was little or no hope that you could follow me, I should have dealt plainly with you, and should have disabused your mind of all vain hopes. But there is room (Luke xiv. 22), and you may follow—John xiii. 36]; **for I go to prepare a place for you.** [We are familiar with the thought that the going, or death, of Jesus prepared a way for us by providing a fountain for the cleansing of our sin, and by rending the veil of the temple, "thus signifying that the way into heaven is now open." But the thought here is different. Jesus departed to prepare places for his own in the Father's house.] **3 And if I go and prepare a place for you, I come again, and will receive you unto myself; that where I am,** *there* **ye may be also.** [The cause for the departure becomes the assurance of the return.] **4 And whither I go, ye know the way.** [My manner of life leads to the Father's house, and as ye know that manner of life, ye know the way.] **5 Thomas saith unto him, Lord, we know not whither thou goest; how know we the way?** [Thomas looked for a way wherein one might walk with his feet.] **6 Jesus saith unto him, I am the way, and the truth, and the life: no one cometh unto the Father, but by me.** [God is not approached by physical motion. Being spirit, we must draw near to him by spiritual simplicity, and this is revealed to us fully in the person of Christ, and an energizing power is imparted by Christ to enable us to attain unto it.] **7 If ye had known me, ye would have known my Father also** [the unity of nature and of character is so perfect that to know the Son is to know the Father also] **: from henceforth ye know him, and have seen him.** [This saying is the outgrowth of what is said in the sixth verse. Since we can only come to the Father's likeness by the imitation of Jesus, then the truth here uttered follows; viz.: that to see Jesus is to see the Father.] **8 Philip saith unto him, Lord, show us the Father, and it sufficeth us. 9 Jesus saith unto him, Have I been so long time with you, and dost thou not know me, Philip? he that hath seen me hath seen the Father, how sayest thou, Show us the Father?** [As Thomas asked for a physical instead of a spiritual way of approach to God, so Philip asked for a physical instead of a spiritual revelation of him. The answer of Jesus tenderly rebukes Philip. The excellency of God is not physical, but spiritual. Righteousness, truth, love, holiness, etc., are all spiritual. A physical revelation of God, if such a thing had been practicable or even possible, would have been of little or no benefit to the apostles. All the physical demonstrations at Mt. Sinai did not prevent the manufacture and worship of the golden calf.] **10 Believest thou not that I am in the Father, and the Father in me? the words that I say unto you I speak not from myself: but the Father abiding in me doeth his works.** [The question of Jesus is a mild rebuke because Philip had been so slow to learn and to believe what the Lord had taught; viz.: his unity with the Father (p. 486), and that he did and taught by the will of his Father and not of himself—p. 456.] **11 Believe me that I am in the Father, and the Father in me: or else believe me for the very work's sake.** [To ask Jesus to reveal the indwelling Father was much the same as to ask a man to reveal his own soul. Therefore Jesus asks Philip to take his word for that great fact, or, if that were not deemed sufficient, to believe it because of the works which Jesus wrought. Divine works testify to the presence of a divine spirit and power.] **12 Verily, verily, I say unto you, He that believeth on me, the works that I do shall he do also; and greater *works* than these shall he do; because I go unto the Father.** [Jesus while in the world manifested sufficient supernatural power to give credibility to the statement that the Father worked through him. But he here declares that his return to the Father will be followed by yet fuller tokens and evidences of his union with the Father. The first of these evidences enumerated is the larger sphere of power granted to the believer. By this the Lord does not mean that the disciples shall perform greater miracles, but that they shall produce moral and spiritual revolutions which are intrinsically more divinely wonderful than miracles. For instance, at his death Jesus had converted about five hundred disciples, but at Pentecost the apostles converted three thousand in one day. The converts of Paul also greatly outnumbered those of Christ's own ministry.] **13 And whatsoever ye shall ask in my name, that will I do, that the Father may be glorified in the Son. 14 If ye shall ask**

anything in my name, that will I do. [The second token of Christ's union with the Father would be manifested in the efficacy of prayer made in his name. Hitherto prayer had not been thus made (John xvi. 24). God would glorify himself through Christ by answering prayer thus made.] **15 If ye love me, ye will keep my commandments. 16 And I will pray the Father, and he shall give you another Comforter, that he may be with you for ever, 17** *even* **the Spirit of truth: whom the world cannot receive; for it beholdeth him not, neither knoweth him: ye know him; for he abideth with you, and shall be in you.** [The third token of Christ's union with the Father would be the sending of the Holy Spirit (Acts ii. 33). Since, however, the worldly-minded could neither receive nor behold the Spirit, the promise to send him to the disciples is prefaced by an appeal to them to keep his commandments, and thus avoid a worldly spirit such as would be incompatible with the reception of the Holy Spirit. The word "Comforter" does not fully translate the Greek word *Paraklete:* no English word does. The word "Advocate" may be used, and "Helper" is as good if not better than "Comforter." He is called the Spirit of truth because of his many relationships to the truth (John xvii. 19; I. Cor. ii. 4; I. Thess. i. 5; Acts ii. 4; v. 32; Heb. ii. 4). That the gift of the Holy Spirit is conditioned upon belief and obedience is also taught elsewhere (John vii. 38; Acts ii. 38; v. 32). We should observe that by the use of the word "another" Jesus shows that he himself had been and would be a *Paraklete.* But earthly fellowship with him was about to be cut short, and therefore the Holy Spirit would come, with whom fellowship would never be interrupted. We should note, too, the distinction between the present "abideth with you," and the future "shall be in you." The Spirit, being present in the person of Christ, had been abiding with the apostles who followed him. Hereafter the intimacy of the relation would be increased, and the Spirit should abide within them.] **18 I will not leave you desolate** [Literally, orphans. The expression breathes the spirit of a father, as at John xiii. 33]:

I come unto you. **19 Yet a little while, and the world beholdeth me no more** [the next day the world crucified him and sealed him in the tomb, and since then has seen him no more] **; but ye behold me** [the present tense here indicates a continued vision; it can not therefore refer to the appearances of Christ after the resurrection, for they terminated at the end of forty days]: **because I live, ye shall live also. 20 In that day** [we may take this either as the day of Pentecost, or the period which began on that day] **ye shall know that I am in my Father, and ye in me, and I in you. 21 He that hath my commandments, and keepeth them, he it is that loveth me: and he that loveth me shall be loved of my Father, and I will love him, and will manifest myself unto him.** [The fourth and all-convincing token of Jesus' union with the Father would be his return in the spirit which is here described. It was not his temporary return after the resurrection, as is shown above, neither was it his final return to judgment, because it was one in which the world would not behold him, and at his final return "every eye shall see him." Jesus, therefore, speaks of his return in the spirit, and his inward manifestation of himself to his disciples wherein he energizes them with his own life. A coming, however, which, like that of the Holy Spirit, is conditioned upon the loving obedience of the disciples. The writings of Paul abound with expressions illustrating the nature of this coming of Christ. It is not to be confused with the coming of the Holy Spirit, though doubtless wholly concurrent with it.] **22 Judas (not Iscariot)** [who had gone out. See table of apostles, p. 222, for this Judas, or Thaddæus] **saith unto him, Lord, what is come to pass that thou wilt manifest thyself unto us, and not unto the world?** [The form of his question betrays the apostle's bewilderment. Expecting that Jesus would soon be an earthly king, he could not imagine how Jesus could so have changed his plans as to thus withdraw himself utterly from the world. The answer of Jesus gave Judas but little present light.] **23 Jesus answered and said unto him, If a man love me, he will** keep my word : and my Father will love him, and we will come unto him, and make our abode with him. 24 He that loveth me not keepeth not my words : and the word which ye hear is not mine, but the Father's who sent me. [Jesus contents himself by pointing out to Judas the fact that loving obedience is the means by which the blessed indwelling is obtained. It was better that Judas should busy his heart and will about the *means* of blessing rather than his head about the mysterious and incomprehensible *manner* of it.] 25 These things have I spoken unto you, while *yet* abiding with you. 26 But the Comforter, *even* the Holy Spirit, whom the Father will send in my name, he shall teach you all things, and bring to your remembrance all that I said unto you. [The word "spoken" of the twenty-fifth verse stands in contrast with the word "teach" of the twenty-sixth. Jesus had uttered the truth, but because the divine plan of salvation through the death, burial, resurrection and ascension of our Lord was yet incomplete, all the words which he had spoken were but dimly understood, since they were related to and founded upon this incompleted plan. When the plan was completed the Holy Spirit would reveal or teach the meaning of the words by bringing them to remembrance after full comprehension of the plan to which they related.] 27 Peace I leave with you ; my peace I give unto you : not as the world giveth, give I unto you. Let not your heart be troubled, neither let it be fearful. [This legacy of peace is by no means to be confined to the period of doubt and fear which accompanied the crucifixion ; in fact, it seems to overstep that period, and to begin after it, and continue throughout all the troubled ministry of the apostles. The breadth of the legacy also to be noted : 1. The quality of it ; it was not the absolute unshaken peace of God, but the peace which Jesus himself possessed while upon the earth—peace with all things save the devil and his powers. 2. The nature of it ; it was not peace from without, but from within. It was not such as promised to pacify and quell the persecutors, but a promise of inner calm amidst the storm. 3. The manner of it; it was no stinted, measured store such as the wo.ld bestows, but a full, free gift from the overflowing bounty of God.] **28 Ye heard how I said to you, I go away, and I come unto you. If ye love me, ye would have rejoiced, because I go unto the Father: for the Father is greater than I.** [The departure of Jesus was not wholly a humiliation, as it might appear to them; but a real exaltation at which they might well rejoice, and that the more readily and freely since it would not mean to them the total separation which they anticipated, because he would return in the spirit. The word "greater" as here used does not refer to any difference in the nature or essence of the Son as related to the Father. It may be true that there has been a certain subordination of the will of the Son to the will of the Father from all eternity, but even that, if it exists, is not referred to here. Jesus has in mind the utter humiliation to which his mediatorial office had brought him, and to even lower depths to which it was about to bring him. From all this his departure to the Father would in a large measure free him, restoring him in some degree to that state of equilibrium in glory, power and authority from which he had descended—Phil. ii. 6.] **29 And now I have told you before it come to pass, that, when it is come to pass, ye may believe.** [Jesus had told them fully of his return to the Father, that when they received the subsequent manifestations of it they might firmly believe it.] **30 I will no more speak much with you, for the prince of the world cometh: and he hath nothing in me; 31 but that the world may know that I love the Father, and as the Father gave me commandment, even so I do.** [In a few hours the earthly teaching of Jesus would be interrupted by the coming of Satan and would never be resumed save in occasional fragments. Satan would come in the persons of his servants and emissaries, but he would find nothing in Christ which would give him either right or reason to exercise power over him. The sorrows and sufferings of Christ would be entered upon of his own free will because by enduring them for our sakes he would please the Father and carry out his commandments, and thus manifest to the world the love which he bore the Father.] **Arise, let us go hence.** [Some think that Jesus then left the room, and that the next three chapters of John's Gospel contain matters spoken on the way to Gethsemane. But it is likely that the words of these chapters were spoken in the upper room after they had risen from the table and prepared to depart, and that John xviii. 1 marks the leaving of the upper room as well as the crossing of the Kidron.]

XV. 1 I am the true vine, and my Father is the husbandman. 2 Every branch in me that beareth not fruit, he taketh it away: and every *branch* **that beareth fruit, he cleanseth it** [by pruning], **that it may bear more fruit.** [The use of the word "true" shows that Jesus refers to a typical vine. The Jewish people had been such a vine (Isa. v. 1; Ps. lxxx.; Jer. ii. 21). Yet it was but "a figure of the true" (Heb. ix. 24). God had now in Christ planted the true vine, and would dissever and cast off all that did not derive life from him, and would prune all that did. This vital connection with Christ is set forth by Paul under the figure of a body and its head (Eph. v. 23; Col. ii. 19). The fact that Jesus had just given them the fruit of the vine to drink as the symbol of his blood made the transition to this figure easy and natural, for the branches derive their juices from the vine.] **3 Already ye are clean because of the word which I have spoken unto you.** [It is God in Christ who cleanseth the soul, but this cleansing is effected through hearing, believing and obeying the Word. The Word tells us what to do that we may be cleansed and saved— Eph. v. 26; Jas. i. 28.] **4 Abide in me, and I in you. As the branch cannot bear fruit of itself, except it abide in the vine; so neither can ye, except ye abide in me. 5 I am the vine, ye are the branches: He that abideth in me, and I in him, the same beareth much fruit: for apart from me ye can do nothing. 6 If a man abide**

not in me, he is cast forth as a branch, and is withered; and they gather them, and cast them into the
fire, and they are burned. [The whole parable is intended
to teach us Christ's relationships. 1. Toward the Father—
Husbandman and Vine. 2. Toward man—Vine and branches.
3. Toward good works—Vine, branches and fruit. 4. The
negative condition, or *lack* of relationship—the Vine, the dis-
severed branches, the fire.] 7 If ye abide in me, and my
words abide in you, ask whatsoever ye will, and it
shall be done unto you. [Though this verse stands somewhat in contrast to the warning in verse 6, it is rather a statement of causation than a promise of reward. If by communion and the study of the word we abide in Christ, our prayers
will be of such a nature that it will fully accord with the divine
counsel to answer them, for they will be prayers tending
toward fruitfulness.] 8 Herein is my Father glorified,
that ye bear much fruit; and *so* shall ye be my disciples. [The spirit of Christ leads to those deeds which
cause men to glorify God (Matt. ix. 8; Luke xvii. 15), and
whoso does those deeds causes such glorification (Matt. v. 16).
Moreover, the spirit of Christ leads to abundant fruitfulness,
and he who has it, not only performs charitable deeds, but
converts the sinner and begets a spirit of goodness in those
about him (Matt. xiii. 8-26; Phil. iv. 17); and this fruitfulness
becomes an evidence or demonstration of true discipleship.]
9 Even as the Father hath loved me, I also have loved
you: abide ye in my love. 10 If ye keep my commandments, ye shall abide in my love; even as I have kept
my Father's commandments, and abide in his love.
[From the *outward* evidence of union with Christ, shown by
the fruit, Jesus now turns to that *inward* bond of union which
is the cause of the fruitfulness. That bond is love. Love is,
as it were, the sap which passes back and forth between the
Vine and branch, and that love is kept active and vital by
the most practical of means—obedience to commandments, a
means which the Lord himself does not hesitate to describe as
efficient between himself and the Father, only claiming for

himself the love of the Father because of a like obedience to that which he prescribed. "And our obedience must be impartial," says Jay; "we must do 'whatsoever' he commands us."] **11 These things have I spoken unto you, that my joy may be in you, and *that* your joy may be made full.** [He had spoken the words of this discourse that the disciples might have a joy corresponding to his own. By perfect obedience he enjoyed a consciousness of the Father's presence and approval. By a like obedience the disciples might have a like sense of his presence and approval, and hence a like joy.] **12 This is my commandment, that ye love one another, even as I have loved you. 13 Greater love hath no man than this, that a man lay down his life for his friends.** [Jesus gives, as his supreme commandment, this law of love. The disciples are to love *one another* as intensely as Jesus loved them, and the measure of the intensity of his love is prophetically set forth by an allusion to his death on their behalf. But he died for his enemies as well as for his friends—Rom. v. 6.] **14 Ye are my friends, if ye do the things which I command you. 15 No longer do I call you servants; for the servant knoweth not what his lord doeth: but I have called you friends; for all things that I heard from my Father I have made known unto you.** [The commandments of Jesus were not to be obeyed in the spirit of bondmen, but in that of friends. Jesus had shown his friendship by receiving his apostles into confidence as to the things which he had heard from his Father.] **16 Ye did not choose me, but I chose you, and appointed you, that ye should go and bear fruit, and *that* your fruit should abide: that whatsoever ye shall ask of the Father in my name, he may give it you.** [Jesus shows the stability of the friendship existing between him and the disciples in that the origin of it lies in himself and not in them. For he chose them as friends before they chose him, gave them their high places as apostles without their solicitation, prepared them to bring forth lasting fruits, and gave them the privilege of supplementing their per-

sonal deficiencies by prayer made effective through his name.]
17 These things I command you [this includes all the
precepts from the beginning of chap. xiii.], **that ye may love
one another. 18 If the world hated you, ye know that
it hath hated me before** *it hated* **you.** [While teaching
the fullness and richness of love which is to exist within the
circle of discipleship, Jesus warns them that in opposition to it
the outer circle of unconverted and sensual—that circle known
as the world—would manifest a spirit of hatred. Since this
world-spirit hated him, the disciples need not be surprised to
find that it hated them when manifesting his spirit.] **19 If
ye were of the world, the world would love its own:
but because ye are not of the world, but I chose you
out of the world, therefore the world hateth you. 20
Remember the word that I said unto you, A servant
is not greater than his lord.** [John xiii. 16.] **If they
persecuted me, they will also persecute you; if they
kept my word, they will keep yours also.** [The apostles
could rest assured that the messengers would receive like
treatment with him who sent them. When, therefore, they
found the world rejecting their message they could cheer
themselves with the expectation that a few at least would
receive it, since a few had always received the words of the
Master.] **21 But all these things will they do unto you
for my name's sake, because they know not him that
sent me.** [Christians in the early ages were persecuted for
bearing the name of Christ by those who were ignorant of
God. But this name, hateful to the world, was sweet to the
disciples. For opposition to the name see Acts v. 28; I. Pet.
iv. 14; Rev. iii. 8. For joy in it see Acts v. 41; II. Cor. xii.
10; Gal. vi. 17.] **22 If I had not come and spoken unto
them, they had not had sin: but now they have no excuse for their sin. 23 He that hateth me hateth my
Father also. 24 If I had not done among them the
works which none other did, they had not had sin: but
now have they both seen and hated both me and my
Father. 25 But** *this cometh to pass,* **that the word**

may be fulfilled that is written in their law [Ps. xxxv. 19; lxix. 4], **They hated me without a cause.** [Though the great proof of the hatred of Christ was yet to come, it is spoken of as if it had passed. Jesus does not mean to say that the world would have committed no sin at all if he had kept away from it. The meaning is that it would not have been guilty of the sin of rejecting Jesus. They would have been excusable.] **26 But when the Comforter is come, whom I will send unto you from the Father, *even* the Spirit of truth, which proceedeth from the Father, he shall bear witness of me: 27 and ye also bear witness, because ye have been with me from the beginning.** [One of the principal offices of the Spirit is to testify of Christ (John xvi. 13-15). The Spirit testified through the apostles and other messengers (Acts ii. 4), so that in a sense the apostles were double witnesses. They themselves could testify as to what they had seen and heard. The Spirit could aid them to testify accurately, and with a full intelligence as to the real meaning of things. The Spirit also gave attestation to apostolic testimony by enabling the apostles to work miracles.]

XVI. 1 These things have I spoken unto you, that ye should not be caused to stumble. [Jesus warned his disciples of coming persecutions in order that those persecutions might not shake their faith.] **2 They shall put you out of the synagogues** [see pp. 466, 467]**: yea, the hour cometh, that whosoever killeth you shall think that he offereth service unto God.** [Persecutors would not only take away religious privileges, but even life itself, and they would do this as a religious act, esteeming Christians such enemies of God that God would take pleasure in their death. Paul gives us an illustration of this fanatical zeal—Acts xxvi. 9; Gal. i. 13, 14.] **3 And these things will they do, because they have not known the Father, nor me. 4 But these things have I spoken unto you, that when their hour is come, ye may remember them, how that I told you.** [The disciples being but few, and finding the vast majority of the nation against them, and being but unlearned

Galilæans, and finding the leaders—the wise, the cultured, the mighty—against them, would be tempted to doubt the correctness of their course, and to ask, "May we not, after all, be mistaken : may not those who know more be better judges in this matter than we who are so ignorant ? " To forestall and prevent such questioning, Jesus asserts that the ignorance is with the rulers. Knowledge of himself and of his Father is the great and supreme knowledge, and the apostles having this were wiser than those with all other learning. It would also strengthen their faith to remember that the Lord's divine wisdom had foreseen all this trouble.] **And these things I said not unto you from the beginning, because I was with you.** [While he was with his disciples they were in no danger, for he himself bore the brunt of persecution. In the beginning, therefore, of his ministry he did not deem it expedient to dishearten his disciples by foretelling trials which were then remote. When he began to announce his approaching death, then he also began to declare that the disciple must be willing to lose his life if he would find it. See pp. 414-417. Some think that Matt. v. 10-12 forms a contradiction to our Lord's statement here. While the words in Matthew were spoken early enough to be classified as "from the beginning," their import is too general to permit of their being brought into contrast with this direct and personal prediction of persecution.] **5 But now I go unto him that sent me ; and none of you asketh me, Whither goest thou ? 6 But because I have spoken these things unto you, sorrow hath filled your heart. 7 Nevertheless I tell you the truth: It is expedient for you that I go away ; for if I go not away, the Comforter will not come unto you ; but if I go, I will send him unto you.** [The disciples had asked the Lord whither he was going (John xiii. 36; xiv. 5), but their question had a very different meaning from that which Jesus here suggests to them. They asked it to ascertain whether his departure would involve a separation or whether it would be a withdrawal from the world in which they could accompany him. The question which he suggests has reference to the place to which he was about to journey, that place being the home and presence of his Father. The question asked was selfish, as if the apostles had asked, "What will your departure mean to us?" The question suggested was generous, intimating that the apostles should have asked, "What will this departure mean to you?" Viewing his departure from a selfish standpoint filled their hearts with sorrow; but viewing it from a generous standpoint would have filled them with sympathetic joy, because of the supreme happiness which it would bring to their Master (John xiv. 28). But even from a selfish standpoint the apostles would have had reason to rejoice because of the advantage which would accrue to them through the Lord's departure, for that departure would result in the advent of the Holy Spirit. Space does not permit us to discuss why the Spirit could not come until the Lord had departed, but the verses which follow give us one good and sufficient reason, for they show that his work had to do with the conviction of human hearts through the preaching of a completed gospel, and the ascension or return of Christ to heaven, and his enthronement in glory there, are essential parts of that completed gospel.] **8 And he, when he is come, will convict the world in respect of sin, and of righteousness, and of judgment** [It would be the work of the Holy Spirit to take the truths respecting Christ, and, using the apostles as mouthpieces (Acts ii. 1-37), to convince the world as to these truths. This convincing work was entirely in relation to Christ, the sin of disbelieving him, the righteousness revealed in him, and the power of judgment conferred upon him]: **9 of sin, because they believed not on me; 10 of righteousness, because I go to the Father, and ye behold me no more; 11 of judgment, because the prince of this world hath been judged.** [Sin, righteousness, and a day of judgment with its reward upon one and its punishment upon the other, are three cardinal doctrines of the gospel. The Spirit convinces the world that disbelief in Christ is its fatal sin, for belief in Christ leads to forgiveness, and to the unbelieving there is no forgiveness. The least sin is a sin unto death, and is a sin eternal unless forgiven. The greatest sin, if forgiven, becomes harmless and is as if it had never been. Until the world is convinced of this great truth it feels no need of a gospel. Again, Christianity teaches that righteousness is prerequisite to the attainment of the presence of God. Without righteousness we can never behold him, nor can we ever hope to stand before him. But this required righteousness was found in Jesus, for he returned to the Father, and abides with the Father, being seen by us no more. The Holy Spirit convinces the world that those who are found in Christ, having his righteousness, shall attain unto the presence of the Father (Phil. iii. 3-14). Lastly, the Spirit convinces the world that Jesus is commissioned as its judge. Our Lord's resurrection is the assurance of this fact (Acts xvii. 31). The resurrection is such an assurance because it is an evidence of the judgment and condemnation of Satan, the head and leader in sinful rebellion against God, and he that hath power to judge the head thereby shows he has power to judge the body. Satan held the power of death over humanity, but Jesus judged him and brought him to naught by taking away this power (Heb. ii. 14, 15). The cross of Christ as the source of life asserted his superiority over all other powers (Col. ii. 14, 15), which implies an ability to judge them.] **12 I have yet many things to say unto you, but ye cannot bear them now.** [The doctrines of the gospel were necessarily obscure and largely incomprehensible to the apostles until time had developed the gospel facts. Jesus, therefore, forbore to speak of many things at this time, lest by doing so he should confuse the minds of his followers.] **13 Howbeit when he, the Spirit of truth, is come, he shall guide you into all the truth : for he shall not speak from himself ; but what things soever he shall hear, *these* shall he speak : and he shall declare unto you the things that are to come. 14 He shall glorify me : for he shall take of mine, and shall declare *it* unto you.** [The Holy Spirit was to bring no absolutely new teaching. The Son of God here claims for himself all that the Spirit taught even to the declaration of things to come.

The Spirit would bring to mind and republish in the *minds* of the apostles all the words which Jesus had spoken, and would add those things which, being now in the mind of Jesus, were really part of his teaching, but which he at this present forbore to utter, the apostles not being able to bear them.] **15 All things whatsoever the Father hath are mine : therefore said I, that he taketh of mine, and shall declare *it* unto you.** [The Son's unity of interest with the Father made him possessor of all the Father's truth, as well as all the Father's counsel as to the future. As Jesus, therefore, might at this time have uttered all which the Holy Spirit subsequently taught, he rightfully claimed all the teaching of the Spirit as his.] **16 A little while, and ye behold me no more; and again a little while, and ye shall see me.** [Having finished his digression about the Holy Spirit, Jesus here returns to his point of departure, the theme of verse 5 above. Of course the apostles would see Jesus after his resurrection, but the seeing here spoken of refers more especially to that spiritual communion with him previously mentioned—John xiv. 19-23.] **17 *Some* of his disciples therefore said one to another, What is this that he saith unto us, A little while, and ye behold me not ; and again a little while, and ye shall see me: and, Because I go to the Father?** [John xiv. 28.] **18 They said therefore, What is this that he saith, A little while? We know not what he saith.** [Having been unable to entertain the idea of our Lord's burial and resurrection, no wonder the apostles were mystified by these allusions to it.] **19 Jesus perceived** [by his divine insight —John ii. 24, 25 ; vi. 61 ; Matt. ix. 4] **that they were desirous to ask him, and he said unto them, Do ye inquire among yourselves concerning this, that I said, A little while, and ye behold me not, and again a little while, and ye shall see me? 20 Verily, verily, I say unto you, that ye shall weep and lament, but the world shall rejoice : ye shall be sorrowful, but your sorrow shall be turned into joy.** [The death of Jesus *truly* brought gladness to his enemies (Luke xxii. 5), and sorrow to his friends (John xx. 11), but the sorrow was indeed turned to joy—Matt. xxviii. 8]. **21 A woman when she is in travail hath sorrow, because her hour is come: but when she is delivered of the child, she remembereth no more the anguish, for the joy that a man is born into the world.** [The simile here is very apropos, according with Scriptural ideals—Col. i. 18; Rev. i. 5.] **22 And ye therefore now have sorrow: but I will see you again, and your heart shall rejoice, and your joy no one taketh away from you.** [Luke xxiv. 52, 53. The joyful hopes which come to us through the resurrection of Jesus are beyond the reach of the despoiling hand of man.] **23 And in that day ye shall ask me no question.** [The coming of the Spirit would make all things clear, and the mysteries about which the apostles now questioned would then be fully explained.] **Verily, verily** [these two words give emphasis and introduce a new thought], **I say unto you, If ye shall ask anything of the Father, he will give it you in my name. 24 Hitherto ye have asked nothing in my name: ask, and ye shall receive, that your joy may be made full.** [Having spoken of his departure, and of what the Spirit would do during his absence, he now speaks of the work which he would himself do while absent. He entered heaven as our high priest (Heb. ix. 24), and part of his priestly office is to make inter-cession for his people (Heb. vii. 24, 25). The use of Christ's name for intercessory purposes was new to the apostles, since it was only thus employed after his ascension.] **25 These things have I spoken unto you in dark sayings: the hour cometh, when I shall no more speak unto you in dark sayings, but shall tell you plainly of the Father.** [This closing discourse was full of dark sayings which the disciples did not understand, but when the gospel facts were completed and when the Spirit came on the day of Pente-cost, then Christ through the Spirit made all things plain to them.] **26 In that day ye shall ask in my name** [fullness of knowledge would lead them to look readily to Christ as inter-cessor]**: and I say not unto you, that I will pray the Father**

for you; 27 for the Father himself loveth you, because ye have loved me, and have believed that I came forth from the Father. 28 I came out from the Father, and am come into the world: again, I leave the world, and go unto the Father. [Birth and death are alike beyond our control. That Jesus had a divine as well as a human nature is shown by the fact that his entrance into and exit from the world were both governed by his own volition, as was also his resurrection (John x. 17, 18). While the apostles did not believe in the voluntary exit of Jesus, it having not yet taken place, they did believe that he had come into the world as a divine being, and for this belief the Father loved them, and this love of the Father was not to be lost sight of in considering the mediatory work of Christ. In short, the Father must be looked upon as one who does not need to be interceded with because of a lack of love. Though, according to the divine plan and order, Jesus is intercessor (I. Tim. ii. 5; I. John ii. 1, 2), yet the office is not self-assumed for the purpose of counteracting any spirit of severity in the Father, but is, on the contrary, undertaken by direct appointment of the Father, made because of the Father's love (John iii. 16). Failing to recognize the Father as the fountain and source of grace, love and mercy has led the Roman Church into gross errors. The Father being suspected of undue rigor, a like suspicion arose also as to the Son because of his nearness to the Father. Therefore the Virgin Mary was called in to intercede with and soften the obduracy of the Son. Since the deification of the Virgin Mary in 1853, she also has been looked upon with growing distrust, and the tendency has been to call upon Joseph to intercede with Mary to intercede with the Son to intercede with the Father. Thus that wonderful love of God which passes all understanding is made less than that of mere mortals who never manifested a measure of philanthropy above what is common. Against such errors Jesus guards us by causing us to understand that, if the love of the Father alone were to be considered, there would be no need for him to intercede at all.] **29 His disciples say, Lo, now speakest thou**

plainly, and speakest no dark saying. [They now clearly understood that as Jesus came from heaven so would he return to heaven, but they did not understand the process by which this return would be effected.] 30 **Now know we that thou knowest all things, and needest not that any man should ask thee: by this we believe that thou camest forth from God.** [The miraculous manner in which he had just read their thoughts caused them to boldly declare their faith in his divinity.] 31 **Jesus answered them, Do ye now believe? 32 Behold, the hour cometh, yea, is come, that ye shall be scattered, every man to his own, and shall leave me alone: and *yet* I am not alone, because the Father is with me.** [He contrasts the faith which his disciples then professed with that utter lack of it which they would manifest in a few hours. All their confidence in his divinity would vanish when they saw him arrested, etc., and they would seek their own safety, leaving him to his fate. Much as he would feel their desertion, he would not be left utterly comfortless, because the Father would be with him. Paul speaks in a similar strain—II. Tim. iv. 16-18.] 33 **These things have I spoken unto you, that in me ye may have peace. In the world ye have tribulation: but be of good cheer; I have overcome the world.** [Christ's return to the Father and his throne is the Christian's source of peace. As none of the accumulations of evil which came upon Christ prevented him from attaining his goal, so the Christian feels that in the conquering power of Christ he too shall rise superior to all his troubles, and this feeling brings him peace.]

CXXII.

THE LORD'S PRAYER.

(Jerusalem. Thursday night.)

ᵈ JOHN XVII.

ᵈ **1 These things spake Jesus ; and lifting up his eyes to heaven** [the action marked the turning of his thoughts from the disciples to the Father], **he said, Father, the hour is come** [see pp. 116, 440] **; glorify thy Son, that the Son may glorify thee: 2 even as thou gavest him authority over all flesh, that to all whom thou hast given him, he should give eternal life.** [The Son h re prays for his glorification, viz.: resurrection, ascension, coronation, etc., that through these he may be perfected as a Saviour and be enabled to give that eternal life unto millions, the bestowal of which will redound unto the glory of the Father. Moreover, the glorification of Christ revealed his divine nature, and the Father was glorified by its thus becoming apparent that he had bestowed upon the world so priceless a gift. The gift of authority was bestowed after his resurrection (Matt. xxviii. 18). All humanity was given into his hands that he might give life to that part of it which yielded itself to him in true discipleship.] **3 And this is life eternal, that they should know thee the only true God, and him whom thou didst send, *even* Jesus Christ.** [God is revealed in Jesus Christ: Jesus has just prayed for his glorification that the Father may be fully revealed in him. The revelation of God is the first step toward the attainment of eternal life. The inner reception of that revelation by a daily conformity to it is the second step. As we actually live God's life we come to know him ; but we cannot attempt to live his life without a revelation.] **4 I glorified thee on the earth, having accomplished the work which thou hast given me to do. 5 And now, Father, glorify thou me with thine own self with the glory which I had with thee before the world was.**

[As the hour for finishing his work had arrived, Jesus speaks of it as already finished. As he had finished that for which he had emptied himself of his glory and entered the world, he asks that now, on his departure from the world, he may be reinstated and permitted to assume again that which he had laid aside. Paul's words are a commentary on these two verses (Phil. ii. 5-11). Thus Jesus ends the first division of his prayer which is a petition for himself, for the glory of the Father, and the good of the world. The second division which follows is a fourfold plea for the disciples which he then had, followed by petitions in their behalf.] **6 I manifested thy name unto the men whom thou gavest me out of the world : thine they were, and thou gavest them to me** [As a first plea or reason why the Father should bless the disciples of the Son, the Son urges that they are his property by gift of the Father. The Father is possessor of all humanity as the Creator; the Son by gift from the Father possesses the believing portion of humanity as its Redeemer]**; and they have kept thy word. 7 Now they know that all things whatsoever thou hast given me are from thee: 8 for the words which thou gavest me I have given unto them; and they received *them*, and knew of a truth that I came forth from thee, and they believed that thou didst send me.** [As a second reason for blessing the disciples Jesus pleads their reception and retention of the truth which the Father had sent him to reveal, and the resulting knowledge and faith. The truth revealed by Jesus was so palpably divine that the disciples could know that its bearer came from heaven. But whether that bearer came of his own volition or as a commissioned messenger of the Father they could not know. But where knowledge was impossible they trusted to Jesus and believed.] **9 I pray for them: I pray not for the world, but for those whom thou hast given me ; for they are thine : 10 and all things that are mine are thine, and thine are mine : and I am glorified in them.** [As a third plea he urges the joint possession which the Father held with him in the disciples, and the further fact that the Son was glorified in the disciples.] **11 I am no more in the world, and these are in the world, and I come to thee.** [As a last plea he urges the necessity of the Father's care over the disciples since the Son will be no longer in the world to care for them.] **Holy Father, keep them in thy name which thou hast given me, that they may be one, even as we** *are.* [Our Lord's first petition grows out of his last plea. His departure would tend to scatter the disciples; they had been united by faith in the name of Christ, that is, by the divine power given of God and revealed in Christ (Ex. xxiii. 21 ; Isa. ix. 6 ; Jer. xxiii. 6), and Jesus asks that they may be still so kept, and that their unity may be as perfect as that subsisting between the Father and the Son.] **12 While I was with them, I kept them in thy name which thou hast given me : and I guarded them, and not one of them perished, but the son of perdition** [literally, son of perishing]**; that the scripture might be fulfilled.** [Ps. xli. 9. Jesus emphasizes the fervency of his petition by urging his own conduct as to that which he asks. He asks the Father to care for those for whom he had himself been so painstakingly careful that not one had been lost save him whom it was impossible to save, and whose loss the Scripture had predicted—a loss in no way chargeable against the loving fidelity of the Good Shepherd.] **13 But now I come to thee ; and these things I speak in the world, that they may have my joy made full in themselves.** [Being about ready to depart from the world, Jesus had taught and prayed for his disciples that they might be brought into a oneness with the Father similar to that which he himself enjoyed, that the consequent joy which filled his own life might in some measure fill theirs also. This also was part of his care for them.] **14 I have given them thy word ; and the world hated them, because they are not of the world, even as I am not of the world.** [An additional reason for the Father's care is here presented. The reception of the Father's word had brought upon them the hatred of the world, thereby increasing their need of a heavenly blessing, as a counter-balance to the curse of the world. Jesus as advocate gives potency to his petitions as to the sufferings of his disciples by suggesting that he has himself shared them—Heb. ii. 10-18.] **15 I pray not that thou shouldest take them from the world, but that thou shouldest keep them from the evil** *one*. [The care which he asks is protection in, and not removal from, the world. It is best both for the Christian and for the world that he should remain in it. The world is blessed by the Christian's presence (Matt. v. 14-16), and abiding in the world affords the Christian an opportunity of conquest and reward—Rom. viii. 37; Rev. ii. 26; iii. 21.] **16 They are not of the world, even as I am not of the world. 17 Sanctify them in the truth: thy word is truth. 18 As thou didst send me into the world, even so sent I them into the world. 19 And for their sakes I sanctify myself, that they themselves also may be sanctified in truth** [To sanctify means to set apart to a holy use. As Jesus himself had been set apart as God's messenger to the world, so he had set apart the apostles as his messengers to it. This setting apart was not a formal, empty act, but was accomplished by God's imparting or developing a fitness in the one sanctified to perform the duties for which he was set apart. Fitness in this case would be imparted by imbuing the apostles with the Spirit of truth. Jesus had set himself apart (Heb. ix. 14), that the apostles might follow his example—II. Cor. v. 14-17 (and also the church—Phil. ii. 5; Rom. xii. 1, 2), that thereby the world might be saved. Our Lord's prayer as to the apostles is, therefore, a threefold petition; viz.: that they may be kept in unity, kept from the world and the devil, and that they may be set apart and equipped for the gospel service. We come now to the third division of the prayer wherein he asks for blessings upon future believers.] **20 Neither for these only do I pray, but for them also that believe on me through their word; 21 that they may all be one; even as thou, Father,** *art* **in me, and I in thee, that they also may be in us: that the world may believe that thou didst send**

me. [Here again the first petition is for unity, and again the
unity subsisting between the Father and the Son is designated as
the kind desired. That future disciples may understand the
nature of this unity Jesus sets it forth in an amplified statement, which reveals the fact that he does not ask for a unity
similar to that subsisting between the Father and the Son, but
for that very unity itself enlarged and extended so as to
become a triple instead of a dual unity by the comprehension
of the disciples within its compass. As a reason why the
Father should bring about this unity (and a reason also why all
Christians should work for it), our Lord states that its attainment will result in the conversion of the world to the Christian
faith.] **22 And the glory which thou hast given me I
have given unto them ; that they may be one, even as we**
are **one** [Jesus here states that to bring about the unity which
he here prays for he had bestowed upon the disciples the glory
which the Father had bestowed upon him. The glory mentioned was that of being the Son of God (Matt. iii. 17; John i.
14; Heb. i. 5; iii. 6), which glory Jesus imparts to his followers (John i. 12; I. John iii. 1). In other words, he made
us his brethren that we might be united in one great household
(Rom. viii. 29; Eph. i. 10; ii. 19; I. John iii. 9, 10; iv. 8, 16).
A true comprehension of the Fatherhood of God and our
brotherhood in Christ must result in unity] ; **23 I in them,
and thou in me, that they may be perfected into one ;
that the world may know that thou didst send me, and
lovedst them, even as thou lovedst me.** [He here
states that the perfect unity of the church and the putting forth
of its power in harmonious effort to convert the world will be
equivalent to a demonstration of the truth of his divine mission. Verse 21 above asserts that the initial stages of unity
will produce faith in the world, and this verse adds that the
perfection of that unity will lead the world beyond faith into
the realm of actual knowledge as to the divine mission of
Christ. The context suggests that this unity will result in gracious manifestations of the Father's love. Possibly these manifestations may be of such a nature as to aid in bringing about

the state of knowledge mentioned.] **24 Father, I desire that they also whom thou hast given me be with me where I am, that they may behold my glory, which thou hast given me: for thou lovedst me before the founda· tion of the world.** [While Jesus prays that his disciples may enter the heavenly state, that state is not expressed as the end desired. He wishes them to be in that state that they may behold his glory. The glory of Christ is his Sonship, and the love which accompanies that relationship. To behold this is the height of spiritual exaltation. To know God is life eternal, and to behold God is joy ineffable. God is truly be held subjectively. We must be like him to see him as he is (I. John iii. 2). The second petition of Jesus, therefore, in no way savors of a vainglorious desire that his disciples may be hold him to lead them to admire him, but a wish that they may participate in the heavenly state, and know the Sonship of Jesus and all its attendant blessedness by, in some measure, par ticipating in it.] **25 O righteous Father, the world knew thee not, but I knew thee; and these knew that thou didst send me; 26 and I made known unto them thy name, and will make it known; that the love where with thou lovedst me may be in them, and I in them.** [In these closing sentences Jesus blends his present and his future disciples. To his present disciples he had made known the Father's name, and to the future ones he would make it known. The knowledge which he had of the Father had been imparted to the disciples, and they had received it, and had thereby been in some measure fitted for the revelation of the glory for which he had just prayed. The world, on the contrary, had rejected Christ's revelation, and had refused to know God, and had thus become unworthy of the privilege here asked for the disciples. Jesus had revealed the Father while on earth that men might attain to the revelation of God in the hereafter, thus participating in the love which the Father has for the Son because the Son is spiritually in them. It is a significant fact that two of the five petitions of this prayer are for Christian unity. It may be said generally of all the petitions that they ask the Father to complete that which the Son has already begun and completed to the limit of his present circumscribed power.]

CXXIII.

GOING TO GETHSEMANE, AND AGONY THEREIN.

(A garden between the brook Kidron and the Mount of Olives. Late Thursday night.)

ᵃ MATT. XXVI. 30, 36-46; ᵇ MARK XIV. 26, 32-42; ᶜ LUKE XXII. 39-46; ᵈ JOHN XVIII. 1.

ᵈ**1 When Jesus had spoken these words** [the words contained in John xiv.-xvi.], ᵃ**30 And when they had sung a hymn** [the shadow of the cross did not quench the spirit of praise in Christ], **they went out** ᶜ**39 And he came out, and** ᵈ**he went forth with his disciples** ᶜ**as his custom was,** ᵈ**over the brook Kidron,** ᵃ**into {ᵇunto} the mount of Olives.** ᵈ**where was a garden, into which he entered, himself and his disciples. {ᶜand the disciples also followed him.}** ᵃ**36 Then cometh Jesus with them** ᵇ**32 And they come unto a place which was named {ᵃcalled} Gethsemane** [The name Gethsemane means *a place of oil-presses*, and hence it accords well with the name of the mountain at whose base it was situated. But the place was now a garden. It is about half a mile from the city, and from what Luke says here and elsewhere (Luke xxi. 37), it seems that Jesus often resorted to it while in Jerusalem at the festivals. Compare also John xviii. 2], ᶜ**40 And when he was at the place, he said {ᵃsaith} unto his disciples, Sit ye here, while I go yonder and pray.** ᶜ**Pray that ye enter not into temptation.** [As the hour of trial and temptation came upon Jesus he fortified himself against it by prayer. And he bade his disciples do likewise, for his arrest would involve them also in temptations which he foresaw that they would not be able to withstand.] ᵃ**37 And he took {**ᵇ**taketh} with him Peter** ᵃ**and the two sons of Zebedee,** ᵇ**James and John, and began to be greatly amazed,** ᵃ**sorrowful and sore troubled.** [While seeking heavenly aid in this hour of extremity our Lord also manifested his desire for human sympathy. All the eleven apostles were with him in the garden, and the three most capable of sympathizing with him were stationed nearer to him than the rest.] ᶜ**41 And he was parted from them about a stone's cast** [one hundred and fifty to two hundred feet]; ᵇ**34 And** ᵃ**38 Then saith he unto them, My soul is exceeding sorrowful, even unto death:** ᵇ**abide ye here, and watch.** ᵃ**with me.** [The sequel shows that the phrase "even unto death" was no figure of rhetoric. The nervous prostration of Jesus was such as to endanger his life, and the watching of the apostles may have been doubly needful. Not only did he require their sympathy, but he may also have looked to them to render him assistance in the case of a physical collapse.] **39 And he went forward a little,** ᶜ**and he kneeled down** ᵇ**and fell on the ground,** ᵃ**and fell on his face, and prayed,** ᵇ**that, if it were possible, the hour might pass away from him.** [This posture was expressive of the most intense supplication.] **36 And he said, {**ᵃ**saying,}** ᵇ**Abba,** ᵃ**My Father, if it be possible, let this cup pass away from me:** ᵇ**all things are possible unto thee;** ᶜ**if thou be willing, remove this cup from me:** ᵇ**howbeit** ᵃ**nevertheless, not as {**ᵇ**what} I will,** ᵃ**but as {**ᵇ**what} thou wilt.** ᶜ**not my will, but thine, be done.** [Much of mystery is found in all life, so it is small wonder if the dual nature of Jesus presents insoluble problems. It perplexes many to find that the divine in Jesus did not sustain him better during his trial in the garden. But we must remember that it was appointed unto Jesus to die, and that the divine in him was not to interfere with this appointment, or the approaches to it. For want, therefore, of a better expression, we may say that from the time Jesus entered the garden until he expired on the cross the human in him was in the ascendant; and "being found in fashion as a man," he endured these trials as if wholly human. His prayer, therefore, is the cry of his humanity for deliverance. The words "if it be possible" with which it opens breathe the same spirit of submissive obedience which is found in the closing words. Reminding the Father of the limitless range of his power, he petitions him to change his counsel as to the crucifixion of the Son, if his gracious purposes can be in any other way carried out. Jesus uses the words "cup" and "hour" interchangeably. They are both words of broad compass, intended to include all that he would undergo from that time until his resurrection. They embrace all his mental, moral, physical and spiritual suffering which we can discover, together with an infinite volume of a propitiatory and vicarious nature which lies beyond the reach of our understanding. The submission of Jesus was no new fruitage of his character; the prayer of the garden had been the inner purpose of his entire life—John v. 30 and vi. 38.] **43 And there appeared unto him an angel from heaven, strengthening him. 44 And being in an agony he prayed more earnestly; and his sweat became as it were great drops of blood falling down upon the ground.** [Commentators give instances of bloody sweat under abnormal pathological conditions.] **45 And when he rose up from his prayer, he came {ᵃ cometh} unto the disciples, and findeth {ᶜ found} them sleeping for sorrow, 46 and said unto them, Why sleep ye? rise and pray, that ye enter not into temptation.** [The admonition which had at first been addressed to all the eleven is now spoken to the chosen three] ᵃ **and saith unto Peter,** ᵇ **Simon, sleepest thou? couldest thou not watch one hour?** ᵃ **What, could ye not watch with me one hour? 41 Watch and pray, that ye enter not into temptation: the spirit indeed is willing, but the flesh is weak.** [Peter, having boasted of his loyalty, has his weakness pointed out and is further warned to be on his guard, since the weakness of his nature will not stand the coming strain. The slumber of the disciples was not through indifference; but was

caused by the prostration of grief. When we remember the
excitement which they had endured that night, the tender
words spoken by Jesus, the sadness of which was intensified
by the atmosphere of mystery which pervaded them, the
beautiful and touching prayer, and lastly this agony in the
garden, it is not to be wondered at that the apostles, spurred
by no sense of danger, should succumb to the long-borne ten-
sion and fall asleep. Had they comprehended how much the
Lord needed their *wakeful* sympathy as he came again and
again seeking for it, they would probably have kept awake.]
b 39 **And again ᵃa second time he went away, and
prayed, ᵇ saying the same words. ᵃ saying, My Father,
if this cannot pass away, except I drink it, thy will be
done.** [Jesus here speaks of draining the cup. The "cup"
was a common Hebrew figure used to denote one's divinely
appointed lot or fortune—Ps. xxiii. 5; lxxv. 8; Isa. li. 17;
Ezek. xxii. 31.] **43 And he came again and found them
sleeping, for their eyes were ᵇ very heavy; and they
knew not what to answer him.** [They were ashamed of
the stupor which had come upon them and knew not what
apology to make for it.] ᵃ **44 And he left them again, and
went away, and prayed a third time, saying again the
same words. ᵇ 41 And ᵃ 45 Then cometh he to the
disciples, ᵇ the third time, and saith unto them, Sleep
on now, and take your rest: it is enough; ᵃ behold, the
hour is at hand, {ᵇ the hour is come;} ᵃ and ᵇ behold,
the Son of man is betrayed into the hands of sinners.
42 Arise, let us be going: behold, he that betrayeth me
is at hand.** [Our Lord's words are paradoxical. In our
judgment the saying is best understood by regarding the
first part of it as spoken from the Lord's viewpoint, while the
latter part is spoken from the disciples' viewpoint. It is as if
he said, "So far as I am concerned, you may sleep on and take
your rest, for the time to be of comfort or assistance to me has
wholly passed. But so far as you yourselves are concerned,
you must arise and be going, because Judas with his band of
temple police is upon us."]

CXXIV.

JESUS BETRAYED, ARRESTED AND FORSAKEN.

(Gethsemane.   Friday, several hours before dawn.)

ᵃ MATT. XXVI. 47-56 ; ᵇ MARK XIV. 43-52 ; ᶜ LUKE XXII. 47-53 ;
ᵈ JOHN XVIII. 2-11.

ᵈ2 Now Judas also, who betrayed him, knew the place : for Jesus ofttimes resorted thither with his disciples. [See p. 672.] 3 Judas then, having received tñe band *of soldiers*, and officers from the chief priests and the Pharisees, cometh thither with lanterns and torches and weapons. ᵇ43 And straightway, while he yet spake, ᵃ lo, Judas, one of the twelve, came, {ᵇcometh,} ᵃand with him a great multitude with swords and staves, from the chief priests ᵇand the scribes and the elders. ᵃof the people. ᶜbehold, a multitude, and he that was called Judas, went before them [The presence of Judas is mentioned by each Evangelist.   His treachery made a deep impression upon them.   The arresting party which accompanied Judas consisted of the band of officers and men from the temple guard or Levitical police, Pharisees, scribes, servants, chief priests, captains of the temple and elders.   They were well supplied with lights, for while the passover is always held when the moon is full, the moon at this time of night would be near setting, and the valley of the Kidron, in which Gethsemane lay, would be darkened by the shadow of the adjoining mountain] ; ᵈ4 Jesus therefore, knowing all the things that were coming upon him, went forth, and saith unto them, Whom seek ye ? 5 They answered him, Jesus of Nazareth. Jesus saith unto them, I am *he*.   And Judas also, who betrayed him, was standing with them.   6 When therefore he said unto them, I am *he*, they went backward, and fell to the ground.   7 Again therefore he asked them, Whom seek ye ?   And they said, Jesus of

Nazareth. 8 Jesus answered, I told you that **I am** *he;* if therefore ye seek me, let these go their way: **9 that the word might be fulfilled which he spake, Of those whom thou has given me I lost not one.** [John mentions the foreknowledge of Jesus to remind us that he could have avoided the arrest had he chosen so to do. Even the foreknowledge of Elisha was difficult to deal with (II. Kings vi. 8-12). Jesus asked, "Whom seek ye?" (1) To openly and manfully declare his identity; (2) to make the Jewish rulers fully conscious that they were arresting him, an innocent man; (3) to confine the arrest to himself and thus deliver his disciples. The older commentators regard the falling to the ground as a miracle, but modern scholars look upon it as a result of sudden fear. Jesus merely manifested his dignity and majesty, and the prostration followed as a natural result.] ᵃ**48 Now he that betrayed him gave** {ᵇ **had given**} **them a token,** ᵃ**a sign, saying, Whomso-ever I shall kiss, that is he: take him.** ᵇ **and lead him away safely.** ᶜ**and he drew near unto Jesus to kiss him. 48 But Jesus said unto him, Judas, betrayest thou the Son of man with a kiss?** ᵇ**45 And when he was come,** ᵃ**straightway he came to Jesus, and said** {ᵇ **saith,**} ᵃ**Hail, Rabbi; and kissed him. 50 And Jesus said unto him, Friend,** *do* **that for which thou art come.** [Some place this event before the preceding paragraph. It comports better with the fitnesss of things to place it here. Jesus made Judas feel his utter nothingness, and his worthlessness even as a betrayer. Before Judas can in any way identify Jesus, the Lord has twice declared himself to be the party whom they sought. When he approaches to carry out his contract, the Lord's question exposes him before all as a betray-er, and not a disciple as he wished to appear to be (for kissing was the common mode of salutation between men, especially be-tween teacher and pupils), and when Judas brazenly persists in completing the sign, Jesus bids him do it, not as a friend, but as a traitor. Little did the betrayer think that the kiss of Judas would become a proverb in every nation.] **Then they came**

and laid hands on Jesus, and took him. [The sight of Judas touching him no doubt reassured them, and they laid hands on Jesus.] ᶜ**49 And when they that were about him saw what would follow, they said, Lord, shall we smite with the sword?** ᵇ**47 But** {ᵃ**51 And**} **behold,** ᵈ**10 Simon Peter** ᵇ **a certain one of them that stood by** ᵃ**that were with Jesus** ᵈ**therefore having a sword** ᵃ **stretched out his hand, and drew his sword, and smote** {ᵈ**struck**} ᵃ**the servant of the high priest, and struck** {ᵈ**cut**} **off his right ear.** [We have seen that the apostles were but scantily armed, there being only two swords in their possession. See p. 657. Peter evidently carried one of these, and stood ready to make good his boast that he would suffer, and, if need be, die, in his Lord's service. He evidently struck a downward blow at Malchus' head, and Malchus would have been killed had he not dodged.] **Now the servant's name was Malchus.** [John knew the household of the high priest (John xviii. 16). He knew Malchus by name, and he also knew his kindred—John xviii. 26.] ᶜ**51 But Jesus answered and said, Suffer ye** *them* **thus far. And he touched his ear, and healed him.** [Some think that Jesus spake these words, "Suffer ye thus far," to those who held him, asking them to loose him sufficiently to enable him to touch the ear of Malchus. But the revision committee by inserting "them" make Jesus address his disciples, commanding them not to interfere with those who were arresting him, making it a general statement of the idea which the Lord addressed specifically to Peter in the next sentence.] ᵃ**52 Then** ᵈ**11 Jesus therefore said** {ᵃ**saith**} ᵈ**unto Peter,** ᵃ**Put up again thy** {ᵈ**the**} **sword into the sheath:** ᵃ**its place: for all they that take the sword shall perish with the sword.** ᵈ**the cup which the Father hath given me, shall I not drink it?** [By the healing of Malchus' ear and the words spoken to Peter, Jesus shows that the sword is not to be used either to defend the truth or to advance his kingdom. Had he not thus spoken and acted, Pilate might have doubted his word when he testi-

fied that his kingdom was not of this world (John xviii. 36).
While we know better than to rely upon the aid of the sword
for the advance of truth, we are often tempted to put undue
trust in other "carnal weapons" which are equally futile.
Wealth and eloquence and elaborate church buildings have
but little saving grace in them. It is the truth which wins.
By using the word "cup" John gives us an echo of the agony
in Gethsemane, which suggests that he expects his readers to
be conversant with the other Gospels. The other Evangelists,
having shown that Jesus had fully resolved to drink the cup,
do not regard it as necessary to repeat these words.] ᵃ **53 Or
thinkest thou that I cannot beseech my Father, and he
shall even now send me more than twelve legions of
angels? 54 How then should the scriptures be fulfilled, that thus it must be ?** [Jesus still addresses Peter.
Had it accorded with the divine purpose that Jesus should resist this arrest, angels and not men would have been his proper
and infinitely more effective rescuers. But, on the contrary, it
was God's purpose that he should be arrested, as the Scripture
had foretold.] **55 In that hour ᵇ Jesus answered and said
unto them ᵃ the multitudes, ᶜ the chief priests, and captains of the temple, and elders, that were come against
him, Are ye come out, as against a robber, with swords
and staves? ᵃ to seize me ? ᶜ 53 When ᵃ I sat {ᵇ was}
daily with you in the temple teaching, ᶜ ye stretched
not forth your hands against me : ᵇ and ye took me
not : ᶜ but this is your hour, and the power of darkness. ᵃ56 But all this is come to pass, that the scriptures of the prophets might be fulfilled.** [The party
which came to arrest Jesus was large. The word "band"
used by John to describe part of it is *speira*, which is the
Greek name for the cohort, a division of the Roman army
which in the time of Augustus contained 555 men. Ten
cohorts, or a legion, were usually quartered in the castle An-
tonia, at the northwest corner of the temple enclosure. That
the whole cohort was present is not likely (Matt. xxvii. 27),
but there was a large enough body to represent it. The

Evangelists therefore properly style it a great multitude. Moreover, it was a motley crowd. Its strength and diversity suggest the fear that Jesus might miraculously defend himself. Each part of the crowd found courage in the strength possessed by the other part, the priests relying upon the solidity of the soldiers, the soldiers superstitiously trusting to some spiritual power residing in the priests, etc. Now, because of these fears, the preparation was as great as if some band of robbers was to be taken. The questions of Jesus, therefore, show two facts: 1. By their extensive preparation the rulers bore an unintentional testimony to his divine power. 2. By their failure to arrest him openly in the temple, they bore witness to his innocence. With his divinity and his innocence, therefore, Jesus challenges them, referring to their own conduct for testimony thereto. In conclusion he cites them to the Scriptures which they were fulfilling. Our Lord's dual reference to the Old Testament at this sacred time should cause us to handle them with awe and reverence.]
ᵇ 50 And ᵃ Then all of the disciples left him, and fled. ᵇ 51 And a certain young man followed with him, having a linen cloth cast about him, over *his* naked *body:* and they lay hold on him ; 52 but he left the linen cloth, and fled naked. [All the predictions of Jesus had failed to prepare the apostles for the terrors of his arrest. Despite all his warnings, each apostle sought his own safety. The young man who fled naked is usually presumed to be Mark himself, and it is thought that he thus speaks impersonally after the manner of Matthew and John. The manner of his description shows that he was not an apostle. As Mark's mother resided in Jerusalem (Acts xii. 12, 25), Canon Cook advances the theory that the Lord's Supper was eaten in the upper room of her house, and that when the disciples retired with Jesus from thence to Gethsemane Mark slipped from his bed, threw his sindon about him, and followed after them. The sindon, or linen vestment, was very costly, not being worn even by the middle classes: no apostle would be thus attired.]

CXXV.

FIRST STAGE OF JEWISH TRIAL. EXAMINATION BY ANNAS.

(Friday before dawn.)

ᵈ JOHN XVIII. 12-14, 19-23.

ᵈ **12 So the band and the chief captain, and the officers of the Jews, seized Jesus and bound him, 13 and led him to Annas first; for he was father in law to Caiaphas, who was high priest that year.** [For confusion in the priesthood, etc., see pp. 64 and 528.] **14 Now Caiaphas was he that gave counsel to the Jews, that it was expedient that one man should die for the people.** [See p. 528. John restates this fact to remind the reader that Jesus was about to be tried by those who had prejudged him and decided upon his death.] **19 The high priest therefore asked Jesus of his disciples, and of his teaching.** [We should note that John calls Annas high priest. The high priesthood was a life office. According to Moses, Annas was high priest, but the Romans had given the office to Caiaphas, so that Annas was high priest *de jure*, but Caiaphas was so *de facto*. As high priest, therefore, and as head of the Sadducæan party, the people looked to Annas before Caiaphas, taking Jesus to him firsᵗ The influence of Annas is shown by the fact that he made five of his sons and sons-in-law high priests. Annas is said to have been about sixty years old at this time. He questioned Jesus for the purpose of obtaining, if possible, some material out of which to frame an accusation.] **20 Jesus answered him, I have spoken openly to the world; I ever taught in synagogues, and in the temple, where all the Jews come together; and in secret spake I nothing. 21 Why askest thou me? ask them that have heard *me*, what I spake unto them: behold, these know the things which I said.** [Jesus indeed spoke some things privately (Matt. xiii. 10, 11), but he did not do so for the purposes of concealment (Matt. x. 27). Jesus was the light of the world; addressing his teachings to all flesh, he chose the most public places to utter them—places, however, dedicated to the worship of the true God. He who had said that heaven and earth would pass away, but that his word would not pass away, did not suffer his teaching to be held in contempt; he did not permit it to be made matter for cross examination. On the contrary, it was to be taken cognizance of among the things universally known and understood. The very officers who had arrested him could tell about it— John vii. 45, 46.] **22 And when he had said this, one of the officers standing by struck Jesus with his hand, saying, Answerest thou the high priest so? 23 Jesus answered him, If I have spoken evil, bear witness of the evil: but if well, why smitest thou me?** [Jesus was then under arrest, and as the trial had not yet opened there was ample time to add new matter to the charges against him. If, in addressing the high priest, he had just spoken words worthy of punishment, the officer who struck him should, instead, have preferred charges against him and had him punished in a legal manner. If the officer could not do this (and the point is that he could not), he was doubly wrong in striking him. Thus the Lord calmly rebuked the wrong-doer. Compare his conduct with that of Paul under somewhat similar circumstances (Acts xxiii. 1-3). Jesus exemplified his teaching at Matt. v. 39. "Christ," says Luther, "forbids self-defense with the hand, not with the tongue."]

CXXVI.

SECOND STAGE OF JEWISH TRIAL. JESUS CONDEMNED BY CAIAPHAS AND THE SANHEDRIN.

(Palace of Caiaphas. Friday.)

ᵃ MATT. xxvi. 57, 59-68 ; ᵇ MARK xiv. 53, 55-65 ; ᶜ LUKE xxii. 54, 63-65 ; ᵈ JOHN xviii. 24.

ᵈ **24 Annas therefore sent him bound unto Caiaphas the high priest.** [Foiled in his attempted examination of Jesus, Annas sends Jesus to trial.] ᵇ **and there come together with him all the chief priests and the elders and the scribes.** ᵃ **57 And they that had taken Jesus led him away to** *the house of* **Caiaphas the high priest,** ᶜ **and brought him into the high priest's house.** ᵃ **where the scribes and the elders were gathered together.** [It is very likely that Annas had apartments in the same palace with Caiaphas, and that from these apartments Jesus was led into some hall large enough to hold the Sanhedrin, which had now convened. But this was not its formal session as a court ; it was more in the nature of a caucus, or committee of the whole.] ᵇ **55 Now the chief priests and the whole council sought** ᵃ **false witness against Jesus,** ᵇ **to** {ᵃ **that they might**} **put him to death; 60 and they found it not, though many false witnesses came.** ᵇ **56 For many bare false witness against him, and their witness agreed not together.** ᵃ **But afterward came** ᵇ **57 And there stood up certain,** ᵃ **two,** ᵇ **and bare false witness against him,** ᵃ **61 and said,** {ᵇ **saying,**} ᵃ **This man said, I am able to destroy the temple of God, and to build it in three days.** ᵇ **58 We heard him say, I will destroy this temple that is made with hands, and in three days I will build another made without hands. 59 And not even so did their witness agree together.** [What Jesus

had really said will be found at John ii. 19-22. Though his words
were misunderstood at that time, being applied, not to his
body, but to Herod's temple, yet it is not unlikely that the
Jewish rulers, hearing our Lord's prediction that he would rise
from the dead after three days (Matt. xxvii. 62, 63), came to
understand the import of his words. If so, the record itself
shows the willingness of the Sanhedrin to receive false witness against Christ, for its judges received testimony which
they knew to be utterly immaterial if rightly construed.
The accounts of the two Evangelists, moreover, show how the
witnesses failed to agree. A man could only be condemned
on the testimony of two witnesses agreeing as to some fact or
facts constituting a ground for condemnation—Deut. xvii. 6;
xix. 15.] ª **62 And the high priest stood up,** ᵇ**in the
midst, and asked Jesus,** ª **and said unto him,** {ᵇ **saying,**} **Answerest thou nothing? what is it which
these witness against thee?** ª **63 But Jesus held
his peace.** ᵇ **and answered nothing.** [While the testimony then before the court might be used to show that
Jesus was recklessly boastful, it was insufficient to justify a
sentence of blasphemy. A threat to destroy the temple
might be thus construed (Jer. xxvi. 9-11; Acts vi. 13, 14); but
a promise to rebuild the temple, if destroyed, was altogether
different. The high priest, knowing this, sought to extort
from Jesus some additional evidence. With great cunning and
effrontery he assumes that the testimony is all that could
possibly be desired, and demands of Jesus what he has to say
in answer to it. But our Lord did not suffer himself to seem
so easily deceived. He gave no explanation, since the future
would explain his meaning, and speak the real truth to all who
had ears to hear it.] ª **And** ᵇ **Again the high priest asked
him, and saith** {ª **said**} **unto him,** ᵇ **Art thou the Christ,
the Son of the Blessed?** ª **I adjure thee by the living
God, that thou tell us whether thou art the Christ, the
Son of God.** [Seeing that Jesus was not to be lured into an
answer, and well knowing his perfect frankness, Caiaphas
resolved, in his desperation, to question Jesus plainly and

bluntly. His question is twofold: 1. Art thou Christ? 2. Art thou the Son of God? The latter of these would constitute blasphemy, and the former, by showing a boastful spirit, would tend to confirm the charge. Perhaps, too, Caiaphas anticipated the future, and foresaw how useful this claim to be the Messiah would prove when a hearing was had before Pilate (Luke xxiii. 2). Originally the Messiah was recognized as the Son of God (Ps. ii. 7), but if the Jews had ever generally entertained such an idea, they had lost it before Jesus' day. The Messiah might of course be called the Son of God in that secondary sense in which Adam was thus called (John i. 49; Luke iii. 38). But Jesus had used the term in an entirely different sense, and his usage had been extremely offensive to the Jews (John v. 17, 18; x. 30-39; Matt. xx. 41-46). Caiaphas evidently wished Jesus to answer this question in that new sense which the Lord had given to the words. Caiaphas had no legal right to ask either of these questions. No man can be compelled to testify against himself, but he knew the claims of Jesus, and realized that if Jesus repudiated them he would be shamed forever, and if he asserted them he could be charged with blasphemy. Taking advantage, therefore, of the situation, Caiaphas put the question with the usual formula of an oath, thus adding moral power to it, for, under ordinary circumstances, one was held guilty if he refused to answer when thus adjured (Lev. v. 1). When their own witnesses failed these rulers called the "faithful witness"—I. Tim. vi. 13; Rev. v. 1.] ᵇ **62 And Jesus said, {ᵃ saith} unto him, Thou hast said: ᵇ I am: and ᵃ nevertheless I say unto you, Henceforth ye shall see the Son of man sitting at the right hand of Power, and coming on {ᵇ with} the clouds of heaven.** [Jesus freely confessed the truth which his church is called upon to confess. "Right hand of Power" was commonly understood to mean the right hand of God. By the words "nevertheless" and "henceforth" Jesus brings his present state of humiliation into contrast with his future state of glory. Hard as it might be for them to believe it, the day would come when he should

sit in judgment and they should stand on trial before him.]
63 And ᵃ65 Then the high priest rent his garments,
{ᵇclothes,} and saith, {ᵃsaying,} He hath spoken
blasphemy: what further need have we of witnesses?
behold, now ye have heard the blasphemy: 66 what
think ye? [Though Jesus had given the very answer which
the high priest was longing to hear, yet he hypocritically pre-
tends to be shocked at it, and rends his clothes and feigns
horror. Evidently he feared the effect of the clear, calm
answer of Jesus and sought to counteract its influence on his
colleagues.] They answered and said, He is worthy of
death. ᵇ And they all condemned him to be worthy of
death. [This was not the final, formal sentence, but the
mere determination of the council at the preliminary hearing.]
ᶜ63 And the men that held *Jesus* mocked him, and
beat him. ᵇ65 And some began to spit on him, and to
cover his face, ᵃ67 Then did they spit in his face and
buffet him: ᶜ64 And they blindfolded him, ᵃand some
smote him with the palms of their hands, 68 saying,
{ᵇand [began] to say unto him,} ᵃProphesy unto us,
thou Christ: who is he that struck thee? ᵇand the
officers received him with blows of their hands. ᶜ65
And many other things spake they against him, reviling him. [To spit in the face has been an insult in all ages
and in all lands. See Num. xii. 14; Deut. xxv. 9; Job xxx.
10. Jesus, having stood out for examination, is now given
back to the officers to be led away into the council chamber.
These officers received Jesus with many indignities. They
seek to make his high claims contemptible, and to make it
appear that instead of being divine he is hardly worthy to be
regarded as human.]

CXXVII.

PETER THRICE DENIES THE LORD.

(Court of high priest's residence. Friday before and about dawn.)

ᵃ MATT. XXVI. 58, 69-75 ; ᵇ MARK XIV. 54, 66-72; ᶜ LUKE
XXII. 54-62; ᵈ JOHN XVIII. 15-18, 25-27.

ᵃ **58 But** {ᵈ **15 And**} **Simon Peter followed Jesus**
[leaving Jesus in the palace of the high priest, we now turn
back to the garden of Gethsemane at the time when Jesus
left it under arrest, that we may follow the course of Simon
Peter in his threefold denial of the Master], **and** *so did* **another disciple.** [This other disciple was evidently the apostle John, who thus speaks of himself impersonally.] **Now
that disciple was known unto the high priest, and
entered in with Jesus into the court of the high priest**
[John's acquaintanceship appears to have been with the household as well as with the high priest personally, for we find that
it is used as a permit at the doorway. It is likely that the
high priest knew John rather in a business way—Acts iv. 13] ;
ᵇ **54 And Peter had followed him afar off,** ᵃ **unto the
court of the high priest,** ᵈ **16 but Peter was standing
at the door without. So the other disciple, who was
known unto the high priest, went out and spake unto
her that kept the door, and brought in Peter.** ᵇ **even
within, into the court of the high priest** [For courts of
houses see p. 182. It is still customary to have female porters
at the houses of the great or rich. See Acts xii. 13. John
would have shown a truer kindness to Peter had he let him
stay out]; ᵈ **17 The maid therefore that kept the door
saith unto Peter, Art thou also** *one* **of this man's disciples? He saith, I am not.** ᵃ **and** [Peter] **entered in**
[The doorkeeper evidently recognized John as a disciple, and
was therefore suspicious of Peter. The cowardly "I am not"
of Peter is a sad contrast to the strong "I am he" of Jesus],

ᵈ18 Now the servants and the officers were **standing** *there*, having made a fire of coals; for it was **cold; and** they were warming themselves: and Peter also **was** with them [they were gathered around a little smokeless charcoal fire], ᶜ55 And when they had **kindled a fire in** the midst of the court, and had sat down together, Peter ᵃ sat with the officers, ᶜ in the midst of **them.** ᵃto see the end. [Though his faith in Christ was shaken, he still loved him enough to desire to see what would **become of** him.] ᵇand he was sitting with the officers, **and** warming himself in the light *of the fire.* ᶜ56 And •69 Now ᵇas ᵈSimon Peter ᵃwas sitting {ᵈstanding} ᵃ without ᵇbeneath in the court, there cometh {ᵃcame} unto him, ᶜa certain ᵇone of the maids of the **high** priest; 67 and seeing Peter ᶜas he sat in the light *of the fire,* ᵇwarming himself, she looked {ᶜand looking} stedfastly upon him, said, {ᵇsaith, ᵃsaying,} Thou also wast with Jesus the Galilaean. ᵇthe **Nazarene,** *even* Jesus. ᶜThis man also was with him. ᵃ70 But he denied before them all, saying, I know **not what** thou sayest. ᵇI neither know, nor understand **what** thou sayest: ᶜWoman, I know him not. ᵈ**They said** therefore unto him, Art thou also *one* of his disciples? He denied, and said, I am not. ᵇand he went out into the porch; and the cock crew. ᵃ71 And when he was gone out into the porch, ᶜafter a little while another saw him, and said, Thou also art *one* of them. But Peter said, Man, I am not. ᵇ69 And ᵃanother ᵇthe maid saw him, and began again to say {ᵃsaith} **unto** them that were there, ᵇthat stood by, This is *one* of them. ᵃThis man also was with Jesus of **Nazareth.** ᵇ70 But {ᵃ72 And} again he denied ᵇit. ᵃwith **an** oath, I know not the man. [Peter's second denial was of a quadruple nature. He denied to four different parties, but in such quick succession that the event is regarded as **one.**] 73 And after a little while ᶜafter the space of about one hour another confidently **affirmed, saying, Of a**

truth this man also was with him; for he is a Galilaean. 60 But Peter said, Man, I know not what
thou sayest. ᵇAgain they that stood by ᵃcame and
said to Peter, Of a truth thou art *one* of them; ᵇfor
thou art a Galilaean. ᵃfor thy speech maketh thee
known. ᵈ26 One of the servants of the high priest,
being a kinsman of him whose ear Peter cut off, saith,
Did not I see thee in the garden with him? ᵇ70 But
ᵈ27 Peter therefore denied again: ᵃ74 Then began he
to curse and to swear, I know not the {ᵇthis} ᵃman.
ᵇof whom ye speak. 72 And straightway ᶜimmediate-
ly, while he yet spake, ᵇthe second time the cock crew.
[Exasperated by the repeated accusations, Peter loses his
temper and begins to emphasize his denial by profanity. Desire to make good his denial is now supreme in his thoughts
and the Lord whom he denies is all but forgotten.] ᶜ61 And
the Lord turned, and looked upon Peter. And Peter
remembered ᵇAnd Peter called to mind the word, ᶜof
the Lord, ᵃwhich Jesus had said, ᵇhow that Jesus
said unto him, ᵃBefore the cock crow, ᵇtwice, ᶜthis
day, thou shalt deny me thrice. 62 And he went out,
ᵇAnd when he thought thereon, he wept. ᶜbitterly.
[When Peter remembered the loving tenderness of Jesus manifested when he foretold Peter's crime it formed a background
against which the sin appeared in all its hideous enormity.]

CXXVIII.

THIRD STAGE OF JEWISH TRIAL. JESUS FORM-
ALLY CONDEMNED BY THE SANHE-
DRIN AND LED TO PILATE.

(Jerusalem. Friday after dawn.)

ᵃMATT. XXVII. 1, 2; ᵇMARK XV. 1; ᶜLUKE XXII. 66-XXIII.
1; ᵈJOHN XVIII. 28.

ᵃ1 Now when morning was come, ᶜ66 And as soon
as it was day, ᵇstraightway ᶜthe assembly of the

elders of the people was gathered together, both chief priests and scribes ; and they led him away into their council, ª all the chief priests and {ᵇ with} the elders ª of the people ᵇ and scribes, and the whole council, held a consultation, and ª took counsel against Jesus to put him to death [Since blasphemy was by no means a criminal offense among the Romans, the Sanhedrin consulted together and sought for some charge of which the Romans would take notice. As we follow their course it will become evident to us that they found no new ground of accusation against Jesus, and, failing to do so, they decided to make use of our Lord's claim to be the Christ by so perverting it as to make him seem to assert an intention to rebel against the authority of Rome]: ᶜ saying, 67 If thou art the Christ, tell us. But he said unto them, If I tell you, ye will not believe [as experience had already proven—John viii. 59 ; x. 31]: 68 and if I ask *you*, ye will not answer. [Thus Jesus protests against the violence and injustice of his trial. His judges were asking him whether he was the Christ without any intention of investigating the truth of his claim, but merely for the purpose of condemning him by unwarrantedly assuming that he was not the Christ. They therefore asked in an unlawful spirit as well as in an unlawful manner. Jesus had a good right to ask them questions tending to confirm his Christhood by the Scripture, but had he done so they would not have answered—Matt. xxii. 41-45. Jesus appeals to them to try the question as to who he was, but they insist on confining the inquiry as to who he claimed to be, assuming that the claim was false.] 69 But from henceforth shall the Son of man be seated at the right hand of the power of God. [See p. 698.] 70 And they all said, Art thou then the Son of God? And he said unto them, Ye say that I am. [The Hebrew mode of expression, equivalent to "Ye say it, because I am."] 71 And they said, What further need have we of witness? for we ourselves have heard from his own mouth. [Thus they unconsciously admit their lack of evidence against Jesus.]

1 And the whole company of them rose up, ᵃ2 and thᴄy bound ᵇ Jesus, and carried {ᵃled} him away, ᵈ28 They lead Jesus therefore from Caiaphas into the Praetorium: ᶜand brought him before Pilate. ᵇand delivered him up to Pilate. ᵃthe governor. ᵈand it was early; [The Sanhedrin could try and could condemn, but could not put to death without the concurring sentence of the Roman governor. To obtain this sentence they now lead Jesus before Pilate in the early dawn, having made good use of their time.]

CXXIX.

FIRST STAGE OF THE ROMAN TRIAL. JESUS BEFORE PILATE FOR THE FIRST TIME.

(Jerusalem. Early Friday morning.)

ᵃMATT. XXVII. 11-14; ᵇMARK XV. 2-5; ᶜLUKE XXIII. 2-5; ᵈJOHN XVIII. 28-38.

ᵈand they themselves entered not into the Praetorium, that they might not be defiled, but might eat the passover. [See p. 641.] 29 Pilate therefore went out unto them, and saith, What accusation bring ye against this man? 30 They answered and said unto him, If this man were not an evil-doer, we should not have delivered him up unto thee. [The Jewish rulers first attempt to induce Pilate to accept their verdict and condemn Jesus upon it, and execute him without a trial. If they had succeeded in this, Jesus would have been put to death as a blasphemer. But as Pilate had insisted upon trying Jesus, and as blasphemy was not a capital offense under the Roman law, Jesus was condemned and executed as the King of the Jews.] 31 Pilate therefore said unto them, Take him yourselves, and judge him according to your law. The Jews said unto him, It is not lawful for us to put any man to death: 32 that the word of Jesus might be fulfilled, which he spake, signifying by what manner

of death he should die. [As the Jews insisted on their own verdict, Pilate bade them pronounce their own sentence, declining to mix jurisdictions by pronouncing a Roman sentence on a Sanhedrin verdict. But the Jews responded that it is not in their power to pronounce the sentence for which their verdict called, since they could not put to death. Jesus could only be sentenced to death by the Roman court, and crucifixion was the mode by which its death sentence was executed. Jesus had predicted all this in the simple statement that he should die by crucifixion (John xii. 33, 34), but he also gave the details of his trial—Matt. xx. 18, 19; Mark x. 33, 34.] ᶜ **2 And they began to accuse him, saying, We found this man perverting our nation, and forbidding to give tribute to Caesar, and saying that he himself is Christ a king.** [The Jews now profess to change their verdict into a charge, they themselves becoming witnesses as to the truth of the matter charged. They say "We found," thereby asserting that the things which they stated to Pilate were the things for which they had condemned Jesus. Their assertion was utterly false, for the three things which they now mentioned had formed no part whatever of the evidence against Jesus in their trial of him. The first charge, that Jesus was a perverter or seducer of the people, was extremely vague. The second, that he taught to withhold tribute from Cæsar, was a deliberate falsehood. See p. 599. The third, that he claimed to be king, was true, but this third charge, coupled with the other two, was intended to convey a sense which was maliciously false. Jesus was a spiritual King, and claimed to be such, and as such was no offender against the Roman government. But the rulers intended that Pilate should regard him as claiming to be a political king, which he had constantly refused to do—John vi. 15.] ᵈ **33 Pilate therefore entered again into the Praetorium, and called Jesus,** ᵃ **11 Now Jesus stood before the governor** [Jesus is called from the guards who have him in custody and stands alone before Pilate that the governor may investigate his case privately]: ᵇ **2 And Pilate** ᵃ**the governor**

asked him, ᵈand said unto him, {ᵃsaying,} **Art thou the King of the Jews?** [The Gospels are unanimous in giving this question as the first words addressed by Pilate to Jesus. The question expresses surprise. There was nothing in the manner or attire of Jesus to suggest a royal claimant. The question was designed to draw Jesus out should he chance to be a fanatical or an unbalanced enthusiast.] **And Jesus** ᵇ**answering saith** {ᶜ**answered him and said,**} ᵇ**unto him, Thou sayest.** ᵈ**Sayest thou this of thyself, or did others tell it thee concerning me?** [Using the Hebrew form of affirmative reply (see p. 698), Jesus admits that he is a king, but asks a question which forms the strongest negation that he is a king in the sense contained in the Jewish accusation. Had he been a king in that sense, Pilate would have been the one most likely to know it. The question also, by an indirect query as to the accuser, reveals to Pilate's mind that no Roman had accused him. He was accused of the Jews, and when had that restless, rebellious people ever found fault with a man who sought to free them from the galling Roman yoke?] **35 Pilate answered, Am I a Jew?** [The strong, practical mind of the Roman at once caught the drift of Christ's question, and perceived that the title "King of the Jews" had in it a double meaning, so that it might be construed in some unpolitical sense. What this sense was he could not tell, for he was not a Jew. The mysteries of that nation were of no interest to him save where his office compelled him to understand them.] **Thine own nation and the chief priests delivered thee unto me: what hast thou done?** [Pilate concedes that the accusation against Jesus comes from an unexpected and suspicious source, and he asks Jesus to tell him plainly by what means he had incurred the enmity of the leaders of his people.] **36 Jesus answered, My kingdom is not of this world: if my kingdom were of this world, then would my servants fight, that I should not be delivered to the Jews: but now is my kingdom not from hence.** [Jesus answers Pilate's question indirectly. He had done something to incur the enmity of the rulers, and that was to have authority with and exercise influence over the people (John xii. 19). They objected to his kingly claims (Matt. xxi. 15, 16; Luke xix. 38, 39), but Jesus shows Pilate that these kingly claims, however distasteful to the Jews, were no offense to or menace against the authority of Rome. Further than this, Jesus did not define his kingdom, for Pilate had no concern in it beyond this. It was sufficient to inform him that it made no use of physical power even for purposes of defense. Such a kingdom could cause no trouble to Rome, and the bare fact stated by Jesus proved that it was indeed such a kingdom.] **37 Pilate therefore said unto him, Art thou a king then? Jesus answered, Thou sayest that I am a king.** [See p. 698.] **To this end have I been born, and to this end am I come into the world, that I should bear witness unto the truth. Every one that is of the truth heareth my voice.** [Jesus here enlightens Pilate as to the nature of his kingdom. He, the King, was the incarnation of truth, and all those who derive the inspiration of their life from truth were his subjects. For the purpose of thus bearing witness to and revealing truth Jesus had been born, thus entering a new state of being, and he had come into the world in this changed condition, thus entering a new sphere of action. The words clearly imply the pre-existence of Christ and no doubt aroused that state of uneasiness or fear which was increased by the words of the Jewish rulers—John xix. 7, 8.] **38 Pilate saith unto him, What is truth?** [This question has been regarded as an earnest inquiry (Chrysostom), the inquiry of one who despaired (Olshausen), a scoffing question (Alford), etc. But it is evident that Pilate asked it intending to investigate the case of Jesus further, but, suddenly concluding that he already knew enough to answer his purpose as a judge, he stifles his curiosity as a human being and proceeds with the trial of Jesus, leaving the question unanswered.] **And when he had said this, he went out again unto the Jews, and saith unto them, ᶜ unto the chief priests and the multitudes, I find no fault in this man. ᵈ no crime in**

him. [The pronoun "I" is emphatic; as if Pilate said, "You, prejudiced fanatics, demand his death, but I, the calm judge, pronounce him innocent."] ᵇ **3 And the chief priests accused him of many things.** ᵃ **12 And when he was accused by the chief priests and elders, he answered nothing.** [When Pilate left the Prætorium to speak with the Jewish rulers, it is evident that Jesus was led out with him, and so stood there in the presence of his accusers.] ᵇ **4 And** ᵃ **13 Then** ᵇ **Pilate again asked him, {ᵃsaith unto him,}** ᵇ **saying, Answerest thou nothing? behold how many things they accuse thee of.** ᵃ **Hearest thou not how many things they witness against thee?** ᵇ **5 But Jesus no more answered anything;** ᵃ **14 And he gave him no answer, not even to one word:** ᵇ **insomuch that Pilate** ᵃ **the governor** ᵇ **marvelled.** ᵃ **greatly.** [Pilate was irritated that Jesus did not speak in his own defense. He had already seen enough of our Lord's wisdom to assure him that it would be an easy matter for him to expose the malicious emptiness of all these charges—charges which Pilate himself knew to be false, but about which he had to keep silent, for, being judge, he could not become our Lord's advocate. Our Lord's silence was a matter of prophecy (Isa. liii. 7). Jesus kept still because to have successfully defended himself would have been to frustrate the purpose for which he came into the world—John xii. 23-28.] ᶜ **5 But they were the more urgent, saying, He stirreth up the people, teaching throughout all Judaea, and beginning from Galilee even unto this place.** [The Jews cling to their general accusation of sedition, and seek to make the largeness of the territory where Jesus operated overshadow and conceal the smallness of their testimony as to what his operations were.]

CXXX.

SECOND STAGE OF THE ROMAN TRIAL. JESUS BEFORE HEROD ANTIPAS.

(Jerusalem. Early Friday morning.)
ᶜLUKE XXIII. 6-12.

ᵗ6 **But when Pilate heard it** [when he heard that Jesus had begun his operations in Galilee], **he asked whether the man were a Galilaean. 7 And when he knew that he was of Herod's jurisdiction** [Herod was tetrarch of Galilee—Luke iii. 1], **he sent him unto Herod, who ̄himself also** ["also" includes both Pilate and Herod, neither of whom lived at Jerusalem] **was at Jerusalem in these days.** ["These days" refers to the passover season. Pilate had come up from his residence at Cæsarea to keep order during the passover, and Herod had come from Tiberias to keep in favor with the Jews by showing respect to their festival. Hearing that Jesus was a citizen of Herod's province, Pilate saw an opportunity to do two things: first, by sending Jesus to Herod he would either shift or divide the grave responsibility in which he was placed; second, he would show a courtesy to Herod which might help to remove Herod's enmity towards him; a courtesy which perhaps might be the reverse of the discourtesy which likely caused the enmity—Luke xiii. 1.] **8 Now when Herod saw Jesus, he was exceeding glad: for he was of a long time desirous to see him, because he had heard concerning him; and he hoped to see some miracle done by him.** [As to Herod's previous knowledge of Christ, see Luke ix. 7-9.] **9 And he questioned him in many words; but he answered him nothing. 10 And the chief priests and the scribes stood, vehemently accusing him.** [The rulers felt that their case had well-nigh failed before Pilate, so they became the more urgent in the presence of Herod, since Herod had less reason to fear them than Pilate. In the midst of this, Jesus stood silent, answering neither question nor accusation. Herod, as sated ruler, adulterer and murderer, wished Jesus to turn juggler for his amusement; but the Son of God had nothing but silence for such a creature. The only contemptuous word which Jesus is recorded to have spoken had reference to this ruler—Luke xiii. 31, 32.] **11 And Herod with his soldiers set him at nought, and mocked him, and arraying him in gorgeous apparel sent him back to Pilate.** [Herod took vengeance upon the silence of Christ by treating him with abusive contempt. But, finding nothing in Jesus worthy of condemnation, he returned him to Pilate.] **12 And Herod and Pilate became friends with each other that very day: for before they were at enmity between themselves.** [Thus Pilate gained but half his desire: Herod was now his friend, but the case of Jesus was still on his hands.]

CXXXI.

THIRD STAGE OF THE ROMAN TRIAL. PILATE RELUCTANTLY SENTENCES HIM TO CRUCIFIXION.

(Friday. Towards sunrise.]

ᵃ MATT. XXVII. 15-30; ᵇ MARK XV. 6-19; ᶜ LUKE XXIII. 13-25; ᵈ JOHN XVIII. 39-XIX. 16.

ᵃ **15 Now at the feast** [the passover and unleavened bread] **the governor was wont {ᵇ used to} release unto them ᵃthe multitude one prisoner, whom they would. {ᵇ whom they asked of him.}** [No one knows when or by whom this custom was introduced, but similar customs were not unknown elsewhere, both the Greeks and Romans being wont to bestow special honor upon certain occasions by releasing prisoners.] ᵃ **16 And they had then ᵇ7 And there was ᵃa notable prisoner, ᵇone called Barabbas,** *lying* **bound with them that had made insurrection, men who in the insurrection had committed murder.**

[Josephus tells us that there had been an insurrection against Pilate's government about that time caused by his taking money from the temple treasury for the construction of an aqueduct. This may have been the affair here referred to, for in it many lost their lives.] **8 And the multitude went up and began to ask him** *to do* **as he was wont to do unto them.** [It was still early in the morning, and the vast majority of the city of Jerusalem did not know what was transpiring at Pilate's palace. But they came thither in throngs, demanding their annual gift of a prisoner. Pilate welcomed the demand as a possible escape from his difficulties.] ᶜ **13 And Pilate called together the chief priests and the rulers of the people** [He did not wish to seem to take advantage of our Lord's accusers by releasing him during their absence. Possibly he knew of the triumphal entry the Sunday previous, and thought that the popularity of Jesus would be such that his release would be overwhelmingly demanded, and so called the rulers that they might see that he had released Jesus in answer to popular clamor. If he had such expectations, they were misplaced], ᵇ **9 And** ᵃ **17 When therefore they were gathered together,** ᵇ **Pilate answered them, saying,** {ᶜ **14 and said**} **unto them,** ᵇ **Will ye that I release unto you the King of the Jews?** ᶜ **Ye brought unto me this man, as one that perverteth the people: and behold, I, having examined him before you, found no fault in this man touching those things whereof ye accuse him: 15 no, nor yet Herod: for he sent him back unto us; and behold, nothing worthy of death hath been done by him.** ᵈ **39 But ye have a custom, that I should release unto you one at the passover:** ᶜ **16 I will therefore chastise him, and release him.** ᵈ **Will ye therefore that I release unto you the King of the Jews?** ᵃ **Whom will ye that I release unto you? Barabbas, or Jesus who is called Christ? 18 For he knew** {ᵇ **perceived**} ᵃ **that for envy they** ᵇ **the chief priests had delivered him up.** [Though Jesus had been declared innocent on the joint finding of himself and Herod,

Pilate did not have the courage to deliberately release him. He sought to please the rulers by scourging him, and the multitude by delivering him to them as a popular favorite, and himself by an adroit escape from an unpleasant situation. But he pleased nobody.] ᶜ18 **But they cried out all together, saying, Away with this man, and release unto us Barabbas:— 19 one who for a certain insurrection made in the city, and for murder, was cast into prison.** [We see from Matthew's account that though the people had a right to name their prisoner, Pilate took upon himself the liberty of choosing which one of two it should be. By doing so he complicated matters for the Jewish rulers, asking them to choose between Jesus, who was held on an unfounded charge of insurrection, and Barabbas, who was notoriously an insurrectionist and a murderer and a robber as well. But the rulers were not to be caught in so flimsy a net. Without regard to consistency they raised their voice in full chorus for the release of Barabbas and the crucifixion of Jesus.] ᵃ19 **And while he was sitting on the judgment-seat, his wife sent unto him, saying, Have thou nothing to do with that righteous man; for I have suffered many things this day in a dream because of him.** [This message of Pilate's wife suggests that the name and face of Jesus were not unknown to Pilate's household. Pilate would be much influenced by such a message. The Romans generally were influenced by all presages, and Suetonius tells us that both Julius and Augustus Cæsar attached much importance to dreams.] ᵇ11 **But** ᵃ20 **Now the chief priests and the elders persuaded** {ᵇ stirred up} **the multitude,** {ᵃ multitudes} ᵇ **that he should rather release Barabbas unto them.** ᵃ **that they should ask for Barabbas, and destroy Jesus. 21 But the governor answered and said unto them, Which of the two will ye that I release unto you? And they said, Barabbas.** ᵈ40 **They cried out therefore again, saying, Not this man, but Barabbas. Now Barabbas was a robber.** ᶜ20 **And Pilate spake unto them again, desiring to release Jesus;** ᵇ12

And Pilate again answered and said {ᵃsaith} unto
them, What then shall I do unto Jesus who is called
Christ? ᵇhim whom ye call the King of the Jews?
ᶜ21 but {ᵇ13 and} they cried out {ᶜshouted} ᵇagain,
ᶜsaying, Crucify, crucify him. ᵃThey all say, Let him
be crucified. ᵇ14 And Pilate said unto them, ᶜthe
third time, Why, what evil hath this man {ᵃhe} done?
ᶜI have found no cause of death in him: I will therefore chastise him and release him. ᵃBut they cried
out exceedingly, saying, ᵇCrucify him. ᵃLet him be
crucified. [Finding the mob cruelly persistent, Pilate boldly
declines to do its will and turns back into the Prætorium declaring his intention to release Jesus. But he retires with the
demands of the multitude ringing in his ears.] ᵈ1 Then
Pilate therefore took Jesus, and scourged him. [Carry-
ing out the program which he proposed, Pilate had Jesus
removed from the Prætorium to the place of scourging, and
inflicted that punishment upon him. We learn from Josephus
and others that the law required that those about to be crucified should first be scourged. But Pilate hoped that scourging would suffice. He believed that the more moderate
would take pity upon Jesus when they viewed his scourged
body, for scourging was so cruel a punishment that the condemned person often died under its infliction. The scourge
was made of thongs loaded at the extremity with pieces of
bone or metal. The condemned person was stripped and
fastened to a low post, thus bending the back so as to stretch
the skin. Blood spurted at the first blow.] 2 And the
soldiers platted a crown of thorns, and put it on his
head, and arrayed him in a purple garment; 3 and
they came unto him, and said, Hail, King of the Jews!
and they struck him with their hands. [The soldiers
had no special malice against Jesus, but the Roman military
system made men hard of heart. The occasion gave to these
foreign legionaries a much-enjoyed opportunity to show their
contempt for the Jews by mocking Jesus as their King. It is
not known which one of the many thorny plants of Palestine

was used to form the Lord's crown. See p. 330. The robe
was also designed to give Jesus a mock appearance of royalty,
and it was likely some cast-off military coat or state garment
of Pilate's. Pilate winked at the conduct of the soldiers since
it favored his plan. If Jesus could be made sufficiently pitiable and contemptible, his enemies might relent. But Pilate
little understood the venom of those enemies: they mocked
and taunted Jesus even upon the cross.] **4 And Pilate
went out again, and saith unto them, Behold, I bring
him out to you, that ye may know that I find no crime
in him.** [Those having our modern sense of justice would
have said that Pilate brought Jesus out thus *because he had
found crime in him.* But scourging was little thought of in
that place and day (Acts xxii. 24). If Pilate had found Jesus
guilty, he would have condemned him at once. As it was, he
sought to return Jesus to the Sanhedrin as having committed
no crime of which the Roman law could take note.] **5 Jesus
therefore came out, wearing the crown of thorns
and the purple garment. And *Pilate* saith unto them,
Behold, the man!** [It was Pilate's original proposition to
scourge Jesus and let him go (Luke xxiii. 16). Having already scourged him, he now hoped to effect his release. Presenting our Lord in this state of abject humiliation, he feels
that he has removed from him every suspicion of royalty. He
speaks of Jesus as no longer a king, but a mere man. Pilate's
words, however, have a prophetic color, somewhat like those
uttered by Caiaphas. All those of subsequent ages have
looked and must continue to look to Jesus as the ideal of manhood. The "Ecce Homo" of Pilate is in some sense an
echo of the words of the Father when he said, "This is my
Son, my chosen: hear ye him." In Jesus we behold the true
man, the second Adam.] **6 When therefore the chief
priests and the officers saw him, they cried out, saying, Crucify *him*, crucify *him!*** [Thus Pilate's expectation
came to naught, for not one of the Jewish rulers ever wavered
in their demand for crucifixion.] **Pilate saith unto them,
Take him yourselves, and crucify him: for I find no**

crime in him. [In this sentence "ye" and "I" are both emphatic; for Pilate wishes to draw a contrast between himself and the Jewish rulers. His words are not a permission to crucify, but a bit of taunting irony, as if he said: "I the judge have found him innocent, but ye seem to lack the wit to see that the case is ended. If ye are so much superior to the judge that ye can ignore his decision, proceed without him; crucify him yourselves."] **7 The Jews answered him, We have a law, and by that law he ought to die, because he made himself the Son of God.** [Perceiving that Pilate was taunting them, and practically accusing them of attempting to put an innocent man to death, they defended themselves by revealing the fact that in addition to the charges that they had preferred against Jesus they had found him clearly guilty and worthy of death on another charge; viz.: that of blasphemy (Lev. xxiv. 16). They had made no mention of this fact, because Pilate was under no obligation to enforce their law; but they mentioned it now to justify their course. They probably felt sure that Jesus himself would convince Pilate of the truth of this latter accusation if Pilate questioned him.] **8 When Pilate therefore heard this saying, he was the more afraid** [The words of Jesus at John xviii. 37 (see p. 707) and the message from his wife had already filled Pilate with fear, and this saying added to it because the Roman and Grecian mythologies told of many incarnations; and, influenced by the calm presence of Jesus, Pilate readily considered the possibility of such a thing]; **9 and he entered into the Praetorium again** [taking Jesus with him for private examination], **and saith unto Jesus, Whence art thou? But Jesus gave him no answer.** [Pilate sought to know whether Jesus were of heaven or of earth; but Jesus did not answer, for the motive of the question was not right. Pilate did not wish an answer that he might give or withhold worship; but that he might know how strenuously he should defend Jesus. But innocent life is to be defended at all hazards, and it matters not whether it be human or divine. Pilate, therefore, already knew enough to enable him to discharge his duties.] **10 Pilate therefore saith unto him, Speakest thou not unto me? knowest thou not that I have power to release thee, and have power to crucify thee?** [Pilate intimates that Jesus should treat his questions with more courtesy since his good will and favor are not to be despised. But the words lay bare the corrupt heart of Pilate, and form a prophecy of the sin which he committed. Judges must hear and give sentence according to truth, uninfluenced by good will or favor. But Pilate, to please the Jews, crucified Jesus, reversing the sentence which he here suggests that he might render to please Jesus.] **11 Jesus answered him Thou wouldest have no power against me, except it were given thee from above: therefore he** [Caiaphas] **that delivered me unto thee hath greater sin.** [Judas is spoken of as having delivered Jesus—John xviii. 2, 5 (the same word being translated both "betrayed" and "delivered"), but Judas did not deliver to Pilate, so Caiaphas as the representative of the Sanhedrin is here meant; and Pilate's sin is contrasted with that of the rulers. Both of them sinned in abusing their office (the power derived from above—Ps. lxxv. 6, 7; Isa. xliv. 28; Rom. xiii. 1); but Pilate's sin stopped here. He had no acquaintance with Jesus to give him the possibility of other powers—those of love or hatred, worship or rejection. The members of the Sanhedrin had these powers which arose from a personal knowledge of Jesus, and they abused them by hating and rejecting him, thereby adding to their guilt. Pilate condemned the innocent when brought before him, but the Sanhedrin searched out and arrested the innocent that they might enjoy condemning him.] **12 Upon this Pilate sought to release him** [As we have seen, Pilate had before this tried to win the consent of the rulers that Jesus be released, but that which John here indicates was probably an actual attempt to set Jesus free. He may have begun by unloosing the hands of Jesus, or some such demonstration]: **but the Jews cried out, saying, If thou release this man, thou art not Caesar's friend: every one that maketh himself a king speaketh against Caesar.**

[Whatever Pilate's demonstration was it was immediately met by a counter one on the part of the rulers. They raise a cry which the politic Pilate can not ignore. Taking up the political accusation (which they had never abandoned), they give it a new turn by prompting Pilate to view it from Cæsar's standpoint. Knowing the unreasoning jealousy, suspicion and cruelty of the emperor, Pilate saw at once that these unscrupulous Jews could make out of the present occasion a charge against him which would cost him his position, if not his life.] **13 When Pilate therefore heard these words, he brought Jesus out, and sat down on the judgment-seat at a place called The Pavement, but in Hebrew, Gabbatha.** [Pilate had already again and again declared Jesus innocent. He now mounts the judgment-seat that he may formally reverse himself and condemn him. The apostle as an eye-witness fixes by its two names the exact spot where this awful decision was rendered.] **14 Now it was the Preparation of the passover** [see p. 647] **: it was about the sixth hour.** [It is likely that John uses the Roman method of counting time, and means six A. M. See p. 142. John notes also the exact day and hour.] **And he saith unto the Jews, Behold, your King!** [As he had tried to waken their compassion by saying, "Behold, the man!" so he now made a final attempt to shame them by saying, "Behold, your King!"] **15 They therefore cried out, Away with *him*, away with *him*, crucify him! Pilate saith unto them, Shall I crucify your King? The chief priests answered, We have no king but Caesar.** [Carried away by the strong emotions of the moment, the official organs of the Jewish theocracy proclaimed Cæsar to be their only king, thus yielding with Jesus their claims to independence and their hopes in a Messiah. This is a most significant fact. When their ancestors rejected Jehovah as their king (I. Sam. xii. 12), their faithful prophet, Samuel, warned them what the king of their choice would do, and what they should suffer under him. Thus Jesus also foretold what this Cæsar of their choice would do to them Luke **xix.** 41-44 ; xxiii. 27-31). They committed themselves to the tender mercies of Rome, and one generation later Rome trod them in the wine-press of her wrath.] ᶜ **23 But they were urgent with loud voices, asking that he might be crucified. And their voices prevailed.** [They overcame Pilate's weak resistance by their clamor.] ᵃ **24 So when Pilate saw that he prevailed nothing, but rather that a tumult was arising, he took water, and washed his hands before the multitude, saying, I am innocent of the blood of this righteous man ; see ye** *to it.* **25 And all the people answered and said, His blood** *be* **on us, and on our children.** [Pilate's act was symbolic, intended to show that he regarded the crucifixion of Jesus as a murder, and therefore meant to wash his hands of the guilt thereof. The Jewish law made the act perfectly familiar to the Jews (Deut. xxi. 1-9). Had the Jewish rulers not been frenzied by hatred, the sight of Pilate washing his hands would have checked them ; but in their rage they take upon themselves and their children all the responsibility. At the siege of Jerusalem they answer in part for the blood of Christ, but God alone determines the extent of their responsibility, and he alone can say when their punishment shall end. But we know that it ends for all when they repentantly seek his forgiveness. The punishments of God are not vindictive, they are the awards of Justice meted out by a merciful hand.] ᵇ **15 And Pilate, wishing to content the multitude,** ᶜ **gave sentence that what they asked should be done.** ᵃ **26 Then released he unto them Barabbas ;** ᶜ **him that for insurrection and murder had been cast into prison, whom they asked for ; but Jesus he delivered up to their will.** ᵈ **16 Then therefore** ᵇ **Jesus, when he had scourged him** [Mark mentions the scourging to show that it preceded the crucifixion, but we see from John's account that the scourging took place somewhat earlier in the proceeding], ᵈ **he delivered him unto them to be crucified.** [Pilate delivered Jesus to their punishment, but not into their hands ; he was led forth and crucified by Pilate's soldiers, who first mocked him, as the next paragraph shows.] ᵇ **16 And** ᵃ **27**

Then the soldiers of the governor took Jesus, ᵇ led him away within {ᵃ into} ᵇ the court, which is called the Praetorium; and they called together ᵃ and gathered unto him the whole band. 28 And they stripped him, and put on him a scarlet robe. ᵇ 17 And they clothe him with purple, ᵃ 29 And they platted {ᵇ platting} a crown of thorns, [and] they put it on him; ᵃ upon his head, and a reed in his right hand; and they kneeled down before him, and mocked him, ᵇ 18 and they began to salute him, ᵃ saying, Hail, King of the Jews! 30 And they spat upon him, and took the reed ᵇ 19 And they smote his head {ᵃ smote him on the head.} ᵇ with a reed, and bowing their knees worshipped him. [After the sentence of death the soldiers take Jesus back into the Prætorium, and renew the mockeries and indignities which had been interrupted that Pilate might exhibit Jesus to the people as John shows us. Moreover, the whole band, or cohort, are now gathered, where at first but a few took part. It is likely that the mock robe and crown were removed when Jesus was brought before Pilate to be sentenced, for it is highly improbable that a Roman judge would pronounce the death sentence while the prisoner was clothed in such a manner.]

CXXXII.

REMORSE AND SUICIDE OF JUDAS.

(In the temple and outside the wall of Jerusalem. Friday morning.)

ᵃ MATT. XXVII. 3-10; ₑ ACTS I. 18, 19.

ᵃ 3 Then Judas, who betrayed him, when he saw that he was condemned [Judas, having no reason to fear the enemies of Jesus, probably stood in their midst and witnessed the entire trial], repented himself, and brought back the thirty pieces of silver to the chief priests and elders, 4 saying, I have sinned in that I betrayed inno-

cent blood. [There are two Greek words which are translated "repented," the one properly so translated, *metanoeo*, which means literally "to know after" and which therefore means a change of mind or purpose; and the other, *metamellomai*, which is used here and which means literally "to care after," indicates a sorrow for the past. The first should be translated "repent;" the second, "regret." Trench draws the distinction thus: "He who has *changed his mind* about the past is in the way to change everything; he who has an *after care* may have little or nothing more than a selfish dread of the consequences of what he has done." Considering the prophecy which had been uttered with regard to Judas' act (Matt. xxvi. 24), he had good reason to fear the consequences. While he testifies as to the innocence of Jesus, he expresses no affection for him.] **But they said, What is that to us? see thou *to it*.** [The rulers did not share with Judas the wish to undo what had been done. They have been censured for not receiving the testimony which Judas gave as to the innocence of Jesus. But as they condemned Jesus upon his own testimony, any evidence which Judas might give would be, from their standpoint, irrelevant and immaterial. Could Judas testify that Jesus was indeed the Son of God? If our Lord's own testimony to this effect was regarded as blasphemy, nothing which Judas could say would change the case. But the testimony of Judas, in the free, untechnical court of public opinion, is of vast weight and importance. It shows that one who had every opportunity of knowing Jesus, and who was sordid enough to betray him, was yet forced for conscience' sake to admit that there was no reason why he should have done so.] **5 And he cast down the pieces of silver into the sanctuary, and departed** [Judas found the chief priests in the sanctuary. Having obtained from Pilate the condemnation of Jesus, they hastened back to the temple to discharge their morning duties. This gave the soldiers time to mock Jesus, and Pilate time to order and prepare the crucifixion. And so, though Jesus was sentenced at six o'clock in the morning (John xix. 14), he was not crucified until the third hour, or nine o'clock (Mark xv. 25). Thus the priests were enabled to be present at the crucifixion, or at least very soon after the crosses were erected. Judas, finding that they would not receive his money, cast it down before them that his hands might be no longer burnt by holding it]; **and he went away and hanged himself. 6 And the chief priests took the pieces of silver, and said, It is not lawful to put them into the treasury, since it is the price of blood.** [The law of God made no provision as to the uses of blood money; it was the tradition of the elders which thus forbade to put it into the treasury. Theirs was a strange conscience indeed, which could take out the Lord's money (and, under the then existing Jewish theocratic government, all public money was the Lord's money) and spend it for blood, but when it was so spent they could not put it back! Moreover, theirs was a strange admission. If the money given to Judas was properly expended for the arrest of a real criminal, it was justice money, and not blood money at all.] **7 And they took counsel, and bought with them the potter's field, to bury strangers in.** [That is, the foreigners who died in Jerusalem. Whether rich or poor, they were not wanted in Jewish graveyards. The potter's field, being excavated for clay, would be of little value, and would sell cheap.] **8 Wherefore that field was called, The field of blood, unto this day.** [This mark of time shows that Matthew's Gospel was written a good many years after the crucifixion.] **9 Then was fulfilled that which was spoken through Jeremiah the prophet, saying, And they took the thirty pieces of silver, the price of him that was priced, whom *certain* of the children of Israel did price; 10 and they gave them for the potter's field, as the Lord appointed me.** [This quotation is not found in any writings of Jeremiah which we have, and as there are no other indications of lost writings of that prophet, it is reasonable to suppose that Matthew refers to Zech. xi. 12, 13; and that early transcribers miscopied the name, which, in the Greek, could be done by changing only two letters; viz.: i for

z and m for r. The prophecy is one of the third class described on p. 51.] ᵉ **18 (Now this man obtained a field
with the reward of his iniquity; and falling headlong,
he burst asunder in the midst, and all his bowels
gushed out.   19 And it became known to all the
dwellers at Jerusalem; insomuch that in their language that field was called Akeldama, that is, The
field of blood.)** [This parenthesis contains the words of
Luke inserted in the midst of a speech made by Simon Peter
to explain the meaning of his words. His account of Judas'
death varies in three points from that given by Matthew,
but the variations are easily harmonized. 1. Evidently Judas
hung until his abdomen was partially decomposed; then his
neck giving way, the rope breaking, or something happening
which caused his body to fall, it burst open when it struck the
ground. 2. Judas is spoken of as purchasing the field, and so
he did, for the priests bought it with his money, so that legally
it was his purchase. 3. The field was called "The field of
blood" for two reasons, and each Evangelist gives one of
them.]

CXXXIII.

THE CRUCIFIXION.

Subdivision A.

ON THE WAY TO THE CROSS.

(Within and without Jerusalem.   Friday morning.)

ᵃ MATT. XXVII. 31-34; ᵇ MARK XV. 20-23; ᶜ LUKE XXIII. 26-33;
ᵈ JOHN XIX. 17.

ᵃ **31 And when they had mocked him, they took off
from him the ᵇ purple, ᵃ robe, and put on him his garments** [This ended the mockery, which seems to have been
begun in a state of levity, but which ended in gross indecency
and violence. When we think of him who endured it all we
can not contemplate the scene without a shudder. Who can
measure the grace of God or the depravity of man?], ᵈ **17 They
took Jesus therefore: ᵇ And they lead him out, ᵃ and led**

him away to crucify him. ᵈand he went out, bearing the cross for himself, ᵃ 32 And as they came out, ᶜwhen they led him away, ᵃthey found a man of Cyrene, Simon by name: ᵇone passing by, coming from the country, the father of Alexander and Rufus, ᵃhim they ᶜlaid hold upon { ᵇcompel ᵃcompelled} to go *with them*, that he might bear his cross. ᶜand laid on him the cross, to bear it after Jesus. [Cyrene was a flourishing city in the north of Africa, having in it a large Jewish population, and Simon shows by his name that he was a Jew. The Cyreneans had one or more synagogues in Jerusalem (Acts ii. 10; vi. 9; xi. 20). There were many Cyreneans afterwards engaged in spreading the gospel (Acts xiii. 1), and since the sons of this man are spoken of as well known to Mark's readers it is altogether likely that Simon was one of them. This Rufus may be the one mentioned by Paul (Rom. xvi. 13). The Roman soldiers found Simon entering the city, and because he was a stranger and they needed a man just then, they impressed him after the manner mentioned on p. 245.] 27 And there followed him a great multitude of the people, and of women who bewailed and lamented him. [Only the women bewailed him. They were not Galilæans, but women of Jerusalem.] 28 But Jesus turning unto them said, Daughters of Jerusalem, weep not for me, but weep for yourselves, and for your children. [Some of these women, and the children of others, would survive till the terrible siege of Jerusalem and suffer in it. Jesus bore his own suffering in silence, but his pity for those upon whom these days of anguish would come caused him to speak.] 29 For behold, the days are coming, in which they shall say, Blessed are the barren, and the wombs that never bare, and the breasts that never gave suck. [The proper blessedness of a matron is motherhood, but the horrors of the siege would reverse even so fixed a law as this.] 30 Then shall they begin to say to the mountains, Fall on us; and to the hills, Cover us. [This language is figurative, describing one in extreme terror seeking impossible

refuge.   But there is a touch of literalness in the fulfillment,
for Josephus tells us that at the end of the siege those in Jerusalem hid themselves in the subterranean recesses of the city,
and that no less than two thousand of them were buried alive
under the ruins of these hiding-places—Wars vi. 9. 4.]   **31
For if they do these things in the green tree, what
shall be done in the dry?**   The language here is obscurely
proverbial.   Here, as elsewhere (Luke xix. 43; Matt. xxiv.
15), Jesus refers to the sorrows which the Romans were to bring
upon the Jews, and the meaning may be, If the fiery persecution of Rome is so consuming that my innocence, though again
and again pronounced by the governor himself, is no protection
against it, what will that fire do when it envelopes the dry,
guilty, rebellious city of Jerusalem?   Or we may make the
present and the future grief of the women the point of comparison, and interpret thus: If they cause such sorrow to the
women while the city is like a green tree, how much more
when, like a dry, dead tree, it is about to fall.   **32 And
there were also two others, malefactors, led with
him to be put to death.**   b **22 And they bring him
unto the place** d **which is called in Hebrew Golgotha:**
b **which is, being interpreted, {** a **that is to say,} The
place of a skull** [Where this place was, or why it was
so called, are matters of conjecture.   All that we know certainly is that it was outside of, yet near, the city—Heb. xiii.
12; John xix. 20], c **33 And when they came unto the
place which is called The skull,** a **34 they gave {** b **of-
fered} him wine** a **to drink mingled with gall:
{** b **myrrh:} but {** a **and} when he had tasted it, he
would not drink.** b **he received it not.**   [This mixture of
sour wine mingled with gall and myrrh was intended to dull
the sense of pain of those being crucified or otherwise severely
punished.   The custom is said to have originated with the
Jews and not with the Romans.   Jesus declined it because it
was the Father's will that he should suffer.   He would not go
upon the cross in a drugged, semi-unconscious condition.]

Subdivision B.

JESUS CRUCIFIED AND REVILED. HIS THREE
SAYINGS DURING FIRST THREE HOURS.

(Friday morning from 9 o'clock till noon.)

ᵃ MATT. XXVII. 35-44 ; ᵇ MARK XV. 24-32 ; ᶜ LUKE XXIII. 33-43 ;
ᵈ JOHN XIX. 18-27.

ᵇ **25 And it was the third hour, and** ᶜ **there** {ᵈ **18
where**} ᶜ **they crucified him,** ᵇ **27 And** ᵃ **38 Then are
there crucified** {ᵇ **they crucify**} ᵃ **with him** ᵈ **two others,**
ᶜ **the malefactors,** ᵃ **robbers, one on the right hand, and
one** {ᶜ **the other**} **on the** {ᵇ **his**} **left.** ᵈ **on either side
one, and Jesus in the midst.** [These were doubtless robbers of the class of Barabbas. They were those who, led on
by fanatical patriotism, had become insurrectionists and then
outlaws. Large numbers of them were crucified during the
Jewish wars (Jos. Wars, xiii. 2. 3). These two may have
been crucified at this time for convenience' sake, but the fact
that Jesus was placed between them suggests that they were
crucified with him to heighten his shame and indignity. For,
though Pilate had no personal ill will toward Jesus, he wished
to show contempt for Judah's King.] ᶜ **34 And Jesus said,
Father, forgive them ; for they know not what they do.**
[Our Lord's prayer here reminds us of the word at Isa. liii.
12. It accords with his own teachings (Matt. v. 44), and it
was echoed by Stephen (Acts vii. 59, 60). Peter and Paul
both speak of the Jewish ignorance (Acts iii. 17 ; I. Cor. ii. 8).
Ignorance mitigates, but does not excuse, crime.] ᵇ **24 And
they crucify him,** ᵈ **23 The soldiers therefore, when
they had crucified Jesus, took his garments and made
four parts, to every soldier a part** [A quaternion or band of
four soldiers did the work of the actual crucifixion. The
Roman law awarded them the garments of the condemned
as their perquisites] ; ᵇ **and part** {ᵃ **parted** ᶜ **parting**} ᵇ **his
garments among them, casting** {ᶜ **they cast**} **lots.**

ᵇ **upon them, what each should take.** [The sandals, girdle, outer robe, head-dress, etc., of Jesus were divided into four parts and lots were cast for the parts.] ᵈ **and also the coat: now the coat was without seam, woven from the top throughout.** [This was the tunic or undergarment. It reached from the shoulders to the knees. Ordinarily it was in two pieces, which were fastened at the shoulders by clasps; but Josephus tells us that the tunic of the high priest was an exception to this rule, being woven without seam (Ant. iii. 7. 4). Thus, in dividing the Lord's garments, they found a suggestion of his high priesthood.] **24 They said therefore one to another, Let us not rend it, but cast lots for it, whose it shall be: that the scripture might be fulfilled, which saith, They parted my garments among them, And upon my vesture did they cast lots.** [See Ps. xxii. 18.] **25 These things therefore the soldiers did.** [Even their small part was the subject of minute prophecy.] ᵃ **36 and they sat and watched him there.** [They were on guard to prevent any attempt at rescue.] ᵈ **19 And Pilate wrote a title also, and put it on the cross.** ᶜ **over him,** ᵃ **37 And they set up over his head** ᵇ **the** {ᶜ a} **superscription** ᵇ **of his accusation** ᵃ **And there was written,** ᶜ **THIS IS** ᵃ **JESUS** ᵈ **OF NAZARETH** ᵇ **THE KING OF THE JEWS.** [It was a well-established Roman custom to thus place a writing above the heads of the crucified to indicate the cause for which they died. Pilate writes the accusation so as to clear his own skirts before Cæsar and so as to show his contempt for the Jewish people. They had forced him to crucify an innocent man, and he retaliates by giving to that man the title which his enemies accused him of professing.] ᵈ **20 This title therefore read many of the Jews, for the place where Jesus was crucified was nigh to the city; and it was written in Hebrew, *and* in Latin, *and* in Greek.** [These three languages were respectively those of religion, law and philosophy; but Pilate made use of them because all three were spoken by people then in Jerusalem.] **21 The chief priests of the Jews therefore said to**

Pilate, Write not, The King of the Jews; but, that he said, I am King of the Jews. 22 Pilate answered, What I have written I have written. [The rulers smarted under this title which Pilate had tauntingly written. They had insisted that Jesus' kingship was dangerous enough to justify his crucifixion; but now (if politically and temporally interpreted) they admit that his kingship was an idle claim, a mere matter of words.] ᶜ35 And the people stood beholding. [The scene had an awful fascination which they could not resist.] ᵃ39 And they that passed by [Jesus was evidently crucified near the highway] railed on him, wagging their heads, 40 and saying, ᵇHa! thou that destroyest the temple, and buildest it in three days, 30 save thyself, ᵃif thou art the Son of God, ᵇand come down from the cross. 31 In like manner also the chief priests ᶜAnd the rulers also scoffed at him, ᵇmocking *him* among themselves with the scribes ᵃand elders, said, {ᶜsaying,} He saved others; ᵇhimself he cannot save. ᶜlet him save himself, if this is the Christ of God, his chosen. ᵃHe is the King of Israel; let him now come down from the cross, and we will believe on him. ᵇ32 Let the Christ, the King of Israel, now come down from the cross, that we may see and believe. ᵃ43 He trusteth on God; let him deliver him now, if he desireth him: for he said, I am the Son of God. ᶜ36 And the soldiers also mocked him, coming to him, offering him vinegar, 37 and saying, If thou art the King of the Jews, save thyself. [Thus one and all unite in mocking Jesus, using both word and gesture. They bring forth brief echoes from the trial of Jesus and take other incidents from his life, little dreaming the deep significance of what they utter. They reminded Jesus of his words about destroying the temple, when they were committing that very act. They speak of his building it again when Jesus was about to die that he might rise. They taunt him with saving others, yet being unable to save himself, which is the great truth of the atonement which the Lord was then making. They promised to believe if he will come down from the cross, yet his being lifted upon the cross was the very act which would convince them—John viii. 28.] ᵃ**44 And the robbers also that were crucified with him** ᵇ**reproached him.** ᵃcast upon him the same reproach. ᶜ**39 And one of the malefactors that were hanged railed on him, saying, Art not thou the Christ? save thyself and us. 40 But the other answered, and rebuking him said, Dost thou not even fear God, seeing thou art in the same condemnation? 41 And we indeed justly; for we receive the due reward of our deeds: but this man hath done nothing amiss. 42 And he said, Jesus, remember me when thou comest in thy kingdom. 43 And he said unto him, Verily I say unto thee, To-day shalt thou be with me in Paradise.** [It seems that at first both the robbers reviled Christ, but one repenting spoke in his favor and prayed to him. It is not likely that this robber had any conception of the spiritual kingdom of Jesus, but he somehow arrived at the conclusion that Jesus was the Messiah, and would come into his kingdom despite his crucifixion. Jesus answered his prayer by a solemn promise that they would, that day, be together in that portion of the invisible world where those who are accepted of God await the resurrection. Many thoughtlessly make this dying robber the model of death-bed repentance, arguing that others also may be saved in this irregular manner. But Christ had not yet died, and the new testament or covenant was not yet sealed. Jesus then could change its terms to suit the occasion. It is therefore no evidence whatever that after his death and in his present glorified state our Lord will in any way change the covenant so as to do away with a single one of the terms required for obtaining remission of sins (Heb. ix. 15-18). Moreover, the example of the penitent robber is a difficult one to follow: he professed faith in Christ and his kingdom when there was no other voice in the whole wide world willing to do such a thing. Any one having such a faith in Christ will not put off his confession until the hour of death.] ᵈ But there were standing by the cross of Jesus his mother, and his mother's sister, Mary the *wife* of Clopas, and Mary Magdalene. [For comment on these four women, see note on p. 225.] 26 When Jesus therefore saw his mother, and the disciple standing by whom he loved, he saith unto his mother, Woman, behold, thy son! 27 Then saith he to the disciple, Behold, thy mother! And from that hour the disciple took her unto his own *home.* [By using the title "woman" Jesus addressed his mother at this the end of his ministry with the same word which he had used at its beginning (John ii. 4). Thus he cut her off from all parental authority over him. In this his last hour our Lord bestows upon his helpless mother the disciple whom he loved, who was then in the flower of his young manhood. All of Christ's disciples are thus appointed by him protectors of the helpless, but few recognize the behest as John did.]

Subdivision C.

DARKNESS THREE HOURS. AFTER FOUR MORE
SAYINGS JESUS EXPIRES. STRANGE
EVENTS ATTENDING HIS DEATH.

ᵃ Maᴛᴛ. xxvii. 45-56; ᵇ Mᴀʀᴋ xv. 33-41; ᶜ Lᴜᴋᴇ xxiii. 44-49;
ᵈ Jᴏʜɴ xix. 28-30.

ᶜ44 And it was now about the sixth hour, ᵇ 33 And ᵃ 45 Now ᵇ when the sixth hour was come, there was ᶜ a darkness came ᵃ over all ᵇ the whole land ᵃ from the sixth hour ᵇ until the ninth hour. ᶜ 45 the sun's light failing [The darkness lasted from noon until three o'clock. It could not have been an eclipse, for the moon was always full on the first day of the passover. Whether the darkness was over the whole world, or simply all of Palestine, is uncertain, as, according to the usage of Bible language, the words would be the same]: ᵇ 34 And at {ᵃ about} the ninth hour Jesus cried with a loud voice, saying, Eli, Eli, {ᵇ Eloi, Eloi,} lama sabachthani? which is, {ᵃ that is,} ᵇ being interpreted, My God, my God, why hast thou forsaken me? [We can imagine what it would mean to a righteous man to feel that he was forsaken of God. But the more we feel and enjoy the love of another, the greater our sense of loss at being deprived of it. Considering, therefore, the near and dear relationship between the Son and Father, it is evident that we can never know or fathom the depth of anguish which this cry expressed. Suffice it to say, that this was without doubt the most excruciating of all Christ's sufferings, and it, too, was a suffering in our stead. The words of the cry are found at Ps. xxii. 1. Eli is Hebrew, Eloi Aramaic or Syro-Chaldaic for "My God." The former would be used by Jesus if he quoted the Scripture, the latter if he spoke the language of the people.] **35 And some of them that stood by, {ᵃ there,} when they heard it, said, ᵇ Behold, he {ᵃ this man} calleth Elijah. ᵈ 28 After this Jesus, knowing that all things are now finished, that the scripture might be accomplished, saith, I thirst. 29 There was set there a vessel full of vinegar: ᵃ 48 And straightway one of them ran, and took a sponge, and filled it with {ᵇ and filling a sponge full of} vinegar, ᵃ and put it on a reed, and gave him to drink. ᵈ so they put a sponge full of the vinegar upon hyssop, and brought it to his mouth. ᵇ saying, {ᵃ 49 And the rest said,} Let be; let us see whether Elijah cometh ᵇ to take him down. ᵃ to save him.** [Jesus had now been upon the cross for six hours, and fever and loss of blood and the strain upon the muscles of his chest had rendered his articulation difficult and indistinct. For this reason some of those who stood by, though perfectly familiar with the language, misunderstood him and thought that he called upon Elijah. Immediately afterwards Jesus speaks of his thirst, and vinegar is given to him to remove the dryness from his throat. Those who give the vinegar and those who stand by unite in saying "Let be." This phrase has no reference to the vinegar; it is a general expression, meaning "Let us do nothing to prevent him from calling upon Elijah, or to prevent Elijah from coming."] ᵇ 37 And ᵈ 30 When Jesus therefore had received the vinegar, ᵃ Jesus cried again with {ᵇ uttered} a loud voice, ᵈ he said, It is finished [He had come, had ministered, had suffered, and had conquered. There now remained but the simple act of taking possession of the citadel of the grave, and the overthrowing of death. By his righteousness Jesus had triumphed in man's behalf and the mighty task was accomplished] : ᶜ 46 And Jesus, crying with a loud voice, said, Father, into thy hands I commend my spirit [Ps. xxxi. 5] : and having said this, ᵈ he bowed his head, and gave up {ᵃ yielded up} ᵇ the ghost. ᵃ his spirit. [None of the Evangelists speak of Jesus as dying; for he yielded up his spirit voluntarily—John x. 18.] 51 And behold, the veil of the temple was rent in two ᶜ in the midst. ᵇ from the top to the bottom. [The veil was the heavy curtain which hung between the holy and the most holy places in the sanctuary. By shutting out from the most holy place all persons except the high priest, who alone was permitted to pass through it, and this only once in the year, it signified that the way into the holiest—that is, into heaven— was not yet made manifest while the first tabernacle was standing (Heb. ix. 7, 8). But the moment that Jesus died, thus making the way manifest, the veil was appropriately rent in twain from top to bottom, disclosing the most holy place to the priests who were at that time offering the evening incense in the holy place.] ᵃ and the earth did quake ; and the rocks were rent ; 52 and the tombs were opened ; and many bodies of the saints that had fallen asleep were raised ; 53 and coming forth out of the tombs after his resurrection they entered into the holy city and appeared unto many. [The earthquake, the rending of the rocks and the consequent opening of the graves, occurred at the moment Jesus died, while the resurrection and visible appearance in the city of the bodies of the saints occurred "after his resurrection," for Jesus himself was the "first-born from the dead" (Col. i. 18). Matthew chooses to mention the last event here because of its association with the rending of

the rocks, which opened the rock-hewn sepulchres in which
the saints had slept.   There has been much speculation as to
what became of these risen saints.   We have no positive information, but the natural presumption is, that they ascended to
heaven.   These resurrections were symbolic, showing that the
resurrection of Christ is the resurrection of the race—I. Cor.
xv. 22.]   ᵇ **39 And when the centurion, who stood by**
ᵃ **watching Jesus,** ᵇ **over against him, saw that he so**
gave up the ghost, ᵃ **saw the earthquake, and the**
things that were { ᶜ **what was} done, he glorified God,**
saying, { ᵇ **he said,}** ᶜ **Certainly this was a righteous**
man. ᵃ **54 Now the centurion, and they that were**
with him feared exceedingly, saying, Truly this ᵇ **man**
was the Son of God. [The conduct of Jesus upon the
cross and the disturbances of nature which accompanied his
death convinced the centurion that Jesus was a righteous man.
But knowing that Jesus claimed to be the Son of God, and
this claim was the real cause for which the Jews were crucifying him, he concludes, since he concedes that Jesus is righteous, that he is also all that he professed to be—the Son of
God.   There is no just reason for minimizing his confession,
as though he had said "A son of the gods;" for he said nothing of that kind, and those err as to the use of Scriptural language who think so.   Like the centurions of Capernaum
(Matt. viii. 10) and Cæsarea (Acts x. 1, 2), this Roman surpassed in faith those who had better opportunities.   But in this
faith he was not alone.]   ᶜ **48 And all the multitudes that**
came together to this sight, when they beheld the
things that were done, returned smiting their breasts.
[The people who had acted under the influence of the priests
now yielded to superior influences and began to experience
that change of sentiment which led so many to repent and
confess Christ at Pentecost.]   **49 And all his acquaint-**
ance, ᵃ **55 And many women** ᵇ **also** ᵃ **were there** ᶜ **the**
women that { ᵃ **who} had followed** ᶜ **with** ᵃ **Jesus from**
Galilee, ministering unto him: ᶜ **stood afar off,** ᵃ **be-**
holding from afar, ᶜ **seeing these things.** ᵇ **among**

whom were both Mary Magdalene, and Mary the
mother of James the less and of Joses, and Salome;
ᵃ the mother of the sons of Zebedee. ᵇ 41 who, when
he was in Galilee, followed him, and ministered unto
him; and many other women that came up with him
unto Jerusalem. [John has already mentioned this group
of women (see p. 729) and has shown that he stood with them.
The women, being unable to bear arms in an insurrection,
had little to fear. They were not likely to be complicated in
the charges against Jesus. But the men were conspicuously
absent. They appear to have stood quite close to the cross
at one time just before the darkness. Probably they feared
violence in the darkness, and so withdrew and viewed from
afar off the scene as lighted by the torches which the Roman
soldiers would be obliged to procure in order to effectually
guard their prisoners (Acts xvi. 29). The synoptists, who
make mention of the women toward the close of the crucifixion, do not mention the mother of Jesus as any longer
among them. It is likely that she had withdrawn with John,
being unable longer to endure the sight. As to the ministering of these Galilæan women, see pp. 297, 298.]

Subdivision D.

JESUS FOUND TO BE DEAD. HIS BODY BURIED
AND GUARDED IN THE TOMB.

ᵃ MATT. XXVII. 57-66; ᵇ MARK XV. 42-47; ᶜ LUKE XXIII. 50-56;
ᵈ JOHN XIX. 31-42.

ᵈ 31 The Jews therefore, because it was the Preparation, that the bodies should not remain on the cross
upon the sabbath (for the day of that sabbath was a
high *day*), asked of Pilate that their legs might be broken, and *that* they might be taken away. [According to
rabbinical writing a few hours before the Sabbath were called
the Preparation; but afterwards the term was applied to the
entire day preceding the Sabbath. The Romans left the
bodies of criminals hanging upon the cross until beasts and
birds of prey, or putrefaction, removed them. But the Jewish

law forbade that a body should hang over night; for a dead
body was accursed, and so the day following might be polluted
by the curse which attached to it (Deut. xxi. 23; Josh. viii.
29; x 26; Jos. Wars iv. 5. 2). The context suggests that the
Jews had grown lax with regard to this law on account of the
trouble of obtaining the consent from the Romans required to
carry it out. But as the Sabbath in this instance was that of the
passover week, and as they were ready enough to do anything to
show that Jesus was an extraordinary criminal, they asked
Pilate that their law might be observed. Instead of killing
the criminals, they broke their legs, which rendered recovery
impossible, since putrefaction almost immediately set in.] **32
The soldiers therefore came, and brake the legs of the
first, and of the other that was crucified with him: 33
but when they came to Jesus, and saw that he was
dead already, they brake not his legs: 34 howbeit one
of the soldiers with a spear pierced his side** [to insure
death in case they might be mistaken], **and straightway
there came out blood and water. 35 And he that hath
seen hath borne witness, and his witness is true: and
he knoweth that he saith true, that ye also may believe.** [Many able men have argued learnedly that this flow
of blood and water was evidence that Jesus died of a ruptured,
or literally broken, heart; but they confess themselves involved
in difficulties, for it is hard to reconcile the idea that Jesus
died a voluntary death with the idea that he died of any
natural cause whatever. Can anything be at once natural and
supernatural? However, John's asseveration that he was an
eye-witness of this shows that he attached importance to it.
To him the body of Jesus gave evidence that it differed from
other dead bodies. We enter with hesitancy the realm
of symbolism, knowing how flagrantly it is abused, but we offer
this as a suggestion. Jesus died for our sins, and his death
was therefore to provide a means for the cleansing of sin.
But, under the terms of his gospel, sins are visibly and physically washed away by water, and invisibly and spiritually by
blood (Heb. x. 22). Now, since both these means were seen

by a faithful witness to issue from the side of our crucified
Lord, contrary to the ordinary law and course of nature, we
have additional reason to believe that things out of the course
of nature, namely, the cleansing of sin, etc., were accomplished
by his crucifixion.] **36 For these things came to pass,
that the scripture might be fulfilled, A bone of him
shall not be broken.** [Ps. xxii. 18.] **37 And again an.
other scripture saith, They shall look on him whom
they pierced.** [Zech. xii. 10. Even after his death divine
power went on fulfilling the prophecies concerning Jesus. He
hangs upon the cross as one of a group of three, yet, in the
twinkling of an eye, he is separated from the other two by the
fulfillment of a brace of prophecies which point him out as the
chosen of God.] **38 And after these things ᵇ when even
was now come, because it was the Preparation, that
is, the day before the sabbath, ᶜ behold, ᵃ there came a
rich man from Arimathaea, ᶜ a city of the Jews,
ᵃ named Joseph, ᵇ of Arimathaea, ᶜ who was a councillor,
lor, ᵇ of honorable estate, ᶜ a good and righteous man
(51 he had not consented to their counsel and deed᾿,
ᵇ who also himself was looking for the kingdom of
God; ᵃ who also himself was Jesus' disciple: {ᵈ being
a disciple of Jesus,} but secretly for fear of the Jews**
[John xii. 42, 43], **ᵃ 58 this man ᵇ boldly went in unto
Pilate, and asked for the body of Jesus. ᵈ asked of
Pilate that he might take away the body of Jesus**
[Joseph's town has been variously identified with Ramleh in
Dan, Ramathaim in Ephraim (I. Sam. i. 1) and Ramah in
Benjamin (Matt. ii. 18). It was in fulfillment of prophecy
that the one who buried Jesus should be rich (Isa. liii. 9). It
is strange that those who were not afraid to be disciples were
afraid to ask for our Lord's body, yet he who was afraid to be
a disciple feared not to do this thing]: **ᵇ 44 And Pilate
marvelled if he were already dead** [instances are cited
where men lived one whole week upon the cross, and men
rarely died the first day]: **and calling unto him the centurion, he asked him whether he had been any while**

dead. **45 And when he learned it of the centurion,** ᵃ **Then Pilate** ᵇ **granted the corpse to Joseph.** ᵃ **commanded it to be given up.** ᵈ **and Pilate gave** *him* **leave. He came therefore, and took away the body. 39 And there came also Nicodemus, he who at the first came to him by night** [John iii. 1]**, bringing a mixture of myrrh and aloes, about a hundred pounds.** [Myrrh was a resin and the aloe was pulverized wood. Both were aromatic—Ps. xlv. 8.] ᵃ **59 And Joseph** ᵇ **bought a linen cloth** [a sindon—see p. 693]**,** ᶜ **53 And he took** ᵃ **the body,** ᶜ **down,** ᵇ **and taking him down, wound him in the linen cloth,** {ᵃ **and wrapped it in a clean linen cloth,**} ᵈ **40 So they took the body of Jesus, and bound it in linen cloths with the spices, as the custom of the Jews is to bury.** [As to the swathing of dead bodies see p. 526, also Acts v. 6. The spices were wrapped between the folds of the linen in order to partially embalm the body. Thus two members of the Sanhedrin unite to bury Jesus, each showing his reverence in his own way: Joseph by buying a sindon instead of cheaper cloth, and Nicodemus by a wonderful wealth of spices—twelve hundred ounces. Possibly the heart of Nicodemus smote him for his tardiness in honoring Christ, and he desired to appease his conscience by giving the Lord a royal burial—II. Chron. xvi. 14.] **41 Now in the place where he was crucified there was a garden** [belonging to Joseph]**; and in the garden a** {ᵃ **his own**} **new tomb, which he had** {ᶜ **that was** ᵇ **which had been**} ᶜ **hewn in stone,** ᵇ **out of a** {ᵃ **the**} **rock:** ᵈ **wherein was never man yet laid.** {ᶜ **where never man had yet lain.**} [To the sindon Joseph adds the honor of a burial in his own tomb. The unused state of the tomb is mentioned to show that there is no shadow of doubt as to whose resurrection opened it.] **54 And it was the day of the Preparation, and the sabbath drew on.** ᵈ **42 There then because of the Jews' Preparation (for the tomb was nigh at hand) they laid Jesus.** ᵃ **and he rolled a great stone to** {ᵇ **against**} **the door of the tomb.** ᵃ **and departed.** ᶜ **55 And the**

women, who had come with him out of Galilee, followed after, ᵃ61 And Mary Magdalene was there, and
the other Mary, ᵇthe *mother* of Joses ᵃsitting over
against the sepulchre. ᶜand beheld the tomb, ᵇwhere
ᶜand how his body was laid. 56 And they returned,
and prepared spices and ointments. And on the sabbath they rested according to the commandment. [As
Jesus died about three o'clock in the afternoon, and as all
work had to stop at sunset, which was the beginning of the
Sabbath, Joseph was much hurried in his efforts to bury Jesus.
The context, therefore, shows that our Lord was not completely
embalmed by him. The body of Jesus might have been kept elsewhere until after the Sabbath; but because the tomb was near
it appears to have been used temporarily, and the preparation of
spices by the women shows that even that part of the burial
was not, in their estimation, completed. This unfinished
burial led the women back to the tomb early on the first day
of the week, and thus brought to the disciples the glad news of
the resurrection without any needless delay.] ᵃ62 Now on
the morrow, which is *the day* after the Preparation,
the chief priests and the Pharisees were gathered together unto Pilate [This was not the whole Sanhedrin, but
members of it. When did they come to Pilate? Meyer,
Cook, etc., say that the Greek word translated "morrow" pre-
cludes any other idea than that it was after daylight Saturday
morning, but Michaelis, Paulus, Kuinoel, etc., say that they
came Friday night, and we think their view is correct. The
word translated "morrow" also means "the next day." As
the Jewish day began at sunset, we know of no other Greek
adverb by which Matthew could have expressed the beginning
of a day. Had it been the Sabbath morning there is no reason why Matthew should not have said so. By mentioning,
instead, the Preparation, he draws the mind back to what we
would call Friday night. It is highly improbable that the Jews
would leave the tomb of Jesus unguarded for one whole night.
Their gathering thus to Pilate in the shades of the evening presents a grewsome picture], 63 saying, Sir, we remember

that that deceiver said while he was yet alive, **After three days I rise again.** [For this saying see John ii. 19; Matt. xii. 39, 40.] **64 Command therefore that the sepulchre be made sure until the third day** [Had the phrase "after three days" meant three full days to them, they would have said "until the fourth day." For the Jewish method of counting days see p. 306], **lest haply his disciples come and steal him away, and say unto the people, He is risen from the dead: and the last error will be worse than the first.** [The marvelous signs accompanying the death of Jesus appealed to men's fear rather than to their love, and were, therefore, calculated to make a far deeper impression upon his enemies than upon his friends. We find, therefore, these Jewish rulers full of active interest in the dead Christ while his apostles and friends are listless in despair. They, of course, did not think it possible that Jesus could indeed rise, but, seeing the profound impression which the portents attending the crucifixion had made upon the multitude (Luke xxiii. 48), and judging the disciples of Jesus by themselves—full of all subtlety and cunning—they grasped at once the idea that the disciples could make a great stir among the people by stealing the body and proclaiming the predicted resurrection. The apostles, on the other hand, when the actual resurrection had taken place, did not learn for fifty days what use to make of it, thus showing that they could not have planned a pretended resurrection.] **65 Pilate said unto them, Ye have a guard** [The Greek here may be the indicative or the imperative; it is clearly the latter. If the Jews had possessed a guard, they would not have asked for one. Pilate consents to their request by saying, "Have ye a guard:" thereby fully sanctioning their idea]: **go, make it *as* sure as ye can. 66 So they went, and made the sepulchre sure, sealing the stone, the guard being with them.** [They sealed the stone by drawing a string or tape across it and fastening the ends with wax or clay to the surface of the rock on either side. If either seals were broken, that fact would show that the tomb was entered from without.]

PART EIGHT.

OUR LORD'S RESURRECTION, APPEARANCES AND ASCENSION. JUDAEA AND GALILEE. TIME, FORTY DAYS. SPRING A. D. 30.

CXXXIV.

ANGELS ANNOUNCE THE RESURRECTION TO CERTAIN WOMEN. PETER AND JOHN ENTER THE EMPTY TOMB.

(Joseph's Garden. Sunday very early.)

ᵃ MATT. XXVIII. 1-8; ᵇ MARK XVI. 1-8; ᶜ LUKE XXIV. 1-8, 12; ᵈ JOHN XX. 1-10.

ᶜ 1 But ᵃ 1 Now late on the sabbath day, ᵇ 1 And when the sabbath was past, ᶜ on the first day of the week, {ᵃ as it began to dawn toward the first *day* of the week,} ᶜ at early dawn, ᵈ while it was yet dark, cometh {ᵃ came} ᵈ Mary Magdalene early, ᵃ and the other Mary ᵇ the *mother* of James, and Salome, ᶜ unto the tomb, bringing {ᵇ brought} ᶜ the spices which they had prepared. [Luke xxiii. 56.] ᵃ to see the sepulchre. ᵇ that they might come and anoint him. ᵃ 2 And behold, there was a great earthquake; for an angel of the Lord descended from heaven, and came and rolled away the stone, and sat upon it. 3 His appearance was as lightning, and his raiment white as snow: 4 and for fear of him the watchers [the Roman soldiers on guard] did quake, and became as dead men. [The angel sat upon the stone that the Roman guards might make no attempt to reclose the tomb.] ᵇ 2 And very early on the first day of the week, they come to the tomb when the sun was risen. 3 And they were saying among themselves, Who shall roll us away the stone from the door of the tomb? ᶜ 2 And they found the stone rolled away from

the tomb. ᵇ4 and looking up, they see {ᵈ[Mary Magda-
lene] seeth} ᵇthat the stone is rolled back: {ᵈtaken
away from the tomb.} for it was exceeding great. ᶜ3
And they ᵇentering into the tomb, {ᶜentered in,} and
found not the body of the Lord Jesus. [John mentions
Mary Magdalene alone, though she came with the rest of the
women. As she was the one who reported to John and Peter,
he describes her actions, and makes no mention of the others.]
ᵈ2 She runneth therefore, and cometh to Simon Peter,
and to the other disciple whom Jesus loved, and saith
unto them, They have taken away the Lord out of the
tomb, and we know not where they have laid him
[Though Mary came with the other women, she departed at
once, while the others tarried, as the sequel shows. The narrative proceeds to tell what happened to the other women
after Mary had departed.] ᶜ4 And it came to pass, while
they were perplexed thereabout, behold, two men
stood by them in dazzling apparel: ᵇthey saw a
young man sitting on the right side, arrayed in a white
robe; and they were amazed. ᶜ5 and as they were
affrighted, and bowed down their faces to the earth,
they said unto them, {ᵇhe ᵃthe angel} answered and
said unto the women, Fear not ye; ᵇBe not amazed:
ᵃfor I know that ye seek Jesus, ᵇthe Nazarene, who
hath been crucified: ᶜWhy seek ye the living among
the dead? 6 He is not here, but {ᵃfor} he is risen,
even as he said. ᶜremember how he spake unto you
when he was yet in Galilee, 7 saying that the
Son of man must be delivered up into the hands of
sinful men, and be crucified, and the third day rise
again. 8 And they remembered his words [For the
words referred to see Matt. xvii. 22, 23. The angel continues
his speech as follows], ᵃ Come, ᵇbehold, the place where
they laid him! ᵃsee the place where the Lord lay.
[Here was a double wonder, that men should put the Son of
God in a grave, and that he should consent to be put there.]
ᵇ7 But {ᵃ7 And} go quickly, and tell his disciples,

ᵇand Peter, ᵃHe is risen from the dead; and lo, he goeth before you into Galilee; there shall ye see him: ᵇas he said unto you. ᵃlo, I have told you. [The women were told to hasten, for the disciples were not to endure their sorrow a moment longer than was needful. Peter was mentioned by name that he might know that he was not cast off for his denial. The Lord appeared to some chosen few in Judæa, but the large body of his disciples were to see him in Galilee; see Section CXLI. Jesus had appointed a place of meeting; but we are not told where it was nor when he appointed it.] 8 And they departed quickly ᵇ8 And they went out, and fled from the tomb; ᵃwith fear and great joy [fear, because of the heavenly messengers; joy, because of their message], and ran to bring his disciples word. ᵇfor trembling and astonishment had come upon them: and they said nothing to any one; for they were afraid. [They told none whom they met, but reserved the message for the apostles.] ᶜ12 But Peter ᵈtherefore ᶜarose, ᵈwent forth, and the other disciple, and they went toward the tomb. ᶜand ran unto the tomb [John shows that he and Peter started for the tomb as soon as they received the message of Mary Magdalene given above, but Luke is less exact, blending her message with that of the other women, as will be seen in the latter part of Section CXXXV.]; ᵈ4 And they ran both together: and the other disciple outran Peter [it is generally accepted that John was younger, and hence more active than Peter], and came first to the tomb; 5 and stooping and looking in, he seeth the linen cloths lying; yet entered he not in. 6 Simon Peter therefore also cometh, following him, and entered into the tomb; ᶜand stooping and looking in, he seeth ᵈand he beholdeth the linen cloths lying; ᶜby themselves; ᵈ7 and the napkin, that was upon his head, not lying with the linen cloths, but rolled up in a place by itself. ᶜand he departed to his home, wondering at that which was come to pass. [The impulsive, thoroughgoing nature of Peter was not content with a mere look; he entered the tomb, neither reverence nor awe keeping him out. The sight which he saw puzzled him. Why should those who removed the body pause to unswathe it? why should they unswathe it at all? why should they fold the napkin and place it aside so carefully? But Peter left the tomb with these questions unsolved.] [d]8 **Then entered in therefore the other disciple also, who came first to the tomb, and he saw, and believed. 9 For as yet they knew not the scripture, that he must rise again from the dead. 10 So the disciples went away again unto their own home.** [Assured that the grave was now empty, and emboldened by the example of Peter, John now entered it, and as he looked upon its evidences of quietude and order, the truth flashed upon his mind that Jesus himself had removed the bandages, and had himself departed from the tomb, as the firstborn from the dead. Here, then, was the first belief and the first believer in the resurrection; and it is important to note that the Scripture did not suggest the fact, but the fact illumined the Scripture. Ps. xvi. 10 and Isa. liii. 10, and many other passages, set forth the resurrection of our Lord; his own words, too, had plainly foretold it, yet among the disciples it was so much beyond all expectation that the prophecies had no meaning until made clear by the event itself. Yet these are the men whom the Jews accused of inventing the story of a resurrection!]

CXXXV.

FIRST AND SECOND APPEARANCES OF THE RISEN CHRIST. THE RESURRECTION REPORTED TO THE APOSTLES.

(Jerusalem. Sunday morning.)

[a]MATT. XXVIII. 9, 10; [b]MARK XVI. 9-11; [c]LUKE XXIV. 9-11; [d]JOHN XX. 11-18.

[The women, having received the message of the angels, and remembering that the message accorded with the words of Jesus himself, made haste] ᶜ9 **and returned from the tomb,** ᵇ9 **Now when he was risen early on the first day of the week, he appeared first to Mary Magdalene, from whom he had cast out seven demons.** [Mark here agrees with John that Mary separated from the other women. As to Mary Magdalene, see pp. 291, 297. After telling Peter and John about the empty tomb, Mary followed them back to it, and evidently reached it after they had left it. She found no one at the tomb.] ᵈ11 **But Mary was standing without at the tomb weeping: so, as she wept, she stooped and looked into the tomb; 12 and she beholdeth two angels in white sitting, one at the head, and one at the feet, where the body of Jesus had lain.** [This picture is intensely natural. The Lord's death had been sorrow enough, but to be deprived of the poor privilege of embalming the body seemed a veritable sorrow's crown of sorrow; and so Mary wept. But it suddenly occurs to her that in her haste she had not yet looked into the tomb at all, having jumped to the conclusion that it was empty because she saw it open : she therefore looks in. Her grief at the loss of the Lord is so great that she forgets to be frightened at the angels; just as a mother in her anxiety for the sick child forgets to fear its fever, no matter how virulent. The angels were placed like the cherubim upon the ark, as though the grave of Christ was a new mercy seat, which indeed it was.] **13 And they say unto her, Woman, why weepest thou ? She saith unto them, Because they have taken away my Lord, and I know not where they have laid him. 14 When she had thus said, she turned herself back, and beholdeth Jesus standing, and knew not that it was Jesus.** [Before the angels can speak the glad news to Mary Jesus himself becomes his own messenger. That Mary did not recognize him may be due to her grief, for tears blind our eyes to many of the tender providences of God; but to reason by analogy it seems more likely that her eyes "were holden" (Luke xxiv. 16), lest the shock of his sudden appearance might be too much for her, as it was for even his male disciples (Luke

xxiv. 37). Conversation with him assured her that he **was** not a disembodied spirit.] **15 Jesus saith unto her, Woman, why weepest thou? whom seekest thou? She, supposing him to be the gardener, saith unto him, Sir, if thou hast borne him hence, tell me where thou hast laid him, and I will take him away.** [Christ's first question expressed kindly sympathy; the second suggested that he knew the cause of her grief, and might be able to help her find what she sought. Thus encouraged, Mary at once assumes that the gardener himself had removed the body, probably under instructions from Joseph, and hope lightens her heart. In her offer to remove the body, she doubtless counts upon the help of her fellow-disciples.] **16 Jesus saith unto her, Mary.** [Her eyes and ears were no longer holden: she knew him. It was the same way he used to speak, the same name by which he used to call her. The grave had glorified and exalted him, but had not changed his love] **She turneth herself, and saith unto him in Hebrew, Rabboni; which is to say, Teacher.** [Seasons of greatest joy are marked by little speech; Jesus and Mary each expressed themselves in a single word.] **17 Jesus saith to her, Touch me not; for I am not yet ascended unto the Father: but go unto my brethren, and say to them, I ascend unto my Father and your Father, and my God and your God.** [This passage is one of well-known difficulty, and Meyer or Ryle may be consulted by those wishing to see how various commentators have interpreted it. We would explain it by the following paraphrase : "Do not lay hold on me and detain yourself and me ; I have not yet ascended; this is no brief, passing vision; I am yet in the world, and will be for some time, and there will be other opportunities to see me ; the duty of the moment is to go and tell my sorrowing disciples that I have risen, and shall ascend to my Father." Jesus does not say "our Father." Our relation to God is not the same as his. While, however, our Lord's language recognizes the difference between his divine and our human relationship to the Father, his words are intended to show us our exaltation. We have reason to believe that next to our Lord's title as Son our title as sons of God by adoption is as high in honor as any in the universe.] **18 Mary Magdalene cometh and telleth {ᵇwent and told} ᵈthe disciples, ᵇthem that had been with him, as they mourned and wept.** [The poignancy of the disciples' grief, even after the intervention of the Sabbath day, explains why the Lord and his angels were so eager to bring them word of the resurrection.] **ᵈI have seen the Lord; and** *that* **he had said these things unto her. ᵇ11 And they, when they heard that he was alive, and had been seen of her, disbelieved.** [It is likely that Mary brought the first word, for we shall see below that Luke places her first in the catalogue of witnesses. The narrative now turns back to take up the account of the other women.] **ᵃ9 And behold, Jesus met them, saying, All hail.** [This was a customary salutation. But the old formula took on new significance, for it means "rejoice."] **And they came and took hold of his feet, and worshipped him.** [This delay, permitted to them, and denied to Mary, probably explains why she became the first messenger, though the other women were first to leave the tomb.] **10 Then saith Jesus unto them, Fear not: go tell my brethren that they depart into Galilee, and there shall they see me.** [The repetition may be due to the reticence of the women remarked by Mark in the last section by the words "they said nothing to any one." The women may have been hesitating whether they should tell the disciples. Thus Jesus reiterates the instruction already given by the angel. This is the first time that the word "brethren" is applied by our Lord to his disciples.] **ᶜand [they] told all these things to the eleven, and to all the rest. 10 Now they were Mary Magdalene, and Joanna, and Mary the** *mother* **of James: and the other women with them told these things unto the apostles. 11 And these words appeared in their sight as idle talk; and they disbelieved them.** [Lamar well says that this very incredulity on the part of the apostles "enhances the value of their testimony to *the fact* of the resurrection. They were not expecting it; they were no visionary enthusiasts, prepared to welcome and credit any story that might be told them; nor would they be satisfied with any proof short of palpable and ocular demonstrations.''']

CXXXVI.

SOME OF THE GUARD REPORT TO THE JEWISH RULERS.

ª MATT. XXVIII. 11-15.

ª **11 Now while they were going** [while Joanna and the group of women with her were on their way to tell the apostles that they had seen Jesus], **behold, some of the guard** [not all] **came into the city, and told unto the chief priests all the things that were come to pass.** [Esteeming it folly to guard an empty tomb, the soldiers went to their barracks, while their officers returned to those who had placed them on guard to report what had happened. They rightly judged that the plain truth was their best defense. They could not be expected to contend against earthquakes and angels. Their report implies that they saw Jesus leave the tomb, and after the angel opened it.*] **12 And when they** [the chief priests] **were assembled with the elders, and had taken counsel, they gave much money unto the soldiers, 13 saying, Say ye, His disciples came by**

---

*NOTE.—We fail to see any such implication. In our opinion Jesus had already departed from the tomb when the angel came. The tomb was not opened to let the Lord out, but to let the disciples in, that they might see as soon as possible one of the chief evidences of his resurrection (John **xx.** 8; Matt. **xxviii.** 6). Jesus did not need that one open doors for him (John **xx.** 19, 26), but the disciples had such a need (Mark **xvi.** 3). But it seems to us contrary to Scripture precedent that these unbelieving soldiers should see the risen Christ, for he did not appear to the unbelieving so far as the record shows, and the implication is that the same principle which made Jesus refuse the testimony of demons made him also decline to let unbelievers become witnesses to his resurrection (Acts **x.** 40, 41).—P. Y. P.

night, and stole him away while we slept. [This was evidently not a full, but a select, council of the Sanhedrin hastily summoned. They willfully shut their eyes to the fact that Jesus had risen, and proceed to purchase a lie to subvert the truth. Unrepentant, despite the many evidences that they had done wrong, they proceed to further invoke the wrath of God. Their lie is doubly apparent upon its face. 1. It would have been practically impossible for men to have rifled such a tomb without waking a guard set to protect it. 2. It is absolutely impossible for men to have known what had occurred while they were asleep.] **14 And if this come to the governor's ears, we will persuade him, and rid you of care.** [It was a capital offense for a Roman soldier to sleep while on guard; therefore, if Pilate heard that they had done this thing, it would require "persuasion" to make him overlook the offense. Possibly the Jews thought that Pilate was sufficiently involved with them to be ready to aid them to hush the story of the resurrection, especially if they confessed to him that they themselves had invented the lie which the soldiers told.] **15 So they took the money, and did as they were taught** [the lesson was short and simple; the reward, large and desirable]: **and this saying was spread abroad among the Jews,** *and continueth* **until this day.** [The words seem to indicate that it was published more largely than simply within the walls of Jerusalem. In his dialogue with Trypho, which was written about A. D. 170, Justin Martyr says that the Jews dispersed the story by means of special messengers sent to every country. The fear which they expressed to Pilate (Matt. xxvii. 64) lends credibility to this statement.]

CXXXVII.

THIRD AND FOURTH APPEARANCES OF JESUS.

(Sunday afternoon.)

ᵇ MARK XVI. 12, 13; ᶜ LUKE XXIV. 13-35; ᶠ I. COR. XV. 5.

ᵇ **12 And after these things he was manifested in another form** [*i. e.*, another manner] **unto two of them, as they walked, on their way into the country.** ᶜ **13 And behold, two of them were going that very day to a village named Emmaus** [Several sites have been suggested, but the village of Emmaus has not yet been identified beyond dispute. Its location is probably marked by the ruins called el Kubeibeh, which lies northwest of Jerusalem], **which was threescore furlongs from Jerusalem.** [el Kubeibeh is distant seven and thirteen-sixteenths of a mile, or sixty-two and one-half furlongs, from Jerusalem.] **14 And they communed with each other of all these things which had happened. 15 And it came to pass, while they communed and questioned together, that Jesus himself drew near, and went with them. 16 But their eyes were holden that they should not know him.** [Jesus himself designedly restrained their vision, that, unlike John (John xx. 8, 9), they might see the resurrection of Jesus in the Scriptures before they saw it in reality.] **17 And he said unto them, What communications are these that ye have one with another, as ye walk? And they stood still, looking sad.** [Our Lord's abrupt question brought them to a standstill. We may well imagine that they considered his interruption very unwelcome. But his kindly mien won their confidence and they tell him all.] **18 And one of them, named Cleopas, answering said unto him, Dost thou alone sojourn in Jerusalem and not know the things which are come to pass there in these days?** [Of Cleopas nothing further is known. It has been suggested that the other disciple was Luke himself.

This is possible, for the other Evangelists mention themselves thus impersonally. The preface to Luke's Gospel in no way forbids us to think that he had a personal knowledge of parts of Christ's ministry. Cleopas marveled that there could be a single man in Jerusalem who had not heard concerning the crucifixion, etc.] **19 And he said unto them, What things? And they said unto him, The things concerning Jesus the Nazarene, who was a prophet mighty in deed and word before God and all the people: 20 and how the chief priests and our rulers delivered him up to be condemned to death, and crucified him. 21 But we hoped that it was he who should redeem Israel.** [To Cleopas, redeeming Israel meant freeing the nation from the Roman yoke.] **Yea and besides all this, it is now the third day since these things came to pass. 22 Moreover certain women of our company amazed us, having been early at the tomb; 23 and when they found not his body, they came, saying, that they had also seen a vision of angels, who said that he was alive.** [Rationalists might see their own reflection in these two disciples, who suppressed the statement of the women that they had seen the Lord as too idle to be repeated, and told the least marvelous part of their story—that about the angels—as too visionary to be credited. Thus the renowned Renan held that the resurrection was a story or fabrication which grew out of the hallucinations of Mary Magdalene. But these two men on the way to Emmaus had less use for feminine hallucinations than even M. Renan. But in the end they believed in the resurrection because they themselves had substantial evidence of it.] **24 And certain of them that were with us** [Peter and John] **went to the tomb, and found it even so as the women had said: but him they saw not.** [The last clause unconsciously suggests the omitted fact that the women had professed to see Christ.] **25 And he said unto them, O foolish men, and slow of heart to believe in all that the prophets have spoken! 26 Behooved it not the Christ to suffer these things,**

and to enter into his glory? 27 And beginning from
Moses and from all the prophets, he interpreted to
them in all the scriptures the things concerning himself. [The counsel of the Father revealed in the Scriptures
shows that Jesus should enter into his glory through suffering.
The books of Moses foretell Christ largely in types, such as the
passover, the rock in the wilderness, Abraham's sacrifice of
Isaac, the day of atonement, etc., but the prophets show him
forth in clear-cut predictions and descriptions. Jesus evidently applied both these divisions of Scripture to himself, making it plain
to these two who were both thoughtless in mind and slow in
heart. Those lacking in a knowledge of the Christology of the
Old Testament are slow to believe in it. Those who know that
Christology, and yet doubt the Old Testament, do so because
they lack faith in the Christ therein portrayed.] 28 And they
drew nigh unto the village, whither they were going:
and he made as though he would go further. 29 And they
constrained him, saying, Abide with us; for it is
toward evening, and the day is now far spent. [They
were loth to part with this delightful stranger who by his
wonderful use of the Scriptures revived their failing faith and
hope in Jesus.] And he went in to abide with them.
30 And it came to pass, when he had sat down with
them to meat, he took the bread and blessed; and
breaking *it* he gave to them. 31 And their eyes were
opened, and they knew him; and he vanished out of
their sight. [While he was breaking the bread to supply
their bodies he opened their eyes and revealed to them that it
was he also who had just been feeding their hungry hearts
with the truth and consolation of the divine word.] 32 And
they said one to another, Was not our heart burning
within us, while he spake to us in the way, while he
opened to us the scriptures? [Thus they admit to each
other that the joy of beholding the risen Lord was but the con-
summation of a joy already begun through a right understanding of the truth contained in Scripture. The sight of the Lord
was sweeter because it was preceded by faith that he ought

thus to rise.] **33 And they rose up that very hour, ᵇ 13 And they went away ᶜand returned to Jerusalem** [their news was too precious to keep, they could not sit still till the disciples in Jerusalem knew it], **and found the eleven gathered together, and them that were with them** [the women and some of the one hundred and twenty —Acts i. 15], **34 saying, The Lord is risen indeed** [his resurrection is not an hallucination of the women], **and hath ᶠappeared to Cephas; {ᶜSimon.}** [Paul and Luke both mention this appearance, but we have none of the details of it.] **35 And they rehearsed the things** *that happened* **in the way, ᵇand told it unto the rest: ᶜand how he was known of them in the breaking of the bread.** [This does not mean that they knew Jesus because of any peculiar way in which he broke the bread: it means that he was revealed at the time when he broke it.] ᵇ**neither believed they them.** [They now believed that Jesus had risen, but they did not believe that these two had walked and talked with him without recognizing him.*]

CXXXVIII.

FIFTH APPEARANCE OF JESUS.

(Jerusalem. Sunday evening.)

ᵇ MARK XVI. 14 ; ᶜ LUKE XXIV. 36-43 ; ᵈ JOHN XX. 19-25.

ᵇ**14 And afterward ᶜas they spake these things** [while the two from Emmaus were telling their story], ᵇ**he was manifested unto the eleven themselves as they sat at**

*NOTE.—Here again we dissent. So general a statement of *unbelief* would not be used when there was a mere doubt as to some of the *narrated details*. We prefer our original comment to this substitution, and it was this: Mark shows us that little dependence can be placed upon the apparently strong admission which Luke records. Unable to contradict the testimony of Peter, they said, "The Lord is risen indeed;" but their hearts were, nevertheless, full of doubt. Luke himself shows this in the next section, for these professedly believing apostles took Jesus for a spirit when they saw him.

meat; [d] 19 When therefore it was evening, on that day, the first *day* of the week, and when the doors were shut where the disciples were, for fear of the Jews, Jesus [c] himself [d] came and stood in the midst, [c] of them, and saith unto them, Peace *be* unto you. 37 But they were terrified and affrighted, and supposed that they beheld a spirit. [His entrance through a bolted door lent weight to their idea that he had no corporeal body. They knew nothing of the possibilities of a resurrected body.] [b] and he upbraided them with their unbelief and hardness of heart [here, as in the previous section, Jesus shows that the heart has much to do with the belief], because they believed not them that had seen him after he was risen. [They had had the testimony of three men and perhaps half a dozen women; they had not lacked evidence.] [c] 38 And he said unto them, Why are ye troubled? and wherefore do questionings arise in your heart? 39 See my hands and my feet, that it is I myself: handle me, and see; for a spirit hath not flesh and bones, as ye behoid me having. 40 And when he had said this, he showed them his hands and his feet. [d] and his side. [These members not only showed that he was not a disembodied spirit, but they served to identify his body with that which they had seen crucified, and hence the person who now spoke was the Jesus whom they had known and lost.] [c] 41 And while they still disbelieved for joy, and wondered, he said unto them, Have ye here anything to eat? 42 And they gave him a piece of a broiled fish. 43 And he took it, and ate before them. [Thus at last satisfying them that he was not a ghost.] [d] The disciples therefore were glad, when they saw the Lord. 21 Jesus therefore said to them again, Peace *be* unto you: as the Father hath sent me, even so send I you. 22 And when he had said this, he breathed on them, and saith unto them, Receive ye the Holy Spirit: 23 whose soever sins ye forgive, they are forgiven unto them; whose soever *sins* ye retain, they are retained. [Now that the apostles knew their Master, he repeats his blessing, and as the New Testament is now sealed in his blood according to the commission under which he came, he, in turn, commissions the twelve to go forth and proclaim its provisions. Symbolic of the baptism which they were to receive at Pentecost, he breathes upon them, and, having thus symbolically qualified them, he commissions them to forgive or retain sin, for this was the subject-matter of the New Testament.] **24 But Thomas, one of the twelve, called Didymus** [see p. 224], **was not with them when Jesus came. 25 The other disciples therefore said unto him, We have seen the Lord. But he said unto them, Except I shall see in his hands the print of the nails, and put my finger into the print of the nails, and put my hand into his side, I will not believe.** [The apostles had undoubtedly seen and talked with some one, but the question was, Who? They said that it was Jesus, and Thomas, holding this to be impossible, thought that it must have been some one else whom they mistook for Jesus. But *he* would not be deceived; he would thoroughly examine the wounds, for these would identify Jesus beyond all doubt—if it were Jesus.]

CXXXIX.

SIXTH APPEARANCE OF JESUS.

(Sunday, one week after the resurrection.)

d JOHN xx. 26-31 ; f I. COR. xv. 5.

d **26 And after eight days again his disciples were within, and Thomas with them.** f then *he appeared* to **the twelve;** d **Jesus cometh, the doors being shut, and stood in the midst, and said, Peace** *be* **unto you.** [He came in the same manner and with the same salutation as formerly, giving Thomas a like opportunity for believing.] **27 Then saith he to Thomas, Reach hither thy finger, and see my hands ; and reach *hither* thy hand, and put it into my side: and be not faithless, but believing.**

[Thomas had proposed an infallible test, and Jesus now cheerfully submits to it.] **28 Thomas answered and said unto him, My Lord and my God.** [We have here the first confession of Christ as God. It should be said in Thomas' favor that if his doubts were heaviest, his confession of faith was fullest. He had more doubts as to the resurrection because it meant more to him; it meant that Jesus was none other than God himself.] **29 Jesus saith unto him, Because thou hast seen me, thou hast believed: blessed *are* they that have not seen, and *yet* have believed.** [Thus, while rejoicing in the belief of Thomas, Jesus pronounces a beatitude upon the countless numbers of believers in his resurrection, who are not witnesses of it.] **30 Many other signs therefore did Jesus in the presence of the disciples, which are not written in this book: 31 but these are written, that ye may believe that Jesus is the Christ, the Son of God; and that believing ye may have life in his name.** [This sounds like an ending to the Gospel, but it is like some of Paul's apparent but not real endings. Starting it with the proposition that Jesus, as the Word, was God, he comes here to the climax of Thomas' confession that Jesus is God, and the beatitude of Jesus upon those of a like faith. He then declares that he has written his book that men might have this faith, and the eternal life to which it leads.]

CXL.

SEVENTH APPEARANCE OF JESUS.

(Sea of Galilee.)

d JOHN XXI. 1-25.

^d **1 After these things Jesus manifested himself again to the disciples at the sea of Tiberias; and he manifested *himself* on this wise. 2 There were together Simon Peter, and Thomas called Didymus, and Nathanael of Cana in Galilee** [see p. 111]**, and the *sons* of Zebedee, and two other of his disciples. 3 Simon**

Peter saith unto them, I go a fishing. [As usual, Peter was the leader.] **They say unto him, We also come with thee. They went forth, and entered into the boat; and that night they took nothing.** [These apostles, thinking that their apostleship had terminated, had returned to their old life as fishermen.*] **4 But when day was now breaking, Jesus stood on the beach: yet the disciples knew not that it was Jesus. 5 Jesus therefore saith unto them, Children, have ye aught to eat?** [Jesus does not use the affectionate *teknia*—"children," but the familiar and colloquial *paidia*—"boys." His question was like that of a stranger, or neighbor, who wished to buy fish.] **They answered him, No.** [Their brevity bespeaks their disappointment at having a purchaser, but nothing to sell him.] **6 And he said unto them, Cast the net on the right side of the boat, and ye shall find. They cast therefore, and now they were not able to draw it for the multitude of fishes.** [The movements of large bodies of fish in the waters of Galilee are frequently visible to one standing on the shore. Supposing that the stranger thus saw fish upon the right side of the boat, the disciples readily obeyed his command, without suspecting who it was that gave it.] **7 That disciple therefore whom Jesus loved saith unto Peter, It is the Lord.** [Even the wonderful draught of fishes did not at once arouse all the disciples to realize that a miracle had been wrought, and that Christ stood upon the shore. But John, having believed in the resurrection of Jesus even before

---

*NOTE.—We can not agree to this: Jesus had said too many things indicating his future need of the apostles for them to think that he was through with them (Matt. xvi. 19; xxiv. 9-13; Luke xxii. 32; John xv. 16, 20, 27; xvi. 1-3). He had told the apostles to go to Galilee, and that he would appear to them there; they had done this and were waiting for his appearance. Peter, because of his denials, may have wavered in his loyalty, but the others surely did not. By going a-fishing they did not mean to abandon their apostleship; they were merely putting in the time, while they awaited developements; but by thus returning to their old occupation they were subjecting themselves to strong temptation (Luke ix. 62).—P. Y. P.

he had seen the risen Lord, may rightly be presumed to have had a livelier expectation of meeting him in Galilee, and this expectation made him more alert for signs of the Lord's presence. During the night he had probably thought much of that other night when they took nothing, and of the day which followed and on which the Lord filled their nets for them. At any rate, the similarity of the two occasions now flashed through John's mind and he recognized that it was Christ who had but now bade them cast the net.] **So when Simon Peter heard that it was the Lord, he girt his coat about him (for he was naked), and cast himself into the sea.** [The arduous task of fishing had caused Peter to lay aside his upper garment; but as he prepares to meet the Lord he puts it on, moved by reverence and respect for the Master, though it encumbered him greatly in his efforts to swim.] **8 But the other disciples came in the little boat (for they were not far from the land, but about two hundred cubits off), dragging the net *full* of fishes.** [The other disciples restrained their emotions, and attended to the duties of the hour. They were about one hundred yards from the land.] **9 So when they got out upon the land, they see a fire of coals there, and fish laid thereon, and bread.** [This sight gave a new meaning to the Lord's question in verse 5; he had not come to buy, but to supply.] **10 Jesus saith unto them, Bring of the fish which ye have now taken. 11 Simon Peter therefore went up, and drew the net to land, full of great fishes, a hundred and fifty and three: and for all there were so many, the net was not rent.** [Peter, being already wet, could lend material assistance in bringing the net to shore. John tells us the exact number of the fishes to show the magnitude of the miracle, both as to the catch and as to the unbroken nets. The latter form a sharp contrast to the broken nets of Luke v. 6. Possibly when the hour approached when they would become fishers of men, Jesus meant to show them that a greater and fuller miraculous power would attend and bless their efforts.] **12 Jesus saith unto them, Come *and**

**break your fast. And none of the disciples durst in-
quire of him, Who art thou? knowing that it was the
Lord.** [It was not, as some suppose, because they stood in a
new and special awe of him, that they durst not question him,
but it was the nature of the question itself. They feared a
mild rebuke like that once administered to Philip—John xiv.
9.] **13 Jesus cometh, and taketh the bread, and giveth
them, and the fish likewise.** [Thus he gave to them
when he fed the multitude and thus it may be hundreds of
times he had given to them when they sat at meat together—
Luke xxii. 17-20; John xiii. 26.] **14 This is now the
third time that Jesus was manifested to the disciples,
after that he was risen from the dead.** [It was his
seventh appearance, but his third appearance to a *group* of
disciples, and the third appearance witnessed by John. John
counts as follows: 1. An appearance to the apostles without
Thomas; 2. an appearance to them with Thomas; 3. this
appearance.] **15 So when they had broken their fast**
[after the eating of a meal together had calmed and quieted
the excitement of the disciples, and made them susceptible of
teaching], **Jesus saith to Simon Peter, Simon, *son* of
John, lovest thou me more than these?** [Jesus here
means: Do you love me more than these fishes and the fishing
business.*] **He saith unto him, Yea, Lord; thou knowest that I love thee. He saith unto him, Feed my
lambs. 16 He saith to him again a second time,
Simon, *son* of John, lovest thou me? He saith unto
him, Yea, Lord; thou knowest that I love thee. He
saith unto him, Tend my sheep.** [For if you love me

---

*NOTE.—Here again we dissent. See Hengstenberg, Alford, Meyer,
etc., and especially Godet. Peter had boasted of a love toward Jesus
superior to that of any of the other disciples (Matt. xxvi. 33; Mark
xiv. 29; John xiii. 37), and by refusing to have Jesus wash his feet, by
being the first to draw a sword in his Master's defense, and by even
now conspicuously deserting the others to swim to meet Jesus, he had
endeavored to prove his boast. Jesus therefore asks him if it is indeed true that his love is greater than that of his fellow-disciples—"Do
you love me more than these love me?"—P. Y. P.

better than fishing, you are a fisherman no longer, but a shepherd.*] **17 He saith unto him the third time, Simon, *son* of John, lovest thou me? Peter was grieved because he said unto him the third time, Lovest thou me? And he said unto him, Lord, thou knowest all things; thou knowest that I love thee. Jesus saith unto him, Feed my sheep.** [The Greek here has subtle shades of meaning which the English does not express. In the first two questions addressed to Peter our Lord uses the strong verb *agapan*, and Peter replies by the weaker verb *philein*. See p. 519. Peter, as we have seen, had professed the most unparalleled devotion for the Master, but when the Lord now asks him if he has that devotion, he humbly describes his love as of a far weaker order—a mere instinctive affection or strong attachment, but nothing approaching adoration. In his third question Jesus drops the *agapan* and takes Peter's own word—*philein:* as if he said, "Peter, are you even sure that you have a high regard for me?" It grieved Peter to have the Lord thus apparently doubt that he had even a tender regard for him, and he appealed to Christ himself as a searcher of hearts to bear witness that, poor and meager as his love was, it was at least as intense as he had represented it to be. In response to each of Peter's professions of love Jesus lays a command on him, as if he said, "If you love me as you say, prove it thus." These three commands also contain subtle linguistic distinctions which, however, are fairly represented by the English. Lambs and sheep are to be fed, and sheep are to be tended. The former means that young and old in the church are to be provided for, and, since the word "tends" means to be shepherd unto, the latter may mean that Peter is to play the shepherd to the wandering and the erring, bringing them into the fold. Before leaving this scene we should note that it has close relationship to other incidents in the life of Peter: 1. Jesus here calls him by the name

---

*NOTE.—Rather, "If you love me better than the others do, take the place which I have assigned you as chief servant of the flock."—Matt. xvi. 18, 19; Luke xxii. 26.—P. Y. P.

by which he had first called him, noting the more honorable name which he had given him. 2. Jesus recalls Peter under circumstances very similar to his first call. Compare verses 1-14 with Luke v. 1-11. 3. In a group around a fire of coals Peter here thrice professes his love for Christ, thus revoking the threefold denial which he had made under similar circumstances—Luke xiv. 54.] **18 Verily, verily, I say unto thee, When thou wast young, thou girdedst thyself, and walkedst whither thou wouldest** [Peter had just shown this freedom by girding himself and plunging into the sea]: **but when thou shalt be old, thou shalt stretch forth thy hands, and another shall gird thee, and carry thee whither thou wouldest not.** [Thus our Lord, by delicate but unmistakable suggestion, shows Peter that the freedom which he now enjoyed would be taken from him, and that he would lift his hands to permit others to bind him that they might lead him to martyrdom to which his flesh (though not his spirit) would go unwillingly.] **19 Now this he spake, signifying by what manner of death he should glorify God.** [John, who wrote after Peter's death, tells us what the words of Christ meant. His words show that tradition is true in saying that Peter suffered martyrdom, but it is no voucher that tradition is true as to the time (about thirty-four years after this), place (Rome), or manner (crucified head downward) of Peter's death. There is certainly no trustworthy evidence that Peter was ever at Rome.] **And when he had spoken this, he saith unto him, Follow me.** [This saying bore the usual double sense in which Jesus employed it. Peter was to follow him now (and he did arise and follow), and he was also to follow Jesus to a violent death and a glorious immortality.] **20 Peter, turning about, seeth the disciple whom Jesus loved** [John] **following; who also leaned back on his breast at the supper, and said, Lord, who is he that betrayeth thee?** [John xiii. 25.] **21 Peter therefore seeing him saith to Jesus, Lord, and what shall this man do?** [Peter and John were near friends (Acts iii. 1), and understanding that the

Lord had prophesied a violent death for himself, Peter was naturally interested in the fate of his dear companion.] **22 Jesus saith unto him, If I will that he tarry till I come, what *is that* to thee? follow thou me.** [It was none of Peter's business whether John's earthly lot was easier or harder than his own; his business was to be faithful in the pathway whither the Lord led him.] **23 This saying therefore went forth among the brethren, that that disciple should not die; yet Jesus said not unto him, that he should not die; but, If I will that he tarry till I come, what *is that* to thee?** [Our Lord's words were a puzzle when John wrote his Gospel, and to many they are a puzzle still. For an able treatment of the various interpretations of this difficult passage see B. W. Johnson's Commentary on John. There is no question that John died. The site of his grave at Ephesus was well known to early Christians. The coming of the Lord for which he tarried was that in the isle of Patmos, of which he tells us in the Book of Revelation. This passage, therefore, shows that John wrote his Gospel before his exile in Patmos.] **24 This is the disciple that beareth witness of these things, and wrote these things: and we know that his witness is true. 25 And there are also many other things which Jesus did, the which if they should be written every one, I suppose that even the world itself would not contain the books that should be written.** [Since the "we know" differs from the "he knoweth" of John xix. 35, most of the critics hold that this verse was added by the elders of Ephesus to whom John committed his Gospel, and that it is the attestation of the church there to the truth and authenticity of the Gospel. But the first person singular, "I suppose," of verse 25 is hard to account for on such an hypothesis. Besides, none of the elders at Ephesus could suppose any such thing. Only an eye-witness who saw the fullness of our Lord's ministry would be led to pen these words. We find in the first Epistle of John a condition of affairs similar to these two verses. The first chapter opens with and continues to use the editorial plural, while the second chapter drops in the first person singular. We think, then, that John finished his own book. Considering the wilderness of literature which has accumulated around the sayings and doings of our Lord contained in the brief Gospels, it is little wonder that John thought a full record of the Lord's life would fill the world with books.]

CXLI.

EIGHTH APPEARANCE OF JESUS.

(A mountain in Galilee.)

ᵃ MATT. xxviii. 16, 17; ᵇI. COR. xv. 6.

ᵃ **16 But the eleven disciples went into Galilee, unto the mountain where Jesus had appointed them. ᵇ6 then he appeared to above five hundred brethren at once, of whom the greater part remain until now, but some are fallen asleep; ᵃ17 And when they saw him, they worshiped *him*; but some doubted.** [Though Matthew speaks of only the eleven being present at this appearance, yet as it was the oft-promised meeting by appointment and as the women and disciples generally shared in this promise (Matt. xxviii. 7-10), we have no doubt that it was the meeting mentioned by Paul the account of which we have here blended with Matthew. As to the doubts, we may explain them in three ways: 1. Among so large a number as five hundred some would likely be skeptical. 2. It would take Jesus some time to draw near enough to all to convince each one of his identity. Some, therefore, would doubt until they were thus convinced by Jesus coming to them and speaking to them, as the first clause of the next section shows that he did. 3. Matthew records no other appearance to the apostles save this one, and it seems to us reasonable to think that he here notes the doubts of Thomas, and connects them with the appearance of Jesus generally. He could not well say *"had* doubted," for he records no other appearance where they had opportunity to doubt. The history of the eleven sustains this view, for there were no doubters among them at Pentecost. According to Paul, many of these brethren were still alive when he wrote his epistle to the Corinthians, which is commonly accepted to have been in the spring of A. D. 57.]

CXLII.

THE GREAT COMMISSION GIVEN.

(Time and place same as last section.)

^aMATT. XXVIII. 18-20; ^bMARK XVI. 15-18; ^cLUKE XXIV. 46, 47.

^a**18 And Jesus came to them and spake unto them, saying, All authority hath been given unto me in heaven and on earth.** ^b**15 And he said unto them, Go ye** ^a**therefore,** ^b**into all the world, and preach the gospel to the whole creation.** ^a**and make disciples of all the nations, baptizing them into the name of the Father and of the Son and of the Holy Spirit: 20 teaching them to observe all things whatsoever I commanded you:** ^b**16 He that believeth and is baptized shall be saved; but he that disbelieveth shall be condemned.** ^c**Thus it is written, that the Christ should suffer, and rise again from the dead the third day; 47 and that repentance and remission of sins should be preached in his name unto all the nations, beginning from Jerusalem.** [The verses from Luke are taken from a later conversation, which will be handled in our next section. They are inserted here because they are an indicative statement of the commission which Matthew and Mark give in the imperative, and a section professing to embrace the commission would be imperfect without them. The first word of the commission is significant, and should be remembered. We have no right to wait for sinners to come and hear the gospel, we must carry it to them. The "therefore" with which it opens shows that Jesus rests this command on his divine authority; but neither the word "power"

nor the word "authority" adequately translate Christ's word. It means all the right of absolute authority, and all the force of absolute power. It is a most transcendent claim which Jesus utters here. All authority in heaven! Paul's qualification of these words, or their counterpart in Ps. viii. 6 (I. Cor. xv. 27, 28), magnifies instead of detracting from their wonderful import, for he deems it necessary to state that the Father himself is not subject to the Son. Surely in connection with this marvelous celestial power his dominion over our tiny earth would not need to be mentioned if it were not that we, its inhabitants, are very limited in our conception of things, and require exceedingly plain statements. The command calls for the Christianizing of all nations. If we realized better that authority with which Christ prefaces his commission, the conquest of the nations in his name would seem to us a small matter indeed, and we would set about it expecting to witness its speedy accomplishment. The structure of the sentence in the original Greek shows that it is the disciples and not the nations who are to be baptized; according to the commission, therefore, one must be made a disciple before he can be baptized. Baptism brings us into divine relation to God. Being a part of the process of adoption, it is called a birth (John iii. 5). The baptized Christian bears the name into which he is baptized (Rom. ii. 24; Jas. ii. 7). Luke sums up the whole commission by recording the words of Christ, wherein he states that he suffered that it might be preached to all nations that if men would repent God could now forgive (Rom. iii. 26). From Luke's record we also learn that the preaching of these glad tidings was to begin at Jerusalem.] ᵇ 17 And these signs shall accompany them that believe: in my name shall they cast out demons; they shall speak with new tongues; 18 they shall take up serpents, and if they drink any deadly thing, it shall in no wise hurt them; they shall lay hands on the sick, and they shall recover. [The Book of Acts gives examples of each one of these signs except the fourth, and though we have no record of a disciple escaping the effects of drinking poison, there is little doubt that in the many persecutions such cases did occur.] ᵃ and lo, I am with you always, even unto the end of the world. [This is a promise not of bare companionship, but of full sympathy and support (Isa. xliii. 2; Ex. xxxiii. 15; Josh. i. 5). The duration of this promise shows that it is intended for all disciples.]

CXLIII.

NINTH AND TENTH APPEARANCES OF JESUS.

(Jerusalem.)

ᶜ LUKE XXIV. 44-49; ᵉ ACTS I. 3-8; ᶠ I. COR. XV. 7.

ᶠ 7 then he appeared to James [of this appearance also we have no details]; then to all the apostles; ᵉ 3 to whom he also showed himself alive after his passion by many proofs, appearing unto them by the space of forty days, and speaking the things concerning the kingdom of God [this shows us that Jesus spoke many things at his appearances beside the brief words which are recorded]: 4 and being assembled together with them, he charged them not to depart from Jerusalem, but to wait for the promise of the Father, which, *said he*, ye heard from me [John xiv. 16, 26; xv. 26]: 5 for John indeed baptized with water; but ye shall be baptized in the Holy Spirit not many days hence. [This promised baptism came ten days later, at Pentecost.] ᶜ 44 And he said unto them, These are my words which I spake unto you, while I was yet with you, that all things must needs be fulfilled, which are written in the law of Moses, and the prophets, and the psalms, concerning me. [That is, these recent events are simply what I told you should come to pass according to the Scriptures, but ye did not understand. The phrase, "while I was yet," etc., shows that in the mind of Jesus he was already parted from them, and his presence was the exception and not the rule.] 45 Then opened he their mind, that they might under-

stand the scriptures [some think that this illumination was of a miraculous nature, and confound it with what the Lord is said to have done at John xx. 22; but the next verse suggests that he did it by discourse, just as he had done it already to the two on the way to Emmaus—Luke xxiv. 27]; **46 and he said unto them, Thus it is written, that the Christ should suffer, and rise again from the dead the third day** [Both the written prophecy and the unwritten nature of things required that Christ should do as he had done. The saying forms an important credential for the Book of Jonah; where else have we the period of three days fixed as the time between our Lord's burial and resurrection?—Matt. xii. 38-40]; **47 and that repentance and remission of sins should be preached in his name unto all the nations, beginning from Jerusalem.** [See previous section.] **48 Ye are witnesses of these things. 49 And behold, I send forth the promise of my Father upon you: but tarry ye in the city, until ye be clothed with power from on high. °6 They** [the apostles] **therefore, when they were come together, asked him, saying, Lord, dost thou at this time restore the kingdom to Israel?** [Despite all that they had seen and heard, the apostles were still expecting that Jesus would revive the old Jewish kingdom, and have himself enthroned in Jerusalem as the heir and successor to David.] **7 And he said unto them, It is not for you to know times or seasons, which the Father hath set within his own authority. 8 But ye shall receive power, when the Holy Spirit is come upon you: and ye shall be my witnesses both in Jerusalem, and in all Judaea and Samaria, and unto the uttermost part of the earth.** [Jesus enlightens them as to their duty, and not as to the kingdom; Pentecost would make all clear as to the nature of Christ's rule and dominion.]

CXLIV.

THE ASCENSION.

(Olivet, between Jerusalem and Bethany.)

ᵇ Mark xvi. 19, 20 ; ᶜ Luke xxiv. 50-53; ᵃ Acts i. 9-12.

ᵇ 19 So then the Lord Jesus, after he had spoken unto them, ᵃ9 And when he had said these things, ᶜ he led them out until *they were* over against Bethany: and he lifted up his hands, and blessed them. 51 And it came to pass, while he blessed them, he parted from them [it is significant that our Lord's gesture, when last seen of men, was one of blessing], and ᵃas they were looking, he was taken {ᶜcarried ᵇreceived} ᶜup into heaven. ᵃand a cloud received him out of their sight. ᵇ and [he] sat down at the right hand of God. ᶜ52 And they worshipped him, ᵃ10 And while they were looking stedfastly intc heaven as he went, behold two men [angels in human form] stood by them in white apparel; 11 who also said, Ye men of Galilee, why stand ye looking into heaven? this Jesus, who was received up from you into heaven, shall so come in like manner as ye beheld him going into heaven. [Thus the angels add their testimony to the sureness of our Lord's promise that he will return.] 12 Then returned they unto Jerusalem from the mount called Olivet, ᶜ with great joy; 53 and were continually in the temple, blessing God. ᵇ20 And they went forth, and preached everywhere, the Lord working with them, and confirming the word by the signs that followed. Amen.

CXLV.

OUR LORD APPEARS AFTER HIS ASCENSION.

ᶠI. Cor. xv. 8.

ᶠ8 and last of all, as to the *child* untimely born, he appeared to me also. [Since Paul reckons this among the bodily appearances of our Lord, we have included it in our work; but it borders upon those spiritual appearances which belong rather to apostolic history and may be classed with the vision of Stephen (Acts vii. 55) and John (Rev. i. 9-17), to which it was near kin. Accounts of the appearance will be found in the ninth, twenty-second and twenty-sixth chapters of Acts. For completeness' sake we might also add the words of Jesus at Acts xx. 35, viz.: **It is more blessed to give than to receive.** These words quoted by Paul are not found in the gospel. The earthly life of Jesus shades off into the celestial, but we think that we have now given all that may rightly be included in the former.]